MARCEL TABUTEAU

MARCEL TABUTEAU

*How Do You Expect to
Play the Oboe If You
Can't Peel a Mushroom?*

LAILA STORCH

INDIANA UNIVERSITY PRESS

BLOOMINGTON AND INDIANAPOLIS

This book is a publication of

Indiana University Press
601 North Morton Street
Bloomington, IN 47404-3797 USA

http://iupress.indiana.edu

Telephone orders	800-842-6796
Fax orders	812-855-7931
Orders by e-mail	iuporder@indiana.edu

The paper used in this publication meets the minimum
requirements of American National Standard for Information
Sciences—Permanence of Paper for Printed Library Materials,
ANSI Z39.48-1984.

Manufactured in the United States of America

Library of Congress Cataloging-in-Publication Data

Storch, Laila.
   Marcel Tabuteau : how do you expect to play the oboe if you
can't peel a mushroom? / Laila Storch.
      p. cm.
   Includes bibliographical references (p.   ) and index.
   ISBN-13: 978-0-253-34949-1 (cloth : alk. paper)   1. Tabuteau,
Marcel, 1887–1966.   2. Oboe players—Biography.   I. Title.
   ML419.T125S76 2008
   788.5'2092—dc22
   [B]
                              2007025642

1 2 3 4 5 13 12 11 10 09 08

IN MEMORY OF MY MOTHER

Juanita Storch

Contents

CONTENTS

PREFACE

For almost forty years music lovers, students, connoisseurs, and fellow musicians were enthralled by the unique artistry of Marcel Tabuteau. They listened to his phrasing, his elegance of style, and to his silvery tone as it would spiral and float seemingly without effort to the top rows of the balcony of the Academy of Music in Philadelphia. During the time that Tabuteau was the solo oboist of the Philadelphia Orchestra, he also taught at the Curtis Institute of Music. To his own oboe students he passed on the best elements of the French woodwind tradition, at the same time establishing such new standards of finesse in orchestral blending, variety of tone color, and nuance of phrasing that what is now known as the "American school of oboe playing," or, more specifically, the "Tabuteau style," has become the accepted and expected norm for oboists in all American symphony orchestras. Through his conducting of woodwind ensembles, his influence reached the players of all other wind instruments. In later years he coached string groups and led an orchestra. Many violinists, violists, cellists, and pianists have said that they received their most valuable musical knowledge in Tabuteau's classes at Curtis.

How did an orchestral musician, someone who only rarely appeared in the capacity of a soloist, and who in his thirty years at the Curtis Institute did not teach more than fifty-seven oboists there, come to have such a far-reaching impact on the development of musical performance in our country? It may be easier to understand through a brief look at some of the ways in which Tabuteau thought about music. His conception of technique was not speed of fingers, although he would emphasize brilliance when it was called for. To him, oboe technique was the total control of all the elements required to most ideally express the life of a musical phrase. This meant a coordination of the use of one's wind, the embouchure, variety of tone color and nuance, articulation, and, above all, imagination and personality. While conducting the string ensemble at the Curtis Institute, he once said to the students, most of whom practiced for long hours with the single-minded idea of a virtuoso career, "You must be open to everything—learn from everything. The more you take from the world, the more you can give to the world. Develop your personality and do more than 'shroom' and scratch ten hours a day!" Tabuteau repeatedly stressed the idea of having "something to say." "It is not the golden pen or the silver pencil that writes the novel—not the platinum flute or the diamond oboe that plays the melody. You must have something to say!"

In speaking of his philosophy of music, Tabuteau often referred to the "laws of nature." To explain his concept of the "life" of the notes and of the "up and down impulses," he used illustrations ranging from the movement of the earth around the sun to the motion involved in our own normal respiration or the way one must lift the foot before being able to put it down. He also evolved his "number system" as a way to impart in an extremely precise manner his ideas of rhythm, dynamic range, and the shaping of musical phrases. However, applying numbers to explain the minute gradations of intensity and nuance in a line of music did not preclude his use of colorful examples to help put across a point. Sometimes it was by means of the "golf player": "He can have the cap and the pants and better clubs and hit the ball. He looks like a golf player—but the real one—the professional, knows exactly where the ball is going. Every note must be placed like the ball in golf—in the hole. You must not miss—it is a game!" Or again: "Perfection is like the point

PREFACE

of a needle—it is easy to hit all around it." And in a warning against monotony: "Your playing is like saltwater taffy. You see all the beautiful colors—red, blue, yellow—but they all taste the same."

In 1950 when I came to play in the Bach Festival at Prades and for the first time heard Pablo Casals as he conducted every rehearsal and described in meticulous detail what he wanted us to do, it all sounded very familiar. Casals has been quoted as saying, "Variety is a great word—in music as in everything; variety is a law of nature. Good music has never monotony. . . . We must give to a melody its natural life." And further, "Each note is like a link in a chain—important in itself and also as a connection between what has been and what will be."[1] These were the strongly held views of Marcel Tabuteau as well.

Tabuteau, who retired in 1954, missed by a few years the time when he could easily have been caught "in action" by television or video camera. With his volatile temperament (explosive outbursts were often followed by observations full of wit and humor, all delivered with an intonation that made his English sound more like French), he would have been more persuasively represented by himself than by the imitations and the "Tabuteau stories" that continue to circulate to this day. In once criticizing the degree of sound he wished a student to produce, he said, "Your forte is like near-beer—during Prohibition—not the real thing." It is perhaps an indication of the force of his personality that even though contact with the "real thing" is no longer possible, the fascination continues, and many people wish to hear more about Tabuteau.

I have always felt that the life of Marcel Tabuteau could not be portrayed in the silent pages of a book. The complexity of his character may be compared to the plant that bound him to his life's work—the reed cane Arundo donax. He spent endless hours making reeds for the oboe, constantly battling the fact that as in all of nature's forms, no two pieces of cane are ever exactly alike. One can no more draw a completely satisfactory picture of his complicated personality than one can find a simple solution for the elusive oboe reed. The answer to each question may literally depend on which way the wind is blowing.

Tabuteau left no written "reminiscences," nor did he often speak extensively about his early years. I have had to reconstruct an outline of his varied experiences from fragmentary records surviving in the libraries

PREFACE

and archives of Compiègne, Paris, New York, San Francisco, and Philadelphia. And, fortunately, many of his colleagues and students have been able to make significant contributions to his story. For the latter part of this account, I have drawn on the letters I wrote during my student years at the Curtis Institute of Music, feeling that they give a more vivid and accurate picture of what it was like to study with him than anything I could reconstruct today. This book, therefore, combines biographical material with a record of my personal contact with Marcel Tabuteau. I hope that it will bring to life, even in a small way, some aspects of the character and musical contributions of this unique artist.

PREFACE

ACKNOWLEDGMENTS

I would like to express my appreciation to the archivists and librarians who have provided much valuable information: Robert Tuggle and John Pennino, Metropolitan Opera; JoAnne E. Barry, Philadelphia Orchestra; Elizabeth Walker, Curtis Institute of Music; Mlle Andrée Durieux, Hôtel de Ville, Compiègne; Fran Barulich, Special Collections, the New York Public Library for the Performing Arts: John Gibbs, School of Music, University of Washington; Matthew W. Buff, San Francisco Performing Arts Library and Museum; Jason Gibbs, Art and Music Center of the San Francisco Public Library; the staff at the University of Pennsylvania Van Pelt Library Special Collections; Centre d'Accueil et de Recherche des Archives Nationales, Paris; Teri A. McKibben, Cincinnati Symphony Orchestra.

I could not have written this book without the help of my friends and colleagues, including many I did not know personally, but all of whom generously responded to my telephone calls, questions, and requests to visit. They gladly shared their memories of Marcel Tabuteau, thus adding important breadth to my search. Their names, unfortunately including many who are no longer still with us, appear in the context of the book. My gratitude to the International Double Reed Society and former president Terry Ewell for the material support of a research grant. A special thank-you to the many members of the society who, through the devoted efforts of Norma Hooks and Evelyn McCarty, made additional contributions to the completion of the project. Those who read parts or all of the manuscript and helped me to "keep going," include John Minsker, John de Lancie, Daniel Stolper, Marc Mostovoy, John Mack, Naomi and Gary Graffman, Linda Strommen, Claus Johansen, Otto Lang, June Campbell, Melinda Bargreen, Ann McCutchan, Sara Blum, and John Friedmann.

My former student Tad Margelli was always ready to identify an obscure composer or piece of music. Ongoing expressions of interest during the past ten years from Geoffrey Burgess, Timothy Clinch, Carlos Coelho, Gerald Corey, Marion Davies, Birthe Gorton, Alain de Gourdon, Ann Ferguson, Michael Finkelman, Arthur Grossman, Richard Killmer, Helen Lawser, Patrick McFarland, Wayne Rapier, Gail Warnaar, David and Vendla Weber, Barbara Wilson, Hiroshi Yoshimizu, and Liangong Yu were all very encouraging. I wish to express my warm appreciation to Nancy Toff, who, while working on her book about Georges Barrère, generously shared the many sources of early history he had in common with Marcel Tabuteau. From outside the world of winds, I am happy that my son-in-law, pianist Jon Kimura Parker, has become an enthusiastic advocate of the Tabuteau story. Naomi Pascal, editor-at-large at University of Washington Press, has been supportive of my project from its beginnings in 1995 to the present. Author Robert Conot offered his expertise in situating me historically into my California background. My apologies to those I may have failed to mention.

Members of the Tabuteau family—François Létoffé, Claude Narcy, Guy Baumier, Denise Budin, and Dr. Jacques Budin—provided invaluable old photographs and personal anecdotes. A special thank you to Gary Louie, recording technician at the School of Music, University of Washington, for his patience and care in editing the Tabuteau-Wolsing tapes into a listenable CD. It has been a pleasure working with Indiana University Press editors Jane Behnken, Bethany Kissell, and Neil Rags-

ACKNOWLEDGMENTS

dale. I would also like to thank copyeditor Jane Curran for her help and thoughtful suggestions.

Above all, to my immediate family, my husband Martin Friedmann and daughter, Aloysia, my gratitude for their confidence in believing that I would eventually complete the book.

—Orcas Island, Washington, 2006

ACKNOWLEDGMENTS

INTRODUCTION

February 20, 1915, saw the opening in San Francisco of the Panama-Pacific International Exposition, the celebrated world fair that heralded the completion of the Panama Canal and the city's reconstruction from the devastating earthquake and fire of 1906. It attracted visitors and notables from all over the world including Thomas Alva Edison and Henry Ford, who together with the great horticulturist Luther Burbank from nearby Santa Rosa formed an intimate trio. The musical world was represented by John Philip Sousa and Camille Saint-Saëns. The renowned French composer braved the ever-more hazardous Atlantic crossing—a German U-boat sank the liner Lusitania with the loss of almost twelve hundred lives on May 7—to honor the exposition with a composition, Hail California! A fellow countryman, Marcel Tabuteau, who had been called to the colors for three months in the fall of 1914, escaped the carnage on the Western Front by being mustered out because of a heart condition. He came to San Francisco as principal oboist of the Exposition Orchestra.

My maternal great-grandfather Jaroslav Bohuslav Storch, a mining engineer born in Prague, capital of Bohemia, had arrived in the San

Francisco Bay area with his family in 1880. Fifteen years earlier, economic opportunity connected with diplomatic events of the turbulent times had drawn him first to the American Far West and then in 1870 to San Dimas in the Sierra Madre of Mexico, center of the famed "Silver Belt." My grandfather Hugo, born in San Dimas in 1873, later became an innovative architect, one of the first in California to integrate Spanish-inspired motifs into his work. With nostalgia for his childhood, in 1895 he named his first-born child, my mother, Juanita. Poor health forced Hugo out of his dark San Francisco offices to seek fresh air and sunshine in Rincon Valley near Santa Rosa, a small town sixty miles to the north in Sonoma County. In 1915 he sold his substantial East Bay residence and purchased a nine-acre ranch containing some two thousand chickens. The venture proved disastrous. Raising chickens is a specialized field of which he knew little or nothing, and two years after relocating, he died. My grandmother and mother were left to fend for themselves. My mother, an aspiring artist, felt isolated, and following a brief marriage that was as unsuccessful as her family's chicken farm, she divorced and reassumed her maiden name. I grew up on the little "ranch" that was now reduced to less than two acres. My mother used her artistic talents and dribbles of money from here and there to scrape by. Although I had only the most limited opportunity to listen to music, I was fascinated by it. When I was seven years old, some friends who owned a hamburger shop lent me a violin. For the next two years I took lessons from a blind violinist, Professor Theroux, whom my mother drove from school to school in compensation. But then the proprietors of the shop moved to another county, taking the violin with them. Under our constrained finances, purchase of another instrument was out of the question. So the next four years turned into a musical dark age for me, when my exposure was limited largely to turning the hand crank on the phonograph in the once-weekly music-appreciation class in our country grammar school. Entering Santa Rosa High School shortly before my fourteenth birthday in February 1935 seemed to me a wonderful opportunity, as the school had an orchestra. Somehow I knew I was already too old to resume serious study of the violin, but what instrument could I play? The orchestra's director, Josef Walter, handed me an oboe. Since the high school's instrument was sitting idle,

INTRODUCTION

its previous player having graduated, I became the new oboist by default.

If what Mr. Walter, a violinist, could teach me from an oboistic standpoint was limited, he nevertheless drew the attention of his students to musical events which took place in San Francisco, and told us about the famous concert artists of the day. Occasionally he would take some of us for what was at that time a slow and cumbersome trip by car and ferry to the Bay Region. So it was that one of the first musical "greats" I heard was Mischa Elman playing the Tchaikovsky Violin Concerto with the University of California Symphony Orchestra in Berkeley. The oboe solos which caught my attention were played by fourteen-year-old John de Lancie. At that time Pierre Monteux had just begun his leadership of the San Francisco Symphony Orchestra. On another trip I heard their oboist, Julien Shanis, in the Brahms Second Symphony. That was a deciding moment for me: if the oboe could sound like that, it was worth "sticking with it" no matter what the difficulties. When I heard Beethoven's Emperor Concerto and Brahms Concerto No. 2 for the first time as played by Artur Schnabel, the experience was beyond what I could comprehend musically, but the impression of "nobility" stayed with me forever. We were there, too, for Igor Stravinsky conducting his own Symphony of Psalms. But when the Philadelphia Orchestra came to San Francisco on its 1936 coast-to-coast tour, there was no way our Depression-era pocketbooks could stretch to the ticket price for this special event. However, Josef Walter showed us the glossy brochure with pictures of the orchestra's eminent first chair players, and this was how I first saw and heard the name of Marcel Tabuteau.

From then on, in my mind, Tabuteau, the Philadelphia Orchestra, and the Curtis Institute of Music became the symbol of the ultimate in musical accomplishment. Everything I read only served to reinforce this conviction. In 1938, Life magazine published an impressive article featuring the Curtis Institute. There was a full-page photo of ten-year-old piano prodigy Gary Graffman at his lesson with Isabelle Vengerova and a series of photographs of Marcel Tabuteau conducting the woodwind ensemble. Even his sneering glance and threatening gestures directed toward an erring oboe player did not alter my conviction that this was without doubt the fabled Shangri-la for music students.

INTRODUCTION

In 1939 I began to take lessons from Julien Shanis, the fine oboist I had heard in the San Francisco Symphony Orchestra. His father, Jean Shanis, an excellent Belgian clarinetist, had played with Marcel Tabuteau during the 1915 Panama-Pacific International Exposition in San Francisco. In 1923 he decided to send his son to Philadelphia to study with Tabuteau. It was before the beginning of the Curtis Institute, and Shanis had private lessons for about one year. During the Philadelphia Orchestra's 1936 transcontinental tour, John de Lancie, a Shanis student, auditioned for Tabuteau in San Francisco and was accepted to study at Curtis. Now, a few years later, Mr. Shanis suggested that I also should "go East" and try to enter the Curtis Institute. He sent a letter of recommendation to Tabuteau, who eventually answered with a few lines on a Christmas card saying that the Curtis Institute of Music did "not encourage feminine students of oboe." When I wrote directly to the school, the secretary of admissions replied that "Mr. Tabuteau is reluctant to accept women students."

Despite the statement in the opening pages of the catalog, "The Curtis Institute of Music welcomes students of all nationalities, races and creeds," this official policy apparently did not include women wind players. Or perhaps they were simply not deemed a viable risk for such a high level of education in the music profession. No conductor would hire a woman for the oboe section of a major or even a minor symphony orchestra, and the Curtis Institute was not in the business of training people either to play in community orchestras or to be teachers. At that time there existed a deep chasm between the music education given in the three or four top conservatories and that being offered in the leading universities of the country; it was out of the question to gain first-class instrumental expertise in academic institutions. Several decades later, when the conservatories had produced a greater number of highly skilled players than could be absorbed into the orchestras of the country, the situation changed dramatically. Many universities are now able to boast of outstanding music departments or schools of music with world-class teachers providing a completely professional education. But in 1940, if one had any hope of ever playing in a symphony orchestra, one had to aim for the Juilliard School, the Curtis Institute of Music, or the Eastman School of Music. The Curtis Institute, which had the

INTRODUCTION

smallest enrollment and accepted all students on a scholarship basis only, was the most selective and the most difficult to enter. And it had Marcel Tabuteau, already renowned for his decades as solo oboist of the Philadelphia Orchestra and for the accomplishments of his students. I noted that the school did not forbid me to come and play an audition, but had simply discouraged me from making the long trip with little chance of a favorable result. Every audition for Curtis had to be played in person. When with reluctance the school finally granted me an audition date and time, an additional word of discouragement was included, in the form of a warning that Mr. Tabuteau preferred younger students. Not to be stopped now, I boarded a Greyhound bus and, after the five-day cross-country trip, arrived in Philadelphia in early April 1941. One of the Curtis secretaries told me that when Marcel Tabuteau heard I was really coming, his response was "Oh, my God!"

The audition took place in one of the spacious, richly carpeted studios on the second floor of the Curtis Institute. I was dimly aware that I was the only girl among more than a half dozen boys all trying out for the one vacancy; more had played on other days. I was struck by the penetrating, direct look of Tabuteau's steely blue-gray eyes. Despite my nervousness I managed to play half of the first movement of the Haydn Concerto and the Barret études he asked for, and to sight-read the first page of the Guilhaud Concertino, a work I had never seen. In a letter to Mr. Shanis, I reported that "Tabuteau was very polite, looked at my reed and said, 'Who teaches you to make reeds like that?' He asked me three times how long and with whom I had studied. Then he said that I had possibilities but it was so sad that young ladies want to study the oboe. I told him I already realized what an uncertain situation it was, but I don't think that made any difference to him. He still thinks it's sad. He beamed all over when I gave him your best regards, asked me how far I had come and that was that." At one point during the audition, Tabuteau asked if I minded if he looked at my teeth, which made me feel like a horse. When he saw a very crooked lower tooth, he exploded, saying: "You can't play oboe with teeth like that!" I immediately told him that I would get them straightened, even though they had already been done once and had moved out of line. I had no way of knowing then that I was not alone in being subjected to this "dental examination."

INTRODUCTION

Almost sixty years later, pianist Jacob Lateiner told me he remembered once accompanying entrance examinations for oboe, and on that occasion Tabuteau had made all the applicants show their teeth.

After the auditions, we had to wait in the elegant foyer. Finally I was called by a secretary who said I must have made quite an impression as he had listened to me for so long (at least ten minutes). Then she told me that a boy who had already auditioned three times (I later learned it was William Criss) had been chosen for the one available scholarship. She added that if any vacancy should occur during the coming school year, Tabuteau would be willing to accept me as a student. I did not find this decision particularly cheering. Midyear openings almost never happened at Curtis. So rather sad and discouraged, I returned to Santa Rosa on the Greyhound bus.

Having heard nothing during the fall, I again wrote to Curtis asking if I could come and re-audition in the following spring, but the institute said no, Mr. Tabuteau would consider me "along with the other applicants." I felt it was impossible that he could remember me a year later. Then in April, like a miracle, a telegram arrived: "TABUTEAU WILL ACCEPT YOU FOR SEASON FORTY TWO FORTY THREE PLEASE ADVISE AS SOON AS POSSIBLE VIA WESTERN UNION IF YOU ARE INTERESTED." Interested? My joy at this news, however, was short-lived. Only a few weeks later a letter from Curtis brought the bad news that due to loss of income the whole wind department was to be eliminated for the coming fall—and, of course, me along with it. The prospect of study at the Curtis Institute now seemed lost forever. Although our limited funds would make another trip to Philadelphia very difficult, the fact that Tabuteau had accepted me for the school gave me the courage to ask him for private lessons, something I otherwise would not have dared to do. I wrote him a letter but received no reply. Helen Reynolds, a friend I had made at the time of my audition, felt it was foolhardy to come without knowing if Tabuteau would really teach me. By telephone she finally reached Madame Tabuteau, who said: "Oh, that man, he never answers the letters!" After this conversation, Tabuteau grudgingly agreed that I could come to Philadelphia. And so, encouraged by my mother, I again set out by Greyhound bus for Philadelphia. It was in

INTRODUCTION

the middle of winter, January 1943. I hoped to manage to stay for about three months.

The hoped-for three months eventually became three years and then stretched to a lifetime's journey largely dominated by the thought of Marcel Tabuteau. There have been detours and byways where I learned to appreciate other admirable musicians and feel their influence, but the road always led back to Tabuteau. In the summer of 1995 at the John Mack Oboe Camp in North Carolina, James Oestreich interviewed several of the participants for a feature article on the oboe that he was preparing for the New York Times. One day as we sat around the lunch table, he casually commented, "If Marcel Tabuteau was so important, why isn't there a book about him?" I admitted to having thought of such an idea and said that I had saved a lot of material about him throughout the years—programs, photographs, notes on his teaching—all stuffed into a "Tabuteau drawer." But where would one begin? It seemed to me that only the talent of a novelist like Balzac could succeed in describing such a mercurial character. Moreover, how would I fill in the pieces of the important two-thirds of his life that had gone by before I began to study with him? Soon I began to realize that I already knew a good deal about Tabuteau's days at the Paris Conservatoire from my earlier re-search on his teacher, Georges Gillet. But what of Tabuteau's early years in America after he arrived in 1905 at age seventeen? Fortunately, the Walter Damrosch Archive in New York answered many questions on this barely explored period. From the basement of the Metropolitan Opera to the cramped third-floor Philadelphia Orchestra Archive in the Academy of Music, from Paris to San Francisco—during the next few years I began to fill in some of the missing details. In my own "Tabuteau drawer" I found the old family photographs that his relatives in Compiègne had given me, some of which now appear in the pages of this book. After Tabuteau's death in 1966, I stayed in touch with his relatives and accumulated many more notes and bits of history. The pages gradually began to pile up. While at first I hesitated to use the word "book," the project has now reached the point where the story must "appear for its audition" and go out into the world.

INTRODUCTION

MARCEL TABUTEAU

1 COMPIÈGNE AND THE TABUTEAU FAMILY

It was in mid-September of 1951 that I saw the French city of Compiègne for the first time. The Tabuteaus had invited me to accompany them on their drive to visit his relatives, the Létoffés. To reach Compiègne from Paris one travels slightly northeast for about an hour. The route passes through well-cultivated plains bounded by the peaceful, poplar-lined Oise River. Modern concrete-block-and-glass apartment buildings soon announce the approach to the outskirts of the town. But on arriving in the center of Compiègne, one is immediately aware of the vestiges of its rich and colorful past. The Hôtel de Ville, an imposing late Gothic edifice, still dominates the central square. Its façade boasts a flamboyant alcove that shelters a statue of Louis XII on horseback. Directly facing the famous king, *le père du peuple* (father of the people), Joan of Arc, leaning forward from the confines of her imposing bronze monument, triumphantly holds aloft an unfurled flag. The earlier church of Saint-Jacques stands nearby, only steps away from the half-timbered houses that survive from the medieval era. For centuries Compiègne was a witness to significant events in French history. At present in the *département* of Oise, in Roman days the city was known by its Latin name of Compendium after the shortcut running through the area. During the Middle Ages, drapers and cloth merchants came from Belgium, Germany, and many regions of France to the famous mid-Lent fairs. In 1430, during the Hundred Years' War between France and England, Joan of Arc was taken prisoner by the English in Compiègne. Louis XV met the fifteen-year-old Marie Antoinette in the royal château when she arrived in France in May 1770 to be married to the Dauphin, the future Louis XVI. During the period of the Revolution in 1794, sixteen nuns from Compiègne were arrested and sent to Paris, where they were condemned to death and executed by the guillotine. It was this incident that Poulenc commemorated in his opera *Les Dialogues des Carmélites.* A plaque near the entry of the elegant, recently restored Théâtre Impérial marks the tragic site of the Carmelite convent.

Tradition has it that in 1810, Napoleon I, while awaiting the arrival of his fiancée, the Austrian princess Marie-Louise, ordered a five-kilometer-long strip of the forest behind the château to be razed. According to the romantic story, he wished to please her by creating a vista resembling the one she knew at Schönbrünn in Vienna. Throughout the nineteenth century there were state visits to the château. Louis Philippe received the ambassador of the Shah of Persia in the palace. During the Second Empire in 1868 a visit by the Prince of Wales, later to become Edward VII of England, was an occasion for pomp and celebration.

By the time the railway arrived in 1847, the population of Compiègne had reached 8,895 persons. Under the reign of Louis-Napoleon III and Empress Eugénie, the court took up residence at the palace in order to be near the forest of Compiègne, long a favorite spot for the royal hunting season. Those who visit the château today can still see reflections of this brilliant period in the elegant state rooms with their silken wall coverings, brocade drapes, and fine inlaid wood furniture. The last royal visit to Compiègne took place in 1901 when Czar Nicholas II and Empress Alexandra of Russia, along with the president of the Republic of France, drove by the flag- and flower-garlanded buildings on their way to attend a grand review of troops.

During World War I Compiègne was occupied and bombarded by the Germans, and its citizens were forced to flee. It was in the forest of

Compiègne, just a few kilometers northeast of the town, that the Armistice of November 11, 1918, was signed in Marshal Foch's private railway car. Only two decades later, in 1940, again in the path of the advancing German army, the historic heart of the city suffered much destruction. On a sad day in June 1940, Hitler insisted on using the same railway coach as the site for signing the new "Armistice" between France and Germany. Finally, after the hardships of the war years, Compiègne was liberated by the Americans on September 1, 1944.

Our visit on that Sunday in 1951 took place at the home of Tabuteau's nephew, François Létoffé. I enjoyed the Létoffé hospitality of a superb luncheon, followed by a visit to the château with its memories of two Napoleons. François was the son of Marcel Tabuteau's older sister, Charlotte. Throughout the next forty years I made periodic visits to Compiègne. Each time François Létoffé shared some of his childhood memories and old photo albums with me. Thus I gradually learned something of the Tabuteau family history.

Marcel's father, François Tabuteau, born on February 3, 1851, was a Gascon from the small town of Saint-André-de-Cubzac about twenty kilometers north of Bordeaux in the *département* of Gironde. He was the eldest of six children of Étienne Tabuteau Guérineau and his wife Jeanne Landreau. Throughout his life, François would always use both names, "Tabuteau Guérineau," when signing any legal paper. Marcel Tabuteau had the two names engraved on his Premier Prix medal from the Paris Conservatory. Was it done to distinguish their family from other Tabuteaus? No one has ever given a reason, but Tabuteau once remarked that Guérineau was a "better" name.

François Tabuteau became a highly skilled clockmaker and jeweler. He had three brothers: Jean, also a clockmaker, who remained in Saint-André-de-Cubzac; André, a teacher; and Octave, a *curé* or parish priest. His two sisters were named Anna and Blanche. Anna married a M. Babin, and Blanche a M. Gautier. Of all these uncles and aunts, the only one I ever heard mentioned was the *curé*. It was in May 1955 after Tabuteau had retired and was living at his home, La Coustiéro, in the south of France. I happened to be there one day when they invited the *curé* from the nearby village of Le Brusc to come for lunch. After he left I heard Madame Tabuteau say almost jokingly, "After all, there *was* a *curé*

COMPIÈGNE AND THE TABUTEAU FAMILY

Tabuteau's father, François Tabuteau-Guérineau, as a young man in velvet jacket about 1872. Photo by A. Guillerot, Compiègne

in your family!" It was customary for good nineteenth-century French families to designate one of their members for the religious orders. Having a *curé* in the family also indicated a distinct level of education. According to François Létoffé, "*l'oncle abbé*," as the family called him, was not the most pious priest. He rode a bicycle, played the flute, kept a little mechanical train on top of his piano, and was even seen attending a theater in Bordeaux. That his musical bent was matched by inventive talents is evidenced by a letter he wrote to the famous flutist Paul Taffanel in 1899. Giving his word as a priest as recommendation, Abbé Tabuteau offered to demonstrate his invention of rubber pads for the flute by redoing and returning one of Taffanel's own instruments within eight days.[1]

Before becoming established in the profession as an independent clockmaker, François Tabuteau had to make his "*tour de France.*" In the

Octave Tabuteau (d. 1927), priest in Bordeaux. Known to the family as l'oncle abbé, *he shows a definite resemblance to his nephew Marcel.*

mid-nineteenth century the *tour de France* was far from the bicycle race known by that name today. Rather, it was a type of working trip undertaken by an artisan as one of the stages of apprenticeship in his field of expertise. He had to go from town to town with recommendations, staying in each place for several months or a year depending on the local needs. This was the way to qualify for the title *compagnon* (fellow workman; the completion of the time of service as a journeyman was known as *compagnonnage*) and was the equivalent of being accepted into a trade guild. But before receiving this title, the candidate was required to create a *chef d'oeuvre* in his chosen métier, which would then be examined by other *compagnons* in the same sphere of work. Tabuteau's father fashioned a handsome clock that was to remain an object of importance in the family for many decades.

COMPIÈGNE AND THE TABUTEAU FAMILY

Tabuteau's mother, Pauline Malaquin (1858–1945) at age nineteen or twenty.

It was while making his *tour* that François stopped in Compiègne and met Pauline Malaquin. Pauline was from the small town of Landrecy in the *département du Nord,* about a hundred kilometers from Compiègne, not far from the Belgian border. Her mother, Marie Julienne Grumiaux, born in 1837, was a *marchande de marée* (fishmonger) who married François Vital Malaquin, a tailor three years her senior. They had two daughters, Pauline Victorine, born February 28, 1858, and Aimée Julienne, born June 20, 1864. Marie Julienne had several brothers, all in working-class professions: Jules, a locksmith, and Alfred, a journeyman, born in 1849 and 1850, respectively. Another brother, Gustave, "uncle of the bride, a brewer age 42," appeared as a witness at Aimée Julienne's wedding in 1888, along with François Tabuteau, "brother-in-law of the wife."[2]

François and Pauline's wedding date has not survived in the family records, but on April 17, 1877, when he was twenty-six years old and she was nineteen, their first child, Pauline Charlotte (called Charlotte), was born. Three years later, in 1880, another daughter arrived, Esther Henriette (known as Germaine). Germaine, married at age seventeen to Camille Auxenfans, died in 1916 during World War I. The couple's little daughter, Suzanne, is seen in some early family photos.

In 1887 the handwritten records in the Compiègne city hall give the following information under entry No. 316:

> Tabuteau Guérineau, Marcel Paul
> The year 1887 on July 4 at 11 o'clock in the morning. Before us, Alphonse Désiré Chovet, mayor and *officier de l'État civil* of the city of Compiègne, Chevalier of the Legion of Honor, there appeared at the City Hall, François Tabuteau Guérineau, age 36, a clockmaker residing in Compiègne, presenting a male infant born the day before yesterday, July 2, at 7 o'clock in the evening at his home, 8 rue Magenta, to him and to Pauline Victorine Malaquin, his wife age 29 years, without profession, residing at the same address, and declaring his wish to name the baby Marcel Paul. This presentation and declaration was made in the presence of Victor Dufour, age 47, a carriage-builder, and Léopold Leseur, age 47, a wheelwright, both residing in Compiègne, who after reading the document have all signed it.

With the birth of another boy, André, on May 5, 1889, the Tabuteau family was complete. From the professions listed by the witnesses who signed the birth records of the four children, it is evident that the Tabuteau milieu consisted largely of Compiègne's manual laborers, craftsmen, and artisans. A new influence came into the Tabuteau family with the marriage of Marcel's seventeen-year-old sister Charlotte to Émile Létoffé, a well-trained violinist over twenty years her senior. Their wedding in Compiègne on September 4, 1894, was followed by a festive dinner at the Hôtel de L'Enfer.

Émile Létoffé would affect everyone in the Tabuteau family, but his impact on the life of his young brother-in-law (Marcel was only seven years old while his new relative was thirty-eight) was to be particularly strong. Létoffé had received a prize in violin in 1882 and was said to have studied with Dancla.[3] He owned several good violins, including a J. B. Vuillaume and a Nicolas Amati *aîné*. As a result of trouble with his eyes he had an operation that obliged him to give up playing for a time.

COMPIÈGNE AND THE TABUTEAU FAMILY

Marcel playing the violin; André, clarinet, and their niece Thérèse, mandolin, in 1898.

Later on he continued to teach violin in his home, always having difficulty finding the glasses he needed. He wanted everyone in the family to play a string instrument, but insisted that first they must study the solfège vocal system. His wife Charlotte played violin, their daughter Thérèse, the cello; both Marcel and his brother André studied violin. In 1896, with the formation of the Harmonie Municipale, which replaced the earlier Harmonie Jeanne d'Arc (a group of young musicians known as the Enfants de Compiègne), more wind players were needed. Marcel was drafted to play the oboe, and André, the clarinet. In the same band their father played the *grosse caisse* (bass drum). Decades later, the two brothers still remembered the time father François missed a cue from the band leader and came crashing in at the wrong moment. In the mid-1950s I heard Marcel and André tell the story. Reminiscing about their father and the *grosse caisse* still made them roar with laughter.

According to local census records for the year 1891, the Tabuteau family consisted of François, *chef* (head of family), age forty; Pauline,

MARCEL TABUTEAU

Father Tabuteau playing the bass drum in the Compiègne town band. He is standing in the middle of the main square below the statue of Louis XII on the façade of the Hôtel de Ville.

COMPIÈGNE AND THE TABUTEAU FAMILY

André and Marcel in 1956 laughing about the time their father missed a beat while playing la grosse caisse *(the bass drum). Photo by Laila Storch.*

wife, age thirty-three; daughters Charlotte, fourteen, and Germaine, eleven; and the two boys, Marcel, age four, and André, age two. When the Tabuteau family was photographed standing in front of their corner home at 8 rue Magenta, the ground floor was the Horlogerie, François' clock shop. The famous *chef d'oeuvre* clock hung in the front window. Today the same window displays the beauty products and drugstore items of the Pharmacie Saint-Jacques.

Also in 1891 the school run by the monks at the Impasse des Minimes became the communal École Pierre Sauvage, named after a benefactor of Compiègne. This primary school provided education for boys only, aged six to fourteen. For Marcel and his brother André, it was a walk of less than ten minutes from their home, around the back of the church of Saint-Jacques, to the school. In the fall of 1989, wandering alone into the church, I was surprised to hear the haunting sounds of an oboe. While observing the splendid altar and a golden statue of the Virgin Mary, I saw that Saint-Jacques himself, carved in wood and portrayed as a pilgrim on his way to Compostela, stood above the organ.

The Horlogerie (clockshop), Tabuteau's first home at 8 rue Magenta, Compiègne, in the mid-1890s. Today, the same corner building is a pharmacy. From left are François Tabuteau, Émile Léfoffé (Charlotte's husband and little Marcel's brother-in-law), Marcel, his sister Charlotte Létoffé, and on the far right, his mother, Pauline, with brother André.

COMPIÈGNE AND THE TABUTEAU FAMILY

The two brothers André and Marcel Tabuteau at about ages nine and eleven. Courtesy Claude Narcy.

Someone was playing using the double-reed stop—which explained the sound of the oboe echoing through the aisles.

By the end of the nineteenth century, Compiègne was a town of about sixteen thousand inhabitants. Daily life there for the Tabuteau family was rather uneventful but not without simple amusements and distractions. There were Sunday concerts in the park and outings on bicycle or by foot into the nearby great forest of Compiègne. The goal was often no more than having a lemonade at the inn Au Bon Accueil in Vaudrampont.[4] Sometimes it was to look for mushrooms or to go fishing in the numerous streams and pools. Deer were still plentiful in the forest. There was a spring at the hamlet near Le Vivier Frères Robert, a pond established by the monks for raising fish. Marcel's father would take a huge demijohn and go by tricycle to carry back fresh water. Another excursion point was the historic village of Saint-Jean-aux-Bois,

A Compiègne Sunday outing. From left: Émile Létoffé's cousin Albert Georges, Tabuteau's grandmother Jeanne Landreau (mother of François), Thérèse, Charlotte, Tante Berthe (wife of Jean Tabuteau). Father François is pedaling the tricycle, 1901.

which still conserved traces of its thousand-year-old abbey. A bit more excitement was offered by the annual *jour de fête de Compiègne* when the enormous bell in the belfry of the Hôtel de Ville would ring out at 8:00 a.m. to proclaim the opening of the fair. This meant there would be shooting galleries, lotteries, and a merry-go-round. (The same bell would ring briskly for a fire, but tolled slowly and repeatedly when there was a death in the town or, more ominously, when war was declared in 1914.)

During their childhood Marcel and André spent long hours at 17 rue de la Madeleine, the residence of their brother-in-law, Émile Létoffé. There, the atmosphere was less rigid than in their own home, where family life ran on the more modest scale of an artisan. They played with their niece Thérèse, who was close enough to their age to seem more like a cousin. Their older sister, Charlotte, always wore elegant dresses

COMPIÈGNE AND THE TABUTEAU FAMILY

and had her hair piled high in an elaborate coiffure. Émile would do things "for fun," such as dressing up for an amateur theatrical performance in the garden. He also experimented with photography, developing films and printing the pictures himself. Many of the family photographs that date from the early 1900s were taken by Émile in the Létoffé garden. The Létoffés and Tabuteaus also gathered for music-making in the courtyard of the home of Émile's cousin Albert Georges, who was better known by the nickname Vieux Beurre ("Old Butter"). His large and distinctive house with its hexagonal domed skylight can still be seen at 40 rue de Paris. A talented man, he had studied fine arts, made excellent drawings, and played the mandolin. But he was something of a busybody who worked his way into every family photograph and managed to annoy various family members. Marcel and André were expected to come to dinner on Thursdays, where they were criticized for their restlessness. They hated sitting on the delicate chairs and wanted to leave as soon as possible.

When Marcel showed a special talent for the oboe, it was Émile Létoffé who could be helpful, perhaps even making the first contact with the famous oboe professor Georges Gillet. Tabuteau told an interesting story in 1959, when he was interviewed by members of the Philadelphia Woodwind Quintet on their series for public television, *200 Years of Woodwinds*. He mentioned that as a young boy he was first oboist of the Harmonie, which he described as "a little band in Compiègne," whose bandmaster was a nephew of Jules Massenet. "I had the opportunity to meet *Cavalier* Massenet," and the great composer then "advised his nephew that I should be sent to the Conservatoire in Paris."

In July 1898, around the time of Marcel's eleventh birthday, there was some excitement for the inhabitants of Compiègne. The local paper recorded that "on Tuesday night towards 9:30 to the northwest of Compiègne, one could clearly see a magnificent comet in the sky a little below the Big Dipper. With its very intense and luminous white tail, it seemed to be falling straight down, but its path went away from the observers and after passing behind a ribbon of clouds, the celestial projectile appeared on the horizon and burst into a magnificent ball of fire." Later in his life while teaching or speaking of movement in music, Tabuteau would often refer to the stars in the heavens. Whether or not

Looking out the window at 40 rue de Paris, Compiègne, the home of Émile's artist cousin, Albert Georges. From left: Unknown woman, Tabuteau, Thérèse, Charlotte, Albert Georges standing.

he saw this particular comet, the night skies above Compiègne in those days must have been clear and easy to observe.

Archery was a popular pastime in Compiègne, and there were occasional huge tournaments. The greatest enthusiasm of the populace, however, was reserved for military parades and especially those of the colorful and courageous dragoons. In one old postcard image, members of the Fifth Regiment of Dragoons are shown trotting smartly down the avenue on horseback while playing a fanfare on their trumpets. One can imagine the young boys' excitement on seeing the "handsome dragoons of Compiègne, pressed into their sky-blue jackets fastened by loops and frogs over highly arched breast-plates, their smart mustaches and their elegant helmets each crowned by a horse-tail flying in the breeze."[5] Learning about the dashing dragoons helped me to understand that during my studies, when Tabuteau had called me a "dragon," he was referring not to a fire-breathing mythical beast, but rather to a dragoon—it was not the insult I had imagined.

COMPIÈGNE AND THE TABUTEAU FAMILY

During one of my visits to Compiègne after Tabuteau's death, his nephew François pointed out places of importance in their family history. We drove through the forest of Compiègne, where he was reminded of the story about the mushrooms that he had heard from his uncle Marcel. *Père* Tabuteau had found a spot where especially good mushrooms were growing. Marcel told cousin Vieux Beurre about it, which made his father very angry. He scolded his son and gave him a slap for giving away the "secret." "So you've gone and told the Vieux Beurre where I found the mushrooms—and now he'll be coming here to get them himself!" If Tabuteau's father was a strict disciplinarian in the manner of nineteenth-century parents, he was nevertheless very supportive when his son needed help with items required for his oboe study. He used his watchmaking skills to make reed shapers and many of the other tools necessary for preparing oboe cane.

Marcel maintained close ties with his family after his departure for the United States in 1905. On two return trips to France he spent time in the army, first in 1906–7 to comply with compulsory French military service and then again in 1914 at the beginning of World War I. Slightly differing versions were handed down in the family about what happened at that time. One had Tabuteau's father writing his son a letter saying, *"Ton pays t'appelle!"* (Your country calls you). In the other version, the father sent a telegram saying, "Come back, war has been declared!" After his return to France in 1914, Tabuteau served in the army for a short time but was released when he failed a medical examination. These two periods of French military service were to cause trouble for Tabuteau soon after the beginning of his musical career in America.

Following the declaration of war and the German advances in 1914, some members of the Tabuteau family were forced to leave Compiègne as refugees. With Charlotte's daughter Thérèse, by then a young woman of nineteen, driving the car, they made the 640-kilometer trip south to the ancestral home at Saint-André-de-Cubzac. After a month or two they found a place to live in Bordeaux and stayed there until the end of the war. On returning to Compiègne, they were unable to have their former rented home back again. In 1920 Émile Létoffé located a little row house in the Rue de Clamart that he was happy to be able to buy. It became home to Émile and Charlotte, as well as to Marcel's

Tabuteau's father preparing oboe cane with tools he made for Marcel. Charlotte and her daughter, Thérèse, are looking on.

father and mother, for the rest of their lives. François Létoffé would live in the same Rue de Clamart house for seventy years.

Marcel Tabuteau's family, his childhood impressions, and his early musical training were all associated with Compiègne; during the initial years of his American career, he returned to Compiègne each summer. Coming into town by train, the first thing he saw at the railway station was the name "Tabuteau" on a piece of his father's craftsmanship. It was the large clock that stood next to the corridor where the passengers descended from the platform.[6] I once heard Tabuteau say that the elegant ancient châteaux of France held little interest for him. This was difficult for me to understand. But much later, after visiting Tabuteau's hometown, I recalled his muttering that he had "seen enough old stones growing up alongside the Château of Compiègne."

By the 1930s Tabuteau's summer visits to Compiègne were becoming more of a quick dash from Paris to visit his mother and the other relatives. The day spent at home was always the occasion for an elaborate and festive meal. Good food played an important role in their lives, and no effort was spared to prepare special treats for Marcel. One time

COMPIÈGNE AND THE TABUTEAU FAMILY

Louise André Tabuteau and Marcel in Compiègne to visit his mother, Pauline. Late 1930s.

he tasted some wine the family had bottled from a big jug they brought from Dijon. He promptly declared, "You must save this wine for me— I am the one who will drink it!" Not surprisingly, they would all go to sleep after so much eating, but Tabuteau would wake up refreshed and ask, "Shall we go for a drive in the beautiful forest? Are there still mushrooms? Any snails? You must fix some for my next visit."[7] *Père* Tabuteau took this request to heart, and before Marcel visited again, he traversed the forest in all directions looking for the precious delicacies. Finally he found about five hundred escargots which he prepared himself *à la Bordelaise*—that is, in his own southern French home style. Tabuteau ate five dozen or more, the number increasing throughout the years with various retellings of the story. François remembered Tabuteau as *"un personnage."* "There was no one like him. To us with his hat and cigarette, he was *'le type Américain.'*" In America, he was, of course, seen as a typical Frenchman.

Both Émile Létoffé and Tabuteau's father died during the 1930s. In June 1936 Tabuteau had just arrived in Paris and was staying at the Hôtel Louvois in Paris when he received an urgent telephone call from his nephew. He was able to reach Compiègne and see his father once more

Mme Tabuteau and M. Tabuteau enjoy a lunch in Compiègne at the home of their nephew, François Létoffé (Charlotte's son), and his wife Hélène, in the 1950s. Courtesy Anne Claude Narcy.

before he passed away at the age of eighty-five. During World War II, the remaining relatives were again evacuated. François' wife, Hélène, took Tabuteau's mother, Pauline, and his sister, Charlotte, to Molineuf (near Blois), where they stayed with Tabuteau's sister-in-law, Denise Budin. François, serving in the French army, was taken prisoner during the early days of the war and did not return home until 1945. Tabuteau used to call him "*le guerrier*" (the warrior) and told Madame Tabuteau to "do what you can for *le guerrier*." She sent many packages from a special section of Gimbel's department store in Philadelphia, which had been set up for mailings to soldiers. Although only a few of the boxes got through to him, he never forgot the coffee, cigarettes, and even a cowboy shirt that came from "Tante Chocolat" (Madame Tabuteau's nickname because of her love of chocolate). In looking back, I realize that in the 1940s, when I was a student in Philadelphia, I had no real comprehension of what it meant to the Tabuteaus not to see any of

COMPIÈGNE AND THE TABUTEAU FAMILY

their family for so many years. World War II dragged on and on. I remember hearing the sadness in Tabuteau's voice when one day he said that his mother had died before he could visit her again. It was in November 1945, and although the war had officially ended, travel from America to France was still impossible.

Several years after the end of World War II, François Létoffé saw the famous family clock sitting in a local shop window. At some point it had been sold, and now, so much later, François managed to buy it back. He took it to La Coustiéro, where Tabuteau was then living, and told his uncle that he had a surprise for him—something from his childhood. "Where did you get it?" exclaimed Tabuteau delightedly, and immediately hung the clock on the wall. After Tabuteau's death it was returned to his nephew's home in Compiègne, and there it remained for the rest of François' life.

2 PARIS CONSERVATOIRE

Tabuteau's Studies with Georges Gillet,
1902–1904

It is impossible to write about Marcel Tabuteau without considering the degree to which he was influenced by his own teacher, Georges Gillet (1854–1920). Until the end of his life Tabuteau spoke of what a great man Gillet was and gave him credit for everything he himself knew about music and the oboe. On many occasions he said that "Gillet was the greatest musician I have ever known." He continued to think of the things Gillet had told him to observe, such as the rebound of a ball after it was bounced on the ground, or the point where fireworks burst and turn before coming back down to earth. Another was the way each phalange or joint of a finger is linked to the hand, the hand to the wrist, going on to the elbow and finally forming the arm—the whole becoming one unit, but within this unit each individual section having its own importance. Using these ideas as a springboard, Tabuteau developed his concepts of motion, line, and inflection in the phrasing of music. In the mid-1940s Tabuteau said, "After thirty years there is not a day that I don't think fifty times of what my teacher told me. Only now I really profit from what he advised—to get a little rubber ball—to be phrased music must respond to the fundamental laws of nature—it must be scaled and rebound, less and less, like the ball does." The single most admired aspect of Tabuteau's playing was always his phrasing; it was on a level not ordinarily encountered in the era when simply a pleasant sound and adequate finger facility were sufficient to secure an oboist's career. Whatever work Tabuteau played, one had the feeling of hearing its essence distilled into three or four measures of the oboe line. His complete control of the wind, which he used to express every nuance, was based on his lifelong dedication to the principles first pointed out to him by Georges Gillet. When Tabuteau retired and returned to France, he arranged for a plaque to be placed on Gillet's grave in the Cimetière Montmartre in Paris with the inscription "Au grand maître Georges Gillet 1854–1920, ses admirateurs" (To the great teacher Georges Gillet, 1854–1920, from his admirers).[1] From those who came to study with Tabuteau in the last decade of his life, we know that he was still thinking and speaking about the inspiration he had found in Gillet's observations.

By the time young Tabuteau began to play the oboe in Compiègne, Georges Gillet had been a professor at the Paris Conservatoire for almost twenty years. He was acclaimed as a brilliant soloist, and his reputation as a chamber music player had been well established through his participation in Paul Taffanel's Société de Musique de Chambre pour Instruments à Vent during the entire fifteen seasons (1879–93) of its existence.[2] In 1887 Gillet made what was for that time a historic tour to St. Petersburg with flutist Taffanel, clarinetist Charles-Paul Turban, and Camille Saint-Saëns. Woodwind players were not often heard in solo roles, so it was a distinct tribute to these French artists that Saint-Saëns composed the *Caprice sur des Airs Russes et Danois* for flute, oboe, and clarinet for them and played the brilliant piano part himself.

Many works performed during the Société's years under Taffanel's leadership were to become part of the standard woodwind repertoire. The two Mozart *Serenades for Wind Octet,* the Beethoven *Octet*, Opus 103, the Mozart and Beethoven quintets with piano, and Mozart's *Serenade for Thirteen Winds* were all played frequently. The Société's second season (1880) opened with the *Serenade*, Opus 44, by Dvořák. Two of Mozart's principal compositions for oboe were listed as *premières*

MARCEL TABUTEAU

auditions, presumably for France: on March 29, 1888, the F Major *Oboe Quartet* and on February 21, 1889, the *Symphonie Concertante* for solo winds and orchestra, written more than one hundred years earlier for Paris musicians but never performed there. Gillet played in every solo and chamber work of the six concerts given every season. Only once, in March 1889, on a rare occasion when each piece on the program required oboe, did someone else play a first oboe part.[3]

A number of significant premières took place during the 1880s. In 1883 Richard Strauss's *Serenade for Thirteen Winds,* Opus 7, was given shortly after its composition; in 1884 came the first performance of the Bernard *Divertissement;* and on April 30, 1885, Gounod's *Petite Symphonie* was played while it was still in manuscript. Surely Gounod had Taffanel himself in mind when he wrote the expressive, flowing solo for flute in the *Andante cantabile* movement. The Paris première of the Thuille *Sextuor* took place on March 20, 1890, the same day that Gillet gave the first performance of the three pieces he had arranged from Bach flute sonatas. Other novelties of the 1890 season were Mozart's *Adagio and Rondo for Glass Harmonica* and the *Trio,* Opus 61, for piano, oboe, and horn by Brahms's friend Heinrich von Herzogenberg. Certainly all oboists would love to have heard the Beethoven *C Major Trio,* Opus 87, played in February 1891 by Gillet and his two recent Premier Prix students, Georges Longy and Louis Bas.

In his orchestral position as solo oboist with the Société des Concerts du Conservatoire, Gillet played all the major symphonic works beginning with Haydn and Mozart and continuing to late nineteenth-century masters such as Franck and Wagner. In the mid-1890s he played in the first performance in France of Schubert's great *C Major Symphony.* He experienced audience whistles and cries of "*Chut!*" (Hush up) directed against Brahms's *Second Symphony.* He took part in path-breaking performances of Bach's music, and from 1895 until 1904 he was solo oboe at the Paris Opéra. Louis Bleuzet, a student of Gillet's who followed him as professor at the Conservatoire, had the highest praise for his teacher. It was during Gillet's long tenure at the Conservatoire (1881–1919) that the distinguished sound and style of French oboe playing was firmly established. Bleuzet wrote the following about Gillet: "One can say without question that M. Gillet is the most

— 23 —
PARIS CONSERVATOIRE

extraordinary virtuoso of the oboe who has ever lived. The delightful quality of his sound had a finesse and a clarity which at the same time did not exclude power. With all that, he had a 'perfect *mécanisme*' [technique] and a prodigious facility of articulation."[4] One had only to hear Gillet play in an orchestra to be aware of his outstanding artistry. "Monsieur Gillet not only gave the oboe this beautiful and powerful sonority which is actually the characteristic of the French oboe, he also gave his instrument a great treasure in resurrecting the great classic masters. He took the lead to set the example and play in a superior manner the sonatas and concertos of Handel and even movements of the sonatas for flute, or violin and piano of Bach, the Quartet by Mozart, and the Trio of Beethoven. And he has succeeded in giving to France this constellation of oboists who are admired by every foreign guest conductor who comes to direct the French symphony orchestras."

During the greater part of the nineteenth century, the favored solo material for the oboe consisted of pieces the professors composed for the *concours* examinations and works featuring variations on melodies from famous operas. The great composers of the baroque and classical eras had lost their popularity and disappeared from the repertoire. So Gillet, in his way, was doing for the oboe what Ysaÿe accomplished for the violin and Casals for the cello, when they rediscovered the music of Bach. Gillet played the extensive oboe solos in Bach's *Cantata No. 21, Ich hätte viel Bekümmernis,* and when after long neglect the oboe d'amore was again fabricated, he used this instrument according to Bach's wishes in the *B Minor Mass.* The Handel *G Minor Concerto* was the oboe solo Gillet performed most frequently. As late in his playing career as March 1899, it was included on the regular series of the Société des Concerts du Conservatoire. Tabuteau probably never had the opportunity to hear Gillet play the Handel *Concerto,* but he followed his teacher's example; beginning with his first season in the Philadelphia Orchestra, Tabuteau gave more performances of this concerto than of any other solo work for oboe.

With the plethora of music from the Baroque period now available to us, it is difficult to realize that one hundred years ago this was not the case. Thus, Bleuzet saw Gillet's championship of Handel and Bach as deserving of special recognition. In my own student days in the 1930s

MARCEL TABUTEAU

and 1940s, the Handel sonatas were almost the only baroque oboe pieces to be found in print, and they were played with piano; at that time a harpsichord was still an exotic rarity. When Tabuteau suggested that I study the Bach sonatas for violin and piano, he was following the advice of Georges Gillet. Gillet, however, was not only interested in bringing back the music of the past. He was also looking to the future. In writing the *Studies for the Advanced Teaching of the Oboe* (1909), he recognized the greatly expanded range of difficulties facing future generations of oboists. The new French composers were pushing the capacities of woodwind players into untried areas. Gillet's twenty-five *Studies*, his lasting contribution to the teaching literature, remain as essential today as when they were first published.

Gillet became oboe professor at the Conservatoire in 1881. For the first few years he continued to use the traditional solos by former professors, especially Gustave Vogt and Charles Colin, for the annual *concours*. Soon, however, he began to invite contemporary composers to contribute new works, many of which are still played today. Numerous compositions, both *concours* solos and others, were dedicated to Gillet by Guilhaud, Colomer, Dallier, Godard, Ropartz, Barthe, and Lefebvre. Even Apollon Marie-Rose Barret (1804–79), of the famous oboe method, dedicated a solo piece to young Gillet. After retiring from his position at the Italian Opera in London in 1874, Barret returned to spend the last years of his life in Paris.[5] He probably heard Gillet play in the Théâtre Italien or with the Société des Concerts du Conservatoire and in 1877 dedicated *O! Ma Tendre Musette* to him. Another work dedicated to Gillet was the *Concerto in D Minor* by the Comtesse de Grandval. Gillet played it many times with either piano or orchestra, and at least one of his students, Alfred Barthel, performed the de Grandval piece after he came to America to be solo oboist of the Chicago Symphony Orchestra.

Already by the early 1900s, Gillet's students were becoming successful both in France and in the United States. Georges Longy had joined the Boston Symphony Orchestra in 1898, and Alfred Barthel went to Chicago in 1903. In France, Louis Bas, Charles Gaudard, Louis Bleuzet, Fernand Gillet (Georges' nephew), and Maurice Mercier had their careers well under way. In 1976, more than fifty years after Gillet's

PARIS CONSERVATOIRE

death, the few of his remaining students I was able to find all spoke of him with the greatest respect and admiration. If his aloof and uncompromising manner inspired awe rather than affection, he nevertheless had more concern for his students' welfare than they realized. He tried, for example, to keep in touch with those who served at the front in World War I. I still remember the impression it made on me when I heard Tabuteau read a letter he had received from Gillet over twenty-five years earlier, in 1918. Tabuteau had apparently written to Gillet about his fear of playing a solo with the Philadelphia Orchestra, and Gillet had replied with advice and encouragement. Tabuteau then spoke of what a great artist Gillet was, which prompted me to write in my notebook, "He really worships that man."

It is thanks to the Paris Conservatoire's careful preservation of its records that we have information about Marcel Tabuteau's progress during the period of his studies. These archives, which include the professors' written reports and the published accounts of the *concours*, also enable us to assess where he stood in comparison to other oboists in his class. Tabuteau's name first appears in Conservatoire records on November 14, 1900, when, at the age of thirteen years and three months, he was the youngest of twelve students auditioning for the class of Georges Gillet. (The exact age of each applicant was listed in years and months as of October first.) Again a year later, on November 7, 1901, Tabuteau played in the *concours pour l'admission* (competitive examination for admittance). Two boys who would eventually be his classmates, Gaston Longatte and Jules Pontier, also tried out both times.[6]

Sol Schoenbach once heard from Tabuteau himself about his early attempts to enter the Conservatoire.[7] In 1996 Schoenbach recounted, "Tabuteau always told me that when he came to try out for the Conservatory the judges *laughed* and *laughed* amongst themselves because of this ridiculous kid playing the oboe—they made so much fun of him." I asked Sol if he knew the reason for such treatment, and he said, "Well, he was so young, about eleven or twelve years old (actually thirteen) and he was from the north—Compiègne.[8] He was practically in tears, you see, and then the great teacher, Gillet, came over to him and said, 'Young man, I will teach you, and if you cannot be at the Conservatory, I will give you lessons. You just come on.'" I expressed my surprise at

MARCEL TABUTEAU

this account, which I had never heard before, and Sol continued, "Yes, Tabuteau told me the whole story and said, 'Imagine those people just laughing at me like I was a clown or some kind of freak.'" But clearly Gillet saw the promise in this young lad, even if some others did not.

So for two years before his official acceptance into the Conservatoire, Tabuteau traveled back and forth from Compiègne to Paris for his lessons with Gillet. The train passed by the famous racetrack at Chantilly. As a very young and impressionable boy, Tabuteau would overhear the jockeys on the train talking about "fixing the races." He later said this was how he had learned the world was dishonest and that it was his fellow passengers on those same trips who taught him to gamble.[9] Both the oboe and gambling were to remain his lifelong passions.

After this period of private study with Gillet, in November 1902 Tabuteau played for the third time in the examination for the *aspirants aux classes d'instruments à vent* (those aspiring to enter the wind instrument classes). His age was now noted as fifteen years and three months. The Conservatoire records state that he was admitted to the class of Georges Gillet on November 13, 1902.[10] There were seven competitors for one available place in the oboe class. Four of the auditioners played solos by Colin, and one played the Guilhaud *Concertino*. Tabuteau and Gaston Longatte both played the *Solo* by Émile Paladilhe which had been the required piece for the annual *concours* only four years previously. Written comments by the jury for Tabuteau were "*bon son*" (good tone), while Gaston Longatte, the other Paladilhe performer, was rated "*moins bien que Tabuteau*" (not as good as Tabuteau).

The competitors ranged in age from thirteen to seventeen, which placed Tabuteau, at fifteen, exactly in the middle. Most of the students in the class he now entered were considerably older and had already spent an average of three years at the Conservatoire. One young man, age twenty-two, had been there for five years. It is in this light that one must consider the notes written by Gillet following the first examination Tabuteau was required to play at the end of January 1903, less than three months after he entered the Conservatoire. At the age of fifteen and a half he was competing with oboe students who were eighteen to twenty-two years old. Each exam was heard by a committee that included professors of other instruments. Some of them, such as Gillet's colleague the clarinetist Turban, made harsher judgments than the major teacher. Other Conservatoire professors wrote lengthy and flowery comments about their own pupils. The pianist Louis Diémer, writing in thick blue pencil, praised almost all of his students in great detail. When Adolphe Sax taught at the Conservatoire, he simply drew a bracket around his list of saxophone students and made the single comment, "They all did very well."

This was not Gillet's way. In his elegant handwriting, so fine as to resemble etching, Gillet wrote very succinct and terse assessments. His remarks were varied, but always astute, concise, and to the point. Comments on his students who played in this exam (Tabuteau's first at the Conservatoire) included "bad pupil, bad musician"; "bad embouchure that may change but will never be correct, had a poor start"; "continues to make perceptible progress"; and simply "progressing." There was a "lazy student." Another was "impossible, has not accomplished a thing the whole year." One pupil was called a "fair student." Out of the ten there was a single unqualified "*bon élève*" (good student). But Tabuteau, after only a few months at the Conservatoire, received the following words from Gillet for his performance of the *Adagio* and *Finale* of Gustave Vogt's *Fourth Concertino*: "*Élève d'avenir—a un temperament artistique*" (student with a future—has an artistic temperament). For no other boy in the class is there mention of these key words—*future, artistic, temperament.* Compared to what was said of the much older students, it is a glowing endorsement, and we can only conclude that the qualities that would characterize Tabuteau's future musical accomplishments were already clearly in evidence.

Gillet's oboe class was held three times every week for two hours, on Tuesday, Thursday, and Saturday. The students were required to be there for the entire period of each session to benefit from listening to the others play and from hearing Gillet's suggestions. Attendance records were scrupulously kept, and thus we know that Tabuteau missed only one class in his two years at the Conservatoire. On June 22, 1903, at the end of his first school year, there were more examinations, and the students played other pieces from the oboe repertoire of the day. Tabuteau performed the *Allegro moderato* movement from one of Gillet's favored works, the *Concerto* by Comtesse de Grandval. Of the nine students

MARCEL TABUTEAU

Marcel Tabuteau at age sixteen in 1903.

who played this time, Tabuteau was the only one to be singled out by Gillet as a "very good student." The brief comments on the others were "studious," "mediocre," or "progressing," with a couple of "good students." Again, it is the sparseness of his praise that lends significance to the adjective *very*. Tabuteau also received favorable marks from other members of the 1903 examining committee: "great promise," "has verve in his execution," "good sight-reading." In July 1903 Tabuteau, the youngest student in the class, was allowed to take part in the prestigious annual *concours*.[11] The required piece was the *Fantaisie-caprice* by Dallier. Tabuteau did not gain any award in this *concours*, but twenty-two-year-old Maurice-Constant Mercier received a first prize and Jean-Arnaud-Marcel Balout, age nineteen, a second prize.[12]

By the time of the midyear exams in January 1904, Gillet gave most of the students slightly more favorable ratings, such as "very conscientious student," "accomplished student," "progressing," or "has made real progress." But again in a few words, Gillet made an extraordinary statement not seen in his other evaluations. Of Tabuteau's performance of the *Pièce en si bémol* by Busser, Gillet wrote, "*Nature exceptionelle d'hautboiste; très bon élève*" (exceptionally gifted nature for the oboe; very good student). It is interesting to compare these words with notes Gillet made some twenty years earlier about one of his most famous students, Georges Longy. Although at first expressing reservations about his sound and sight-reading and complimenting him only on "exactitude and conscientiousness," Gillet eventually credits Longy with great improvement in tone quality and ranks him as a "student with a future." This prediction came true even if Gillet's observations were generally more reserved than those he made about Tabuteau at the same age.

Most of the students in Tabuteau's class were also enrolled in the solfège courses at the Conservatoire. They were graded as stringently in this subject as for their major instrument. As there is no sign of Tabuteau's name in any of the solfège examination records, it is probable that the thorough drilling he had received from his violinist brother-in-law in this subject enabled him to be exempted from the class work. Considering that the wind players would be making their living by playing in orchestras, there was surprisingly little training for this profession at the Conservatoire. However, during the years of Tabuteau's studies, Paul Taffanel conducted the student orchestra, so the musical approach is sure to have been on a high level. One more exam remained before the *concours* of 1904. On June 21 the same ten students who had played in January again performed their Colin, Handel, Guilhaud, and Vogt solos. Tabuteau played the *Fantaisie* by Colin. Again they were ranked by Gillet as "studious," "conscientious," "making progress," "satisfactory," or "continues to make progress." Only Tabuteau was rated "*très bon élève*" (very good student).

The annual *concours* of the Paris Conservatoire, which took place in the middle of each summer, was an event avidly followed by the public and a source of national pride to the highest government authorities. It attracted an amount of attention that is today bestowed only on major competitions. For a modest fee the public could attend the performances, a custom that has continued to the present. The names of those "admitted" to participate were published beforehand in music magazines

MARCEL TABUTEAU

along with the pieces to be performed. Afterward, the results were reviewed in the newspapers with critiques of the participants. On June 30 the name of Marcel Tabuteau appeared in *Le Monde Musical* as one of the competitors to appear in the 1904 oboe *concours*.

To envision the Conservatoire National de Musique as it appeared when Tabuteau was a student, one must peel back two layers of its existence in Paris, pass over the sparkling modern buildings at the Cité de la Musique, move to the more somber halls of the rue de Madrid, home of the Conservatoire beginning in 1911, and return to the ninth *arrondissement,* corner of rue Bergère and rue du Conservatoire. Here, alongside the rue du Faubourg-Poissonnière, stands the edifice which during almost all of the nineteenth century and into the early years of the twentieth saw one of the greatest concentrations of musical accomplishment on the European continent. The elegant small concert hall, despite several modifications, retains the general proportions and aspect from the period of its construction in 1811 to plans of the architect, Delannoy. The entrance hall has scarcely changed since its 1865 redecoration in the Pompeian style popular at that time. One can still admire the three tiers of narrow balconies that encircle the main body of the *salle,* their façades painted in soft shades of green, blue, and ocher. Portraits of famous composers and classical playwrights alternate with Grecian lyres surrounded by stars, fantasies of swirling flowers, and formal abstract patterns. This is the hall where in the 1820s Habenek conducted the orchestra of the Société des Concerts du Conservatoire in the first performances of Beethoven's symphonies in France.[13] Chopin, Liszt, Berlioz, Sarasate, Saint-Saëns, and Clara Schumann were only a few of the great artists who played here. The students entering through the imposing columns of the dignified foyer shared a sense of their exalted lineage and the obligation to uphold the lofty traditions of the Conservatoire.

Long after the Conservatoire moved to its second home in the rue de Madrid, the yearly *concours* continued to be held in the historic hall of the Faubourg Poissonnière. On my first visit to Paris in the summer of 1948, I listened from the cramped upper balcony while seventeen violinists, one after the other, played their *concours* solo, Lalo's *Symphonie Espagnole.* I experienced the atmosphere and feeling of intimacy of the old Conservatoire as described by one of the professors who taught there for sixty years: "With its narrow corridors and stairways, its small rooms, ancient walls and courtyard, it did not have the vast appearance of the new conservatory, rue de Madrid, where everything is large, grand, spacious, stately, but of a cold and glacial atmosphere, without any charm for the eyes. At the Faubourg Poissonnière, life was more familial and there was a feeling of togetherness; one touched elbows."[14] On *concours* days there were the nervous students, the mothers, and the tension-filled air while waiting for the votes. The jury sat in the Imperial Box at the center of the rear of the auditorium and deliberated the results in the former private salon of Napoleon III.

Today the old Conservatoire, rue Bergère, houses only the section of dramatic arts, but in July 1904 all attention was centered on the young musicians who were taking part in the *concours* and the professors who would be judging them. Some *concours* were held *à huit clos* (behind closed doors) in the Petite Salle, but the 1904 *concours* for winds (flute, oboe, clarinet, bassoon) was announced as an event to be held *en public Grande Salle—à midi* (open to the public in the large theater—at noon).[15] The music review *Le Ménestrel* singled out Thursday, July 28, as a "day of exceptional brilliance."[16] The jury for woodwind instruments was headed by the director of the Conservatoire, Théodore Dubois, with a representation of professors from other disciplines: the clarinetist Mimart; Louis Bas, already a well-known oboist; the flutist Lafleurance; Georges Pfeiffer from composition; and the eminent piano professor and indefatigable member of the Société de Musique de Chambre pour Instruments à Vent, Louis Diémer. Diémer's composition, *Légende,* was to be the *solo de concours* for this year. He had also written a short *Moderato* for oboe and piano to serve as the obligatory sight-reading test. While not at all a "flashy" piece, it contains enough alternating triplets, syncopations, and eighth notes, along with ritardandos, changes of dynamics, and accidentals to challenge anyone's accuracy of interpretation on sight.

One way in which Tabuteau prepared for this crucial test was to begin buying reeds at the beginning of the year and putting aside the very good ones. The Lorée oboe was the "official" instrument used at the Paris Conservatoire; all the students were expected to play Lorée

MARCEL TABUTEAU

oboes and also to buy reeds that Gillet made and sold at the Lorée shop. By stocking up well in advance, Tabuteau made sure to have the best reed possible in time for the *concours*. It evidently served him well.[17]

Eight oboists took part in the 1904 *concours*, of whom six had already played in earlier years and had received honorable mentions or, in the case of Jean-Arnaud-Marcel Balout, a second prize. Tabuteau was the eighth and final contestant. Half of the competitors were over twenty years of age; Tabuteau, who had just turned seventeen on July 2, was the youngest. The critics were generous in their praise: "Last year M. Tabuteau did not even place in the *concours;* this year only a First Prize could reward the excellent intonation, the nuance and perfect sonority that were demonstrated in his playing. His artistic and beautifully felt performance earned him a great and well-deserved success. Next to him the other contestants paled a little, except for M. Balout who knows how to bring forth the best of the oboe. We should nevertheless mention M. Henri, who was without doubt nervous and did not do his best in the beginning, but improved, to end with an excellent performance, and M. Pontier, who was able to show some feeling." Both Henri and Pontier were awarded a second prize. This was the normal path most students had to follow: through a second accessit (certificate of merit), then a first accessit, to the second prize, before finally arriving at the ardently coveted highest award of Premier Prix. The jury at the Paris Conservatoire voted by a secret ballot using small, billiard-type black and white balls. Their decision was unanimous: After only two years at the Conservatoire, Marcel Tabuteau, skipping all the lower levels, had jumped directly to the first prize. In total, six out of the eight competitors received official recognition.

The first prize consisted of an impressively large and heavy silver medal inscribed on one side, "Mr. TABUTEAU-GUERINEAU 1er PRIX DE HAUTBOIS 1904," encircled by the words "Conservatoire National de Musique et de Declamation." On the reverse two mythic-looking female figures draped in flowing Grecian-style garments represented the arts of music and drama. Except for its inclusion at the 1979 Tabuteau Day exhibit at the Curtis Institute in Philadelphia, this medal always remained with the descendants of Tabuteau's Létoffé relatives in

PARIS CONSERVATOIRE

Compiègne. Since the death of Tabuteau's nephew François in 1995, it resides in Nantes with Nicole Baumier, granddaughter of Tabuteau's older sister, Charlotte. Nicole's son, Guy Baumier, an oboist and conductor in the town of Paimboeuf near Nantes, along with his sisters, continues the musical traditions established so long ago by the Létoffé family.

I often heard Tabuteau play sections of the Paladilhe *Solo de Concours* from the year 1898, but never a note of the Diémer. Nor did he ever mention the piece with which he earned his Premier Prix. Why, one can only guess. When I eventually "discovered" this little-known *concours* solo, I found it to be an unusual and fascinating work, and one that I felt it would be appropriate to play in 1979 on one of the "Tabuteau Day" celebration concerts.

There were other outstanding performers in the 1904 *concours*. The obligatory piece for flute was *Cantabile et Scherzo* by the *jeune maître* (young master) Georges Enesco. Two first-prize winners who would later become known in the United States were the clarinetist Gaston Hamelin, who joined the Boston Symphony Orchestra, and the bassoonist Louis Letellier, later of the New York Philharmonic. Another young student who received lavish praise from the critic A. Mangeot in *Le Ménestrel* was Mlle Nadia Boulanger. She was awarded first prizes in organ, piano accompaniment, and fugue. In the previous year, before reaching the age of sixteen, she had already won a first prize in composition. M. Mangeot expressed the opinion that the Conservatoire had never had such a brilliant student and predicted that "Mlle Boulanger is certainly destined for a great future."

Another important event took place on the day that Tabuteau won his Premier Prix. His teacher, Georges Gillet, was awarded the Cross of the Legion of Honor, presented by M. Chaumié, the minister of Public Instruction and Fine Arts.

For Tabuteau in July 1904, with the achievement of his Premier Prix, the equivalent of graduation, formal schooling came to an end. What did he do until he left for the United States in May 1905? According to a biographical sketch that appeared in April 1954 in *Arpeggio*, a publication of the Philadelphia Musicians' Union, Marcel Tabuteau "landed his first professional job at *Les Variétés* in 1904." I found this sole reference

Georges Gillet visits Compiègne, probably in 1904. Seated from left: Gillet, Charlotte, Émile Létoffé. Standing: Mme Gillet, Tabuteau's father, and brother André.

to a musical engagement in Paris intriguing but puzzling. Unexpectedly, I stumbled on a clue in Henry James's *Parisian Sketches,* which consists of a series of letters written for the *New York Tribune* in 1876. Reporting on current life in Paris, James calls the Variétés "that dreary, flimsy burlesque of the events of the year, which is the pretext for so many bad jokes and undressed *figurantes.*" This did not sound musically very promising. However, a footnote giving the address of the theater as 7 Boulevard Montmartre seemed a clue worth following, and in May 1998 it led me to Les Variétés. Sandwiched between the busy restaurants of the crowded boulevard, it could be easily overlooked if not for the nearby historical plaque. Only on closer observation is one's attention drawn to the façade with its double row of Grecian-style columns. In order to see the interior, I bought a ticket for a play by Sacha Guitry; through the program booklet I learned that Les Variétés had been the site of far more significant theatrical events both before and after the period of Henry James's reports.

The theater was founded in 1807, and its first few decades were dedicated to plays by well-known writers, such as Scribe, Dumas, de Musset, and Sand. The première of Murger's *La Vie de Bohème* (which later became the model for Puccini's popular opera) took place at this theater in 1849, but its greatest glory came in the 1860s with the operettas of Jacques Offenbach: *La Belle Hélène, La Grande Duchesse de Gérolstein,* and *La Périchole.* Sarah Bernhardt rented the Variétés during the Exposition of 1889 and performed there in *La Dame aux Camélias,* one of her most famous roles. The beginning of the twentieth century at the Variétés was again largely devoted to operetta. In the Collection Rondel at the Bibliothèque de l'Arsenal in Paris, among the few surviving full-season sets of programs for the Théâtre des Variétés, is that of 1904–5, exactly when Tabuteau would have been there. In April 1904 there was a production of Johann Strauss's *La Chauve-Souris (Die Fledermaus).* Beginning in November, however, the repertoire featured French operettas by composers Messager, Lecocq, and Offenbach, and the lesser-known Lacome, Vasseur, and Planquette, including *La Fille de Madame Angot, Les Cent Vierges,* and *Le Petit Duc* of Lecocq; *Monsieur de la Palisse* by Claude Terrasse; *Barbe-Bleu* in three acts and four tableaux by Offenbach with text by Meilhac and Halévy, and *La Jolie Parfumeuse,* also by Offenbach. Whether or not Tabuteau was already there for *Die Fledermaus,* it is tempting to think that he may have first played this music in the red plush and brocaded jewel-box elegance of the Théâtre des Variétés. I remember the enthusiasm with which he once coached me on the little oboe solos in the overture.

In 1998, with my ticket for the Guitry play in hand, I entered through the small but tasteful lobby with its finely painted Corinthian columns and bas-reliefs of mythological subjects. Coming into the main auditorium, one is immediately transported back to an era and atmosphere well suited to lighthearted but elegant entertainment. Above the proscenium arch, the founding date of 1807 proclaims its proud heritage. Three levels of horseshoe-shaped balconies are dominated by a huge multi-tiered chandelier hanging from the middle of the ceiling. A mural offering tribute to Offenbach's greatest successes forms a border around the upper rim of the top balcony, while the décor of the middle level features a lyre worthy of Orpheus himself. Tabuteau would certainly not have been ashamed to mention that he played in such a theater. I squeezed into the narrow box, reflecting that it was surely designed for smaller people than today's theatergoers. There was no orchestra in the pit, but a hundred years fell rapidly away, and it was not difficult to imagine the strains of an Offenbach overture signaling the start of a joyous evening at Les Variétés.

As well as playing operettas, Tabuteau was beginning to make his way as a "freelancer" in Paris. On December 22, 1904, his name appears in a program of the Association des Concerts Alfred-Cortot at the Nouveau Théâtre, 15 rue Blanche. This first performance in France of Beethoven's *Messe Solennelle* was under the direction of Cortot, who, after after winning his Premier Prix in 1896 in the piano class of Louis Diémer, was becoming increasingly active as a conductor. Tabuteau was listed as second oboe to R. Bourbon, an older Conservatoire graduate of 1899, while Taffanel's famous student, Louis Fleury, was playing first flute.[18] A later program booklet of the Philadelphia Orchestra, containing brief biographical "portraits" of the players, gives a tantalizing reference to Tabuteau's early steps in the profession. On receiving his first prize from the Conservatoire, he is said to have been "promptly offered two jobs—one in New York with Walter Damrosch, and the

PARIS CONSERVATOIRE

other in Berlin." I once heard him make a passing remark wondering what his life would have been like "if he had gone to Berlin." Nothing more seems known of this early prospect. In the spring of 1905 Marcel Tabuteau accepted the offer from Walter Damrosch and sailed for New York.

MARCEL TABUTEAU

3 ARRIVAL IN AMERICA

Walter Damrosch and the New York
Symphony Orchestra, 1905–1908

At the beginning of the twentieth century, the number of full-fledged symphony orchestras in the United States could easily be counted on the fingers of one hand. There was the orchestra in Chicago that had been created by musical trailblazer Theodore Thomas. An orchestra had existed in Cincinnati since 1895, and the still struggling New York Philharmonic could boast of its early foundation in 1842. Then there was the Boston Symphony Orchestra, founded in 1881, with its prestigious pedigree of eminent European conductors and outstanding players, all made possible by the generous support of the banker Henry Lee Higginson. Philadelphia had formed its own orchestra only in 1900.

At the turn of the century in New York, the young Walter Damrosch was trying to carry forward the pioneer work begun by his father, Leopold, whose sudden death had left the opera, symphony, and chorus in the hands of his twenty-three-year-old son. Walter was anxious to create an ensemble that could rival the Boston Symphony Orchestra, but he was limited by union restrictions to use whatever players were available locally.[1] He envied the ability of the non-union Boston organization to import fine musicians from Europe. Damrosch felt that the string and brass sections of his New York Symphony were quite acceptable but that his woodwinds were weak. He chafed under the unfavorable comments they received in the newspapers.

This was an era during which German musicians formed the greater part of the personnel of most American symphony orchestras. Germans were also patrons and supporters of the major U.S. musical institutions. However, in the area of woodwind playing, the French school was gaining worldwide renown. Paris Conservatoire graduates and experienced French and Belgian wind players were in high demand. Gillet's pupil Georges Longy in Boston was one of the leading exponents of this style of playing.

Damrosch, young and enterprising, was determined to make improvements in his orchestra. In April 1905 he went to France to look for excellent wind players. He stayed in mid-Paris, just around the corner from the Place Vendôme at the small but elegant Hôtel de France et de Choiseul on the rue Saint-Honoré. A hotel favored by artists of varied professions, it is a spot where Damrosch would probably still feel at home if he were to return today.[2] With overstuffed velvet-covered sofas filling the softly lit corner lounges and hallways hung with darkly imposing portraits, it evokes an earlier era. In the spring of 1905 Damrosch proceeded to recruit and contract the musicians he needed for his orchestra.[3] Among them were the instrumentalists whose "importation" to America was to become something of a cause célèbre. The "famous five" were Georges Barrère, flute; Léon Leroy, clarinet; Marcel Tabuteau, oboe and English horn; Adolphe Dubois, trumpet; and Auguste Mesnard, bassoon. Tabuteau, still several months short of his eighteenth birthday, was the junior member of the group. It was less than a year since he had received his Premier Prix, and it was his teacher, Georges Gillet, who had recommended him to Damrosch. The other four, each about ten years older than Tabuteau, were all players with considerable orchestral and solo experience. Georges Barrère, Premier Prix from the Paris Conservatoire in 1895, was a former pupil of the renowned Paul Taffanel and already had a well-established career in Paris. He was first flutist at Concerts Colonne and the Opéra and also a member of the board of directors of the musical union of Paris.[4] Léon Leroy, who had studied clarinet with the eminent Professor

Rose, was awarded his Premier Prix in 1897. He became a professor at the Conservatoire of Versailles and was a solo player in the Garde Républicaine Band under Gabriel Parès.[5] Adolphe Dubois, the only one of the five whose musical education was not at the Paris Conservatoire, had received his first prize in trumpet and cornet from the Royal Conservatory of Belgium at the age of fourteen. By 1882 he was already playing professionally, and in the 1890s he became solo trumpet with the Orchestre Lamoureux in Paris. He played at Bayreuth under Richter and Mottl before joining the Royal Opera in Brussels, the Théâtre de la Monnaie.[6] The bassoonist, Auguste Mesnard (who incidentally lived to the age of ninety-nine), was a Premier Prix at the Paris Conservatoire in 1897, the same year as Leroy. Mesnard was a regular member of the Orchestre Lamoureux, where he performed under such guest conductors as Weingartner, Richter, Mahler, and Richard Strauss.[7] He did not arrive in the United States at the same time as the other four, but only in October, immediately before the beginning of the fall symphony season.

Tabuteau, Dubois, and Barrère crossed the Atlantic together. They embarked on May 6, 1905, at Le Havre on the French steamship *La Savoie* and arrived in New York on May 13. Barrère remembered their landing as taking place on "one of those oppressive mornings, half-foggy, warm and humid."[8] The "Manifest of Alien Passengers for the United States Immigration Office" lists Tabuteau as a single musician, age twenty (his true age of seventeen was crossed out), a citizen of France, of French "race," and with Paris as his last residence. It further states that he has paid his fare himself, is carrying $50.00, and will be staying at the Hotel Lafayette on Fifth Avenue.[9]

Almost immediately a storm of protest broke over the heads of the newly imported musicians. As Damrosch later recounted, "When the Frenchmen arrived, the rage among the members of the New York Union knew no bounds. I had a summer engagement for the orchestra on one of the roof gardens, but the Union refused to let them play with us except as 'soloists,' and I determined to take the matter higher up to the annual convention of the National Federation of Musicians, which was held in Detroit in the summer of 1905."[10] Letters and telegrams flew back and forth between the New York Symphony, Damrosch, and

ARRIVAL IN AMERICA

union officials, climaxing in Damrosch taking the train to Detroit, where he presented his case. Addressing representatives of the National Federation of Musicians, Damrosch made an eloquent defense of the musicians he had imported. He emphasized the rivalry between Boston and New York, saying that "Mr. Higginson of Boston and many ladies and gentlemen interested in music in this city [New York] have always asserted that a first class symphony orchestra could not be maintained on union lines. If you tie our hands in the matter of these few instruments you will prove that these people are right." Passionately envisioning the triumph of New York, he spoke in heroic terms: "While if you enable us to develop an orchestra of highest excellence we will be the strongest battering-ram for you to use in storming the Boston fortress."

Damrosch asserted that the opposition to his new musicians came either from persons in rival organizations wishing harm to the New York Symphony or from those who were not chosen for the vacant positions. He continually hammered at the question of rivalry. "I maintain that there are not any musicians to be found in New York among those free to accept engagements who are of such merit as to be able to stand the test of comparison with, for instance, our rival, the Boston Symphony Orchestra, which, as you know, is a non-union orchestra . . . I would be perfectly willing to have this point established by a competitive test among any applicants for the positions of solo flute, solo clarionet [clarinet], English horn, solo trumpet and solo bassoon." And speaking of his French recruits, "They are magnificent players, have passed the examination satisfactorily, and have taken out their first citizenship papers. . . . They have not been brought over as 'pauper musicians' nor for the purpose of lowering the wages of musicians in this country." He then pulled out all the stops: "The exclusion of these gentlemen who are well-known abroad would give our union a terrible reputation there as well as here. It would hold our country up to ridicule and contumely and lay us open to the suspicion of refusing artists admission to our shores because we feared their superior musical attainments." In reference to the special difficulty of finding outstanding wind players, he noted, "Symphony orchestras need distinguished soloists among the wind instruments and these cannot always be obtained here as they are rare the world over."[11]

MARCEL TABUTEAU

On May 20 Damrosch received a telegram from the National Federation instructing the New York local to allow his new men to play on a temporary basis pending the decision of the convention. Whether they would be permitted to become union members and permanent orchestra players in the United States was still uncertain. Damrosch took the precaution of presenting them to the public as soloists, *not* regular orchestra members. Barrère made his début on May 20 at the New York Theatre Roof Garden, playing two solos, *Madrigal* from *L'Enfant Prodigue* of Wormser and *Scherzo* by Widor, accompanied at the piano by Damrosch.[12] Tabuteau was also about to take the first step of his career in the New World. Appropriately enough, Dvořák's *New World Symphony* was featured on the May 22 concert, and Tabuteau, in his new role as English horn soloist, played the famous *Largo* in the second movement. Dubois followed with a trumpet solo on May 23, and Leroy performed the Weber *Concertino* for clarinet on June 7.

The decision eventually handed down by the convention allowed the four applicants to be immediately enrolled as members of New York Local 310, with Mesnard, the bassoonist, to be admitted on his arrival. However, the AFM decided that Damrosch had not made the exhaustive efforts he should have to locate musicians in the United States. He was therefore considered to have broken union rules and was required to pay a fine of $1,000. The receipt for this amount was signed in New York City on May 31, 1905, by Joseph Weber, AFM president. On June 1 the whole problem was summed up in an article in the *New York Times* with headlines stating, "Damrosch Fined $1000; Didn't Consult Union," and in smaller type, "Thought He Had Right to Hire Five Musicians from France," then in bolder letters again, "Tried to Get Them Here." The *Times* reported Damrosch's reply to the union officers: "that he had gone over the field here with a fine-toothed comb and had failed to find men of sufficient experience in symphony playing for his purposes." The question was resolved for the moment, but bitter exchanges were to continue between Damrosch and Weber for years afterward, resurfacing whenever there was a personnel crisis in Damrosch's orchestra. As late as 1944, on the occasion of a memorial speech he gave after the death of Georges Barrère, Damrosch would hark back to the situation of forty years before. Again he spoke of the rivalry with

Boston and of his efforts to improve the New York Symphony. He recounted his trip to Detroit to put his case before the AFM and how his plea was contested by the New York delegates: "I remember as if it were yesterday, how one of them, a German by birth said, 'Ve don't vant to have our pisness spoiled by those foreigners.'" Damrosch, himself German-born, was now fully involved in developing and defending musical life in America.

Tabuteau's contracts with Damrosch have not survived, but from those signed by the other musicians in May 1905 one can gain an idea of the range of their salaries. For the first year's employment, Barrère would earn $2,000 and Dubois was to receive $1,400; Tabuteau, hired for English horn and second oboe, would probably have received less than the older and more experienced trumpet player. The contracts were already prepared and signed in France, to become effective once the musicians became members of the Musical Mutual Protective Union of New York. It was spelled out that the musicians would be expected to play not only in the concerts of the New York Symphony Orchestra, but in programs of every kind, public or private, also chamber music, whenever and wherever required "by the party of the first part" (Walter Damrosch). In his own hand Damrosch added the scale of prices for individual concerts, whether in town, out of town, on tour, at festivals, winter or summer, with hotel expenses at $1.50 per day or $10.00 a week. Every detail was covered. The party of the first part could make deductions if the player missed any rehearsal or concert due to his own fault or illness.[13] The contracts included a provision for giving lessons at the Institute of Musical Art. For the first season, the rate for Barrère was $2.00 a lesson. Later it was raised to $3.00. In 1906 a separate teaching contract was offered to all the solo wind players. This excluded Tabuteau, as the first-chair oboist was Cesare Addimando. The contract was signed by Walter Damrosch and his brother Frank, who was director of the Institute of Musical Art. Not surprisingly, it stated that any teaching activities "shall not conflict with the engagements of the said players in the New York Symphony Orchestra."[14]

Now that the initial hurdle with the union had been cleared, Barrère, Tabuteau, Leroy, and Dubois were able to plunge fully into the busy 1905 summer schedule of the Damrosch orchestra. The first regular

MARCEL TABUTEAU

engagement was for five weeks in June and July at Ravinia Park near Chicago. Tabuteau would again be playing Dvořák's *From the New World,* then still a relatively new work. Sometimes it was announced simply as "slow movement from *America Symphony.*" Other programmed works with important solos for English horn were Rossini's *William Tell Overture* and Berlioz's *Roman Carnival.* Damrosch made sure there was variety in his concerts; he once had the *Andante* from the Mendelssohn *Violin Concerto* played by all the first violins.

A frequent soloist during the Ravinia season was principal oboist Cesare Addimando. A native of Italy, Addimando was born in Foggia and had studied in Naples.[15] Most of the solos he played were pieces based on popular nineteenth-century operas: Donizetti's *Linda di Chamounix,* Auber's *Massaniello,* Verdi's *Rigoletto* and *Ballo in Maschera.* Along with Barrère and Leroy, he also took part in the *Capriccio on Danish and Russian Airs* by Saint-Saëns with Walter Damrosch at the piano. It was not until July 21, the last concert of the Ravinia season, that Tabuteau's name finally appeared on a printed program. The famous Beethoven *Trio in C Major,* Opus 87, for two oboes and English horn was presented as a work for oboe, English horn, and clarinet, in that order, featuring Addimando, Tabuteau, and Leroy. Damrosch must have had a special liking for this work, as it would often appear on his programs sandwiched between numbers for full symphony orchestra.[16]

It probably was not easy for the youthful Tabuteau to sit in the second oboe or English horn chair and listen to playing of a very different style from that in which he had been trained. Echoes of his unflattering opinion of Addimando were heard decades later. During the Philadelphia Orchestra's transcontinental tour in 1936, Julien Shanis invited his fellow San Francisco Symphony oboists to a dinner in honor of Tabuteau, with whom he had studied. The English horn player, Leslie Schivo, brought a bottle of wine made by Addimando, who was by then a longtime resident of the Bay area, where he had come to occupy the position of solo oboe with the San Francisco Symphony under Alfred Hertz. After tasting the wine, Tabuteau is said to have ungallantly remarked, "Sour, just like his playing."[17]

Despite Tabuteau's unfavorable opinion of Addimando, he must have been a valued member of Damrosch's orchestra, whether due to

ARRIVAL IN AMERICA

his thorough musical background, or simply because of the dearth of competent oboists. Damrosch's supportive attitude toward Addimando, however, had its limits. In May 1906, when Addimando, no doubt aware of the higher amounts being paid to the recent French imports, threatened to break his contract unless his previous year's salary of $1,300 was doubled, Damrosch called his request "too preposterous even to admit of discussion."[18] Again in 1908, when Addimando gave notice that he would stay only if he received $500 more per season, Damrosch simply engaged someone else. It is perhaps not surprising that Tabuteau also would look for opportunities to better his own situation, but before many years went by, he too would learn the consequences of trying to extricate himself from agreements made with Walter Damrosch and his orchestra.

Now, still in the first summer of his new employment, Tabuteau proceeded from Ravinia Park to Willow Grove Park in the Chelten Hills about seventeen miles north of Philadelphia, where for seven years the New York Symphony was contracted by the Philadelphia Rapid Transit Company to play a three-week-long season. The concerts at Willow Grove had begun before the Philadelphia Orchestra came into existence and were one of Damrosch's earliest and most cherished educational projects. Although the programs were designed to be entertaining, Damrosch hoped to introduce the pleasures of classical music to a broader public. To this end, between the lighter fare of Strauss waltzes, ballet music by Delibes, and single movements of Mozart, Beethoven, or Tchaikovsky symphonies, every week he gave a regular symphony concert and an all-Wagner program. For these summer concerts the orchestra was reduced to about fifty players, considerably smaller than its winter format. Programs for "Symphony nights" were nevertheless of an uncompromising nature; for example, Brahms's *Symphony No. 3 in F Major* was among the works played in 1905. Popular concerts took place every day, a two-part program in the afternoon and another at night. Between the two short sections of each concert, the music lovers were entertained by an electric fountain display that lasted for two hours in the afternoon and one and a half hours in the evening. As advertised in the program booklet, the break allowed time to enjoy a "light lunch" at the Rustic Pavilion near the midway. Willow Grove, primarily

MARCEL TABUTEAU

an amusement park, was a popular Philadelphia family destination for many decades. Although the second half of the night concerts began at the late hour of 9:30, there was no problem in returning to the center of Philadelphia. A "Special Willow Grove Express" left for the Reading Terminal downtown station until 11:05 p.m.

The four new French wind players were introduced as soloists to the Willow Grove audiences. Tabuteau's main solo continued to be the *Largo* from the *New World Symphony*. Dubois played a trumpet solo, *Mandolinata* by Paladilhe, and Barrère and Leroy played the Saint-Saëns *Tarantelle* for flute and clarinet. Preserved among Tabuteau family papers in Compiègne was a handwritten account, the French translation of a review entitled "Willow Grove Park—The Triumph of Damrosch and His Orchestra despite the Bad Weather." After referring to the crowd of thousands who rushed to occupy the seats in the open air as soon as the weather permitted, the article described the first Symphony Evening on Monday, August 7, 1905, which included the overture to Gluck's *Iphigenia in Aulis* and the *New World Symphony* by Dvořák. An underlined section must surely be one of the earliest critiques calling attention to Tabuteau, who had just turned eighteen: "The Symphony was admirably interpreted; the *Largo*, of such high and moving inspiration, was especially outstanding, due to the talent of the English horn of Mr. Tabuteau, a young French artist, already an accomplished musician, who is certainly destined to become a celebrity. His playing, full of warmth, is characterized by great sonority allied to an incomparable clarity of execution." The article also gives Damrosch credit for his accompanying at the Steinway piano as well as for his interpretation of the orchestral numbers.

The orchestra played in a shell of Damrosch's own design, which preserved the outdoor atmosphere for the audience of fifteen to twenty thousand listeners.[19] Speaking about his work at Willow Grove Park, Damrosch paid tribute to the public, saying that in all his years there, he had never seen a disturbance of any kind. He felt that this testified to the general discipline maintained in the park as well as the self-respecting Philadelphia community.

The last engagement for Damrosch and his orchestra in the summer of 1905 was at the Pittsburgh Exposition. From August 30 through

ARRIVAL IN AMERICA

September 9 they played much of their earlier repertoire. The Beethoven *Trio,* again with the names of Addimando, Leroy, and Tabuteau printed on the programs, appeared twice in this short period. There was no indication of which movements were played.[20]

As fall approached, Tabuteau could anticipate the beginning of his first full-time symphonic engagement. The regular 1905–6 winter season of the New York Symphony was heralded by announcements of an "Orchestra of 90, comprising the best players of New York strengthened by the addition of the following artists," and here Damrosch listed the names of his five French wind players with their former distinguished orchestra positions. "Mons. Marcel Tabuteau, English horn" was simply noted as "premier prix at the Conservatoire Nationale, Paris." There would be a series of eight concerts on Sunday afternoons and eight on Tuesday evenings in Carnegie Hall, all to be directed by Damrosch except for four concerts in January and February conducted by "Herr Felix Weingartner who will visit America by invitation of Mr. Damrosch." Soloists were to include the soprano Emma Eames, violinist Jan Kubelik, pianists Rudolf Ganz and Raoul Pugno, plus other artists less well remembered today.[21] There was a projected repertoire of standard works—Beethoven, Brahms, Haydn, and Mozart symphonies—with the Berlioz *Symphonie Fantastique,* Debussy's *L'après-midi d'un faune,* and Tchaikovsky's *Romeo and Juliet* overture providing special interest for English horn. Damrosch must have felt vindicated for his efforts when he saw the *New York Times* review of the November 14 opening concert, with its enthusiastic support for the new orchestra members: "The wind instrument players who were brought over from Paris by Mr. Damrosch last Summer, and who were heard at that time in the popular concerts, have very materially strengthened it [the orchestra], and the wood wind choir can offer a beauty of tone and a finish of execution such as have not been heard from resident players for a long time. . . . The tone of the orchestra is good, homogeneous, and in the main well balanced, and much of the roughness that characterized its playing last season has been refined away." Brahms's *Third Symphony* was on the program, and "Debussy's prelude, concerning which Mr. Damrosch was moved to deliver some brief explanatory remarks, was heard here for the first time. It is a most insubstantial fantasy; but from

Tabuteau in a portrait from his early New York years. Note the neatly parted hair, very high collar, bow tie, and stylish (for that era) suit jacket with matching vest. Courtesy Guy Baumier.

ARRIVAL IN AMERICA

this gossamer web of orchestral tone has been spun a delicate tapestry of singular poetic fancy, dimly suggesting the Grecian landscape, the recumbent faun blowing upon his pipes of Pan."

It is not surprising that these French wind players banded together to play chamber music. Coming from Paris, they had certainly attended concerts of Taffanel's Société de Musique de Chambre pour Instruments à Vent, or they would have been aware of, and influenced by, the performance level established by this elite group. In Boston, too, the eminent French oboist Georges Longy had founded the Longy Club to further music for woodwinds. Now something similar was being attempted in New York. The "First Program of the New York Symphony Wind Instrument Club" presented French woodwind chamber music, including two larger works, the Caplet *Suite Persane* and the Gounod *Petite Symphonie*. In each of these numbers Barrère was the flutist and Tabuteau played second oboe to Addimando, who had a prominent role for oboe in Pierné's *Prelude and Fugue* and Théodore Dubois's *Two Pieces in Canonic Form.*[22] Thirty years later Tabuteau would conduct the Caplet and the Gounod in his woodwind ensemble concerts at the Curtis Institute of Music. We may wonder if he thought back to his early days as second oboe listening to Addimando and Barrère play the solos. The personalities of Addimando and Barrère apparently did not harmonize well, and Addimando soon took a dislike to playing with Barrère. In early February 1906 he wrote to tell Damrosch that he could no longer belong to the Wind Instrument Club. Aside from his objections to Barrère, he added, "Time to me is money, therefore I cannot afford to waste any."[23] This did not sit well with Damrosch, who reminded him that his contract provided that he should play chamber music concerts whenever called upon to do so, and requested that he continue to attend rehearsals.

In the spring of 1906 the New York Symphony made a tour of the East Coast, including Wilkes-Barre, Pennsylvania, Wilmington, Delaware, and Washington, D.C., and then south to Raleigh, Memphis, Birmingham, Nashville, and St. Louis—all places Tabuteau was seeing for the first time but not the last. Years later, with the Philadelphia Orchestra, he would visit and revisit these same towns, but no longer as English horn player in the *William Tell Overture*. The Willow

MARCEL TABUTEAU

Grove season began earlier than the previous summer, with the orchestra leaving New York on May 26 at 7:50 a.m. to arrive in the Philadelphia suburb of Jenkintown a little more than two hours later. The concerts did not vary greatly from those of the year before, but now for the first time Tabuteau's name appeared on a Willow Grove program as a soloist. He was featured on the first half of an evening concert playing *Romance* for English horn, a piece by Philippe Gaubert dedicated to Louis Bas. Whether it was performed with orchestra or piano is not stated.

After Willow Grove ended on June 17, the orchestra went to Ravinia, where Tabuteau again played his usual *William Tell* and Addimando his ration of operatic solos. On the Fourth of July, *William Tell* and *Selections from Rigoletto* shared the program. The next day a return appearance of the Beethoven *Trio* showed Addimando, Leroy, and Tabuteau on the printed program. We can therefore be reasonably sure that Tabuteau was in the United States in the summer of 1906. Things were to change in the following year. During Damrosch's 1907 Ravinia season, a July 23 program has Addimando playing his *Rigoletto,* but a new name appears in a *Duet for English Horn and Violoncello* by Glinka. The soloists are Messrs. Labate and Rogovoy. It is a curious and little-known fact that Marcel Tabuteau and Bruno Labate, later to become famous as the solo oboists of the Philadelphia Orchestra and the New York Philharmonic, respectively, should both have played English horn for Walter Damrosch in the early years of the century.[24]

Tabuteau always said that he played two seasons with Walter Damrosch, yet it was common knowledge that he entered the orchestra of the Metropolitan Opera in 1908, and there was no question that he had arrived in the United States in May 1905. The numbers simply did not add up. Now, as the evidence of letters between Damrosch, the attorney Guernsey Price, AFM president Joseph Weber, and official French Army records will show, we can safely say that the mystery of the missing year has been solved. After playing for one season in the New York Symphony Orchestra, Tabuteau returned to France to enter the army. France required an obligatory period of military service from all its young men, and Tabuteau was a nineteen-year-old French citizen. On

Niece Thérèse sits in the Létoffé family car, her eyes on her two uncles, André and Marcel, in uniform, 1907.

October 7, 1906, he was enrolled in the 45th Infantry Regiment, Compiègne, *département* of Oise, for a period of three years. A few months later, on February 25, 1907, he became a "military musician" and was able to join the 45th Infantry Regimental Band. An official act of July 11, 1892, giving special consideration to graduates of the Conservatoire made it possible for Tabuteau to be demobilized on October 7, 1907, after exactly one year of service. There are two contrasting photos from the days of his army service. In one he is wearing fatigues and appears to be sweeping up garbage. In the other, a smartly uniformed Tabuteau, with a slightly aloof and superior expression, is standing in the middle of a military band holding his oboe. In both photos he sports a finely pointed goatee, never to be seen in later pictures.

At the conclusion of his year in the French military, Tabuteau returned to New York in time for the 1907–8 season, where he had to face problems with the New York union for the second time. A letter written by one of Damrosch's representatives to attorney Guernsey Price in September 1907 speaks of the difficulties surrounding Tabuteau's return to

Tabuteau sweeping the floor while doing K.P. in the French Army, 1907.

the United States. The Musicians' Union was trying to expel Tabuteau on a technicality concerning the break in his continuous U.S. residence following the filing of his first citizenship papers. Damrosch asks, "Could Tabuteau get an injunction against the Musicians Mutual Protective Union preventing it from expelling him until the courts have decided that it has this right, so that he can in the meantime earn his living?"[25] Price replied the next day with a long and detailed letter saying that he had talked with an officer in the Naturalization Bureau and had written to the Department of Commerce and Labor to find out if Tabuteau's absence of a year broke the residency requirements. He referred to a statute providing "that the petition for citizenship must be filed not more than seven years after the first papers . . . so that if Tabuteau should come back in October" and begin another five-year

ARRIVAL IN AMERICA

The 45th Infantry Regimental Band of Compiègne, 1907, where Tabuteau fulfilled his obligatory year of military service. He is holding his oboe, in the back row, sixth from the left.

wait, it would be completed in 1912, the year in which Tabuteau eventually did become an American citizen. Price's conclusion was that as the question of Tabuteau's continuous residency could not be definitely settled, quite possibly an injunction against the union could be obtained. In a handwritten postscript he added that he would like to know "whether Tabuteau did take an oath in France on entering the Army" but was of the opinion that it would not affect the situation at hand.

At the beginning of October Damrosch was having other problems. He needed a new solo cellist, and in a long letter to Joseph Weber, he discusses both this question and the one pertaining to Tabuteau. As the two subjects continue to be linked in later letters, they merit a summary. On October 5, Damrosch recalls the promise he had made to Weber back at the 1905 Detroit convention to let him know if a time arose when he could "not find a solo instrument of the highest rank in this country." He now faces such a situation, as his solo cellist, Leo Schulz, "has been suffering during the summer from a kind of nervous prostration" and has had to give up orchestra playing for the present.

Damrosch is worried, as his season is about to begin. He tells Weber, "Unless you can suggest some great artist who is 'lying around loose' so to speak, we will have to see what we can get from the other side." He doesn't want to have difficulties with the Federation, but says he has been unable to fill the position because "the few cellists of high rank in this country are already under contract." In the same letter he says, "I hope the case of Tabuteau" has been amicably settled and "that he is entitled to the full protection of the Union of which he is a member." As the rest of the letter clearly shows, Damrosch was doing whatever he could to help Tabuteau. "I presume that you have heard from the State Department regarding his case. The answer I received both from the State Department as well as from the Department of Commerce and Labor are absolutely favorable to him. The boy is exceedingly anxious to continue his life and work in America and I am sure that after having made due examination of his case you will, in justice to him, enable him to do so." Weber responded immediately on October 9: "Permit me to advise you that in the case of Tabuteau I have ascertained that his serving in the French Army does not annul his declaration to become a citizen of the United States. Therefore the incident is ended in so far as the Federation is concerned, and I have so notified Local 310."

As to importing a solo cellist, Weber admonishes Damrosch that "in the interest of the true furthering of art in this country, it becomes your duty to give an opportunity to home talent which in my opinion, with good will on your part, you will find it possible to do." He does not easily drop the subject of importation, and again on October 21 writes to Damrosch about both the cello situation and Tabuteau. "I am pleased to hear that you have found a solo cellist. Now permit me to enlist your good services to develop American talent." He assures Damrosch that in this way there will be no clashes with the Federation. Nailing down his final point, Weber concludes, "As an example, permit me to call to your attention the fact that you found it possible to replace Mr. Tabuteau during his entire absence in Europe without ever finding it necessary to request permission to import a substitute for him."[26]

The season of 1907–8, which would be Tabuteau's second and last in the New York Symphony, held the promise of musical events more exciting than those of previous years. Tabuteau had missed the well-

ARRIVAL IN AMERICA

publicized November 1906 U.S. debut of his fellow countryman Camille Saint-Saëns playing his own colorful piano concerto, *Afrique*, but now he would experience his first collaboration with the famous soloists Fritz Kreisler and Josef Hofmann, artists with whom he would be associated for decades to come. The season culminated in a long-planned tour to the West Coast for the orchestra. It would also bring a major career change for Tabuteau, though one fraught with much discord and acrimony.

However, first came the regular series of concerts in Carnegie Hall—more performances of the ever popular symphony *From the New World*, relieved by an unexpected appearance of the Gounod *Petite Symphonie*. To give the woodwind section such prominence on a regular concert testifies to Damrosch's appreciation of the caliber of his wind players. In January they were off to Detroit and Cincinnati, with Kreisler playing Lalo, and on February 1 Damrosch was able to realize his ambition to present the American première of Tchaikovsky's opera *Eugene Onegin* in a concert version. In his enthusiasm for this music he was years ahead of the Metropolitan Opera, where it was not performed until 1920. The month of March 1908 was taken up by a Beethoven cycle. It included all nine symphonies and the four *Leonore-Fidelio* overtures. H. E. Krehbiel, the respected New York critic, writing especially for the occasion, hailed Beethoven's opus in exalted terms as the "Musical Holy Writ . . . the embodiment of all that was to come, has come and is still to come." Subscription prices for the whole series of concerts ranged from $2.50 in the rear balcony to $75 for a first-tier box. Aside from the major works, some odd bits of Beethoviana surface in these programs: the *Scotch Folk Songs,* the *Turkish March,* and an aria, "Call of the Quail." We can be grateful for Damrosch's devotion to the oboe trio, as it again gives us proof of Tabuteau's participation in these events. For the opening concert of the series on March 1 at Carnegie Hall, the *Trio (Adagio* and *Presto* movements only) was finally presented in its original form for two oboes and English horn. The performers were Addimando, Labate, and Tabuteau. Why Labate did not play the second oboe part a few weeks later at the Academy of Music in Philadelphia, when the trio reverted to its oboe, clarinet, and English horn version, remains an unanswered question.

MARCEL TABUTEAU

In early May 1908 Damrosch and the New York Symphony Orchestra set out for the long-hoped-for tour of the western states. It began in the South with concerts in Mississippi, Alabama, and Louisiana. The orchestra reached Los Angeles by way of Dallas, El Paso, and Tucson. It must have been a welcome respite from the constant train travel to spend almost a whole week in San Francisco, a city still recovering from the devastation of the 1906 earthquake. There was time to present varied repertoire, including a Wagner Night and, on May 19, an all-Beethoven program featuring the *Eroica* symphony—and the famous *Trio* played by the ever ready Addimando, Leroy, and Tabuteau. During my Curtis years I made a note that Tabuteau told me he had been in San Francisco with Damrosch and had played English horn in the Beethoven *Trio* with Addimando as first oboe. He added that "Addimando was oboe King in New York; he played like a trumpet and had terrible schooling." Tabuteau remembered the occasion as being in 1906; no doubt the after-effects of the earthquake had impressed him with that date. It must, however, been in 1908, which was the only coast-to-coast tour during the time he played with Damrosch. After two concerts at the University of California in Berkeley, the orchestra headed for the Northwest. A "Grand Wagner Night" with excerpts from six operas was presented in Seattle. Damrosch could scarcely have imagined that this city would one day be the site of a successful Wagner Ring Cycle Festival.

The few times I heard Tabuteau refer to touring with Damrosch, he did not speak of Wagner. He said that when the orchestra reached Seattle, he was so excited by seeing the husky dogs and the ongoing signs of gold rush fever that he wanted to leave the tour then and there. He added that he was so young and eager for adventure, he would have been ready to head for Alaska or the Yukon.[27] Was Tabuteau's imagination simply stimulated by what he saw, or did he actually take the more serious step of trying to find out if he could earn a living with music in this still untamed corner of the country? A curious document in the Damrosch Archive can only make us wonder. It is a sheet of pink paper, the carbon copy of a letter dated October 31, 1908, apparently written by a member of the administration of the Damrosch orchestra and addressed to "The Manager of the Seattle Symphony Orchestra."

ARRIVAL IN AMERICA

Dear Sir:

Representing the Symphony Society of New York, Mr. Walter Damrosch Conductor, I wish to inform you that this Society has with Mr. Marcel Tabuteau a contract for his services as English Horn and oboe player for 46 consecutive weeks, beginning October 1, 1908, it being agreed therein that Mr. Tabuteau shall accept no other engagements for musical performances, without the permission of the Society. It is possible that Mr. Tabuteau may seek to obtain engagements with your orchestra, and if he should so attempt, the Society and Mr. Damrosch will deem it a courtesy if you will send word at once to either them or myself. Mr. Tabuteau has been made plainly to understand that the Society and Mr. Damrosch insist upon his carrying out his contractual obligations and that they will take all legal steps necessary to this end. I am sure you will agree to hold artists to their agreements is to the advantage of all concerned.

Requesting that you treat this letter as confidential,

I am Respectfully,

Whether Tabuteau actually did write to inquire about the Seattle Symphony Orchestra or whether he only talked of doing so, the letter indicates that the administration of the New York Symphony had reason to believe he might have such an idea in mind. This is only one of the many problematic circumstances surrounding the beginning of the next stage in Tabuteau's career.

With concerts in Bellingham, Tacoma, and Spokane, Washington; Victoria and Vancouver, British Columbia; and Portland, Oregon, the tour was coming to an end. Between May 5 and June 5 the orchestra had played thirty-one concerts. Forty years later, in 1948, Tabuteau traveled to the West Coast for the last time with Eugene Ormandy and the Philadelphia Orchestra. Did he ever look back on that youthful adventure of so long ago? If so, he said not a word about it, even to colleagues who knew him well.

4 THE METROPOLITAN OPERA

Singers and Conductors of the "Golden Age,"
1908–1914

Marcel Tabuteau entered the orchestra of the Metropolitan Opera House at the beginning of one of its most brilliant and artistically productive periods. The fall season of 1908–9 marked the first year of the reign of the new general director, Giulio Gatti-Casazza, and the conductor he brought with him from Italy, forty-one-year-old Arturo Toscanini. One of Gatti-Casazza's stipulations for taking over the direction of the Met was that the orchestra be improved and enlarged. For Tabuteau, this presented an opportunity of advancement from his position as second oboe and English horn with Walter Damrosch. However, the move from the New York Symphony to the orchestra of the Metropolitan Opera proved to be a far from simple transition.

Already in the spring of 1908 Damrosch must have had suspicions that Tabuteau was looking around for other employment. In a memo sent in June, Damrosch refers to some of his orchestra musicians as "the naughty children." He mentions that Tabuteau, "second oboe, one of the Frenchmen for whom we made the great fight compelling the Union to admit him, received an offer from the Metropolitan Opera House as first oboe. He intended secretly to accept it and calmly continue to draw his salary from us until November. I found this out and told him that the Symphony Society would hold him strictly to his written contract which lasts another year." Damrosch also complained to Andreas Dippel, the administrative manager of the Metropolitan, and received a promise that musicians under contract to his orchestra would not be recruited.

At this point Cesare Addimando, the first oboist of the New York Symphony, thinking that Tabuteau's action would put Damrosch in a hole, gave two weeks' notice and asked for $500 more a year. Damrosch informed Addimando that he had broken his contract as it did not contain a two-week-notice clause. After firing Addimando, Damrosch promptly proceeded to hire "Monsieur Debucher, said to be the finest oboe in the country who came to Cincinnati three years ago, and I think we are safe."[1] The final item in Damrosch's memo points to the keen competition for acquiring French or Belgian wind players. He explains how he had notified the second flute player "that the Symphony Society would not reengage him for another year because at a Nordica Concert on tour he had put the orchestra into convulsions by openly imitating her gestures while singing.[2] He is furious but we are well rid of him as he is one of the old guard who do not like the new order. I have a splendid Belgian in his place."[3]

According to James Collis, Tabuteau was so anxious to be accepted at the Metropolitan that he allowed the conductor, Alfred Hertz, who interviewed him, to assume he was a Belgian.[4] Furthermore, he dropped casual remarks about knowing the music so well that he did not even have to count bars.[5] When he realized that the Met was interested in him but was hesitating because of his lack of experience, Tabuteau went even further and said he had played at the famous Théâtre de la Monnaie in Brussels.[6] Later, looking back on the day when he eventually found himself in the pit having to read difficult operas at sight, he said, "I paid dearly for my sin."

After the end of his second and last season with Damrosch (1907–8), Tabuteau went to France for the summer. In the fall of 1908 a series of telegrams and letters flew back and forth concerning his return transportation to the United States. André Tridon, the manager of the New York Symphony Society, both cabled and wrote to Tabuteau

MARCEL TABUTEAU

in September about his boat ticket. He addressed Tabuteau at the old family home in Compiègne, 8 Rue Magenta, saying that a second-class cabin had been reserved for him on *La Provence,* a steamship of the Compagnie Générale Transatlantique, sailing from Le Havre on October 17. He asked Tabuteau to come to his office immediately on the day of his arrival in New York. In a letter of October 7, the Compagnie Générale Transatlantique wrote to confirm the Symphony Society's payment of $67 for the ticket that would be delivered to Tabuteau. Then on October 20 the Symphony Society asked the Compagnie Générale Transatlantique when *La Provence* "will make dock this week. One of our French artists is coming over, and it is of the utmost importance that someone from our office meets him at the landing." Was the Damrosch organization now aware of Tabuteau's imminent "defection" to the Met, or were they simply doing him the courtesy of meeting him at the dock in the assumption he was to continue with the New York Symphony Orchestra? From the fragmentary surviving correspondence it is impossible to guess, but the major events of the next few weeks can be traced.

On November 9 the Metropolitan Opera Company addressed a polite but directly to-the-point letter to the New York Symphony Society. It stated that the Met recognized Mr. Tabuteau's contractual obligations with the New York Symphony, but that when they had engaged him they had known nothing about his other contract. The letter continued, "We need him as a first oboe player. We request the New York Symphony to release Mr. Tabuteau of his contract." The stage was now set for the final round, which would involve legal action.[7]

On November 12, the lawyer Guernsey Price, who a year earlier had helped Tabuteau with his immigration and citizenship problems, wrote to Walter Damrosch:

> Re: MARCEL TABUTEAU CONTRACT
> Enclosed herein I send you [a] check on my attorney account for $181.47, being the amount paid by Marcel Tabuteau, and general releases to yourself and to the Symphony Society.

Two identical, notarized "General Release" documents dated November 12, 1908, were directed to Walter Damrosch and to the Symphony

THE METROPOLITAN OPERA

Society of New York. Each of the addressees paid the amount of $1.00 to Marcel Tabuteau, thereby releasing him from all further obligation or liability to their organizations. Sol Schoenbach believed that Damrosch, even as he had done with Addimando, threatened never to let Tabuteau play anywhere again. As a form of "blackmail," this could have helped Tabuteau to legally extricate himself from his predicament.

In the early part of the twentieth century, opera in New York held the place that films, radio, television, and recordings fill today. Every Sunday, opera was front-page news in the weekly magazine sections of the New York papers. There were full-page pictures of the "star" singers and the conductors, with detailed reports of their comings and goings. Scarcely a day passed without some newspaper story about the prima donnas Lillian Nordica, Luisa Tetrazzini, Geraldine Farrar, or Marcella Sembrich, describing their jewels and telling how many trunks were necessary to carry their elaborate wardrobes. Another continually favorite subject was the popular tenor Enrico Caruso.

The program booklet for the 1908 season took care that its title page, a swirling design of eight flowingly garbed harp players entwined in a Tiffany-style pattern, specified "*Grand* Opera." It contained well-organized information for "Rules of Traffic" with the admonition, "Carriages can deposit their passengers at the Broadway, 39th Street and 40th Street Entrances." The ads advised the opera lovers that Tecla pearls, Pongee silk suiting, and kid gloves were "established as the correct adjunct to refined dressing with new shades and lengths for street and evening wear." Pages were devoted to jars of "Vanishing Cream" for 25 cents, teachers of Singing, and Egyptian Deities: The Best Cigarette of All, with "special attention directed to the After-Dinner Size. Not for the average smoker or average purse." The Café de France, 38th Street near Broadway, as the closest French restaurant, offered a special supper for $1.00 with "music by Signor Bendelari's Quartette." A Melville Clark Apollo Player Piano was pictured with an attractive pinch-waisted "Gibson Girl" seated in front of its keyboard. G. Schirmer advertised: "Just published, *Love's Torment,* a Gipsy Waltz by Enrico Caruso, and [*in smaller print*], Richard Barthelemy, for voice and piano, high or low 75¢." On a more mundane level, "The Invincible Electric Renovator, a Portable Suction Cleaning Machine attachable to any

MARCEL TABUTEAU

electric light socket," was shown standing in the middle of a Victorian parlor ready to suck up the dust from the heavily draped surroundings. Turbaned and gowned, satin-slippered ladies riding on camels contributed to the exotica in these booklets—whether intended to appeal to or to reflect the tastes of the opera-going public is not clear.

The famous gold curtain had been installed in 1906, and for the fall of 1908 a new orchestra pit had been constructed. *Aida,* the opera given on opening night, November 16, was staged by scenic artists who had visited the Egyptian collections at the British Museum and the Turin Museum, assuring a fresh authenticity in the production. The stellar cast of singers included Enrico Caruso as Radamès; Emmy Destinn, making her Metropolitan debut as Aida; Louise Homer in the role of Amneris; and Antonio Scotti singing Amonasro.[8] When Gustav Mahler was conducting, later in the season, this sophisticated approach to stage production continued, with four folk dancers imported from Prague for the American première of *The Bartered Bride.* And to prepare *The Marriage of Figaro,* Mahler was given an unheard-of twenty rehearsals.

Now just a few days after the crucial date of Tabuteau's release by Walter Damrosch, he was free to begin the Met season. Almost sixty years later, in October 1965, Tabuteau told his last student, Rowland Floyd, how he had "played at sight, without rehearsal, *Aida* under Toscanini at the Met on a bad reed he had just made."[9] The reviewers were unanimous in their enthusiasm for the new régime. Much of the credit for the success of *Aida* was given to Toscanini.[10] The performance "thrilled with the magnetism of Arturo Toscanini, the conductor, who made his first American appearance." The famous critic Henry E. Krehbiel wrote that "in the best sense he is an artist, an interpreter, a re creator. Without such men music is as lifeless to the ear as it is on the printed page." According to Richard Aldrich in the *Times,* "the spirit that pervaded it was clearly instilled by the new conductor. . . . He is a dominating power, a man of potent authority, a musician of infinite resource." Although he did not single out individual players, Aldrich added, "Seldom has the orchestra sounded of greater richness and fullness."[11]

Aida was the first opera performed in the new season, but when Toscanini had begun rehearsals with the orchestra on October 19, four

THE METROPOLITAN OPERA

weeks before opening night, it was for *Götterdämmerung*. This massive opera, which concludes Wagner's Ring Cycle, was not scheduled for performance until December 10, four weeks into the season, but Toscanini felt that it would require the most work. He conducted standing up for four hours, which nobody had done at the Met since Anton Seidl in the 1890s.[12] The largely German orchestra was impressed that an Italian could show such command of a Wagner opera, and the men were astonished by his ear and memory. In a rare reference to his Metropolitan Opera days, Tabuteau spoke of the difficulty of joining the Met when he was so young and immediately having to face the five-hour-long *Götterdämmerung*. As he came into the orchestra well after these rehearsals had begun, he again felt himself in almost a "sight-reading" situation. Then as now, there was little opportunity for an orchestral musician to gain opera experience before actually playing the repertoire. Tabuteau had taken part in the all-Wagner concerts Walter Damrosch programmed so frequently, but playing excerpts is not the same as playing the entire opera. Tabuteau said he had the feeling that the German musicians in the orchestra were waiting for him, "the young French fellow, to break his neck" (traditional Franco-German hostility evidently extended into the orchestra pit). To prepare himself, he began to study the complete scores of the operas in bed at night. And more than just *looking* at the music, he painstakingly copied by hand, in pen and ink, pages and pages of the oboe parts. When I graduated from the Curtis Institute of Music in 1945, Tabuteau gave me a stack of crumbling, yellowed, and soot-smudged pages of manuscript that had long been lying on his studio shelves. I recognized a few passages from Brahms symphonies, but realized only much later that most of the music was the repertoire from his years at the Met. There were lengthy passages from all of the Ring Cycle—*Das Rheingold, Die Walküre, Siegfried,* and *Götterdämmerung*—as well as from *Tannhäuser, Die Meistersinger, Tristan und Isolde,* and *Parsifal.* He had copied out parts of Humperdinck's *Königskinder* and *Hänsel und Gretel*, every note of the *Dance of the Hours* from *La Gioconda*, and extensive sections of *Aida, Otello,* and *Pagliacci.* Tabuteau obviously did not depend for long on sight-reading but prepared these demanding scores in the most thorough way.

Who were the singers Tabuteau heard on the stage above him as he began his first season in the orchestra pit of the Metropolitan Opera House? They were among the most luminous personalities in operatic history: the legendary Marcella Sembrich, Johanna Gadski, Olive Fremstad, Geraldine Farrar, Louise Homer, Enrico Caruso, and Pasquale Amato sang in *La Bohème, Faust, Die Walküre, Madama Butterfly, La Traviata, Tosca, Rigoletto,* and *Parsifal* under conductors Arturo Toscanini and Alfred Hertz. In early December 1908 the Met audience heard Toscanini's *Carmen* and *Götterdämmerung* for the first time. Just before Christmas, it was *Tristan und Isolde* under the direction of Gustav Mahler, who would not agree to let Toscanini do this opera until after his own production from the previous spring had been given.[13]

During his three seasons at the Met, Mahler also conducted *The Marriage of Figaro, The Bartered Bride, Don Giovanni, Fidelio, Die Walküre, Siegfried,* and the first performance in America of *Pique Dame.*

On January 10, 1909, a special concert was given to benefit the victims of a tragic earthquake that had hit Messina, Sicily, a few days previously. Despite the high ticket prices, which netted the sum of $14,000, the event attracted the largest audience of the season to the Metropolitan Opera House. All three of the Met's major conductors took part in the program. Hertz was on the podium for Liszt's *Les Préludes,* while the *Press* reported that "led by that great Italian conductor, Arturo Toscanini, the Funeral March from *Götterdämmerung,* one of the most wonderful compositions in German musical literature, became a dirge for the Italian nation. . . . Toscanini knew he was expressing a country's woe; so did his great body of players." The other musical pinnacle of the evening was Beethoven's *Leonore III Overture,* conducted by Gustav Mahler, whose reading of this masterpiece "held the audience spellbound. Fortunate is the city that can boast of two such giants of the baton as Mahler and Toscanini." Vocal "giants" also contributed to this concert. Caruso sang the *Miserere* from *Il Trovatore.* Other stars were Frances Alda, Destinn, Amato, Fremstad, Sembrich, Homer, Scotti, and Farrar.[14] Another extraordinary concert took place on February 21, when Toscanini conducted Verdi's *Messa Da Requiem* with an orchestra of 150 players and a chorus of 200 singers.

THE METROPOLITAN OPERA

These had to be exciting musical experiences for a very young French oboist.

That same year a new production of Verdi's *Falstaff,* conducted by Toscanini, premiered in Philadelphia on March 16. In April the Met performed eighteen different operas in fifteen days in Chicago and added four more performances on a three-day stop in Pittsburgh on the way back home to New York. That season was heavily laden with Wagner. Every opera of the Ring Cycle was given several times, as well as *Tannhäuser, Parsifal,* and *Die Meistersinger.* Most of the Wagner was in the hands of the respected conductor of German repertoire, Alfred Hertz, who would later play an important role in the development of the San Francisco Symphony Orchestra. Martin Mayer sums up the glories of Toscanini's (and Tabuteau's) first season at the Met: "One year in the hundred stands out for the quality of its performances, the drama of the processes by which they came to the Metropolitan's stage, and the strength of its influence on subsequent seasons. The 1908–9 season, the year of the Metropolitan's twenty-fifth anniversary, was the year when the opera house acquired the leadership that would guide it for the next quarter of a century."[15]

Tabuteau's second season at the Met was, if anything, even more intensive than his first, as Gatti-Casazza was expanding both his roster of singers and the repertoire. There were more novelties and new productions. High points were *Otello* under Toscanini with Leo Slezak in the title role and Gluck's *Orfeo ed Euridice* with Louise Homer, Johanna Gadski, and Alma Gluck. I once heard Tabuteau refer to "the beauty of playing Gluck under Toscanini." Toscanini now took on more of the Wagner repertoire, most frequently *Tristan und Isolde* and *Die Meistersinger.*

With the debut of Anna Pavlova and her partner, Mikail Mordkin, ballet began to play an important role at the Met. Tchaikovsky's *Swan Lake* entered the repertoire in 1911. American, world, and Metropolitan Opera premières, plus a number of works from different European milieus, added spice and variety to the standard Italian and German repertoire. From France, a "modern" opera, Dukas's *Ariane et Barbe-Bleu,* was given its U.S. première, contrasting with the lighter fare of

Lecocq's *La Fille de Madame Angot*, a reminder of Tabuteau's Paris days at Les Variétés. There were some unusual works from Germany, including Lortzing's *Zar und Zimmerman* and, as a change from Humperdinck's ever popular *Hänsel und Gretel*, the world première of his new opera, *Königskinder*. Although few were able to hear it, in early 1910 an experimental radio broadcast took place from the Met stage. The season ended with a greatly extended tour of the Midwest and South; then there were several weeks in Paris for which the orchestra was left behind.

A major event of Tabuteau's third season with the Met was the December 10, 1910, world première of Puccini's new opera, *La Fanciulla del West*. Toscanini conducted, with Caruso and Destinn creating the leading roles. John de Lancie remembered Tabuteau once telling him about the rehearsals: "The masses did not have money to go to the opera in New York, so the public would attend dress rehearsals. There were many Italian immigrants. As rehearsals with Toscanini were conducted in Italian, of course they could understand him. Puccini was in the audience. He stood up and spoke to Toscanini about something. Toscanini turned around and said, "I know your music better than you do. Just sit down!" (This incident was probably only one of many that contributed to the deteriorating relations between Toscanini and Puccini toward the end of Puccini's life.)

Many oboists who studied with Tabuteau later expressed the regret that they had never asked him about the days when he played for Mahler, Toscanini, Caruso, and Farrar, but this was not easy to do. In his opinion, a pupil had no business posing questions. Perhaps because Tabuteau so seldom spoke of that period, the few things I heard him say remained clearly in my mind. In the season of 1944–45, Tabuteau conducted an orchestra of Curtis students for a series of Sunday morning broadcasts on radio station KYW in Philadelphia. Once, while we were rehearsing excerpts from *Carmen*, he stopped and said, "I will never forget when we did *Carmen* with Toscanini at the Metropolitan—every measure was like a different landscape." He also became particularly animated when we played the ballet music from *Aida*, and I remember receiving a rare word of praise for the rather tricky trills.

Unfortunately, Tabuteau did not reminisce or talk about Mahler, nor did he mention the many historic operatic premières in which he had taken part. Except for his few references to Toscanini, he only spoke of the intense work required to learn all the operas. Occasionally he would recount some trivial occurrence of orchestral life. One incident that still amused him after forty years was the story of the contra-bassoon player who had an attachment connected to a foot pedal that would allow him to play the forty-two measures of low B-flat at the beginning of *Das Rheingold* without running out of breath. As Tabuteau told it, some pranksters in the woodwind section detached the rubber tube, and "you know, the floor of the pit of the Metro-po-lee-tain which had not been broomed for years—he got a big mouthful of dust! Ha, ha, ha!" I found this a rather fanciful story, but in 1993 an article appeared in the *Journal of the International Double Reed Society* concerning the "Aerophor," a tone-sustaining device for wind instruments invented in 1911 in Germany. It was indeed operated by a foot pedal, which pushed air through tubing into the player's mouth. The inventor, Bernard Samuels, a flutist, claimed that many passages, especially in the works of Wagner, could not be played as intended unless one used the Aerophor. In 1914, none other than Alfred Hertz had written a testimonial asserting that he "would not rest until each wind instrument player of the Metropolitan Opera House uses one." Now I could finally believe Tabuteau's story![16]

Other glimpses of Tabuteau's operatic period occasionally came to light. Ten years after he had retired and returned to France, I wrote to ask him about some notes in the opening of *Madama Butterfly* that were giving me trouble. He replied with detailed instructions of how to practice the passage, suggested fingerings to use, and noted that "it is not a sin to attack the high D# mordant." John Mack told me of his experience with Tabuteau and opera. It was in the spring of 1952, and Mack had just returned from a tour with the Sadler Wells Ballet. He received an unexpected telephone call from Philadelphia asking him to play second oboe with Tabuteau for a week and a half at the May Festival in Ann Arbor, Michigan. The programs were to include music from *Die Walküre*. Describing his impression of Tabuteau, Mack said, "He was so excited. It was going to be a concert performance and that wonderful Set Svanholm was singing and Ormandy was conducting.

MARCEL TABUTEAU

Tabuteau's note in 1964 to Laila Storch explaining how to practice a difficult passage in the opening of Madama Butterfly. *He has turned it into a Christmas greeting and adds, "In 1909 found it very difficult."*

Tabuteau was hopping up and down with excitement. Of course he'd played this stuff when he was a kid at the Met. He really knew that music. It was as if he'd been given a youth drug, and I thought, I've never seen Tabuteau like this. It was totally different than anything he was doing now and it was absolutely as if he couldn't contain himself. He was so full of joy."

THE METROPOLITAN OPERA

Mack remembered another little Met anecdote. While he was playing in the Juilliard Orchestra in the 1940s, he was asked by Professor Frederick Jacobi, the composer, if he had by any chance studied with Marcel Tabuteau. When Mack said yes, Jacobi, who had been a coach at the Met, said, "Young man, let me tell you something. When your teacher arrived in this country, he sounded like every other French oboe player, but not for long . . . not for long!" Reflecting further on Tabuteau and the Met, Mack concluded, "In my heart I feel one thing: that Marcel Tabuteau, with his very concentrated training, finding himself in the opera pit which was totally international—Russians, French, Germans—all these people tossed together, and the singers, and all the different composers and conductors! It was the perfect place to absorb all these influences, and someone like Marcel Tabuteau, with his brilliant talent, could not help but respond."

In the archives of the Metropolitan Opera House, a few documents survive from the time Tabuteau worked there. Contracts made between the Metropolitan Opera Company and the Musical Mutual Protective Union of New York were headed with the dates of the season followed by "United States of America, Canada, Cuba and Mexico," and contained very exact conditions. Aside from the stipulations concerning basic salary and extra performances, there were provisions for free rehearsals, which "may exceed three hours once each week if entire rehearsal is for work performed for the first time that season, if only one opera or concert programme is rehearsed, and only one conductor officiates." The management also claimed the right of "not more than six Sunday rehearsals for operas, and other free rehearsals for the Sunday concerts, none of these to exceed two and a half hours."

The contracts specified an interesting scale of extra compensation for single performances outside "Greater New York": in Philadelphia, $2.00; for Baltimore and Albany, $3.00; for Boston, $5.00; but in the event of two consecutive performances "in the same city, like Philadelphia, Baltimore, Boston, etc. . . . $5.00." The musician would be paid $1.00 "hotel indemnity" in the event it was necessary to stay overnight and $3.00 for each fraction of an hour in which a performance exceeded four hours from the beginning of the overture. When one notes the frequency with which Wagner operas appeared in the schedule, it is clear that there would have been many $3.00 bonuses! For tours lasting one or more weeks, the payment was an extra $2.00 per day.[17]

Each of Tabuteau's existing contracts (there are none from his first three years) is based on a season of twenty-three weeks. Between the 1911 and 1912 seasons, Tabuteau's salary jumped from $50 to $70 a week. From the 1930s to the 1960s, a first-desk oboe player was usually one of the highest paid members of an orchestra, but this was not the case during Tabuteau's years at the Met. For the 1913–14 season, the first horn, Frank Corrado, was paid $117 a week, which was more than the concertmaster, Eugene Boegner, who earned $105. First bassoonist Leopoldo Bucci received $100, to be equaled in the following seasons by the harpist, Carlos Salzedo. All of these salaries were considerably higher than that of first oboist Tabuteau. He ranked along with the timpani player, August Kircher, and first trombonist, Justus Pfeiffen-schneider, whose pay rose from $50 to $70 a week at the same time as Tabuteau's. The rank-and-file string player or a second chair in the wind section was still getting $56 a week. Tuba and horn player Harry Fricke was low man on the roster with a salary of $27, which, however, was augmented by "three dollars extra when required to wear stage dress."

Tabuteau's contract as first oboe for the 1912–13 season states that his salary will be $70 with an extra $10 for anything above seven per-formances in a week. (Contrast this schedule with that of today, when the musicians of the Metropolitan Opera Orchestra play only four times per week.) For the following two seasons his basic salary was to be $84 with $12 each for extra performances. However, the total in-come was sure to exceed this amount, as in each of these three contracts there is a clause in which the "the Musician agrees to place himself at the disposal of The Company for rehearsals in New York beginning on October 22 or 27," the date varying according to the year. For prelimi-nary rehearsals the company agrees to pay "the Musician at the rate of Twenty-five Dollars for six day rehearsals per week. Evening rehearsals to be paid the same as performances [$12]."

On February 24, 1912, a "letter of agreement" was sent to Marcel Tabuteau at 532 West 146th Street, New York City. It was signed by Gatti-Casazza and offered him the position of "first oboe player in the orchestra of the Metropolitan Opera House and for the tours to be undertaken by said company at a guaranteed salary of $12.00 (twelve dollars) per performance with a guarantee of 8 (eight) performances including a Sunday night concert per week, for the seasons of 1912–13, 1913–14, 1914–15. Tabuteau accepted the "engagement," which differed from the contracts made and executed each spring between the Metropolitan Opera Company and "the Musician." Whether or not the conditions of the Gatti-Casazza letter were fulfilled, by the 1913–14 season Tabuteau would have been earning approximately $96 a week. On April 15, 1914, he signed his contract for the coming year, but the current 1913–14 season, Tabuteau's sixth, turned out to be his last at the Metropolitan.

In the latter years of Tabuteau's tenure at the Met, there were only two other players in the oboe section: Lambert Schoof, second oboe, and Romeo Boninsegna, English horn and third oboe. By 1910 the large orchestra of 135 players that Gatti-Casazza had demanded when he became general director of the Met had been dissolved. While the Met had the equivalent of two orchestras, it cannot be determined in exactly which performances Tabuteau took part. But from the time the oboe section consisted of only one person for each position, it can safely be assumed that Tabuteau played in almost every opera or concert. The last three seasons Tabuteau spent at the Met saw many novelties and premières. In 1911 there was the opera *Lobetanz* by Ludwig Thuille, a composer best known to woodwind players for his *Sextet for Piano and Winds*. For the first time, an American opera, *Mona*, by Horatio Parker, was given a world première, and in 1913 Alfred Hertz led the world première of *Cyrano* by Walter Damrosch, the conductor of Tabuteau's first years in America. The brilliant coloratura soprano Luisa Tetrazzini made her Met debut, and the much admired contralto Ernestine Schumann-Heink returned after a long absence. Two of the most important American premières in 1913 were *Boris Godunov* under Toscanini and *Der Rosenkavalier*, directed by the diligent and versatile Alfred Hertz.

MARCEL TABUTEAU

On the eve of World War I, enthusiasm for Wagner's music was at an all-time high. Besides ongoing frequent productions of each of the operas of the Ring Cycle, all the other major Wagner operas were scattered throughout each season. Programs with vocal and orchestral excerpts from his operas had also become popular. These were often featured in the Sunday evening concerts, one of the less well known activities of the Metropolitan Opera Orchestra. Works played ranged from overtures and arias to Strauss waltzes and serious symphonic repertoire. Internationally known instrumental soloists also took part in these concerts. Fritz Kreisler appeared several times, as did the violinists Mischa Elman, Carl Flesch, Eugène Ysaÿe, and Efrem Zimbalist. Once, after a performance of Saint-Saëns's *B Minor Concerto* with Mischa Elman, Tabuteau was quite outraged by a music critic's comment that he had "equaled the beauty of the violin solo in the slow movement." With the same youthful bravura displayed at the time of his Met audition, Tabuteau said he felt he had easily outdone Elman. But in telling this story he laughed at himself.[18]

The most brilliant pianists of the era appeared as soloists with the Met Orchestra: Josef Hofmann, Ferrucio Busoni, Teresa Carreño, Sergei Rachmaninoff, and Leopold Godowsky. Although the names of many of the conductors are not remembered today, there were also concerts conducted by Toscanini or Alfred Hertz. For example, on April 13, 1913, Toscanini gave his first purely symphonic concert in America. He led the orchestra of the Metropolitan Opera in a program of Wagner's *Eine Faust Overture,* Strauss's tone poem *Til Eulenspiegels Lustige Streiche,* and Beethoven's *Ninth Symphony.* Thus, while working under conductors Toscanini, Mahler, and Hertz, and being surrounded by the great voices of the "Golden Age" of the Metropolitan Opera, Tabuteau was also collaborating with the outstanding instrumental soloists of the day and learning major symphonic repertoire. In only a few years after joining the Philadelphia Orchestra, he would be playing with almost all these solo artists again.

The rich experiences of his early years at the Met, working in company with extraordinary conductors and singers, undoubtedly made a significant contribution to Tabuteau's musical development. During each of Tabuteau's six seasons at the Met, Enrico Caruso and Geraldine

THE METROPOLITAN OPERA

Farrar were leading singers, while Toscanini and Hertz were the principal conductors. Thirty years later, the only framed and autographed photographs of famous musical personalities to be seen in Tabuteau's studio were those of Toscanini and Stokowski hanging above his reed desk and, on the opposite wall, Geraldine Farrar.

5
SAN FRANCISCO INTERLUDE

*The Panama-Pacific International
Exposition Orchestra, 1915*

John de Lancie, who grew up in the Bay Region of California, remembered that the first time he heard the name Marcel Tabuteau was in connection with the 1915 Panama-Pacific International Exposition: "It was during the early 1930s. I was only nine or ten years old and was just beginning to study the oboe with Gus Apel, a German who came to San Francisco around 1900. He was a trumpet player, but he took up the oboe in order to get more work. My father used to bring me to my lessons in Oakland, and I remember how Apel told us that during the 1915 Fair he arrived at a rehearsal one day and heard this beautiful oboe sound. It was the little solo in the *Marsch Militaire* of Schubert. He got up from his chair to look around and asked somebody who was playing. 'Oh, a new fellow who's just arrived from the East Coast.' It was Tabuteau."

I once spoke with a ninety-six-year-old retired flutist in Seattle, Brooks Parker, who had played in the San Francisco Symphony Orchestra during its first season of 1911–12. He told me that he had worked with Tabuteau during the 1915 Exposition. I asked him if he remembered how Tabuteau had sounded, and he answered, "Indeed yes—beautiful. He played beautifully." He also recalled that the other members of the oboe section were Apel and Bertram. At that time I was under the false impression that they were all part of a band.[1] I was to discover, instead, that they were members of a full-size symphony orchestra that had been especially organized for the exposition in San Francisco. Tabuteau's participation in the Panama-Pacific International Exposition constituted only a brief, but nevertheless fascinating, interval in his early career. Again, as with Damrosch and the Metropolitan, he rarely spoke of those days. But I *did* remember his mentioning how much he had liked being in San Francisco for about six months—how he found it a wonderful place, which still retained something of its older, wild "Barbary Coast" atmosphere, and how he had often gone fishing in the Bay and up to Mt. Tamalpais. I believed he was there to play during the fair, but he never said a word about either the music or the exposition itself, that festive event celebrating the completion and historic opening of the Panama Canal. Now, over eighty years later, it would be a challenge to see if any *facts* concerning Tabuteau and the 1915 Fair were still to be found.

The first real clue turned up in Philadelphia. Tabuteau had written a letter, in his rather deficient English, to the management of the Philadelphia Orchestra from a San Francisco address of 1600 California Street.[2] Dated August 10, 1915, it was addressed to Mr. Louis A. Mattson, the assistant manager of the orchestra:

Dear Sir,

Excuse me if I have been so long to answer at your question but I was very busy lately with the rehearsals and concerts of the Beethoven festival. Please do no make any comment on story by the photo wich I sent you yesterday as a french reservist as I fear it may *give me troubles!*

YOURS VERY TRULY,
MARCEL TABUTEAU

The picture shows a still youthful-looking Tabuteau wearing a heavy, double-breasted coat and high laced boots. He is standing alongside an army tent and is holding a huge World War I army rifle. On the back of the photo he had written: "Reservist in french army. Released last

MARCEL TABUTEAU

december—and glad of it!!" The last four words were scratched out with pen or crayon. The letter and picture place Tabuteau in San Francisco during the summer of 1915, while "released last december" helps to explain his whereabouts in the beginning of the 1914–15 musical season. Although Tabuteau had signed his principal oboe contract for the Met in April 1914, it is evident that he did not play the 1914–15 season (Toscanini's last). We recall the family stories about the message from his father, "*Ton pays t'appelle!*"(Your country is calling you), when war broke out in August 1914. Tabuteau duly returned to France where, as in 1906, he had to report to the 45th Regiment of Infantry in his hometown, Compiègne. According to official military records of the Département of Oise, he was discharged with a medical diagnosis of endocarditis (inflammation of the heart lining) on December 14, 1914, after only a short period of service. The note on the back of the photograph he sent to the Philadelphia Orchestra expresses his relief at his release, but the possibility remained that he would still have to serve in the French military. Army records show that on July 7, 1915, he had to undergo another medical examination at the Consulat Général of France in San Francisco. A diagnosis of rheumatic endocarditis with systolic heart murmur (*endocardite rhumatismal avec souffle systolique*) resulted in the continuation of his earlier discharge.[3] John de Lancie remembered hearing Tabuteau grumble about his return from his 1914 military venture because he was unable to get back into the Met. Finding himself without work, he understandably looked toward San Francisco, where an orchestra of symphonic proportions was being assembled for the Panama-Pacific International Exposition. The crucial letter of August 1915 indicated that Tabuteau was indeed in San Francisco at that time, but when I began to look into the musical events of the exposition, I found no sign of a Beethoven festival. In the hope of finding records that would confirm Tabuteau's participation in the exposition and in a Beethoven festival, I decided to investigate further.

I began by looking for 1600 California Street. From this location, one block east of Van Ness Avenue at the corner of Polk and California Streets, it would have been an easy trip to the fairground at the marina. A low, four-story brick apartment house of uncertain age stands on the corner today. The route of the historic California Street cable car, which

SAN FRANCISCO INTERLUDE

Tabuteau with musket in the French Army at the beginning of World War I, 1914.

runs close by, has changed but little. On the way to my oboe lessons in the late 1930s, I remember passing the ornate Palace of Fine Arts with its distinctive lagoon and colonnade. Not far from the Golden Gate Bridge, it is the only building that survives on the site of the Panama-Pacific Exposition. In 1915 it was one of a series of domed palaces that graced the beautifully landscaped grounds. The Palace of Horticulture was able to boast of a dome larger than that of the U.S. Capitol or St. Peter's in Rome. Festival Hall, where most of the concerts took place, "reflects the best mood of the French Renaissance. The great dome, encircled by smaller corner domes, suggests the *Théâtre des Beaux Arts* in Paris."[4] The famed 433-foot-high Tower of Jewels at the entry to the exposition grounds was covered with cut glass in colors of ruby, amethyst, turquoise, emerald, and flashing white diamonds, which sparkled by day in the sunshine and by night in the light of spotlights. Although not located on the fairgrounds, another important building, the Exposition

MARCEL TABUTEAU

Auditorium, erected at a cost of $2 million, was intended as a gift to the city of San Francisco and in 1915 was lauded as the "finest structure of its kind in America." Now known as the Civic Auditorium, it has been in use ever since.

Architecturally, the buildings of the exposition were largely based on European models, but in keeping with California's Mediterranean heritage, the color scheme ran through shades of yellow, terra cotta, red, and pink to cerulean blue. The 365-acre space was divided into three sections. On the eastern side was the amusement area known as the Zone, and in the west, the pavilions of foreign nations and the various states. In between were eight exhibition palaces separated by spacious courtyards, all reflecting the influence of Rome and the Italian and Spanish Renaissance, plus a racetrack to provide some excitement.

The Zone boasted a reconstruction of the quaint medieval center of the German town of Nuremberg, a working model of the Panama Canal, a presentation of the Creation based on the biblical book of Genesis, and "The Battle of Gettysburg, a Painted History of the Century's most Blood-stained Tragedy." If certain of the Zone displays were quite high-minded, there were also such diverting attractions as Miss Lea Lelio Kuli, a hula dancer who was described by the *San Francisco Call and Post* on March 5 as wearing "a garment of leaves and grass. Her chief adornments are her wonderful dusky hair, her white teeth, tempting smile and her brown eyes with their drooping lids." Only a few days later, on March 19, the same newspaper reported less cheerful news from the Zone: "Princess Zehia Eddie, a dancer in the Circassian Theater, is dead today." She was shot by her brother, Isaac Eddie, who said "he killed his sister because she refused to give up café dancing." On a happier note, the official fair booklet predicted that based on the previous twenty-seven years of weather records, nothing but pleasant days could be expected for the entire ten months of the exposition.

The U.S. vessel *Jason*, arriving on April 12 via the new Panama Canal, had encountered anything but smooth sailing on the Atlantic round trip to bring the valuable art objects that would complete vacant spots in the exhibits. The ship had left five months earlier loaded with Christmas gifts for the children of the European countries already at war. Not only was it battered by violent storms, but it also had to thread its way

SAN FRANCISCO INTERLUDE

through mine-filled waters. On its return voyage to the United States, the *Jason* carried a cargo of treasures insured for $3.5 million, everything from 104 cases of ancient statuary to postimpressionist paintings, loaded at the ports of Piraeus, Genoa, Marseille, Barcelona, and Bristol.

The Panama-Pacific International Exposition was one of the most lavish and opulent displays of its type in the early part of the century. "Music was of the soul of the place, a permeating beauty. . . . You heard it wherever you went. . . . From February 20 to December 4, the Exposition was a great music festival. Besides symphonies, choruses, orchestras, led by celebrated conductors, and daily recitals by the world's greatest organists on one of the world's greatest organs, there were bands playing almost continuously somewhere in the grounds, and sometimes at the rate of twelve concerts in a single day. Music attended all the public functions and pervaded the entire life of the Exposition, and a great and satisfying abundance of it was as free as the sight of the sculptures or the palaces, or the colors that spread themselves in succession over the gardens."[5] The sheer number of performances is impressive by the standards of any day. Of over 2,000 concerts, 575 were given by the Exposition Orchestra. Of the 368 organ recitals, 100 were given by Edwin Lemare of London, considered by many to be "the greatest living organist." One wonders if he considered it a gesture toward California when his programs included "In North Dakota," a movement of his own symphonic poem "From the West."

There were band concerts galore. Aside from the official Exposition Band, ten other wind groups came from the United States and from as far away as France and the Philippines. Altogether they played over a thousand concerts, without counting those given by visiting nonprofessional bands. The Exposition Orchestra "made many fine events possible. It was, as it had been designed to be, the central structure of the Exposition musical scheme." The great choral works could not have been given without this orchestra, and "even the visit of Saint-Saëns depended on it." Music lovers termed it "the best orchestra ever heard in San Francisco." It was praised for "fineness, power, and easy precision that are rare in orchestras, no matter how long drilled."

Negotiations concerning salaries had gone on for eight months between the American Federation of Musicians, San Francisco Local 6,

MARCEL TABUTEAU

and Mr. George W. Stewart of Boston, who had been appointed director of music for the fair. The national union took the position that, based on the minimum of $45 a week paid at the 1904 World's Fair in St. Louis, the musicians should now earn not less than $50–$55, especially as the San Francisco Exposition would be open for seven days a week instead of the six in St. Louis, with Sunday being an especially heavy playing day. Mr. Stewart had reserved the right to select solo players from AFM members anywhere in the country, but not to exceed fifteen from outside San Francisco. However, Local 6 eventually agreed to a minimum scale of the lower fee, $45 a week.

The long planned and much heralded visit of Camille Saint-Saëns was without doubt one of the most momentous occurrences of the exposition. Saint-Saëns had composed a piece of music especially for the occasion, appropriately entitled *Hail California!*[6] The three Saint-Saëns concerts of June 19, 24, and 27 were deemed sufficiently important to warrant the inclusion of the names of the personnel of the Exposition Orchestra in the printed program, something not ordinarily done. Here we find Tabuteau and Apel listed as the oboe section, along with a Mr. A. Bertram on English horn. Without question Marcel Tabuteau was the principal oboist of the official Exposition Orchestra. Already on February 23, 1915, a newspaper item had stated with a certain bravado that "the most remarkable orchestra ever heard in this city is now playing nightly at the Old Faithful Inn . . . soon the people will throng to hear Max Bendix and his eighty instrumentalists with much the same enthusiasm that they manifest in Baden-Baden or Hamburg when a Weingartner or a Nikisch directs a great orchestra." The article told how "San Francisco has furnished her quota of the orchestra, some twenty-six of the men being members of our Symphony Orchestra, the balance are furnished by proud Boston, haughty New York and epicurean New Orleans." The unknown reviewer praised the various sections of the orchestra: "the wood wind is pure . . . and in the brass one notes a dignity and splendor unwonted in trombones and French horns and trumpets on the coast." He predicted that the high quality of this orchestra and the authority of its conductor, Max Bendix, "will prove such an artistic stimulus to San Francisco as will mark the beginning of a new and better era in the orchestral life of San Francisco."

When one reads the names of the musicians in the Exposition Orchestra, it is not surprising that enthusiasm for its accomplishments ran so high: principal bass, Anton Torello from Barcelona, Spain; solo horn, Anton Horner; first bassoon, Richard Krueger from Germany. These men were already members of the Philadelphia Orchestra. The first trumpet, Harry Glantz, would go to Philadelphia the next season, along with Tabuteau. The principal cellist, Horace Britt, had formerly held that same position in Philadelphia and would have a long career in both orchestral and chamber music. Tabuteau's roommate and fellow poker player during the fair was Paul Whiteman of the viola section, who was to become famous in the 1920s and 1930s for the elegant style of his jazz orchestra and his championship of the music of George Gershwin.[7]

Max Bendix, Richard Hageman, and Auguste Bosc shared the podium of the Exposition Orchestra. Bendix and Hageman had been conductors at the Met and would have been familiar to Tabuteau from his time there. Bendix had directed many of the special concerts and ballets in the 1909–10 Met season, and Hageman had served as both pianist and conductor. Seven years had passed since the convoluted events of Tabuteau's disputed departure from the New York Symphony Orchestra and his engagement at the Met. However, it was probably just as well that by the time of Walter Damrosch's guest appearance with the Exposition Orchestra in September, Tabuteau had apparently left for Philadelphia.

In preparation for Saint-Saëns's visit, the score to *Hail California!* was brought over in advance by M. Gabriel Parès, the noted former *chef de musique* of the Garde Républicaine Band. France had released sixty-five men from the army in order to provide the personnel for this French Band, as it was called during its eleven-week engagement at the fair. A frequent soloist with the band, who a couple of years later would become Tabuteau's colleague in the Philadelphia Orchestra, was the clarinetist Daniel Bonade. On January 28, 1915, a month before the opening of the fair, the noted critic of the *San Francisco Examiner,* Redfern Mason, wrote: "Camille Saint-Saëns is to be with us. The old man eloquent of French music has rounded out his three score years and ten, but is still one of the world's young men, and, unlike Hans Richter, the Atlantic has no terrors for him.[8] Not only will Saint-Saëns make the voyage to this Paris of the West, but he is engaged in composing a work

In this photo from Tabuteau's 1915 San Francisco year, one can see his oboe with no left-hand F key and a short scrape reed. Courtesy Guy Baumier.

SAN FRANCISCO INTERLUDE

in one of the larger forms which shall celebrate in enduring fashion the completion of the Panama Canal. The directors of the exposition have given him a free hand. The first thought was that he should write a commemoration march; but, bearing in mind, perhaps, the melancholy result which followed Wagner's attempt to write a *Centennial March* to order, George Stewart and his colleagues gave him to understand that he must allow Pegasus to bear him where it wished."

"Pegasus" led Saint-Saëns to the composition of *Hail California!* a work for the combined forces of a symphonic orchestra, organ, and a band, which turned out to be none other than that of the famous John Philip Sousa. Redfern explained: "Who will play the work when Saint-Saëns comes to conduct it? . . . It will be played by the Exposition Orchestra, a body of eighty instrumentalists recruited from among the best musicians of the country. . . . Throughout the whole term of the exposition the orchestra will give concerts, classical indeed, but inclining to the works of the masters in their lighter moods rather than to the ponderous compositions, beloved of music-lovers in their most exclusive art-worship." The general atmosphere is well expressed by a June 10 announcement stating that the official Exposition Orchestra led by Max Bendix would play light music by Grieg, Delibes, Boccherini, and Waldteufel, with the reminder to the public: "Don't miss the reproduction of Old Faithful Geyser in the Spectatorium under the Big Mountain and Yellowstone Falls, every hour on the hour." Other programs, however, featured works one would hear in the world's leading concert halls: the *Leonore Overture No. 3*, the *Fifth Symphony* and *Seventh Symphony* of Beethoven, symphonies by Schumann and Tchaikovsky, Strauss's *Don Juan*, the Dvořák's *New World*, Glazounov's *C Minor Symphony*, Opus 58, in its San Francisco première, and several all-Wagner concerts. The Union Pacific Railway Company, which owned the Yellowstone Park concession, was praised for its role in making the orchestra possible. Many of the concerts were given in the Old Faithful Inn, and no effort had been spared to provide for the comfort of the conductors and musicians. There were ample washroom facilities and a large room containing individual lockers for all.

Shortly before the much anticipated arrival of Camille Saint-Saëns, another, somewhat more sober but musically significant event was unfolding. This was the visit of the Boston Symphony Orchestra, which made a special trip to the West Coast to play thirteen concerts at the exposition. They performed under the leadership of their highly regarded conductor, Dr. Karl Muck, from May 14 to 25. Although the concerts took place so soon after the May 7 sinking of the *Lusitania,* the United States was not yet involved in the European war. The "patriotic" hysteria that fueled rumors Muck had been seen signaling to offshore U-boats, which eventually led to his arrest and internment, was still several years in the future.[9] Now, in San Francisco, he presented programs of the most uncompromising level, ranging from the music of Bach, Beethoven, Mozart, and Brahms to that of Sibelius and Richard Strauss. Indeed, one program featured Strauss's *Also sprach Zarathustra.* During an all-French program that featured his *Organ Symphony No. 3,* Saint-Saëns was recognized sitting in Festival Hall. At the conclusion of the work, applause and calls of "Saint-Saëns!" resounded from all sides of the auditorium. Dr. Muck and the orchestra led in the acclaim that would not cease until the eighty-year-old composer rose and bowed. Another French musician who took part in these concerts was Georges Longy, the solo oboist of the Boston Symphony. He had joined the orchestra in 1898 and was undoubtably the most famous of Gillet's students in America at that time. It is regrettable that we do not know what contact, if any, Tabuteau may have had with him in San Francisco.

Saint-Saëns had arrived on May 21 and expressed delight at being able to come to the exposition, as well as astonishment at the beautiful night illumination. A day later, Sousa's band of sixty-five men came for the beginning of an eight-week engagement at the fair. The three Saint-Saëns concerts at the end of June included several of the composer's best known works: the *A minor Cello Concerto,* the symphonic poem *Omphale's Spinning Wheel, Suite Algérienne,* and *The Promised Land.* The last-named work made use of the Exposition Chorus of three hundred voices in a première performance for America. Saint-Saëns conducted it himself but shared the leadership of other numbers with Richard Hageman. However, the creation everyone was waiting for was *Hail California!* Subtitled *Symphonic Episode,* it consisted of four sections: I, *Entrée à l'Exposition,* II, *California, Land of Flowers and*

Fruits, III, *Spanish Airs,* IV, *Military March.* Redfern Mason's program notes tell us something about the varied elements of the composition. The first movement uses "La Marseillaise" to help evoke the joyful opening of the exposition. The second section paints an idyllic tone picture of California as it was when first seen by Fra Junipero Serra, founder of the missions. Then come the spirited rhythms of the Spanish era. The work ends with a trumpet introducing the "Star Spangled Banner," followed by an interlude for organ and an episode for band alone. Finally, all groups join together, adding "La Marseillaise" again for good measure and thereby putting a French accent upon California's mostly Spanish history. One would like to know what Tabuteau thought while playing in this extravaganza! With Sousa's band playing and Saint-Saëns conducting, it truly must have been a mega-event. Saint-Saëns and Sousa were photographed, arms linked together. The earnings from the Saint-Saëns concerts exceeded the estimated budget, while the Boston Symphony came close to meeting the $62,303.75 it had cost to bring them.

In July a rather exotic collaboration took place between the Exposition Orchestra and the colorful and innovative American dancer Loïe Fuller, or as she was billed, La Loïe Fuller. She had recently performed before a hundred thousand people in Athens, and none other than the great sculptor Auguste Rodin had proclaimed, "Her creations will live forever!" At the exposition, La Loïe chose compositions from the standard symphonic repertoire for her dances: *A Night on Bald Mountain,* the *Peer Gynt Suite,* and Debussy's *Nocturnes* alternated with the orchestra alone playing Rimsky-Korsakov's *Capriccio Español* and *Scheherazade,* along with *Afternoon of a Faun, Le Roi d'Ys* overture, and Borodin's *Dances* from *Prince Igor.* With important oboe solos in all of these works, Tabuteau was rapidly expanding his orchestral experience.

The Beethoven Festival to which Tabuteau referred in his letter to the Philadelphia Orchestra management took place on August 6, 7, and 8, but it was not a part of official exposition events. An orchestra of one hundred musicians was hailed as "the largest symphony orchestra ever assembled in San Francisco." For this special occasion the program again included the players' names. Tabuteau was principal oboist for all three of the concerts, which were given in the new Civic Auditorium at Larkin and Grove Streets. The conductor was none other than Alfred Hertz, for whom Tabuteau had so recently been playing at the Metropolitan Opera. With the Beethoven concerts serving as Hertz's introduction to the city, it would be his role to lead the San Francisco Symphony into that "new and better era" hoped for by the critics. The *Ninth Symphony* was performed with the collaboration of the famous singers Ernestine Schumann-Heink and Paul Althouse. No explanation was given for the fact that the second concert of the Beethoven Festival consisted entirely of the music of Wagner. However, the *Männerchor* of New York did present a statue of Beethoven to the city of San Francisco at an unveiling ceremony in Golden Gate Park.

The preface of the official fair booklet, written several months before the opening of the exposition, referred to the "grim irony" of the outbreak of "what may prove to be the greatest war in history." At the same time, it expressed confidence that there would be little detrimental effect on the exposition or its exhibits, and that fair attendance would actually increase. In August 1915, on the peaceful shores of San Francisco Bay, the war in Europe must still have been seen as a matter to be settled by distant foreign nations, and the Beethoven Festival came to an end with a performance of Wagner's *Kaisermarsch*.

6 THE PHILADELPHIA ORCHESTRA

The Stokowski Years, 1915–1940

LEOPOLD STOKOWSKI'S SEARCH FOR A FIRST-CLASS OBOIST

There are at least three versions of how Marcel Tabuteau came to be engaged as principal oboe of the Philadelphia Orchestra. One story is that in the spring of 1915, while Tabuteau was in San Francisco, he heard of the oboe opening from some of the Philadelphia Orchestra men who were playing with him in the Panama-Pacific International Exposition. This sounds plausible, but there is good evidence that Tabuteau had already written to the Philadelphia Orchestra in the fall of 1914. Then there is the question of what part Alexander van Rensselaer, the respected president of the Philadelphia Orchestra Association, may have had in the choice of Tabuteau. As a fervent supporter of the orchestra and a confidant of Stokowski, he could make suggestions, even concerning personnel, that were taken very seriously. On one of the Met's visits he had apparently come down to the edge of the orchestra pit, asked to speak to Tabuteau, and offered him the position. But as Tabuteau said, "In those days I was very happy in New York.

Philadelphia was a small town and I turned it down."[1] In the *New Grove Dictionary* no less an authority than Philip Bate states that Stokowski decided to hire Tabuteau after hearing him play in a performance of *Tristan und Isolde*.[2] The Met gave six performances of *Tristan* during the 1913–14 season, with Toscanini conducting, all in New York except for one in Philadelphia on January 6, 1914. It would have been quite possible for Stokowski to attend any of these performances. A statement I heard from Tabuteau himself in 1945 confirms that this was indeed how he was hired.[3]

For several years Stokowski had been looking for a new solo oboist. Since the beginning of his Philadelphia tenure in 1912 during the orchestra's thirteenth season, he had made a number of significant personnel changes. He was happy with some of the original players who had been with the orchestra since its foundation in 1900, especially the horn player Anton Horner, the timpanist Oscar Schwar, and violinist Thaddeus Rich. Many others, however, he found inadequate.[4] Stokowski had certain aims for his orchestra in the realm of interpretation. If his solo players later became known as outstanding individual artists, it was not merely because they were all superbly trained masters of their instruments. Stokowski encouraged the expression of individuality. The result was not artistic anarchy, as all the players were blended into Stokowski's tonal vision of the music, but at the same time one could admire the special qualities of each solo instrumentalist as his own talents unfolded. Later in his life, Stokowski stated:

> In working with the Philadelphia Orchestra, my dream was, and we partly achieved that dream, to express to the utmost the spirit, the inner spirit, of every kind of music. I say "every kind" because every composer as an individual, as his life develops, produces—creates, different kinds of music. . . . And, of course, the differences between two composers who lived in the same period, like Brahms and Wagner, are like the difference between the North Pole and the equator. . . . In order to do all that with the Philadelphia Orchestra, I begged the players to notice all those differences and I said to them, "Each one of you must be a poet as well as a great player of your instrument, and through your poetic feeling, you can express every kind of music." . . . Do not permit yourselves to become, as is the tendency in the world today, standardized, so that you all think and feel the

THE PHILADELPHIA ORCHESTRA

same way. . . . Give your personality, all your inner feeling, give that expression through the music. Do not all be alike. Be different as you really are in your natures. No two violins are alike. No two bows are alike. No two hands are alike. No two nervous systems are alike. No two minds are alike. No two emotional characters are alike. You are all different. Be different! Don't standardize yourself. And put all those differences, all that richness of different coloring of personalities into music." They finally did that and the orchestra became so flexible and so extraordinary![5]

Under a conductor with such a goal, it is not surprising that the players *did* become so greatly admired as individuals. Tabuteau once said that Stokowski could afford to encourage this attitude as his own personality was so colorful and magnetic that there was no danger he would be outshone by anyone in the orchestra.[6] When I remember the intensity with which Tabuteau worked to find the specific tonal quality and style of expression demanded for each different composer, I realize that whether or not he originally had these concepts, he was actively fulfilling Stokowski's vision. The interaction of conductor and player during the Stokowski years created such a synthesis that one cannot always say who influenced whom. Philadelphia Orchestra musicians who remember this era have said that Stokowski would often stay after a rehearsal and ask Tabuteau to play a particular phrase over a number of times. The next morning Stokowski would propose that same phrasing to the whole violin section. For Tabuteau, to have his search for color and imaginative interpretation not only encouraged and appreciated by the conductor, but recognized, must have affected his lifelong striving to make the exact reed he needed—painstakingly scraping the cane to a point that would best allow the expression of his musical ideas and at the same time have the particular quality of sound he envisaged for Mozart, Brahms, or Wagner.

But before Stokowski could begin his quest for such elevated and poetic musical standards, he had first to find an excellent oboe player. The archive of the Philadelphia Orchestra contains letters exchanged between Stokowski and Andrew Wheeler, the secretary of the orchestra's administrative board, which indicate that Stokowski, almost from the time of his arrival, was looking for a new "first class" oboist. Although

MARCEL TABUTEAU

fragmentary, this correspondence from the period of 1912–15 is sufficient to illuminate some aspects of Stokowski's search.

A decade had now elapsed since the Damrosch era, but certain issues had not changed that greatly. A major problem for conductors continued to be how to secure that rare and highly valued commodity, a good Belgian or French oboe player. In fact, there already was a French oboist in the Philadelphia Orchestra. Alfred Doucet held the principal oboe position from 1902 to 1913. He had won his Premier Prix at the Paris Conservatory in 1881 and thus would have graduated in the final year of the professorship of Charles Colin, just before the appointment of Georges Gillet. On January 5, 1910, Doucet was a soloist with the Philadelphia Orchestra in the series of "popular concerts" conducted by Carl Pohlig. He played the *Légende Pastorale,* the first of the three *Scènes Écossaises* the composer Benjamin Godard had dedicated "to his friend," Georges Gillet. Doucet was born in 1862. In 1913 he would have been fifty-one, in those days considered rather old for an oboe player.[7] No record remains of the manner in which Doucet came to the end of his employment in Philadelphia, but letters exchanged between Andrew Wheeler and Stokowski in May and June 1913 (the conclusion of Stokowski's first full season with the orchestra) make it clear that negotiations were already under way to engage the Belgian Henri de Busscher, solo oboist of the Queen's Hall Orchestra in London.[8] Almost immediately, problems arose with the Musicians' Union, as had happened in the case of the 1905 Damrosch imports.[9]

Stokowski was spending the summer of 1913 in Munich. On May 29 Wheeler wrote to let him know that de Busscher had already been lured to Philadelphia. "Mr. de Busscher arrived here about two weeks ago, and after consultation with us and with some friends in New York, he decided that the only thing for him to do was to apply for admission to the Union in this city. If he joined in New York it would be impossible for him to get a transfer under six months, and his only course was to join here. He was taken down to see them by Mr. Hall of our Orchestra, and I understand made a good impression. He has signed preliminary papers, and his case will be finally acted on about July 6th. . . . I think the chances of securing de Busscher are good, but if we talk too much about the vacancy in the first oboe they [the union] may put two and two together."[10]

THE PHILADELPHIA ORCHESTRA

Wheeler wrote again on June 25th, referring to Stokowski's reply of June 11 (which has not survived):

> In regard to Debusscher, I am afraid we are in trouble with the Union and that nothing can be done with him for this year at least. I am enclosing a letter from Weber received yesterday which speaks for itself. Somebody has evidently leaked, although we did our best to make the application seem regular and in order, and apparently at the time of his application there was no suspicion regarding him. I am particularly sorry for him, as he has made three trips to Europe in one month [quite an extraordinary feat in the era of travel by ship]. He came over here the latter part of May, made his application and went back to London early in June. He only stayed five days in London, and has now come back with his wife and thinks that everything is coming all right. I have not seen him for a couple of days to tell him of this letter of Weber's, which I am sure will be a great shock to him. In the meantime we will probably have to look elsewhere for an oboe for the coming year, and you know under the rules of the Union we must take one for a whole season. I am sending you a lot of letters regarding a man named Marchetti, who seems to be very well recommended and is anxious to come. I will not do anything definitely with him till I hear from you, and in the meantime there is a bare possibility that Debusscher may join the Union in some other city; but even then he could not get a transfer to this city under six months. I am sure that the position has been very carefully watched through friends of Mr. Doucet, and anything like a man coming over from Europe would be subject of great comment and suspicion.

These letters make it clear that Joseph Weber, president of the AFM, was ever on the alert for "suspicious" Europeans being slipped into a U.S. orchestra via the back door. It is interesting that not even the conductor (let alone a committee) necessarily listened to prospective new members of the orchestra. Interviews, recommendations, and opinions of trusted associates were all called upon in looking for new players, even those needed to fill key positions.

The de Busscher matter continued to occupy Stokowski's attention during the summer of 1913. On July 5 he wrote to Wheeler expressing his mounting anxiety about the oboe situation. In his distinctive handwriting, replete with frequent emphatic underlining, Stokowski acknowledged "the six shirts . . . and six extra cuff links which arrived . . . from Charvet.

MARCEL TABUTEAU

They are very smart"; and then he immediately commented, "I am deeply disappointed about Debusscher. It is a very serious matter for us. It will be *too late to wait till my arrival,* as Mr. Watts writes [to] Mr. Weber. . . . My feeling is that we should inform the Union that we have tried honestly our best to find a *first class oboist* but cannot. That if the Union cannot show a *1st class oboist* free in U.S.A. to fill our serious need, we demand of their permission to import one. But we insist on a *1st Class man.* . . . Regarding Marchetti—he is *good*—but not *1st Class.* The only other man who is free that I know of is Philip Kirchner—6 East 118 St. New York. He is about the same class as Marchetti. Either of these would do as a *make-shift* for *one year.* But I hope we can do better with the Union. Don't touch E. Devaux—he drinks."[11] All this maneuvering and Stokowski's repeated insistence on a "1st class oboist" reminds us of Damrosch's 1907 struggle with the AFM to find a "first class cellist" for *his* orchestra.

The management in Philadelphia was also growing nervous about the oboe situation for the upcoming season. Stokowski's July 5 letter expressing his reservations about Marchetti and pleading for a "1st class oboist" could not yet have arrived when two days later, on July 7, Wheeler again wrote to Stokowski in Munich: "I cabled you today in regard to the oboe player, Marchetti. It seems that he must have an answer immediately in case we want to secure him, as he has an offer from the Chicago Opera Company which he proposes to accept within the next few days. The De Busscher matter seems to be closed for us for this year, and we must supply ourselves at the earliest possible moment. From all accounts Marchetti is a very good man and ought to fill the bill for us for one year at least, after which we can probably get De Busscher." Using the familiar tactic of another job offer (which, of course, he may really have had), Marchetti was trying to force the decision. On July 22 Wheeler announced to Stokowski:

> Today I am able to give you further reports on the oboe question.
> Mr. De Busscher had an interview with Weber yesterday and came to
> see me in the afternoon to report. He states that the objection to him
> on the part of the Union is that he made the gross mistake of applying
> for a position, or stating that he wanted to apply for a position, before
> he was actually a member of the Union. This, according to Weber,
> would debar him from ever joining the Union. He, however, explained

THE PHILADELPHIA ORCHESTRA

satisfactorily to Mr. Weber that it was done entirely through ignorance of the rules, and Mr. Weber seemed convinced that he was innocent in the matter, and finally told him that he would write to the members of the Executive Committee to see if an exception could not be made in his case. This will take a week to ten days, or possibly two weeks, and it is doubtful even then whether they will let him join in this city. As I have told you, I feel very sorry for him and his wife, as they have brought their household furniture over here and fully expect to settle down in this country. He is a helpless sort of individual and she has the brains of the two. In the meantime we have had a call this morning from Mr. Marchetti, and I must say that Mr. Braun [a member of the orchestra's board of directors] and I were very favorably impressed with him. He studied under a notable professor, whose name I have forgotten for the moment, but whose pupils are occupying first positions all over Europe. He plays a modern French instrument, and in the style of the French school. He has played in opera at Roma under Richter and Toscanini, and four seasons at Buenos Ayres under Toscanini. He has also played at Rome under Mengelberg in symphony, and the Ninth Symphony in Rome under Mahler, and was personally complimented by Richter. He is willing to come, and we have told him that we would let him know definitely in a week. If by the end of a week nothing is heard from Weber in the Debusscher matter we will engage Marchetti for the coming season.

This letter must certainly stand as a masterpiece of recommendation by hearsay. Wheeler's impressions were seemingly based on a personal interview, but no matter how astute an administrator he may have been, he would hardly have been capable of assessing the qualities of tone and instrumental expertise that Stokowski desired from his solo oboist. However, Stokowski evidently already had some knowledge of Marchetti's capacities. His July 5 letter had stated that he would consider Marchetti only as a "makeshift" or interim solution. It was perhaps an indication of the scarcity of even "good" oboe players, let alone those in the "first class" category, that the businessman prevailed and Marchetti was hired as first oboist of the Philadelphia Orchestra for the 1913–14 season. In such a way were important positions filled in 1913.

But Stokowski did not give up so easily on the question of his solo oboist. In the summer of 1914, by which time Marchetti had already been in the orchestra for a year, Stokowski continued his efforts to acquire Henri de Busscher. On September 2, 1914, he wrote to assistant manager Louis Mattson, asking him to send an orchestra list marking the men affected by the start of the war—a real worry at a time when so many of the musicians were from Europe. He added an urgent request: "Please exert every means to find whereabouts of *Henri* Debusscher, recently oboe with Cincinnati Orch. Telegraph Wunderle for Debusscher's address. Failing that try Hase. Failing that try Leipniker. Don't apply direct [*sic*] Cincinnati Orch."

Like a spider at the center of a web, Stokowski kept careful track of all threads leading to potential recruits for his orchestra. He was obviously aware that de Busscher had played the 1913–14 season in Cincinnati, not as solo oboist but as a member of the section. His brother Albert, then the first oboist in Cincinnati, had probably helped find a way to tide Henri over after the job in Philadelphia failed to materialize. In his own former position as conductor of the Cincinnati Orchestra, Stokowski would naturally seek to cover the appearance of poaching on their personnel A day later, on September 3, 1914, Mattson replied to Stokowski at his address of Pelham Manor, New York: "Enclosed I am sending the requested list of the musicians who are, to the best of our knowledge, now in Europe, also letter from Mr. Tabuteau to Mr. Mackey."[12] He told Stokowski that he had wired Wunderle and had managed to get an address for de Busscher in Atlantic City. The major interest his letter holds for us, however, is the first official mention in Philadelphia Orchestra annals of the name of Marcel Tabuteau.

A few days later, Ralph Edmunds, a new member of the Philadelphia Orchestra management, wrote to Stokowski, stating among other things that "I have had a letter from Mr. De Busscher, in which he tells us that he has signed with the New York Symphony Orchestra for next season." With this letter the name of Henri de Busscher disappears from the files of the Philadelphia Orchestra. After several seasons with Walter Damrosch and the New York Symphony Orchestra, in 1919 de Busscher became the respected first oboist of the Los Angeles Philharmonic, where he remained until 1946. He also gave both oboe and voice lessons well into his nineties. In Philadelphia,

Marchetti continued as the principal oboist for a second season, 1914–15. In the same letter Mattson referred to what proved to be a defining event in solidifying the future reputation of Stokowski and the Philadelphia Orchestra: "If you are still desirous of doing the Mahler Symphony, you could easily arrange to have the chorus parts photographed and printed." The historic first performance of Mahler's *Eighth Symphony* in the United States would take place in the spring of 1916.

Tabuteau was hired by the Philadelphia Orchestra six months after Mattson's letter, in the spring of 1915. Taking into consideration Stokowski's tenacity in following every lead and keeping track of the whereabouts of good oboists, it is not surprising that he remembered hearing Tabuteau play in *Tristan* with the Met in early 1914. In Tabuteau's letter of August 1915 from San Francisco, he apologized to Mattson for the delay in replying to his "questions." In the one-page form that he filled out for the Philadelphia Orchestra Association, he gave "April 1915" as the date he was engaged for the orchestra. Other questions included the usual ones of name, place, date of birth, marital status (which he answered by "married"), with spaces for education and symphony orchestra experience. In his own words: "At the age of six I began musical education with my brother-in-law a well knowed violinist. When 13 years old became a pupil at the Paris Conservatory in the class of Mr. Georges Gillet the famous master of the French oboe school with wich[13] I studied five years.[14] In 1904 I have been awarded the first prize at the Paris Conservatory." Under symphony orchestra experience, he stated: "Mr. Gillet recommended me to Mr. Damrosch who advised me to come in this country. Have played few seasons with Mr. Walter Damrosch and since 1908 played with Toscanini at the Metropolitan Opera House." In response to the question concerning soloist experience, Tabuteau wrote his frequently quoted lines: "do not want any! as much as an oboe player can have!!!" My own interpretation of this statement is that although not at all anxious to play solos, he felt he could safely add the second line as the dearth of concert-caliber material for oboe made extensive solo performance a quite unlikely event.

MARCEL TABUTEAU

Tabuteau had now arrived in the city with which his name would be permanently associated. The opening concerts of the 1915–16 season took place on October 15 and 16, Friday afternoon at 3:00 and Saturday evening at 8:15, a pattern that would vary little during the thirty-nine years that Tabuteau was to play in Philadelphia. His first concert began with the *Leonore Overture*, No. 3, then Beethoven's *Seventh Symphony*, with Mendelssohn's *Midsummer Night's Dream Music* and Wagner's *Rienzi Overture* following the intermission. Tabuteau's fellow principal wind players in that season were flutist Daniel Maquarre, clarinetist Robert Lindemann, bassoonist Richard Krueger, and horn player Anton Horner. The third pair of concerts, on October 29 and 30, included such standard fare as Brahms's *Second Symphony* and Strauss's tone poem *Don Juan*, but in the fourth pair Tabuteau was introduced to Stokowski's adventurous programming with the first U.S. performance of Schoenberg's *Kammer Symphonie*.

At this time the war in Europe was intensifying and broadening in scope. In an era when a high percentage of both orchestra players and soloists came from European countries, it was inevitable that musical life would soon be affected. A note in the Philadelphia Orchestra program of November 1915 states that "the war in Europe having prevented the arrival of M. Rosenthal [Moriz Rosenthal, the famous Polish pianist], his place on the program for next week will be filled by Mr. Ernest Hutcheson." Hutcheson performed the Liszt *E Flat Concerto* on the fifth pair of concerts, November 12 and 13. The same program featured a recent work, Ippolitov-Ivanov's *Caucasian Sketches*, listed under its French title as *Esquisses Caucasiennes*. Since Ippolitov-Ivanov, who was born in 1859, lived until 1935, he was a contemporary composer of the time. Unlike some of his fellow Russians, he introduced no clashing new harmonies into his music but, inspired by the years he spent in Tiflis, wrote colorful and attractive works based on authentic folk melodies. Stokowski had included these pieces in his inaugural concert in Philadelphia, October 11, 1912, along with Brahms's *First Symphony* and the *Leonore Overture*, No. 3. The *Caucasian Sketches*, with its evocative solos for viola, English horn, and oboe, remained a

Stokowski favorite. He seemed especially fond of the *March of the Sardar,* recording it as early as 1922. More than twenty years later, when Tabuteau chose *In the Village* from the *Caucasian Sketches* for us to play with the orchestra he was conducting at the Curtis Institute, I did not realize that this piece, which few of us had ever heard, was for him an old friend.

The music of Wagner had not yet been banished from American symphonic programs as it would be after the United States entered the war in April 1917. At the end of November 1915, Stokowski presented excerpts from all four operas of the Ring Cycle—familiar territory for Tabuteau after his Met years. In the middle of his first season with the Philadelphia Orchestra, the rarely played overture to *Anacréon* by Cherubini appeared on one of the concerts. Tabuteau once had me practice a phrase that he felt could help one learn to make a smooth connection between intervals without awkward maneuvering from note to note. I found it extremely difficult, if not impossible, to play this group of notes to his satisfaction. He told me it was from the overture to *Anacréon,* and I wondered why this obscure little solo seemed so important to him. Years later, when I saw the 1915 Philadelphia Orchestra program, I felt I had found the answer. We all tend to remember challenging musical passages from the early years of our careers, and in this respect it would appear that Tabuteau was no different.

Works with prominent parts for oboe followed quickly one upon the other during that season, Tabuteau's first with the orchestra. In mid-February, the Mendelssohn *Scotch Symphony;* the next week, the Brahms *Violin Concerto* with Albert Spaulding as soloist. It was the first of the approximately one hundred times that Tabuteau would play the matchless oboe solo in this concerto. At some point in their careers, almost every noted violinist of the first half of the twentieth century— Fritz Kreisler, Efrem Zimbalist, Georges Enesco, Carl Flesch, Jascha Heifetz, Bronislaw Huberman, Oscar Shumsky, Yehudi Menuhin, Joseph Szigeti, Erica Morini, Nathan Milstein, and Zino Francescatti—stood waiting at the beginning of the second movement while Tabuteau played the noble opening theme. There are oft-told stories of the violin soloist (whose name varies with the telling) who forgot to play after hearing the wonderful introduction given by the oboist of Boston,

Philadelphia, or New York. According to John Minsker, it really did happen to Fritz Kreisler. Minsker knew two people who were there: his friend Joe Melnicoff and Robert Bloom. "They both told me how during the Brahms *Concerto*, Tabuteau was playing this long solo and my God, how he could play it! Joe said Kreisler was just standing there listening, shaking his head, and then realized he had missed his entrance. They had to do it all over again. That came from two sources. Bloom, who was in the orchestra then, was the first to tell me the story." Tabuteau thought highly of Kreisler, and it seems that the admiration was mutual.

Whether or not Kreisler actually did miss that entrance, there were others who thought they might do so. Of all the great soloists with whom Tabuteau played the Brahms *Concerto*, the sole one still alive at the end of the twentieth century was Oscar Shumsky. Only fifteen at the time of his 1932 performances with Stokowski and the Philadelphia Orchestra, Shumsky studied at the Curtis Institute of Music, first with Leopold Auer and later with Efrem Zimbalist. I asked him if he had any memory of the oboe solo at the beginning of the slow movement of the Brahms *Concerto*. Almost before I could finish the question, he interjected, "Not only do I have the memory of it, I've never forgotten how Tabuteau played it. There's no one who shaped it in the way in which he did. I just felt like not coming in when it was time for the violin soloist to appear." Shumsky also remembered receiving a compliment from Tabuteau, who "mumbled a few words of approval after the Brahms rehearsal and then said, 'You know, you are the only violinist who has ever taken my A the way I've given it.'"[15]

A momentous event in Philadelphia Orchestra history took place in Tabuteau's first season with the orchestra: the performance in the spring of 1916 of Gustav Mahler's *Eighth Symphony*. Stokowski had become acquainted with this monumental work during the summers he spent in Munich. In 1910 he had heard it conducted by Mahler himself. He subsequently conceived the idea to present it for the first time in America and was able to realize this dream in Philadelphia on March 2–4, 1916. Although the program was scheduled for nine performances, the demand for seats was so great that five extra performances had to be added.

On April 9 the whole production was taken to the Metropolitan Opera House in New York. It was necessary to transport 58 trunks of instruments, 110 orchestra players, two choruses of 400 members each, and a children's choir of 200. The logistics were daunting and required two special trains of eighteen cars. For a relatively new orchestra, this production was a courageous undertaking. Over two weeks before the concerts every seat had been sold. On April 10 the *New York Sun* spoke of the "presiding genius of all . . . Leopold Stokowski, the gifted and accomplished young conductor of the Philadelphia Orchestra." Music celebrities of the day were in the New York audience: Ignace Jan Paderewski, Pablo Casals, Mischa Elman, Fritz Kreisler, Leopold Godowsky, Percy Grainger, and Tabuteau's former Metropolitan Opera colleagues Marcella Sembrich, Emma Eames, and conductor Alfred Hertz. This much heralded event succeeded in putting the name of the Philadelphia Orchestra on the map as the news spread across America and to Europe. The famous photograph taken on the stage of the Academy of Music, its space stretched to the ultimate to hold the twenty-four tiers of choruses deployed behind the orchestra, and Leopold Stokowski standing in front holding a baton (which he still used at that time), hung over the desk where Tabuteau made his oboe reeds until the day in 1954 when he closed his studio and left Philadelphia.

The oboe section in 1915–16 consisted of Marcel Tabuteau, Edward Raho, and Peter Henkelman. Max Lachmuth, an oboist in the orchestra's initial 1900–1901 season, was brought back, but with his name listed in italics, presumably to play when more players were needed. For the Mahler *Eighth,* Lewis Raho, Edward Raho's son, was added as an extra, and the end of the season showed John Lotz as extra oboe and English horn. At the beginning of the next season, 1916–17, more double reed instruments, an oboe d'amore and a Heckelphone, were added to the orchestra.[16] This departure from the standard distribution can only have been Stokowski's idea, and it did not become a permanent feature. There was another first American performance of a work by Mahler, *Das Lied von der Erde,* and a curious suite by Ernest Schelling, entitled *Impressions from an Artist's Life.* In the latter work, each variation was headed by a set of initials. The program notes stated that "the

MARCEL TABUTEAU

names of the people or places which inspired Mr. Schelling are veiled," but "it is possible in certain cases to reveal the individuals or the localities to whom they belong." Thus, "K. M." was Karl Muck, conductor of the Boston Symphony Orchestra, and "G. L.," whose initials headed the "seventh variation for oboe solo and pianoforte," was identified as Georges Longy. If Tabuteau was in any danger of forgetting the fact, there were periodic reminders of Longy's well-established reputation as the leading oboist in the country. William Kincaid, principal flute of the Philadelphia Orchestra from 1921 to 1960, told of a time in the early 1920s when the orchestra was performing the Beethoven *Violin Concerto* in Carnegie Hall.[17] Whether Stokowski mentioned that Longy was in the audience or whether Tabuteau actually saw him come down the aisle to his seat, it resulted in Tabuteau becoming sufficiently rattled to play an F natural instead of F sharp in the opening oboe theme.[18]

In the middle of his second season Tabuteau addressed a handwritten letter to Stokowski. He was by now twenty-nine years old and was learning some negotiating skills. He knew that Stokowski had spent many of his summers in Europe studying scores and learning German. Accordingly, in attempting to better his financial situation, Tabuteau appealed to Stokowski's appreciation of devoted study and the dignity of the artistic profession.

> Phila. 3-12-16
> Mr. Leopold Stokowski
> Conductor of the Philadelphia Orchestra
>
> Dear Mr. Stokowski,
> You will be surprised at the contents of this letter, as my position has been assured for a term of years and it is my entire desire to fulfill the contract to your entire satisfaction.
> To be able to meet my financial obligations I am obliged to play extra engagements during the season and had to accept work in summer at the seashore all of wich have a tendency to lower the artistic work wich you expect from me and wich I desire to give. The extra work of last season and the summer engagement that I played amounted to 720 dollars. This is about what I am able to make each year in choosing the extra work. I could increase this amount by accepting all the engagements that are offered me. I am telling you all

this to say that if it is possible for the Association to increase my contract to a minimum of $500 per season I could refuse all outside engagements and give my time during and after the season to the study of my instrument and above all to keep the dignity of my position wich I feel is very much lowered.

I would like you to understand that I am not dissatisfied but I want to get away from the "jobs," and this is the only way I can do it and meet the demands made on me, both artistically and financially.

Hoping that you will give this matter favorable consideration,
I am,
        Yours truly
        Marcel Tabuteau[19]

I once heard Tabuteau say that he used to play "side jobs in New York theaters and with the Brooklyn Guards" (probably when he was at the Met), and "during the last war [World War I], summers at Willow Grove with Victor Herbert." The above letter indicates that it was a serious issue for him. On December 7, 1916, Stokowski wrote to Arthur Judson, who was now the manager of the orchestra, saying that he told Tabuteau that he would put the matter "before those who have the finances of the Orchestra in hand" and that he hoped Judson would "be able to arrange matters that Tabuteau will be satisfied, as he is a very good man, and playing in bands in the summer is certainly disadvantageous for him." A note scribbled at the bottom of Stokowski's letter indicates the recommendation of an increase of $10 a week. Although no records of Philadelphia Orchestra salaries for the early seasons have survived, it is unlikely that Tabuteau would have earned less than he did at the Met. If we assume a salary of approximately $100 a week for the twenty-five weeks of the season of 1916–17, and if Tabuteau did indeed receive the $10 raise, it would have come to half the amount of his request.

By the summer of 1917, the United States had been involved in the world war since April, and Stokowski was becoming alarmed by personnel problems caused by the draft. On August 27, 1917, Judson wrote to Stokowski in Seal Harbor, Maine: "I am enclosing [for] you a list of the men who because of age are subject to draft, and who have, of course, registered and have had their numbers drawn. A great many men were drawn in such high numbers that they will not be drafted until the second or third call. As you will see, I took immediate action when the law was passed and kept in close touch with it up to date. It is a little difficult to get absolutely authentic news because you can make no guess as to what will happen until the man is actually drafted. The men themselves are presenting their exemption claims to the local boards, and if there seems reason for it, will take their claims to the General Board of Exemption Appeals. I will keep you posted on the matter." Tabuteau's name appears on this list, followed by the comment. "Number drawn in the 47th hundred. Will claim exemption because of physical disability and because of dependents."[20] It is probable that "disability" refers to the same heart ailment that was responsible for his release from the French Army in 1914. But who were the dependents Tabuteau claimed? In the 1915 questionnaire for the Philadelphia Orchestra, he had listed himself as "married," but his wife at this time was not the Mme Tabuteau we all knew several decades later.

A few old-timers remembered that in his Metropolitan Opera days Tabuteau had lived with (or was possibly married to) a ballet dancer. This would seem to be confirmed by something I heard him say on a dreary day in his studio during World War II. In an unusual moment of personal reminiscence, he spoke of "someone in France who wanted me to stay there." As I understood it, when he returned to France after the outbreak of World War I, a young woman he had been very fond of in his Conservatoire days had asked him not to go back to the States but to stay in France and marry her. His next words to me were that he "did not want to disappoint the 'little dancer,'" so he came back to the United States, and the friend in France became a "famous tragedienne at the Comédie-Française known as Mme Delvair." I jotted down the name on a back page in my lesson notebook, where it remained for over half a century. When I began research on Tabuteau's early years, I found "Delvair, Jeanne-Louise, born in Paris, 10 December 1877: Comédie-Française," in the *Dictionnaire des Lauréats,* a part of Constant Pierre's epic history of the Conservatoire National de Musique et de Déclamation. At first it seemed a promising lead, but noticing a birth date that made her ten years older than Tabuteau, I dismissed the idea. Finally, in October 2003 I decided to inquire directly at the Comédie-Française to see what, if anything, they could tell me about "Mme Delvair." The archivist's immediate response was that Jeanne Delvair had indeed been an eminent tragedienne. Additional information came later by e-mail: Jeanne-Louise Deluermoz, known as Delvair, worked at the *maison de couture* Lanvin before she entered the Conservatoire in 1897. After her first prize in *tragédie* and her debut in 1899, she became a regular member of the Comédie-Française in 1910. She retired in 1937 and died in 1949. After World War I she married Georges LeRoy (born in 1885), a colleague at the Comédie-Française who later became a famous professor at the Conservatoire.[21] It seemed to me that if Mme Delvair had eventually married someone eight years younger than herself, an age difference of two more years would not have precluded a possible relationship with Marcel Tabuteau. But the rest of the story will have to remain in the realm of romantic conjecture.

During the fall of 1917 Judson and Stokowski continued to exchange letters expressing their worry about the draft. On September 11 Judson wrote that "Winterstein, who sits in the back of the second violins, has been drafted, and I am afraid we cannot get him released. Tabuteau has been drafted and has filed an exemption claim, but we do not know whether he will succeed. Have you personally any influence at Washington which we could use to get these men free?" And just a few days later, on September 14: "I am having Mr. Van Rensselaer look very carefully into the matter of exemption from military duty for the entire Orchestra. I do not know what the result will be, but I have canvassed the situation very thoroughly and I think that we are pursuing the only course that promises any success. Perhaps I will have good news about it in a few days." Stokowski answered quickly on September 16: "I am terribly anxious about the fifteen men who may be drafted from the orchestra as everyone of these men is of high quality. I am especially anxious about Tabuteau and Glantz. I know so little about these matters that I cannot think what course to comply with. I wish that I might see Mr. Fels [a member of the orchestra's board of directors], who is now in Philadelphia and ask his advice.[22] Some of the men among the fifteen on the list, are absolutely not to be replaced under present conditions, so you can judge of my anxiety."[23] In the same letter Stokowski wrote about hearing a trombone player, Walter Lillebak. "He is the best man that I can see that is available at present." Hiring and firing practices are

MARCEL TABUTEAU

illuminated by Stokowski's suggestion "to put him [Lillebak] in the orchestra for a few weeks and let him play and show his qualities. He says he is willing to accept an engagement on a weekly basis, so I would advise engaging him on trial basis of a weekly salary, with the understanding that if he is not satisfactory, a weeks notice on either side will terminate the agreement." On September 19 Judson wrote again to say he had made the arrangements with Lillebak. "In the matter of the draft," he went on, "things stand as follows":

> Cailliet is exempted on account of dependents.
> Josef Chudnowsky and Antonio Ferrara, exempted on account of physical disability.
> Glantz has informed me that he will certainly not be drafted in the first army, and I have an idea that he will be exempted for physical reasons.
> Betz, our assistant baggage master, and Winterstein, one of the second violins, will probably have to go, although I may be able to save Winterstein.
> I have taken up with the proper persons, notably the one that you mention in your last letter, the question of these men, and I am quite sure that Mr. Tabuteau will be exempted. From what I know, I do not think you need to worry about him. I have had no word from the other men, and since I have notified them to let me hear at once in case they are taken, I can only assume that they are all right.

The draft caused ongoing grave concern. However, a year later, on August 20, 1918, Judson addressed a reassuring letter to Tabuteau, who was now living and probably playing for the summer in Ocean City, New Jersey. Judson returned Tabuteau's draft card and told him that "Mr. Fels . . . believes that no action will be taken in the matter for at least a year." He therefore advised Tabuteau "to rest easy in the matter."[24] Having been released from the obligation of further military service in France, Tabuteau must have been relieved to hear that the odds of his being drafted into the U.S. Army were very slight. And soon the war would be over.

Only a few months later, in October 1918, it is matters of personnel that take precedence. In a letter from Judson to Stokowski, "special terms" are specified in the contracts of several men: "Maurice Eisenberg—to study with Kindler" . . . "Lewis Raho—to study with

THE PHILADELPHIA ORCHESTRA

Tabuteau." No reason is given for these conditions. Did Stokowski hire these players with the understanding that they improve themselves through study? Other comments, such as, "Max Olanoff—to study with Rich and get a new violin," would seem to indicate that continued employment was dependent on some upgrading of skill and equipment.[25] Early in the 1918 season two pairs of October concerts had to be postponed due to a ban on public gatherings necessitated by the severity of the influenza epidemic. On November 15 and 16, shortly after the armistice was proclaimed, the *Dirge* from Edward McDowell's *Indian Suite* was played "as a tribute to the memory of our soldiers and sailors who have fallen in the War." There were other somber announcements to follow. In 1924 the black-edged programs for February 8 and 9 stated that "in memory of Woodrow Wilson, The Funeral March from *Götterdämmerung* will be played before the Symphony." And on February 29 and March 1, the program carried an appeal from Cosima Wagner, widow of the great composer, asking for assistance in the "restoration of the Bayreuth Festival Theater at Bayreuth [Bavaria] which has slumbered since the awful events of 1914." Richard Wagner continued to cast a mighty shadow in the music world of the 1920s. He was still spoken of as "the Master," and explaining that the perpetuation of the Festspielhaus at Bayreuth was one of his greatest desires, "the committee solicits support for this project as well as for his widow, daughter of Franz Liszt, now past eighty, an invalid and nearly destitute."

FIRST PERFORMANCES

The accomplishments of Leopold Stokowski and the Philadelphia Orchestra are well documented in numerous articles and books. One can read detailed accounts of his first performances of the then controversial new compositions of Stravinsky, Schoenberg, Berg, Varèse, and Shostakovich, as well as those of many lesser known composers. His experiments in orchestral seating and recording and his fascination with new instruments (such as the Ondes Martenot),[26] electronic techniques, and music of other cultures are all well known. Marcel Tabuteau was a part of this exciting wave of modernity.

MARCEL TABUTEAU

Shortly after the monumental Mahler *Eighth* came another gargantuan work—Richard Strauss's *Alpensymphonie*. Then in 1922 Stokowski took the courageous step of giving the American première of Stravinsky's *Rite of Spring*. We can only imagine the orchestra players' experience of rehearsing and performing this score for the ballet that only nine years earlier had scandalized the Paris music world. In future seasons Philadelphia would hear Stravinsky's *Oedipus Rex* (1931); Schoenberg's *Die Glückliche Hand* (1930), *Gurrelieder* (1932), and *Violin Concerto* (1940); and Shostakovich's *Symphony No. 1* (1928) and *Symphony No. 6* (1940). This new music presented an enormous challenge to the conductor and players alike. In considering first performances in which Tabuteau participated, we should think back to the era before Stravinsky's complicated rhythms and unfamiliar sonorities had been absorbed into general practice. Today, his major works pose no insurmountable difficulties even to youth symphony orchestras. After a performance of the Ravel *Trio* by pupils at the Curtis Institute of Music in the 1950s, the director of the school, Rudolf Serkin, remarked that students were easily negotiating rhythmic and harmonic elements that only a few decades earlier had caused trouble for professional musicians.

Other first performances in which Tabuteau took part were Sibelius's *Symphony No. 5 in E-Flat* (1921) and *Symphonies No. 6* and *No. 7* (both in 1926); Manuel de Falla's *El Amor Brujo* (1922); Stravinsky's *Symphonie d'instruments à vent à la mémoire de Claude Achille Debussy* (1923); Varèse's *Amérique* (1926); and Berg's *Wozzeck* (1931). The Philadelphia Orchestra had a long association with Sergei Rachmaninoff and played the world premières of his *Piano Concerto No. 4* (1927) and *Rhapsody on a Theme* by Paganini (1934), both with Rachmaninoff himself as soloist, and in 1936, his *Symphony No. 3*.

In 1921 Richard Strauss made a two-and-a-half-month tour of the United States as accompanist to the soprano Elizabeth Schumann. For orchestral performances as conductor of his own works, he chose to use the Philadelphia Orchestra. From the end of October until after Christmas, in concerts in New York at Carnegie Hall and the Metropolitan Opera House, Strauss conducted his seven tone poems, *Til Eulenspiegel, Don Juan, Tod und Verklärung, Don Quixote, Also sprach Zarathustra, Ein Heldenleben,* and *Symphonia Domestica*. After his opening concert on

October 3, he wrote to his wife, Pauline: "A storm of applause after each item. The orchestra of the very first rank and enthusiastic—about my short rehearsals."[27] Following the successful Carnegie Hall concert, Strauss led the orchestra in a series of three evenings at the Metropolitan Opera House. On November 15 he began the program with *Also sprach Zarathustra*, continued with *Salome's Dance*, and after a more gentle interlude of five of his songs sung by Elizabeth Schumann, ended with *Tod und Verklärung*. Soloists featured in the other two Met concerts were the Philadelphia's principal cellist Michel Penha, playing *Don Quixote*, and Bronislaw Huberman, in Strauss's rarely performed *Violin Concerto in D Minor*, Op. 8. By now fifty-eight years old, Strauss gave no lofty musical reasons for making this exhausting tour of over forty recitals and concerts. His savings had been confiscated in England during the war, he could not count on a pension, and he worried that if anything happened to prevent his conducting, he would have only the royalties from his works to fall back on. He wrote to Franz Schalk, his co-director at the Vienna Opera, "I am not going for pleasure. . . . Even operatic successes are unreliable—if the royalties fail . . . I shall be a beggar and shall leave my family in 'poverty and shame.' I must free myself from this worry."[28] The grand finale of the tour was the pair of concerts at the Academy of Music in Philadelphia on December 23 and 24, 1921, which began with *Ein Heldenleben* and ended with the suite *Der Bürger als Edelmann*. In between, Paul Kochanski played the Vivaldi *A Minor Violin Concerto*, the only non-Straussian work on all the orchestral concerts. It is tantalizing to imagine what it must have been like to play all these Strauss works with the composer himself. Tabuteau seems never to have said one word about the experience. However, anyone who heard Tabuteau play the oboe solos in *Don Juan, Tod und Verklärung*, and *Don Quixote* will never forget those nostalgic phrases and the almost bittersweet tone quality with which he brought Strauss's heroes to life. His coloring and inflections at the closing of the solo in *Don Juan* remain unique.

During Tabuteau's first ten years in the orchestra, there were novelties and first performances, but the major part of Stokowski's symphonic repertoire between 1915 and 1925 was amazingly predictable. A liberal number of Beethoven, Brahms, and Tchaikovsky symphonies were programmed every season. There was always Mozart, although

MARCEL TABUTEAU

only the last three symphonies: *No. 39 in E-Flat, No. 40 in G Minor,* or the *Jupiter, No. 41 in C Major.* The Franck *D Minor Symphony* was played every season and Dvořák's *From the New World* every year but one. Although Schumann does not immediately come to mind as a Stokowski specialty, the conductor chose his symphonies quite frequently, usually *No. 2 in C Major* with the deeply expressive oboe solo. The Mendelssohn *Scotch Symphony* was performed many more times than the popular *Italian.* The *Unfinished Symphony* and the "Great" *C Major No. 9* of Schubert were played again and again. There was an occasional Bruckner *Seventh* and Chausson *B-Flat Major.*

IMPORTANT SOLOS IN ORCHESTRAL WORKS

Along with the standard repertoire of the major symphonies, tone poems, overtures, suites, and concertos, and the many challenging new works, there were compositions with outstanding solos for oboe. Tabuteau's close to one hundred performances of the solo in the Brahms *Violin Concerto* have already been mentioned. In the early 1920s two pieces with important oboe solos were programmed for the first time: Satie's *Gymnopédies* in October 1921 and Henry Eichheim's *Japanese Nocturne* in March 1923. Fortunately both of these works were later recorded on 78-rpm disks (now reissued on CD) and have been avidly listened to by oboists ever since. Henry Eichheim, an American violinist and composer born in Chicago in 1870, made a number of trips to the Far East between 1915 and 1930. He was a pioneer in experimenting with the exotic colors of Asian music, and he accumulated an extensive collection of indigenous instruments long before ethnomusicology became a respected subject for study in American schools and universities. When Stokowki, ever curious about other cultures, took a sabbatical year off from the Philadelphia Orchestra to immerse himself in world music, he benefited from the company and guidance of Henry Eichheim during the Asian segment of his trip. Eichheim's own works were based on Asian subjects using harmonies derived from Debussy and Scriabin. The *Japanese Nocturne,* popularized by Tabuteau's characteristic interpretation of the extensive solo, is from a set of seven pieces, *Oriental Impressions.* Some of the sketches were dedicated to well-known personages of the time: the *Korean Sketch* to pianist Josef Hofmann, the *Japanese Sketch* to Mrs. F. S. Coolidge, the *Siamese Sketch* to Eva Gauthier, and *Entenraku* to his good friend, the violist and composer Charles Martin Loeffler.[29] Less well known was the recipient of the dedication of the *Japanese Nocturne*, Ethel John Lindgren. She was the young daughter of gifted pianist Ethel Roe Lindgren, the widow of a Chicago banker, who became Eichheim's wife in 1917. Ethel John Lindgren later became a respected researcher and writer on folklore.

Tabuteau first played Ravel's *Le Tombeau de Couperin* with Stokowski on February 4 and 5, 1921. Ten years later, in mid-November 1931, there were four more performances in Philadelphia and New York with Fritz Reiner conducting. Tabuteau subsequently played *Tombeau* during the 1930s, 1940s, and early 1950s under Eugene Ormandy. The eminent clarinetist Mitchell Lurie told me about a high point of his student years at the Curtis Institute. He vividly remembered "the night in April 1942 when I got to hear Tabuteau play *Tombeau de Couperin.* Ormandy was having a terrible ego battle with him at that time but there was nothing he could do about it but let Tabuteau come up to the front of the Orchestra and take three bows. He had to keep bringing him back. The applause just wouldn't stop." Lurie roundly contradicted the false rumor that Tabuteau had never played *Le Tombeau de Couperin,* saying, "I heard it and I will never forget it!" Almost exactly four years earlier in 1938 an all-Ravel program was performed in memory of the composer, who had died just three months earlier in Paris. It was repeated three times in Philadelphia, March 25, 26, and 29, always beginning with *Tombeau.* Eugene List then played the *G Major Piano Concerto,* followed by four of Ravel's popular orchestral pieces: *Rapsodie Espagnole, La Valse, Alborado del gracioso,* and *Bolero.*

Ibert's colorful and evocative *Escales* did not appear on Philadelphia concerts until the Ormandy era. I had never heard *Escales* in San Francisco, and the lengthy oboe solo came as a total surprise. Tabuteau had been playing snatches of it in the Studio for over two weeks, but I did not recognize it. On the concert of November 5, 1943, there he was sitting on the stage, changing oboes, enough to make even the listener nervous, but "when he struck out on it, so smoothly and creepy, it made your flesh crawl (like *Salome's Dance*). Ormandy had him take a well-deserved bow at the end. After the concert he said he didn't know which oboe he wanted to use and when he finished, he wasn't playing on the one that he thought he was!"[30] To hear Tabuteau play as often as possible, I usually attended both the Friday afternoon and the Saturday night concerts. With a repeat on Monday, I heard the exciting *Tunis-Nefta* solo three times. A few years later, in 1947, *Escales* was programmed by guest conductor Dmitri Mitropoulos. A commotion occurred at the end of the weekly broadcast when the announcer read, "and the violin solo in the Max Reger was played by Alexander Hilsberg." As soon as the sign came that they were off the air, Tabuteau bellowed, "Hey, Norris! Who played the oboe?" (There had been about five measures of violin solo in the Reger piece, while Tabuteau had played the lengthy *Tunis-Nefta*.) It was quite a scene, with "Mitropoulos trying to calm Tabuteau, and Norris West, the announcer, wishing he could vanish!!"[31] From Kansas City, I heard that concert on the radio and made my only long-distance telephone call of the winter to tell Tabuteau how impressed I was by his "African" style in *Escales*. His response: "And you know, I have never been in Tunisia!"[32]

One of the great favorites in both the Stokowski and Ormandy eras was *Scheherazade*. Tabuteau played it over one hundred times—in the regular series, in children's concerts, in youth concerts, in out-of-town series, on tours (November 1916 in Columbus, Cleveland, Buffalo, Lima, and Detroit), and for the Philadelphia visit of the Ballets Russes in the1930s. It appeared in pension fund concerts, for broadcasts, at the Worcester Festival, and in June 1949 at Royal Albert Hall, London. Stokowski recorded sections of *Scheherazade* as early as 1919 and then did the complete work twice for RCA Victor with "his" Philadelphia Orchestra, in 1927 and again in 1934. All of the wind solos are brilliantly played in the 1934 version. Despite the limited recording capabilities of the time, something of Tabuteau's concept of the oboe phrases can be discerned.[33] Rossini overtures did not play an important role in Philadelphia Orchestra concerts, but *L'Italiana in Algeri* was programmed by Pierre Monteux in 1928 and by Eugene Ormandy in 1942. Tabuteau must have practiced it as thoroughly as he did every other work. In 1964 toward the end of his life, he played the opening solo over and over into the tape recorder that Waldemar Wolsing

THE PHILADELPHIA ORCHESTRA

brought to Nice. The Johann Christian Bach *Sinfonia in B Flat Major*, with its lovely solo for oboe in the slow movement, opened the concerts of March 26 and 27, 1943. I was lucky to be there. Another work I heard for the first time was Respighi's *Gli Uccelli* (The Birds). With Tabuteau, each section became a dramatic vignette, whether the haunting melody of the dove or the humorous hen flapping her wings.

Tabuteau's interpretation of these prominent orchestral solos made a lasting impression not only on wind students but on all who heard him. In June 1999 Henry Pleasants spoke with me by telephone from London. Pleasants, who studied voice at the Curtis Institute in the late 1920s, was later the music critic for the *Evening Bulletin* and author of books on historical and modern singers. When I asked him about Tabuteau, Pleasants said, "I could sing it for you now, the way he played the opening solo of the slow movement of the Brahms *C Minor Symphony*. No one ever approached what he did. And when you had Kincaid and Tabuteau in *Afternoon of a Faun!* Those are indelible memories." Then he *did* sing the trumpet trio from Debussy's *Fêtes* as it comes from the distance and recedes, saying it was Stokowski's "fantasizing that made the music so wonderful." Of the famous conductors of the past sixty years, Pleasants commented, "I've heard them all—Furtwängler, Klemperer, Karajan, to name just a few—and I've come to the conclusion that Stokowski was the greatest of them all. He knew how to make the most of those soloists!"

ENGLISH HORN

At the time Tabuteau was trained in France, it was standard procedure for the first oboist of an orchestra to also play the major English horn solos. There are at least two documented occasions of Tabuteau taking over this role in the period following the 1925 departure of the Philadelphia Orchestra's outstanding English horn player, Peter Henkelman, who had been much appreciated by Stokowski. In 1926 the Philadelphia Orchestra was designated as the "Official Orchestra" of the Sesquicentennial Exposition. A concert conducted by Stokowski on September 18 began with *Finlandia* and ended with the Dvořák *New World* symphony. Samuel L. Laciar in his review for the *Public Ledger*

MARCEL TABUTEAU

discussed the performance movement by movement. When Tabuteau played with Walter Damrosch at Willow Grove in 1905, he had received his first public recognition in the United States for his playing of the *Largo* from the *New World*. Now twenty-one years later that same "young French artist . . . certainly destined to become a celebrity" played the same *Largo* only a few miles distant from Willow Grove. This time, having fulfilled the prediction, he was praised as "the solo oboe of the Orchestra who took the English horn part and played . . . with great artistry, feeling, beauty of tone and perfection of phrasing. Mr. Tabuteau was applauded to the echo at the conclusion of the movement." It was fortunate that the fireworks from the Hawaiian show (this was an exposition, after all) were not set off until the last movement, and even then were almost unnoticed due to the "immense amount of tone" produced by Stokowski and his orchestra.[34]

A recording, said to be of Tabuteau playing the English horn solo in the Sibelius tone poem *Swan of Tuonela*, became almost the stuff of legend. For years one heard stories of somebody who possibly owned a copy of the fragile disk, but it was nowhere to be found after the end of the 78-rpm era. It was eventually reissued on CD by Grammofono 2000, still without Tabuteau's name on the label, but his distinctive phrasing makes it recognizable beyond any doubt.[35] John de Lancie remembered Tabuteau's story of how the record came to be made in May 1929. "Stoki called him up one morning and said, 'I would like to record the *Swan* tomorrow.' Tabuteau didn't even have an English horn. He got on the train and went to New York to rent an instrument. He came back to Philadelphia the same evening, sat up all night long in his studio making English horn reeds, then went in the next morning and recorded it."

John Minsker, who played English horn in the Philadelphia Orchestra from 1936 to 1959, is one of the few who can remember the oboists and English horn players from the early Stokowski years. "I think I've known every English horn player who has been in the orchestra! Lachmuth I met out in the tennis courts; Henkelman, down in New Orleans when we were on tour. Another was Leoncavallo, from 1926 to 1928, a very nice fellow. Then there was Joseph Wolfe for one season. We used to see him in New York frequently and in Paris when we were there in

THE PHILADELPHIA ORCHESTRA

1955. Max Weinstein often played English horn between 1930 and 1932, although not officially listed as such. Bob Bloom was there from 1930 to 1936, first as assistant oboist for two years and then as solo English horn. Louis Rosenblatt, who followed me in the orchestra, had been my pupil, and now there is Betsy Starr, also a pupil while I was teaching chamber music at Curtis." Minsker described how he had met Max Lachmuth one summer when he was playing tennis in Fairmount Park. Lachmuth was working in the field house arranging the schedules of who would play on which court. Thinking the name sounded familiar, Minsker learned that Lachmuth had been the English horn player in the orchestra's first season, 1900–1901. The Dutch player, Peter Henkelman, came in the second season and stayed until 1925. Sol Schoenbach, who heard Henkelman in New York, remembered that "he had a dark sound—rather heavy, and sometimes he had a problem making attacks as we all do, but after he left, Stoki was getting a new English horn player every year."[36] It was during the period of these various short-term players that Tabuteau was called upon to revive his early English horn skills and step in to save the day.

GUEST SOLOISTS

Tabuteau was a great admirer of Fritz Kreisler. He often said that Kreisler was the only violinist who knew how to use his bow to create a truly subtle range of nuance and style. Kreisler had been a soloist with Walter Damrosch's orchestra in the earliest years of Tabuteau's career. From that period comes a story told to John Mack by a New York oboist, Irving Cohn. While Kreisler was playing the Brahms *Concerto,* a pad fell out of the F key of Cesare Addimando's oboe during the opening of the second movement. Tabuteau, who was then sitting in the second oboe and English horn chair, had to play the oboe solo when it returns for the second time. At the end of the movement, Kreisler is said to have remarked, "That's the way it should be played." A few years later, Tabuteau again played with Kreisler in the Sunday concerts of the Metropolitan Opera Orchestra, this time the complete solo. After he joined the Philadelphia Orchestra, Tabuteau played for Kreisler's appearances during another quarter of a century. The many other violinists with whom Tabuteau played have already been mentioned, but there was yet another for whom he reserved one of his rare compliments. This was Ginette Neveu, the French violinist, who died at the tragically young age of thirty in the crash of a Constellation aircraft while returning to the United States for the 1949–50 concert season. In October 1948 I was in the audience in Philadelphia when she played the Beethoven *Concerto* to a standing ovation. As Tabuteau was leaving the Academy of Music after the concert, I heard him say, "She puts all the men in the shade. I am glad that girl does not play the *oboe!*" The "pronouncement" he made during her first rehearsal with the orchestra was considerably more colorful. At the end of the second movement he turned to John de Lancie, who was sitting next to him, and said, "*Ça m'emmerderait bien si une femme jouait le hautbois comme ça!*" (It would really annoy me if a woman played the oboe like that).

Among cellists, Hans Kindler, the orchestra's principal from 1916 to 1920, held a virtual monopoly on concerto roles for his instrument. After he left the orchestra he returned as a soloist in a total of thirteen out of the fifteen seasons between 1915 and 1930. Beginning in the late 1920s, Gregor Piatigorsky became a popular visitor, returning periodically throughout the whole time Tabuteau was in the orchestra. I remember Piatigorsky's impressive performance of *Don Quixote*, especially the way he expressed the poignancy of the Don's death at the end of the tone poem. Emanuel Feuermann, cut off in 1942 at age thirty-nine from the long career he should have had, played with the orchestra only a few times, beginning with the 1938–39 season. He fortunately left a Philadelphia recording of the Brahms *Double Concerto* with Jascha Heifetz, conducted by Eugene Ormandy. When Feuermann played this same concerto with Joseph Szigeti on a May 1940 concert in Ann Arbor, it became the occasion for another of Tabuteau's outbursts. Always worrying about pitch, he had been complaining that Feuermann played sharp, and at the conclusion of the concert he yelled loudly, "Bravo, Szigeti!"[37] Considering his great fame, Pablo Casals played very few times with the Philadelphia Orchestra, in part, perhaps, due to his absence from the United States after 1928. He was a soloist in 1917–18 and again in 1920. When Tabuteau met him in 1950 at the Bach Festival in Prades, he saw how Casals was venerated after his long years of self-imposed exile. People were coming from all over the world to hear him play and conduct at the advanced age of seventy-three, which led Tabuteau to remark, "And to think I remember his playing to half-empty halls in New York in the 1920s!"[38]

Up until the mid-1930s, the legendary pianist Josef Hofmann was soloist with the orchestra almost every season. In 1937 Fritz Reiner led the Curtis Orchestra with participation of the first-chair Philadelphia wind players for a grand jubilee at the Metropolitan Opera House to celebrate the fiftieth anniversary of Hofmann's childhood debut in America (see chapter 8). After this gala event, the name of another pianist, Rudolf Serkin, began to appear in Philadelphia programs almost as frequently as Hofmann's had earlier. Artur Rubinstein followed closely in number of performances. Long before the harpsichord became a common sight and sound, Wanda Landowska came to Philadelphia as a soloist three times in the 1920s. In January 1927 she performed the *Concerto* for harpsichord, flute, oboe, clarinet, violin, and cello that Falla had recently written at her suggestion. In that same 1926–27 season, the celebrated German pianist Walter Gieseking made his first appearance with the orchestra, and the Romanian Clara Haskil came as a young woman to play the Schumann *Concerto,* not to return to the United States again until the mid-1950s. Vladimir Horowitz, less reclusive in the early part of his career, was a soloist with the Philadelphia Orchestra almost every season between 1927 and 1934. Electrical instruments made their debut in the 1930–31 season with the announcement of Maurice Martenot as a soloist. In the late 1940s, Clara Rockmore, sister of the well-known pianist Nadia Reisenberg, played the theremin with the orchestra.

If instrumental soloists have been named here to the exclusion of the great singers who appeared with the Philadelphia Orchestra during the Tabuteau years, it is merely because the concertos for violin, cello, and piano contain many of the major orchestral solos for the oboe. But Tabuteau had a great interest in voice production. He used to tell us to observe the way singers planted their feet firmly on the floor, never slouching, as they produced their sound from the ground up. He must have enjoyed being on the stage with vocal artists ranging from Philadelphia's own Nelson Eddy and Marian Anderson, Ernestine

Schumann-Heink and others from his Met days, to Kirsten Flagstad and Lauritz Melchior, the magnificent Wagnerians of three decades later.

OPERA

The season of 1934–35 saw the Philadelphia Orchestra's short-lived experiment of staged opera at the Academy of Music with Fritz Reiner and Alexander Smallens conducting all the performances. An impressive roster of works was given, including Shostakovich's controversial *Lady Macbeth of Mzensk,* Gluck's rarely performed *Iphigénie in Aulide,* and the more standard fare of Wagner (*Tristan, Die Meistersinger*), Verdi (*Falstaff*), as well as *Marriage of Figaro, Der Rosenkavalier, Carmen, Hansel and Gretel,* and *Boris Godunov.* Except for the Shostakovich, it was all familiar territory to Tabuteau from his Metropolitan Opera days. This was also the season in which Fritz Reiner fulfilled his desire to present an uncut version of *Tristan* for the first time in America. The October 1934 matinee began at 1:00 p.m. and ended about six hours later. When Tabuteau emerged from the darkness of the Academy of Music orchestra pit, through the stage door, and into the light of Locust Street, he spotted Boris Goldovsky, to whom he made his oft-quoted remark: "Tell me, mon cher, is Roosevelt still President?"[39]

CONDUCTORS

The only notable conductors of the first half of the twentieth century with whom Tabuteau did *not* play were those few who stayed in their own countries, or who for personal or political reasons did not come to the United States. Among those who did travel, there was one famous maestro, Wilhelm Furtwängler, who came to the United States in the 1920s but did not conduct in Philadelphia. Otherwise, the list of visiting conductors reads like a Who's Who in the world of the baton. The real profusion of guest conductors began in the season of 1927–28, when Stokowski took his year off to travel and study the musical cultures of other lands. Up until this time he had rarely been absent from the podium, but now the season was divided among seven conductors.

THE PHILADELPHIA ORCHESTRA

Fritz Reiner and Pierre Monteux each had three months, Reiner at the beginning of the season and Monteux at the end. In between, Ossip Gabrilowitsch, Willem Mengelberg, Frederick Stock, and Sir Thomas Beecham each led a set of concerts. Ernest Schelling was in charge of the children's concerts. Earlier in the 1920s Gabrilowitsch, Mengelberg, and Stock had conducted an occasional concert, but other guests were primarily composers: Vincent d'Indy, Darius Milhaud, Richard Strauss, Igor Stravinsky, Georges Enesco, and Ottorino Respighi had all made Philadelphia appearances. Following the 1927–28 season, other world-renowned conductors came to Philadelphia: from England, Eugene Goossens; from Austria, Clemens Krauss; from Italy, Arturo Toscanini, Bernardino Molinari, and Tullio Serafin; from Poland, Emil Mylnarski; from Russia, Issay Dobrowen; and from Germany, Otto Klemperer. More composers came as well: Carlos Chavez, Paul Hindemith, and Nadia Boulanger. The name of Eugene Ormandy first appeared on the roster in 1931. In 1936 he became co-conductor with Stokowski and in 1938 was given the title of music director. However, Stokowski did not completely break the ties to "his" orchestra until after the 1940–41 season.

What were Tabuteau's opinions of some of the conductors with whom he played? From Tabuteau himself, I heard only a few comments. Once in his studio while he was playing excerpts from *Lohengrin* in preparation for an upcoming concert, he remarked in a disdainful manner that Ormandy "did not even know the tempi of the operas," perhaps not a surprising reflection from someone with Tabuteau's years of experience at the Metropolitan. Another time, when I complained of some problems I had in Houston while playing for guest conductor Ernest Ansermet, Tabuteau said not to worry and gave his opinion that "Ansermet is a big piece of cheese. He should have gone in the dry cleaning business . . . If you play well he wants it some other way. He is a pest."[40] But when Ansermet had conducted in Philadelphia, Tabuteau was very complimentary. It is possible that the negative comments made to me came after he saw an interview in *Woodwind* magazine where Ansermet spoke in glowing terms about Kincaid but rather brushed off Tabuteau.[41] In the 1960s Tabuteau told Marc Mostovoy that he had enjoyed playing for Igor Stravinsky. He felt that Stravinsky

MARCEL TABUTEAU

expressed the inner rhythmic propulsion of his own works in a very special way: "He 'shouldered' the notes (*pushing a bit forward with his shoulders*), and gave the dotted notes their inner value."[42] I also remember experiencing Stravinsky's particular portrayal of rhythmic pulse when I played for him in Houston.

When I was first about to enter a symphony orchestra, Tabuteau cautioned me never to be trapped into expressing my opinion of a conductor, even by a casual question a fellow musician might ask, such as, "What did you think of tonight's performance?" "There are stool pigeons everywhere," he said, and told me to mind my own business and not be drawn into intermission conversations. "Spend the time fixing your reeds!" It was good advice, which he almost certainly did not always follow himself. But I was well trained to keep quiet and never repeated his remarks until these many decades later when both he and the conductors are gone.

Was Tabuteau himself interested in conducting? When John Minsker was a student, he remembered seeing Tabuteau with the score to *Prince Igor* and knew he had conducted it at a Philadelphia Orchestra rehearsal. Stokowski was looking for a new assistant, and anyone from the orchestra who wished could try out. Minsker recalled that about that time Saul Caston got the job as assistant conductor, but added, "Oh, Tabuteau was thinking about conducting; yes, I'm sure of that. He liked to conduct." An old newspaper clipping announces his formation of an orchestra, "The Philharmonic of Philadelphia."[43] How long this orchestra survived is unfortunately not known.

Tabuteau respected Fritz Reiner, with whom he had ample occasion to play, both during Reiner's long term as a guest conductor in the 1927–28 season and then later, when he conducted opera in Philadelphia. In 1931, before the year of the "experiment" with the uncut *Tristan*, Reiner had led a staged performance of *Elektra* with the orchestra and an international cast of singers. Richard Strauss wrote to Reiner to wish him "good luck" and said he was glad that "you will conduct *Elektra* with the Philadelphia Orchestra, whose extraordinary achievements still linger in my memory." Reiner's presentation of *Elektra*, over a year before it was performed at the Metropolitan, made a powerful impression. Tabuteau said he considered it to be the greatest feat of conducting

he had experienced in his entire life.[44] The music critics of the time reacted in a similar way. Olin Downes wrote about Reiner's "complete
mastery" of the score and his "dramatic fire," concluding that his "reading is one of the memorable experiences of twenty-five years of review-
ing musical performances."[45]

There are several versions of a story involving Ossip Gabrilowitsch.
One came from Tabuteau himself, one from William Kincaid, and another was told by John Minsker. In March 1931, during the Easter season, Gabrilowitsch was conducting three performances of the *St.
Matthew Passion*. He had very definite ideas about protocol and insisted
that his name be pronounced "Gabril-*oh*-witsch," with the accent on the
o, never on the syllable *bril*. To leave no doubt as to the seriousness of
the occasion, "Sacred Concert" was printed at the top of the program,
and at the bottom, "The audience is respectfully requested not to ap-
plaud." For these concerts, he also demanded that the entire orchestra
be seated and remain silent for five minutes before he came on the stage.
According to John de Lancie, "You can imagine Tabuteau—the 'ultimate noodler'—when he heard this! Another request from Gabrilowitsch was that in keeping with the solemnity of the event, all attire be
extremely sober. On Friday, Tabuteau came on stage wearing a colored
necktie. Gabrilowitsch refused to let him play and had Di Fulvio take
over. There was a small 'scene' and Judson [the manager] told Tabuteau
to leave."[46] In the audience, John Minsker, then a student, heard that
"something had happened on Friday—that Tabuteau had worn a red
necktie." Minsker attended almost every concert of the Friday, Saturday,
and Monday series. He remembered that the St. Matthew Passion was
given at Philadelphia's Metropolitan Opera House at Broad and Poplar
Streets. He later heard Tabuteau grumbling and expressing his anger
about the way he had been treated, swearing that he would "take a picture
of Gabrilowitsch and hang it in his bathroom."[47] Kincaid's account dif-
fered considerably: "You will recall that the orchestras in the *Passion* are
divided. Apparently during a rehearsal while the two orchestras were
playing, one orchestra was a measure off and Gabrilowitsch didn't notice. When they reached the end of the movement it became painfully
obvious as the first orchestra continued to play for an extra measure.
Tabuteau responded with a huge guffaw heard by everyone! This was

followed by Gabrilowitsch's request at the last rehearsal that the attire be sober and Tabuteau arrived Friday afternoon wearing a brilliant red tie."[48] How often a story is handed down in different ways, each one containing perhaps some element of truth. But in any event this same Gabrilowitsch performance had a serious impact on one young listener. Almost seventy years later John Bitter, who studied conducting at the Curtis Institute in the 1920s and 1930s, told me it had been the source of his lifelong devotion to the *St. Matthew Passion*.

Following these guests, all of them indisputable stars in the galaxy of classical conductors, there suddenly appeared on the regular subscription series of November 27 and 28 and December 1, 1936, the name of Paul Whiteman. For this extraordinary event his own orchestra was combined with the Philadelphia Orchestra to play a concert of music by Jerome Kern; William Grant Still; Handy's *St. Louis Blues* in an orchestral version with a harp solo played by Curtis student Casper Reardon; a Ferde Grofé suite, *Tabloid* (*Pictures of a Modern Newspaper—Run of the News, Comic Strip, Going to Press*); Rodgers and Hart, *All Points West;* and ending with Gershwin's *Rhapsody in Blue*. Roy Bargy, a well-known popular pianist, played the piano solo. There were spoken "program notes" delivered by Deems Taylor, the popular commentator of the New York Philharmonic Sunday broadcasts. One would like to have witnessed Whiteman's reunion with his old "buddies" from the 1915 San Francisco Exposition Orchestra: Anton Horner, Anton Torello, and Marcel Tabuteau. Fifteen-year-old John de Lancie had just arrived in Philadelphia that fall to begin his studies at the Curtis Institute. He attended the concert and always remembered the striking picture on the stage: Whiteman's orchestra members attired in midnight-blue shirts and white full dress suits, in opposition to the traditional formal white tie and black tails of the Philadelphia Orchestra men. In the context of symphony concerts of the 1930s, to hear "jazz" resounding to the rafters of the venerable Academy of Music must have been earthshaking, especially for staid Philadelphia. But it may be considered to have presaged the "crossover" concerts that became common happenings in the 1990s.

In the mid-1940s Bruno Walter was a frequent guest. I heard the concert of the first week of January 1946, when, in his noble manner, he conducted Brahms's *Tragic Overture*, Haydn's *Oxford Symphony No. 92*,

THE PHILADELPHIA ORCHESTRA

and Mahler's *Symphony No. 4* with soprano Desi Halban. Henry Pleasants said he could still hear Tabuteau's playing of Brahms' *First Symphony* ringing in his head. I can say the same for Tabuteau's unique interpretation of the Mahler and the charm of inflection and rhythmic incisiveness he gave to each characteristic phrase.

Other conductors Tabuteau played with before his retirement were George Szell, Guido Cantelli, Leonard Bernstein, and Eduard Van Beinum (whom he liked). Cantelli was in Philadelphia in the spring of 1949, not long before the orchestra left for a tour of England. Tabuteau seemed to find it amusing that Cantelli was supposedly the only pupil of Toscanini. Cantelli, who was very young, began to throw a temper tantrum, exactly mimicking Toscanini's behavior on the podium. John de Lancie recalled what happened next:

> We had a nice fellow in the Orchestra, A. A. Tomeii [Tony Tomeii], the assistant first horn and president of the local Musician's Union, a very interesting character known as a rough and tough kind of guy. What had made him famous was that one time, during the era of big orchestras in the movie houses, when he was playing in the Stanley Theater, somebody sitting in the first row started making fun of the musicians. Tony jumped out of the pit, assaulted the fellow, and knocked him out. Tony spoke Italian. So when Cantelli started beating his arm with the baton against the side of his leg, Tony stood up and said in Italian, "Maestro, I don't know what you're used to, but I can tell you that if you expect to talk this way and treat the orchestra like this, one more outburst and you're going to see one hundred men get up and walk off the stage." After that, Cantelli was like a lamb, so you can see what an act it all is.

Tabuteau was playing only the first half of the season when the elderly French conductor Paul Paray came to conduct in Philadelphia. John de Lancie, who was playing the other half, convinced Tabuteau to come to hear Paray and described his reaction. "He walked out of that concert and said, 'You know, in my life I only had admiration for two men, my teacher and Toscanini, but now I have to include Paul Paray.'" Such extravagant praise was followed a few years later by one of Tabuteau's contradictory changes of heart, mind, or mood. It was after Paray had retired and moved to Monte Carlo. Tabuteau was in Monte Carlo when

MARCEL TABUTEAU

de Lancie asked him one day, "Have you had a chance to see Paul Paray?" He replied, "You know, I heard him conduct the Beethoven *Ninth* on the radio. It was terrible and I didn't want to see him again.'"[49]

Tabuteau's admiration for Toscanini dated from the years he spent with him at the Metropolitan Opera. While I was studying at the Curtis Institute, Tabuteau spoke of Toscanini in almost reverential terms. In 1944 Sol Schoenbach was able to convince Toscanini to come to Philadelphia to conduct a concert for the benefit of the orchestra's pension fund. Toscanini wanted to do an all-Beethoven program, and as Sol saw it becoming longer and longer, he said something about union limitations on time. Toscanini "flew into a fury in which he denounced all the officials of the union, living and dead, and carried on like a maniac. . . .'People think that I'm old, that I'm sick! I'll show them! I'll conduct more than two men!'" His program was to include the Egmont Overture, the *Pastoral Symphony,* the *Septet,* and the *Leonore Overture.* Sol continued, "When he came for the rehearsals, we put in a supply of champagne and at the first rehearsal Tabuteau made a speech in French and Toscanini answered in his bad French. Every rehearsal was just wonderful—a love feast—until the last one, when Toscanini blew his top. It was in the *Septet.* When I had asked him why he wanted to do the *Septet,* he said that as a young boy, it was the first score he had bought with his own money. He hadn't eaten lunch for a week to save up the money for it and it was still his favorite piece."

At the intermission of the final rehearsal, as the musicians started to leave the stage, Tabuteau called them all back. He made another short speech telling Toscanini how much they appreciated his coming to conduct them and presented him with a scroll. Toscanini immediately unrolled it and spoke warmly to the orchestra. There was general applause. After Toscanini's evident pleasure at this gesture, it came as a shock when following the break, he went into a rage, shouting and hurling insults during the rehearsal of the Beethoven *Septet* because the violins had rushed some of the eighth notes. Again, it was Tabuteau who came to the podium, put an arm affectionately around Toscanini's shoulder, and asked if he would like another rehearsal just before the concert. Tabuteau understood that Toscanini's apparently irrational anger reflected his intense desire to reach the realization of his vision of the music, which he

THE PHILADELPHIA ORCHESTRA

seemed unable to communicate in a less excitable manner. Everyone agreed to the rehearsal, and the performance, which I heard on February 6, 1944, was spectacular. Schoenbach summed it up in these words: "The Beethoven concert! I'll never forget Tabuteau after it was over. He said, 'Now I can die.' That program was absolutely the end as far as every detail was concerned. It was prepared with great heat, and presented with great illumination and everything went right. . . . I think this was the greatest performance he did with us."[50]

TABUTEAU AND STOKOWSKI

Marcel Tabuteau's interaction with Leopold Stokowski is a fascinating but complicated subject. It was during the long Stokowski reign that Tabuteau came into prominence as a musician and oboist of premier rank. From all accounts, during most of Stokowski's tenure with the orchestra, Tabuteau regarded him highly and made every effort to fulfill his exigent demands. Tabuteau respected and admired Stokowski's level of culture, his knowledge of foreign languages, and his imagination. Many writers have addressed Stokowski's phenomenal ability to tell a story in music and to evoke a color or an atmosphere. If it required insisting that a bassoonist try dozens of reeds until reaching the exact feeling of "drab and desolate" he wanted to establish the atmosphere in the *Boris Godunov* synthesis, it would be done. Sol Schoenbach remembered other conductors asking for many things, but no one else who so persisted in searching for a precise color or nuance to portray the drama of a particular piece of music.[51]

When Tabuteau was teaching us the important orchestral passages for oboe, he always insisted that we memorize them thoroughly. He said we must be able to keep our eyes glued on the conductor and never be looking down into the music stand. He no doubt based this advice on his long experience with Stokowski. Many people have spoken of the degree to which Stokowski conducted by means of his powerful eye contact. Some have even suggested that the maestro used mystical or hypnotic powers to pull such a wide range of effects from the orchestra players. In a speech on the occasion of the Stokowski Centennial celebration in 1982, Edna Phillips, Philadelphia Orchestra harpist from

MARCEL TABUTEAU

1930 to 1946, recalled what it was like to play for Stokowski. She contrasted the orderly rehearsals with "what would happen at performance time, when the beauty and power of the orchestra could transcend normal limits and reach the stars," and she attributed that image to Marcel Tabuteau.[52] Another person who credited Tabuteau with a "celestial" statement about Stokowski was Benjamin de Loache, who took the role of the speaker in the 1932 American première of Schoenberg's *Gurrelieder*.[53] He remembered how "Stokowski walked on stage. His swift elegance and the mystery of his power enmeshed me. . . . Perhaps Marcel Tabuteau expressed it best: 'No conductor ever rose to the realms of the angels as does Leopold Stokowski.'"[54]

From many conversations with John Minsker, I learned about his years in the Philadelphia Orchestra. Minsker, who had his ninety-fifth birthday in January 2007, had distinct memories of what it was like to rehearse with Stokowski: "It was an era of discipline. When he stopped, every man in that orchestra stopped. Nobody played a quarter note after that. He had the orchestra under such control. . . . If he looked your way and you didn't have your eyes on him, I think he would have thrown you out. . . . Stokowski had the ability to get what he wanted with his hands and with his facial expression and with that certain hypnotism he had. And he had the complete attention of every member of the orchestra all the time." I suggested there may have been an element of fear or tyranny as well as discipline in all of this. Minsker agreed, noting that when he joined the orchestra,

> we had a yearly contract, but not too long before that, a man was here today and gone tomorrow. I mean he would be dropped right in the middle of a rehearsal—out. I heard those stories too many times. They had to be true. When Stokowski would stop and start again in a rehearsal, there was no fooling around. He didn't say, "four bars, let's see, four bars after letter G," and everybody would look for G and count four bars. With us, when it was *his* orchestra, everybody knew where G was . . . and could figure four bars very quickly. He never wasted a second of rehearsal time. He'd stop the orchestra, say what he had to say, "Four after H," and start again. He undoubtedly did that so that everybody was constantly aware of what was going on. Nobody fell asleep at a rehearsal, and he could do just what he wanted at the concert. Friday was one thing, Saturday another. It wasn't the

THE PHILADELPHIA ORCHESTRA

same concert. He was creative, and he didn't need another rehearsal to change something. He just did it.

Minsker described his first impressions on entering the orchestra: "I had played in the Dell a couple of times in 1934 and in 1936, the same year that I joined the Orchestra.[55] But Stokowski had a Sunday-night broadcast before the season began. He played *Afternoon of a Faun, The Holiday in Seville* [Albéniz, *Fête Dieu à Seville,* from *Iberia* orchestrated by Stokowski] and the slow movement of the *New World* symphony . . . I was, of course, scared to death. When I heard the orchestra begin to play, I was even more frightened because it was different from playing at the Dell. With Stokowski, everything was just enlarged and the sound of the orchestra and the way the players—*everybody*—Guetter, the bassoon, Tabuteau, and Kincaid—they'd get a tone and they'd go—and go and go and travel with it, and I was just sitting there, and . . . I was so frightened. I thought I'd better go back home!"

Minsker spoke at length about Stokowski's conception of pitch:

> Stokowski was very fussy about tuning. That was one of the remark-able things about him. He was very smart in that he realized you had to start with a low, dark sound. The quality of sound that he got from the orchestra was so completely different from any other orchestra in existence. There's never been anything like it since. Now, all the string players like to tune sharp. They want a brilliant sound but . . . when you have white—white, the presence of all colors, is bright. If you start with white, where do you go? When you start with black, then you can add everything on to it: the brown, the purple, the blues, and finally you get into the reds and the yellows. You can add all those colors and, of course, that is what Tabuteau did with his oboe and that's what Stokowski did with the orchestra. If there was any little friction in intonation he would stop the orchestra and tune. *Never once* in all the time I was there, did Stokowski tell anyone to go higher. It was always *down,* and we tuned to A = 438. We didn't tune to 440. We pumped the box at 438.

The box Minsker referred to was a tuning apparatus that had been or-dered by Stokowski. About a foot square, it fit under the music stand and included the frequencies from 435 to 440. There were buttons la-beled for each pitch level. After pressing the one chosen, Di Fulvio then

MARCEL TABUTEAU

pumped with the foot pedal. "The box made a sound like a street player's organ. Once when Toscanini came and heard the sound of the A from this 'organ box,' he said, 'No! I want to hear the A from the oboe!' Tabuteau beamed and felt that was a real boost to him."[56]

Rehearsals in the Stokowski years were scheduled for three hours but at times would end after two hours and forty-five minutes. There were fewer rules and regulations then, and sometimes Stokowski would ask the men if they wanted to stay a little longer on Thursday and not have any rehearsal on Friday morning just before the afternoon concert, and, of course, everybody agreed. By the time Minsker joined the orchestra, they would not have permitted the rehearsal to go beyond three hours. He remembered that "while I was a student, Tabuteau was always working for a *big* sound—to get more and more and more tone. In those days Stokowski wanted a tremendous lot of tone. So much tone! That's what I was trying to work on, too, on the English horn. . . . Stokowski wanted a tremendous range—the most pianissimo pianissimo, and the most fortissimo fortissimo."

Stokowski asked Minsker a few times to come to his apartment on Rittenhouse Street to play for him. This was a standard Stokowski practice. When he came to Houston in the early 1950s to conduct *El Amor Brujo*, I had to go to his hotel and play all the solos for him. I remember his asking me if I had ever heard *cante hondo* and the gypsies in Spain. Then he insisted that I play more and more on one of the big solos.

Minsker described how Stokowski

> wanted this big sound but he also wanted the "fade out." In the end of the prelude to *Tristan* where you play that low A-flat, it was "less, less." He would have me play it three or four times and I'd miss it a couple of times. He wanted still less. You kept trying to play less, and no matter what he asked for, you *did* it. You didn't argue about it. . . . On the other hand, if you had a harmony note, very, very low and extremely hard to play without being too loud, he'd give it to the bassoon. Or if an oboe had to play a very soft, low C-sharp, he'd give it to the English horn. He wanted to get results, and he didn't care how he got them. If Stokowski said, "Do this or that," and a player said, "It's impossible," he replied, "Well, you go home and try it." If he didn't have it the next day, that player was gone. . . . Playing for him was difficult but it was rewarding. When you walked out of a concert with

THE PHILADELPHIA ORCHESTRA

Stokowski, do you know how Tabuteau would be? It was like, "Didn't we show them something?" Later, after Stokowski left, I never had that feeling. . . . In 1960, when Stokowski came back after the twenty years he'd been away, I had already left the orchestra, but I was an extra for his concert. I'll never forget it. He didn't say a word, but he changed the sound of that orchestra within ten minutes. None of the dragging they were doing. Everything was precise. There was no question about where the beat was or about playing with it. It was the most miraculous thing I've ever experienced in my life. And the sound! There is a place in *El Amor Brujo* where there are three very dark chords and the sound that came out! I looked over at de Lancie, and he looked at me. We couldn't believe what we were hearing. It was something you can't explain.

Despite all this "magic," sometime in the mid-1930s Tabuteau began to show signs of disenchantment with Stokowski. Whether rightly or wrongly, he became convinced that Stokowski wanted to get rid of him. As incredible as it may seem in our present era of committees, controls, and protection for musicians, there was nothing to prevent Stoki's capricious treatment of orchestra members. Once during my student days Tabuteau spoke of how hard he had to work to satisfy "that madman." He asked if I thought he kept his position because he played so well. Of course, that is exactly what I thought. "No," he said, and told me that one time he was so distressed when Stokowski had summarily fired a cellist who had a family to support that he went to see Stoki, clenched his fists, and shook the desk that stood between them, saying, "Mr. Stokowski, if you ever try to do anything like that to *me*, I will tear you apart from limb to limb." Then in an aside to me, "And you know, at that time I was quite a strong fellow. Stokowski turned white." We were walking from Curtis to Hans Moennig's shop. I still remember the street corner where Tabuteau abruptly stopped to recount this story. I wondered what to believe: Was it possible that someone of the musical stature of Marcel Tabuteau could find it necessary to threaten the conductor with brute force to feel sure of his job? Was Tabuteau being theatrical to make a good story or was it at least partly true? Emmet Sargeant, a cellist in the Philadelphia orchestra from 1929 to 1944, remembered Stokowski's methods: "When I joined the orchestra in 1929, he fired fourteen or fifteen members every year, a big turnover. I think

MARCEL TABUTEAU

he liked playing with people like a cat with a mouse. . . . He fired me one year. When there were tryouts, I came and played for him again. He liked that. It had never happened to him before. Since then, I was in his favorite quartet, often playing for him backstage."[57]

It is not surprising if the uncertainty of keeping one's job under Stokowski could create a feeling of paranoia, even among his top-caliber musicians. There was a persistent, although never proven, story that at one point Stokowski was thinking of hiring Robert Bloom for first oboe.

Another ongoing rumor was that Tabuteau was responsible for pro-hibiting the eminent French oboist Myrtile Morel from landing in New York when he arrived for promised employment.[58] Before my first trip to France in 1948, Tabuteau warned me that if I should happen to run into Myrtile Morel, I should absolutely not mention that I had been his (Tabuteau's) student. I did not understand this puzzling admo-nition, but, of course, when I did "run into" Morel at the Montmartre shop of the oboe maker Charles Rigoutat, I said nothing. Only much later I learned that all the French oboists had heard about Morel being turned back from entering the United States sometime in the 1920s.[59] Although it is not known where Morel was headed, or exactly what was done to obstruct his arrival, the situation was blamed on Tabuteau and helped to make him very unpopular in France. In light of his own prob-lems on entering the United States in the Damrosch era, it is certainly possible that he might have alerted the Musician's Union about the ar-rival of yet another French oboist. When I next met Morel in 1976, it was to talk about his great teacher, Georges Gillet. In the course of the conversation, he himself told me about giving up his job, selling his fur-niture, and losing everything, believing that he would work in the United States. Again, I kept mum about Tabuteau. Finally, in the summer of 2002, I spoke with oboist and composer Patricia Morehead, who had been witness to the potentially explosive meeting of Tabuteau and Morel in 1960. She was in the Lorée shop at 4 rue du Vert Bois at the same time Morel happened to be there. Someone saw Tabuteau coming in the front door, and Robert de Gourdon quickly said, "Get him out!" But it was too late. The two oboists had seen each other and actually shook hands, after which Morel started to pound Tabuteau and call

THE PHILADELPHIA ORCHESTRA

him every bad name in the book.[60] Tabuteau's response to this meeting is unknown, but it is hard to imagine that the breach was mended. Although this incident does not put us any closer to knowing what really happened, it confirms the decades-long rumor of a serious problem between Myrtile Morel and Marcel Tabuteau.

Tabuteau repeatedly said that the only two musicians he ever admired in his life were his teacher Georges Gillet and Toscanini, but there is little doubt that at one time he would also have included Leopold Stokowski. This is confirmed by a story told by Fritz Reiner. In 1941, at the end of de Lancie's first season as solo oboe with the Pittsburgh Symphony Orchestra, he was invited to meet with Fritz Reiner. After Reiner had asked de Lancie about his summer plans and said that he would like him to come back in the fall, the conversation turned to Tabuteau and Stokowski. Reiner was very surprised when de Lancie mentioned the derogatory manner in which Tabuteau was speaking of Stokowski, even to the point of calling him a faker. Reiner responded with a story of how "one night in the late 1920s or early 1930s, after we had played a concert in New York, Tabuteau and Kincaid came to my hotel room and we sat up all night eating and drinking. We spent the whole night discussing conductors and Tabuteau said that Stokowski was the greatest in the world." By the early 1940s, however, Tabuteau had changed his tune and was praising only Toscanini. Feeling so sure that Stokowski was against him, he began to refer to Stokowski as "that son of a bitch."[61]

Once Tabuteau remarked that Stokowski had the "redeeming feature of a certain sense of humor" and that he could accept a joke without anger. To illustrate, Tabuteau spoke of a period when he felt that Stokowski had been riding the orchestra too hard. Tabuteau came to the Academy of Music early enough before a morning rehearsal to locate some props stored underneath the stage from the previous night's performance of *Aida*. He found a yoke from the scene where the Ethiopian prisoners are paraded by to become the slaves of the Egyptians. After hauling the wooden yoke up to the stage, he then linked it around the whole oboe section. "You know, when Stokowski came in to begin the rehearsal and saw us, he got the idea!!" Tabuteau was convinced that his little joke had not been taken amiss.

MARCEL TABUTEAU

Stokowski's good humor surely had limits, however. When Tabuteau left from the stage-door exit after the regular Saturday night concerts, a group of admiring students was always waiting to see him and hear his pronouncements on the evening's music making. John de Lancie remembered how "he'd come out and give a big lecture about this and that, and talk about what was good and bad, and most of the time everything was bad. When I was a student, Stoki was still the conductor of the orchestra. Tabuteau would go into this business about how *we* pull the strings and he's like a puppet up there and he just follows what we do and on and on. Tabuteau just couldn't be realistic. He insulted everybody. There's no question in my mind that is what caused the rupture between Stoki and Tabuteau. There was so much rivalry in the orchestra—jealousy and factions—and I'm sure someone must have gone to Stokowski and said, 'You should hear the way he talks about you outside of the orchestra, about pitch, and about this and that.' I mentioned this one day to Minsker. He agreed and said, 'You're right. I remember, I remember.'"[62]

On the same question John Minsker observed, "I think he [Tabuteau] always had some feeling of—I wouldn't want to say inferiority, because God knows there was nobody who could even approach his playing—but a little feeling of paranoia, as though somebody was crawling up his back or trying to get his job away from him. He was always rather outspoken. You know how he would say the conductors make everyone think that the Magic Stick does it all—things like that—and some of it must have gotten back to Stoki and maybe he even thought about replacing Tabuteau. I have no firsthand knowledge of it. He never mentioned it to me. All I know is that when I was in school, Stokowski was God Almighty to Tabuteau. He couldn't have raved more about him. And then after I came back to play in the orchestra, he gradually began denigrating Stokowski. So in the meantime, I think something had happened. It might have been in the two years when I was away playing in Detroit."[63]

Someone else who could conceivably have had a sense of when the break occurred was William Kincaid. Many years later he told John de Lancie how he knew that things were no longer the same between

THE PHILADELPHIA ORCHESTRA

Stokowski and Tabuteau. Stokowski had always treated Tabuteau with respect. In their early years he would never speak to Tabuteau from the podium but would get down and walk over to the music stand. Kincaid then reminded de Lancie of a time in 1939 when de Lancie was still a student at Curtis and was suddenly called to come in and substitute with the orchestra as Tabuteau was sick. De Lancie recalled the occasion quite clearly. He assumed he would be playing second oboe, but on reporting to the personnel manager he was told, "Just wait for a minute, young man. Mr. Stokowski wants you to play first oboe." De Lancie was in such a state of shock that he played through the whole first part of the rehearsal, Tchaikovsky's *Sixth, Pictures at an Exhibition* (Stokowski's arrangement), and the *Passacaglia in C Minor,* before he realized that he was sitting in the position of the first-desk second violins. He was accustomed to playing first oboe with Reiner at Curtis, but now suddenly found himself in Stokowski's unorthodox seating arrangement without even being conscious of it. Two days later Tabuteau came in on crutches with very bad gout. Stoki was sitting up on his podium. Tabuteau came up to Stoki with a radiant smile and shook hands in a rather obsequious manner. Kincaid, who by now had been in the orchestra for eighteen years, said that this was the first time Stokowski did not get off the podium and come down to shake hands with Tabuteau. "Never did I see Stoki talk to him from the podium. When I saw that, I knew something was wrong." De Lancie had therefore been present at this major sign of a rift without recognizing its significance. In looking back, however, de Lancie himself felt the incident must have been a manifestation of a break that had begun sooner; based on what Minsker had said, perhaps in 1936 when Robert Bloom left the orchestra, or maybe in 1937 when Stoki was beginning the routine of doing half the season and Ormandy the other half.[64]

Sol Schoenbach had somewhat different thoughts about Tabuteau and Stokowski. He felt that Tabuteau had become disappointed because "with Stokowski he felt he had the right person with whom to really make music and that he was able to reach Stokowski and give him a lot of his ideas. Stokowski was the kind of man who would take everything he could from you, and then he would disown you because he didn't want everybody to know where he got it. . . . He didn't want people to

MARCEL TABUTEAU

know that Tabuteau had such influence over him. You know, we would have a Monday-morning rehearsal and Stokowski would go out in the audience and listen to what Tabuteau did, and then when he came back and we would go into it again, he would always say, I want this and that, so he was obviously getting ideas." When I told Schoenbach I thought some people today might find this hard to believe, he responded, "Well, I must say that Stoki had some ideas of his own and maybe he got them from somebody else, but mainly I would say that the orchestra was shaped by Tabuteau." This observation became very generally accepted.

Years after Stokowski had left Philadelphia, Tabuteau spoke to his student Alfred Genovese about the legendary conductor's good and bad points. Tabuteau appreciated that "one thing about Stokowski was I could play the same piece twelve times, and twelve different times change a little of the phrasing here or there, and Stokowski always recognized the change. With others, it would just go by them—they wouldn't understand the subtleties of it." On that score he was absolutely clear: "Stoki had a talent and the ear to hear all these fine variations." But the time of Tabuteau's great admiration for Stokowski was long past, and now, in considering him as an adversary, he said, "The lion will never lie down with the lamb. They are natural enemies."[65]

It was in 1950 that I first experienced the intensity of Tabuteau's reaction to the mention of Stokowski's name. We were in France, in the village of Prades, to play for Pablo Casals's Bach Festival. Famous musicians were descending from all parts of the world to witness the reappearance of the master cellist, and Tabuteau heard the rumor that Stokowski might be among the visitors. I knew nothing then of their clouded relationship and was puzzled and alarmed when Tabuteau became very agitated, threatening to leave if Stokowki should turn up. Fortunately, Stokowski never did come, or we might not have Tabuteau's recordings of Bach's *Brandenburg Concerto No. 1*, the *C Major Suite* or the *Concerto for Oboe and Violin*. Around that same time I remember Tabuteau voicing the opinion that if you had elements of Toscanini and Stokowski rolled into one, you would have the greatest conductor of all time. He credited Stokowski for being "above all, an *artist*, and no matter in what field he might have worked, even outside of music, he would have been extraordinary."

In December 1954, in the middle of the symphony season in Houston, I wrote to the Tabuteaus about the sadness our whole orchestra felt at the departure of the impressive Hungarian conductor Ferenc Fricsay. I received a sympathetic reply from Tabuteau noting that "the only salvation and possible happiness for an orchestra player is to develop the technique to admire without reservation *le chef d'orchestre*, otherwise it is unbearable!"[66] Was he perhaps thinking back to his days of unreserved admiration for Stokowski? A few months later, in May 1955, I heard more about Stokowski from both Tabuteaus. They were perhaps inspired to openly express their opinions on learning I had decided to leave Houston just before Stokowski was to become the next conductor there. Mme Tabuteau said that Stokowski was "a rotten egg, but that Tabuteau could stand him at first, as there was an element of gamble in his [Tabuteau's] nature and that you never knew *when* Stoko. might do something really great. That from time to time he did—being unpredictable." Tabuteau himself said that he "was once so fed up with him [Stokowski], he wanted to go study in Germany and become a conductor himself—but finally decided to 'idealize' the situation in his own mind and accept it." He said he "often wanted to be in a room alone with him and just wring his neck!"[67]

Despite all the negative comments in his letters, only a year later, toward the end of 1956, Tabuteau allowed himself one final backward glance to the days of his admiration for Stokowski. From Vienna, where I was then living, I sent Tabuteau a newspaper clipping with a picture of Stokowski, who had recently appeared there. Tabuteau replied from Toulon with the following rather strange words, the last I would ever hear from him on the subject of Stokowski:

"The family is always glad to receive news. Those of this morning made me sad—the decaying Stoko!—when he was young and in top form there was already a feeling of the cadavre, what must it be like now! In all honesty I have to admit that in my half century of experience with conductors, he was the most gifted of all, but he was possessed of such a power of destruction that he could neither escape nor be saved from it."[68]

In 1960, when Stokowski returned to conduct the Philadelphia Orchestra after his nineteen-year absence, John de Lancie, who was by then the solo oboist, found it an exciting experience. In attempting to tell a not-too-receptive Tabuteau about the concerts, he said, "But the color—" Rather grudgingly Tabuteau agreed, "*Oui, ça il en avait*" (Yes, that he had).

7

TABUTEAU AS SOLOIST WITH THE PHILADELPHIA ORCHESTRA

1915–1954

SOLO OBOE PERFORMANCES

Shortly into his first season with the Philadelphia Orchestra, Tabuteau made his debut appearance as a soloist, albeit in an "out of town" popular concert. On November 15, 1915, at the Playhouse in Wilmington, Delaware, he played the Handel *G Minor Concerto,* a work familiar to him from his student days with Gillet, and one that he continued to perform throughout his career. He played it again on January 31, 1916, at the Philadelphia High School for Girls with Thaddeus Rich, the concertmaster and assistant conductor, on the podium. On November 17, 1917, Tabuteau made another more "informal" solo appearance with Rich as conductor. This time he played the *Andante and Tarantelle* by Lefebvre at the auditorium of the Stetson Hat factory on Montgomery Street below Fifth in Philadelphia. In 1918 Tabuteau joined with Thaddeus Rich and two other Philadelphia Orchestra principal string players, violist Emile Ferir and cellist Hans Kindler, to perform the Mozart Oboe Quartet at the Bellevue-Stratford in a concert for the Chamber Music Association. One newspaper reviewer recognized

Tabuteau in a formal Philadelphia portrait from the mid-1930s.

the difficulty of the quartet "full of rapid staccato and legato runs and skips of intervals of nearly two octaves, calling for great sureness of embouchure and absolute co-ordination of lip and fingers. Mr. Tabuteau's artistic work as first oboe of the Philadelphia Orchestra is well known. . . . Not only in the clearness of his technique but also in great beauty of tone . . . as well as by his good taste, Mr. Tabuteau proved himself to be an artist of the highest rank." According to another writer, Tabuteau "handled the instrument with rare facility . . . the rapid passages in the allegro and the final rondo were delivered with perfect precision" and "the exquisite theme of the slow movement was descanted with expression and a rounded fullness of tone."[1] These were but the first of the glowing comments Tabuteau would receive for playing a work that was soon to appear in a new version.

THE MOZART QUARTET AS CONCERTO

In the prospectus of the regular Philadelphia series for the 1919–20 season, Tabuteau is listed for the first time as one of the season's soloists

TABUTEAU AS SOLOIST

along with such major artists as Alfred Cortot, Sergei Rachmaninoff, Harold Bauer, and Fritz Kreisler. On April 30 and May 1, 1920, with Stokowski conducting, Tabuteau played the Mozart *Oboe Quartet,* Opus 30. No Köchel numbers were used then! Stokowski had arranged the *Quartet* as a concerto for oboe and small orchestra. Tabuteau shared the solo honors for these concerts with a singer, Estelle Hughes, winner of a local vocal competition and Stokowski Medalist for 1919. The headlines of all the reviews mention "Two Soloists," first Estelle Hughes and then Marcel Tabuteau. The critic of the *Press,* Clarence K. Bawden, headed his column with the twenty-three-year-old singer: "Estelle Hughes, Soprano, Wins Cordial Reception on Her Premier— Marcel Tabuteau Oboist, Gives Splendid Exhibition of His Skill."[2] After a lengthy essay on the "promise in this naive little girl from the mountains" (Hughes was from the small town of Pen Argyl near the Delaware Water Gap), he proceeded to laud Marcel Tabuteau in a rather homey manner: "We are mighty lucky that we have him as first oboe player of the Philadelphia Orchestra." He credited Tabuteau with making the presentation of this Mozart work "one of transcending importance. The possibility of tedium is removed, the layman finds a well-spring of melodic and rhythmic fascination, while the musician who is acquainted with reed instruments may marvel at the accomplishments of this superior Frenchman." He was evidently not very well informed about the tonal range of the oboe. Rarely has an oboist been given so much praise for the final high F, which Mr. Bawden stated was a third higher than the oboe is supposed to be able to play: "in some mysterious manner Mr. Tabuteau managed to reach the unique tone— but another proof of his virtuosity."

No fewer than seven newspapers reviewed Tabuteau's Mozart performances. Linton Martin of the *North American* wrote about "Marcel Tabuteau, that sterling artist who is first oboist of the orchestra. Mr. Tabuteau's virtuoso skill and distinguished artistry in playing his instrument were most felicitously revealed in the Mozart Quartet, Opus 30, which was arranged and re-scored expressly for the occasion . . . by Conductor Stokowski. Mr. Stokowski, who supplied spoken program notes from the stage for the Mozart work, has happily preserved and enhanced the idyllic spirit and pastoral simplicity of the number. . . . And

MARCEL TABUTEAU

with fluent technique, Mr. Tabuteau combined a loveliness of tone attesting the artist of the first order."[3] Another paper, the *Record*, said that "Mr. Tabuteau is a master of his lovely-toned instrument, and has the further gift of playing in a style that suggests improvisation, so joyous and free of spirit are the notes he produces . . . The audience reveled in Mr. Tabuteau's playing, which was probably of as general appeal as anything offered during the season."[4] In a fourth newspaper, the *Public Ledger*, the anonymous critic wrote, "Marcel Tabuteau, most unassumingly but marvelously well, played Doctor Stokowski's clever arrangement of Mozart's Oboe Quartet as a concerto with flute, clarinet, bassoon, two horns and strings."[5] Then in recognition of the man who dominated oboe playing in the first decades of the century in the U.S., he added, "Not since Longy played a Handel concerto with the Boston Orchestra, about a decade ago, have we had the oboe as soloist. It was music utterly delightful. Never a rasping or faltering note came from the reeded tube in the burbling gayety or the alternate tender melancholy of Mozart's inimitable score. Mr. Tabuteau was applauded to the echo."

The critic of the fifth newspaper, the *Evening Ledger*, was unstinting in his praise of Tabuteau and Mozart, but in commenting on the scarcity of solo works for oboe, he had some harsh words for Handel.[6]

> The second soloist was Marcel Tabuteau . . . one of the finest artists in the country; indeed, it may well be doubted if any oboist anywhere plays the oboe better that Mr. Tabuteau, in technique, tone or in artistry. He played the Mozart Quartet arranged by Mr. Stokowski . . . It was an excellent choice, for about the only thing in original oboe concertos is an impossibly unmusical and dry work by Handel. Mr. Tabuteau's performance was a masterpiece of interpretation as well as of oboe playing. The graceful runs were taken with ease and dignity and the pathetic slow movement with wonderful beauty of tone. The composition is exceedingly difficult, being written uncomfortably high and full of long "skips," which are always dangerous on this treacherous instrument. Nevertheless it was taken without an error and always with a reserve that indicated a vast amount of unused possibilities.

Still more praise came from the *Philadelphia Inquirer*. The Mozart was "admirably played by Mr. Marcel Tabuteau, with a lovely quality of tone and an impeccably perfect execution and thoroughly well deserved was the hearty applause which it elicited."[7] A final review in the *Evening Bulletin* stated that "Mr. Tabuteau plays his reedy plaintive-voiced instrument in a highly facile and expressive manner, and it is not too much to say that he literally charmed his listeners."[8] With these reviews, which go beyond mere appreciation of his excellent oboe playing, Tabuteau, now nearing his thirty-third birthday, was becoming publicly recognized for his style and musicality.

Stokowski's orchestration of the Mozart *Oboe Quartet* is housed with his other scores at the University of Pennsylvania's Van Pelt-Dietrich Library, Division of Special Collections. There are no individual parts. An ink manuscript of the score by an unknown copyist contains Stokowski's carefully penciled-in additions of one flute, one clarinet, one bassoon, and two horns in the first and last movements. He also added a second violin part, which is mainly a doubling of the existing violin line. The wind instruments are employed to reinforce the strings in the short tutti sections. However, the flute is often given a leading melodic line in place of the original violin. The two horns are used in a very idiomatic, Mozartian style. Little is changed in the Adagio movement except that the top line of the viola double stops is given to the second violins. In the middle of the last movement the violin double stops are divided into first and second violin parts. Articulations, dynamics, and phrasings are all meticulously indicated in Stokowski's delicate and finely etched notation, which contrasts surprisingly with the bold handwriting of his signature. Eight measures before the rapid oboe passage in 4/4 time, Stokowski cuts out the strings altogether and gives the winds a four-measure interlude. From this score it is not clear what Stokowski intended for the brilliant section of running sixteenth notes, but the sequence of quarter notes on each first beat of the four measures before the return to the main theme has been condensed into a space of two measures. It is possible that in 1920 an accurate edition of the Mozart *Quartet* score was not available. The Stokowski arrangement enabled Tabuteau to perform this incomparable work with orchestra at a time when there was no Mozart *Oboe Concerto*. It would be thirty years before the *D Major Flute Concerto* would be definitely established as Mozart's "lost concerto" in C Major for the oboe.

Tabuteau's next quasi-solo appearance took place in the 1922 season, when he played the first of his many performances of Bach's *Second Brandenburg Concerto*. Given thirty times between 1921 and 1952, this work must certainly qualify as a "Philadelphia favorite." When I heard it in 1945, the other soloists were Alexander Hilsberg, violin; William Kincaid, flute; and Saul Caston, trumpet. Tabuteau's earliest performances in 1921 were pre-Kincaid, with flutist André Maquarre, violinist Thaddeus Rich, and trumpeter Ernest Williams. In 1928 the soloists featured both in Philadelphia and New York were the same as in 1945 except for the concertmaster of that time, Mischa Mischakoff.

On February 1, 1922, Stokowski presented a children's concert that featured all members of the higher double reed instruments. Tabuteau played *Danse* for oboe and orchestra, a movement of the *Pastorale et Danses* by Guy Ropartz.[9] Obviously with the intention of acquainting the children with the lesser-known double reeds, Lewis Raho played the first movement of Beethoven's *Moonlight Sonata* arranged for oboe d'amore and orchestra, and Peter Henkelman played Saint-Saëns's *Le Cygne (The Swan)* for English horn and orchestra. The pièce de résistance was surely *Il Sogno (The Dream)* by Bartaletto performed on the Heckelphone by Edward Raho. As Tabuteau had acquired a bass oboe for the Philadelphia Orchestra in 1917 (see chapter 8), Raho almost certainly used that instrument. Why Stokowski persisted through several seasons in referring to it as a Heckelphone is a mystery. According to Michael Finkelman there were fewer than a half-dozen Heckelphones in North America at that time, and perhaps it seemed a more exotic name to Stokowski.[10]

In the 1923–24 season, Stokowski continued to showcase his wind players in the series of three Thursday afternoon concerts he gave for public school pupils at the Academy of Music. On March 27, 1924, Tabuteau played the *Légende Pastorale* from the *Scènes écossaises* (1893) by Benjamin Godard in the version with orchestral accompaniment. Godard and Ropartz had both dedicated their compositions to Tabuteau's teacher, Georges Gillet: Godard with the wording "to my friend" and Ropartz, more formally, "to Monsieur Georges Gillet." In choosing

Philadelphia Orchestra in the season 1945–46. Eugene Ormandy is conducting with the woodwinds directly in front of him. In the middle, solo flutist William Kincaid with Albert Tipton on his right as second flute. Next to Kincaid is the oboe section I heard during my years at the Curtis Institute: Marcel Tabuteau as first oboe, Luigi Di Fulvio, second, and John Minsker, English horn. In back of Tabuteau is first clarinet Ralph MacLean and Jules Serpentini, second. George Goslee is the first bassoon. The program lists Sol Schoenbach as "On leave–in the service of the United States." Photo by Adrian Siegel.

these pieces, Tabuteau was staying close to his Paris Conservatoire roots. Ippolitov-Ivanov was again in the spotlight as Stokowski conducted the *March of the Caucasian Chief* with its important passages for English horn and clarinet. In that same season, there was also a focus on the winds in a series of four lecture-concerts given for the Philadelphia Forum at the Academy of Music. For Tabuteau it was again the Handel *G Minor Concerto* on December 12, 1923, and on January 26, 1924, clarinetist Rufus M. Arey played a movement from the Mozart *Clarinet Concerto*. Although Walter Guetter was listed as principal bassoon beginning in 1922, Ferdinand Del Negro was the bassoon soloist in this series.

THE MOZART SINFONIA CONCERTANTE

If ever the term "dream team" could be applied in the world of woodwinds, surely it would be for the group of four players who united to play the Mozart *Sinfonia Concertante* in the 1927 season. These men, each one of whom has rightfully been called legendary, had already been playing together in the Philadelphia Orchestra for a number of years. To see the program for October 21 and 22, 1927, announcing the "Quartette Concertante for Oboe, Clarinet, Horn and Bassoon" (as it was then called), with Marcel Tabuteau, Daniel Bonade, Anton Horner, and Walter Guetter, can only make any wind aficionado long to be transported back in time. Fritz Reiner was on the podium, as this was the season that Stokowski took off to travel and study the music of the Far East. Even as the *Concertante* was being played in Philadelphia, newspapers with a New York dateline of October 21 stated that "Leopold Stokowsky [*sic*] famous conductor of the Philadelphia Orchestra, is on the high seas bound for the Orient whose wierd [*sic*] music he expects to bring back to the United States." Stokowski was ahead of his time in his wish to explore non-western music. Use of the term "weird" instead of the more acceptable "exotic" would indicate a certain lack of public appreciation for his ideas.

Some knowledge of the uncertain history of the *Concertante* is shown by H. T. Craven's review in the *Record*. He writes that it was "unknown in this country until about twenty-five years ago," and after mentioning the three "gracious and melodious movements," says: "It would be difficult to conceive of a more enchanting performance than that which was accorded to this gem by Marcel Tabuteau, oboist; Daniel Bonade, clarinetist; Anton Horner, French horn, and Walter Guetter, bassoon, four of the finest instrumentalists in the orchestra. Mr. Reiner conducted with much delicacy and affectionate appreciation of the beauties of the work, blending the orchestral backgrounds delightfully with the quartet. The audience responded with clearly genuine enthusiasm which the four chief artists were especially compelled to acknowledge."[11] Samuel L. Laciar of the *Public Ledger* remarked on the "grace and beauty of the music . . . the Philadelphia Orchestra is exceedingly fortunate to have four such artists at the first desks of these important instruments. The

TABUTEAU AS SOLOIST

playing was superb in every detail, quality of tone, precision and execution . . . like all of Mozart's works, it has to be played in a peculiarly fluent and easy sounding manner. And there are all sorts of difficulties, trills for the oboe, extremely rapid passages for all the instruments, very high and extraordinarily difficult passages for the horn. But each of these great artists surmounted immense difficulties with apparent ease and with splendid musicianship and artistry throughout. Especially interesting was the 'cadenza' in the first movement, when after the customary six-four chord, the solo instruments entered into a brief but beautiful development of part of the movement." Laciar concluded that "it is doubtful if there is another orchestra in the world whose 'firsts' could have performed this concerto (for it is virtually one) in the manner in which Messrs. Tabuteau, Bonade, Horner and Guetter did yesterday. At the close they were recalled many times by the delighted audience."[12]

These symphony men did not have the rest of the concert "off " on the day they appeared as soloists, for in writing of the Brahms *Second Symphony,* which concluded the program, Mr. Laciar mentioned the "beautiful work done by Anton Horner in the exquisite coda of the first movement and by Marcel Tabuteau in the lovely oboe melody in the scherzo." Linton Martin of the *Inquirer* gave most of his space to Reiner's outstanding conducting of Brahms' *Second,* finding the Mozart to be "a work of mixed merits" but recognizing that the four soloists "played with the fine sense of ensemble which marks a chamber organization of intimate association."[13] *The Evening Bulletin* was generous in its praise for the "four supreme solo players of the orchestra. . . . They fairly rivaled one another, but so much does each excel in his own field that there was glory enough for all. Mr. Tabuteau's amazingly fine work with his oboe is familiar to orchestra patrons; Mr. Bonade is a veritable King of Clarinetists, with a facility and a tone that scarcely could be surpassed, while Mr. Horner, with his horn, and Mr. Guetter, with his bassoon, complete an incomparable quartet of artists. . . . The four men seemed almost embarrassed yesterday by the applause that compelled them to rise and bow, and then to do it again and again, even after they had sought their accustomed seats and let the audience shower still more applause upon them. But they deserved every bit of it."[14] The

MARCEL TABUTEAU

October 29 issue of *Musical America* reviewed this concert with the headline of "Mozart Novelty Played by Reiner" and called it "the most engaging and artistically stimulating program thus far this season."

Leon Lester, who was a student at the Curtis Institute in the 1920s, heard these four artists play the *Concertante*.[15] In 1999 he told me of his impressions: "You were sitting there and you heard the clarinet—Bonade. Oh, he's the greatest! And then the bassoon would come in—Walter Guetter. He would outshine them all. What a joy to hear him play the bassoon; there's never been bassoon playing like that. And then Tony Horner, who was at his height. Oh, how he played that horn, it was just glorious, and Tabuteau—whichever one was playing at the moment—that's the closest thing to heaven I ever got—to hear those four. No wonder they had those great names."

There is no doubt that this must have been a superb performance. However, with the general improvement in the standards of wind playing in the United States during the past seventy-five years, it is unlikely that any reviewer would now express such astonishment at the expertise of the soloists. Today the four first-chair wind players of any major orchestra would be routinely expected to give a creditable performance of this work, while in 1927 it was regarded as a unique accomplishment. The change is no doubt due in large part to the long years these four remarkable musicians devoted to teaching, as well as playing, their respective instruments.

In 1940, some thirteen years after playing the *Sinfonia Concertante* with his contemporaries, Tabuteau performed it again with his much younger colleagues, Bernard Portnoy, clarinet; Mason Jones, horn; and Sol Schoenbach, bassoon. Portnoy and Jones had only recently been students in Tabuteau's ensemble classes at the Curtis Institute. In 1997 I was able to ask them what they remembered about the *Concertante*. Each one had vivid recollections of the experience. Both Jones and Schoenbach spoke of being on the boat returning from the 1940 South American tour of the All-American Youth Orchestra and finding themselves seated at the same lunch table with Stokowski. As Jones recalled, "he would ask questions of people; he was always a glutton for information and he asked what concertos there are for my instrument. I told him there was Mozart and Richard Strauss and I said there was

TABUTEAU AS SOLOIST

also a piece by Mozart that includes four wind instruments. He took it all in but didn't say a word. That fall the *Concertante* was on the program of the Philadelphia Orchestra and later we recorded it."

Sol Schoenbach recounted in his inimitable way, "Well, Stokowski casually mentioned to me that it was the 137th year of Mozart's birth or death or something like that and it would be a good time to do the *Concertante* . . . So, lo and behold, a few months later, all of a sudden there it was. Tabuteau asked us to get together in a hurry, because now we had these concerts coming up. We put in a little time and Tabuteau made some remarks, very, very, deep remarks, and then we found ourselves with Stokowski playing it and later doing the recording." I asked if they had performed it together before, and Sol said, "No, never. That's the way it was. Everything was like that in those days. Nobody told you ahead of time to rehearse it. Tabuteau was the only one we could turn to for that."

They played the *Concertante* on the regular series (Friday afternoon, Saturday night, and Monday night) of November 22, 23, and 25, 1940. Later in the week there was an additional performance of the last movement, Andantino—Theme and Variations, for a youth concert. Sol Schoenbach, Bernard Portnoy, and Mason Jones all remembered how Stokowski suddenly asked each one of them to improvise a cadenza. According to Jones: "I think we only played the last movement. There was applause and then Stokowski said, 'Well, they'd like to hear some more music so this time I want each one of you to play a cadenza.' Of course, they were very short, these little cadenzas. I don't remember what I did; I think I took one of the themes and went to a different key, came back to it, and put in a trill." Portnoy described it in greater detail: "When we finished and were walking off the stage after taking a bow, we got inside the wings and Stokowski with his crazy ideas, said, 'At the end right before the finale, there's a fermata. We'll start a few bars before that and then each of you will take a cadenza.' We were just standing there. What do you mean a cadenza? What a mess that was. I started playing—I don't know what—arpeggios. It wasn't as if we were a jazz band and improvised all the time. Tabuteau went back to the opening of the theme. Then Sol was the last one to come in and he was playing chords and kept going up and up and up and Stokowski kept standing higher on his toes, putting on an act as if he was reaching for the sky. Finally Sol resolved the note and we all came in on the finish, but it was a very frustrating moment, I can tell you that!" These cadenzas even attracted the attention of the newspaper reviewers who, without knowing the inside story, gave their impressions of the unusual display. In the *Record* of November 28, Arthur Bronson told how "Stokowski announced that he had asked Tabuteau to play a few cadenzas in the work, but it wasn't sure that he would. Monsieur Tabuteau was such a temperamental person, he said." When the last movement was repeated as an encore "the doughty soloists let loose. Oboist Tabuteau suddenly decided he would play a cadenza. And bassoonist Schoenbach concluded that he too, might try. Then clarinetist Portnoy, and French Hornist Jones—each followed the other with cadenzas of their own devising, or running right into the other's solo, so that Stokowski seemed utterly taken aback."

Henry Pleasants of the *Evening Bulletin* referred more sedately to the responsive and enthusiastic atmosphere of the youth concerts, with Stokowski being in "top form and high spirits fulfilling his multiple obligations as master of ceremonies, guest of honor and principal entertainer." He credited the four wind soloists as getting into the spirit of the evening "to the extent of improvising their own comic cadenzas." According to the *Inquirer* it was these cadenzas that stole the show. "Four members of the Philadelphia Orchestra 'went temperamental' last night . . . taking musical matters right out of Leopold Stokowski's shapely hands and into their own. Their antics made the maestro himself, the players and the youthful audience laugh fit to beat the band, or in this case, the Philadelphia Orchestra."

In 1999 I chanced to meet Harry Peers, a retired trumpet player from the Metropolitan Opera Orchestra. While a student at Curtis in 1940 he had attended the famous "concert of the cadenzas." He told me how he remembered it: "Stokowski announced that in Mozart's day it was the custom to improvise at the performance. He surprised the orchestra by saying 'We will do this for you tonight—we will play cadenzas.' Then he started the piece and there were no cadenzas other than the written ones. When it was finished, and everyone was clapping, Stoki turned around, snapped his fingers, and said 'Oh, we forgot the cadenzas. We'll do the

TABUTEAU AS SOLOIST

last movement over again with cadenzas.' Every time there was a six-four chord Stoki pointed to one of the soloists and the orchestra stopped playing. When it came to the bassoon, Sol would modulate and trill and go off into a different key. He did this three or four times and finally Stoki broke up with laughter. He was laughing his head off and couldn't conduct. So he just gave a final chord and that was that. That ended it." I had heard the story from three of the players, but had never known anyone who was in the audience. "Well," Harry said, "I was there!"

Fortunately, on December 22, 1940, these four artists recorded the *Concertante,* issued on RCA Victor as Album 269 on 78-rpm disks. It was the last recording Stokowski made with the Philadelphia Orchestra until he returned twenty years later in 1960. About that recording session, Sol Schoenbach said: "In those days when you made records you couldn't do anything over. It had to be flawless in order to pass. If anybody made a mistake you had to go back to the beginning and do it again. It was a very exhausting experience and I was amazed that it came out so well." When I told him how grateful we are to have that beautiful recording, Sol replied, "It was a miracle wasn't it? Absolute miracle." Bernard Portnoy had similar memories: "We made the *Variations* in one take, believe it or not, in wax. It took up two sides. We went through it once and that was all—and it was perfect." Perhaps not completely perfect, according to Jones: "There's a little place at the end where it's in 6/8 time and I never realized until I heard the recording that I played it with the grace note and Tabuteau does two even notes. It's just a small detail—something we never rehearsed or talked about." About the difficulties for the horn, Jones added, "In a *Concertante* performance you have to keep cool and calm. It doesn't go especially low but it goes up to high E-flat. There's a lot of continuous playing and that run in the last movement. No amount of rehearsal will do that for you. You just have to feel it right at the performance." The oboist who can be heard in all the orchestral tuttis is John Minsker.

There was yet another story from Sol Schoenbach, a follow-up to the *Concertante* undertaking. "They didn't really have to pay anybody but then the producer, that man from Victor—his name was Charles O'Connell—came around one day and said, 'you know, we got the most wonderful reviews everywhere for that recording. I can't thank you

MARCEL TABUTEAU

enough,' and Tabuteau said, 'Well, thanks is not enough. If it's so good, how come we didn't get a bonus of some kind?' So O'Connell replied, 'You're absolutely right.' The next week we got fifty dollars each. Ha, ha, ha! If we hadn't spoken up we would never have gotten anything. From the fifty dollars they sent us they took off fifty cents which was the Social Security tax in those days, so I thought I could turn this into an idea for getting Social Security for the entire orchestra. I was trying all the time to get us covered by Social Security, but they told us it didn't apply for nonprofit organizations. So I said, 'But Victor is not a nonprofit organization.' Then I went to their highest man in New York, and it was again 'No, the law does not cover it.'" Sol said he often felt like giving up but that Tabuteau would keep fighting. "When Tabuteau got onto a subject, he never left it."

The *Sinfonia Concertante* was the only complete recording of a Mozart work Stokowski made during his years in Philadelphia. Long unavailable, it has now been reissued on CDs by two companies. One, Boston Records, BR1021, which also includes excerpts of Tabuteau's playing from the Stokowski years, is minus the orchestral introduction. The complete version on Cala Records (CACD0523) was reviewed in early 1999 by both the *American Record Guide* and *Gramophone*. Sixty years after its original release this recording received compliments for both the orchestral sound and high level of the playing. The *Guide* cites the almost nonexistent surface noise and further states that "the orchestral playing is gorgeous, and the soloists are wonderful in every respect: virtuosity, tone, and musicianship. The sound of the orchestra is richer, more 'romantic' than we expect in Mozart; but after all, this is Stokowski! The performance is tasteful and musical. Both the work and the recording are beguiling." The *Gramophone* is no less warm in its praise of "this enchanting account . . . the tone is predominantly mellow; the line, smooth yet malleable, and the tempos are generally broad. Among the soloists, oboist Marcel Tabuteau is the star act, but the other section leaders are hardly less distinguished." At the time of these reissues, three of the four soloists, Tabuteau's very young colleagues when the recording was made, were still living.[16]

As a student, I used to listen to the 78-rpm *Concertante* over and over. One time I mentioned to the Tabuteaus what a fine example of his

TABUTEAU AS SOLOIST

recorded playing I felt it was. RCA Victor had sent him the album, but it sat in his apartment for five years. The Tabuteaus did not own a phonograph, and they had never heard it. Finally, one day in October 1945, I persuaded Madame Tabuteau to come to my place and listen to it. She became so enthusiastic that she sent a telegram to Tabuteau, who was on tour with the orchestra. After he returned, I borrowed a better machine from my violist friend, Karen Tuttle, and the Tabuteaus climbed the steep steps to my fourth-floor room in the Hannah Penn House to hear the *Concertante*. In a letter to my mother I described this "event" in detail. "Last night at 6:00 p.m. they came. Tabuteau was really pleased. Imagine, he'd never heard those records at all. It was fun to see him listening up in my attic—conducting phrases here and there—cursing Stokowski's tempos in the Mozart—smiling when one of his phrases came out just so." If he was not happy with Stokowski's tempi, which he felt were too slow, it is not evident in the life and color with which he filled every phrase of the first movement, nor in the long floating lines he spun out in the Adagio. The statement of the theme in the Finale and the arpeggiated variation no. 8 present a perfect example of Tabuteau's ability to play a series of articulated notes, avoiding sounding either too short and "pecky" or too long and mushy. He gives each individual eighth or sixteenth note its exact place in the total pattern with an appropriate length and inflection, all adding up to a uniquely satisfying shaping of the complete phrase. This recording remains a testament to Tabuteau's belief in the oboe as an unrivaled medium for musical expression.

Tabuteau's last performance of the *Concertante* took place in 1948 and was the only one I heard in person. The symphony season in Kansas City where I was playing English horn was so short (twenty weeks) that I could be in Philadelphia by March 5 for the concert. Ormandy had initiated a "Viennese" series with music by Johann Strauss, Schubert, and Mozart. In a nod to orchestra history, Linton Martin of the *Philadelphia Inquirer* pointed out that Tabuteau was the only soloist surviving from both the 1927 and 1940 performances and that of the other three players—Ralph McLane, clarinet; Sol Schoenbach, bassoon; and Mason Jones, horn—only the clarinetist had not been in the 1940 performance led by Stokowski.

HANDEL G MINOR CONCERTO

The Handel *G Minor Concerto* was the first solo work Tabuteau played, soon after he joined the Philadelphia Orchestra. During the next fifteen years he performed it many times but always on an out-of-town or children's concert. Not until the 1931–32 season did it appear in the regular orchestra series in the concerts of December 11 and 12, 1931, conducted by Alexander Smallens. The *Evening Bulletin* praised "the voice of the solo instrument, played with remarkable skill and the refinement of artistry for which he is justly famous by Marcel Tabuteau, the distinguished first oboist of the orchestra. Mr. Tabuteau, with characteristic modesty, yesterday acknowledged the applause that called him back several times after his brilliant performance." Most of the critics were more concerned with the Shostakovich *First Symphony* than the Handel. Henry C. Beck of the *Record* headed his review: "Orchestra Offers Blaring Program." His reference to Tabuteau commenced with "The orchestra pretended that all was to be mild and mellow by beginning with the Handel *Concerto Grosso in G Minor*." He cited Tabuteau's "excellent breath control and tone shading," and added that he "was accorded a reception which all but flustered his modest personality." He dismissed the Shostakovich by "refraining to use valuable space in the discussion of nothing." The *Inquirer* mentioned that "Marcel Tabuteau played the solo oboe part beautifully in the Handel concerto grosso," but again gave more space to the symphony with its "blaring brass and pounding percussion" by the "Russian revolutionist with the jaw-shattering name of Szostakowicz" (a reasonable transliteration of his name had not yet been decided upon).

In the four papers that reviewed the Handel, only Samuel L. Laciar of the *Public Ledger* covered it in some detail. He devoted almost half of his article to the Concerto, noting that "the work had not appeared before at the regular symphony concerts of the Orchestra . . . although it has been performed by the Philadelphia String Simfonietta, also with Mr. Tabuteau." (Blending the terms *symphony* and *sinfonietta*, the full name of this group was Philadelphia Chamber String Simfonietta.)[17] In a paragraph headed "Tabuteau Surpasses Himself," Laciar mentioned that all those who attend the Philadelphia Orchestra concerts "have long been familiar with the beautiful tone and artistic phrasing which grace all the passages written for the first oboe as played by Mr. Tabuteau. Yesterday, however, he had a solo part virtually from beginning to end of each of the three movements. He has never played better, exhibiting a tone of amazing variety of color, immense flexibility and exquisite quality in every register. Mr. Tabuteau was greeted with warm applause upon his first appearance on the stage, and at the close was deservedly recalled half a dozen times." About Shostakovich, the "youthful composer of the Soviet regime," Laciar considered the symphony to be a work of promise even though "irregular in matter of musical quality" with "a considerable tendency to 'lumpiness' in several of the themes."

Tabuteau consistently garnered critical praise for his style and the apparent ease of his performances, but few people realized the agonies he suffered with reeds. John Minsker remembered being backstage in the Green Room one time just before Tabuteau had to go on to play the Handel *Concerto* at a student concert. Tabuteau pulled a reed out of his case, and it came off the tube. "It was as though he didn't realize what was happening, almost as if he'd gone into a coma. He was so distressed . . . I thought he was going to cry. He evidently didn't have another reed ready and he had to go out there and play a solo. He asked, 'Do you have a reed?' I gave him the reed that I'd been playing and he went onstage and sounded great—it was remarkable, and nobody ever knew anything had happened, proving that a great deal was *how* he blew. Nevertheless, he spent most of his time in the studio working on reeds."

THE MOZART QUARTET AGAIN

During the 1939 season five first-chair members of the orchestra were featured as soloists: Marcel Tabuteau, flutist William Kincaid, violist Samuel Lifschey, concertmaster Alexander Hilsberg, and bass player Anton Torello. On October 22, several days before Tabuteau's first performance, an extensive but rather fanciful article appeared in the *Record*. The writer, who signed only his initials E. H. S., had evidently made some effort to be informed about the oboe.[18] He began by raking over the old stories that "all oboe players go more or less balmy," with the qualification, however, that this superstition was current "a generation ago." Then he noted that "Tabuteau's only eccentricity after some forty years of oboing is a tendency to laugh uproariously at his own jokes, which, after all, is an amiable weakness, especially since M. Tabuteau's jokes are generally less than six months old and he seldom laughs alone." He included tributes to Tabuteau's gifts as a gourmet cook and a roulette player, and to his being a chevalier of the Légion d'Honneur. "One of the world's truly great oboe players who for the past 24 years has been the bright particular star of the Philadelphia Orchestra's galaxy of virtuoso first-desk players . . . the genial and popular M. Tabuteau will be soloist for the first time in entirely too many seasons playing the Mozart *Quartet for Oboe and Strings* in the arrangement by Leopold Stokowski." After indulging in a colorful description of how Mozart wrote the quartet for Friedrich Ramm, his drinking partner "in the taverns and streets of Mannheim," the writer continued to trace the history of the oboe from Greek and Egyptian days up until the French School of Tabuteau's teacher, Georges Gillet. "If you will glance at the personnel lists of the world's leading orchestras you will more than likely find the tenants of the oboe department bearing Gallic names." And to make sure that it was not forgotten: "One of the most famous in this country was the late Gustave Longy, of the Boston Symphony."[19] Mr. E. H. S. closed by discussing the manufacture in Paris of the highly prized Lorée oboes with late 1930s prices of $200 to $275. "Lorée makes about one hundred instruments a year. . . . They are the Stradivari of the oboe world."[20] Hans Moennig, Philadelphia's great woodwind artisan, was quoted as saying that about five hundred instruments (including the anonymous ones made in Germany or France) were sold in the United States per year, mostly for bands. The last word in debunking the "oboists going balmy legend" was given to Moennig: "There's nothing to it. They get to be English horn players and most of them who do business with me are no crazier than a fox."

The *Inquirer*'s lengthy "preview" article about Tabuteau's upcoming solo appearance included the biographical information from the questionnaire he had filled out in 1915 for the Philadelphia Orchestra files. Tabuteau's response to the question "Soloist Experience" ("Do not want

TABUTEAU AS SOLOIST

any!!!") was quoted verbatim including its three exclamation points.[21] In 1939 the *Quartet* appeared with its correct Köchel listing of K. 370. Again, the reviews were enthusiastic. Edwin H. Schloss of the *Record* begins with "Tabuteau Hailed as Oboe Soloist with Orchestra" and noted that this was "his first solo appearance here in seven years. . . . Not since M. Tabuteau was made a Chevalier of the Legion of Honor by the French government on the same stage two years ago has he been the center of so much acclaim. The applause yesterday was tremendous, recalling the affectionate tempests of last week's 'Kreisler reception' and leaving no doubt in anyone's mind as to the place M. Tabuteau occupies in the esteem of Philadelphia music lovers. And for his part, the smiling M. Tabuteau responded with a performance of Mozart's Quartet which left no doubt as to the place he has long occupied in the oboe world—a place, of course, a great many ledger lines above the staff." After more about the *Quartet* and the Stokowski arrangement, Schloss wound up with, "It is music well suited to the oboe's happiest moods and equally well suited to M. Tabuteau's gifts for perfect phrasing, his infallible taste and the pluperfect quality of his tone production."

If there were no longer seven newspaper reviews as in 1920, there were at least still four. This was a time when major U.S. cities were served by several daily papers, each with its own music critic. There was not a dissenting voice in the praise of Tabuteau's Mozart performances: if anything, only increased recognition and appreciation by all for the beauty of his phrasing and sound. The program had included a Purcell-Cailliet Suite from *Dido and Aeneas* and the popular Franck *D Minor Symphony,* but Tabuteau was given priority in the heading of every article. Besides being "Hailed" by the *Record,* Tabuteau was "Acclaimed" in the *Evening Bulletin,* and in the *Evening Ledger* he "Scores as Soloist." The *Inquirer's* caption had "Mozart Oboe Opus Sandwiched between 2 Symphonic Offerings."[22] According to Linton Martin of that paper, "There are oboes and oboes. But there's only one Marcel Tabuteau. That was demonstrated when the Philadelphia Orchestra's first oboist appeared as soloist at the concert in the Academy yesterday and was acclaimed with fervor and affection. The occasion, coincidentally, signalized Mr. Tabuteau's silver anniversary year with the orchestra, showing that he is by no means a wandering oboist." After speaking of the "symphonic sandwich" in which "the piquant flavor was provided by the solo number," he said that the "cool, clean, clear, bitter-sweet timbre of the solo part stood out always against the supporting string tone and Mr. Tabuteau's spirited performance, contrastingly gay and grave, was a delight. There was never a deviation from pitch, never a faltering tone or a blurred note in a performance of sustained elegance and charm."

Mr. Laciar of the *Evening Ledger* referred to the very special place that the Franck *D Minor Symphony* holds with Philadelphia audiences, chosen in voting almost every season for the Request Program, and said that despite the excellent performance it had received, "the feature of yesterday afternoon's concert . . . was the playing of an oboe solo by Marcel Tabuteau. Mr. Tabuteau's performance of the work was literally perfection and showed that he is one of the greatest oboists in the world and probably the greatest. His tone possessed all throughout that limpid beauty which is always associated with his rendition of his many important solo parts in orchestral works while his phrasing was of the utmost artistry and his interpretation music only, to the last degree."

Henry Pleasants added to the accolades and wrote with special understanding of Tabuteau's qualities: "The orchestra's veteran first oboist is one of this generation's great musical artists, condemned to a relative obscurity simply because his favorite instrument happened to be the oboe rather than the violin or the piano." Pleasants regretted that there was so little literature for this instrument and doubted that it would ever be much larger as "the oboe is not cast in an expansive or heroic mold." But he felt that Mozart wrote "affectionately" for the oboe and "thoroughly understood" it. "Mr. Tabuteau's playing was a happy and rare combination of interpretive insight and complete technical mastery. The audience paid the soloist a handsome tribute of applause which was not unmixed with a sincere personal regard. Mr. Tabuteau, for his part, seemed very happy, but just a little embarrassed by his unwonted prominence."[23]

On November 7, 1939, a week after the October 27 and 28 Philadelphia concerts, Tabuteau played the Mozart in Carnegie Hall in New York. If in Philadelphia it might be expected that Tabuteau would be

Rehearsal in fall of 1939 for the Mozart Oboe Quartet (as Concerto). Tabuteau is seated in front of concertmaster Alexander Hilsberg. Eugene Ormandy is the conductor. Courtesy Dr. Jacques Budin.

lauded as a popular and respected "local personality," no such partiality could be awaited from the New York critics. Five papers wrote in praise of Tabuteau. The respected critic Olin Downes portrayed Tabuteau in terms that many a world-renowned concert violinist or pianist would have been delighted to add to his or her résumé. Downes's eulogy of Tabuteau's performance extends from his opening statement that last night's concert of the Philadelphia Orchestra in Carnegie Hall "contained one work which in itself would have made the concert worth the journey" to his conclusion: "At the end the audience applauded the little piece of Mozart as they would have applauded under other circumstances some reverberating modern tone-poem—and perhaps with better reason." Downes showed his appreciation of the finer points of Tabuteau's art. Praising his tone,

> slenderer than the thicker tone that oboists of other schools than Mr. Tabuteau's affect, and by so much the truer to the essential quality of the instrument; also, the better for Mozart's music. Then comes an astonishing technique, which is the vehicle of the phrasing of a most sensitive and admirable musician. Mr. Tabuteau can play a florid passage almost with the agility of a flute, and as cleanly, and he can sing on his reeds like the Pied Piper of Hamelin. Above all, he has infallible taste. That is a quality for which Mozart furnishes the supreme test and in which respect it will expose a second-class artist quicker than by almost any other means . . . each small tone, each sustained phrase, made for beauty and delight. . . . The slow movement has a quality of melancholy, yet not too deep or too intense for the frame of the whole piece. The movements are short. When they are finished everything has been said, and without an instant's lapse into the formal repetitiousness . . . often discovered in the writings of even the greatest masters of the period.[24]

Downes was less enthusiastic about Ormandy's interpretation of Brahms's *Second Symphony*, where he found a deficiency of style.

Several Curtis oboe students came to New York to hear the Mozart. For John de Lancie, the Brahms *Symphony* was equally impressive. "I remember it to this day, the way Tabuteau played that third movement of the Brahms *Second*. It was one of those transcending moments." About the *Oboe Quartet:* "He played it sitting down. As I remember, he came onto the stage in a wheelchair."[25] None of the laudatory New York reviews mentioned that Tabuteau had to come out in a wheelchair. Rather, a newspaper in Toledo, Ohio, sent a "special" to the Philadelphia *Evening Ledger* with the flamboyant headline "Crippled Oboist Defies Pain to Play." "In spite of a sprained ankle, Marcel Tabuteau . . . will continue the tour of Mid-Western cities with the Orchestra. Tabuteau hobbled to his place on the stage of the Auditorium Theater, Chicago, Tuesday night, but by the end of the concert he was in great pain." He was advised by a doctor to take an ambulance to the train and return to Philadelphia, but in the tradition of "the show must go on," he

TABUTEAU AS SOLOIST

continued to Toledo, Fort Wayne, Milwaukee, and Pittsburgh. In Toledo "he was rolled to his place on the stage in a wheelchair, with an understudy, Adrian Siegel, ready to take over if need be." Gout (almost surely the problem) was not mentioned, perhaps seeming less "heroic" than the idea of battling a sprained ankle.[26]

Back in 1904 when Tabuteau was awarded his Premier Prix in the Conservatoire *concours*, the opinion of a reviewer was that "next to him the other contestants paled a little." Now, almost forty years later, two New York critics considered that the impact of his Mozart overshadowed performances of Beethoven and Brahms on the same program. Irving Kolodin of the *New York Sun* wrote: "If one can conceive of so plaintive an instrument as the oboe in terms of bravura, this was the word for Mr. Tabuteau's playing of the racy finale. Here his phrasing of turns and other ornaments was agility itself, adding the final touch of comprehensiveness to the exposition of the instrument's capacities." After the "moving adagio which the soloist sang with magnificent artistry," Kolodin stated, "This coincidence of virtuosity and taste somewhat overshadowed the other music of the evening, which comprised two symphonies: The first of Beethoven and the second of Brahms. Were it not that all the evidence of the performance indicated otherwise, one might almost remark that Mr. Tabuteau's participation in the playing of the work seemed an afterthought, so casually did he rise from his seat in the orchestra and take his place in the chair beside the podium occupied by Eugene Ormandy. However, once he began to play, all that was evident was the most penetrating forethought, so carefully was each note intoned, shaded and joined to its successor." Kolodin also praised the Stokowski version of the score, the "charming moments . . . in which an interchange of phrases between oboe and flute introduced a new color into the texture and refreshed the ear for the additional oboe passages to come."[27]

The "Music of the Day" section of the *Brooklyn Eagle* carried a bold double headline: "Ovation for Tabuteau; Ditto for Jan Peerce." Tabuteau would have been amused (if he even saw the review) to find the name of the famous tenor following his own with a "ditto." They had not appeared in the same concert; Jan Peerce was making a Town Hall debut. Miles Kastendieck, who reviewed the "Philadelphians,"

MARCEL TABUTEAU

said flatly in his opening sentence, "Had it not been for the performance of Mozart's *Quartet in F for Oboe and Strings* with Marcel Tabuteau as soloist, the second concert of the Philadelphia Orchestra in Carnegie Hall last night might have been dismissed as routine." After listing his complaints about the rest of the program, he added, "Mozart and Tabuteau saved the evening. . . . Mr. Tabuteau's playing revealed how much of an artist an oboe player can become. The various qualities of the instrument's tone were knowingly modulated while the music was impeccably phrased. Soloist and musicians caught the irresistible spirit of the work with the result that every one had a good time."

Pitts Sanborn of the *World Telegram,* in his comments on the three movements of the Mozart *Quartet,* focused especially on "the level of importance attained by the intervening Adagio. The deeply expressive lyricism of this interlude provides the chief artistic excuse for transcribing the quartet along larger lines. Marcel Tabuteau, the man Mr. Stokowski had in mind in making his edition, was the soloist last evening. Such were the surpassing quality of his tone, his technic, and his taste, that the great audience not only applauded his performance but actually cheered it, a show of enthusiasm most richly deserved."

The Mozart in Carnegie Hall had become a triumph for Tabuteau. The critic of the *Herald Tribune,* Jerome D. Bohm, wrote: "Mr. Tabuteau's delivery of the solo part was nothing short of astounding. The oboe is generally acknowledged to be the most difficult of orchestral instruments to master. Mr. Tabuteau has not only mastered its technique in extraordinary fashion, but his musicianship is no less compelling than his virtuosity. Such sheer tonal loveliness as he imparted to every measure of the composition, coupled with such sensitivity and depth of feeling are rarely encountered in any instrumentalist." Finally, a November 10 article in the magazine *Musical America* linked Tabuteau and Kreisler in its heading. The review of the Philadelphia October 20 and 21 concerts, in which Kreisler had played the Schumann *Fantasie in C for Violin and Orchestra* and the *Viotti Concerto in A Minor,* was immediately followed by mention of the concerts of October 27 and 28 when "Mr. Tabuteau's superb solo playing in the Mozart" was the "outstanding pleasure of the program. . . . The work is replete with lovely music from first note to last and one can not imagine a more artistically defined and balanced performance than was attained. A prolonged ovation, in which Dr. Ormandy and his colleagues participated, signified great delectation and approval, the soloist being recalled many times."

HOWARD HANSON PREMIÈRE

One of the only times that Tabuteau played anything other than a Handel, Bach, or Mozart solo in a regular Philadelphia subscription series was the October 20 and 21, 1950, première performance of Howard Hanson's *Pastorale*. A highlight of the fourth general meeting of UNESCO in Paris in the fall of 1949 was a special concert in commemoration of the Chopin Centennial. Composers representing eleven countries were commissioned to write works for the occasion, among them Lennox Berkeley from Great Britain, Florent Schmitt and Jacques Ibert from France, Bohuslav Martinů of Czechoslovakia, Carlos Chavez from Mexico, and the international Alexander Tansman. The *Pastorale* was America's contribution. In the Paris concert it was played by oboist Jules Goetgheluck with Hanson at the piano. Hanson then made the arrangement for oboe and strings, which he reserved for a first performance in Philadelphia a year later. On a concert including a Mozart symphony and the Berlioz *Fantastique,* which Max de Schauensee described as "an unusually well balanced musical menu," "the novelty was Howard Hanson's *Pastorale for Solo Oboe, Strings, and Harp,* the solo part entrusted to the talented and popular Marcel Tabuteau. Dr. Hanson's piece is brief and charming. It is music of mood and atmosphere, scored with the sure hand of the practiced technician, an offshoot of the musical impressionists of 40 years ago . . . The effect is distinctly pleasant. Mr. Tabuteau played the well written solo line beautifully; which of course, was to be expected from this sterling artist. His phrasing and sense of style are impeccable, his tone lovely and relaxed. Fortunate was Dr. Hanson to have had such a performer."[28] Linton Martin also had complimentary words for the composer and soloist: "The oboe was undoubtedly the ideal solo instrument for a composition of this character . . . this 'Pastorale' gave the audience an opportunity to enjoy some superlative solo work by Marcel Tabuteau, who justly shared the applause with Ormandy and the orchestra, as well

Tabuteau is featured in a 1950 newspaper cartoon as "The greatest master of phrasing in the world." Courtesy John Minsker.

TABUTEAU AS SOLOIST

Caricature of Marcel Tabuteau, as drawn by Alfred Bendiner.

as the composer for the skill, displayed in evoking atmosphere."[29] The *Philadelphia Daily News* offered yet another tribute: "Marcel Tabuteau, principal oboist for the Philadelphia Orchestra and probably the world's greatest executant of that instrument, displays his superior virtuosity in the performance of Howard Hanson's *Pastorale for Solo Oboe, Harp and String Orchestra* . . . on the program the Philadelphia Orchestra is presenting this weekend."[30]

LAST MOZART IN PHILADELPHIA

Twelve years after Tabuteau's New York triumph with the Mozart *Oboe Quartet,* he played it again in Philadelphia. His 1951 performances were in the context of a pre-Christmas holiday Viennese program conducted by Eugene Ormandy. There were Strauss waltzes, polkas and galops, as well as Schubert's early *D Major Symphony.* The concert opened with the "Lullaby—*Gott Weiss Alles,*" a Viennese carol especially orchestrated for the occasion by the composer and manager of the Philadelphia Orchestra, Harl McDonald. It was also Harl McDonald's arrangement of the Mozart *Quartet* that Tabuteau used this time. By now, Stokowski had severed all his relations with the Philadelphia Orchestra and had presumably taken his scores with him. McDonald's version was considerably less sophisticated than Stokowski's. He added two clarinets, two horns, and divided the violin line into two parts. The winds are simply used to reinforce the short tutti sections. The discrepancy in the number of measures in the last movement was corrected, but in general the arrangement lacks the interest of Stokowski's earlier score with its subtle and imaginative touches.[31]

Again, Tabuteau received critical acclaim. From Max de Schauensee of the *Evening Bulletin:* "Mr. Tabuteau tossed off the little work with great charm and ease. His phrasing was a model of clarity and his entire performance was permeated by a graciousness, characteristic of the artist." Linton Martin of the *Inquirer* referred to "our own peerless oboe artist, Marcel Tabuteau, who delighted his listeners with his beautiful tone and triumphant technique." Credit was given to McDonald for his contribution: "The work in this form was virtually ideal for Tabuteau's talents, as shown by the fact that he maintained interest throughout, not an easy thing for an oboe soloist." I received a letter from Madame Tabuteau, in which she wrote about his most recent performance: "A marvel, the Mozart—better than in Perpignan.[32] Ideal atmosphere. I was with Mrs. Ormandy on Friday and Saturday I sat in *my* usual seat. For me, I preferred the reed of Friday. An extraordinary warmth of tone. Too bad that so many idiots didn't understand anything. *Tant pis pour eux.* [Too bad for them.] After the concert the Curtis students came to present their wishes and bottles of Rhine wine. The apartment was straightened up and your mother's *crèche* was in the place of honor."

THE SOLO SITUATION FOR OBOISTS

During the first half of the twentieth century few oboists aside from Léon Goossens performed as soloists. There were several reasons for this situation. The rich repertoire of oboe concerti by seventeenth- and eighteenth-century composers was still lying dormant on back shelves of European libraries, many of them in private castles. Aside from musicologists, few people knew of the oboe concertos by Vivaldi, Telemann, and

TABUTEAU AS SOLOIST

Albinoni or those of Mozart's contemporaries, J.C. Bach, Lebrun, and Fiala. The Mozart *Concerto* itself, considered lost, had not yet been rediscovered and released from its disguise as the *D Major Flute Concerto.* Richard Strauss and Bohuslav Martinů had not yet composed their concertos for oboe, nor Poulenc, his sonata. Not only was there a lack of repertoire, but also in the United States there was simply no tradition of oboists playing solos. The economics of paying for an orchestra to record a solo performance compounded and discouraged oboe solos. Oboe students concentrated on études and the orchestral repertoire; they learned very few solos: the Saint-Saëns *Sonata,* a couple of Handel sonatas and concerti, the dubious Haydn *Concerto,* and perhaps a few Paris Conservatoire *concours* pieces. The Mozart *Oboe Quartet* was considered the ultimate challenge. The day of the university music department requiring a series of full recitals in order to qualify for a degree was still in the future. In light of all these factors, the number of Tabuteau's solo appearances with the Philadelphia Orchestra, even spaced at infrequent intervals, represents a significant accomplishment. Admittedly, many times he was one of four soloists in the *Second Brandenburg Concerto,* but it was always considered a solo engagement. During my years in Philadelphia the *Brandenburg* was usually an occasion for a photograph of Tabuteau, violinist Alexander Hilsberg, flutist William Kincaid, and trumpet player Saul Caston to appear in the newspaper.

Tabuteau played at least 67 solo performances of the following repertoire with the Philadelphia Orchestra: Handel, *G Minor Concerto,* 12; Mozart, *Quartet,* 8; *Sinfonia Concertante,* 10; Bach, *Brandenburg No. 2,* 30; Lefebvre, *Andante and Tarantelle,* 1; Godard, *Légende Pastorale,* 1; Ropartz, *Danse,* 1; Hanson, *Pastorale,* 2. There were other occasions when he took part in children's concerts or where he was featured in Bach obbligati at either the Bethlehem or Worcester Festivals.

When I visited Tabuteau in France after his retirement, I never saw a piece of music in his home. However, when I once showed him the recently published Mozart *Concerto,* he appeared to be familiar with it and gave me some valuable suggestions for practicing the opening measures. Toward the end of his life he began to practice the Cimarosa

Concerto and can be heard on a tape playing the opening of the second movement over and over in every possible combination of skeletal patterns. It would only be years later that I learned how he had acquired this score as well as several baroque concerti and why he was practicing them.

CHAMBER MUSIC

Several photographs from the early 1920s show Tabuteau seated along with the other formally dressed members of a wind quintet. The group, known as the Philadelphia Orchestra Ensemble, consisted of Tabuteau and his fellow first chair players: William Kincaid, flute; Walter Guetter, bassoon; and Anton Horner, horn. Between 1922 and 1925 there were three different principal clarinetists in the orchestra, a new one every season. First was Georges Grisez, then Rufus Arey, and finally, Daniel Bonade. Each one in turn played in the quintet. Although Guetter is always listed as the bassoonist, Ferdinand Del Negro appears in one of the pictures. It is probably from the same 1922–23 season when Del Negro played a solo on the Philadelphia Forum concerts in place of Guetter. Little is known of the activities of this ensemble except through a few announcements in Philadelphia Orchestra programs. Occasionally they played on a series in the ballroom of the Bellevue-Stratford Hotel, and they gave concerts for the Germantown Cricket Club Chamber Music Association. Their programs included works that Tabuteau would later drill into each new class of students in his Curtis Institute Woodwind Ensemble—notably, the four-movement Beethoven *Quintet,* Opus 71, and the *Suite* by Charles Lefebvre with its opening canon.

At the end of September 1922, Tabuteau joined with several French woodwind colleagues to play in the Berkshire Festival of Chamber Music. The program lists August(e) Mesnard, bassoonist from the early Damrosch Orchestra, and Georges Grisez, clarinetist, playing with Tabuteau in a Suite by Brescia dedicated to Mrs. F. S. Coolidge. A string quartet from San Francisco with Louis Persinger as first violin played the Ravel *Quartet* and joined with the winds for the Schubert *Octet.*

Philadelphia Orchestra Ensemble, 1923. Standing: Ferdinand Del Negro, bassoon; Marcel Tabuteau, oboe; Anton Horner, horn; Seated: Rufus Arey, clarinet; William Kincaid, flute. With frequent changes of clarinetists, the quintet played concerts during the 1920s and early 1930s. Photo by Kubey-Rembrandt Studios, Philadelphia. Courtesy Dr. Jacques Budin.

RECORDINGS

According to Preben Obberby, "Stokowski's work with the Philadelphia Orchestra is one of the peaks in the performance of music and one of the great chapters in the history of recording. Together, his recordings with this orchestra are nothing less than a historical document." Long before the CD era he cites David Hall, then head of the Rodgers and Hammerstein Archives, on the "cultural obligation" to perpetuate this body of work in long-playing form and how "until now, RCA Victor has not lived up to this responsibility."[33] Fortunately, Stokowski recordings continue to reappear in CD format under many labels, recently in the elegant albums from Andante. In all of those with the Philadelphia Orchestra we can hear the playing of Marcel Tabuteau. Less fortunate is that the early recording methods rarely do justice to the oboe. Tabuteau himself was not at all happy with the way he sounded on the old 78s. In 1962 in a letter to Marc Mostovoy he said, "About recordings . . . in the old days they could only reproduce a shadow of what was performed. The men at the controls were only interested in obtaining a perfect neat line, *c'est à dire* [that is to say], amplifying the soft expression 'piano' and subduing the climax 'forte.' Nothing of the in-between was considered and, as you know, the in-between is *my aim*. That's the reason why I was not at that time interested in recording. I am happy now the technique has improved. As for the inflexion and form . . . distribution, what do you expect from them? To understand now as it will probably be done by the majority in—2175?"[34] Tabuteau's own opinion was corroborated by bassoonist John Shamlian, who played in the Philadelphia Orchestra from 1951 to 1982: "In those early days, when you sat in the orchestra and listened to Tabuteau, you heard the great phrasing and the way he tapered things off, but on the records, it just wasn't there. I believe it was the lack in the recording technique of that time. It did not catch the subtlety of the oboe—a disappointing thing. You had to be on the stage listening. Posterity will just have to believe what we say!" Even Charles O'Connell, who was for many years the head of RCA Victor's Red Seal Division, had some doubts about how well the oboe was being recorded. He remembered suggesting to Toscanini his concern that the oboe playing of "the principal theme of the first movement in the Schubert *C*

TABUTEAU AS SOLOIST

Major Symphony" was not prominent enough.[35] "Marcel Tabuteau's tone and ultra-subtle nuances are notoriously difficult to record. Sometimes they cannot be apprehended even in concert performance, but conductors, as a rule, are so beguiled by the beauty and finesse of this great artist's work that they leave him severely alone."

Fifty years later, for Tabuteau's colleagues John Minsker and Sol Schoenbach, the problem of the gap between what they heard and what came through on the recordings was still a worrisome subject. Although releasing a CD of excerpts of his playing from the Stokowski era was a laudable idea (Boston Records BR1017CD), they both considered it to be a disservice. Nevertheless, I feel that a few examples in this collection give a fairly realistic idea of Tabuteau's artistry: Henry Eichheim's *Japanese Nocturne* recorded in 1929; Erik Satie's *Gymnopédies* from 1937; and the solo at the end of Mussorgsky's *A Night on Bare Mountain* recorded in 1940.[36] The historic recording of the Mozart *Sinfonia Concertante*, mentioned earlier, also captures both Tabuteau's sound and phrasing to a reasonable degree.

In the mid-1930s an anonymous series of 78-rpm recordings was sold in supermarkets and through the newspapers with a title of *The World's Greatest Music.* I managed to acquire these heavy multi-disk albums of the *Brandenburg Concerto No. 2,* Brahms's *Second Symphony,* and the Mozart *G Minor Symphony.* Were they copies of standard recordings made by the Philadelphia Orchestra or were they done especially for popular release? And which other works were in the series? The oboist in the *Brandenburg* is without doubt Tabuteau. One has only to listen to the Andante to recognize the inflection of the phrases and the shimmer of his tone in the high notes. No one else in the 1930s sounded like that! Another rare item is Bach's *Cantata No. 78, Jesu, der du meine Seele,* a RCA Victor Red Seal record set released in 1946 of the "Bach Choir of Bethlehem and Orchestra" conducted by Ifor Jones.[37] Violinist Alexander Zenker contracted a small group of Philadelphia Orchestra musicians, always including the solo wind players for this annual event. Tabuteau plays the oboe obbligato to the aria "Nun du wirst mein Gewissen stillen" sung by bass soloist Mack Harrell in English, as "O Lord, my conscience." In the same cantata, William Kincaid is heard in the flute obbligato to the tenor aria, "Das Blut, so meine Schuld durchstreicht." Both arias are accompanied by piano; harpsichords, authentic performance practice, and complete sets of all the cantatas were still far in the future. The noted critic of the *San Francisco Chronicle,* Alfred Frankenstein, dedicated a lengthy review to Cantata No. 78, calling it "the first significant recording of that portion of the literature which is the heart and soul of Johann Sebastian Bach." There is no other known recorded example from the many seasons that Tabuteau participated in the Bethlehem festivals. Every year he played the *B Minor Mass,* always on the oboe. Oboes d'amore were neither commonly used nor readily available. As the month of May and the Bethlehem dates approached, I would hear him in his studio going over and over Aria No. 9, the *Qui sedes* obbligato. The transposition from the original d'amore version meant starting on B-natural, not a favorite note for most oboists, and despite the descent into the very low register of the oboe, it always sounded warmly beautiful and convincing. Throughout the Bethlehem years, Tabuteau played not only most of the cantatas with important oboe solos but also the *Suites for Orchestra* and the *Brandenburg Concertos.*

When we consider that Stokowski's initial recording career with the Philadelphia Orchestra stretched over a period of little more than two decades, from the pioneer efforts in 1917 to the technically sophisticated sound track he made for the film *Fantasia* in 1940, we must be grateful for the wealth of repertoire represented. However, one can only regret that there are no recordings of works he often performed that give the oboe a very important role. There is no Schumann *C Major* and no Mendelssohn *Scotch* Symphony. Of the Beethoven symphonies, no *Eroica,* but only Nos. 7 and 9. In the Philadelphia Orchestra Centennial Collection, one can hear the very experimental 33⅓-rpm recording of the Beethoven *Fifth* made in 1931. As for the recordings made in 1941 with Toscanini, which include the Schubert *C Major* and *La Mer,* belated attempts to salvage the deteriorated metal masters had only minimum success. The most recent complete set of three CDs digitally remastered and issued by Musical Heritage Society in 2006 gives us the best representation of Toscanini's collaboration with the Philadelphia Orchestra. The booklet includes a well-known photo of Tabuteau and Toscanini looking at a score.[38]

In the early days of recording, the few minutes that could fit on each side of a 78-rpm disk, plus considerations of what the record companies thought would sell, accounted for the proliferation of short works and arrangements. There was also Stokowski's predilection for his own Bach transcriptions, which showed off the rich tonal palette of the orchestra. When he did record whole symphonies, it was all four Brahms symphonies, Sibelius No. 4, the César Franck *D Minor*, Shostakovich Nos. 1, 5, and 6, the Dvořák New *World*, and Tchaikovsky Nos. 4 and 5. There is outstanding playing from the winds in the remarkable excerpts from Wagner operas and Stokowski's "symphonic synthesis" of Mussorgsky's *Boris Godunov. Scheherazade*, Stravinsky's *Firebird*, and the Schubert *Unfinished* were each recorded twice. Except for those of Rachmaninoff, there were no piano or violin concertos recorded during the Stokowski era. *Le Tombeau de Couperin*, which Tabuteau played many times, unfortunately never found its way to wax or shellac. It is perhaps fitting that Tabuteau's only true solo recording with the Philadelphia Orchestra was the Handel *G Minor Concerto*, the work he had performed during his first season and on many subsequent occasions. Two years before he retired, on April 5, 1952, he recorded the Handel *Concerto* as a part of the set, *First Chair*. Featuring solo performances by the principal players of the Philadelphia Orchestra and conducted by Eugene Ormandy, the recording was made as a contribution to the orchestra's pension fund. With the release of this album in 1953, Tabuteau's thirty-six years of recording experience extended from 1917 until well into the era of the LP.

HONORS

In 1937 Marcel Tabuteau became a chevalier of the Légion d'Honneur. The presentation was made by the French consul, M. de Verneuil, on the stage of the Academy of Music during the intermission of the October 15 Friday afternoon concert. The Légion d'Honneur, originally created by Napoleon as a military recognition, has been subsequently awarded to those in other fields who have made significant contributions to French culture. With the decoration of red ribbon, medal, and diploma, Tabuteau joined the ranks of his distinguished compatriots in the arts. He was not given to talking about special awards that came his way, but on formal occasions he did wear the discreet red lapel ribbon of

On the stage of Curtis Hall at the 1952 graduation ceremonies Tabuteau received the degree of Doctor of Music. Looking on somewhat amusedly are Mary Louise Curtis Bok Zimbalist and Efrem Zimbalist.

the Légion d'Honneur. And he must have felt some satisfaction in receiving this particular honor, which had been awarded to his teacher, Georges Gillet, on the day in July 1904 when Tabuteau won his Premier Prix.[39] On the centenary of Tchaikovsky's birth, celebrated in the concerts of April 19 and 20, 1940, Tabuteau was given the traditional watch, a gift each orchestra man received after twenty-five years of service. Frances Wister, the steadfast long-time chair of the Women's Committee, in her famous hat and dress which ignored any change of fashion, made the presentation on the academy stage.

In May 1952, at the nineteenth graduation commencement ceremonies of the Curtis Institute of Music, the honorary degree of Doctor of Music was conferred on Marcel Paul Tabuteau-Guérineau; it was one of the few times his full name appeared in print since his own "graduation" almost fifty years earlier. He was photographed in cap and gown standing at the corner of the small Curtis stage facing Eugene Ormandy, Mus. D., who was presenting the degree. With his almost

TABUTEAU AS SOLOIST

sheepish grin and twinkling eye, Tabuteau provoked a chuckle from Mary Louise Curtis Bok Zimbalist and Efrem Zimbalist, who were looking on from their seats in the middle of the stage. William Morris Kincaid received the same degree that day, thus keeping "Tabuteau and Kincaid" linked academically even as they were musically.

TOURS

Touring was always an important part of life for the Philadelphia Orchestra, and Tabuteau spent a good deal of time "on the road." A series of five, and in later years up to eight, concerts per season in Washington, D.C., Baltimore, and Wilmington and ten in New York was a Philadelphia tradition. Already in Tabuteau's first season with the orchestra, there was a seventeen-day tour that extended as far as Buffalo, Cleveland, and Detroit. For several years, from 1916 through the 1922–23 season, the orchestra played five pairs of concerts in Pittsburgh. In the late 1930s the orchestra began to spend a week in May at the Ann Arbor May Festival in Michigan. From 1944 to 1957 another yearly event was the October week at the Worcester, Massachusetts, Music Festival. As early as 1925 there were plans for more extensive tours, both to the West Coast of the United States and to the major cities of Europe, but they did not materialize. A coast-to-coast tour was one of Stokowski's dreams. In 1936 it finally took place, sponsored by the RCA Victor Company. The large, glossy program book prepared for the 8,000-mile tour announces: "Stokowski and the Philadelphia Orchestra"; the maestro is shown in dramatic profile, outlined in eye-catching blue-green color against a stark black background. The middle fold provides a cleverly drawn map of the tour, the routing clearly indicated by a flag planted on each city where the orchestra would play between April 13 and May 18. There are photos of Stokowski in his various conducting poses—one with a caption, "Trombones—Achtung!" no doubt an authentic quote from the repertoire of foreign expressions Stokowski affected in addressing his "Or*chest*er."

The text informs us about the qualities of his music making: "a synthesis of architecture and sculpture; power and sensitiveness; of visible rhythm and audible color; of Olympian majesty and of human under-

Tabuteau and William Kincaid in front of their Pullman cars on tour with the Philadelphia Orchestra in the 1930s.

standing." It goes on to describe the sounds, colors, and voices of the many lands where "he has walked intimately with statesmen and merchants, princes and children and philosophers, with Asiatic lamas and village priests and Indian mystics." Clearly the music lovers of Little Rock, Arkansas, Lincoln, Nebraska, and Salt Lake City, Utah, could expect a mind-expanding treat; in the mid-1930s, before international air travel and mass tourism, how many had visited "other lands," let alone conferred with an Asiatic lama or Indian mystic? The brochure included two pages of portrait-style photographs of sixteen of its principal players with their instruments and a few words about their other interests or hobbies; thus, "The Woodwind Section is especially proud of Marcel Tabuteau, one of the world's best oboe players, and the orchestra's finest cook."

TABUTEAU AS SOLOIST

The orchestra headed up through Hartford, Connecticut, to Springfield, Massachusetts, and Boston, then crisscrossed the Midwest, and traveled south to Atlanta and New Orleans, stopping in Dallas, El Paso, and Phoenix before reaching the three California stops: Los Angeles, Santa Barbara, and San Francisco. Charles O'Connell conducted the concert in Springfield, his hometown, where in the final number on the program, a *Chorale and Fugue in D Minor* by Zemachson, the audience was surprised to hear the magnificent tones of the imposing pipe organ being played by Leopold Stokowski himself. A full third of the tour concerts consisted of the music of only two composers—Bach and Wagner; the Bach performed, of course, in Stokowski's transcriptions. The *Japanese Nocturne* with its exotic oboe solo was played as an encore in Chicago and San Francisco, but in Santa Barbara it figured on the printed program, no doubt in recognition of its composer, Henry Eichheim, Stokowski's travel companion in the Far East, who was now established in that southern California city along with his collection of Javanese musical instruments. The reviews of the concerts were ecstatic, and RCA Victor recordings of the Philadelphia Orchestra, which were already popular, became more than ever the centerpiece of any serious record collection. In Santa Barbara the whole orchestra was photographed standing in front of their private Pullman cars. It was in Arizona that Tabuteau had his cowboy "encounter" with the white horse, immortalized in a photograph first printed in the résumé booklet of the 1935–36 season and reproduced many times since. From his pose as a seasoned cowboy, we may wonder if Tabuteau was finally realizing a dream he had cherished since he had read dime westerns during his boyhood in France. But it was only a few moments later that disaster struck. Just before mounting the handsome steed replete with splendid silver harness, Tabuteau said to Kincaid, who was also about to ride, "'Beel, I do not lak thees 'orse!' . . . A moment later, with a cow-hand's hat flying in one direction and a long Gallic cigarette holder in another, 'thees 'orse' disappeared at full gallop around the corner of the barn bearing a reluctant and vociferous Tabuteau. Fortunately the horse was caught before anything was injured except dignity."[40]

A year later there was another coast-to-coast tour from April 20 to May 23, this time with two conductors at the helm: Eugene Ormandy

On the Philadelphia Orchestra coast-to-coast "far west" tour of 1936, Tabuteau was photographed in "cowboy style" on the horse that bolted. Photo by Don Keller, Phoenix, Arizona.

and José Iturbi. The war years prevented more extended touring until the spring of 1946. Tabuteau had been suffering from gall bladder problems and was now scheduled for surgery. As it was considered too risky for him to go on this transcontinental tour, John de Lancie, recently returned from military service in France, played in Tabuteau's place. The last long tour of the United States that Tabuteau made with the orchestra was in the spring of 1948. Assistant manager Joseph Santarlasci, whose job it was to make travel arrangements and see to the transportation of the instruments, remembered him as "giving no problems. Of course he could be a little demanding. Tabuteau was somewhat of an idol. All those principal players were a bit egotistical. We had sleeper cars and I had to be very careful where I put him. I would venture to say we had a sort of mutual respect for each other. In fact, he was very nice to me as a young man. (I had just come out of the service when I started with the orchestra in 1945.) On some of the trips we

TABUTEAU AS SOLOIST

would have lunch together. Another thing, he always sent a barrel of cane back from France, and one of my duties was that in the fall I would have to go down to the port—it would come in by boat; no planes then—and I would clear it through customs for him and make arrangements to have the barrel delivered to his apartment. It was hard to explain to a customs agent what it was!" Santarlasci described the way the orchestra traveled in those days. "We had our own special train with six sleepers, diner, a baggage car, and a coach for recreation where they played cards. After the concert we'd start out for the next town. Most of the travel was done at night. We played in a lot of university towns and they were always kind enough to let the orchestra members use the facilities, like the gymnasium and the showers. That was difficult on a train even when there were compartments. Sometimes we would make arrangements for a group of hotel rooms, which the men would share."[41] On that 1948 tour the orchestra played an average of six concerts a week from Buffalo and Detroit to Atlanta and New Orleans, on to four cities in Texas, followed by the whole West Coast, and returning via Colorado, Omaha, and Chicago. It was in San Francisco on this tour that my mother met Tabuteau for the only time. Exactly forty years had gone by since Tabuteau made his first cross-country tour of the United States with Walter Damrosch and the New York Symphony Orchestra in May 1908. Tabuteau's last trip with the orchestra was their first "international" tour to England in May 1949. But this is a later story that coincided with the time when the Tabuteaus were beginning to make serious plans for retirement.

MARCEL TABUTEAU

8 TABUTEAU AT THE CURTIS INSTITUTE OF MUSIC

1924–1946

From the time of its opening in the fall of 1924, one of the major aims of the Curtis Institute of Music was to train first-class orchestral musicians in all instruments. Although some effort was already being made in this direction—for example, at the Institute of Musical Art in New York—American symphony orchestras were still largely dependent on players imported from Europe. The first Curtis catalog emphasized the distinguished piano, violin, and voice faculty, consisting of such artists as Josef Hofmann, Carl Flesch, and Marcella Sembrich, but it also included a paragraph headed "Orchestra." Here, mention was made that the institute had engaged the "soloists of the various choirs of the Philadelphia Orchestra: W. M. Kincaid, Flute; Marcel Tabuteau, Oboe; Anton Horner, Horn; and others." The orchestra training would be under the direction of Leopold Stokowski. If Tabuteau's name was deemed worthy of inclusion from the very first season, it was not long before the "others" would also be dignified by appearing in print. The 1925–26 catalog carried a full-page announcement under the heading "Courses in Orchestral Instruments":

There is in the United States a serious lack of players of woodwind, brass and percussion instruments qualified to hold posts in the many symphony orchestras scattered through the country. There exist today more excellent positions, waiting to be worthily filled, than there are players ready to fill them. Especially is this true now that the present immigration laws have practically cut off Europe as a source of such players. It is the plan of the Curtis Institute of Music to build a school to supply this demand . . . For teachers of double-bass, flute, oboe, clarinet, bassoon, French horn, trumpet, trombone, tuba, timpani and other instruments of percussion it offers artists who hold in the Philadelphia Orchestra the posts of solo players of these various instruments. Each is a master of great reputation.

To the earlier three are now added the names of Daniel Bonade, clarinet; Walter Guetter, bassoon; Anton Torello, bass; Oscar Schwar, tympani; as well as the first-chair brasses of the Philadelphia Orchestra. All of these musicians, with the exception of William Kincaid, had been trained in Europe. But Kincaid, too, inherited French schooling from his famous teacher Georges Barrère, who, as mentioned earlier, had come to America in 1905 on the same boat with Tabuteau. Now they would all pass on the best of their European traditions and help to "supply the demand." They would succeed only too well, so that before the end of the century the situation would be reversed, with the existence of more excellent players than available positions.

This same catalog carried a statement by Mary Louise Curtis Bok, the founder of the Curtis Institute, whose generous endowment made possible the creation of the school: "It is my aim that earnest students shall acquire a thorough musical education, not learning only to sing or play, but also the history of music, the laws of its making, languages, ear-training and music appreciation." She continued to emphasize the "background of quiet culture, with the stimulus of personal contact with artist-teachers who represent the highest and finest in their art." The former Drexel mansions with their richly appointed interiors—pictured in exquisite drawings throughout the early catalogs—provided a genteel setting in keeping with the aims of Mrs. Bok. In her earlier work with Settlement Music School she had seen promising young talents forced to abandon their careers because of lack of means. Mrs. Bok wanted the new school at the corner of Locust Street and Rittenhouse

Square to give its students a musical and cultural education, stressing quality rather than quantity, and "to make a distinct contribution to the musical life of America." The material aspects of life were also addressed, with the suggestion that "at least $10 a week ought to be reserved for food, if proper consideration is to be given to the nourishing and well-balanced diet that a student needs." A tearoom on the premises offered "substantial lunches at 25, 35 and 45 cents. Ample portions of the best food, well-cooked, are served." There is the pleasant prospect of sitting at the same table with faculty members, which can help "bridge the gulf which too often separates pupil from teacher." In those lavish pre-Depression days, Steinway grand pianos were installed in students' living quarters; in the summers many were sent on a yacht up to Maine to continue their studies in Rockport or Camden. It was a rarefied type of musical "retreat" where they mingled with star faculty members, Josef Hofmann, Efrem Zimbalist, and other guests of Mrs. Bok.

In the early 1920s, there was no area of performance more in need of high-level training and development than that of the orchestral wind instruments. By taking advantage of the splendid Philadelphia Orchestra players literally at its doorstep, Curtis made a decision, the effect of which could hardly have been predicted at the time. Marcel Tabuteau's classes created new standards of musicality for wind players as well as for all others who came under his influence. The 1926 Philadelphia Orchestra programs carried a series of dignified "announcements" of Curtis Institute activities, in every one of which Tabuteau figures. In March we read that classes would be given in "Orchestral solfège, aptly named by Mr. Stokowski, who suggested the course," and that Marcel Tabuteau would be the teacher. The Philadelphia Orchestra program book for the weekend of October 22–23 tells of the start of the Curtis Institute's orchestra work under the "personal direction of Dr. Leopold Stokowski, who has as his associate Dr. Artur Rodzinski. . . . The orchestra begins with a membership of eighty-three . . . Messrs. Tabuteau, Fisnar, Horner and Cohen, personally coach and assist the oboe, bassoon, horn and trumpet sections."[1] For a number of years, until highly competent students of the more rare instruments were developed, several Philadelphia Orchestra men also played in the Curtis Orchestra.

TABUTEAU AT THE CURTIS INSTITUTE OF MUSIC

The third time a Curtis Institute announcement appeared in the 1926 Philadelphia Orchestra programs, it was with a formal statement detailing the exact number of students (twenty-eight) registered in the Department of Orchestral Instruments: "Mr. Kincaid has six young men studying the flute; Mr. Tabuteau, four students in oboe: Mr. Bonade, six in clarinet; Mr. Cohen, two in trumpet; Mr. Simons, four in trombone;[2] Mr. Schwar, one in tympani; while five are studying double bass under Mr. Torello." No mention was made of the other string instruments that form part of an orchestra. Were the string students primarily aiming for solo careers, and only incidentally (and often reluctantly) impressed into orchestra rehearsals and concerts? Curtis catalogs from 1924 through 1927 tell us that the first head of the violin department was Carl Flesch, teacher of many internationally known soloists. He was assisted by Sacha Jacobinoff, Michael Press, Frank Gittelson, Emanuel Zetlin, and later, Lea Luboshutz. Louis Bailly, formerly a member of two famous early string quartets, the Capet and the Flonzaley, taught the violists, while the cello instructor was the English soloist Felix Salmond, who had played the first performance of Sir Edward Elgar's *Concerto for Cello.*

The 1926–27 Curtis catalog emphasizes the importance of its orchestral training by referring to the fact that "Dr. Leopold Stokowski, the salient figure among the great conductors of today, personally trains and drills the student orchestra. In other words, the students of The Curtis Institute of Music receive the training which has made the Philadelphia Orchestra the foremost in the world." On the same page we learn that there are classes conducted by Marcel Tabuteau that concentrate on the technique of orchestral playing, classes in which "phrasing, rhythm, delicate points of shading, and dynamic variety are worked out on the different orchestral instruments." When one considers the degree of Marcel Tabuteau's influence on the oboe in America, it may come as a surprise to note that during his thirty years at the Curtis Institute of Music, he taught a total of only fifty-seven students. Of this number, the seventeen oboe students who graduated with diplomas in performance all became active and well-known performers. Another group of eleven remained long enough in Tabuteau's classes to build significant playing careers even without graduating. Six went into other

MARCEL TABUTEAU

fields of music. Of the remaining twenty-three—almost half the total number—many did not stay in school for more than a year. Some left after only a few months, and as far as is known, none continued with music as a profession. The majority of those who withdrew did so in the first ten years of the existence of the Curtis Institute. This may indicate that as the school and Tabuteau, as well as the level of accomplishment expected, became better known, there was a consolidation of the oboe class with less attrition.[3]

In the early years of Curtis, candidates for violin were expected to play Kreutzer studies and de Bériot and Vieuxtemps concertos, while the pianists had to be able to perform a liberal amount of Bach, Beethoven, and Chopin. We can gain an idea of the generally low level of wind students at that time when we learn that Tabuteau auditioned, accepted, and taught boys who had no previous oboe training. There were no specific entrance requirements for the various woodwinds; all were lumped together under "Orchestra Instruments." The 1927 catalog states simply that "an applicant must have at least an elementary knowledge of music and be physically fitted for the instrument." The original generous age limit was thirty, but by 1938 applicants who wished their major subject to be "Orchestra Playing" "should not be over twenty-five years of age." It was not until 1939 that flute, oboe, clarinet, and bassoon were listed in a group with the specified requirements of a "good ear, a keen sense of rhythm, and the ability to read at sight." Now, applicants were asked to play two pieces of standard repertoire, but no particular works were named. Some details changed every year. In 1940 there was a rather general statement that "except under unusual circumstances, *preference will be given to applicants between the ages of sixteen and twenty-four*" (original emphasis), and the pieces were to be played from memory. Only a year later the age preference for woodwinds had descended to "those under twenty-one."

EARLY STUDENTS

In 1999 I visited with Leon Lester, bass clarinetist of the Philadelphia Orchestra from 1938 through 1966. He confirmed that "things were totally different then. I came from a poor background musically and

TABUTEAU AT THE CURTIS INSTITUTE OF MUSIC

I guarantee you plenty of the others did also." He described how he happened to audition at the Curtis Institute in April 1928. "You won't believe this. My father bought me a clarinet. We lived in a little one-horse town in West Virginia. My mother read the newspaper. She believed everything she read in the papers. She saw that the Curtis Institute would be giving free scholarships and insisted I should go and try out. I did not want to but I could only get rid of her by going to play the audition, fail, and get a letter of refusal. Tabuteau and Bonade were the examining committee and they were speaking in French while I was playing and of course I couldn't understand one word. Then I went home and was sure that would be the end of it. You know what happened? I got that letter. Please report in the fall. I still have it. I was accepted." About auditions in general: "The standards were very low. I looked at recent entrance trials for clarinet. The things they have to play to audition now are what we played to graduate. I never played the Mozart Concerto until the end." In a 1980s master class in Seattle, Julius Baker made similar remarks about auditions for flute.

Musicians other than wind players spoke of the first years of Tabuteau's classes. In a conversation with Robert Gomberg, Tabuteau gave one reason for the development of his number "system." (Robert Gomberg, an early violin student at the Curtis Institute, joined the Philadelphia Orchestra in 1931 and became a good friend of Tabuteau. They roomed together on tours, and he was able to talk more freely with Tabuteau than many others could.) Gomberg asked, "Maestro, why do you use all these numbers? Why don't you just explain aesthetically what you want the students to do?" Tabuteau said that the string players already came in better prepared, but that he had to accept students from the Midwest and other places where an oboist might have done nothing more than play in a high school band. He had to build them up from uncultivated backgrounds. To explain how to make a line, he couldn't just speak in musical terms about the aesthetics of expression. They wouldn't understand. So instead he gave them numbers such as 1,1234, 2345, and so forth, to show them how to make a crescendo and how to build a phrase. With the numbers they could understand the loops and the surge of the music. It was a means to an end. Another time Gomberg asked, "Marcel, why do you seem to always be so hard on your students?" Tabuteau replied, "Bob, you know, if I am so hard on my stu*dents*, it's because I want them to be prepared to play for a son of a bitch like Stokowski."[4]

The eminent violinist Oscar Shumsky, who studied with Leopold Auer and then Efrem Zimbalist in the late 1920s, told me he used to sneak in to listen to Tabuteau's classes whenever he could. "They were enormously creative and I learned a lot. I have never forgotten them."[5] Zadel Skolovsky, a concert pianist, entered Curtis at age eleven as a double major on both violin and piano, eventually becoming a student of the demanding Mme Vengerova. When his classmate, clarinetist Bernard Portnoy, told him about the many hours the wind students spent with Tabuteau each week, Skolovsky's comment was, "That's teaching!" And his overall opinion of Tabuteau? "Oh, he was a genius. He is probably one of the greatest things that ever happened at the Curtis. Look at his output—all those fantastic wind players!"[6]

In the mid-1920s, Tabuteau taught large classes of both winds and strings that were first called "Orchestra Training" and later, simply "Orchestra Class." "Woodwind Ensemble" was soon added, and it was this group that gave such memorable concerts during the 1930s and 1940s. Through lessons, Woodwind Ensemble, and the orchestra class, the oboe students had at least six and a half hours every week with Tabuteau. During the four school years, 1930–31 through 1933–34, he also held a reed-making class for one hour a week. Leon Lester, Arthur Statter, and John Minsker—all in their nineties when I spoke with them—were among the few wind players who could remember Tabuteau's classes from the 1920s and early 1930s.[7] Leon Lester described how the classes were run. "In my second year at Curtis on Saturday mornings Tabuteau had a class of flute, oboe, clarinet, bassoon, and horn in Knapp Hall where the harps were—a huge room in the basement. It must have been the spring of 1930. He would have us sit around in a semicircle and he would point, 'you,' and you had to come up and stand in front of the group. Then he would say, 'Susten for me a nutt.' So he'd pick on this poor bassoon player, Adelchi Angelucci.[8] Angelucci would play one note, "duh, duh," and Tabuteau said, 'Why you want to be a moosicienne? Why you don't be a plumber?' After another sustained note, 'Why you don't be a dahntiste?' And so it went

TABUTEAU AT THE CURTIS INSTITUTE OF MUSIC

on, 'a fie-er man?' We'd all sit there and hope we wouldn't be called next." One time Angelucci tried to defend himself by saying he couldn't understand why his reed didn't play because "it worked so well at home." Tabuteau responded with, "Pack up boys! We're all going to Angelucci's house."[9]

Once when Tabuteau asked who could play the piano accompaniments for the little melodies in the Lemoine solfège book he used for practice in phrasing, Leon Lester volunteered. "While someone was playing either flute or oboe, Tabuteau was right behind me looking over my shoulder at the notes. At the end of a page I flipped two pages instead of one. It ruined everything and he hit me smack on the head. It didn't hurt me. I survived." No thought in those years of a student objecting to this type of physical "discipline." It did not happen often, but from time to time Tabuteau's students were either threatened or actually "whacked." Leon played in a quintet with Harold Gomberg, but in those early years there were only rehearsals, no concerts. He had a few chamber music classes with the famous violist Louis Bailly, played in the student orchestra under Emil Mylnarski and Artur Rodzinski, and recalled seeing Leopold Auer, "a decrepit old man at that time, who would come to the concerts in Casimir Hall and sit up in the box."[10]

Trumpet player Arthur Statter was also in Tabuteau's classes in the early 1930s. Although he studied with Saul Caston, he said, "Whatever I know about playing the trumpet I learned from Marcel Tabuteau. He was the greatest of all teachers. His concepts of music were universal and fit all instruments, even the keyboard."[11] Statter remembered the same Saturday morning classes of which Leon Lester had spoken. "The very first year that I got there the new wind players at Curtis were put in a class where Tabuteau began to give them his ideas on numbers—all these things that I still remember. My first job in New York was as solo trumpet in the Radio City Music Hall. It was a full symphony orchestra and quite strenuous work, especially during the holiday seasons when we had to play five shows a day. After having played all day and night, sometimes I found myself the next morning in rehearsal with swollen lips and difficulty getting the notes out. Then I remembered how Tabuteau said that you should play with this [points to his head] so well that you can play even when you have a bad reed. That's the way he

MARCEL TABUTEAU

described it. Everything must be in the mind and if that is right, you don't have to worry, and that is how I could keep playing." Statter confirmed that it was not only the oboe students who hung on to Tabuteau's every note in the Academy of Music. When I asked what he remembered about Tabuteau's playing, he cited "the little phrase at the end of *Fêtes* [from Debussy's *Trois Nocturnes.*] That stayed in my mind. All of us at Curtis worshipped him. We went to the Philadelphia Orchestra concerts specifically just to hear our Tabuteau." Statter later played first trumpet for the Voice of Firestone broadcasts, and after making the historic, six-week, cross-country tour with Toscanini and the NBC Symphony Orchestra in 1950, he became a regular member of that orchestra.[12]

John Minsker spoke of the two sides of Tabuteau's personality, which he described as "Manichean." "How he would lay you out in class or at your lesson. In the woodwind class or orchestra class, I would get it as much or more than anybody else. Sometimes you were almost in tears. In fact, I think I might have gotten it even more, because the students knew that I had the key to his studio and that we were pretty close. There was that rough side, but then he would be like a father to me. You'd go out and he'd take you by the arm. You walk down the street and he'd invite you to lunch and it's as though the other never happened. You don't talk about it. It's completely forgotten. That was Tabuteau—he would just be a completely different person."

Tabuteau always had one student whom the others referred to as "the studio slave," a term he probably would not have appreciated had he heard it. The "position" entailed having a key to his studio, doing various errands, and being ready to carry out any requests he might make. In the early 1930s the designated person was Minsker. How well Tabuteau placed his trust is evidenced by a colorful episode concerning which Minsker kept quiet for over six decades. It took place during the Depression when there were rumors of financial crisis. In Minsker's own words:

Well, about the gold coins—there were several bags of them. It must have been in 1933, just before Roosevelt declared that embargo on gold. I never told anybody for years. I guess it doesn't matter now although I wouldn't want to tell Janet Reno.[13] She'd probably have me put in jail. I always waited for Tabuteau at the stage door and walked

TABUTEAU AT THE CURTIS INSTITUTE OF MUSIC

with him back to the Drake. One night at the corner of Fifteenth and Locust he met somebody he knew—I don't know who the man was but he spoke to Tabuteau about the banks closing and said that things were looking awfully bad. So we went over to Tabuteau's apartment and he said, "Monday we'll go to Montreal." He had accumulated a considerable amount of gold and wanted to get it out of the country. He called in sick to the orchestra, and Sunday night we took the train to Montreal. I don't know exactly how many bags there were, but several. Well, he needed some excuse for going to Montreal. It was for a vacation to relax a little bit and he was taking me along. This was a story for the customs and the conductor on the railway. We had a private room . . . not a drawing room but it had two beds, an upper and a lower. There was a metal piece that fit around the bottom of the toilet so you didn't see the plumbing. He pulled that out and stuffed a couple of bags in there, and there was another bag in his big black briefcase that I was carrying. I don't think he was concerned about the Canadian customs, but the American customs came through and they started to look around. The inspector touched the briefcase—My God, I thought I was going to die—and he said, "Oh, it's just a briefcase" and didn't open it up. I don't know how suspicious they were, but they didn't look any further. We got into Montreal and checked in at the hotel. Then Tabuteau sent me to walk around the town and I thought I'd freeze to death. It was so cold. It was during March—dead winter. The bitter icy-cold wind was blowing like the devil and I'm freezing out there. I walked around awhile and then came back to the hotel and just sat in the lobby. Of course, in the meantime he had gone to the bank and put the gold in a safe-deposit box. Then we took the Monday night train back to Philadelphia and on the way we got the same conductor. He said, "You going back already?" and Tabuteau said, "Yes, things look so bad, very bad, and we have to go back." I'm sure it was that very day that the embargo was declared.

Minsker's memory served him well, as it was on Monday, March 6, 1933, that Roosevelt closed the banks and ordered the embargo on gold. That year at the end of the orchestra season Tabuteau sailed back to France from Canada and took the gold with him.

Beginning in 1926, the "Students' Orchestra" at Curtis presented concerts under the direction of Leopold Stokowski or Artur Rodzinski. At first, the concerts featured only single movements of symphonies or concertos, but they soon developed into full-fledged programs. The

MARCEL TABUTEAU

names of the students in the violin section read like a page from a future Philadelphia Orchestra program. But the lack of advanced wind students is evidenced by Marcel Tabuteau's name as first oboe along with Louis Di Fulvio, the second oboist from the Philadelphia Orchestra. Other first-chair Philadelphia Orchestra wind players performed in the student orchestra—except for flutists, who were always plentiful. By 1929 the whole Curtis Orchestra consisted of students, with Robert Bloom as the first oboist. In 1929 the Curtis opera class was able to present a performance of Eugène D'Albert's *Tiefland* under Rodzinski's direction using a full orchestra of students.

For some very special events, such as the November 28, 1937, concert commemorating the fiftieth anniversary of Josef Hofmann's childhood debut in New York, Tabuteau and the other Philadelphia first-chair winds once again played in the student orchestra. As explained in the Curtis publication *Overtones,* "Curtis Institute's orchestra instrument teachers *en bloc* signified their desire to participate in the celebration of Dr. Josef Hofmann's Golden Jubilee and volunteered to join forces with The Curtis Symphony Orchestra for the Metropolitan Opera House concert." The article then named the musicians who would "appear on this occasion with their Director and his piano under Mr. Fritz Reiner's baton." They would be joined by a number of their former students who were by now playing in top-ranking U.S. orchestras, such as NBC, Cleveland, Philadelphia, and Cincinnati. Bernard Portnoy, who was a member of the student orchestra, remembers the performance as "quite an event. We rehearsed and rehearsed and then went to New York. There were opening remarks by Walter Damrosch; Reiner conducted us in Brahms' *Academic Festival Overture,* and Hofmann played the Rubinstein *D Minor Concerto.* Afterwards, we went to Steinway Hall for a party and it was 'Who's Who in Music in America.'" In 1992, this concert became available on a CD as a part of the complete recordings of Josef Hofmann. We can hear the voice of Walter Damrosch telling of being present in 1887 at the nine-year-old Hofmann's debut. We realize that Tabuteau is sitting on the stage and cannot help wondering whether, after the manner of his departure from Damrosch's orchestra thirty years earlier, any reconciliation ever took place between the two men.

TABUTEAU AT THE CURTIS INSTITUTE OF MUSIC

Although orchestral, piano, and string playing were beginning to flourish at Curtis, it was not until 1930 that "Students of Mr. Tabuteau in Wind Ensemble" could be featured during a season that included recitals by students of other eminent faculty members, "Professor Auer, Mr. Bailly, Madame Sembrich, Mr. Salzedo, and Mr. Hofmann." The date was February 10, 1930, and it would mark the beginning of that unique yearly event, the Tabuteau Ensemble Class Recital. Appropriately enough, the concert opened with the Beethoven *Quintet in E-Flat Major,* Opus 71 (originally for wind sextet), which would remain a Tabuteau favorite throughout many years. Those of us who studied with him in the 1940s remember beginning all our rehearsals with this work, and for week after week getting no further than the opening bars of the Adagio. He used to call it our little "prior," or maybe it was "*prière*" (prayer). No one ever dared to ask.

This first concert also featured compositions by De Wailly, Tansman, and Pierné. The oboist for every work was Robert Bloom. He was joined by flutist Maurice Sharp and clarinetist Robert McGinnis. The February issue of the Curtis publication *Overtones* took notice of the concert among "Student Activities, Casimir Hall."[14] It mentioned that "a Wind Ensemble, under the direction of Marcel Tabuteau, made its debut in the following unusual programme," and then listed the works of the lesser-known composers. The next month's *Overtones* again wrote of a concert given for the Agnes Irwin School by a group described as a "Wood Wind and Brass Quintet," consisting of the standard wind quintet conformation: flute, oboe, clarinet, bassoon, and horn. This news item mentioned that the quintet was rehearsed by Marcel Tabuteau and that the concert was "unique" because it marked the first occasion on which wind instrument players had been "engaged for a Chamber Music recital outside of the Institute." In April the same wind students participated in a program of chamber music as part of a series of Curtis radio concerts on the Columbia Broadcasting Network. *Overtones* again referred to the works they played as "unusual." To the De Wailly *Aubade* and Pierné *Pastorale variée* of the Woodwind Ensemble's debut recital was added the *Passacaille* by Barthe; all these were traditional short French pieces.

Along with his mother, the violinist Lea Luboshutz, Boris Goldovsky came to the Curtis Institute in the early 1930s.[15] He had only recently arrived from Budapest and did not yet speak English. Already interested in conducting, he asked to attend some of Tabuteau's classes to learn more about the way in which a great wind player worked with his students. He had been warned that Tabuteau did not like outsiders at his rehearsals, so he entered the room very quietly and sat in a far corner. By the intonation of Tabuteau's words he soon realized that he was speaking French but could not make out what he was saying. He thought to himself, "What a sophisticated country! They even teach classes in French!" He moved a little closer and soon realized that he was mistaken and that Tabuteau was speaking English, but an English in which every word was pronounced as if it were French. Goldovsky was, however, tremendously impressed by the manner in which Tabuteau was explaining phrases with numbers. He thought that perhaps even the subtle phrasing concepts of his own teacher, Ernst von Dohnányi, which he had found very mysterious and inimitable, might be analyzed by such a method of numbers. In his book *My Road to Opera*, Goldovsky wrote that "Marcel Tabuteau was a master educator—and not simply in the realm of oboe playing. He was a great connoisseur of all the woodwinds, as well as of horns and other brasses, and the way he taught his students to attack and mold a phrase was a marvel to behold as well as hear."[16]

In February 1931 Robert Bloom took part in a concert featuring "Artist-Students" of the Curtis Institute under the direction of Dr. Louis Bailly, the renowned violist, who was head of the Department of Chamber Music. The Swastika String Quartet (named after Mary Louise Curtis Bok's Merion estate)[17] was on the first half of the program, and Bloom played in the Mozart *Quintet in E-Flat Major* K. 452 with pianist Joseph Levine, a student of Josef Hofmann. The other wind players were James Collis, clarinet; Theodore Seder, horn; and William Santucci, bassoon.

The program presented by "Students of Mr. Tabuteau, in Wind Ensemble" in May 1931 was considerably more expansive than their "debut" just a year earlier. By now, there were more students who could come closer to Tabuteau's performance standards, and it was possible to

TABUTEAU AT THE CURTIS INSTITUTE OF MUSIC

do works for larger ensembles. The concert opened with Gounod's *Petite Symphonie* for nine winds and closed with Richard Strauss's *E-Flat Major Serenade,* Opus 7, for thirteen players. The name of Harold Gomberg appears for the first time in two movements of the Handel *Sonata No. 1.* One movement only, the Adagio, from Beethoven's *C Major Trio for Two Oboes and English Horn* was on the program. Tabuteau must have remembered his frequent performances of this work in his Walter Damrosch days. The concert was dutifully reported in *Overtones,* this time without being described as "unusual." The winds were becoming accepted as contributing to the musical stature of the Curtis Institute.

The "famous" Beethoven *Quintet* again opened the 1932 concert, and larger works on the program included the *Double Quintet,* Opus 54, by Florent Schmitt and the Nováček *Sinfonietta,* Opus 48, for eight winds, a work first performed by the Société de Musique de Chambre pour Instruments à Vent in Paris in 1889. There were two Handel solos on this lengthy program: the *C Minor Sonata* was played by Rhadames Angelucci, and the *Concerto in G Minor* listed Harold Goldblum as the performer. One must assume that the latter was a mistake, as there was no one by that name in the oboe class. *Isadore* Goldblum played in all the ensemble numbers on the program, and lacking other evidence, it is probable that Harold *Gomberg* was the soloist for the Handel *Concerto.* In featuring these Handel works, Tabuteau was following in the footsteps of Georges Gillet, who had moved on from the romantic repertoire of the nineteenth century to resurrect Bach and Handel for the oboe. Even as late as the 1930s, very few oboe compositions of the baroque period were available.

All of the music on the May 1933 Wind Ensemble concert was by French composers: Gabriel Pierné, André Caplet, Camille Saint-Saëns, and Emile Bernard. Shortly after he arrived in America, Tabuteau had played second oboe in the Caplet *Suite Persane* with the New York Wind Instrument Club. On the Curtis program, the names of Arno Mariotti and John Minsker were now added to those of Rhadames Angelucci and Harold Gomberg. The Stravinsky *Pastorale* appeared on a Tabuteau ensemble concert for the first time in 1936 with flutist Julius Baker and Rhadames Angelucci, who was still the oboist for all seven of the other works on the program. The Stravinsky was performed again in 1937, but now the oboist for the whole concert was Harry Shulman. Jorge Bolet, who would play for many of Tabuteau's future programs, joined the wind players in the Beethoven *Quintet*, Opus 16, described in the program as "for Piano and Woodwind."

Until the 1934 season Tabuteau gave forty-five minute lessons to an average of four to six pupils. In 1935, however, the enrollment suddenly jumped to ten oboists. For the 1936–37 season, there was a class of twelve students, the largest in Curtis oboe history. This was the only time that Tabuteau experimented with group lessons. He taught six pupils in a two-hour class every week, and the other six had individual thirty-minute lessons. John de Lancie, who came to Curtis as a fifteen-year-old student in the fall of 1936, remembered the ordeal of the class lessons. "That was a nightmare, being ridiculed and attacked in front of your peers. There was one poor fellow—we laughed—we shouldn't have laughed, but in those days the style was for big pants. He was not very tall, and when he would stand up to play, his legs would be shaking in the wide pants and it would make us nervous too." Sixty years later, de Lancie could still name all his fellow-sufferers: Don Cassel, Livingston Gearhart, Marty Fleisher, Harry Shulman, Perry Bauman, Bob Kosinski, Billy Kosinski, Charlie Gilbert, Joe Lukatsky, Bill Vitelli, and Edmund Jurgenson. Several of these students soon dropped out. "That class diminished rapidly. Lukatsky left. Vitelli left. Gearhart went to Paris. Don Cassel left, but went on playing in Nashville, Tennessee. Fleisher stayed, and Shulman was there two years with me." From then on, except for a medium large class in 1938–40, there was an average of four pupils a year. Lessons became shorter, usually lasting forty minutes, and in Tabuteau's final few years at Curtis, at times they were only thirty minutes long. My own memory is that the intensity of thirty or forty minutes with Tabuteau could seem like an eternity. Once when there was no lesson, I wrote to my mother that I felt I had missed "the weekly dynamiting." John de Lancie expressed a similar feeling when he said that the whole four-year period he spent with Tabuteau at Curtis was like sitting out in an orchard during a lightning storm wondering when it would hit you.

Several wind students remembered how the orchestra class functioned in the mid-1930s. John de Lancie reminisced:

TABUTEAU AT THE CURTIS INSTITUTE OF MUSIC

Generally Tabuteau would take one piece from the works the Philadelphia Orchestra was performing that weekend. Jorge Bolet played the string parts on the piano, and we would go through the piece. That was the only way we ever had any opportunity to get some idea of repertoire. We didn't play anywhere, we didn't have records, and we didn't have "Good Music Radio Stations." The only way you heard music was to go to a concert. You went down to the Academy of Music on Saturday night and you heard the piece we'd been working on. Sometimes Reiner would ask Tabuteau to work on a piece we were preparing for a broadcast he was conducting. We didn't play concerts but we *did* do broadcasts. Once Reiner had scheduled the *Swan of Tuonela*. Charlie Gilbert was playing English horn—we were going through it in class, and Charlie sounded good. Then the next week we played the *Swan* again, and Charlie was obviously having trouble with his reed. Tabuteau stopped and said, "Last week it sounded purty good. What happened to that reed you were playing?" Charlie said, "Well, I still have it but I'm saving it for Mr. Reiner." We all ducked. *We* thought Charlie was being practical and was right. He was honest, but after a scathing lecture from Tabuteau, Charlie had to take out that good reed and play and play and play!

Everyone learned a lot, but it was often like coming too close to a high-tension wire. Once the Kosinski brothers were playing *Tombeau de Couperin.* For the opening oboe solo, Tabuteau was experimenting with different divisions of the rhythm, using three groups of two for each beat rather than the printed two groups of three. After singing it over several times, he announced, "Let's *try* it!" Bobby Kosinki spoke up and said, "Mr. Tabuteau, don't you think if Ravel had wanted it that way, he would have written it?" Tabuteau walked over from where he was standing to the front of Bobby's music stand, leaned over the edge, and in his most threatening tone of voice, shouted, "Young man, when I want musical advice, you will be the *last* person I will ask!"

If some of us now regret the many things we might have asked Tabuteau, thinking back on this type of experience reminds us why we decided to say as little as possible.

Perry Bauman, one of the students in the large class, remembered the Kosinski brothers, Bobby and Billy, as "a couple of characters. They were so destitute, and the story was that they had only one suit between them so they could never go out together. I suspect it could have been

MARCEL TABUTEAU

true, but knowing them, I can't verify it! They looked alike but were not twins. I think their only contact with the oboe was a few lessons with Bloom. Tabuteau took them on as a sort of experiment to see how much he could teach someone who had no prior training. They were always trying to play little jokes. They would pretend to be hiding behind the piano with a reed knife and were going to 'do away' with Tabuteau when he came into the room. Bobbie was the older and a very talented boy. Billie later played English horn in Pittsburgh with Reiner and eventually went to Los Angeles. Bobbie gave up the oboe and worked in a gas station." Bauman also spoke of his own lessons. Although he had studied for a short time with Philip Kirchner in Cleveland, he felt that he had not learned much about the oboe before he came to Curtis. Tabuteau kept threatening to ship him back to Ohio. But Bauman remembered how "once Bob Bloom dropped in unexpectedly at the studio, and Tabuteau asked me to play the E major étude from the fifteen big studies in Barret. I had memorized it, and it was the one I played the best. He introduced me and apparently wanted to impress Bloom on how well he taught." Immediately after graduation in 1942 Perry left to play first oboe in the Toronto Symphony Orchestra. Tabuteau's parting words were, "If anything happens that you can't handle the job, don't blame me!" Perry remained steadfast in his admiration for Tabuteau, and later on, in the summers when Tabuteau went to Canada, they shared a love of fishing.[18]

Many non-oboist wind players and also string players were influenced by Tabuteau. Bernard Portnoy, whose career would encompass playing first clarinet in the Philadelphia and Cleveland Orchestras as well as teaching at Juilliard and at Indiana University, spent six years in Tabuteau's classes in the mid-1930s. His memories were similar to de Lancie's. "Tabuteau taught orchestra class for three hours. We had all the woodwinds and percussion and brass with Jorge Bolet filling in for the strings. We'd do the music that the Philadelphia Orchestra was playing that week. If it was a Brahms Symphony or a Beethoven Symphony— he'd point [to indicate] which one of us should play here and there—the second or first part. The brasses learned a lot in that class too." Portnoy also described the chamber music sessions. "The way it functioned, we

TABUTEAU AT THE CURTIS INSTITUTE OF MUSIC

learned to attack a note for a whole semester and then we were allowed to go on to the quintet. Everything was in order. You were a beginner and then gradually you moved up. He would have everybody there in the woodwind class and he'd pick you out and say, 'All right, you play the first movement, you play the second movement'—but you never were allowed to leave the class. You had to sit there and listen to the others play. You were playing in front of your colleagues, and you were listening to him correct everybody. Sometimes he didn't call you—but it was a three-hour class—three hours of woodwind quintet."

In 1937, when the Curtis Woodwind Ensemble made its only commercial recording, Bernard Portnoy was the clarinetist, along with Rhadames Angelucci, oboe; Julius Baker, flute; Jules Seder, bassoon; and Ernani Angelucci, horn. Portnoy recalled the session vividly.

> That recording was done in New York—I think at 28th Street—for RCA, and there were rugs on the floor. It was the end of the season, and the Philadelphia Orchestra had just come back from a tour. Tabuteau was all ready to go to Europe, and the school decided we should make a record. We went to New York, and he is sitting there waiting. Oh, I'll never forget that session. He was killing us. It was hot. There was no air-conditioning, and he's there with no shirt on drinking water—(he had ham for lunch)—yelling and perspiring. We did the Pierné *Prelude and Fugue,* thank God. We also did the De Wailly *Trio,* but that never came out because we had nothing to fill the other side. He wanted to do the other Pierné that has the beautiful oboe part in the third section, and to change the order to do movements one, three, and then two. Now remember, we're doing it on wax so you have to turn a page while you're playing. Everything is quiet, and we did the beginning—Angelucci played the oboe solo in number three and then I turned the page to go to the second movement where I play duddily, duddily duh, and the music fell on the floor! He said, "All right, we'll do it again." Well, three times something happened, and he started to yell. That was the end. He had enough for the day, so we never finished the other Pierné and they never released the De Wailly.[19]

I asked Portnoy if the oboe players got the worst of Tabuteau's ire, and he replied, "Everybody got it! Look, he chewed me out after that recording in New York because I dropped the music on the floor. He said, 'I never want to *see* you again!' and I went home and lived all summer with that thought. Then when I saw him in the fall he tried to get me a job. He would be hot and bothered, but he did a lot of wonderful things for me."

Clarinetist Mitchell Lurie was in Tabuteau's classes in the late 1930s. When I asked what importance the experience had for him, he replied, "Oh my, that's like saying—What is the meaning of life?" Like most of the other students, he spoke of his feelings of terror, a word that surfaces over and over in memories of Tabuteau's classes. "I learned something that none of our kids have to cope with today—that Tabuteau, like his fellow teachers in that era, taught mostly through terror tactics. One day I caught sight of myself in that huge mirror in the room where he used to teach. He was going after me or somebody else and I saw my face in that mirror. There was a look of fear that I had never seen before. I thought, I've come here clear across the country to this dirty, lousy city, from Los Angeles which was so pretty in those days, and I just couldn't figure out the logic of sitting there in terror. If only I could put that aside and really understand all that this man was trying to get across to us! And it worked, because then I began to soak in the marvelous things he did and said to get us to play music and not simply play our instruments." This type of realization, or as Lurie called it, "a kind of epiphany," was what enabled most of us to stand all of the insults and focus on the important things we were receiving. In Lurie's words, "It was like when you have a terrible temperature and then there is a crisis and the fever breaks." Lurie felt that he had also benefited from the teaching of the solfège professor, Mme Renée Longy Miquelle, who emphasized the need for musicians to think logically.

Lurie's studies were not all overshadowed by fear, as his clarinet teacher, Daniel Bonade, "taught through the best of good humor. I was blessed, because Bonade filled in the gaps and gave me a choice later on when it was my turn—whether I was going to teach through terror or whether I was going to get the best out of my students by keeping them relaxed and able to take in what I had to say. You can be positive but at the same time demanding . . . the iron fist and the silken glove, but if the iron fist is a glove with spikes and nails in it, one doesn't come through very well."

TABUTEAU AT THE CURTIS INSTITUTE OF MUSIC

Lurie agreed that the style we learned in Tabuteau's classes gradually entered into the general fabric of woodwind playing in the major American orchestras: "I think it impregnated itself into the wallpaper. And what is so wonderful is that when you sit down and play with Curtis people from then and from now, the inflections are still there." He remembered the famous Andraud "orange books" and "how we played that same Beethoven quintet over and over and it was never right." There were also "some little variations for each instrument with a purposely fiendishly difficult one given to the clarinet. During the last class of my first year Tabuteau said, 'All right, now we will do this,' and it was my turn to play. I wasn't ready and I really messed it up. Then school was over. I practiced all summer on that one variation and sure enough, first class of the next fall, he says, 'The book!' We turned to that piece and he points at me, 'Variation three. *You play!*' and I just knocked it off. He had nothing to say, only, 'Mmm,' because I had done it. I wasn't going to get caught the second time."

Following his graduation in 1942, Lurie was asked by Fritz Reiner to become the principal clarinetist of the Pittsburgh Symphony. Shortly before the start of the season he was classified 1A by his draft board and became a pilot in the Air Force. During the war when I was writing letters for Tabuteau I remember that he heard from Lurie. When I saw his concern for all the boys who had been in his classes and were now here, there, and everywhere in the armed forces, I realized there were sides to him that we didn't always see. He insisted on replying to every one. On two trips to France in the 1960s, Lurie, to his great regret, missed connections with both Tabuteau and Bonade, the two men who had had such a great influence on his life.[20]

Mason Jones spoke of the classes from the standpoint of a horn player. He also came to Curtis in the 1930s and remembered that the students first had to spend a lot of time on the "drives," which he described as "attacking a note and learning to come in on nothing." He said that Tabuteau deplored the way his horn colleagues in the orchestra would warm up and go down to the low notes, spread and blatting. "It almost killed him. He said they should be doing entrances and precision work." Jones described what it was like preparing for the end-of-the-year Curtis recital.

MARCEL TABUTEAU

We wound up playing the Beethoven piano quintet and then maybe Taffanel. Once in a while he'd bring a contemporary composition or maybe somebody would send him a score. He did a piece by Jacobi that had a million notes for everybody. He could spend fifty minutes on one little eight-bar passage to get all the inflections correct, and then if it wasn't right he would blow up and lose his temper. Once in a while, when he gave you a compliment, it was heaven. With the horn, psychologically, you have to be confident, keep your lip very flexible, and be able to manipulate quickly, and that's what I did in his classes. I played the parts very carefully. One time I had a little trumpet-like group of notes, but I had to wait maybe forty bars to play them. I just sat there and counted. Then I came in, ta-ta-tah, ta-ta-tah, a little fanfare thing, and he stopped me. He liked it, and said, "You've been counting bars and then you came in just exactly right." Of course you have to count the bars; you can't allow yourself to get bored while counting. . . . These days the students don't always want to play in a symphony orchestra. Some winds are going into solo careers and are also playing the valveless horn. There are lots of notes coming out. But in an orchestra you can be just as thrilled by a little phrase played by somebody like Tabuteau or a Horner.[21]

As with so many other students, Jones's memory of a little phrase well accomplished in Tabuteau's class had left a lifelong impression.

Edward Arian, who studied double bass with Anton Torello at Curtis, was one of the many string players who attended Tabuteau's classes as often as he could. "You didn't have to be a woodwind player to learn from him. I remember how he explained the way to play sixteenth notes. One problem for string players is not to rush. He said that most musicians are thinking 1234, 1234, 1234, and in that way it is easy to rush and become unsteady. The secret is to think of going from the second sixteenth note to the first one of the next group, 234-1, 234-1, and it works so magnificently." This was, of course, the first lesson in the woodwind classes, but it was apparently a revelation for string players. The woodwind students used to walk down the street saying "4-123, 4-123, 4," with 4 being the first of the group of sixteenths, or for triplets, "3-12, 3-12, 3." Arian remembered Tabuteau's long cigarette holder (a piece of oboe cane) and how he used it to illustrate the end of a phrase. "'No, you don't finish it by'—and he put his hand down on the table top, you know, flat—bang. 'You don't land down like that.' Then he

TABUTEAU AT THE CURTIS INSTITUTE OF MUSIC

blew out a little smoke and said, 'Now watch,' and as the smoke drifted slowly upward, he said, 'that's the way to finish the note. When the tone fades away, it goes up—it doesn't sink.'"[22]

Other students received the benefit of Tabuteau's educational ideas, both in music and manners. The trumpet player Harry Peers, who was in the orchestra class, recalled how one day he encountered Tabuteau in the hall at Curtis and said, "Hello, Mr. Tabuteau." Tabuteau replied, "Young man, do not say 'hello' to me. Say, 'How do you do, Mr. Tabuteau'; 'Good morning, Mr. Tabuteau'; 'Good afternoon, Mr. Tabuteau.' 'Hello' is what you say to the barge man when you want to cross the river." And John Minsker recollected one time when he went for his lesson: "My shoes were kind of messed up. They weren't shined well, and Tabuteau said, 'You go get a shoeshine before you come to the Curtis.' There were standards. Look how they dress now!"

If the 1938 class recital relied largely on the dependable French favorites of Gounod's *Petite Symphonie,* Caplet's *Suite Persane,* and Saint-Saëns's *Caprice sur des airs Danois et Russes,* it broke new ground in that the Mozart *E-Flat Serenade for Eight Winds* (albeit only two movements) opened the concert. Now the oboists were Martin Fleisher, Perry Bauman, and John de Lancie. Two weeks earlier, the Mozart and Gounod had been played on a Curtis radio broadcast, and by the end of 1938 Tabuteau's Wind Ensemble had reached a level of fame that warranted its inclusion in *Life* Magazine's feature article on the Curtis Institute.

The 1940 woodwind program included four large ensemble works for as many as sixteen players. Two of the numbers were transcriptions by William Strasser after Spanish music by Joaquín Turina. There was also an original Strasser *Fuga* and Hershy Kay's transcription of the Ravel *Sonatine.* "Classics" were not neglected; the Beethoven *Variations on "Là ci darem la mano"* for two oboes and English horn and Mozart's *Quintet in E-Flat* K. 452, with Jorge Bolet as pianist, were on the same program. With the addition of three compositions by Hugues, De Wailly, and Rieti, it was a marathon evening. John de Lancie was the solo oboist in all nine works and must have felt he was truly earning his diploma. Assisting oboists were Perry Bauman, Ralph Gomberg, and Charles Gilbert, English horn. The following year, 1941, saw the last important woodwind recital until after the end of World War II. It was now Ralph Gomberg who played in every number on the program, which aside from the ever recurring Beethoven *Quintet,* Opus 71, included the Mozart *E-Flat Serenade,* finally performed with all movements, and for the first time on these concerts, the Poulenc *Trio for Oboe, Bassoon and Piano.* Flutist John Krell, clarinetist Mitchell Lurie, and horn player James Chambers, who all went on to distinguished careers, took part in this program. Although it was the last in that decade-long evolution of the Tabuteau ensemble recitals, in my experience it was a "first," as it took place on April 10, just a few days after my audition at Curtis. I had never heard wind playing of such high caliber, finesse, and brilliance. It made an indelible impression on me, but I also noted the indignant glances Tabuteau occasionally directed toward the performers. I could not imagine how it felt to have him sitting alongside them on the stage. Almost sixty years later Ralph Gomberg told me about the "terror of that 1941 recital with Tabuteau right there on the stage." Again the word *terror,* the common denominator in almost all memories of Tabuteau wind classes. Ralph was the youngest of the five members of the Gomberg family from Boston, all of whom attended the Curtis Institute of Music. The two oldest, Robert and Cela, were violinists; then oboist Harold; and Leo, a trumpet player. Robert used to take his little brother Ralph along to Tabuteau's ensemble classes. He learned by listening even before becoming Tabuteau's youngest student at age eleven. According to Ralph, "The violin and piano teachers would come in to hear the classes. Tabuteau thought violinistically and often mentioned up and down bows. He had such a vivid imagination and would make comments to explain the music; he always spoke of the line, and the ebb and flow of the music. You had to bring it alive. Not just the bland notes on a white piece of paper with bar lines. What does that mean? The conductors who say they are only doing what the composer has written!"

SPREADING INFLUENCE

The 1930s had seen the flowering of the Curtis Woodwind Ensemble, and it was also during that decade that Tabuteau's oboe students began to enter the nation's symphony orchestras. What an impressive contrast between the late 1920s, when there was not even an oboe student fit to play in the Curtis school orchestra, and only a few years later, when a number of superbly trained oboists were going out to "the excellent positions waiting to be worthily filled," so boldly announced by the 1925 Curtis catalog. This was a time when good oboists were still at a premium and conductors would call Tabuteau, happy to accept whomever he had trained and recommended. The first Tabuteau students played with major orchestras in the East and Midwest. During the next three decades they would spread ever farther westward until the whole country came under the influence of the Tabuteau style of playing.

A brief summary of the main positions held by Tabuteau students begins with Robert Bloom, who played oboe and English horn with the Philadelphia Orchestra from 1930 to 1936, was afterward first oboe in the Rochester Philharmonic Orchestra and the NBC Symphony Orchestra, and then was a long-time member of the Bach Aria Group and professor at Yale University. Harold Gomberg entered the National Symphony Orchestra as principal oboe at the age of seventeen. Following engagements as principal oboe in both Toronto and St. Louis, he joined the New York Philharmonic in 1943 as solo oboe, remaining there until his retirement in 1977. He also taught at the Juilliard School of Music. John Minsker played English horn in the Detroit Symphony Orchestra from 1934 to 1936, when he went to the Philadelphia Orchestra as English horn and oboe, staying until 1959. He taught at the Philadelphia Musical Academy, the Philadelphia Conservatory of Music, and the New School of Music. At the Curtis Institute, he held the Marcel Tabuteau Chair of Woodwind Studies from 1978 to 1985. Upon graduation in 1936, Rhadames Angelucci auditioned for Eugene Ormandy, who was then the conductor of the Minneapolis Symphony Orchestra. After two years playing English horn, Angelucci was appointed principal oboe by Dmitri Mitropoulos, the next music director. He held this position for forty-four years until his retirement in 1982. Arno Mariotti was solo oboe in the Pittsburgh and Detroit Symphony Orchestras, later becoming professor at the University of Michigan. Of students from the end of the decade, Perry Bauman joined the Toronto Symphony Orchestra immediately after graduating in 1942. He was

MARCEL TABUTEAU

the third Tabuteau student to become solo oboe in Toronto, following Harold Gomberg and Martin Fleisher, who were each there for one year. Bauman played with the Toronto Symphony for twenty-three years and also for a few years with the orchestra of the Canadian Broadcasting Company.

Some careers were interrupted by World War II. On graduation in 1940, John de Lancie was engaged as first oboe of the Pittsburgh Symphony Orchestra at age nineteen. In 1946, after five years of military service, he joined the oboe section of the Philadelphia Orchestra as assistant first oboe, becoming associate principal in 1948 and principal oboe when Tabuteau retired in 1954. He remained in that position until 1977, when he was appointed director of the Curtis Institute of Music. At Curtis he taught oboe and wind classes from 1954 until 1985, forming his own distinguished class of students. William Kosinski played English horn, first in Pittsburgh and then, from 1963 to 1973, in the Los Angeles Philharmonic. Harry Shulman was first oboe in the Pittsburgh Symphony before joining NBC in New York. After returning from military service, Ralph Gomberg played first oboe in Baltimore. He was then in New York with the Mutual Broadcasting Orchestra before being appointed principal oboe of the Boston Symphony Orchestra in 1950, where he remained until he retired in 1987. He taught at Boston University and at Tanglewood.

Of the students from the mid-1940s and early 1950s, Martha Scherer entered the Buffalo Symphony Orchestra in 1947, where she played English horn for fourteen years under conductors William Steinberg and Josef Krips. Charles Morris was assistant principal in the Philadelphia Orchestra from 1954 to 1959 and then continued as second oboe until 1986. Marguerite Smith played second oboe in Buffalo and then moved to English horn in Columbus, Ohio. Marc Lifschey was first oboe in the National Symphony Orchestra from 1948 until going to Cleveland as solo oboe in 1950. He remained in Cleveland until 1965 except for the 1959–60 season when he played with the Metropolitan Opera. He was then principal oboe for twenty-one years in the San Francisco Symphony Orchestra, taught at the San Francisco Conservatory of Music, and from 1988 until 1997 was professor of oboe at Indiana University. William Criss was solo oboe with the Metropolitan

Opera for ten years from the 1949–50 season through 1958–59. As for myself, after playing English horn in the Kansas City Philharmonic for two seasons, I became principal oboe in the Houston Symphony Orchestra from 1948 to 1955. I was later first oboe with the Mozarteum Orchester in Salzburg and the Puerto Rico Symphony Orchestra, joining the Soni Ventorum Wind Quintet in 1965 and teaching at the University of Washington in Seattle from 1968 to 1991. Laurence Thorstenberg was solo oboe of the Dallas Symphony Orchestra for the seasons 1951 and 1952, before being engaged by the Chicago Symphony Orchestra in 1953 as assistant solo oboe and later English horn. In 1963 he became solo English horn of the Boston Symphony Orchestra, where he remained for the next thirty years. Louis Rosenblatt played English horn in the Houston Symphony Orchestra in 1954–55 and then four seasons as English horn in the New Orleans Symphony Orchestra until 1959, when he was engaged as oboist and solo English horn of the Philadelphia Orchestra. He retired in 1995 but continued to play and teach at Temple University. John Mack, who was first oboist of the New Orleans Symphony Orchestra from 1952 to 1963 and of the National Symphony Orchestra of Washington, D.C., from 1963 to 1965, joined the Cleveland Orchestra as solo oboe in 1965. He retired from orchestral playing in 2001 after a fifty-year career but continued to play and to teach at the Cleveland Institute and the Juilliard School of Music, as well as at his long-established summer camps in North Carolina and Carmel, California. Alfred Genovese, who in 1953 became the last Tabuteau student to graduate from Curtis, played first oboe in Baltimore and then spent three years, 1956–59, with the St. Louis Symphony Orchestra. He played the 1959–60 season in Cleveland before joining the Metropolitan Opera Orchestra, where he was solo oboe for seventeen years. In 1978 he became associate principal of the Boston Symphony Orchestra and in 1987, solo oboe. Upon retirement in 1998 his career had totaled forty-five years. Felix Kraus, Theodore Heger, and Donald Hefner were in school during Tabuteau's final years at Curtis. Richard Kanter arrived at the beginning of Tabuteau's last season, 1953–54, and stayed on to study with John de Lancie. His career as second oboist of the Chicago Symphony Orchestra extended for forty-one seasons, from 1961 to 2002. After playing

MARCEL TABUTEAU

first oboe in the National Symphony Orchestra, Washington, D.C., for three seasons, 1960–63, Felix Kraus moved to the oboe section of the Cleveland Orchestra. In 1979 he became solo English horn. At the time of his retirement in the summer of 2004, after forty-one seasons in Cleveland, he was the only Tabuteau Curtis student still active in a symphony orchestra.

The war dealt a blow to the continuity of Tabuteau's wind classes and the ensemble concerts. Nonetheless, Tabuteau's influence would continue to grow. His increased work with string players and a new crop of oboe students allowed his teaching to reach an ever-widening circle of young performers. As Jorge Bolet had done earlier, now Abba Bogin, Seymour Lipkin, and Jacob Lateiner played for Tabuteau's classes, filling in any missing orchestral parts from works being studied. During his final ten years at the Curtis Institute Tabuteau conducted the string ensemble classes, and in 1944–45 he was in charge of an orchestra that played a series of radio broadcasts. This took place while I was studying in Philadelphia and will be recounted in more detail from my own memories and letters.

PRIVATE STUDENTS

At least two important aspects of Tabuteau's teaching were not directly linked to the Curtis Institute of Music: the students he taught outside of the school and his important relationship with the Lorée oboe firm. Students came to him during his years in Philadelphia, and some sought him out after he returned to France. Even without undergoing the rigorous three to six years of training at Curtis, all were deeply influenced by Tabuteau. Wayne Rapier worked with Tabuteau over a period of many years both in Philadelphia and later in Nice.[23] For three years between 1951 and 1954 while Wayne was in the U.S. Marine Band, he made the trip from Washington, D.C., for lessons almost every week. After playing first oboe in Baltimore for several seasons, he asked Tabuteau if he could come to France. Beginning in 1960 while he was a member of the Philadelphia Orchestra, he went to Nice for five summers and played for Tabuteau—often it was orchestral repertoire he had been doing at the Robin Hood Dell summer concerts.

TABUTEAU AT THE CURTIS INSTITUTE OF MUSIC

During World War II Tabuteau welcomed young men in the armed services to his studio on South Sixteenth Street. Some were stationed in Washington, D.C., or elsewhere on the East Coast. Often when I had a lesson at the Studio I would see them there in uniform; my impression was that he never turned away any soldier or sailor.

Little is known about those whom Tabuteau taught before 1924 when he became associated with the Curtis Institute of Music. However, it is believed that his first student was Philip Kirchner in New York. Oboist and toolmaker Wally Bhosys was a great admirer of Kirchner and heard from Kirchner an account of his playing in a Broadway show while Tabuteau was at the Metropolitan Opera.[24] As the operas finished later than the shows, Kirchner used to run down and wait at the stage door, take Tabuteau out for drinks, and try to talk him into teaching. It took about six months, but finally Kirchner became Tabuteau's first pupil. In 1919 Kirchner was engaged as solo oboist of the Cleveland Orchestra, where he remained until 1947.[25] I remember seeing Kirchner a few times at Tabuteau's studio. By then he was no longer in Cleveland but had returned to New York, where he was trying to make a living. It was obvious by the way they greeted each other that he and Tabuteau were old friends. Like several other well-known oboists of that era (Bruno Labate, Fernand Gillet), Kirchner was dependent on other people for his reeds. If the source dried up, the oboist was in trouble. John Mack told me that in the late 1940s, Tabuteau asked him "to make some reeds for my good friend Kirchner." Shortly afterward, Tabuteau said to Mack, "I want you to listen to this letter from Kirchner. 'My dear friend Marcel, Thank you so much for the beautiful reeds.'" Then with a secretive smile, Tabuteau handed Mack a ten-dollar bill. One can hear Kirchner's musical playing and stylish phrasing in a 1939 recording of *Scheherazade* with the Cleveland Orchestra under Artur Rodzinski.

There has always been a good deal of curiosity concerning how and when Tabuteau changed the style of his reed making. An interesting photograph taken around 1915, shortly before he went to the Philadelphia Orchestra, shows Tabuteau, still with a fair amount of hair, his easily recognizable heavy eyebrows, and a mustache, wearing a stickpin in his impeccable necktie. He is holding an oboe, and one can clearly see his classic finger position and the reed with its conventional short French scrape. It is generally thought that Tabuteau began to experiment with a longer scrape only after he became interested in the results achieved by Peter Henkelman, the long-time English horn player of the Philadelphia Orchestra and favorite of Stokowski. He would also have been impelled by Stokowski's demands to find a way to blend more completely with the different colors of the other woodwind instruments. According to Wally Bhosys, there may have been an additional impetus for Tabuteau to change his sound and reed style. Bhosys knew some of the wind players from Tabuteau's early years in the United States, including the bassoonist Auguste Mesnard, one of the "famous five" brought over by Damrosch in 1905. He played jobs with Mesnard, who told him stories about how Tabuteau would sometimes crack on the low notes and wobble on high ones with that short French scrape. Whenever Henkelman played a solo on the English horn, Stokowski had him take a bow. Lewis Raho, the second oboe before Di Fulvio, said, "You could see the smoke coming out of Tabuteau's head and he started fooling around with the long scrape." Some believe that Tabuteau was already experimenting with reed changes on his own while he was in New York—that he had been impressed by a German oboist there and tried to combine French fluency with a fatter sound. Bassoonist Ferdinand Del Negro, who remembered Tabuteau's playing from the early 1920s, said that his sound was thinner then but had "flare, like the old French oboists."[26]

In Stokowski's correspondence there is a reference to "special terms" for various orchestra members. Lewis Raho, a member of the oboe section from 1918 to 1924, was advised "to study with Tabuteau." As it is highly unlikely that any "command" from Leopold Stokowski would be ignored, we can assume that Raho did study with Tabuteau. In the 1922 concert when Stokowski featured all the instruments of the oboe family, Lewis Raho played the oboe d'amore. Theodore Heger, one of Tabuteau's last students at the Curtis Institute, remembered Raho. He said that Raho used to play in Trenton and other orchestras in the Philadelphia area and that he had heard him play the English horn solo in the *William Tell* Overture. "He was a nice man and everyone seemed to like and respect him. He played the big shows in town and taught in

TABUTEAU AT THE CURTIS INSTITUTE OF MUSIC

the schools; he believed that voice lessons helped the oboe tone, and he actually sang very professionally." Ernest Serpentini played in the Philadelphia Orchestra from 1924 to 1926 and later in the Cleveland Orchestra. When Heger bought Serpentini's English horn from his sister, she told him that in 1917 while wearing his World War I Navy uniform, Ernest had taken lessons from Tabuteau.[27] John Minsker remembered Serpentini from the early 1930s when he played at Philadelphia's Mastbaum Theater in winter and in Mexico City in the summer. Another oboist who had private lessons from Tabuteau, and upon whom Tabuteau did not hesitate to call if he needed some good Italian food, was Nick Lannutti.[28]

In 1923 Julien Shanis (who later became my main teacher in California) was the first person to make the long trip from San Francisco to Philadelphia to study with Tabuteau. The private lessons he had for about one year influenced his approach to music for the rest of his life. He used to say that Tabuteau knew more about the oboe than anyone else, and this was before the existence of the Curtis Institute when he began to teach on a more organized and regular basis.

Bert Gassman, an oboist with a long and respected career, was also strongly influenced by Tabuteau. He was introduced to Tabuteau in Hans Moennig's shop in the mid-1940s when he came over from New York to have his oboe repaired. Although already an established professional who had studied with Pierre Mathieu (Premier Prix at the Paris Conservatoire in 1907, three years after Tabuteau), he still wished to learn more and improve his own working situation. Tabuteau invited him to come to his studio early on Saturday mornings. Gassman would get up at 6:00 a.m. to arrive in time for a lesson and be back to play with the Metropolitan Opera, where he was then the solo oboist. When he was almost ninety years old, Gassman reflected that "Tabuteau taught me great things. His sound was gorgeous and he was a wonderful teacher. Like Mathieu, he was strict and firm. No nonsense with either one of these great musicians."[29]

William Arrowsmith joined the orchestra of Metropolitan Opera in 1947 as associate solo oboe, remaining through the 1985–86 season for a career of thirty-nine years. In the mid-1940s after studying with Robert Sprenkle at the Eastman School of Music, he moved to

MARCEL TABUTEAU

Philadelphia expressly to take lessons from Marcel Tabuteau. While there, he shared a room with another oboe student and aspiring conductor, Bernie Poland. During the time he spent in the Navy Band, he would see Tabuteau when the Philadelphia Orchestra played in Washington, D.C. Later he continued the contact when the orchestra came to New York. He remembered Tabuteau as "such an enthusiastic person, I think he liked me, perhaps it was because he too, had played at the Met."[30]

Earl Schuster was in a band in Washington, D.C., during the war. Between 1941 and 1945 he went to Philadelphia for lessons almost every month. He used to buy things that Tabuteau wanted from the PX at his military base because "you were worshiping him and glad to do anything." He remembered "the studio-that spooky, dark, and dingy place, and staying over to hear the Philadelphia Orchestra concerts." He considered his copy of the Mozart Quartet with Tabuteau's numbers on it to be "a treasure." Schuster played in the Indianapolis Symphony Orchestra, served as assistant to Ray Still in Chicago for three years and was principal oboe in San Diego for ten years. After travels to Vienna and studies with Jörg Schäftlein, he specialized on the baroque oboe.[31]

Another young man who traveled from Washington, D.C., to study with Tabuteau was Grover Schiltz, who later became the longtime solo English horn player of the Chicago Symphony Orchestra. He was in an army group at the Music School of the Naval Receiving Station in Anacostia in the fall of 1953, Tabuteau's last season in Philadelphia. As Schiltz recalled, "I only had a few lessons with him, but they have remained indelibly in my mind throughout my career."[32]

Daniel Stolper, well known educator, performer, and oboe editor for the International Double Reed Society publications, never forgot the lessons he had with Tabuteau between 1950 and 1952. As a very young boy in Milwaukee, Dan was already playing in youth orchestras and professional groups. His teacher, Florian Mueller, solo oboist of the Chicago Symphony Orchestra, offered to contact Marcel Tabuteau. As Dan described it, "We met on a January evening in the Ludlow Building, a dark, and sort of forbidding place with a creaky elevator. Tabuteau always seemed rather distracted with reeds and trying oboes . . . he had

TABUTEAU AT THE CURTIS INSTITUTE OF MUSIC

two or three out each time I saw him. My dad left me with him . . . and I nervously started warming up—I remember the last movement of the Mozart oboe quartet. Tabuteau gradually paid more and more attention and then said, 'What else can you play?' I mentioned the Handel sonatas, Schumann Romances and the Goossens Concerto. His expression was eloquent . . . like 'I'm sure you can play all that !!!???' Finally he said, 'Young man (he never called me by name), you must learn to play the oboe before you play Mozart!' I spent almost two hours with him. He didn't say much but his gestures and facial expressions were communicative. When he indicated that I could put my oboe away, he said, 'Will you come again? Is you father able to bring you?' I did come again—five more times."[33]

Earnest Harrison studied with John Minsker for several summers before he became the principal oboist of the National Symphony Orchestra in 1951. From then until 1954 he made frequent trips from Washington, D.C., to Philadelphia, where he would spend long Saturday afternoons in Tabuteau's studio watching him work and listening while he endlessly tried reeds. Reminiscing fifty years later he said, "No matter how mean he could be, none of us who heard him play could help but be influenced and inspired by the quality of that man's sound. He not only changed the way we played the oboe, but he changed the whole approach to music in our country. This man was unique."[34]

About the same time, Richard Blair came from Detroit to study with John Minsker. He often accompanied Minsker to the studio and eventually had lessons from Tabuteau. Over half a century later he also told me of the unforgettable experience of hearing Tabuteau play in the Philadelphia Orchestra.[35]

Robert Zupnik took lessons during the war while he was stationed at Carlisle Barracks near Harrisburg, Pennsylvania. He took the train for the 120-mile trip and was Tabuteau's last student before the Saturday night concert. (Zupnik had auditioned for and had been accepted to Curtis in the mid-1930s, but his father was against his becoming a musician.) On his way back to the railway station, he used to walk by way of the Drake with Tabuteau and once mentioned that he had studied medicine for five years. Tabuteau told him if he became a doctor and played oboe on the side he would be "King of the Oboes!" But after

MARCEL TABUTEAU

leaving the Army, Zupnik chose music and became assistant principal oboe of the Cleveland Orchestra from 1946 to 1977.[36]

Robert Lehrfeld was a student of Philip Kirchner in Cleveland before leaving to study at the Eastman School of Music. During World War II while in an army band at Fort Meade, Maryland, he was invited by his friend, trumpet player Harry Peers, to spend the weekend at his home in Philadelphia. When Harry asked, "How would you like to meet Marcel Tabuteau?" Robert replied, "Are you kidding?" He was amazed when they went backstage the next night that Harry "didn't drop on the floor the way the rest of us did at the very thought of Marcel Tabuteau." (Harry had already substituted in the Philadelphia Orchestra as a student. See chapter 17). Following this first contact, for almost two years until he was sent overseas with his band, Lehrfeld made weekly visits to see Tabuteau. He remembered that his lessons were not formally structured, but he would listen for hours as Tabuteau worked on reeds and played through his orchestra solos. Lehrfeld was later first oboe in the Indianapolis Symphony and in Thomas Scherman's Little Orchestra Society of New York.[37]

San Francisco oboist Raymond Dusté was another member of the armed forces whose contact with Marcel Tabuteau would have far-reaching results. It was Dusté who became largely responsible for Tabuteau's influence finally reaching the West Coast in a more "updated" fashion than Julien Shanis brought back twenty years earlier. Although Dusté modestly referred to his meeting with Tabuteau as "just a timely break," he knew how to make the best of a "chance" and how to apply his sense of observation. Ray was playing in the 324th Army Service Forces Band at Aberdeen Proving Grounds in Maryland where General Campbell, the chief of ordnance, wanted to keep his own band for the duration of the war. Dusté used this opportunity to attend concerts in nearby Philadelphia, later saying, "I came home from the Army with the Philadelphia Orchestra completely embedded in my bones. My few encounters with the great man fully converted me to that way of performance." Tabuteau called him "Soldier Boy" and "allowed" him to come to the studio. Occasionally he played some Barret studies for Tabuteau, receiving the usual responses: that he was "playing on a 'slivair' for a reed" with "wire for electricians wrapped around it"; he

TABUTEAU AT THE CURTIS INSTITUTE OF MUSIC

"sounded like a 'trompette' and needed much work on fundamentals" and that Tabuteau had "no time to hear him 'practeece.'" And finally, "Go see Minsker. He has all my secrets." Said Dusté, "He will never know how many 'secrets' I learned just being around and listening. What emanated from him! I felt fortunate enough to be in the same room."[38]

Surely one of the shortest encounters with Tabuteau's teaching must be the one described by A. Clyde Roller. Growing up in a small town in Oklahoma, Roller became intrigued by the local high school band. He was given an oboe the director had picked up for twelve dollars, but found there was no one to teach him. He determined that the next time a visiting orchestra came to play in nearby Tulsa he would seek out the principal oboist. He did not have long to wait. In 1937 the Philadelphia Orchestra was making its second transcontinental tour and was to play in Tulsa on April 27. For Clyde, "a young man with a mission," Marcel Tabuteau's reputation was burning in his mind. He went to the railway station, where the Pullman cars of the special train were parked, and asked someone where he might find Mr. Tabuteau. A window blind went up and Tabuteau, with half-opened eyes, shouted out asking what he wanted so early in the morning. When he heard there was a young man who wished to have an oboe lesson, he snorted, "You can't teach anything in one lesson!" He must have relented, as then he told Clyde to wait and he would come out shortly. After hunting for a hotel with an available room, Clyde unpacked his oboe, and for about forty-five minutes Tabuteau listened while walking around the room, removing his coat—listening some more—removing his tie—then putting tie and coat back on, still listening. Finally he asked for a C-sharp major arpeggio. Clyde felt that he was able "to oblige with great brilliance." But when Tabuteau requested a "low C-sharp very softly," he was less successful. Nevertheless, he was offered a scholarship to the Curtis Institute of Music. To his great regret, even with a scholarship, the difficult economic situation of the 1930s made living in Philadelphia impossible for him. But he never forgot that Tabuteau had said "very good" after the arpeggio he had practiced so diligently and thought that perhaps all was not lost forever.

And indeed all was not lost. Some years later, after A. Clyde Roller had graduated from the Eastman School of Music and was playing and

MARCEL TABUTEAU

teaching in Birmingham, Alabama, the Philadelphia Orchestra came to play a concert. Clyde went backstage during the intermission to look for Tabuteau.[39] He was told on which side of the stage to find Tabuteau and began walking in that direction. By then, Tabuteau was coming toward him. Getting close enough to see Roller clearly, he came up to him and asked, "What happened?" Roller concluded the story of his one lesson with Marcel Tabuteau this way: "He had remembered the Tulsa incident and it still boggles my mind that he could recall all that without my saying a word! He was a Great Person besides being the musician that made him a Giant in the vast Music Profession."[40]

David Ledet had the unusual experience of making his initial contact with Tabuteau by simply looking him up in the telephone book. In the early 1950s while Ledet was teaching at the University of Illinois, he came to Philadelphia for a Music Teachers National Association convention. He reached Mme Tabuteau and told her he wanted to talk to Tabuteau about reeds. (He did not mention oboe study, knowing that "he would rake me over.") When he called back at the hour Madame suggested, Tabuteau told him to come to the studio at one o'clock on Saturday afternoon. He found Tabuteau there gouging cane and grinding the gouger blades. Tabuteau agreed to teach him but said "This lesson in going to cost you $80.00." He must have been surprised when Ledet, an assistant professor who had borrowed money to get to Philadelphia, replied, "O.K." The lesson lasted for five hours and ended at six o'clock with Tabuteau saying, "Let's go downstairs to the bar for a Scotch," and then, "What about tomorrow?" After another long session Ledet went back to Urbana and worked on everything he had learned. A month later he drove all the way to Philadelphia and continued making the trip regularly during the next two years, always having lessons that lasted three or four hours. Tabuteau never again asked for the overpriced fee. After he returned to France, he would send Ledet a cigarette box of six reeds or gouged cane every few months. One summer Ledet went to France to see him and remembered that as they headed for Fréjus and the *marchands de roseaux*, Tabuteau stopped at a butcher shop to buy a leg of lamb, saying, "I want to make sure I get the best cane!" David Ledet's faithful study of cane and reeds led to the publication in 1981 of his excellent book *Oboe Reed Styles*.[41]

TABUTEAU AT THE CURTIS INSTITUTE OF MUSIC

Like his own teacher Georges Gillet, Tabuteau insisted that all his students play the Lorée oboe. As his students spread out across the country, so did the Lorée oboes. Throughout his own lifetime Tabuteau played Lorée oboes exclusively. Long before he began to teach at the Curtis Institute, he either ordered or brought Lorée oboes back from France for his colleagues and friends. Add to this the fifteen other Gillet students who were making their careers in the United States, and one can understand how the ascendancy of the Lorée oboe in America was assured for the better part of the twentieth century. As for those who stayed in France, when I asked Albert Debondue if they were always required to play Lorée oboes, his answer was: "Obligatoire— *Obligatoire!*" (Compulsory!).[42]

Anyone who spends the long years of study necessary to become a professional musician wants to have an instrument of the highest quality. Most pianists wish for a Steinway. Due to the sparse numbers and astronomical prices of the highly prized, centuries-old Italian violins and cellos, a string player's dream is almost impossible to realize. Wind players are more fortunate. From top-level performer to the average good student, every oboist can reasonably hope to own the woodwind equivalent of a Stradivarius. Although prices gradually rose throughout the years, in comparison with bassoons, harps, or old violins, they remained fairly modest. One could pay ten times, a hundred, or even five hundred times more than the standard price, and not get a better instrument.[43] Unlike the strings, where it is possible to become quite proficient on a less than top-quality instrument, the mechanical intricacy of the oboe means that an instrument of inferior caliber prevents progress beyond a certain point. The Lorée became the preferred instrument not only of professional players, but also of every serious oboe student, whether of high school or college age.

For the past two hundred years Paris has been home to fine oboe makers, and in the nineteenth century several manufacturers came to the fore. Founded by François Lorée in 1881, the firm F. Lorée soon became the official purveyor of oboes to the Paris Conservatoire. In the same year Georges Gillet was appointed professor at the Conservatoire.

He played a Lorée oboe and worked closely with François Lorée and later his son Lucien to further improve the instrument. From the very beginning of his business at 5, rue du Dragon on the Left Bank not far from the church of Saint-Germain-des-Prés, François Lorée kept a small notebook; in the elegant penmanship of the era, he meticulously entered the name of each purchaser, the model of the instrument chosen, and whether it was an English horn, oboe d'amore, or *baryton* (bass oboe). The first oboe on Lorée's list, a system No. 5 in *palissandre* (rosewood), numbered A 0, was sold to Rudall-Carte in London.[44] Soon after came Georges Longy, who bought Lorée's sixth oboe, an instrument made *en buis* (in boxwood). The name of Georges Gillet appeared for the first time (still in the year 1881) as having acquired a No. 6 model oboe also *en buis*, numbered A16 in the line of production.

The Lorée oboe and its makers were to play a large part in the life of Marcel Tabuteau. Too young to have known founder François Lorée, who died in 1902, Tabuteau, through long association with Lucien, the son and successor of François, became closely allied with the family. From the beginning of his career, Tabuteau depended on Lucien Lorée for his own oboes and later on for those of his students. When he went back to France in the summers, one of his first visits was always to the Lorée shop to order instruments. He enjoyed social gatherings with the Lorées—lunches in the garden of their home at Le Perreux-sur-Marne in Val de Marne, an eastern suburb of Paris. A photograph from 1936 shows Tabuteau seated under a garden umbrella with the Lorées, young Robert de Gourdon, and his wife Raymonde.[45] I remember Tabuteau's devastation in 1945, toward the end of World War II, when he heard that both Lucien Lorée and his wife had been asphyxiated as the result of a malfunctioning gas radiator in their small Paris apartment. Only much later was I able to comprehend the extent of his loss. After the end of the war, Tabuteau continued the connection with Raymond Dubois, who had become the owner of F. Lorée some years earlier. Throughout the 1950s Dubois began to assign more of the work to his son-in-law, Robert de Gourdon. Today it is *his* son Alain who continues the tradition of the firm now officially known as F. Lorée–De Gourdon.

In 1904, the same year he received his Premier Prix, Tabuteau's name appeared for the first time in the Lorée record books. He had purchased

TABUTEAU AT THE CURTIS INSTITUTE OF MUSIC

a 1900 model oboe, appropriately enough with the serial number T 6. Shortly afterward, he acquired a *cor anglais,* also model 1900, numbered T 25.[46] This was well before his audition for Walter Damrosch in April 1905, when he was engaged to play English horn in New York; he was probably following the French tradition that oboists were also expected to play the major English horn solos in orchestral works.

By the frequency with which their names appear in the books, it is evident that Gillet's students who became well known on both sides of the Atlantic—Alfred Barthel, Louis Bleuzet, Arthur Bridet, Myrtile Morel, Roland Lamorlette, Alexandre Duvoir, Fernand Gillet, and many others—all favored the Lorée oboe. Tabuteau's predecessors in the Philadelphia Orchestra, Alfred Doucet and Attillio Marchetti, as well as his colleague from Damrosch days, Cesare Addimando, were also frequent patrons of Lorée. In 1908, the year he entered the orchestra of the Metropolitan Opera, Tabuteau bought two oboes and an English horn (serial numbers X 96, X 97, and X 98). He often brought back oboes from Paris for other people, but their specific names are seldom mentioned. In 1910 BB 40 was designated for Lambert Schoof, his second oboist at the Metropolitan, and two oboes, BB 42 and BB 77, were indicated for Bruno Labate. From then on, barely a year passes without frequent purchases by Tabuteau, even during the war years of 1915–17. In 1917 he acquired a *Baryton* GG 6, for the Philadelphia Orchestra. In 1918 oboe GG 55 was intended for his first student, Philip Kirchner. Another client of F. Lorée in 1918 was the *Armée américaine* with a purchase of five oboes, Nos. 8–12 in the Series HH.[47]

By 1922 Tabuteau was buying oboes in groups of three at a time (LL 82, 83, and 84). In the 1930s he sometimes bought as many as six or seven oboes in the same year. Without doubt many were sold to his students, but he was also always looking for something more to his own liking and constantly tried new oboes or a combination of sections from different oboes. Even with oboes of a high level of workmanship, there are variations, and Tabuteau wanted to keep the best from each "batch" for himself. There were instances when Tabuteau would "sell" an oboe to a student, then begin to feel that it was better than his own, and pressure the student to accept a different one. In 1948 I experienced the fear

MARCEL TABUTEAU

that I would not be allowed to keep the first Lorée oboe made especially for me by Raymond Dubois.

Donald Hefner told me of an agonizing ordeal while he was a student at Curtis in the early 1950s. He was playing a Rigoutat oboe that Tabuteau disliked. "One day, in my brashness, I said, 'Sir, I may be late for my lesson next week as I am going to try oboes.' It was like the mushroom cloud, and Tabuteau replied, 'Damn fool, I told you I had an instrument for you.' When I had previously asked if he had an oboe I could buy, nothing had come of it. But now, he said he had one, and I was so thrilled at the idea of getting an oboe from Tabuteau that I must have made about fifty reeds and finally came up with a beautiful one as I wanted to please him." Hefner described how he started to play high notes and how seemingly they became only better. Watching Tabuteau, he saw him getting redder and redder. "Tabuteau jumped up, snatched the instrument, and broke the reed, saying, 'It's too good for you!' and I never saw that oboe again." Later, he asked Hefner to come to the apartment on Christmas eve. Tabuteau had bought six oboes and was trying to decide which ones to keep. As Donald recounted, "He went into the bedroom with this armload of oboes and asked, 'What do you think of that one?' 'Very deep,' I said. 'What do you mean, 'deep'? He demanded an evaluation. This went on for about two hours. I was dying to get out of there. Then he said, 'I can't make up my mind. You'll have to wait another week.' At that moment Madame Tabuteau said, 'Monsieur Hautbois' (to me) and to Tabuteau, 'Aren't you going to give him his Christmas present?' I had chipped in fifteen dollars for a case of cognac as a present from all of us students. Tabuteau asked, 'Did you give something for my cognac?'" After the affirmative response, he gave Hefner a nice new reed knife and wished him a *Joyeux Noël.* The following week at his lesson Tabuteau brought in an oboe and said, "It's the one you liked." Then he added, "Did you tell anyone how much you paid?" "To my reply of $500, it was, 'Damn fool!' I didn't know I shouldn't mention the price and finally I asked, 'Why, sir, are you always getting all these oboes?' His answer was, 'I am always trying to find something better.'" Despite the turmoil, Hefner summed up his feelings for Tabuteau by saying, "All in all, it was the most important and significant experience of my whole life—like a father. It helped me through everything."[48]

TABUTEAU AT THE CURTIS INSTITUTE OF MUSIC

After the early 1930s, most of the instruments Tabuteau bought at Lorée appear in the records as *Hautbois 1906 modèle Tabuteau*. Tabuteau's name was never put on these oboes, of which the identifying feature was the added left-hand F key but no F resonance key. He often said that the simple forked F fingering was "the most beautiful note on the oboe" and that it made possible an alternate, softer tone color on what is normally a rather loud and not-too-easy note to control, especially in the lower register. If you want the full sound of a strong F, you use the left-hand key. To add the E-flat key to the forked F was unthinkable, and in passage work (such as broken thirds), never was one allowed to employ the left-side F key. I believe that Tabuteau felt it necessary to retain the flexibility of being able to use the forked fingering. Later, it occurred to me that it is one of the few remaining links of the modern oboe to its early baroque ancestor—although I doubt that this entered Tabuteau's mind in those days as we never saw a baroque oboe—either copy or original.

Throughout the years of World War II, the Lorée records became patchy. Few instruments were made, and if some were sold, the purchasers' names were not entered into the books. When instruments finally began to arrive again in the United States, either through Chiassarini in New York or Hans Moennig in Philadelphia, it was difficult to know exactly which ones went to Tabuteau. Problems arose in the 1950s when a new model was created using John de Lancie's name. With Tabuteau's explosive temperament, disturbances were almost guaranteed. I was once witness to an outburst of his insults in the Lorée shop, which must have been offensive to someone with the quiet and refined nature of Robert de Gourdon. Not long afterward, when I was about to make a visit to Nice, de Gourdon warned me that "*Nous sommes en froid avec M. Tabuteau*" (We are "in the cold"—that is, not on good terms—with M. Tabuteau). It is not surprising if there were periods of *froid*, but even as in a family, differences were forgotten, and the underlying bonds of decades of old friendship won out. For over sixty years, from 1904 until his death in 1966, Tabuteau was linked to the Lorée oboe and its makers. He had known Lucien Lorée, Raymond Dubois, and Robert de Gourdon as friend and customer and had bought between 150 and 200 of their instruments.

MARCEL TABUTEAU

9
LESSONS WITH TABUTEAU
My Arrival in Philadelphia, January 1943

After several futile years of trying to enter the Curtis Institute of Music, I finally arrived by bus in Philadelphia during the cold winter of January 1943, hoping to have a few private lessons with the great master. My San Francisco teacher, Julien Shanis, had talked so much about Marcel Tabuteau that I felt I already knew something of him and of what he expected a student to do musically. However, nothing had prepared me for the shock of my first lessons. I was alternately bewildered, puzzled, or indignant and found that I had no basis at all for understanding a person who was without doubt a supreme artist, but who I felt often acted in an erratic and unreasonable manner. I had never been outside of California and had no knowledge of traditional autocratic European methods of treating pupils, some of which seemed to me to approach cruelty. Even though there were exceptions, most of the teachers who descended from nineteenth-century masters were dictatorial and allowed for no dialogue with their students. I later learned that Tabuteau was not the only Curtis teacher who treated his pupils with disdain. The distinguished cellist Orlando Cole, himself a member of the Curtis faculty for over fifty years, told me about *his* teacher, Felix

Salmond: "Nobody could have been meaner than Salmond. It was awful. Those lessons I had with him in the first semester—it was always, 'Why are you studying cello? You're wasting your time. You're wasting my time. What makes you think you could be a cellist?'" Cole reflected: "It's no way to make music. They put you in such shaking fear. How are you going to play? The very talented kids could survive, but I think there were a lot of less than top talents that were ruined by that approach. They couldn't take it."[1] Another of the "greats" of that era was Anton Torello, who had always appeared to me as quite a benevolent figure. "No way, no way," said his student Roger Scott.[2] "If you weren't careful he would chew you up and spit you out. I think he was a classic example of all the European teachers. They ruled by fear. But after a while you prepared some kind of defense against it, and I took in everything but wouldn't give him the satisfaction of knowing that he had hurt me. You make your face like a type of mask and eventually he would land on somebody else." The famous piano pedagogue Isabelle Vengerova was also noted for her severe methods. Each student who lived through several years of training with these Curtis Institute "tyrants" had to find his or her own method of survival.

Quite soon I came to recognize that there was a strong element of the theatrical in Tabuteau's character and even a sense of humor underlying many of his comments, but this did not make it easier to accept when he shouted and screamed at me. He was unpredictable, so one never knew what would happen next. My former teachers had been strict and demanding but, at the same time, polite and considerate. I had never heard Julien Shanis raise his voice. With Tabuteau, I had to make a constant effort to understand what he was trying to impart to me musically, while attempting to fathom the mysteries of a personality totally unlike any I had ever encountered. I realized he had the key to everything I wanted to learn, and I was grateful that he was willing to teach me, but I reacted against being treated in what I regarded as a humiliating manner. Desperately trying to comprehend what made his playing "different," I seesawed back and forth between dejection and elation, hanging onto a rare word of praise as if it were a ray of light from on high.

MARCEL TABUTEAU

From coast to coast oboe standards had not progressed to what they would become several decades later when Tabuteau's influence had spread throughout the whole country. In 1943 I was still playing on the old short-scrape style of reed. Twenty years earlier in 1923, when Shanis was in Philadelphia, Tabuteau had apparently not insisted that he change from the traditional French style of reed making. Shanis religiously adhered to everything Tabuteau told him: how to practice scales and phrase the Barret Studies. If reed making had been an issue, he would surely have followed whatever Tabuteau wanted him to do. This was now to cause considerable problems for me! The kind of control that Tabuteau demanded and the concepts he presented opened a new world, but I was unable to understand the rationale of his approach. Was there conscious reasoning behind his explosions and insults or were they just spontaneous outbursts triggered by his impatience with my shortcomings? It was small comfort to hear that the students before me had been subjected to the same scathing remarks and upbraiding. Each withering look and sharp-tongued appraisal of my playing cast me into depressions that often lasted several days. During the first year I frequently felt like giving up the oboe altogether, but some dogged stubbornness and determination to "get it" kept me going. Only very gradually I managed to overcome the extreme nervousness I felt as I waited for my lesson and heard his steps in the hallway approaching the door, either at his own studio or later at Curtis. More than a year went by before I was able to play somewhat near my best during lessons. Finally I realized that if I was constantly paralyzed by fear, of course he would find me dreadful. I risked his anger by occasionally making remarks which he might easily have found too "fresh." It required walking a fine line to conform to his ideas of acceptable behavior in a student and at the same time try to keep some sense of independence.

A few years ago I found a footlocker containing all the letters I had written to my mother during the mid-1940s. Perhaps I had foreseen the importance of keeping a record of my experiences, as in June 1943, following my first four months of study with Tabuteau, I wrote home saying: "I haven't had time to keep any kind of diary since I've been here, so these letters are my only day-by-day account of what happens

LESSONS WITH TABUTEAU

and I don't think I've left much out. Please keep them together, if you have room—not that they're so wonderful—but I may want to read them over sometime to see what I did when, and especially to remember my lessons."

A half-century later when I *did* reread those letters, I felt that even with no pretension of being a literary effort, they portray more accurately what it really was like *then* than anything I could reconstruct today, which would inevitably be conditioned by all the years since gone by. These old letters were filled with observations about the weather, the prices of food, ration books (we were in the middle of World War II), the Academy of Music, museums, and concerts (especially those of the Philadelphia Orchestra), but it is the ongoing reports about Tabuteau that take precedence over all else. They are presented in this and the following two chapters as a chronicle of the years of my studies. As such, the letters contain expressions of speech current at that time. With the exception of occasional descriptive interludes, these chapters consist of excerpts from letters to my mother in Santa Rosa, California, and a few to Julien Shanis. They begin several days after my arrival in Philadelphia.

Philadelphia, January 24, 1943

I should have written sooner, but I honestly haven't had a chance. I went to hear the Philadelphia Orchestra Saturday night and spent most of the evening observing Tabuteau. It was a popular concert with Alec Templeton as soloist. They made *Marche Slav, Tales from the Vienna Woods,* music by Jerome Kern, and the more interesting Rachmaninoff 2nd Concerto really sound like something. I was surprised how very different Tabuteau sounds in person than on the radio or records—really so good and he doesn't look like such a bad egg at a distance, but at close range—wow! I phoned him last night—and he wanted me to come down to his studio today. He was really very nice on the phone. I had been practicing scales and Barret but when I got there, what does he want me to play but long notes. He had me scared stiff. I know it's absolutely silly, but the man frightens you to death. He just screams at you and works himself into a tantrum trying to get a point across. My mouth was so dry, I couldn't play a thing decently. It really did sound awful—I don't blame him for screaming, but it petrifies me so I can't play. His so-called studio is really a workshop for making reeds. Sort of a dark hole, but right in central Philadelphia.

MARCEL TABUTEAU

I hope I can get over being so nervous, but I can't imagine ever feeling at ease with the man. He's got a terrific eagle eye. Just glares right through you. I wish I didn't have those bands on, because he wants perfection of tone production—but guess I'll just have to see what I can do.[3] He says I blow all wrong (of course). I have to count up to 9 and back to 0, blowing faster all the time. He made me do this out loud. Coming backwards, I left out "4" and he just screamed "*four!*" After 15 minutes with him, I was totally exhausted and couldn't get out of there too fast. I've never run up against anybody else like that—he's a roaring maniac. However, all that he said musically, I agree with; how I'm going to do it is the only question. I'm supposed to go back Thursday. I'll have to tell him I can't take two lessons a week, but all I could do was agree with him today . . . I am still shaking from this afternoon. I hope things will improve, 'cause I couldn't stand much like that. Before I left, he wanted to look at my reeds again; pinched, squeezed, and poked them all and then asked if I would please have Lym send him a shaper exactly like mine, *immediately.*[4] Ship my gouger as soon as you can. I will have to make dozens of reeds trying to get one that will play from 0 to 9 and back to 0. I hope something good will come out of this someday, but it doesn't look very hopeful. According to him, I just move my fingers and blow—it doesn't mean anything and I guess it didn't the way I blew this afternoon. Well, don't worry—I'll probably live through it.

January 27, 1943

It took me until yesterday to recuperate from my session with Tabuteau, and I don't know if I'm prepared for another one tomorrow. At least no one can say I haven't been trying to do what he said to. I practiced hours yesterday and again today . . . When I was calm enough to go back over what he said, I could realize it was really all exceptionally good, but the terrific way in which he says it!! He's really electrifying. I don't know where I ever got the idea he was short; he is really monstrous. As Mr. Shanis always said—"strong as an ox." Whatever his poor, decrepit old age is, you certainly would never know. He has terrific energy. [In January 1943 Tabuteau was fifty-five!] On Monday, shaking all over and with my mouth dry, I couldn't do anything well. He'd say something that sounded like *Ray-dee* and I thought he was saying in French, "ré" which means "D." I didn't do it right and he'd scream. It finally developed he was saying "Rea-dy"— like "get-set-go." My note would come shaking out with a great whack. He told me a note should be started like a hot rod being sunk into butter—no friction—but mine were all like a hot rod coming

LESSONS WITH TABUTEAU

against metal—friction. Very good simile I thought. I hope every lesson won't be torture. I'll have to write down what he says and then at least I can benefit from it later. Did I tell you Tabuteau either didn't notice or say anything about my bands—I'll have to try to keep my mouth shut.

January 28, 1943

I must report to you on my second lesson from Tabuteau. In the first place today we are having *sleet*. I would call it frozen rain, but it's supposed to be sleet—not hail either. It piles up on the ground white like snow and it is very slippery. I started being nervous this morning despite all good intentions. Then I got calmer, but by the time I arrived at Mr. T's Studio I was jittery all over again. Anyhow, I was way ahead of time and found a sort of hallway near his room where I could take out my oboe and warm up. He is really very nice before and after the actual lesson, but the way he gets wrought up and the antics he goes through!—I wish you could see it! Anyhow, I knew what the Ray-dee was all about this time which helped considerably, though I usually came in either too soon, too late, too loud, or too mushy. He says there is me and "ze o-*boe*"—they should be one—"ze oboe is nozzing." You have to say something from the head. His figures of speech are sometimes quite picturesque, such as—"It eez better to write somesing fine with an old stick of charcoal than nothing with a new fountain pen." He almost has hysterics explaining some things, and he makes faces and imitates one's playing. He says I play like letting all the air out of a balloon—Isn't that wonderful? But I felt quite elated because several times he said "good" and I imagine that is really something when he says good. He expects as soft a tone from the oboe as from a violin—and the spaces between the notes have to be measured just so. According to him, my left hand is o.k., but I have to hold my right wrist differently. He suggests I tape a board onto it, to get used to it (!), and my reed doesn't go in my mouth right. The oboe is supposed to be growing on me just like my ear . . . He said something about the trouble with being talented was you had to work at it all your life—always improving. I wonder if he meant to include me or if that was just him. When I was about to leave, he heaves a big sigh and says how discouraged he is—cane and reeds of course being the trouble. He starts working on them before I'm even out the door. Asked me where I got my cane. I said, "Here and there," and he said, "Already gouged?" When I said no, "Raw," he was quite amazed, and when he found out I did my own gouging, he really had to try to conceal his surprise. He isn't letting me play anything except one note at a

— 222 —

MARCEL TABUTEAU

time and five notes up and down. I thought maybe he would expect me to take two lessons a week, and I asked him when I should come next. He asked me if I had much money to spend, to which I, of course, said no, and he suggested every ten days and I said I thought I could make it once a week, which was o.k. with him. It doesn't seem to make a great deal of difference to him.

February 4, 1943

As this was a "lesson day," there is enough to write about. I got down there, and the elevator man said Mr. Tabuteau says he is "veree sorry" but he lost your number and couldn't phone you, but he left a note on the door. *The note:* "Dear Miss . . . . . . I am sorry but we have an afternoon rehearsal. Cannot see you before *four o'clock.* Marcel Tabuteau." This was about quarter to two. I took the note and am saving it as it proves he can write and has a lovely signature on it. However, you can see he had already forgotten my name. I am enclosing it and will you please put it in with my envelope of oboe notes and pictures for safekeeping. So I had two hours of a sort of dreary, rainy, and foggy Philadelphia day to kill. I decided to drop in at Curtis which was only a few blocks distant and then see the exhibit of photographs by Adrian Siegel, the Philadelphia Orchestra man whose pictures were reproduced in *Life.* They were being exhibited at the Art Alliance near Rittenhouse Square, which is right around the corner from Curtis. When I walked in the doors of Curtis, I spied Miss Hoopes sitting at a desk in the lobby, so went over to speak to her.[5] She asked what I was doing, and then she said, "You know, we're going to have our Woodwind Ensemble again next year and a very small woodwind department." She thought that as I am in Philadelphia I might have a good chance . . . Zimbalist was going to recommend that the teachers give first preference to those who had been accepted but turned away! . . . Anyhow, she said it would be up to Tabuteau and as I was already studying with him, I should ask *him* about it. Well, I didn't say anything today, but I will at the first reasonable opportunity.

Then I finally went for my lesson. He was in a good humor today. Almost nice, and didn't scream *quite* as much. He gave me another exercise, still going from 1—9—1. He said he has an entirely new method of teaching—that he is giving away his secrets that he shouldn't tell. He wants me to play long tones for a *month.* It is really rather interesting though, because it isn't just straight plain long tones, but wind and dynamic control and everything—but it's hard, especially with bands. However, I can see when you get it, it would be a basis for all playing and phrasing. When the lesson is over and I'm

LESSONS WITH TABUTEAU

about to leave, he always says how discouraged he is. Today he said he didn't like music anymore. I asked if he could think of what he would like better and he said a job where they only played about fifteen weeks. Notice still music! I said he should like San Francisco. They only have twelve concerts and starve in the summer. He said that would suit him fine (the twelve-concert part, I imagine). Of course, they do have a terrific schedule here. It must be hard to have good reeds enough for all the concerts. Seven whole months of at least two concerts a week and usually more. Only a person with vitality could do it . . .

When I was leaving the building, the elevator man asked if I gave Tabuteau my telephone number, and I said, "Yes, and he pinned it on the wall where he won't lose it," and the E. man said, 'I'll have to remember that so I can tell him where it is!' Talk about absent-minded professors. I asked the E. man if he (I mean Tabuteau) had been in that building very long and he said, "For years." There are little manufacturing places in it, such as for arch supports, and the halls are very dark, but it's perfectly all right and very centrally located. Oh—Tabuteau said I had improved 1,000 times already. Imagine that!

February 11, 1943

Today Tabuteau came limping in—he had been in bed for three days with the gout, hadn't been able to go with the orchestra on tour, and hadn't had any sleep. He surely looked tired, too. I showed him my gouger, but he didn't really have much time to look at it because he had another pupil coming right after me. Anyhow, he was visibly pleased when he saw it and said what a fine machine it was. He was still more interested in my shaper, and asked if he could borrow it for a few days while he had the man who does things for him, copy it. I couldn't very well refuse, so he lent me one similar to it to use. Today he said "Good" more times than bad. And several times he said "Splendid!" When I went over to hand him the $5.00 (I have to be sure I give it right into his hand else he is likely to leave it there), he said, "I have faith in you and I trust you, so next time please just put the money in an envelope and give it to me." He said he hates to handle money, and that he hates money anyway. I said that suited me fine as I hated it too. [In 1943 Tabuteau's fee for private lessons was ten dollars an hour but he had agreed to give me half-hour lessons. William Kincaid charged fifteen dollars an hour.] I forgot to tell you that before this, when I was getting ready to leave, he made a special point to come over and say that it was very fine, very good, or some such thing. So I said it would surely be better when I was rid of my bands, thinking that would be a good time to let him see them and reminding him that he said I couldn't play with crooked teeth. I told him I put chewing gum over them so I could play, and he said, "Oh God, don't tell me that!" I think he was sort of amused. At least he didn't blow up and say there was no use my studying with them on. Oh, another thing he said during the lesson was that it was too bad I hadn't been practicing right all this time (when I was beginning), but that as I was young and *intelligent* it would turn out all right. So he thinks I'm intelligent; well that's something anyhow.

February 15, 1943

I am taking an hour off to listen to the Philadelphia Orchestra play their children's concert on the radio. I am more and more impressed by Tabuteau, but you really miss about three-fourths of his playing from the radio . . . It's something about making every little phrase sound just a little different and putting one's own individuality into it. Tabuteau's tone is really beautiful, as lovely as any violin you could imagine, and you always get the feeling, as he says, "Before you start to play, all the pressure should be behind the note, just like it's there before you turn on a faucet of water." When he plays you know he's not giving every last drop of tone he can possibly squeeze out. He keeps something for himself—sort of up his sleeve—and I feel like he has a terrific sense of humor in his playing sometimes. His playing is very subtle—never loud. Later I saw him walking down the street with smoke fuming out all around him, so I spoke to him and he was very nice . . . I inquired how he felt (his gout, you know), and he said "*Very* much better." He seems to like to discuss it! I can forgive him anything when he plays oboe like that . . . I am impressed by his tremendous vitality and obvious interest in every note he plays. Never lets anything sound boring or commonplace. He fusses enough about his reeds and trying things out before his solos, but when he starts to play, it's just perfect.

February 18, 1943

A lesson with Tabuteau is surely a strain! I am really a nervous wreck tonight, probably partly because he was in such a stew over his reeds. He's having an awful time—keeps fiddling with the blade in his gouger. He says he has the worst cane in the country, but if you get the gouger just right, everything is o.k. The gouge is everything, he says, and that he can't make a good reed anymore. He said he wouldn't wish on anyone, even his worst enemy, what he goes through . . . I mustered courage to ask him about Curtis before I left,

LESSONS WITH TABUTEAU

not knowing whether he would explode or what. Thought it might make him mad if I presumed to bring it up, but he was very nice and said he was willing to take me—if there's room. I'll have to see at Curtis now, if there'll *be* room. Anyhow, he said I would have to make an application and play an audition, "Just for the record." He sort of mumbled it off, "Just form."

An announcement in the newspaper stated that courses in woodwind instruments will be reinstated for 1943–44 and that auditions will be held at the school in April. "Appointed to the faculty are the Philadelphia Orchestra's William Kincaid, flute, and Marcel Tabuteau, oboe, who will also teach woodwind ensemble and string ensemble."

February 25, 1943, Thursday

Had quite a day, but no lesson. Sort of felt like I'd missed the weekly dynamiting . . . I went to Curtis and as far as anything is definite with them, I guess I can go there next Fall. Then I went downstairs to the practice rooms and located Marion Davies, a cellist from Hayward, California whom I once played with in the San Francisco Conservatory Orchestra at Stern Grove. She raved about Tabuteau and how marvelous his woodwind classes were. Said she attended all of them and the way he bawled out the oboe players was terrific. Evidently whatever oboist is studying with him, gets the worst of it. One thing Mr. Shanis misjudged was when he thought Tabuteau might treat a girl nicer than a boy. If the way he roars and screams at me is nice, I'd hate to be a boy and get any worse than that. But everyone has told me how much Tabuteau is respected around here. I heard that Mitchell Lurie, the clarinetist from Los Angeles, stayed in the school an extra year just for Tabuteau's training, and Marion Davies worships Tabuteau. She said some people consider Pablo Casals and Tabuteau the two greatest instrumental artists in the world. That's quite an exalted opinion. No doubt he is a great artist, but the oboe is such a miserable medium of expression to have to battle. When I see him, he is always in a pickle and stew and sounds so discouraged and says he is unhappy.

March 5, 1943

Had a lesson yesterday. I was sort of shaky and Tabuteau was in a terrific mood. Just set to blow up no matter what I did. He really gave me the devil. Not so much for actual playing but for minor points. In the first place, he expected me an hour earlier, mixed it up somehow, mumbled something about that other girl maybe coming, and said, "She is a nuisance anyhow." Wonder if he says that behind my back?

MARCEL TABUTEAU

Well, I can't give you an adequate picture of how he screamed and carried on. But after I had played twelve scales, two octaves each, I was sort of out of breath and then because I didn't get the oboe in my mouth soon enough, he went off on a great harangue, "Hopeless—what's the use—I tell you . . ." etc. I didn't break down, but kept going. On the slow melodies, I thought surely he'd blow up again, but he didn't. Said they were good. Maybe that's just because he didn't have any more time. He had to be at a rehearsal at 4:00 p.m. Afterwards he calmed down and said, "I can't let you play like you did in San Francisco." I replied rather sarcastically, "When in Philadelphia, do as the Philadelphians do," and he said, "That's right." Then I said I don't see how he could stand giving lessons anyhow, it must be so hard on him when *he* could play everything, and he said, "Oh, I am used to that sort of punishment," or maybe it was "torture." Anyhow, tongue in cheek I said, "Well, we all have to make some *sacrifices.*" Mrs. Reynolds [where I was living] thinks he's just awful. "No manners, inexcusable—a lump of clay," she calls him—but I can't explain to her that in between the explosions he comes through with some explanations that make it all worthwhile.

March 10, 1943

If you can get a hold of a March 8 issue of *Time,* you will surely like the article on Tabuteau. It has a picture of him with his foot up on a chair. He must have been interviewed that week I told you he had the gout. It mentions his "medieval shop." Guess that is where I go for lessons! It's really quite a piece of publicity for him and for the oboe in general, as so many people read *Time.* As His Majesty says in the article, which is incidentally headed, *King of the Reeds,* "For forty years I have play the oboe," confessed Marcel Tabuteau, "and still I never know what is coming out. It is a perpetual anxiety, But maybe this is good—I have never the time to get myself bored." I love the way that is worded. I wish you could hear his accent . . . but he has no trouble expressing himself—except when he is beside himself with fury. Then he just sputters and mumbles "*Mais non, mais non.*"

The "medieval-looking fourth-floor workshop" referred to by *Time* magazine, was known to Tabuteau and all his students as the Studio. At first I was disappointed to be having my lessons in this dingy, soot-encrusted fourth-floor room in the Ludlow Building on South Sixteenth Street instead of in the beautiful former mansion that housed the Curtis Institute. However, as the months went by, I came to appreciate the Studio, and one day I scribbled down a detailed description of the place:

LESSONS WITH TABUTEAU

The walls and ceiling are covered in a dull shade of eucalyptus-aqua-green paint. Large pieces peeling off reveal the light tan plaster underneath. Limp faded dark-blue and orange cretonne curtains droop at the two windows which face out onto a narrow alley. By one of the windows, a large wicker chair with several pieces broken out of the back. The other furniture is an odd assortment of several chests of drawers mostly filled with cane. Above a cubbyhole on the left side of the room, a shelf holds empty Egyptian cigarette boxes stacked precariously high, along with a Chinese ginger jar and a tan pottery jug. Dusty books, Kleenex and paper towels are all piled on top of a dark brown chest over which hangs a framed charcoal sketch of Tabuteau in younger years and a little mirror dulled by layers of soot.[6] Another desk is stuffed with old letters, union papers, ads and pictures, all black with dust, and below it, two shelves of French books.

A cretonne-covered trunk holds the big white basin where cane is soaked, split, and rough gouged; nearby, the cutter, splitter and large flat grind stone. Burlap sacks filled with cane sit on the floor. Another cubbyhole crammed with grimy orchestral scores and solfège books is covered by a cloth embroidered with the motto *Dans la vie faut pas s'en faire.* (In life, nothing is worth worrying about.) A huge inverted glass dome hangs by chains from the middle of the ceiling; its dim bulb provides the only lighting for the room. The rough wooden floor is partly covered by a fringed carpet worn thin by years of use, its design of nondescript colors only barely visible.

But the focal point of the room is the desk where Tabuteau makes his oboe reeds. It is littered with knives, pieces of cane, reed tubes, an ash-tray from Bookbinders restaurant, cigarette boxes, nail polish, sharpening stones, spools of silk—all the essential items of use to an oboe player. A small adjustable lamp with a 40-watt bulb serves for close work. No chair in front of the desk, only a couple of ancient piano stools. On the wall behind the reed desk, autographed photographs of Toscanini and Stokowski and a large one of the Philadelphia Orchestra taken on the occasion of the 1916 performance of Mahler's *Eighth Symphony*. An A-440 bar, a thermometer, and a 1934 calendar complete the "decor." This is only a thumbnail sketch of the room, its real personality being integrally tied up with that of M. Tabuteau.

I later learned from Mme Tabuteau that the Studio had once been a considerably cleaner and more attractive place. She told me that when the cretonne was fresh and the soot less thick, people had been invited

The Studio at 15 South 16th Street, 4th floor of the Ludlow Building in the 1940s. Tabuteau's reed-making desk with photographs of Arturo Toscanini and Leopold Stokowski on the wall. The signed photographs include the following dedications to Tabuteau: from Toscanini, "à Marcel Tabuteau, Souvenir de A. Toscanini, 23-4-1915"; from Stokowski, "à Marcel Tabuteau en admiration de son art."

there for tea. This would have been difficult to imagine when I saw it. She called his "workshop" *La Souricière* (the Mousetrap). John Minsker remembered a narrow dark staircase leading to an attic room where a distinguished-looking elderly man, a goldsmith, Mr. Pierce, had a little shop where he made loving cups and repaired jewelry. Minsker believed that he was the person who made an early version of the planing board that Tabuteau favored for preparing oboe cane.[7]

March 13, 1943

I think I must see Tabuteau from a different angle there in his shop than one would otherwise. Every week I hear how discouraged he is over reeds and everything. How for forty years he's been working at them, and he still doesn't know the secret of what makes a good one. Said he found an old trunk he hadn't opened for about ten years and what did I think was in it? "Cane?" I say, and he said 10 lbs. of it he didn't even know he had! I said that would keep him going for another ten years, and he said if he thought he was going to play the

LESSONS WITH TABUTEAU

Tabuteau sitting at his desk in the studio scraping on a reed. Photo by Zev Pressman.
Philadelphia Orchestra Archives.

oboe for ten more years, he would jump right out that window. He keeps saying he is tired of it and is going to quit—that he hasn't been able to make a good reed since December 15. He certainly is explicit. I wonder what happened on December 15? Ever since then he has been trying to get a "good gouge" by constantly grinding and changing the shape of the blades. Now it seems all his gougers and blades are out of whack and they (the reeds) keep getting worse.

Tabuteau gouging cane. Cane shavings, his micrometer, a plane, corks, a reed case, and knives all cover his desk. Photo by Adrian Siegel.

I had sent him a card after the last concert, which I didn't think he would even notice or remember. The oboe solo was *so* good I said I wanted to stand up and shout "Tabuteau," but remembering he said oboists should be refined, decided to do it by mail instead. Anyhow, soon after I came into the studio he said he received my card and seemed *very* pleased that I had expressed my appreciation. I had sent it before I knew about his write-up in *Time* or I probably wouldn't have. His theory about good playing is very interesting if true. He says "feeling" has nothing at all to do with it. The musician who just plays with "feeling" doesn't know what he's doing—that everything depends on intelligence and control. His playing gives the impression that he has some indefinable secret—he does everything so differently and so beautifully, you'd think it was inspiration, but according to him, it is hard, cold, calculation—knowing just how and where to place the notes and what to do for contrast. He knows *exactly what* he is doing. It's taking infinite care over every detail. If this is right, great playing requires more intelligence, patience, and imagination than musical talent—but still that doesn't explain just what makes one or two people so different. Perhaps the "talent" lies in thinking or knowing *what* to do . . . Probably the majority ignore the hair-line differences.

LESSONS WITH TABUTEAU

Tabuteau "sighting" the line of the guide and bed of one of his gouging machines.
Photo by Adrian Siegel.

[Tabuteau would never cease speaking of playing with understanding and intelligence, but later he would also say much more about the character, the spirit, or the emotional element of a particular piece of music.]

You should hear the way I play scales now. *Slower* than I ever have in my life. Then there are twelve little short exercises in the beginning of Barret that I am having a dreadful time relearning, as before, I played them as a bunch of notes, and he says I don't know the first thing about music. I group the wrong things together. I used to love fast things and would rather practice ten difficult études than one slow melody, but now I have just the opposite problem. I actually play the slow melodies better that the fast studies.

Tabuteau is so complex—certainly a person it would be very difficult to really know. Today he started in on something about how all his pupils sound or play just like he does—all try to copy him—and all the good it does him, is that they'll steal his job away from him. I should have reminded him he wanted to quit anyhow, but I said I hardly thought he had to worry about that, as none of them *were* him.

MARCEL TABUTEAU

He said that's one thing he never did—imitate his teacher. But Tabuteau insists that you *do* play like he does, as nothing else is any good, so he shouldn't blame everyone for imitating him! Then he said, "However, if you can imitate well, that's already something." I wonder if he's logical or not. Then he wishes he were back in France. That's where he belongs, says he. Been here too long He thinks California has a *nice* climate all the time.

I meant to make a note of it if I ever saw him laugh. That is, when I went for a lesson. I've seen him laugh with Kincaid, the flutist, on the stage. Well, he laughed twice Thursday. First, when I told him the trouble I'd just had about practicing, and then when we discussed whether he'd starve if I didn't take a lesson next week. So you see, he does laugh, but at what subjects?! It was because all of a sudden Thursday noon, Dr. Reynolds [where I lived] blew up and said the oboe was driving him crazy and he couldn't stand it anymore. Well, I had to try to get through my next lesson on top of that and then figure out what to do. I'd rather face Tabuteau in his worst temper than go through that again. This is what Tabuteau found very funny! He is very decent though about my not coming for lessons oftener or even regularly. He says, "Just do the best you can."

March 18, 1943

Now I am working nights at Burpees—"Seeds that Grow," which should enable me to continue studying. [I started out on the night shift, 11 p.m to 8 a.m.] Just so I can just keep up enough energy to continue taking a lesson a week as long as Tabuteau is here. One thing about him so far, he is more concerned with quality than quantity, and the music is Barret, so while I have to practically learn it over again, it is not as bad as if I were totally unfamiliar with it.

March 20, 1943

The last two nights I have had a hard time trying to keep awake at work. I had to go to the dentist yesterday morning so couldn't sleep then. He (Dr. Wright) had come back from New York one night on the same train as Tabuteau. He said, "I saw Marcel." Evidently "Marcel" told him I was a fine musician and coming along splendidly. It made me feel very good and it was nice of him to tell me. Tabuteau asked Dr. W. if he were the one putting all "those things" in my mouth, and he had to admit to being the guilty party, and T. said "Beautiful, Beautiful!" whatever he means by that. Anyhow, I was discussed behind my back by my dentist and Tabuteau—quite a unique combination.

— 233 —

LESSONS WITH TABUTEAU

March 24, 1943

Phoned Tabuteau. He was gone as usual, and I got Madame and arranged to take a lesson tomorrow. He is playing a solo in a recital Friday night. Nancy Mae Iden (my flutist friend) and I are going to the orchestra concert Friday afternoon when Piatigorsky is soloist and then have dinner and go to Tabuteau's recital. I asked Mme T. what he was playing and she said she didn't know much about it except it's a modern composition by a girl composer! She asked me how I liked Philadelphia and was very friendly. She says "He always forgets. He forgets everything!" [On the program for the Music Guild, Tabuteau was to play the Handel *G minor Concerto* and a new *Suite* by Vivian Fine.]

March 27, 1943

I guess when last I wrote I was supposed to have a lesson the next day. Well, I went down there and the elevator man said Tabuteau had left about forty-five minutes ago with another Frenchman and didn't say anything about coming back, but I expected he'd turn up a little late. About twenty minutes after three he still hadn't come. I was sitting on the elevator man's stool downstairs (I should find out his name—he is really very nice). It was such a pleasant day, I didn't want to go up to the dark fourth floor. Pretty soon a couple of well-dressed ladies came in and one said, "Are you the young lady?" and it was Madame Tabuteau. He hadn't come home at all the night before and she hadn't been able to give him my message. She said hunting for Tabuteau was really something. When she found out he had been in his studio, she said, "Then at least he is not dead!" (But didn't sound very worried!) He had been in New York with the orchestra. She calls him "Tabuteau" just like everyone else does. She is a nice-looking woman, and very talkative. Blonde hair—probably not natural but it looks pretty anyhow. She said I should get "the man" to let me in so I could practice, but he and I decided that wouldn't be such a good idea without T's permission. He was going to let me into another room so I could wait awhile just in case Tabuteau turned up, but then some man called me to the phone and said Tabuteau was on the line asking if I was waiting—so then I talked to him, and he said he just came back and he could not teach. So I went home. At least I had met Madame, and there was a little excitement anyhow . . .

Saturday was a big day musically. I met Nancy Mae at the Academy and we went to the orchestra concert. T's solo in the J.C. Bach (*Sinfonia in B-flat major*) was great, and Piatigorsky was wonderful. After dinner we went to Tabuteau's recital. I am enclosing a program. Tabuteau is certainly the most many-sided creature. Last night he was an entirely different person. He looked so pleasant—came out smiling and beamed at the audience and looked so neat in dress clothes. Very handsome. Everybody who is anybody musically was there. He played first the Handel *G minor Concerto* that everyone plays—Sargeant, Remington, Lois Wann, Mitchell Miller—ad infinitum.[8] Of course, he played it beautifully—the best I've heard it. He played the fast parts slower than they're usually taken. It was a flawless performance and he was loudly applauded. Mary Louise Bok and Zimbalist were there. He (Z.) seems a very quiet, almost mouse-like man. Then later, Tabuteau played a new composition which had been selected from over one hundred works submitted to the guild. He is very good at making modern music sound like something. The girl (Vivian Fine) who wrote the new piece was sitting near me, and I spoke to her afterwards. She wanted to meet Tabuteau, so I took her back and caught him before he left. Everyone was congratulating him and was he charming! Saying such clever things. How he couldn't play the oboe anymore but he tried to do justice to the music. Laughing—you'd think he was the nicest man in the world when he laughs like that. What a different side I see when I go for my lessons. I see him in his shirt sleeves, fretting over pans of soaking cane, grinding the gouger blades, being discouraged and wishing he were back in France. I must say he has the respect of people in Philadelphia. He is definitely a "personality" here and people who don't know anything about oboe or music know that they have to like everything he does. Of course he has been here since 1915 and is a character.

April 1, 1943

I have just returned from my lesson. He really turned up today—I wondered if he would, it being April Fool's Day. You could feel heat in the sun at last. In fact, it was almost too hot yesterday, and the air seems to lack the freshness of California. Even Tabuteau remarked on the weather. Miss Hoopes from Curtis just this minute called, and said Mr. T was having his auditions on April 26 at 2:00 p.m. and that I should be there. That should be an interesting experience—1943, and my third type of audition. 1941—the real thing. 1942—by mail (long distance type), and 1943, heaven only knows what. Anyhow, I was going to tell you about my lesson. I hadn't had one for *three* weeks! He didn't rant at all today—only raised his voice a couple of times. He was explaining something about this new, original system of his—says it would revolutionize the whole foundation and conception of music and that it is what makes his playing sound *different*—that everyone imitates him, but they don't know the secret so they don't sound the same. It is all

LESSONS WITH TABUTEAU

based on numbers and when you know that, you can actually hear them when he plays. You can hear 1, 1-2, 2-3, 3-4 as plain as day. Every note is placed exactly at a certain spot as if on a micrometer. It seems to me it would take almost a superhuman accuracy and perfection to play like that and you'd think anything so calculated and mathematical would sound cold and dry, but it certainly doesn't the way he does it. He'll have me play five notes over and over to get just the right impulses. Then he also scraped on my reed and tried it on my oboe and he could sound the same as he usually does on my oboe while I can't sound anything like him. He says of course he cannot expect me to change over night. I'm surprised he doesn't expect me to do just that. However, I think his system of thinking of notes by numbers (which is something different again from his reeds), would put a very solid foundation under everything you do and would keep your playing from sounding aimless and pointless. There is such a difference between just blowing an oboe and playing *music* regardless of the difficulties of the instrument. Tabuteau makes you play from the top of your head to the bottom of your feet—not, as he says, "From your neck up." It may not sound any different to the average listener, but it's what makes you feel there is a lot more behind every *note* he plays.

Just before I left, a violinist came in and Tabuteau had to ask my name again so he could introduce me. He asked me to write it down on the envelope (the one with the $5.00 in it) and said he would now remember it for all time—I wonder! Anyhow, he was very pleasant then, and admonished his friend for kicking up the edge of his frayed old rug. The man in the elevator (John, I found out his name, so I will henceforth refer to him thusly) calls everyone who goes up to visit Marcel, "Some Frenchman." He said he took some Frenchman up to see him—the man I had just met was named "Lipkin" a member of the Philadelphia Orchestra.

April 9, 1943

My lesson was a dilly! Tabuteau was just on the verge of being in a very bad humor, I could tell. He was sort of at the explosion point, but I had a pretty good lesson anyhow. He called me "*Stupide!*" and then later tells me "good," "fine." Said it was the best tone he had heard out of me yet and liked the new reed I made. He was counting in French half the time. Wish I had taken more French and less Latin. Then the most unexpected thing happened. As I was packing up my stuff, he asked me if I was good at writing letters and I, of course, said, "Oh yes, very good." He said he had about fifty—no time to answer—would

MARCEL TABUTEAU

like to get rid of them—and he never writes letters. It seems if I will write them he will give me some lessons. I don't know how many lessons it's going to be worth to him, but anyhow, it's a good proposition, I think. He said they aren't to friends of his and the content will show the answer. I hope I can do it right. He wanted to know if I had studied that. I said "No," but I could type, which I guess impressed him enough, as he didn't seem to care how they were written. I'm supposed to go up to his place Sunday about 5:30 and get them. Then I will know more about it. In case you shouldn't get very many letters from me for awhile, you will know it's because I'm writing them for Tabuteau. I really think he *should* have a secretary! Have thought so ever since I never received answers from him and Mr. Shanis didn't either. It really will be wonderful to earn a few lessons that way. However, I hope I'll have time to work another week at Burpee's as I need cash for living and bills too.

April 12, 1943

To show you what a condition I'm in, I just went all over the room looking for my ink bottle, only to find it in my hand! Also, last night at Nancy's I broke a cracker in two unevenly, and said "Excuse me!" On Sunday evening I went over to the Drake. Just asked what number was Tabuteau, and nobody paid the slightest attention to my going up to the fourteenth floor. It wasn't what I had imagined. The Drake is one of the biggest-looking buildings in downtown Philadelphia, but inside the halls were narrow and dark, and it's just like a hotel. Outside their apartment I could hear the radio and their voices. They had some mystery (!) program on and started to argue when I knocked. I don't know whether he had forgotten or what. Anyhow, he let me in and started fussing around, and I could see he hadn't gotten anything together and was in a general mess. The room was so little and cluttered up. I had pictured a spacious big apartment like some I've seen in San Francisco, but I guess he hasn't much time to live in it anyhow. There was a good view of the city, though, such as it is. On the walls were enormous bright modernistic paintings. It all really looked typically French "artiste"—an old oboe standing in one corner and in another, all sizes of empty bottles, maybe from French champagne and wine. It seemed boxes and papers were cluttered all over—twice too much for the size of the room. At least, that was my impression. I didn't look too carefully. The paintings were very abstract, just masses, but certainly colorful. So I suggested I get the letters some other time, which seemed to relieve him, and he wanted me to come back today. Finally he asked me if I wanted a drink (!) before I left. I had visions of myself staggering out of there and of course refused. He was probably just being polite, in his way, anyhow.

April 13, 1943

I went up to T's again. The place looked entirely different. Bigger, and they must have cleaned it up. I had a completely other impression. He actually got about sixteen letters together with the help of Madame, and I wish I could tell you about all of them. Everything under the sun. I have to make a hotel reservation, and answer cane, reed, and oboe inquiries. (I recommended myself to make some reeds for one fellow!—T. doesn't care.) Someone writes from Florida about good cane growing in his back yard, and somebody else wants to know how to become a professional oboist in the shortest possible time. Old friends and distant ones, a Canadian who met him fishing, and even Mitchell Lurie, a clarinetist I know, who wants his picture. One letter was in French, which made my heart sink, but I soon saw I could read it (at least with the aid of a dictionary). I asked him, "Could the man read English?" and he said, "Write in English" (as if I *could* write in French!!!) He assumes I know a lot, it seems to me. I really feel quite honored that he trusts me to do it. Some go as far back as 1941!! He doesn't even really read them and many *are* a waste of his time. I have to be *nice* in all of them, especially to music publishers. And of course the article in *Time* added more letters to his pile. Don't you think this is rather thrilling? Tabuteau's private secretary? He said (jokingly, I think), if I'm no good I'm fired. Madame was very nice and more helpful; gave me paper and will pay for the stamps. He really needs a secretary as many of these letters do require answers. I have done a few already. He wants to see and sign them.

April 16, 1943

Took about ten letters to Tabuteau on Thursday, and he liked them. I only had to do one over, and that's his fault because he didn't read it in the first place. A man from Brooklyn wrote about his sister having visited Lorée, brought back lots of tube cane, and as he doesn't play oboe anymore, offered to send some to Tabuteau. Problem was, T wants it all, not just a sample. He is so rattle-brained. I knew to even get him to sign them would be a problem, so I brought pen, bottle of ink, and blotter, and then had to tell him *where* to put his John Henry when I had it plainly typed at the bottom of the page. I wrote one letter to a boy in the Navy who must be something unusual, as Tabuteau is going to write to him personally and even added a line on this letter.

MARCEL TABUTEAU

In writing to someone who was in his woodwind ensemble for *three years*, I asked him how he called his students, by first or last names and he said, "I don't call them anything. I don't even know their names!"

Mrs. T (or rather Madame—why do they all call her "Madame" and him Mr., not Monsieur?) said that old oboe in the apartment was from *Tibet*.

Later in April, when I still had some of the first batch of Tabuteau's letters to answer, I ran out of Drake stationery and was unable to reach Madame on the phone to get more. Realizing I would not have any "to take tomorrow," I thought, "Maybe I'd better *pay* him for my lesson. I don't want to take advantage of him!" Most of the time I had to try to imagine how Tabuteau would answer a specific letter and then have him check it over. Occasionally, however, he told me exactly what he wanted to write. After the article in *Time* Magazine, he received many letters from young high school students. Only two have survived among my papers. One begins:

> Dear Mr. Tabuteau:
> You are my idol! Why? Because you are a wonderful oboeist. I play a tuba in the school band, but it is my one ambition to play an oboe . . . [after asking where he could buy a second hand oboe, as none is available in his small school, he continues:] Wish you would send me an old reed as a much valued souvenir . . . I am a sophomore in the Galeton high school and am fourteen years old.
>
> SINCERELY,
ROBERT P. MURPHY

The other letter tells how "after I read that you were the world's champion on the oboe, I made it a point to listen to the Philadelphia Orchestra, and the oboe solos sounded marvelous. I am a girl of fourteen. I have studied oboe for one and one-half years and love it!..I am contemplating taking up oboe with the desire to play in some Philharmonic Orchestra . . . [and she asks for his advice about] "the best colleges for such a training."

I kept a copy of Tabuteau's reply to this letter:

> My dear little girl,
> If I were you I would not have any more to do with the oboe than the pleasure of *listening* to it. I have been playing oboe for 45 years,

LESSONS WITH TABUTEAU

and for 44 years my greatest desire has been to give up that very ungrateful instrument. Stop now while you still love it, and when you quit, let me know.

Very fatherly,
Marcel Tabuteau

April 21, 1943

The war is beginning to affect Curtis. They can't even get good *violinists*. I think only about eight auditioned. Next year it will probably consist of boys under eighteen and girls. Even the three 4-F's who were in the school have been inducted into the Army. Of course, there's still as good a faculty as ever, and they aren't compelled to keep up a certain number of enrollments, so perhaps the quality won't suffer too much. However, it won't be anywhere near the same—but then no school is now. Did I tell you I asked Tabuteau what I should do at my audition—saying I didn't want to learn a solo. He just laughed and said, "Formality," that I could play part of my lesson. I discovered they had scheduled the auditions for the Monday after Easter and the Philadelphia Orchestra is playing its usual Friday-afternoon concert then instead of on Good Friday, so Tabuteau had forgotten that, I guess. I mentioned it to Miss Hoopes, who had also overlooked it, so now she has to rearrange it. There is apparently a girl coming from Minneapolis. Remember two years ago when I was the *only* girl who tried out? Poor Tabuteau—he'll be lucky if he even *hears* a *boy* this time. Wonder if he would want *two* girls at once? Probably would prefer boys if he could get them, but he never says anything to me about being a girl, which is quite good for him. Of course, I don't know *what* he *thinks*!

My last lesson was quite good. He only got mad once because my head made a shadow on the music stand. (Maybe I should remove my head!) . . . The way I place my notes on my wind annoys him no end. There has to be a perfect continuity, and you really have to get a mental picture in your head of the *line* of the music. He is always talking about the *Line*. One thing I did pleased him—something he demonstrated first—and he said he couldn't do it any better himself. For him, you can't practice a lesson, and then dismiss it from your mind after you play it, because you have to keep putting the same things into practice, and also, he makes you go back and play the same exercises over in a different key, so there's no forgetting, but it surely takes concentration.

MARCEL TABUTEAU

April 23, 1943

I could have said something to Tabuteau yesterday but I guess it's a good thing I didn't. I suppose it's all according to the mood he's in, but I got to thinking no one else could get away with the way he acts. If it weren't that he is such a fine artist, one wouldn't tolerate it. If you don't understand something he says the *first* time, the second time he invariably shouts it out in a voice you could hear for ten blocks. Yesterday after I played something that he said was "pretty good," and I commented "could be better," off he went on how I didn't have to give *my* opinion—he would do the talking—blah, blah, and on and on. He was really almost beside himself. That made me mad and I talked right back rather loudly and said, "All right, in the future even if I think it's terrible, I'll keep it to myself," and he said, "That's right." And when I was about to leave and was trying to find out about my next lesson, he said, "Don't complicate matters," and bawled me out for replying "O.K." "And don't say Ho. K. to me! If there's anything I can't stand, it's that Ho.K.!" he screams. I almost said, "O.K., I won't say it again"—but instead I said, sarcastically, I hope, "Very well, in the future I shall endeavor to eliminate it from my vocabulary." Then I wasn't able to bring him his letters because I couldn't get any paper . . . but he expects me to do them anyhow. So I paid him cash for yesterday's lesson . . . He's really impossible. He blames Miss Hoopes for scheduling his auditions wrong when he's the one who forgot about the concert! Of course, you have to try and be impervious to the way he acts, because while there are a lot of good points in the lessons, his explosions stand out in your mind afterwards.

Monday, April 26, 11:30 p.m.

Auditions today! They had me on last (sort of an afterthought), and I was able to help some of the even "nervouser" kids by telling them where to warm up their oboes and loaned my Barret to one poor boy who didn't bring a piece of music. I guess my only consolation is that others go through torture too. That kid didn't go to sleep 'til 3 o'clock last night! There were four girls including me, and three boys. Poor Tabuteau—I guess they were quite punk, as he actually smiled and sunk into a chair when I came in. He said it's so sad—they come such distances and have no conception of what it's all about. He doesn't *want* two girls! When I left he didn't know what he was going to do. I *presume* I'm duly accepted again. He just had me play one *short* little simple melody—much less than at my first audition. It was funny—

LESSONS WITH TABUTEAU

Miss Hoopes sits outside and keeps track of the schedule. He asked me what *her name* was!!!, saying "Whoops?" in his special accent. He surely doesn't bother himself much about any other person besides Tabuteau. Of course, the type of nervousness I had today was not like that of the first audition. At least I know what the others went through, but still some of them don't have enough perception to even get nervous for Tabuteau!

Everything winds up this week. The last two symphony concerts and then the orchestra leaves for a ten-day tour. I think Tabuteau does not stay in Philadelphia after that, so I don't know what I'll do next. The almost three months I've studied with him have just been a drop in the bucket and yet I imagine if I could put all I've learned into practice, I'd know a good deal. In the number of pages of music covered, it is *nothing*. I've done about *six pages* in Barret! But *how*!!

April 28, 1943 [on Drake paper]

I have lots to write about from the last two days. Tuesday night I was at Tab's apartment for about an hour. It was very interesting. They argued in French most of the time over what I should write and I walked out with three letters. They could have done them themselves in that time—very funny. He has a fine English horn and first he will sell it, then he won't. I would surely like it myself but of course it's $300! However, that is very reasonable for a practically new one. Then Madame gave me a check to enclose with an order for fishing hooks and flies—$13.10, and didn't even fill in the "Pay to the order of." I had to write in the name of the company. That's trusting me, isn't it? I could have just as easily put in my own. Of course, who would do that—but even so. Also, he had me send a money order he had made out in January to some French boy in Canada. They were just finishing dinner and had bottles of salad oil all over the table and lots of lettuce and artichokes, and he guzzled some tall glass of something down at one gulp! Oh, I had asked Tabuteau about Curtis and he said—this was definite—I was in—unless (Madame T said), a bomb dropped on the school or something. Then at Curtis the registrar told us what courses we would have to take and today I received another formal letter of acceptance.

May 2, 1943

I wanted to attend both final orchestra concerts, Thursday night and Friday afternoon, as it was my last chance to hear Tabuteau this year. I surely hope I had the camera focused right when I snapped his picture after the concert. It took a little nerve to wait at the stage door and nab him, but he was very nice and *posed* for me. You should see how he bows and smiles to passing Philadelphia matrons and old ladies who speak to him. He probably doesn't know them, at least their names, from Adam, but he puts on a charming act.

May 12, 1943

Well, today was my last lesson for a good while I guess. Of course, I have a sort of "let out of school" feeling, relaxed from tension, but I'm really going to miss Tabuteau. I was lucky today and had a good lesson . . . Met a boy, Bill Criss, the one who was accepted when I didn't get in. He is now in the army. He remembered me—or at least that *one* girl had tried out then. He said there were actually about fourteen boys who tried that year, that there was only one vacancy and that it was between the two of us. It really appears I would have been accepted if I'd been a boy. According to Bill Criss, every student with Tabuteau goes through what I've been experiencing—the insults and all. Some have gotten it for saying "O.K., Hello," for not carrying cigarette paper in their cases, or for holding their wrists wrong. This boy says T's main objective is to discipline you à la the European "Master" system, to really break you down before he even teaches you the oboe. I now make a point to read the headlines on the way to my lesson as he always says, "What are the news?" and it seems you're supposed to know! [Tabuteau apparently felt that as the French word *nouvelles* is plural, it should be the same in English.]

To come to today—thank goodness I've had this time to practice as I'd have hated to have a poor last lesson. I have gotten used to the funny, gloomy old building. I remember my reaction the first time— it always seemed to be a dull, dark day too. I said to myself, "And to think I might have taken my lessons in a beautiful Curtis studio instead of in this old hole," but now it's more like, "I'll probably *have* to take them at Curtis instead of here." Anyhow, he really didn't say anything very bad about my playing, and it was, "That sounds *pretty good.*" He has his own special way of saying this. Only once he told me not to play something as if I were about to be seasick. When you are able to change your tone and reeds enough to suit him, then it is phrasing and *how* to play things that he mainly talks about. He really was quite approving today. Possibly the season being over, he feels better. At the end of the lesson, he started comparing the bores of our instruments. He is continually changing his oboes. Puts half of one with half of another. Then he would ask me which sounded best and I'd have to answer, wondering if I was hitting the right one. A couple combinations were so close, he was getting me all confused.

LESSONS WITH TABUTEAU

Finally I said, it all depends what you want, and what type of music you're playing, and I don't know which is *best*. You have to be *careful* what you say with him, but evidently I struck the right "combination," as he said, "That's just it," and that he didn't know either. So we packed up and after a few more comments, parted for the summer. He is so occupied with himself and his oboe problems, I really think you could study with him and not learn anything if he didn't choose to help you.

I was still talking to John [the elevator man] when T. came down and told him to let me in to the Studio after T. left so I could put away his tools. Part of my duties as secretary, I guess. I made sure to *pay* him for today's lesson and also included 25¢ change from postage money he gave me, which he very generously gave me back and said, "Keep that for *yourself*." Wasn't that magnanimous? I really didn't want it, but made some remark about getting a milkshake. I must say, I didn't get many lessons out of the secretary deal (one to be exact!), but I really don't care, as he has been generous with his time, almost always giving me more than half an hour (usually an hour or more), and after all, when I see how he *can* be, he could have charged me $10 a lesson. You just are forced to admit, it's a favor if he teaches you. The letters are very easy to answer, and it's sort of fun. Mr. Shanis says it proves he likes me, but I don't think anything about Tabuteau proves anything. He is absolutely unique. He has—I don't know how to describe it—a characteristic—for instance, I ordered these flies and fish hooks and he received them. They were really for some Frenchman in Canada and I was supposed to write to tell him they had come, but when I read the part of this Frenchman's letter where he says, "They will soon be very scarce," then T. says, "Why should I tell him anything at all? Don't answer the letter—if they are going to be scarce, why should I not keep them for myself?" Isn't he awful? He is that way about cane too—in fact everything. He is interesting though, and an endless topic of conversation among all the students—not only oboists. He is a *character*, and you can't help but think he is part of an era too that is irreplaceable. When he's gone there may be other great oboists and musicians, but there'll be nobody to really take his place. I never could understand Mr. Shanis' worshipful way of speaking of T. and his great admiration for him, but I can see it now. He *gets* you. One could go on and on about him. I definitely feel it is worth almost anything to take advantage of the opportunity to study with him."

MARCEL TABUTEAU

LESSON NOTES

The lessons, as described in my letters, were often close to traumatic experiences, but fortunately I also kept a little notebook in which I wrote down the valuable counsels Tabuteau gave me week by week. If faithfully followed, they provide a basis for control of all the elements necessary to play expressively on the oboe. The notes began on January 25, 1943:

1. Start long tones like an engine, gradually, not sudden, increasing the wind intensity by blowing faster from 1–9, while the lips do the opposite. On the return, 4-3-2-1 must be up, up up inflections before the "down" resolution on 1.

2. There should be no friction—begin the note like a hot rod cutting into butter. The gradations [of sound or intensity] should be as fine as those on a micrometer.

3. In a series of notes separate them but gauge the *space* between the longer notes, decreasing the space as the notes get longer.

4. The oboe should be a part of you. In itself it means nothing. *You* should speak. Beautiful phrasing is more thinking first than anything. Think before you speak or play. Hear the tone in your head before you produce it. (A dark, smooth tone, not shrill.)

5. Practice on one note 1-5-1, sustained and tongued. When changing notes, play between the notes with a perfect legato. Play these five notes as if they are the most beautiful music in the world. Scale-wise passages are the most beautiful.

6. When beginning a note say *Ta* not Blah, and don't sound like the air coming out of a balloon. *Be ready to play.*

7. Silence—and then a tone starting out and coming back to silence is most beautiful. Silence—quiet—is important. Just create more and more disturbance in the air—gradually—not sudden.

8. Be every bit as particular in practice as at lessons.

9. Have something to say, not just moving your fingers and having it sound like an oboe. When the *oboe* talks it means nothing.

All of the above comments were made in my first two lessons. By my third lesson on February 4, I was admonished not to "pump the wind into the notes. No matter how many notes you play, do it with the continuation of the wind, like bowing on a violin."

> Don't force for volume. Be conscious of what you do. Analyze how you finish the last articulated note. In connecting notes, float like

an eagle, don't flap like a duck. In a series of 1-9-1, hold the final attacked note as long as possible, letting air escape through the nose. Between 1 and 0 there must be a mile.

Have the air pressure *there before* you start to play. Like the pressure in a faucet. Analyze what you do when it is good, so you can be sure you know you are doing.

A dark, smooth tone should be velour—like velvet. Not scratchy like sandpaper.

Every reed is different—you must change the position of the lip accordingly.

By February 18, we had progressed to making gradations from 1 to 13 and back to 1. Then we began doing three sets of scales in chromatic sequence, C Major and A minor, D-Flat Major and B-Flat minor, D Major and B minor, as well as the chromatic scale from C to high E, all detached and slurred, with the admonition to change position of lips when going to the high notes and not to play like steps of a staircase but in a spiral.

I began to understand more fully all that I had learned in these first ten lessons and became convinced of the logical base of Tabuteau's "system." I saw that in playing the notes of the 1-9-1 pattern, if you are counting in 4/4 time, the fifth and the ninth will arrive on a downbeat (or down impulse) and the notes in between should be played with "up" inflections, all of which can then be transferred to scales and applied to musical phrases.

After over a month spent on trying to achieve some control over single notes and scale-wise patterns, I finally began the melodies in the Barret book. Now he gave even more attention to inflections, the "up and down" directions, which must be in the right places in the melodic line. Recognizing that the oboe's great possibility is to express the essence of a musical thought, he said, "It is better to practice a few notes carefully than to play one thousand—especially on the oboe." I began to realize that with Tabuteau's approach, as much significance could be condensed into a short phrase as something thinly spread throughout several pages of music. In 1995, fifty years after the days when he played in the Philadelphia Orchestra, John Minsker reminisced about the spot at the end of the 5/4 movement in the Tchaikovsky *Sixth Symphony* where each woodwind instrument repeats a four-note "sighing" phrase. "Tabuteau did something that was so superior to the way everybody else played it. You know, he lifted the dotted eighth and then he came down with color and intensity on the quarter, eighth ending."

SUMMER INTERLUDE

The first few months of my lessons with Tabuteau were coming to an end, but now I could look forward to continuing with him in the fall at the Curtis Institute. The only immediate problem was how to get through the summer. I was lucky to find some work in a photo shop in Germantown near where I lived. In the few weeks that Tabuteau still remained in Philadelphia, I began to see another more "human" side of his nature and also became better acquainted with Madame Tabuteau.

On May 20, 1943, I wrote: "Saw in the paper that Tabuteau had an operation Monday and is in good condition. It just said an abdominal operation and that he is in a Philadelphia hospital. Glad he came through it o.k." Almost sixty years would go by before I learned the full "story" of this "abdominal operation" (see chapter 10).

Two days later, on Saturday, May 22, I wrote: "I have been trying to get Madame Tabuteau on the phone several evenings with no success. Finally reached her this morning. Guess what? I am going with her to the hospital next Wednesday. He wants me to come and answer a lot of letters. I suppose everybody is remembering him there. She said he was getting along very well, but can't be moved for another week anyhow."

Thursday, May 27

Last night Mme Tabuteau had me come up and gave me a big glass of tea and two Chinese cookies. Then we went to the hospital in a taxi. Tabuteau is still flat in bed. She takes him grapefruit and other special fruits. She said he is getting very impatient. No doubt. Patience is not one of his virtues. There was a stack of letters, which I have to answer. She is acknowledging most of the ones which came as a result of his operation, though. He didn't say much—except in French. Mme Tabuteau is a very smart woman and has such a good sense of humor. She certainly liked the photographs I brought her, the 5×7 of him smiling, and of the other she said, "That is more the 'bon vivant' but this—!" She said his relatives, especially his mother, would like a copy and it was one of the best he's ever had. I said, of course he photographs well, and she said he was very "photogénic!" He asked about my practicing. It seems the only thing that really ever amused him was when I told him about it driving Dr. Reynolds crazy. This made him start to laugh again last night, and she said not to make him laugh as he's not supposed to. She says for once she doesn't worry about him as she knows he is so well guarded and taken care of. The hospital is between the prison and Girard College and he has a private room and nurse."

June 5, 1943

I've had the most wonderful evening! I phoned Mme Tabuteau this morning to find out when to return his letters and she said to stop by tonight. He is home from the hospital and up and around, though moves rather slowly. I heard another voice as I approached the apartment, and when I went in, there was a soldier. Madame Tabuteau introduced me, and who do you suppose it was—after all these years—John de Lancie. [Although we had studied with the same teacher in California, it was not at the same time, so I had never met him.] Tabuteau had on trousers, an undershirt, and a towel around his neck! Madame Tabuteau is still raving about the photo I gave her—says it is the best picture she's ever had of him, so natural and full of life. Wasn't I lucky to get it? He doesn't say one word about the photos. Just *looks* at them. John was going over to T's shop to work on reeds and I presume to have a lesson tomorrow. From what they talked about, I gather de Lancie expects to be sent overseas soon. He is in an Army Band at Fort Myer, Virginia. T. was in such a *wonderful* humor. For once he actually sounded human. They had some French letters about stocks that someone had asked them to translate and they decided to do it then so I could take them to type. By this time de Lancie had departed. Madame says that he is Tabuteau's "son" as he has been so much under his influence since he was very young.

The Tabuteaus drink tea in tall glasses, and I know now that's what I saw him gulp down that night (not that he doesn't drink other stuff besides tea, of course). He was telling de Lancie that all he could show the world as a result of his work would be a pile of cane shavings. He said, "Yes—if I had saved all my shavings, it would make a pile as high as the Drake."

The letters were in rather complicated legal language. Tabuteau borrowed *her* glasses and made some joke about how he bought 25¢ ones for reading and then uses hers. I wish you could have seen him—in fact, all of us. Tabuteau sitting there in his undershirt with glasses perched way down on the end of his nose and Madame T. speaking

MARCEL TABUTEAU

French and English a mile a minute. He said, "For writing the letters you can take a lesson next week." Oh Lord—what will I do. He really wants me to and I know what a lesson means! He is a different person then. Anyhow, I certainly enjoyed tonight. They both really have a delightful sense of humor. He had some other letters for me to answer, including one from Robert Bloom, the first oboe of the NBC Symphony, who writes and says, "I met some boys from Philadelphia and learned that you have had an operation recently. I hope you are over the unpleasant part and are feeling well now. There is not much news in N.Y. We have had a quiet season with Stokowski and Toscanini. And we'll have them again next year." Can you imagine that?? A *quiet* season with Stoki and Toscanini!!!

Then there was quite a discussion as to whether I should write his letters in the first person, "I," or as a secretary *for* Mr. Tabuteau. Madame T. thought the latter, and we discussed it pro and con. She said people would wonder when it didn't sound just like him. But he said I should imagine I'm him—and he won out. He said that is the funny part, and seemed to get a great kick out of it. He said the letters he'd seen that I did at first were exactly what he would have written, and I said of course he wouldn't have written them at all otherwise, so there's nothing to compare them to. Then he wanted to see how I signed his name, and he liked it. Said it was better than he could do. [I had practiced writing "Marcel Tabuteau" over and over like a student repeating a misspelled word at the blackboard until I came very close to his signature.] That seems like forgery to me. I always put my initials under it as I think I should for safety, don't you? Although he would as soon just have me write—"Marcel Tabuteau." I had him sign a picture for a boy in Texas who wrote asking for one. Then I wanted to keep it for myself and finally asked him if I sent this, if he'd sign one for me. He said, "Certainly," and then, "You can sign it yourself." I told him what a wonderful dedication I could put on it! He asked me if I found time to write any other letters—to my family—because of doing all his. I said I managed to write my mother, and that was about all. He said *he* would have to write some letters to you for *me* and got a great kick out of that idea. Madame said she wished I'd been around when he received the Legion of Honor as they had such stacks of mail then. I was there until after 10:30!

June 7, 1943

I wrote eight letters for Tabuteau again yesterday and typed their French translations . . . You are right about the "good stroke of luck" that snapshot has turned out to be. So many people want a photo of

Tabuteau, and I have given away several, but Madame T. says they are not for *everyone*—just the *few*. I got up at 6:30 this morning and went over to the camera shop to practice as I hadn't expected to have another lesson until next fall.[9] Especially after I've been writing, "I never teach during the summer."

June 9, 1943

Now I must tell you a story. I was up at Eleanor Mitchel's apartment last weekend and she talked a lot about Tabuteau.[10] First of all, I'm evidently not the only one who's had tooth trouble. There were two boys at Curtis with crooked teeth. Tabuteau didn't explode at one of them until later, and then made it very difficult for him. Eleanor thought I was lucky he'd protested when he did. She was the only girl in his woodwind classes during the past years. She wonders what will happen next season, as he has always had one of his boy pupils do everything he possibly could get them to—hold his coat, tie his reeds, do his shopping at the Reading Terminal Market, etc. She said Madame T. wouldn't consider shopping! One boy was so pleased when Tab told him he would be his apprentice, only to find out he just tied reeds and reeds and reeds and didn't learn a thing, and also how he worried whether Tab would like the groceries he bought. Eleanor said, "Don't get yourself in for anything," and furthermore, "Keep out of Madame Tabuteau's classes [Mme Tabuteau taught French at Curtis] because if you are Monsieur's pupil, she will get you to do things for her also." She wondered though, if he would be gentleman enough not to have a girl do it! Well, I didn't take this too seriously, because I'm already writing his letters, which I suppose is one phase of it, and I certainly wouldn't stay out of Madame T's class, because I want to learn French and I really don't mind doing something for a person I like. And then you get to see more of the "inside" that way. So I just forgot about it—but especially thought the shopping sounded rather far-fetched.

Anyhow, today Mrs. Potter, who runs the camera shop, was going downtown (I guess you know Germantown is about seven miles from central Philadelphia and takes a half-hour via streetcar and subway), but she got a headache and asked if I'd do the errands—take some pictures to be framed, pick up some camera repairs, et cetera. Well, I did go and as I was walking down a side street from the picture-framing place, I spied "Reading Market," so thought out of curiosity I'd look in. It is a monstrous place which is divided into avenues and people seem to rent individual stalls. Meat, vegetables, poultry, fruit, eggs—everything! Very different from a Safeway! So I had walked about one-half block further after coming out of the market and was thinking

MARCEL TABUTEAU

about how Tabuteau would like some cherries I saw in there. I was looking a mile off when suddenly someone said "Hello." I was startled as I didn't expect to run into anyone I know on the street in Philadelphia! It was Madame Tabuteau (!) and she was headed for the Reading Market! She wanted to know what I was doing down there and said if I had a minute she would show me something, adding, "You never know, next winter he may want you to come and get something for him when he is too busy!" So she goes to the meat counter where they know him. The butcher fixes everything especially for him—knows just what he wants and calls him the "Professor." Sure enough, on the package was "Prof." $1.14—14 points." With ration points it complicates things. Then I followed her all around—she seemed to want me to and said I would get educated. We stopped at a French flower and herb stand where she talked to the lady in French which sounded so nice. "Bon jour, Madame," "Merci," and so on. She said she *never* does go shopping, that he always does it *himself,* but while he is sick, she has to. She wouldn't dare pick out a chicken, but only goes where they know what he wants. She says he really is an extraordinary cook! Well, we went from hither to yon, finally did buy a pound of cherries for 60¢ and I observed some of the prices of things which she said I should write to you about. Strawberries 45¢ a basket, blackberries 45¢ a basket. One muskmelon 40¢, lettuce 18¢ a head. One eggplant 30¢, one avocado 30¢, one grapefruit 18¢, and one dozen plums, just ordinary ones like those that drop off our trees, *50¢,* and I thought things were high in California last year. Well, it was quite a shopping expedition. We must have been in there at least one-half hour, and I had to rush to do my other errands and get back to the Photo Studio, but it was fun. Mme Tabuteau was going to cook the dinner tonight as they were having company. They will be here until about June 15, then go to the ocean for a few weeks and then probably to Canada. She said he is not recovering as fast as he was expected to. That is, he gets tired. He thought he would go for trips and long walks after a few days!

It seems Madame already has it figured out that I can pick up his groceries next year. It's all right if they are ordered ahead of time as she said they are, but it would certainly be terrible to have to pick out something. I'd hate to even choose a head of lettuce for him. It wouldn't have struck me so funny if this flutist hadn't just told me about his always having a pupil do all this. Being Tab's pupil evidently entails more than playing the oboe. I know that in his own way, he sort of treats his pupils as his family (not exactly family), but I guess it's just his system. His Majesty and all his little vassals. I don't think

LESSONS WITH TABUTEAU

I would mind to a certain extent, as I really do admire him so much, but would draw the line at holding his coat. Still, when he *commands* you to do a thing, you usually do it. It looks like I am being trained for the job, girl or no girl!

Friday, June 11, 1943

I had my lesson and felt so dumb. Tabuteau shows you things you never even thought of before. I really felt hopeless, but it is so marvelous what he can tell you. Afterwards, I walked a few blocks with him and asked him if there was any hope for me. He said nothing was hopeless if you thought things right in your head first—good playing being more knowing first *what* to do—that it is never an accident if something is good. You have to keep at it all the time. He does, himself, he said.

Tuesday evening, June 16, 1943

I've just been up to Tabuteaus' and had a wonderful time. All three of us composed a letter to his doctor, and Madame T dug out several French books for me to borrow during the summer. He has a *great* sense of humor—sharp as a needle—but can bark too. He also barks at her and has to be waited on. He said he was in a writing mood, so signed two pictures for me. What fun he had thinking up what to put on them. On one he was going to put "To my talented female oboe student," or some such thing. Mme T. and I shrieked, "Horrors, not that." I said perhaps we had better just forget that one and he roared. Later I said, "Anything, but none of that female oboist stuff," and he laughed again. Madame always fixes me a big glass of tea. She was going to loan me a beautiful book of pictures of Paris. He said, "*She will lose it.*" I told him I didn't lose books, but I didn't take it anyhow, as it was valuable and I'd prefer to look at it there rather than have the responsibility of it all summer. He finally wrote on the laughing photo, "à ma fidèle secrétaire, Marcel Tabuteau, June 1943," and on the other (a big 8×10), he said he looked as if he were facing a firing squad and asked for the slip of paper with my name on it, so he could copy it. It had my telephone number [Germantown 7348] and he thought how hilariously funny to put, "Laila Storch Ger7348." So he did. He wrote, "Up against the wall, to Laila Storch Ger 7348 with my sincerest wishes for a successful career, Marcel Tabuteau, June 1943." Isn't that wonderful? [This was the first and only time that Tabuteau wrote my name correctly as "Laila." Never able to pronounce "Li-la," they both soon began to refer to me as "Lola" and that was the way it stayed.]

MARCEL TABUTEAU

I never dreamed I'd get such an inscription from Tabuteau after only knowing him a few months. Mme says he always *means* what he says, and says what he means. I guess I should have asked him if he meant "career" as an *oboist* or just career? Anyhow, we were talking about how long it's taken me to get to Philadelphia to study, and she said she thinks the war will be over and then he will go back to France and not be here next year. "But then you would just have to come to Southern France to study with him. After all, three thousand miles more is nothing," and on it went like that. He said he would be here one more year anyway, but really wants to go back to Europe. He has had enough of America—forty years.

July 1, 1943

At my last lesson John let me in before Tabuteau came. I had my camera and took a wild chance on a couple of exposures. I was lucky to get anything, as I was scared Tabuteau would come at any minute. Here is a description of some of the photos I am enclosing. Tabuteau's desk: this is where I always see him sitting working on reeds. I set *my* oboe on his peg to complete the picture. Note the signed photos of Toscanini and Stokowski above the desk. The corner with the wicker chair is where he sits and insults you. Also, a picture of John the Elevator Man, who took me up for my lessons and was always so nice. So now I have a little record to keep.

On July 4 I wrote, "Rather dull around here without the Tabuteaus." They had finally left to spend the summer in Nova Scotia.

10

MY FIRST YEAR WITH TABUTEAU AT THE CURTIS INSTITUTE

October 1943–May 1944

In the fall of 1943 as the beginning of the school year approached, I had to find a new place to live. Some friends suggested the Hannah Penn House, which was run by the Republican Women of Pennsylvania as their club. The traditional dark red brick colonial building at 250 South 16th Street was almost exactly two blocks equidistant from the four cardinal points that were to mark the borders of my existence for the next two years—west, to the Curtis Institute, north, to Tabuteau's Studio, east, to the Academy of Music, and south, to the Drake Hotel where the Tabuteaus lived. Two of my cellist friends, Marion Davies and Shirley Trepel, were already living there, and it was one of the few places that would rent rooms to music students without too many restrictions on practicing.[1] Marion and Shirley had studied with Emanuel Feuermann until his untimely death in 1942; now they were students of Gregor Piatigorsky. A pianist, Heather Halsted, who was studying with Olga Samaroff at the Philadelphia Conservatory of Music, completed the group of girls in the house. There were also two retired businesswomen, Mrs. Hill and Miss Byrne, who seemed very elderly to us, and Carola Collings, a rather exotic ex-Spanish dancer.

The girls of the Hannah Penn House, 1945: Laila Storch, Shirley Trepel, and Marion Davies.

One room on the fourth floor was available for $20.00 a month that included once a week maid service! As I was now working as a waitress in Stouffers trying to earn enough money to get through the coming winter, the price of rent was an important consideration. Although my Hannah Penn House room resembled an attic, I thought every musician must live in a garret for a time, and it would be a good place to make reeds. Shortly after the middle of September, I stopped in at Curtis and was told that Tabuteau was supposed to be back in town.

September 21, 1943
   Guess what? I just phoned the Drake and Tabuteaus not only were back, but both talked to me, said they had been thinking a lot about me lately as he has a big stack of correspondence and is going to need me very badly. Madame said they had letters from John de Lancie who is in North Africa and that he has met all her relatives there.[2] He says North Africa is much like the country around San Francisco. Tabuteau had a successful fishing trip and feels much better. I could hear him doodling on the oboe when I called. You should have heard

MY FIRST YEAR WITH TABUTEAU AT CURTIS

his voice on the telephone. He just shouts into it—so loud you can barely understand him. Tabuteau, Tabuteau, Tabuteau! Summer is really over *now*. I thought it never would be.

Reading these words more than fifty years later, I could only wonder at such boundless youthful enthusiasm. Then I remembered my 1976 visit with the eminent French oboist Myrtile Morel. He was eighty-seven years old, but when he spoke of his teacher, he said, "All through my life the thought of Gillet was always there. Gillet, Gillet, Gillet! He was my God!" The way Tabuteau dominated his students' minds throughout their lifetimes can only be compared to the impact Georges Gillet had on his pupils.

September 24, 1943
Well, I was at Tabuteaus last night. Their little apartment was piled with luggage and boxes. We spent some time looking at all his fishing pictures with the big 30 lb salmon he caught—loads of them. There were so many letters to answer. One from a boy who asked Tabuteau how he produced his vibrato and as the cane situation was so bad, could he spare any?! T. said to give him a long theory, so I tried to remember everything I'd ever heard about vibrato and it looked good on paper! Tabuteau is very tan and seems much better than when he left Philly. I'm afraid he is healthy enough to have his temper back too, but that is good—he wouldn't be himself if quiet. He is going to play with "The New Friends of Music" in New York on November 7. I must manage to hear that! Madame said for me to put it on his calendar, so he will remember to go! . . . Tabuteau wants to hear me play before school starts!

I had other problems besides the imminence of playing for Tabuteau. My teeth were still being restraightened and my upper wisdom teeth had to be extracted. I could not see how it would be possible to continue working at Stouffers and have enough time to study and practice—but I needed the money to live on. I had a chance to earn $2.00 by playing for a Music Demonstration class run by a Mr. Louis Kazze, but as I wrote to my mother: "I didn't tell Tabuteau I was playing anywhere, as he probably wouldn't approve. It was very funny; after I left from rehearsing with Mr. Kazze and was on my way back to my place, I was thinking about Tab and when I looked up, there he was walking along, fuming—he's always leaving a cloud of cigarette smoke in back of him—and carrying two _big_ bags of groceries. Fortunately he didn't see me, as he probably would have wanted to know where I had been with oboe and music! But imagine running into Tabuteau right around the corner from where I live!"

Because of the war, oboe players were becoming scarce and at the end of September I was offered the chance to play with the Philadelphia Opera Company. This meant traveling for several months. When I stopped by at Curtis, Tabuteau was in the office talking to Miss Hill, the registrar, who invited me in to discuss the opera situation. She told me that "Max Zehr, the manager had called her and practically begged her to let me go! Tabuteau definitely doesn't feel it would be right for me to start touring and says I should _practice_ now. He says you can always get money somehow (?) and I should think of the future. In principle he is right of course, and it would be difficult to break up school right at the beginning." I decided not to take the job despite the uncertainty of how I would manage to get through the winter. That night, I went to meet Max Zehr in the Academy of Music foyer after his opera rehearsal. He told me he had already engaged an oboist from Pittsburgh. Nancy Mae, my flutist friend who was also asked to play the opera, and I were about to leave when we suddenly realized that

> here we were inside the Academy and a concert was going on. Something quite out of the ordinary. It was a Swing concert by Duke Ellington and his band in the _Philadelphia Academy of Music_! Everyone has been talking about it. Well, we went up the back stairs, evaded the ushers, and got in. It was already about 10:00 p.m. so after the intermission we found two lovely vacant plush seats in the first balcony. Expensive seats! It was quite an experience. That man is really fantastic and he has some smooth musicians—very versatile players, not like most jazz one hears. I kept wondering what Tabuteau would think if he knew I was there. It was a little after 11:00 p.m. when we left, making our way through the huge mob of people. As I passed the stage entrance, can you imagine my amazement to see _Tabuteau_ standing in the doorway? I'm sure my mouth dropped right open. Well, I went up and asked him if he'd been at the concert and told him I had too, and that I'd been wondering what on earth he'd think if he'd known I was there. The man with him said, "Why, Mr. Tabuteau was a great admirer of Duke Ellington (since the past ½ hour), and now all Tabuteau's pupils will be talking about his being

MY FIRST YEAR WITH TABUTEAU AT CURTIS

at Ellington's concert." I told Tab I would rest easy now, knowing he'd been there too, and I think he was amused. You should have seen the natty green sport clothes he had on . . . I wish you could have heard those trumpets and saxophones. What an evening this was!

October 2, 1943

Everything seemed to be going along so nicely for me but then what a lesson I had! Two men were there when I arrived at the Studio and Tabuteau introduced me—by my name! Miss Storch—He remembers it! Oh, if I could only tell you everything. He said I am very careless in my playing. Later he said he was very glad I had come to him as I have been careless, but that my playing has not suffered too much—that I hadn't gone backwards. I played quite a lot of a Barret Sonata and he played the bass line with me. In many places he said, "Very good." Guess what? I am really going to be his apprentice now. He said, "You will tie my reeds for me and I will also show you how to prepare my cane." I have to tie six reeds a week for him. Just think of it! Tabuteau having a *girl* assistant!! I remember Mr. Shanis said if he took you into his shop, it was a sure sign he likes you. And he said among other things, "I am pretty sure you are going to be a pretty good oboe player some day," which sounds like quite a qualified statement but for Tabuteau to even suggest that someone might be *good is amazing* and to tell it to your face! He said that of course it depends on what *he* did. I guess meaning if he stays here or not. He told me he had a letter through the Red Cross from his brother and that he is well and also one from his mother who is 87. Imagine him having a mother living! We left the Studio together and it was just like a continuation from last June. Before he packed up his oboe, he said in a very loud voice. "*O.K.,* we will go now." I guess you can imagine how thrilled I am about Tabuteau. Now I don't mind at all when he roars, because it is so wonderful the way he explains things. I can't get over being his "Apprentice." Now I'll be able to continue going to the Studio even though lessons will be at Curtis. Tonight I worked at Stouffers but kept forgetting spoons, water, and everything because I was thinking, "Tabuteau says I'll be a pretty good oboe player." He was trying to get me to "punctuate" the music and said, "You know what it is—punctuations?? I hope you do not punctuate my letters like you do music!"

October 4, 1943

My first day at Curtis! I kept telling myself all weekend and even this morning—"You're not there yet!" I was very careful crossing the

MARCEL TABUTEAU

streets today, as my first class, French with Madame Tabuteau, wasn't until 1:00 p.m. I had a lesson in the middle of the afternoon and it really unhinged me. I was more nervous, I guess, as it was different playing in a Curtis Studio and Tabuteau made me feel like two cents . . . Today he got so mad when I said "Yeah."

[My friend Nancy had decided to accept the Philadelphia Opera tour. I was happy that she] brought her typewriter from Cleveland and is going to leave it with me so I can use it all winter. Now I won't have to worry if His Majesty wants letters done from time to time. I have to bring his attendance record (a box of cards) up from the office and the first thing he asks me to do is deliver a message to Kincaid and even asked when his own classes were over. He also asked when I was supposed to be through with my lesson. I told him 2:40 and he said, "All right, you are through then." Just the way he said it was so funny. [My letter ends with] signed Laila—finally in Curtis—can you believe it?

Now I felt almost as if I were beginning a second year of study. I wrote to my old teacher, Julien Shanis, of my excitement at finally being in Curtis and mentioned that I had asked Tabuteau what we would do in woodwind ensemble. When I received his one-word answer, "Attack!" my visions of playing Mozart and Beethoven quintets promptly evaporated. However, I soon came to realize that teaching us the discipline and control necessary to attack a note at the precise point desired, eliminating as much guesswork as possible and aiming to avoid the feeling of it being just luck if it responded at all, was one of the most valuable techniques Tabuteau imparted to us.

Due to some union dispute, the Philadelphia Orchestra had not yet had a rehearsal and Eugene Ormandy was threatening to call off the first concert of the season. It affected us in that when things were finally settled, they called an afternoon rehearsal for the orchestra, and our eagerly awaited first woodwind ensemble class was canceled. But then another notice went up on the Curtis bulletin board so that on October 7, we did gather in Studio IIB for the beginning of our Thursday afternoon sessions with Tabuteau. Although they would later usually be held in the larger Curtis Hall, the mixture of happiness and dread I felt at actually being there would be forever associated with the red and gold autumn leaves in Rittenhouse Square that I saw from those second-story windows. To my mother I wrote,

MY FIRST YEAR WITH TABUTEAU AT CURTIS

I wish I could tell you how wonderful his class was. I'm sure there's nothing else like it in the world, and I am so grateful that I can be in it. Everyone was absolutely terrified. It was like the first lesson I had with him, only he applied those principles to each one individually, having each person play long tones, counting 1-2-3-4-5-4-3-2-1-0. He told some students they weren't fit to play in ensemble yet and that they would have to learn to attack a note first. The way he explains things and what your attitude toward music should be is terrific. He is so much more than just a superb oboist. He talked from about 4:30 until 6:00 and then I walked home with him. I live right on the way to their place, and one day I walk home with Mme Tab and the next with him.

I made a few additional notes to help me remember some of the things he said in the class:

how he wanted to teach us how to be happy with music as he has been for forty years. He explained about placing the notes on the wind and not *winding* the notes. Also, he defined silence as being beauty. He spoke often of Gillet, who said you would have to practice this way four or five years before it would become a part of you; then it would be in your blood. He told us that Gillet just dropped him a word now and then, which he often didn't understand and he only found the meaning, and applied it years later. He mentioned Mischa Elman; how he gave so much at first and then when he was older and played out, he had nothing to say. Thibaud was God-like but deteriorating from careless living. He said what we might mistake for coldness was really control, and that we must be as careful as if we were counting out each grain from a bag of sugar. Another illustration was to prepare like a tennis player before you begin to play. In the pattern 1-2-3-4-5-4-3-2-1, the notes must have their values gauged—2 must be longer than 1—3 longer than 2, etc. He practices phrasing on long notes and adds the coloring, that is, the melody, later. Or as in the Sibelius 2nd where there is a series of repeated notes, they should all be different. Don't let your notes go down in inflection but up, up, up and only down on 1. The aim is to have fifty levels of contrast. That you must be able to take off and land; these are the most difficult things to do. Some people could fly, but nothing else. He said the instrument means nothing. Like having a gold fountain pen, but it is what you write that counts. Pointing to different students, he said, "You—play a pen. You, a piece of charcoal. You, a pencil. You, a piece of chalk." He said a man like Toscanini would always improve even if he lived to be 2,000. When practicing, you must always have your ideal or goal in mind and work for it. The intelligence must be your guide. As he is always telling me too, you must develop your sensitivity and become conscious of every note. Solfège will help as Miss Soffray teaches his way of phrasing—each note going to the next—having a direction. Today she spoke about rhythm being more important than time. Tabuteau said his teacher told him only a pencil was necessary to make music and illustrated by tapping on the table.

A couple of days later after working all Saturday morning at the Studio preparing Tabuteau's cane, I had my first of many experiences of having to listen to him try oboes and give an opinion. "He kept trying his two oboes. They are practically identical but he tries one and then the other, changes bells and asks me which I like best. He would send me out in the hall to listen. Finally he asked me to play on them. Then *he* went out and I played. His oboes are marvelous—one has the most beautiful tone quality. They are only several years old and he says they are the best oboes he's ever had. But the nervous tension when you're around him is terrific. You just can't feel at ease or completely relaxed— he is ready to take your head off at the slightest excuse. I can understand how he feels, but he makes no effort to control it. I suppose I should consider myself compensated for being allowed to play a few notes on his oboe—or rather ordered to."

Most of my lessons were now at Curtis, usually in an acoustically dead room, cramped in between two pianos. However, after the orchestra had been away on tour, lessons were made up on Saturdays at the Studio. Then I would either have to help with cane preparation or sometimes I could just sit and watch him work on his reeds and listen to him play. On the night of October 9, the same Saturday as the "oboe trying," the Philadelphia Orchestra opened its season. I wrote the following to my mother:

It was wonderful to hear Tabuteau in the orchestra again, especially after the fear that he might not play this year. The theme of the Brahms *Haydn Variations* was a beautiful example of the restraint he talks about. Salome's Dance was terrific. The way he plays that solo makes your flesh creep. After hearing him play like that I think I'd shine his shoes if he asked me to. But this morning over at his Studio, he seemed so ready to jump at me. Really, if it weren't that I worship his

MY FIRST YEAR WITH TABUTEAU AT CURTIS

artistry, I don't think I could put up with it. Did I tell you I had to shop for Kleenex, cotton and paper towels for the Studio and I am supposed to put all his drawers of reed junk in order? I'm practically his vassal: write his letters, prepare his cane, do his shopping, but I keep telling myself it's worth it because there's no one else like him and he won't be here forever. And another thing, by sitting in there hearing him blow for a couple hours, I get saturated with his tone, which helps me to recall it later—there's the worth of it all. Today he played excerpts from the *New World,* the solo from *Benvenuto Cellini,* some Brahms, and the Tchaikovsky 4th. His capacity for taking infinite pains is almost unbelievable. He works hours on a slight difference in tone quality— always trying to satisfy himself. Music is *never* dead when he plays. I can almost hear his preludes and sound ringing in my head. Maybe if I listen to him all winter, I will improve myself—I hope.

October 13, 1943

Tabuteau will play in New York for "The New Friends of Music" on November 7. They are all sold out but I simply have to hear it. Mme T. is to be their guest so she said to write and tell them she was having a friend with her that weekend and could they arrange for another ticket. I hope it works! . . . Sometimes I can't help but think it's almost unreal being here and studying. Marion Davies said too, how much less conscious of the war we are here than in California. Everything seems almost normal here, that is, of course, compared to other phases of life, and to think we can actually be continuing with music—when a year ago I was worrying that Mrs. Roosevelt was going to draft me!

We always played our lessons standing up, but occasionally Tabuteau would sit down, either when he was suffering from gout or recovering from one of his operations. In mid-October, I wrote to my mother:

He had to play sitting down, so I sat down also and once while we were playing, I couldn't help but think, is this really me sitting right beside Tabuteau and playing along with him?[3] Of course he would stop me a lot, and one time he got mad because I stopped when he hadn't told me to. Said it was bad enough when he *didn't stop* me and not to stop anyway . . . Another time, I flipped a page of music and he roared like a lion. He said I almost hit him with it—as if a piece of paper would have hurt him. I sort of laughed and he glared and can he glare at you! I just stared right back at him. He can really be ridiculous sometimes. [In retrospect, I think this was pushing my luck!]

MARCEL TABUTEAU

[In wind class, we were progressing a little beyond attacks.] I had to call Tabuteau tonight to find out about getting music for ensemble tomorrow and he said to take out the Beethoven Quintet from the library. [This was the same Quintet in E-Flat Major, op. 71, that was played on so many of the Curtis programs during the 1930s.] Now the fun should begin. We probably won't get past the first measure. He is very amusing in class, not like at lessons. He is witty, comic, pantomimes, gesticulates—is very animated and vociferous and just fascinating to watch. In string class he told them he would have to bring "that damn little stick, the oboe" and show them what he meant about some phrase. The oboe is just his means to an end—an annoyance no doubt.

October 14, 1943

We played about twenty-five measures of the Beethoven Quintet and Tab said almost all I did was good. We even had a laugh when I tried to play a note and nothing came out. Later when he asked a clarinetist to play and the same thing happened, he said, "It sounds like an *oboe*." After that, some of us had to play in the orchestration class so students could hear how things they had arranged actually sounded. Do you remember the opera in English on the radio? Well, Menotti is the teacher of this class and a very nice youngish man.

Friday night, and another installment. What a break I had this afternoon! I was just leaving school when I saw a student [Seymour Lipkin] with the score to the Beethoven Piano Quintet and then spotted Tabuteau. It turned out they were rehearsing here for the Town Hall performance and I got in to listen to them. The first chair woodwinds of the Philadelphia Orchestra! What a chance to hear Tabuteau play chamber music. He tells the others what to do just as if it were a class. Every note of Tabuteau's playing was so outstanding—his precision, style, everything—it's just beyond what oboists usually do. I can't get over how lucky I was to hear this—just by accident, and I had the score to follow. Tabuteau was very nice about letting us listen. It was Sol Schoenbach on bassoon, James Chambers, French horn, the new clarinetist, Ralph MacLane, and a boy from Curtis played piano in place of Serkin who will play it later.[4] What Tabuteau does with just the fewest or simplest combination of notes is absolutely marvelous and his *tone* was beautiful. It was so much better than hearing him in orchestra. When I hear him play like that, I just can't be bothered about all his oddities and what he's like personally . . . We were there about an hour-and-a-half. If I'd had to work at Stouffers tonight I would have missed this.

MY FIRST YEAR WITH TABUTEAU AT CURTIS

October 16, 1943

I certainly have never known anyone I could feel such a variety of ways about in one day as Tabuteau. I wish I could tell all that went on at my lesson. First of all, he roared because I didn't have a pen for him to sign a check. Said he never heard of a secretary without a pen! My lesson itself went fairly well. A lot he said was "good" and one place in Barret, "*perfect*," *but* then there was loads I didn't do right. Afterwards, I was supposed to stay and shape some cane and tie some reeds for him. First he was talking about how the orchestra sounds more like a brass band to him every day and how much he'd like to quit music and go fishing in Florida. Then he asked if I'd send him some money every month if he retired. I said where would I get any money. He seemed to be quite sure I would make money. (I hope so but I am skeptical.) Anyhow, Tabuteau went on to say I would play well, as well as *any boy*. Those were his words and he added "*if* I practiced like HELL." He keeps telling me how hard I should practice and said I should work doubly hard and make every minute count now because I am losing money by studying (i.e., not playing the opera job). Money seems to carry a lot of weight with him. But imagine him saying I'd play as well as any boy—especially after all the years he has been so against girls. I'd die if he said I'd play *well for a girl.* Anyhow, then Mr. Minsker (the English horn in the Orchestra) stopped in. Tabuteau was complaining about a pupil coming later this afternoon and said he *hated* them. The only thing he liked was that he didn't have to pay income tax on them and said to me, "I have to pay income tax on you" (as I'm part of his Curtis salary). I said, "Maybe you shouldn't have given me the scholarship." I just have to answer him back sometimes, he makes me so mad. He handed me some cane and I made some passing remark about it being rather thick and he told me to "*shut up*" and said to Minsker, "She's as fresh as a boy." If I just acted like a mouse he'd have me shaking and trembling like a leaf. As it is, he intimidates me enough. I can't be myself or at ease when I'm around him. Then I cut through one piece of his cane and he yelled in a perfect fury to Minsker, "What is this stupid girl doing—Ruining all my cane?!!xb#*!!!," and yet he asked me to do it and says if the reeds aren't tied right, he will fire me. It's no picnic working on his cane. I don't much care if he does *fire* me. Minsker is *very* nice and told him to take it easy on me and Tabuteau grumbled something about my being used to it, or that he had to treat them rough. Honestly, sometimes I think he is crazy, surely unbalanced, and has a perverted sense of humor. If one has to go through what he does to be as good an oboe player, I seriously

MARCEL TABUTEAU

question whether I want to do it. Minsker said that even as recently as ten years ago, Tabuteau was working about ten hours a day in that studio on reeds. When he made some remark about playing had never been easier for him than now, Minsker said the forty years experience and his wonderful oboe probably helped. Yet even now, he spends hours and hours in that place unceasingly trying for just what he wants. As much as I want to be a fine musician, I can't face becoming so one-sided, but after you hear Tabuteau play, you don't want to play oboe unless you can at least *try* to do it that well. I guess anyone who spent forty years on reeds would be a little off.

[Occasionally the school gave us tickets to sit in the "Curtis Box." It was on the right side of the proscenium, very close to the stage so that we could look directly down on the musicians.] It is so much nicer than the top Amphitheatre. Tabuteau dominated the whole concert as usual. Everyone agrees to that. There is no question as to his stupendous musicianship. He puts so much energy into every little phrase. They played the Respighi *Antique Dances*. Sometimes the things he does just make you catch your breath. I'm sure he must play better than ever and yet sometimes looking at the stage, you see a tired old Frenchman sitting there. His face is so expressive. I'm sure he gets nervous before his solos. Afterwards, during the applause he looked up and saw us in the box. "Fresh as a boy" as I am, I waved and clapped and forgave him for being such a pill in the afternoon. He smiled and looked *so* pleasant . . . I can't help but think that I'll never hear oboe playing like that again. I feel so sad that he is so old—not that he seems old but you know he won't keep on forever. I just must be grateful I am hearing him this season. I was so afraid for a while he wouldn't play. There was that rumor. I don't want to miss a single concert.

[On Saturdays I would hear Tabuteau play at the Studio and then again at night with the Orchestra.] This morning over at the Studio he played Study No. 15 from Barret and lots of excerpts: Bach *G minor Fugue*, Beethoven *Sixth*, the *New World* and the Elgar *Enigma Variations*. He went over the solo in the second movement of the Beethoven Quintet so many times. He spoke of his teacher, Gillet, and of what a great man he was—what musical understanding. "I wish you could have heard him play." [Gillet's words had remained with Tabuteau during his whole life.] One day in class, he recounted a story of how Gillet had given him just a hint of all these musical ideas and how Tabuteau had said he understood, but then later he told his father that he didn't. His father then talked to Gillet and Tabuteau got a terrific scolding. Gillet had said that one must play as

MY FIRST YEAR WITH TABUTEAU AT CURTIS

if skating on ice. *"Nous avons les patins mais nous ne patinons pas. Nous marchons. Il faut patiner."* (We have the skates but we don't do the skating. We take steps. One must skate.)

Monday morning, October 18, 1943

I took Tabuteau's tied reeds up to the Drake yesterday. I should get a special notebook and record everything I can because I really feel—in fact I know—that he will quit as soon as he possibly can. Yesterday he was already counting the weeks of the season and saying "only twenty-eight weeks to go" and I may be getting in just under the line as far as the advantage of studying with him goes. We talked quite awhile and I heard some amazing stories, such as how the great Tabuteau can be swayed by little things. He was telling Madame Tabuteau about someone's audition and how when the student asked, "Mr. Tabuteau, may I play you one of my own pieces?" it struck his sense of humor, especially when it was followed by Saint-Saëns *The Swan.* They asked what I was doing, and Mme T expressed the thought it would be better to borrow money than take up too much time working now. I just couldn't borrow money without someone telling me it would be all right, and so I asked Tabuteau what he thought, and he said he thought it would be perfectly all right—*just* so I didn't borrow it from *him*! and broke out in gales of laughter. Isn't that a kick, but at least I guess there's no doubt in their minds that I'll make it playing oboe—which as Madame said, would be considerably more interesting than working in Stouffers. Now Madame has a job for me, which I accepted—washing and ironing her blouses every week. $2.00 for about three hours. That isn't bad. She said his socks go with it, but that sort of appeals to my sense of humor. Someday I can say, "I washed Tabuteau's socks." Sometimes I contrasted my situation with that of my cellist friends, Marion and Shirley. The Piatigorskys have them come to lunch and dinner several times a week. You could never see Tabuteaus asking me to dinner. [Yet before long they would do just that.]

Constantly on the brink of "bankruptcy," nevertheless by mid-October I had found it too difficult to work at Stouffers and keep up with all my Curtis studies. I decided to quit Stouffers, noting to my mother: "I won't go broke this week anyhow. With what I still have ($2.00 of Stouffers salary) and with $2.00 from washing Madame Tabuteau's blouses, I will get by another week! I have been eating at Horn and Hardart (the Automat at the corner of 16th and Chestnut

MARCEL TABUTEAU

Streets). There's always a bunch of Curtis kids in there and you can get a pretty good meal for from 40¢ to 60¢ . . . By being careful, you can eat on even less than $1.00 a day. There is a delicatessen right opposite Curtis where you can buy sandwiches, fruit, and cupcakes for lunch and take them back to school."

I continued to be awed by the "luxury" of Curtis—not having to pay for books or music—and even those of us studying only "secondary piano" could use the fine Steinways in all the practice rooms. I wrote to my mother, "I never pull open that big heavy door to Curtis but what I think about it and wonder if I'm actually here. I went to tea Wednesday. They have an enormous silver samovar and a maid to remove the dirty cups and a lady to serve you tea and cookies. Imagine being served tea at school!" Obliged to limit myself to fifteen cents for lunch to keep within my budget, I looked forward to the ritual weekly mid-afternoon Curtis tea as a slight addition to my meager noon rations. Often Mrs. Bok (by then Mrs. Zimbalist), presided at the samovar in the Common Room as we walked by to take our cup of tea and a cookie while attempting to maintain a dignified manner. It was a challenge to acquire one more cookie by going through the line a second time as inconspicuously as possible.

My new job for Mme Tabuteau came with the unexpected advantage of an occasional bit of supper. When Tabuteau was away with the orchestra I began to learn what I had to do for her.

> She has only a few silk blouses (skiddy to iron) and underwear. With plenty of suds and hot water, it isn't hard for $2.00. After this, she will leave the key for me and I will do it when she's at Byrn Mawr. [Madame Tabuteau taught French at the Shipley School.] They have been at the Drake ever since it was built [in 1929] and she says they really like it. Their little apartment has atmosphere. While waiting for the things to dry, she fixed her supper (I was there from about 5:30–8:30), and insisted I have some *salade, fromage* and *thé* with her. The salad had Italian or French olive oil and string beans, that Tab slices lengthwise himself. They grind the pepper, and the cheese was something rather strong, from Canada. [This was my first exposure to some of the elements of finer cuisine—sliced string beans and freshly ground pepper were not common items in most households of the 1940s. The evenings of doing the blouses, especially when she was

MY FIRST YEAR WITH TABUTEAU AT CURTIS

there and he was off with the Orchestra, were a special treat. Sometimes she fixed something more substantial than salad and cheese. Leftover cold roast shoulder of lamb prepared by Tabuteau was slightly flavored with garlic. It was delicate and tender and began to give me an idea of his cooking skills.] She gave me so much, three slices of the roast with toast and butter and salad with real olive oil and she always serves tea in tall glasses. Then I had some nice English seedless raspberry preserve on toast and a fresh pear. It all tasted so good. She said she remembers from her student days how they loved to eat at someone's home and how they ate a lot when they had the chance! She told me that she likes South American and Mexican things and wanted to go to Mexico once but Tab decided to go to Canada instead.

There were about four or five pairs of Tab's socks—wool ones—but they were simple to wash. Not as dirty as mine or at least they were black and did not show. Mme Tab said when they first lived in the Drake, she did not even know how to wash a pan. Had never done it, and he doesn't expect her to do any housework or anything she doesn't like to do. She just teaches because she really enjoys it and she loves going out to Bryn Mawr, which is almost in the country. She was putting away summer hats and showed me the one Tabuteau likes on her. A little affair with a veil with pink dots on it. It seemed to me the kind most men would laugh at. I feel more at ease with her than with Tab. She said I am lucky to know him so well (?) (Do I?) Anyhow, I guess Gillet never was friendly at all to Tabuteau when he was a student. Perhaps the way he acts is partly inherited from Gillet, the Paris Conservatory "Master." I never could figure out what it was Mme called Tab. It is *Pingouin*, French for penguin. I noticed they had pictures of penguins and little figures of penguins in every shape and form sitting all around. That is his name. He loves penguins and his house in France is called *The Pingouinette*. Isn't that quaint? Tabuteau, a penguin. I immediately thought of him in his full dress all puffed up on the stage for symphony concerts and realized he doesn't look so very unlike one after all!

A few years later, an article in the newspaper, primarily about his cooking, contained Tabuteau's own explanation. The writer had noticed the flowers, books and paintings around the apartment, and a "photograph of several penguins. 'That's my nickname' said Tabuteau. 'They called me "Penguin" because I was so impressed by Anatole France's *Penguin Island*.'"[5]

During my years at Curtis I came to know well the two crowded rooms of the Tabuteau's apartment 1405 at "The Drake, Spruce Street West of Fifteenth, Philadelphia."[6] Turning right from a small entryway, one entered directly into the living room. There, the dominant piece of furniture was an oblong dining table pushed against the far wall. It was used not only for meals but also for letter writing and all other paper work. Opposite the table, an overstuffed armchair where Tabuteau dozed after meals, large paintings on the walls, books everywhere, oboe cases stuffed into the top shelf of the hallway coat closet—all contributed to the colorful ambiance. Crammed into another room on the left of the entry were twin beds, side tables, and chests of drawers, all painted a shade of blue-green much favored in French country houses. A minuscule white-tiled, hotel-style bathroom provided barely enough space to do the washing, which I would then iron in the crowded bedroom. The pocket-sized but all-important kitchen was squeezed in back of the dining area. With nothing but small apartment-sized appliances, a built-in stove, under-the-counter refrigerator, and just room for one person to turn around, Monsieur Tabuteau managed to cook delicious meals and create the superb dinners he served to famous guests.

My life went on like a seesaw, from abject misery in lessons to elation after hearing Tabuteau play or explain his musical ideas.

October 23, 1943
We played dreadfully in ensemble Thursday but Tabuteau was in a wonderful humor—perhaps he thought we are hopeless so why bother! But two days later I had the worst lesson ever. My cold was so miserable and I played terribly. Tabuteau said I sounded like a dying chicken or turkey and I told him that's how I felt and he said, 'Then you ought to be buried.' He was so mad. He said it was bad, very bad, amateurish, just blowing. I even cried in the dressing room afterwards. Even when you feel normal, it takes more than average concentration to get through a lesson with him, and if you have any less than that, it's really impossible. I learned one thing—he makes no allowance for how you feel . . . I'm glad that Tabuteau can't hear those turkeys and other country sounds next door to us in California. He might think they've influenced my playing. Yesterday he told the horn and bassoon they sounded like elephants blowing water through their trunks. Colorful, no? But when I listened to Tabuteau's String

MY FIRST YEAR WITH TABUTEAU AT CURTIS

Ensemble after my lesson and it was so good, I had to forgive him. He talked so much about the rebound—the change of direction while playing. That's what the two numbers coming together signify, illustrated by skipping a flat stone on water. He said all the games you might want to play are right there in the music. You aim for a note, glide, hit it, make a loop.

October 28, 1943

I heard the Philadelphia Orchestra woodwinds rehearse the Beethoven Quintet again yesterday and before French class Madame Tabuteau told me there would be a ticket for me for the New York concert. Woodwind class was bad as usual today. Tabuteau said among other things, that every note I played was like an extraction and that I should at least give the listeners Novocain. He says I play from the neck up. I do *try* to play from my stomach or lower. Martha had a lesson at his Studio yesterday and said he shook a boy who was there, really got rough with him and pulled the oboe right out of his mouth. I'd heard he could be pretty wild. I guess I've been getting off easy. I always forget to remember when I see Tab that I washed his socks. Also, his undershirts last time. Isn't that something—or is it?

Fifty years later the many original ways in which he managed to insult our playing may seem amusing, but at the time it was no laughing matter. It is nevertheless not surprising that Tabuteau was exasperated at the low level of the woodwind ensemble class he had to work with in the fall of 1943. There was no comparison with what I had heard in 1941 at the time of my audition. The school year of 1942 when Curtis had eliminated the whole wind department had taken its toll. There were now no carry-over students who had already absorbed some of Tabuteau's approach to music. All of the boys who would ordinarily have remained from earlier class years were by now drafted and in the U.S. Armed Forces. He had to explain all his concepts in almost a pre-beginning way. It also must have been difficult for him to accept that his oboe class now consisted of two other girls besides me: Martha Scherer, a former pupil of Rhadames Angelucci, and Marguerite Smith. One very young boy, Charles Edmunds, completed the class.

During our two years in Curtis together, Martha Scherer was my faithful friend, supporter, and sympathizer as we suffered through our lessons and sought to understand all that was expected of us. Martha's

MARCEL TABUTEAU

memories of Tabuteau were similar to mine. We both recall his commenting, "Say, what is the matter wid' you, you stupide fool," and when things were not going well in wind class, "I should have a big club and I would smash you all." I never saw Tabuteau smash anyone's reed, but Martha spoke of once barely getting through a lesson on a "horrible reed" and giving it to Tabuteau, who said, "Say, I will fix that reed for you." He crushed it on the music stand before returning it, with, "Here, I fixed your reed." Martha also endured what was almost a "routine," or was it more like paranoia? Tabuteau always seemed to feel that the bell from someone else's oboe was better than his. He took Martha's and kept it for weeks, giving her one to use that according to her, "was no gem." Finally she had to beg to get her own bell back. There were lighter moments such as his hilarious pantomime of the driver of a cart sticking a carrot on a pole and hanging it over the donkey's head to make him go. This was intended to help get the music moving as he wished. In the famous long D Major trill étude (No. 3 in Barret), which, like everyone else, Martha had to transpose into three keys, she found that the trills went better if she shook the oboe a little. She did this at a lesson, and "Tabuteau's eyes twinkled as they did at times, and he said, 'Say, you are the pu-peel and you must shake the *finger.* When you are the *teacher,* then you can shake the oboe!'" It was after I left school that Martha heard the story of the guillotine. In illustrating how one should avoid abruptly chopping off the end of a note, Tabuteau said not to "behead the note, 'kou,'" demonstrating how this was done by the guillotine. He spoke of how during his childhood "all the folks and the kids went to the Square on Saturday mornings to see the beheadings." Whether or not he had been one of the spectators was not clear, but as the last execution by guillotine in France occurred only in 1977 in Marseille, it is possible that such an "entertainment" *did* exist in Compiègne in the 1890s.[7]

All three of the girl students had to work in Tabuteau's studio. He said it looked like a factory, and once when he screamed at Martha and Marguerite and yelled, "*Young lady,*" we didn't know who he was addressing. After they left he said, "They are nice girls." Referring to "the little one" (Marguerite Smith), he couldn't see why she wanted to play oboe, "a nice girl like that.'" More often we saw Tabuteau as a threatening presence

MY FIRST YEAR WITH TABUTEAU AT CURTIS

and always remembered one time when we were in the studio laughing while preparing his cane, thinking that he was out of town. Suddenly the shadow of his fedora hat and his cigarette holder appeared behind the opaque glass in the upper half of the studio door. Before we could catch a breath he came in—clump, clump—looming ominously larger than he really was, with eyes red and face contorted in pain from the gout (as we learned later), and loudly berated us for our levity and careless attitude toward the serious business of doing his work. I always had to be very careful when I cleaned and straightened up "the four drawers of his desk with all his reed stuff jumbled in them. What a mess! You never saw so many knives, shapers, and all other oboe tools. I left a note telling him not to worry, I didn't throw out anything but dust, cane shavings and stale cigarettes and I didn't put anything in my pocket. Maybe that will make him mad, but I know as soon as he can't find something, he'll accuse me of dumping it out."

Contrary to common belief, Martha Scherer and I were not the first girl oboists at Curtis. A scant decade earlier, a girl on any wind instrument, even the flute, was an almost shocking curiosity. Leon Lester told me about such an "oddity" arriving at the school. "It was Ardelle Hookins on the flute. She was the very first one and I think it was 1930. She had studied with Barrère before that. She had a little background and I guess some ability. But what a novelty! All the boys said, 'A girl on a wind instrument!!' It was unheard of." I may have been the first woman oboist to get both in and out, but when I auditioned in 1940 there was already a "young lady" studying oboe at Curtis. This had, however, apparently done nothing toward softening Tabuteau's opposition to the idea of teaching girls. Thelma Neft came from a Pittsburgh family of medical people. She had studied some piano and was also "handed a fiddle." When her school made a plea for volunteers to "take" the oboe, the general belief was that "a girl can't do it." In those days it was considered physically too difficult for a woman, and furthermore, there were no opportunities to play. With a metal oboe and a scholarship to study at Carnegie Tech, she was soon noticed by a newspaper critic who drew Fritz Reiner's attention to this unusual fifteen-year-old girl. During the intermission of a Pittsburgh Symphony Orchestra rehearsal Reiner listened to her read through the Beethoven *Pastoral*

MARCEL TABUTEAU

Symphony and recommended that she go to Curtis.[8] Almost certainly she faced the same objections that I met later on, but Randall Thomson, then director of the school, wrote a letter stating that Curtis was not to reject anyone on the basis of sex. In 1939 she sight-read her audition and was accepted.

Sixty years later she spoke of her fellow students in the woodwind class: Ralph Gomberg, MacLean Snyder, Robert Davison, Mitchell Lurie, and Anthony Gigliotti. As a very young girl, her experience was somewhat different than ours a few years later. She was "treated like a little sister. They had to either 'do me in' or take care of me!" Everyone played in front of the others, and never was an unkind word said to her. In woodwind ensemble she sat between John de Lancie and Ralph Gomberg. Given nothing to play, she would turn the pages. Once there was a work that required a drum. Tabuteau was not happy with the way the part was being played and said, "Maybe the little girl can do it!" She remembered how his cigarette ashes were always falling on the floor and that he said they were "good for the rugs and kept the moths away." The genuine Persian carpets at Curtis! Thelma Neft was at Curtis for the two school years of 1939–40 and 1940–41. In the middle of her third year she left to study medicine.[9]

November 1, 1943

Now I am up to Grand Study No. 3 in Barret and slaving on those trills all over again. A boy, Bill Criss, told me that is a dilly to get by Tab. One student was on it four months. Finally he got promoted. Tab let him play the same thing a half tone higher—in D-Flat. The boy about went crazy. I've got my fingers crossed. You'd think it would be dull taking the same things over, but it's about three years since I've done Barret and Tab's approach is so different, it's like studying something entirely new . . . Tabuteau asked me to prepare some cane for him after school Monday and I was over at the Studio until about 7:00. He was tired but in a good mood. He didn't scream at me and even said 'Thank you,' when I handed him pieces of cane and turned the grindstone for him. Very unusual! [Dusk came early on winter afternoons in Philadelphia. His cigarette glowed in the fading light. I tried to avoid the falling hot ashes and sparks that sputtered from the steel gouger blade as he held it against the revolving grindstone.] He is in a grand stew and says he can't make a reed anymore. It's all probably because of this Beethoven Quintet he has to play in N.Y.

— 273 —

MY FIRST YEAR WITH TABUTEAU AT CURTIS

next Sunday. When I went over to the Drake to do Madame's washing (and Monsieur's socks and undershirts), there was an envelope for me with a *loge* seat for the Town Hall concert. A $2.75 ticket—they didn't have to pay for it of course, but it's a wonderful seat, and there was also a brand new $5.00 bill. On the outside she had written, "*Pour le voyage et le concert.*" Isn't that nice? I am getting a key to Tabuteau's studio so I can work there anytime, except he says not to go in at night after the elevator man (friend John) leaves.

November 8, 1943

[November 7 was the big trip to New York for the Beethoven Quintet.] First I went to Carnegie Hall to hear the New York Philharmonic. Bruno Walter was conducting and Harold Gomberg was playing oboe. After that I dashed to Town Hall. There was still another concert going on, so had to wait outside. Saw Tabuteau arrive and the rest of the quintet from Philadelphia. Madame T forgot her ticket and had to get a pass. I was clutching mine wildly. The whole series is sold out, so there's no chance of buying one. Town Hall is lovely. The first modern hall I've seen back here. It is small and really classy. We had seats in the boxes in the very first row of the balcony. Madame T sat next to me. First there were two Beethoven String Quartets played by the Busch Quartet. A boy from Curtis who was there told me that just before the concert began they were in a terrific dither backstage as all the pianos were tuned high to A-444 and Tabuteau refused to play. It would have been impossible. The only one at A-440 was a Baldwin and Serkin will only play a Steinway, so they had to get another piano. The Beethoven Quintet was last on the program so they had time to find one. I bet Tabuteau really was having fits. He couldn't change his reed—and they had *ordered* an A-440 piano. What a mess! Anyhow, the thing went perfectly. Better than when I heard them rehearse it. Serkin was wonderful in the piano part. Everyone was good and Tabuteau was colossal. I wish you could have heard him. Madame T and I just raved about him. You can enthuse over Tabuteau to her as if they weren't even related. I never expect to hear better oboe playing. It was so superior—it just leaves everybody else in the dust, but how he works to get it that way and the reason the quintet was so perfectly balanced was because Tab had coached the whole group for phrasing and ensemble. We went backstage afterwards. George Szell and Artur Schnabel were back there and nobody was speaking English. I wished it weren't over but am so glad I could go. Four of us from Curtis were there. Serkin had given one of his students a train ticket so he could come and hear it and

MARCEL TABUTEAU

turn pages. I was able to speak to Tabuteau and members of the quintet in the Artists Room and tell them how wonderful it sounded.

In November 1996 I asked Sol Schoenbach if he remembered that Beethoven Quintet concert in Town Hall, and he replied, "I may be dying and I'll never forget it." His own account filled in the colorful details of the happenings that had only reached me through backstage hearsay. "Well, you know Tabuteau always put everything onto my shoulders because he thought the other people were nincompoops. There was MacLane and I think Chambers. Mason Jones must have been drafted by then. Anyhow, he said, you tell 'em to be sure the piano is A-440. I wrote letters to Steinway and to the Town Hall and to the manager whose name was Colberg. 'Yes,' they all assured me, 'oh yes, they always tune the pianos.' We got there and the piano was like 450 and Tabuteau said, 'I will not play.' He put on his hat and coat and said, 'Gentlemen, we're going back to Philadelphia,' and I'll never forget how we were walking down 43rd Street, all four of us, and we were going back to Philadelphia and the manager came running after us and all the perspiration even though it was rather a cold day, and Tabuteau said to him, 'You call yourselves Friends of Music? You are *enemies* of music!! *Enemies!*' and all the people in the street were turning around to look. The manager said, 'we have other pianos. Come back. The piano tuner is there.' Of course they had, I don't know, about nine pianos backstage in Town Hall and Tabuteau sent me around with the piano tuner to find one that was 440, and they finally found one piano there that probably had never been used. It was horrible. Tabuteau struck the A key. 'O.K.' he said, 'That's the one.' All the time this was going on, the Busch Quartet, which you probably heard, were playing with that icy, non-vibrato tone and we were making so much noise, they kept saying 'ssh—ssh,' and Tabuteau—he didn't care what they thought. And Serkin, he wasn't even there. We had rehearsed with him over on Park Avenue at his place and everything went swimmingly and he said 'I'll join you later.' You know, he was only going to come at the Intermission. So they pushed out this relic of a piano and Serkin was there just walking around. Finally the time came, and we went out on the stage

MY FIRST YEAR WITH TABUTEAU AT CURTIS

and he played the first chord and you could see the dust come out of the piano and he was so taken aback, he was completely disarmed, and from that point on it was a riot because the piano was all out of tune and notes were missing. Well, you were there." I told Sol that I had thought they all sounded fantastic and that I still have the program. "Well, I haven't," said Sol. "That was the beginning of our association with Serkin, which he also probably never forgot."

Our oboe lessons at Curtis were always on Mondays, so I practiced diligently all of the next morning after returning from New York, but my lesson was postponed. "Tabuteau was in court today but I don't know what for. There is something wrong with him—I overheard snatches of a conversation about not being able to play standing up—even the *Star Spangled Banner*, and Monday night, he just stood and held his oboe and didn't play. There was apparently a question of his getting insurance from some accident. I heard that the judge couldn't understand a word he said (because of his accent), but in the end he got the payment."

When we students heard of Tabuteau's ongoing health problems in the fall of 1943, we had no idea what the trouble was. I had visited him in the hospital in late May, but in those days one's ailments were usually kept a personal matter. The details came to light only sixty years later.[10] A booklet with over a hundred pages of testimony in the Supreme Court of Pennsylvania, Eastern District, had been left behind in Tabuteau's studio. A few excerpts give some idea of the struggle with his insurance company and the court's difficulty understanding exactly what a symphony orchestra oboist *does*. In his written account of the accident Tabuteau stated that "On April 12, 1942 at about 3 p.m., I was walking in the direction of the Philadelphia Museum, on the south side of the street, between 15th and 16th Street, on the Parkway . . . as I had very often on Sunday afternoons." He describes how he slipped or tripped on a brick that was "about one inch higher than the adjoining block." He lost his balance and in attempting to keep from falling, sprained his ankle, and felt a sharp pain in his right groin, which got progressively worse. He was examined by his physician, Dr. Ludwig Loeb, and told to wear a truss. It was eventually concluded that he had

MARCEL TABUTEAU

sustained incomplete inguinal hernias on each side. The surgery in May 1943 was intended to correct this problem.[11]

In April 1926, at the age of thirty-eight, Tabuteau had taken out an accident insurance policy for which he paid an annual premium of $105.60, but now the insurance company was refusing to make any payment for time he had missed from his work. In the initial claim, "Due to pain and discomfort caused by his said injuries the plaintiff was intermittently hindered and prevented daily from practicing, from playing, from teaching, from giving radio and other performances on the oboe; which condition of partial disability . . . will continue in the future requiring an operation." The London Guarantee and Accident Company, Limited, agreed that the policy was in full effect, but "we deny that there is anything due." They maintained that the problem "did not result from an accident, but was the result of faulty development of the body of the plaintiff and in not any way connected with said alleged accident." The insurance company succeeded in having the results of the first trial thrown out. A second trial was scheduled for November 1943.

Tabuteau was duly sworn in and questioned by Attorneys "Thomas F. Kaliner, Esq., For the Plaintiff " and "Thomas E. Comber, Esq., For the Defendant." Kaliner, Tabuteau's attorney, asked, "The next day, at rehearsal, you felt a terrible pain?" Tabuteau's reply: "At rehearsal! I felt a terrible pain as soon as I started to blow my instrument." The Court: "Where was that?" Tabuteau: "In the Philadelphia Orchestra." The Court: "No; where was the pain?" Answer by Tabuteau: "In the right groin." After being asked, "What is the nature of the instrument you play?" Tabuteau answered, "I play what is called an oboe—it is a woodwind instrument. In order to obtain emotion of tone it takes great physical effort. I have been doing it twenty-nine years, and never had any trouble before, but that morning I had terrible pain." (He must have meant twenty-nine years in the Philadelphia Orchestra.) There were more questions about the pain, and Kaliner quizzed Tabuteau about exactly how much he was able to play. "After the accident, you attended the concerts and played at the performances: were you able to play the entire number—your entire part—so far as the physical work

MY FIRST YEAR WITH TABUTEAU AT CURTIS

was concerned?" Answer: "No; I was unable." The Court: "That is too indefinite." Kaliner then asked: "Which part were you able to play?" Tabuteau replied, "Some part of it,—the most important part." To the question of whether it was "a half of your part" or "one third of your work," Tabuteau said it was "difficult to explain." He tried to describe the concept of "a few bars being very exposed, and a few are not so exposed . . . and I had a man with me to play the part." The Court added, "Anyone who attends a concert knows that the man who plays your particular instrument does not play the whole symphony—He comes in at certain times; Is that right?" Tabuteau: "Yes, Your Honor."

This idea caused some consternation, and more explanation was requested. "You were allowed to have a substitute sit in the orchestra, and you also sat there?" "Yes." Question: "Some (one) played your part?" "Yes." Question: "What were you doing there?" "I couldn't play." "What were you doing?" Answer: "I was sitting there." Question: "As the instruments were playing?" Answer: "Yes, Your Honor." When Kaliner asked, "Mr. Tabuteau, as I understood you to say, you played some of the more exposed passages?" the Court, in a display of its superior wisdom, responded: "Do not lead the witness. Some play at certain particular times in a symphony, and when that time comes for a man to play the oboe in the symphony, the director motions to him when he is to begin, and he plays that particular part." When Kaliner said, "Yes," the Court countered: "This gentleman led me to think that he sat there, and when he was told by the director to play, some other man sat there and played the oboe instead of him." Tabuteau was called upon for more clarification. The Court asked: "You did not sit there with an oboe in your hand and play nothing?" Assuming that if this were the case, "you would soon be out of your seat," the Court found Tabuteau's reply that he was unable to perform his duty, was "too general." Tabuteau said his pain was such that "sometimes when the director told me to come in, I couldn't play." The Court: "Then what did you do?" "I gave a sign to my assistant, who was with me to play my part." Question: "You had someone sitting on the side?" "Yes, Your Honor." The Court: "While you were sitting there as a member of the orchestra?" "Yes Your Honor." Question: "So, so far as the director was concerned, you were a member of the orchestra?" "Yes. I had an agreement with a man to help me, and he was willing to do it."

MARCEL TABUTEAU

Question: "Where was he? Was he sitting in the orchestra?" Tabuteau: "He is also in the Philadelphia Orchestra. He was sitting a few feet away from me." And so it continued. Tabuteau was asked about "practicing" and replied, "I would like Your Honor to understand, the preparation time—the preparation of my work is the most essential thing. To make it clear, if you are in a circus, if you are a gymnast, if he doesn't practice he will break his neck. The same with me. I have to prepare my work. When I am feeling fine, I have to play a little passage thousands of times to be sure." The Court seemed to understand "that musicians have to practice constantly between concerts." Kaliner grilled Tabuteau about what he was able to do during the rest of 1942. He cross-examined Dr. Ludwig Loeb about the nature of the condition that led to Tabuteau's operation at the Lankenau Hospital on May 17, 1943. He asked questions about his own medical background and how often and for what other ailments he had seen Tabuteau. When gout was mentioned, Comber, the attorney for the insurance company, sprung at the opportunity to pull out the photograph from *Time* magazine. "That shows you there suffering from the gout?" Tabuteau admitted, "Yes." Comber: "With your foot raised up? . . . That picture was taken when?" Tabuteau replied that it "was taken about 1937—it is an old picture. They are using it, a very old picture, to put in the magazine." Comber questioned the date of the *Time* article—"March 1943?" And tried to lead Tabuteau with "Did you, or did you not, in the interview given by you to them, say that you were chronic—"No; I didn't tell them that,—" Here the court record breaks off with "Balance of reply unintelligible." The second trial eventually came to an end with the verdict in favor of Tabuteau and a settlement of $3,078.

This was the era of Eleanor Roosevelt's "My Day" newspaper columns, and my next letter on November 13 began,

> Another installment in the "My Day with Tabuteau" series. He kept me busy for several hours this afternoon on cane. For doing it, he said he would play duets with me every three weeks (an extra lesson), so then even if he weren't here next year, I would have some background. He was really in a good humor today. He had to go marketing and had me take his oboe to his place so he wouldn't have to carry it around with him. He even gave me the key to the apartment—but I had the jitters for the whole four blocks I had to carry that oboe.

MY FIRST YEAR WITH TABUTEAU AT CURTIS

Sometimes with my friends, Marion and Shirley, we try to ana-lyze Tabuteau but we can't figure him out. He makes so many strange remarks and his attitude toward music and people is so odd. If he weren't such a puzzle we wouldn't think about him and discuss him so much. He is such a paradox. Tonight I was talking to some other students after the concert when he came out the stage door. Several people recognized him and he stopped to speak to them and you should see the immediate transformation and charm he radiates. It almost drips. No wonder people think he's such a good fellow and so pleasant. He is inevitably in a wonderful mood *after* a concert. I mentioned some very tricky little passage, which he played so well, and he said he had fun. 'I always have fun,' he said, 'or I wouldn't do it.' It does look that way when you watch him, but this afternoon in the Studio he was disgusted. I have honestly never known anyone so complicated. I try to just think of his musicianship . . . There must be something way back in his youth or somewhere to explain a lot of his attitudes.

Soon after I wrote to my mother:

Marion and Shirley came home from String Class Monday and said Tabuteau told them he was going to have a flute player from wood-wind ensemble play with them and then he said "and I have a girl who is a good oboe player, that is pretty good, at least I'm trying to make a musician out of her"—or something to that effect. Anyhow, they said he acted very modest about it as if he didn't want to brag and they were sure it must be me and that he is going to have me play a solo with the String Ensemble on a recital. I never expected that. Of course, he hasn't said anything to me about it yet. Yesterday Marion played in a beautiful performance of a Beethoven trio for piano, vio-lin, and cello, the *Archduke*, with Marie Shefeluk and George Walker. They were offered a job by some Women's' Club but as this Negro boy is the pianist, they were told they'd have to substitute someone else—so they refused to do it unless he played. I was very proud of them. He is a fine pianist and everyone likes him so well at school. Isn't that stupid? People are dreadfully prejudiced around this town.

Almost sixty years later Marion Davies remembered being coached on the trio by William Primrose. He backed up their resolve, Curtis stood ground, and George Walker played with them at the club.[12]

I often had colds that winter. On November 17, I wrote:

I only got through my lesson by making a big effort. He kept saying, "What's the matter with you? Come on!" I played all through that third Barret etude doing three trills on each note. He didn't say anything so I don't know what he thought. When he says *nothing* that doesn't necessarily mean it's good! But he told me to take it in D-Flat next time so at least I won't be on it four months like the poor boy of several years ago. He said something about it seemed I was always blowing my nose. The Tabuteaus have an idea that girls are weak anyhow, and it is so annoying for me to prove it . . . The next time I was at Mme Tabuteau's she gave me a lot of instructions about my cold. Fed me rum; at that point I was willing to take anything. Rum with very hot water and a slice of lemon with a couple sugar lumps. I also had a *pheasant* sandwich and she gave me some pills (not together), and some rum in a little bottle to take before going to bed. I did all that but felt just as bad this morning. I *must* be at Woodwind Ensemble tomorrow. Mme Tab said he would wonder what had happened when he sees the bottle 'cause she doesn't drink anything. He will probably curse her for wasting it on me.

Sunday, November 21, 1943

I was still feeling sick, but went to woodwind ensemble Thursday and played badly. Tabuteau said, 'Who is your teacher anyway? He certainly doesn't know much about teaching oboe.' I said he played in the Philadelphia Orchestra and he said 'Well, I think you'd better change!' Then later he told me I'd have to do something about my reeds. He said he wanted to help me all he could—that I must change my gouge and he would give me some cane. He had never talked so nicely. I was really surprised, so asked if I could bring my gouger to the studio and he said, 'Do anything you please, only prepare my cane!' . . . Oh, I forgot, yesterday Tab told me to learn the Handel *G minor Concerto*. Woe is me! It's the one he played last spring—the oboe player's War Horse, and the only time it ever really sounded good was when Tab played it and I can't make it sound like *that*. I never thought he'd consider having me study a solo but I'm afraid he won't be able to stand to hear me play it.

December 2, 1943

I worked over at the Studio during two days while Tabuteau was away with the Orchestra. Practiced for hours on the Handel *Concerto* but I can't make it sound like anything. Of course, Tabuteau is never satisfied with the way *he* plays. He says once about four or five years

MY FIRST YEAR WITH TABUTEAU AT CURTIS

ago he played a few notes that really satisfied him. I saw a couple of old reeds of his lying around and tried them. They were marvelous and I found out how a reed should play. His reeds play *easily*—not stiff at all. Then while looking for something else, I found a French book, which out of curiosity, I opened. I couldn't read it but it had the naughtiest illustrations you could imagine. Of course, I had to look at the whole thing. I always thought I might find something like that in the Studio. Half the pages were uncut as if it hadn't been opened so perhaps I shouldn't think too badly of Tabuteau for having it. Maybe someone just gave it to him. Anyhow—these French! I'm sure I don't know what he'd think if he knew I looked at it. It was lying right under some ads for reed supplies.

We were all looking forward to the party on December 5, which would be a combination celebration for the 20th anniversary of Curtis and Christmas. I described the event to my mother:

There was a big fire burning in the Common Room fireplace. The festivities were in Curtis Hall with Zimbalist as Master of Cere-monies. The Opera Class put on a funny program clowning audi-tions. Then Piatigorsky, Primrose, and Gian Carlo Menotti sang a Trio written by Menotti and accompanied by Zimbalist on the piano. For the libretto, Menotti had taken the catalog of the school and set it to music. Every line was familiar to me! There was a very ominous sounding passage for "Students are on probation during the entire pe-riod of enrollment and may be dropped at any time for failure to progress according to the standards of the faculty." Instead of the usual flute obbligato, Menotti had used a bassoon. Primrose was hi-lariously funny. They were presented with flowers afterwards and all fought over them. Primrose filled in with reading between numbers from a book of chess moves with perfect deadpan English humor un-til Zimbalist would get up and make him stop. The finale was Haydn's *Toy Symphony* directed by Zimbalist and composed of faculty members all playing tin whistles or instruments other than their own. Primrose played violin, Luboshutz, cello, Frederich Schorr (of Met opera fame) a cuckoo whistle. Piatigorsky played the double bass. It was wonderful. Our counterpoint teacher, Constant Vauclain, played drums, the librarian, trumpet; Soffray (solfège teacher), tambourine. Zimmy almost forgot to have them all stand to acknowledge the ap-plause. Tabuteau and other Philadelphia Orchestra members came late as they had played in Atlantic City today. Mme Tab was there

MARCEL TABUTEAU

though and I introduced the other oboists to her as they had not met her . . . Refreshments were potato chips, sandwiches, stuffed eggs, pickles, olives, weenies (with toothpicks in 'em) punch, candy, and cake.

I heard Menotti's clever trio thirty years later in 1975 when it was performed for the Curtis Institute's fiftieth anniversary party at the Bellevue-Stratford Hotel. The three singers were Boris Goldovsky, Orlando Cole, and Alexander McCurdy. To honor Menotti's seventieth birthday in 1981 there was another performance of the trio. This time the already experienced Cole and McCurdy were joined by Felix Galimir with the piano accompaniment played in grand operatic style by Boris Goldovsky.

Saturday night, December 11, 1943

Yesterday, just so you see how my days go, at 8:00 I got up—ate—went over to the Studio and dumped cane in water—came back here and practiced. Back to Studio at 11:00 with Martha and Marguerite, and gouged and split cane until 1:40. Prepared *280* pieces. Our best record so far. Dashed to school. Grabbed a cinnamon bun across the street and just made it to Italian Renaissance class. Dr. Vittorini gives such good lectures and it makes me feel I've missed something by not reading Dante's *Divine Comedy*. At 3:00, came home, got my oboe, went back, rehearsed quintets until 5:00—went to Cosmopolitan Club and waited on tables until 8:30. Had a good dinner there and really needed the $2.00 they paid me, as I didn't work for Mme Tab last week. Had no time. Then until 11:00 o'clock I wrote and typed Tabuteau's letters. Finally got all ten of them done. Four to Canada, one with a $50.00 check for some fellow who takes care of his car and is going to buy him whiskey and Scotch up there.

December 16, 1943

Tuesday morning Martha and I worked in Tabuteau's Studio again. He was in an odd mood. Grumbled, swore, but amused us so, we almost laughed at him. He was talking about selling the whole business to the Devil, etc., etc. and about an hour later he says, "you know the oboe is the most wonderful instrument. When you get it just right, you can express more in just one note, etc." He must really love it but we came to the conclusion there is no such thing as a good reed. Even the best one, by its very physical characteristics, would be bad and changeable. There is a rare item in one of his drawers. His lesson note-

MY FIRST YEAR WITH TABUTEAU AT CURTIS

book with *1904* dates in it. I think it was Gillet's handwriting, but to read the assignments over—Barret, Sellner, scales (all in French of course), octobre, mai, avril, made me feel so strange. Another era, but exactly the same studies we have now.

My mother was painting a special icy scene with a penguin holding an oboe for me to give Tabuteau for Christmas. I was sure it would be different from anything else he might receive, but I wrote her "whiskey seems about the only thing he really likes." After one of my mid-December sessions doing the blouses and socks, I described for my mother how Mme Tabuteau fixed me a big fruit salad, and I saw some of

the things former students send him—or rather their mothers! Davison's mother sends them a turkey every Thanksgiving from her farm. The mother of Minsker, the English horn player in the orchestra, sends them a big Fruit Cake every Christmas and a boy in the Army sent them a crate of oranges and grapefruit from Florida. She gave me some. Just as we finished eating, the siren blew and there was an alert. They shut off the central switch at the Drake so there was no light. Mme Tabuteau lit a little candle and it made fascinating shadows on the wall. Their room is littered with such a variety of things. I could look out the window and see Philadelphia getting dark. She said, "Do you suppose it is the Germans?" and I guess she was serious 'cause then during the whole blackout she talked—mostly about France and how they used to go there every single summer. They shipped their Buick over and drove to Paris, visited their relatives and then went to spend the summer at their house in the country near Toulon. Her home was Blois, and the Germans have ruined it. She said her mother saw the Germans come three times, in 1870, in 1914, and now, during this war, she died with the Swastika over her head. Mme T was there when war started in 1939. He used to be on the boat to France by the first of May and come back the end of September. They never missed a year; I think she said, for seventeen years. She would go over later on account of her teaching, and she said never once did he meet the boat on time—was always a day or two early or late. He would drive about eighty-five miles an hour. Part of the reason that Tab can work such hours at the oboe during the winter must be that he leaves it completely alone in the summer. They must have had a wonderful time. She said everyone in France was always amazed at how much money they spent, but of course they did not see them earning it. She did her shopping in Paris and they hated

MARCEL TABUTEAU

to leave their home in the South just when it began to be so beautiful towards fall. They always barely made the boat and he had to bribe the officials with money to get the car put on. It was surely interesting to hear her tell about it. It was almost midnight when I got home.

By December 20 we were in our Christmas break, but as I wrote my mother that day:

> Tab told me I would have a lesson Tuesday (tomorrow)—so far I'm not having any vacation. [It was a change of pace when] Marion asked if I'd like to go to her lesson and said Piatigorsky wouldn't mind. He is a fine teacher and never raises his voice. I felt lucky to be able to sit in and hear him play. I wish Tabuteau were a little more like him in personality. Piatigorsky even spoke to me when I left. Imagine! I guess Marion and Shirley have told him about me and he said he knew me as "the oboe girl." He is very nice, a lovely person, and very kind too, the girls say.

One time later in the winter I had the amazing experience (for me) of

> playing bridge with Piatigorsky. I haven't played cards of any type for years! He has been sick and wanted Marion and Shirley to come over and play bridge with him. They persuaded me to be the fourth. They plugged me with rules which, of course, I didn't remember, but he was easy-going and not too serious a player. I had wonderful hands of cards and Marion and I beat the other two with a very high score. Piatigorsky is quiet in voice and even called me by my first name right off. He has a very Russian accent and says awfully funny things. Mrs. Piatigorsky came back about 11:30 from working at a psychiatric hospital. She just does it for "*fun*"??

Now it was time to deliver the Christmas present to Tabuteau, and I wondered what his expression would be when he saw the *Pingouin*. "Will he say 'Holy Smoke'? He says that a lot." On December 23, after midnight, I described the evening for my mother:

> I must tell you all about taking the *Pingouin* over. I phoned about 7:00 and he wasn't home yet but she expected him and said I should come soon. He arrived just before I did. I said 'Merry Christmas' and he said, 'Well, Well, Well,' and was very nice. He wanted her to undo it but she made him do it and he seemed really tickled that I'd brought them a package. They admired the Noël paper and the little card and wanted to know where I found it. He kept unwrapping

MY FIRST YEAR WITH TABUTEAU AT CURTIS

and saying, 'My, my,' and when he began to see what it was, he said 'Ah—ha—a-a.' She thought you made it look like him and said how wonderful that was when you'd never seen him! They like the colors and kept saying 'very fine.' It was certainly the perfect gift and you don't know how much pleasure it was for me to be able to give them something they couldn't possibly get anywhere else. I could tell he was really pleased and they wanted you (*votre maman*) to know how much they appreciated your doing it. Then Tab said, 'We must have a drink on that,' and what would I have? He announced what he wanted and she dug behind a lot of books on the shelf and got out a bottle of Scotch. She mentioned a lot of names and I grabbed on 'Port'—any port in a storm! Anyhow, I didn't think I ought to take Scotch but I just couldn't refuse a little wine on an occasion like that.

January 1944 started out a little better with a good session on our Beethoven Quintet in woodwind ensemble and a lesson in which I played the First Sellner Duo with Tabuteau. "We played some parts over a good many times but he didn't stop me at all in the slow movement. Once he said very nicely, 'I play with you because I love to play but you must listen too, to what I do.' Martha had her lesson afterwards and said she had stood outside the door listening. She couldn't believe it was me and couldn't tell us apart. She said she thought he had 'someone *really* good' in there!"

One evening when I went to the Drake to get more letters, I was invited to stay for dinner. "I had already eaten but it was several hours ago and I am always ready for more. He had just cooked a roast and it was honestly the most delicious meat I've ever tasted—just melted in the mouth. Potatoes, gravy (the juice, not thick, starchy, gravy). He fixed a big tossed salad right at the table and we had the usual tea, toast, *fromage,* and even dessert—applesauce, and the fruitcake that Minsker's mother sent them for Christmas. They were talking in French all the time and were quite funny. When Mme Tab's slip showed, he began on that. Said her dress was too short for her. It wasn't at all a short dress so I sided with her."

In an expansive mood after dinner, Tabuteau talked about the woodwind class. Later I jotted down some of his reflections and graphic descriptions:

MARCEL TABUTEAU

The bassoon had made a less than musical sound which he said was "like seeing a well-dressed man on the street and then he stops and blows his nose with one finger on a nostril." Something else reminded him "of a cow kicking over a bucket." Then he made a comparison of his own head which had 'not much hair but plenty *halo* and the student who had plenty hair but nothing around it. He also said if it were thousands of years ago in caveman days, he would have a big club, and we would all be killed by the end of the afternoon. He's always saying "Un-believ-*able*." Tonight he spoke of how he hates to play solo with the orchestra—that his only consolation is to look around and think what stupid fools all the people are. Then he talked about the three uses of number patterns; for rhythm, 4,1234 etc; for placement on the line—distribution; and in the rebound, where two numbers come together, such as 1-1-2, a change of direction. He really swears by it and says it is a marvelous system. Said he played that way even when he was eighteen but he did not make the patterns then. You must go somewhere according to the harmonies and know where the climax is. He said most people always think the highest note is the climax and how stupid that is. You must be able to drive higher on the line to a lower note and travel. Also, the spirit is the last thing to put on the playing. You cannot work from the "spirit" of a piece. It would be like trying to put a flower on canvas and starting with the perfume. But what work it is to play a few notes well—even the beginning of the solo in the Tchaikovsky 4th—it is unbelievably difficult. He said if I ever play a few notes well, it will only be because I came here. True enough.

Tabuteau seemed to be staying in a "good humor" and was "nice" during almost all of January. I was enjoying a respite from the verbal lashings. It was rather amazing, as on January 21 and 22 he was to be a soloist with the Philadelphia Orchestra and that would ordinarily have put him in a frenzy. Perhaps in the end it was all connected with reeds, I suggested to my mother, for

one day over at the Studio, Tabuteau was trying reeds and had several good ones. He really seemed pleased and was playing excerpts from the Tchaikovsky 4th, the Handel *Concerto,* Mussorgsky, and the Paladilhe *Solo.* [All the students were there for his superb performance of the Handel *G Minor Concerto.*] Perfect is the only word for it. I'd rather hear him than anybody on any instrument. He has the most wonderful quality of playing delicately and refined and fragile and yet

MY FIRST YEAR WITH TABUTEAU AT CURTIS

making it sound like there are mountains of power in back of it. Yesterday we (the cellists, Marion and Shirley, and myself,) bought him a pound of nuts in a fancy box (made in France) at Maron's, an elegant French candy store here, which we'll give him after tomorrow night's concert. He loves nuts.

A couple of days later I saw Madame Tabuteau at Zimbalist's recital. I wrote my mother the following account on January 24:

We were supposed to wear long dresses so I did, but most didn't. Madame T says I have been walking on air ever since Saturday because Tabuteau played so well. I can't tell you how perfect he was—every note. We all shouted "Bravo." The opening measure alone was the most beautiful you could imagine . . . Do listen on the radio, even if it's not like hearing him in person. Everyone remarked what a pleasing stage personality he had. He appeared very gracious and modest. We saw him a minute afterwards and he said, "So here are the young ladies!!" We gave him the box of nuts from Maron's and he seemed really pleased. Today at my lesson he thanked me for them and said these were so good and how did I know that he liked nuts? Mme Tab. appreciated the special *box* we got for the nuts. (It cost $1.00.) At Maron's they have their boxes decorated with cats and she loves cats. He was in a *fine mood* and we talked a little about the Handel and he said, "And so you were not disappointed?" He is relieved it is over—says he wasn't nervous at all. He seemed really so nice. I hope it lasts! When I made a mistake, he just said "A-*ha*," instead of screaming.

Tonight I was talking to Abba Bogin who wrote down the grades on Tab's card for him. He said Tab told him to "give Miss Storch an 'A' and the other two 'B's." It seems silly but they *do* give grades in everything. I had no idea how Tab would mark—thought he would be tough. Of course, your main instrument is what counts, so I'm surely glad about the "A."

Abba Bogin, who was a piano student of Isabelle Vengerova, used to listen to Tabuteau's classes and eventually became a type of unofficial "assistant." Tabuteau had little interest in the details of keeping attendance records and marking down grades and was happy to have Abba help him. Other "duties," such as keeping the water pitcher filled, came along with the "job." Over fifty years later in an interview with Melissa Stevens, he described one time when the students decided it should be

MARCEL TABUTEAU

filled with gin instead of water. Abba put the pitcher and glass on Tabuteau's music stand. After a few minutes of working, he stopped and poured a drink. "He picked it up, drank a little and continued working without saying a word. His eyebrows did not even flicker. He went through the whole pitcher . . . When the class was over, he said, 'the time is up. I'll see you next week and Abba, that was a very good pitcher of water. He walked out."[13]

One of the high points of my Philadelphia years came in February 1943 when for the first time I heard Toscanini conduct the Philadelphia Orchestra. I had been an ardent Toscanini fan since my high school days when I listened to all his Saturday night NBC Symphony broadcasts and considered this Sunday February 28 concert as a wonderful birthday present. Linton Martin of the Philadelphia Inquirer wrote a glowing review headed: "Toscanini Is Cheered at Academy. Gilbert: *Comedy Overture on Negro Themes,* Kennan: *Night Soliloquy,* Creston: *Choric Dance No. 2,* Kabalevsky: *Second Symphony,* Schumann: *Manfred Overture,* Mendelssohn: *Reformation Symphony,* Wagner: *Meistersinger Prelude.* It was a program that, on paper, looked like a scrambled musical grab bag. But in performance it was electrifying and magnificent—a memorable occasion of flaming inspiration, given glow and greatness by the maestro's magic. Apparently ageless and certainly incomparable, the vital and vigorous Toscanini had both orchestra and audience on their toes for two hours. The orchestra played for him with an almost unearthly beauty and brilliance of tone and when the thrilling climax and coda of the *Meistersinger* Prelude brought the concert to a close, the capacity audience mingled cheers with the applause that brought Toscanini back to the stage for repeated bows." Cheers were less common in 1943 than now, when even a concert of routine interest can bring an audience to its feet. After my next lesson, "I walked a couple blocks with Tabuteau on my way to a recital at Curtis. He asked if I'd heard Toscanini and said what a wonderful man he is— seemed glad he hadn't had much to play at that concert—so guess there is *somebody* for whom Tabuteau feels awe."

Now one year later Toscanini was to return on February 6 to conduct an all-Beethoven program for the Philadelphia Orchestra Pension

MY FIRST YEAR WITH TABUTEAU AT CURTIS

Foundation. A number of things happened in very quick succession. First, I received a call to go to North Carolina for the weekend to play in an orchestra concert for which I would earn $25.00 plus travel expenses. This would enable me to pay my rent for another month, but my major concern was that "I can get back Sunday night in time for Toscanini—Mrs. Piatigorsky has a ticket I can use and I am so thrilled to see him again." A couple of days later, on February 2, 1944, I wrote excitedly to my mother:

> Here is what Tabuteau sprung out of a clear sky yesterday. He said that he was supposed to have Toscanini for dinner Thursday, but that Ormandy also wanted him that night as Ormandy has to leave for Havana the next day and it would be his only chance to see Toscanini, so as Tabuteau's apartment is too small to have them all and Ormandy's is being done over, they are going to use Hilsberg's (the concertmaster's) apartment for the dinner and Mrs. Hilsberg has a maid but he thought it would be nice to have someone to help carry dishes in and out also and Tabuteau asked if I could or would do it!! And he added he thought it would be a nice chance for me to see the Maestro up close—Tabuteau is going to do the cooking and they are having an Italian make Ravioli for Toscanini—Isn't that terrific? Imagine my seeing him in person—I'm so excited and you know how I've always worshipped him—cut out all his pictures and listened to his programs and it was always one of my main ambitions to see him conduct. To serve Toscanini! It will be something to remember all my life. Tabuteau said something about paying me for my time even, but I'd be willing to pay *him* for a chance like that. Toscanini's presence under any condition is notoriously hard to get into and here I'm just being invited to see him—and of course it will be quite a gathering—two great conductors at one whack!
>
> T-O-S-C-A-N-I-N-I, himself. I am going around in a daze. I was worried about what I should wear but Madame Tabuteau said just any plain dark dress—my brown will be o.k. and maybe they'll have an apron or something . . . I have to leave for North Carolina Friday morning so I am lucky to be able to do this first . . . The kids in my house are all excited and said I should sing a different theme from a Beethoven symphony every time I bring something in. I hope I can keep my mind on what I have to do. I just can't believe it—to think I'd live to actually be in the same room with Toscanini! I'm sure I have a lucky star. Would you ever in your wildest dreams have imagined anything like this? It's just like a story!

The "story" continues in a letter written in pencil two days later on the train:

En route Philadelphia to Washington D.C. February 4, 1944, a.m.
Dear Mother,

At various times I've thought—this is the most exciting moment of my life—but now beyond a doubt, the most wonderful experience I've ever had was last night. Tabuteau had me come to Hilsberg's apartment at 5:45 after Woodwind Ensemble as he said he had mushrooms to peel. Well, here I was in the kitchen—a big basin of string beans in the sink and I helped Tabuteau pick the ends off of them. Then I ran them all through a gadget that slices them lengthwise. I sliced radishes and fixed lettuce, fennel, and endive for the salad. He showed me how to do everything. Mrs. Hilsberg was very nice to me. Their coffee grinder broke and everyone was bemoaning in a different accent how sad it was. Finally, Hilsberg jiggled the right screw and it worked again. Tabuteau fixed an enormous pan of mushrooms. He was so excited. About 7:15 I heard the Maestro arrive. I just about died because I couldn't see him. First, I caught a glimpse of him in the other room though. After the soup (borscht), (but before that they all had champagne), Mrs. Hilsberg asked me to take off the soup plates. I was walking in the air. After awhile I got to bring in the big plate of ravioli and serve Toscanini first. He looked so pleased when he saw those ravioli. Madame Tabuteau had me get him more red wine. After I'd been in and out several times, Ormandy just spoke to me and said, "Don't you go to Curtis?" asked what I played— "Oh—oboe. Are you good?" etc. He was so friendly. Finally he and Hilsberg insisted I sit down and eat salad with them. [Tabuteau would not have presumed to ask to have his student sit down at the table.] After serving Tabuteau's Roast Leg of Lamb, the string beans and mushrooms, I sat at the same table with Toscanini and tried to soak in every word he said. Ormandy came by and said, "You must remember every minute because you're in the presence of the greatest musician in the world." [I included a diagram of the seating arrangement—Toscanini at the head of the table, then Mrs. Ormandy and Madame Tabuteau opposite each other, followed by Mr. Hilsberg and Mr. Ormandy on opposite sides, then Mrs. Toscanini and Mrs. Hilsberg facing each other, with the addition of a card table where I sat across from Tabuteau.]

They had grapefruit with strawberries and Russian cookies for dessert and I had that at the table too and listened to him talk. It was

MY FIRST YEAR WITH TABUTEAU AT CURTIS

way beyond my wildest expectations. I would have given anything just to *see* him, but to be able to hear him and watch him—if I could only tell you. He is so sweet, so lovable, so simple and humble. They talked mostly about music—he speaks of everything with the greatest enthusiasm and is frank and honest in his opinions. He seems ageless. His skin is practically without a wrinkle and has the fresh bright color of a child's. He is the cleanest looking man you ever saw. It looks like he was scrubbed hard—and so neat. Really he is beautiful to look at. I kept feeling like I was in a dream, that it couldn't be me. Later, after I'd taken all the dishes off the table and they had left the table, Ormandy, Hilsberg, Tabuteau and Toscanini were talking together. Ormandy beckoned to me, but I just couldn't go—then finally he came over and insisted I come and listen. I swear I will be grateful to him all my life. Imagine the privilege of being treated that way. I kept feeling overwhelmed at how lucky I was. Toscanini was discussing contemporary music and said, "But this is what is difficult," and he walked over to the piano and with a caressingly soft touch, played a Beethoven melody, saying, "One measure, two measures—three measures—four—five measures—to write a long melody like that," and the way he played it, carrying the phrase along so perfectly! It was the Adagio movement from the Septet, which would be on his Philadelphia concert. He kept playing and singing in his croaky voice and illustrating things—I've already made notes of as much as I could remember of his opinions on many composers and conductors' tempi, etc. Once he and Tabuteau both sang a slow movement of a Mozart Symphony together. That was a rare combination. In short, I was like a guest for the whole evening and stayed until he left about 11:00 p.m. Mme Toscanini asked me to get him a glass of water which I did, and he said "Thank you, my dear." Ormandy said to me, "You know, I was thinking, you have the distinction of being the only real American here," and sure enough I was the only one born in America. Nice of him to think up some distinction for me when I was in such a distinguished gathering. When they left Toscanini even shook hands with me and patted me on the shoulder. The whole evening was really an inspiration for a lifetime . . . Oh—and dear Tabuteau—there were lots of ravioli left and he said, "You must take them home to the girls," so I took home a big pot of ravioli, sauce, mushrooms and cheese, and we had a midnight feed on the ravioli that Toscanini ate. The kids were thrilled and they all touched me and shook my hand! . . . There's no use—I could go on exploding about it all indefinitely. It would take another letter this long to tell all the things I heard him say.

With lots of love,

Laila, "The girl who had dinner with Toscanini."

The "notes" I wrote down late the same night refer alternately to Toscanini's opinions on a myriad of musical subjects and my own wonderment at finding myself in such a lofty gathering where I had actually served him the red wine and ravioli:

Mrs. Toscanini said that he wasn't always as expansive in company, but that evening he talked and sang with great enthusiasm for several hours until he became hoarse. Tabuteau was facing Toscanini, who sat at the piano. They spoke of early Metropolitan days when Toscanini said he used to give the cue warnings to Tabuteau because he was young and new but intelligent. Ormandy joked, "Oh, he was intelligent then!" Asked by Ormandy what he would play on some future radio broadcasts, Toscanini replied that Stokowski had been giving them so much contemporary music that he was going to do Beethoven, and maybe some Schumann or Brahms. "After all, I am an old man—I will give them old music." He mentioned all the fugues in modern music. "When they can't think of anything they write a fugue." Of today's composers, he does not care for William Schumann and Roy Harris. Creston, he likes better. Hindemith he considers "mathematical." He often said, "I am a Latin" or emphasized his Italian feeling. Asked about the Metropolitan Opera, he said he told Caruso to come in 1903 and then later he (Toscanini) came because he heard Mahler had left Vienna for New York. When Steffi (Mrs. Ormandy) said she once heard a complete Mahler cycle conducted by Mengelberg, he said, "Oh yes—all seven." He thinks the Eighth is ridiculous and cited a theme Mahler gives to the trumpets in one place and also his bad taste in using a trumpet in the opening of the Schubert *C Major Symphony*. Toscanini wrote into a score he saw in the New York Philharmonic Library, what a shame it was that such a great man should do such things. He said that he was there and heard Mahler use four bassoons in Mozart's *Marriage of Figaro*. "Two weren't enough for him. Mahler is often banal. Schubert, Beethoven, Verdi are never banal." He often conducted Leoncavallo's *Pagliacci* but "felt ashamed," and he considered Tchaikovsky to be "the Russian equivalent of Leoncavallo." But he likes the little melody

MY FIRST YEAR WITH TABUTEAU AT CURTIS

in the Fourth Symphony, *Andantino in modo di Canzona,* which is simple like a folk song. Ormandy spoke of the way Tabuteau plays that oboe solo. Toscanini said he tried to study the Fourth only last summer, and almost as if to justify his attitude toward Tchaikovsky, mentioned that he had conducted the *Pathétique* in 1898. At the piano while playing the slow movement of the Beethoven *Septet* that he was rehearsing for the Pension Foundation concert, he said that a new member of the orchestra, Ralph MacLane, was the finest clarinetist he had ever heard in America. [The concert included the Overture to *Egmont, Septet in E-Flat Major* with augmented strings, the *Pastoral Symphony No. 6 in F Major,* and the Overture to *Leonore No. 2.*]

My euphoria over Toscanini's music-making did not extend to my oboe lesson of the next day. It was almost as if Tabuteau, who was so happy after the concert, was reminded anew of the level of perfection reached in playing with Toscanini and could not bear to listen to the inadequate efforts of his students. Again he screamed and roared, "My leetle fran (friend), you are care*less*—I have told you, you are care*less*. It is unbeliev*able*. What is da *matter* wid you?? Stupide! You do not know how to pract*eece.*" But I rationalized that "Since Toscanini was here I guess maybe he's decided he's not being particular or hard enough on us," and I still continued to float on air. People would ask if it was really true that I "had dinner with Toscanini? I have the gold top off a champagne bottle as a tangible souvenir of that evening. I should have a locket made out of it!"[14]

During this whole winter I had been writing letters to Tabuteau's former students now serving in the Armed Forces. I knew he wanted to keep in touch with John de Lancie, I explained to my mother, so

> I sent de Lancie the pictures I took of Tab's studio and he wrote so much about them in his letters that Tab said he couldn't understand why *he* hadn't seen them. (I'm sure I mentioned them one time but he wasn't interested.) Now he said, "don't you know you mustn't take *anything* in the Studio, not even pictures?? I have the hardest time convincing those young people I wasn't born yesterday!" and laughed. He's so suspicious. De Lancie had mentioned that he could see the spot where Tabuteau had given him *beaucoup de Hell.*

Sometimes the boys answered directly to me, as I described to my mother:

I had a letter from Robert Davison who is in the Navy. It was about a joke Tab had told me to remind him of, concerning a French word, that he doubted Tab would have explained to me. Something Tabuteau had said years ago when Davison was in school and another oboist was playing his lesson—the slow movement of the second Barret Sonata marked *Lento con espressione*. Tabuteau said the only part the student played well was the "*con*," knowing that Davison, who had studied in France, would understand. It is evidently a word in French Mme Tab won't let me add to my vocabulary. I haven't been able to find out what it means yet. Something bad, no doubt.[15] Speaking of bad words, you should hear Tab swear at his gouger. "God damn son of a bitch." It sounds so funny the way he says it that I almost laugh every time.

One word I *was* able to learn a little more about was *dragon*.

I asked Mme Tab. if she knew I was a "dragoon" as I wanted to try to find out what he really meant when he called me one. He wouldn't tell me, and she said I should guess and that I should know he never said anything mean or unkind!?? Only a few days previously Jane Hill (one of the secretaries at Curtis), had asked me to take a soldier (an oboist in uniform) to the Studio to introduce him to Tabuteau. He was really lucky as Tab was there and was very nice to him—put on a good show and even gave him the reed he was working on. He was talking about conductors. "When you play pianissimo they want forte and when you play forte they want pianissimo. You can't please the bastards!" Then he says, "I can talk like that to you because you are a soldier and she, she is a dragon. You know what is a dragon?" I asked, "Do you mean dragoon?" He says, "Yes. It is a rough and ready branch of the Army." At my last lesson he was harping about how you had to be an aristocrat to play oboe, not a rough and ready girl! Finally he explained they were the brightest branch of the army—and the most colorful. They wear bright plumes and carry swords and ride ahead into battle on beautiful horses. They sound quite dashing so now I don't mind being called one. I said I thought if I were going to be an oboe player, I'd have to be able to take it a little and he sort of laughed and said, "I quite agree with you."

Going to Philadelphia Orchestra concerts was as much a regular part of my life as attending classes at Curtis.

It is awful waiting in line for these Saturday night concerts at the Academy. You almost always get some pigeon droppings on you.

MY FIRST YEAR WITH TABUTEAU AT CURTIS

They all roost there and have no pity on the people down below. It was wonderful to hear Tabuteau play the *Eroica* of Beethoven . . . If you want to hear how wonderful Tab sounds, you should play my record of the last movement of Mozart's *Symphonie Concertante* for four winds with the Philadelphia Orchestra. It is more faithful to his playing than anything I've heard. He's never even listened to it.[16] Says Stoki's tempos were awful and Stoki had the impertinence *not* to follow him (Tabuteau) that day. He hates records. Thinks they are distorting and canned—like when you look in the crazy mirrors at a fair. He said I could make some records for him and he would sign them—like his letters—and laughed. I said I didn't think I'd fool anyone!

February 26, 1944

Did I tell you the other night Tabuteau said he *could* have a job in *Cuba* for me next year? He didn't mean it too seriously I know, and I think it was only a ten weeks thing, but the very idea that he would consider me for a job was pleasing and Cuba is an intriguing idea. I guess because Ormandy has just returned from there, perhaps he told Tab. they need an oboe. Mme Tab. told me once that his students practically always get jobs, as conductors write him from all over asking if he has anyone. He has the reputation now for turning out good pupils and you can't go through Curtis without absorbing *some* musicianship. He is even known in South America, as a friend of hers was traveling there some years ago and a South American man said to her, "Oh—Philadelphia—you have a fine musician there!" The lady naturally expected him to mention Stokowski, but instead he said, "Marcel Tabuteau."

February 29, 1944

Tabuteau said a teacher is like a mother bird. Feeds you a few years but should help you to learn to teach yourself. Then will give a peck on the head and tell you to fly away. He says that not until I think and practice right will he peck me on the head and that he is giving me as much as he can. The last word. My last chance. I must find things and practice right. Play the meaning of the notes and find the character of each little segment. Practice the cells. I must stop and think, I am studying with the person I've always wanted to. It's really wonderful to be so sure and not have to worry and wonder if you'd learn more or do better if you had someone else. For singers and violinists, there are many choices. With the oboe, there is no doubt. I not only have the best oboist in the world for a teacher, but

MARCEL TABUTEAU

he is also such a great musician that all the students at school, no matter who their own teachers are, can learn from him. Regardless of how he acts personally, I have to remember I'm getting what I want. Excuse me if I keep reminding myself!

By the beginning of March my "luck" had run out—Tabuteau's spell of "niceness" was over. Everything began to go as badly as it had seemed to be going well earlier in the year. I explained to my mother:

I don't know what has happened to Tab lately but he is really cracking down. For a while things were going pretty smoothly. I knew it was too good to last. Last week in woodwind ensemble there was water in my reed and he said I sounded like a "singing kewspitter" (cuspidor). I heard that today he kicked a boy out of string ensemble just for looking bored! And I was beginning to think he really had a kind streak under all his exterior—especially after he sent us a kettle of ravioli from Toscanini's dinner! At my lesson today I couldn't play two notes to suit him. "Really, it is terrific. Stupide! My young fran," he says, "you do not know—this—that—etc. etc." It's such an effort to keep calm enough to even play. I talk to myself and tell myself how silly it is—that I'm not playing an audition—that it doesn't help to get nervous, but nevertheless, my heart pounds, my hands shake, and my mouth gets dry. I can well believe he would like to pick up a chair and crash it down on my dome. In Ensemble last week he said the only thing that kept him from tearing me to bits was the fact that I was a girl. If you want to see a facsimile of some of the dirty looks I got, look in that old *Life* magazine about Curtis in my scrapbook. Once he said, "I can see by the way your lips are set, you are all ready to say *pah* instead of *ta*. I look at your lips from the standpoint of an oboe player," at which everybody roared with laughter. It was really funny and then he said, "Well, I can't help looking at your lips." And did I tell you when a clarinetist missed a run, his excuse was that he had a hair on his tongue and Tabuteau said, "that is the limit. It is un-fair. You have hair on your tongue and I don't even have hair on my school." We told him it was "skull" but he pronounced it just like "school." Then he said, "Why do you say fool?" We said that's spelled differently; he was thinking of "cup-fool" and we had to tell him that was cup*ful*. He really was confused.

[The next ensemble class was just as bad.] He picked, roared, and screamed at me the whole two hours. The things he said were so awful that if I believed them all, I'd surely quit playing the oboe today. Even

MY FIRST YEAR WITH TABUTEAU AT CURTIS

Martha said it made her so upset to hear him, she felt like throwing something at him and Marilyn Costello, who was out in the hall awhile, said she couldn't stand to hear him picking on me. It was the way he kept it up that made me so mad, and instead of shaking or anything, I just got so indifferent I couldn't play at all. If that's the way he *used* to be, it must have been hell. I'm sure he's been unusually on edge the last couple weeks because there was a question of our playing for a broadcast. Now, thank goodness, he has decided we are too bad and it is out of the question—otherwise every class would be an Inferno.

By mid-March I felt that "I was getting more, rather than less nervous, playing for Tabuteau. He said, 'What kind of lesson are this? You sound like a squawking turkey! It is amateurish. Don't you practice?' That was the worst thing, and then he said he couldn't understand why I fall apart in places that aren't hard. 'Maybe you are tense?' and he grabbed my arm, which was stiff as anything. Then he *yells*, '*Don't be tense*,' which you can imagine was a big help. Once he said, 'not so bad' but you are care*less*.' There's never *one* lesson but what he mentions the word 'care*less*.' He says there's always something in my playing that gives me away as not being careful enough. It's just like a 'finger print' and from hearing anyone play for *two* minutes, he can tell just what they're like." Years later I learned that he used this term for almost everyone, even signing a photograph for a future famous oboist, "To my talented but careless student." But this did not help me from feeling really badly in 1944!

Practicing longer hours seemed to make little or no difference. In my next lesson, "he said that I haven't made any progress in musical understanding lately. What is the use for me to be here, why do I want to study music, I am hopeless, I am not interested, I can't even play a scale correctly, my attacks are no good, my articulation is no good, in fact nothing was good! It is really a bit discouraging but from what I hear, I guess he's said the same things to everyone. Perhaps I've been getting off easy. I can surely see how he can knock a person's confidence so that it could ruin you. However, he won't get the best of me if I can help it.

Despite my resolve, the incessant "pounding" in March was beginning to affect me. "I have spent the last two days 'dissipating' trying to forget Tabuteau and all my oboe troubles. Last night I went with the

MARCEL TABUTEAU

girls to an old Carole Lombard movie at a tiny twenty-nine cent theater (crowded and stuffy). We bought tremendous bags of popcorn that we munched all evening. Then I tried drowning my sorrows in ice cream sodas. For three days I didn't practice."

It was not a month of total despair. Doing the Tuesday night wash for Mme Tabuteau was actually a pleasant contrast. Sometimes besides Tabuteau's socks, there would be his dress ties, as he did not like them to be starched. For three weeks in a row she fixed a lamb chop for me— broiled and well seasoned. Along with a green salad, cheese, tea, and fruit, this was the Tabuteau standard light supper. Six rib lamb chops were part of their weekly shopping order at the Reading Terminal Market. Another happy occasion was one of my first visits to Hans Moennig's shop. "I found I can't fix my oboe myself as I could in California, 'cause what goes wrong here is caused by the weather changes—wood shrinks, posts move, et cetera. I surely love Mr. Moennig and he is such an honest workman. He fixed it right while I waited and only charged me *40 cents*." Then there were the faculty recitals. "Tonight was Primrose. I would far rather hear him play viola than listen to almost any violinist. His rhythm, technique, phrasing—everything is perfect. Seymour Lipkin, a sixteen-year-old student, played for him." The three eminent Russians on the faculty, Efrem Zimbalist, Gregor Piatigorsky and Isabelle Vengerova, were unforgettable in a program of just two works, the Mendelssohn *D Minor Trio* and the Tchaikovsky *A Minor Trio*. It was the only time any of us ever heard the legendary Madame Vengerova. A little later we had the revelation of the recently arrived Mieczyslaw Horszowski in a recital of eighteenth-century keyboard music.

Tabuteau let up a bit, I wrote to my mother.

I got off a little easier in woodwind ensemble Thursday but he kept after me about the importance of the wind. He said, "I am not a magician—it can be done. The spark must be there." On my way home from the Orchestra concert tonight I was walking along and heard a familiar voice in back of me shouting, "It's getting colder," and then louder—"It's getting colder, isn't it?" I didn't realize he was speaking to me, but that made me turn around. He usually doesn't start conversations that way. He is always nice after concerts and I am inclined to forgive him again. I mentioned how beautifully he had

MY FIRST YEAR WITH TABUTEAU AT CURTIS

sounded in *La Mer*. He said he didn't know how he did it because he never practices. Before he left, he brought up my wind again. He said in a very derisive tone, "*but your wind*—you don't shape it—you play all on one wind." I guess I should be glad he tells me things. I'm just not phrasing with my wind enough and I make triplets sound 1 2 3 4 instead of 1-1 2 3 or down—up, up, down. I don't change the direction of every note. It is not only thinking right, but one must have the technique to express the bound and rebound, 1-123 like a rubber ball, not like a piece of wood, and the notes must be placed at the perfect, exact spot on the circle.

Sometimes there were lighter non-musical moments to describe for my mother:

Sunday night Shirley gave me a feather cut. Everyone said it gave me a new personality and this morning when I was packing up my oboe after my lesson, Tabuteau said, "so you play better with your hair short. Leave it that way." I was so surprised as he never makes any remarks about such things and I said I was glad if it suited him and he said it was much better. "You were looking awful," he said. You should hear the way he says "*owful.*" Martha had come in and said she guessed maybe she'd better get her hair cut too, and he said yes, it was awful the way we wore our hair in such long bushy ways. It's the first opinion we ever had out of Tabuteau about our appearances. I guess he notices everything even if he doesn't say anything. He tried to show us how our hair ought to be by smoothing his back (what little he has,) and I got the idea he liked it smooth and flat. However, I just can't have mine that way. I'll have to compromise on short. I guess that's why Mme Tab. wears hers in a braid around her head, not loose at all. I told him it allowed the air to circulate around my brain better this way and he laughed.

March 21, 1944

Oh frabjous day! Calooh! Callay! I had a good lesson. (The oboe hasn't gone to my head—it's just that I'm reading *Alice in Wonderland*.) Anyhow, a number of things combined to make this the first really good lesson I've had lately. Lessons are always better at the Studio than at school. For one thing, without all those heavy rugs, the acoustics are better and one isn't cramped in between a couple of Steinways. For another thing, I didn't get nervous. Maybe going to those three movies last week instead of practicing, helped! He doesn't shriek at you when you play really well.

This lesson was followed on March 30 by "a marvelous woodwind class. It was really a rare occasion. The best we've had all year. Odd, because all week there was a notice on the bulletin board, 'No woodwind ensemble.' Then this morning we found we'd have it for *one* hour. The clarinet and bassoon had good reeds and I played the one I had my good lesson on a week ago. In an hour we did seven things and often we spend all of two hours on seven *measures*. We were all so happy about it, especially after some of the terrible classes we've had lately and how disgusted he's been with us. It was one of the few times I've really enjoyed playing in ensemble. It's usually torture. We played the last two movements of the Beethoven. Then the Barthe *Passacaille several* times. Once he said 'Bravo' when I finished my solo. Then we did the last two movements of the Lefebvre and two movements of the Pierné all in one hour. When we finished and the string class came in, he greeted them with, 'I wish you could have heard them.' It was a class to remember. If it only would always be like that."

A few days later I described an evening at the Tabuteaus:

> I was over at their place to get some letters and he asked me to come back for supper at 8:15. It was fun and really the first nice time I've had there (aside from with Mme T) since Christmas. He yelled at me, "Peel your potatoes, for Lord's sakes! *Take* some more gravy!" Just like "Longer the G#!!" He had cooked roast chicken and was it good! Also, mushrooms, string beans, salad, cheese, tea, pears, candy. I had one chicken leg and he had the other. What flavor! He said he didn't mind giving away all his oboe secrets (?) but when it came to cooking, he wouldn't tell a thing! I stayed until about eleven. They drag dinner out and then relax with their glasses of tea afterward . . . They really seem to get along well. I think they are quite an ideal couple considering their temperaments. He is really nice to her and vice versa. She spoils him. Last night I felt quite at home and not too uneasy. They were amusing, figuring up how much candy she eats a week—about five pounds—that would come to sixty pounds already this year. And then how many cigarettes he's smoked since Christmas—at least $16.00 worth—forty boxes a month—around twenty-seven cigarettes a day.[17] They listen to a lot of news. He was telling Walter Winchell to "Shut up." Something came on the radio about bombing Rome and he said, "They never *got* me" and that no one "has anything" on him. From the trend of the conversation and mention of the

MY FIRST YEAR WITH TABUTEAU AT CURTIS

Pope, I presume he meant the Catholic Church. Then he was talking about the English language and said because he isn't an imitator he doesn't get the sounds. He said he has been playing professionally for forty years, thirty-nine of them in the U.S.A.

I had been waiting ever since coming to Philadelphia to hear Tabuteau play the Schubert *C Major Symphony.* "He played the slow movement so beautifully and the scherzo just sparkled." Wagner's *Good Friday Spell* was on the same program, and I marveled at his "sound that just spiraled up to the top of the auditorium . . . Marion and I went back afterwards. Abe Kniaz was there too and said, 'You played beautifully tonight.'[18] Right away Tab exploded, 'what do you mean *tonight*? Don't you know that's the worst thing you can possibly say—Don't you know I always try my best?' He really spouted off! I asked him how he liked Marion's short hair and he admired it. I said it was the 'Tabuteau Trim' and at least he got a kick out of that."

The string ensemble was now doing several radio broadcasts. The newspaper listed: "Today 1:00 p.m. KYW Curtis Institute of Music String Ensemble, Marcel Tabuteau, Conductor. Prelude to '*Le Deluge*' Saint-Saëns; *Eine Kleine Nachtmusik,* Mozart." Of course I listened, and one Sunday I was able to go to the station and watch him conduct from the control booth. "It was a riot to watch. He had his coat off, his shirt half open, danced around like a madman and got so warm, he tore half his clothes off. But the musical result was something! During the broadcast he kept pulling up his pants with one hand and almost knocked the music stand over. The people in the control booth feared that with all his exuberance something would happen. I had to get him water afterwards and he dragged out his bottle and poured whiskey in it. What a character!"

The last few weeks of the school year flew by. I described for my mother one time when

> I was over at Tabuteaus to get a stack of his correspondence, and he said that he thought I should go to Curtis another year, but that I *could* have a job in the Havana (Cuba) Symphony next winter. Of course, the way he talked, it doesn't leave me much choice . . . He was really quite nice about it though—told me how cheaply one can live in Havana. I know if I don't take the opportunity of studying with

MARCEL TABUTEAU

him while I have it, I won't get it again. He is at the point now where he says he will quit music before long *even* if he has to stay in this country, and before it was only if he could return to France. It seems there might be a *possibility* I could graduate if I go another year to Curtis. Tabuteau said to practice solfège all summer and that if I worked hard next year on Brod and Gillet, he thought I could do it. He seemed so pleased when I told him I'd been able to get along this year without borrowing money and he said not to worry about next year as I'd probably get more jobs. I'll try to join the Union in the fall and trust in God and Petrillo.[19]

Toward the end of April Tabuteau began to say that I should play the *spirit* of the music and quit worrying so much, that my playing was lifeless as a mummy, and he could just as well teach a robot. I knew I had been thinking form, form, form, and cells, cells, cells. He had so completely drilled into me the idea that I must calculate and think that I was afraid to do anything else. Now he suddenly told me to play with feeling. Things seemed to be falling into place, and I saw that it was a question of balance, and I did not have to find cells and patterns to the exclusion of everything else. He said, "Scale your *feelings!*" when before, it was always, "Scale your givings." "According to Tabuteau, some people do things well without knowing what they do and others have to think and practice. Some do too *much* and some too little; to get the right balance in your phrasing and to know what is just enough is the difficult thing." Lessons were winding up for the season. I was able to play the last five Grand Studies in Barret quite to his satisfaction. "He has forgotten for three weeks to tell me how care*less* I am. The worst thing he called me was a stupid fool. He seemed pleased with almost everything and said he would play a duet with me for my last lesson. We played the first movement of Sellner Duo II. It really is wonderful to play with him but in one place I didn't make the right inflection and he said, 'If my playing doesn't inspire you more than that, it is hopeless.'"

I described for my mother an evening I had spent at the Tabuteaus:

On Wednesday night I went to get some letters and do the honorable washing. Mme was mad at him for coming home so late and said she was practically a widow. He said, "I am an oboe player," and to me, "she does not know how it is to play on bad reeds—before I married

MY FIRST YEAR WITH TABUTEAU AT CURTIS

her I made reeds until 3:00 in the morning." Then she said, "if you hadn't married me you probably wouldn't be here anymore," and on and on they went. I had eaten my dinner already but they offered me some salad and a chicken sandwich. Tabuteau was amazed when I ate everything. He said he thought I said I wasn't hungry. While I was ironing, Tab went to sleep in his big chair. He was looking so harmless when asleep. His mouth was drooping open and his hands were hanging so limply. Later he said something about how I was sure to stay in Philadelphia a long time because I knew he hated to write and I do his letters and I do Mme Tabuteau's ironing. Then he talked about practicing. He lays great importance on the "Grand Studies" No. 3, 12, 15 and 16 in Barret. And about blowing, he reemphasized that you have no control if you play directly into the reed. You should expel all the wind—say Ah-h—Ah-a-a, for 45 seconds, and then attack with the *pressure* of the wind. *Not* with the wind itself. Once you get it, you have it. . . . His sense of humor is quite something. When I left, he said I not only had $2.00, but my supper, candy, and a $25.00 lesson. I asked him if I should make him a refund? They always worry about my walking just around the corner when it is late. Tabuteau doesn't like young girls to be on the streets late at night. You should hear him rant about the kids you see wandering around now. He believes children should respect their parents. He is right of course, but I can imagine what a tyrant he would have been as a father.

On Sunday night, May 14, I went to the Bach Festival, and it was a wonderful way to finish the season. The Philadelphia Choral Festival Society gave two programs of Bach Cantatas on May 13 and 14 at St. James Protestant Episcopal Church. Tabuteau and Kincaid were among the soloists and for the first time I heard some of the greatest Bach solos for oboe. Aside from the *Second Brandenburg*, there was Cantata No. 82, *Ich habe genug;* Cantata No. 21, *Ich hatte viel Bekümmernis* with its beautiful *Sinfonia* and *Aria* for soprano, *Seufzer, Tränen, Kummer, Not,* and the famous Cantata No. 140, *Wachet auf.* What an introduction to these sublime works to hear them played by Tabuteau! For years I kept a scrap of paper where I had scribbled down something he said while he was practicing these obbligati in the Studio. "Bach's music is the essence of what I try to do in playing." I took this to mean the perfection of form and balance unified to the expression of the character, the depth of feeling and spirit of each work.

MARCEL TABUTEAU

As my first year at Curtis came to an end, I wrote the following to my mother on May 16:

> Farewell to Tabuteaus—1944. I went over this evening and did Mme's washing. Tabuteau worked on reeds and played Bach and slept in the big chair. I gave them the letter I wrote to myself for them to send this summer. When he left to go out for a walk, he gave me a beautiful French folding reed knife and said, "Here's a present for you." He asked me to give him a penny in return as otherwise it is bad luck. Fortunately I had a brand new 1944 one.
>
> Before leaving for the summer, Shirley and I went out and walked around Rittenhouse Square about midnight. We took a long look at Curtis. I can honestly say I've never been so happy as during the time I've spent there. It's just gone by too fast. Every minute of it has been wonderful. Even when I walk in the door and down the halls, I think how I love every inch of it—the paintings on the walls, the soft carpets, the beautiful lighting. Miss Hill, Miss Hoopes, and everyone, have been so nice to me. I haven't had any trouble or unpleasantness except for my few bad sessions with Tabuteau. The kids in the Hannah Penn House have been great and I've met so many interesting people. Dinners with Mme Tabuteau have been so much fun. Really, everything seems so much better for me than it has been in times past and I can't be grateful enough.

MY FIRST YEAR WITH TABUTEAU AT CURTIS

11 TABUTEAU CONDUCTS THE CURTIS ORCHESTRA

Fall 1944–Spring 1945

THE CURTIS ORCHESTRA: GRADUATION

The major event of the 1944–45 season at the Curtis Institute, at least for wind and string students, was the creation of a small orchestra to be conducted by Marcel Tabuteau. We were to play a series of Sunday radio concerts sponsored by the Philadelphia Savings Fund Society. My excitement over this news was soon counter-balanced by the agonizing experience of the rehearsals. Despite my resolve to resist nervousness and to "survive" better in lessons, everything soon fell into the same old pattern—only now with the additional stress of the orchestra. It all began in September 1944 before school opened.

> *September 15, 1944*
> Saw Miss Hill and Miss Hoopes. Tabuteau hasn't popped in to Curtis yet but the plans for this year are *terrific*. Philadelphia Savings Fund is sponsoring Curtis broadcasts again—*every one* to be under the direction of His Highness—and to use full groups—both strings and woodwinds. We rehearse together on Thursday nights. Will I ever have to *work*! However, this means that there is a possibility that

my joining the union will be taken care of through the school. They will advance the fee and we will eventually pay it back from playing the broadcasts. Wouldn't that be marvelous? I don't know how it's going to feel to see Tabuteau again. He has such a dynamic personality—it just crushes you. I hope I can stand on my own two feet.

My apprehensiveness at the idea of facing Tabuteau again was growing. On September 17, "Marion saw *Tabuteau* on the street yesterday. I should call them but somehow can't quite get up the nerve. I know he'll want me to answer a stack of letters and I've enough to do for myself."

But shortly thereafter, on September 19, I did contact Tabuteau.

> Last night I got the Tabs on the phone and went over to the Studio to see him today. I was there about two hours listening to him play—Grieg *Norwegian Dance*, Debussy *Fêtes*, Mendelssohn *Scherzo* and *Scotch* Symphony, and *Tombeau de Couperin*. Then parts of the Beethoven Trio and snatches of the Mozart *Quartet*. Also, the last étude in Barret and the cadenza from *Samson and Dalila* as you never heard it before. The opening "A" just shimmers with intensity! He told me that he had played under the influence of his teacher for about fifteen years—then later analyzed what he was doing. He was really quite nice and in a wonderful humor—if it would only last! We were talking about getting to feel one-sided and that music is nothing at all unless you have something to say and bring to it. He said he thought the best thing for me to do was read lots of books!

September 22, 1944

> I went up to see Mme Tabuteau. They were in the midst of supper at 8:00 p.m. as usual. They talked about everything—France, etc. etc. He is worrying about the broadcasts. If he doesn't like the way the woodwinds play, he will hire professionals. Woodwinds will only be used for six or seven out of the thirteen broadcasts, so *if* I do play, I'll just about make enough to pay the union fee! But even that would be something and then the experience too.[1] Of course, he had to give me a bunch of letters to answer. Would you consider sending the typewriter if he'd pay the charges? Some of his letters really require typing and Mme said he should rent one for me but of course he'd never get at that.
>
> [I knew I would have to play for Tabuteau before school started so] I decided to take a chance on finding him at the Studio. I went over about 11:30 and the Studio was empty. I just had my oboe out and hadn't blown a single note when *he* came in. Gave me the old line

again about cleaning and filling the water glasses. I had been practicing a Brod Sonata but he took all my music off the stand and said we wouldn't bother with that. There were Ferling Duets underneath which I haven't even looked at since I left California. I did them with Shanis all the time so fortunately I could play them right off. Of course, he said my reeds were awful, but practically *nothing* about my playing, so I don't know what he really thought. He said 'it wasn't so bad,' and we played the last movement *twice*. We played it fast too, and I really enjoyed it. Afterwards, we had an argument. He said he was going to take it easy and told me how much I was going to do for him. I said I had to do my own work first, as he would be mad at me if I didn't play my lessons well. I don't care if he screams about my playing but I hate to be treated that way about other things. I know I mustn't make him really mad at me, but I don't want him to think he can just run me around so much. He said, "You are still my secretary, you know." Anyway, it is a relief to have the first session of playing for him over with.

Compliments from Tabuteau were always somewhat of a false alarm, as they would inevitably be followed by a devastating thrashing. There was no danger that our young egos would be allowed to become inflated. Our first session of the new orchestra was for woodwinds only and went deceptively well. "Tabuteau was so pleased with the way I played a few measures in *Lakmé*, just the accompaniment for a singer [of] the Introduction to the *Bell Song*.[2] He said it was excellent, well placed rhythmically, and then the biggest piece of praise he has ever given me when he added, 'I couldn't do it any better myself!!' This amazed us all coming from 'Almighty God' himself. It was a red-letter day! When he *does* praise something though, I always wish he hadn't, because then I'm afraid I won't get it right the next time. He stopped and asked, 'Is that the same reed you played this morning?' and when I replied *no* he said, 'Aha, maybe it is one you stole from me.' But it was in a half-joking tone and not too threatening."

Thursday, September 28, 1944

The first orchestra rehearsal with Tabuteau is over! I was a bit worried what he would do to me, because he said so little when I played for him earlier in the week. But luck was with me. Several times he said "Bravo" and "good." He didn't throw anything at me or even threaten to break my neck or call Minsker. (That's what he said—if I

MARCEL TABUTEAU

couldn't do it, he'd get Minsker!) Because this is a sponsored program, we're not playing very profound music, but by the time he gets through with the *Emperor Waltz,* it will be as perfect as if it were Beethoven's *Emperor Concerto.* We worked for *three* hours and have another rehearsal tomorrow at 5:00 p.m. after the Philadelphia Orchestra Friday afternoon concert. He is a demon for work and you should see how he exerts himself. At one point he pulled another of his classic phrases in pronunciation or rather mispronunciation. He was getting exasperated with the whole business and yells out, 'I do not want to be conducteur—I only want to go back to France, to my grapps and pêches trees.'"

Sunday, October 8, 1944

Midnight: If I don't write now, I don't know when I will. I was at Tabuteau's from 7:00 to 11:00 p.m. They asked me to stay for dinner. Wonderful roast, potatoes, string beans, tossed *salade* with olive oil, cream cheese, tea, pears and prunes. They were very nice but what a week it has been. It started off badly on Monday when I didn't take my lesson as scheduled. My oboe has been causing me some trouble and by Monday was so bad I couldn't play two notes, so I took it to Moennig and didn't go for my lesson. Tabuteau called me up to his Studio and gave me Holy Hell. He was furious and really raised the roof. But I knew if I'd taken a lesson with my oboe in that condition, he would have been equally mad! So he says in a very sarcastic voice, "Unfortu*nately*—I know a leetle bit more about the oboe than you do and maybe I could have fixed it." But I've had trouble before and he's never touched a screwdriver to my instrument. He said it was all right in orchestra rehearsal and implied I was just trying to get out of my lesson! I'm still glad I didn't take the lesson because he would have blamed it all on me and not the oboe. On Tuesday, Moennig, who is horribly busy and rushed, started to work on it. You just have to be grateful when he can even look at your oboe. I'd been trying for two weeks to see him but he's had no time. Anyhow, the whole upper joint was leaking like a sieve. He put all new pads on the upper joint and several on the lower and a new cork where they fit together. My oboe is six years old now and could stand a complete going over. Moennig has very few skin pads left, so put on cork ones. He worked on it all day. It cost me $7.50 but now it plays so much better. I was wishing I could tell Tab. just how much *was* wrong with it, and my wish was granted. I saw him on the street waiting for a streetcar and hollered out, "Ten new pads on my oboe." He said, "No!" and looked slightly more agreeable than yesterday.

TABUTEAU CONDUCTS THE CURTIS ORCHESTRA

October, Friday the 13th, 1944

Today I became, as the current joke goes around here, "A *Brother member* of *Local 77*, A. F. of M." We had to spend the whole morning over at the Union getting sworn in. There was the typical type of Union Official you find in every city—cigar and all, and the dirty, smelly, headquarters. The funniest part is where my name goes in the Union Book (the directory). Under *oboes*, it will come right *before* Tabuteau. I will be on the same list with Bloom, de Lancie, Gomberg, and all the famous Curtis boys! The dues and initiation fees come to $62.00, which is paid until April 1945. Then it will be $7.50 twice a year. If we play six broadcasts at $10.00 each, we'll just about break even. As we *rehearse* on *school* time, we are only paid $10.00 for a half-hour rehearsal and the half-hour broadcast.

Now with the first broadcast fast approaching, the kettle began to boil. Our Friday rehearsal was "an absolute nightmare. The next day I felt like a dead turkey." It was to get worse.

Sunday, October 22, 6:00 p.m.

I've never been through such a weekend. Thank God it is over, but there will be more like it. The last three days have been like nothing I've ever been through. Friday night Tabuteau tore every person in the orchestra to shreds. He roared and screamed and we got so nervous we couldn't play. Naturally, there was no spirit and everything sounded terrible. And was he ever mad at me! I felt so discouraged, I was ready to throw the oboe in the river and quit the whole business. I dreaded to even think about Sunday. No one got any sleep that night—everybody felt sick and we talked until 1:00 a.m. Yesterday I was an absolute wreck . . . Finally on Saturday night I went to the [Philadelphia] Orchestra concert and felt a little better. Then I was nervous again this morning. Went to the radio station at 10:00 a.m. Tabuteau was nervous too. He even brought me the reed he played yesterday and told me to try it. That was pretty nice of *him* I guess. Anyhow, he made me play different notes and decided my own sounded better. I was so afraid it wouldn't hold up. It was three weeks old already but I just haven't been able to make any that played better. I didn't feel as nervous when we were actually rehearsing. Fortunately, he didn't give me any too horrible bawling out. He got mad at Marion and her bow shook a little in one place during the broadcast. She feels so awful—like never playing again.

We had to play the whole program through three times—it was dreadful, with Tabuteau yelling, jumping around, dancing, sweating.

The Curtis Orchestra that played a series of Sunday radio broadcasts in 1944–45, conducted by Marcel Tabuteau. Photographed in the KYW Studio, April 22, 1945.
L to R Row 1: Maria Shefeluk, Bernard Eichen, Gaetano Molieri, Janee Gilbert, Shirley Marcus, Norman Carol.
Row 2: Aaron Rosand, Viviane Bertolami, Marion Davies, Shirley Trepel, Betty Shoop, Patricia Trachsel, Kathleen Broer, Charles Joseph.
Row 3: Harold Whippler, Ruth Wehner, Emma Beck, Elaine Shaffer, Laila Storch, Martha Scherer, Nancy Durrett, Deanne Muenzer, announcer Peter Roberts (standing); singer Julia Johns.
Row 4: Hershel Gordon, Eugene Eicher, Thomas Dykton, Stanley Drucker, Robert Cole, Adelchi Angelucci, Abe Kniaz, Zoe Fisher, Thomas Holden.
Row 5: Carl Torello, Harold Rehrig, Samuel Krauss, Robert Harper, Fred Stoll, Benjamin Podemski, (standing) (These six men and Adelchi Angelucci are Philadelphia Orchestra members.) Photo by Tyler Fogg.

I died a thousand deaths wondering if I'd get my pianissimo notes. We had all of a seven-minute intermission to get a drink of water, etc. Then at 1:00 we were on the air. I was in a trance through the overture (*Marriage of Figaro*) and pretty tense for the whole half-hour, but I didn't let myself think for a moment that it was a broadcast and I didn't mess up or miss any of my solos.[3] In such conditions, it's a wonder I didn't completely collapse. Playing under that man!!! I saw him after the concert last night and he told me it was a wonderful experience for me to see what you have to do with reeds and everything

TABUTEAU CONDUCTS THE CURTIS ORCHESTRA

else to play in an orchestra and I suppose he is right. But, if the strain is always that great, I couldn't take it. I feel like I need a week in a rest home. He himself admits he rides us hard. But I'm so glad I got through it because I think I could get through almost anything after that. It really is a unique situation I find myself in. Playing oboe in an orchestra Tab is conducting. And it wasn't as if I had any *big* solos but just a few notes here and there. He is as particular about the smallest phrase as if it were a whole concerto. One gets a new slant on even the same old music, so it is *never* boring. We'll do the *Carmen Suite* next, including the Act IV Entr'acte with the oboe solo.

We had survived the ordeal of the first concert but there was "fallout" the next day. As I wrote to my mother a few days later,

Tabuteau was in an utterly stinking mood for my Monday lesson. Zimbalist came in the room to tell him how wonderful the broadcast was and he became all honey and effusive, saying he would do his best "to hold up the Flag of the Curtis Institute!" Then after Zimbalist left, he immediately lit into me again. "My dear little *fran*. The things you did in that program yesterday! That note— those G's, they should have gone h-up, h-up, h-up and they all went down, down, down.[4] A *duck* could have done better. You should be ashamed, etc., etc., on and on." In the evening I went over to do Mme's stuff. He was out playing a concert and I was still there when he returned and he was *so* nice. They had me stay for bouillon, which turned into cauliflower (French style—cold, like salad, with oil), cold roast veal, crackers, bread (Rye), tea, grapes (big ones). I enjoyed food for the first time in ages. He talked about every soul in the Curtis Orchestra and how they played. He has an opinion on everyone. It was late and so Mme had him walk me home. I said I was honored and he said I should be.(!) She said he didn't see very many people home! He asked me for the thousandth time who lives in our house and I said he must come in and see us some time, so he said he would. "Now would be too late? Wouldn't they be surprised to see me," and he roared with laughter. But just for the record, he shook hands with me. I don't think he ever has before. It was almost as if we were friends. What a contrast in one day!

I forgot to tell you that Friday I saw the President of the U.S.A. (Roosevelt, you know.) He made a tour of Philadelphia, visited the Navy Yard, etc. I was having lunch not far from the route he was traveling, so went out with Heather to watch. I hadn't intended to, even if it were Churchill, Stalin and Roosevelt, all in one, because it was so cold—but after all, I'd never seen a President before. You never saw so many cops, guards and sedans! He looked very good, just as he does in newsreels. Smiling and waving to everyone, he really appeared to be very well and pleasant.

When Tabuteau had to go on tour, he would make up the missed lessons either before or afterward at the Studio. This meant that not a whole week had gone by since the previous pounding when it was Saturday and time for another. I described that day to my mother:

> I went over to my lesson scared stiff. I just decided to tell him I was disgusted and couldn't play, so I did. I figured he couldn't do any worse than tell me to quit the oboe, as I was no good anyhow. Instead, he was almost nice—he didn't scream at all—but said the oboe was a difficult business, that lots of times it had almost gotten him. This was the first I ever heard him admit that. So he dug out some cane and had me try his reed and really tried to be helpful. My reeds have been much too hard to play and he never tells you anything about making them. He said I was working, but on the wrong track—that once in awhile we all get on the wrong path. He didn't blow up and tell me to quit but just said, "Don't worry, in a hundred years all your troubles will be over."

Monday, November 6, 1944

> Tabuteau arrived back in Philadelphia at 7:00 a.m. after being on tour all week. Of course he walks into my lesson with the usual greeting, "I heard you playing some notes as I came up the hall. They were all wrong. You don't know how to blow in that thing. Your 'fondamental' is all wrong, etc., etc." This helps your self-confidence beautifully, so naturally the next notes you play are even worse. Anyhow, he sinks into the chair, tears the bottom out of a paper cup, and said that is the way my playing is, like pouring sand into a cup without any bottom in it—no matter how much you pour, it never gets filled. My playing doesn't go anywhere. No directive, no rebound, no drive, no push, no intensity, no this, no that. He told me I should put the oboe aside and think about "bringing a note back to you." "The troub' with you is you don't understand the laws of physics. You should develop your logic." So he throws things up in the air showing how they reach a point, turn slowly, and then come down fast. That's what you're supposed to do between notes. Anyhow, he did say, as he has before, that my technic is "enough," my intonation "purty good," and my tone is "not bad," but not knowing how to use my wind, is as bad as being a

TABUTEAU CONDUCTS THE CURTIS ORCHESTRA

string player with no bowing technic. "This is what you must practeece," he says. He told Martha today that her reed had a tone like "walking with your bare feet on cut glass." We get together afterwards and hash our lessons all over with everything he said. He told her how disgusted he was with everything—how the only way to be happy was to hang yourself! You can see what delightful little sessions we have.

Wednesday, November 8, 1944

I want to record for posterity the fact that today I had a nice day and was happy—and I have to try to remember it tomorrow and the rest of the week when I can only look forward to the depths of misery and despair. Two rehearsals with Tabuteau tomorrow—one Saturday morning and the works on Sunday . . . But today everyone was nice at school. Dr. Vittorini even cleaned my glasses for me with his clean handkerchief when he saw me fussing around with my jacket sleeve.[5] It seems it is only Tabuteau who is not human. Mme T was nice to me last night when I was there to do her blouses. The Orchestra was in New York. She fixed me a grand dinner and we listened to the election returns while I scorched the ironing board—(not while she was looking!)

We had two main works to prepare for the next broadcast. Tabuteau, not exactly pleased with our style in the Strauss Waltz *Voices of Spring,* remarked, "That sounds like the Voices of the Frozen Moon." A set of excerpts from *Carmen* reminded him of his experience of doing that opera with Toscanini at the Met. "Every measure was like a different landscape and how exciting it was!" Tabuteau called on his own imagination to urge us to play the flavor of this music. He said one section should be like the "little boys who come in a parade following the toreadors."

Seymour Lipkin, who played piano for Tabuteau's classes, remembered those rehearsals from over a half-century ago. During the Smugglers March "Tabuteau bent over pretending to carry a heavy sack on his shoulder. He was looking furtively from side to side and sneaking across the stage like the *contrebandier* with his contraband. It was so colorful."[6] In 1999, I spoke with violinist Aaron Rosand in the Zimbalist Studio where he now teaches at Curtis. He also had vivid memories of the same music from *Carmen:* "I can still see him carrying that sack on his back. That's what he instilled in all of us; playing with imagination and color. The most profound influence in my life was working

MARCEL TABUTEAU

with Tabuteau." But at the same time that Tabuteau acted out the scene to give us an idea of the stealthy atmosphere, he also insisted that all the inner workings of the phrase be exactly in place.

Sunday November 12, 1944

Now the second broadcast is over and I'm so relieved I can't believe it. Thursday afternoon in woodwind class, he said he'd never heard anything so terrible. He was telling me how it was not only the worst he'd ever heard me play, but he'd never heard *anything* from *anybody* so bad, and no matter what I did, it was wrong. Then he made me come up in front so he could glare at my reed and he yelled about how did I dare to play on such a reed! I went home and sawed my reed all to pieces and played it again that night and he said everything was good—so where am I? . . . The *Carmen* broadcast went quite well except for a wrong entrance by the horn player Tabuteau hired from the Philadelphia Orchestra! The Introduction to *Micaela's Aria* [the soprano was again Pierrette Alarie] really had me worried and I hope I don't see that *Aragonaise* again for a *long* time. There was a horrible pianissimo attack to make on a high note in the aria accompaniment and I knew if I didn't get it I could never look Tabuteau or anyone in the face. The only thing that helps is this desperate determination that I just have to do it and I can't break down. In one spot, I had water in a key and I was scared to death my next note would gurgle but it didn't. I tried to forget about everything and just play. After we were finished, Tab was kind enough (for him), to say I played quite well and that it was the best I'd done the *Carmen* . . . —but what torture—I just don't see how I can be an oboist and go through that all the time.

In many ways things seemed more difficult than the year before. The Philadelphia Orchestra was often away on tour and my lessons became almost secondary to the pressure of having to play well for the broadcasts. I had no time to work on Tabuteau's cane and saw less of him informally at the Studio. But I did continue to write his letters.

November 13, 1944

I phoned Tabuteaus about 6:00 p.m. about a letter he wanted me to write. They had me come up and I ended staying until almost midnight for Sunday dinner of spaghetti with wonderful sauce, chop, salad, cheese, tea (about 4 big glasses), and pears. Mme Tabuteau said she liked how I sounded on the radio and that means something to me, as she is a strict oboe critic. Tab was in a kind of stupor the first

TABUTEAU CONDUCTS THE CURTIS ORCHESTRA

part of the evening and after dozing, sort of woke up and became his better self for a while. He *can* be very amusing—he says himself, he should have gone on the stage, and as much as admits that most of his carrying on is all an act—but it's such a good one, it surely fools me. I sat across the table staring at him (while he was looking off in space), and tried to figure out what kind of a man he is, but I can't. What is more his real self? The way he is at home or on the scene?

Despite all the stress, I felt that I was in the middle of "the best two years of my life" and was "afraid *nothing* will ever be this wonderful." Toward the end of November Tabuteau mentioned that "he thought next year I'd be ready for a job." He hoped that he would no longer be in Philadelphia by then and suggested that if I practiced well and learned all the orchestral solos, I should be able to manage by myself. This meant a great deal to me because I felt that "he wouldn't shove anyone out, especially with his name as a teacher, unless he considered one ready."

Our next major project with the Curtis orchestra was to prepare the Mozart *Haffner* Symphony for the December 3 broadcast. Rehearsals began in the middle of November, and it was a great joy to play this music with Tabuteau. I felt that Mozart like this was "better than any tonic," and when Tabuteau shouted "good" after the short solo in the last movement, I thought maybe I was finally getting "just a hint of what it could be like to play oboe really well." He communicated his love for this music to all of us, and I tried my best to get all the throbbing stab-in-the-heart feeling that he wanted put into the B-Flat in the slow movement. Everything went well for that broadcast. The only other works were two Brahms *Hungarian Dances,* and there were no traumatic episodes.

I jotted down some of the things he said in rehearsals. A favorite way of admonishing us was with the mock apology, "You know we have to play well. I am sorry." He had evolved a saying about conductors: "There are three kinds of conductors: Those who let you play. Those who make you play and those who prevent you from playing!" While struggling to get the wind students to form phrases and play with inflection, he rather begrudgingly admitted that other instrumentalists might occasionally succeed despite themselves. "Pianists have two hands—the balance of

MARCEL TABUTEAU

two parts (question and answer) and violinists only one (referring to the bow arm) but they have to push and pull, so sometimes it is accidentally right." In one of his more talkative moods at the Studio, Tabuteau spoke of conducting. He said that he "never cared for glory, reputation or money and that he was lazy. He said he should have been a conductor and that he would rather do that than sit in an orchestra. But he liked the freedom of his summers and had put the oboe completely away for the last twenty-five summers. He also said that hard as he works to conduct, he works twenty times harder to play oboe in the orchestra and that it still makes him nervous after all these years. Sometimes I wondered if he understood nervousness but I'm sure he wouldn't say that if it weren't true."

One of my friends was Sonia Pečmanová, a violin student from Czechoslovakia. "Her teacher, Mr. Galamian (new at Curtis this year), used to teach at the Russian Conservatory in Paris, was born in Persia, is Armenian, but really Russian, if you can figure that out. He looks so nice and is having such success with his pupils here." The string players did not feel as intimidated by Tabuteau as we winds did. Violinist Diana Steiner remembered that "the first performance we did with him was the *Haffner* Symphony. It was in the middle of the war. There were virtually no boys over the age of eighteen and so we had quite a small orchestra. I suspect that anybody who was in Tabuteau's string class and continued in music would still carry that sense of phrasing and flow that he taught us . . . He was so meticulous in his demands—we used to fear Hilsberg terribly—we would shake in our boots—but I don't think we feared Tabuteau in the same way because he could be awfully strict but he also always had that twinkle in his eye.[7] He used to sit on a sort of stool but whenever he got excited he would jump up and be gesticulating and speaking very rapidly. One time, a huge spray of spit came right in my direction. I was a very easily embarrassed teenager and was afraid to let him see what I had to do, which was to wipe off my face when he turned in the other direction. But he saw me out of the corner of his eye and you know how his cheeks would get a little pink and his eyes a little bit beady? He just laughed, turned to me, and said, 'Next time young lady, you bring zee umbrella!'" Diana also "remembered sitting in the Curtis Box at the Academy of Music on Saturday

TABUTEAU CONDUCTS THE CURTIS ORCHESTRA

nights. When he would play his solos—even little things like the five-note phrases in the Tchaikovsky Fourth Symphony, he would always play to the Curtis Box, or sometimes after a beautiful long solo like in the Brahms Violin Concerto, he would look up with a big smile. He knew we were all there. He had his private audience."[8] One of the boys in the orchestra under the draft age of eighteen was Charles Joseph, a violin student of Mme Luboshutz. After a long career of performance in Germany and teaching in several U.S. universities, he remembered "what I learned from Tabuteau was worth more than anything else at Curtis. His ideas of how to approach phrasing were absolutely flawless. Both in my own playing and in my teaching I have used, not exactly his number system, but the *idea*. You can't play on 'zero like a sewing machine. You have to go somewhere.'"[9] Another of the young boys from that orchestra, cellist Hershel Gordon, who later played in the Philadelphia Orchestra, had similar memories. "What Tabuteau taught us about music I never learned from anyone else."[10]

Soon it was time to think of Christmas again. I had shown the Tabuteaus a book of colored sketches made by my mother of scenes around our rural Sonoma County home. I wrote to her with a holiday request:

> They loved your little sketchbook so much. Could you do anything like that for them, just a few sketches, even some with cats and country scenes? What they love is their farm in France—grapevines, peaches. Tab remarked on the rhythm of your drawings. He sees rhythm in everything in the world. From that little book, he thought our place was just what he wanted to go back to, and here I had left it! . . . Essentially, I think they are a lot simpler than they make themselves out to be. I have to mail some things for them to France. They are sending soap, wool for knitting, and chocolate to his mother and sister.

The Curtis Christmas party in 1944 was somewhat less spectacular than the one of the previous year. Carl Sandburg was supposed to be the guest of honor but due to a death in his family, was unable to come,

> so we just had Christmas carols, dancing, refreshments, and the opera class put on a short program. There was a crew of twenty-one French sailors from a submarine at the party and we were supposed

to entertain them . . . I was sort of talking to one of them—that is, I at least found out his home town was Compiègne, at which point I immediately introduced him to Mme Tabuteau. They had a spirited conversation and when Tabuteau came later after the Orchestra concert, he met them. Of course, Compiègne being Tabuteau's hometown, he took an interest in the fellow. We had fancy sandwiches and gallons of punch with sherbet in it and thin cookies and candy. Mrs. Zimbalist was dressed all in white with a beautiful orchid. Mme Tabuteau introduced me as "l'étoile élève" (meaning star pupil!) Marion and I left about 11:30. It was pouring rain and we got our feet soaked. Thank goodness we only live two blocks away. Jacob and Isadore Lateiner, the fifteen and sixteen year old brothers, walked us home.

I was determined to get up early and practice especially after hearing that Georges Gillet would be up and have a dozen reeds made before 8 a.m. even after playing a late night ballet, so I put cane to soak at 5:30 a.m. and then got up at 7:00. Went to the Studio at 8:00 and tried to make a reed before my lesson which was at 10:30. Finally ended up playing on my old one—but had a pretty good lesson; that is, I learned a lot.

We were rehearsing for the December 17 broadcast which would include the Overture to *Mignon,* the Dance of the Sugar Plum Fairy and Arabian Dance from the *Nutcracker,* and *Scènes pittoresques* by Massenet: *Air de Ballet, Angelus* and *Fête Bohème.* It felt festive for the season and reminded me of happy Christmas programs at Santa Rosa High School with much of the same music I had played there. And the best of all was, "He didn't yell at me today." The happiness was short-lived as we had a Sunday broadcast that I described as "terrible."

Tabuteau kept glaring at me all the time and if the piccolo played out of tune, he frowned at me. Afterwards, he came up and screamed and gave me the most horrible looks and told me if he said the nasty things he wanted to, he would never speak to me again. Of course the whole orchestra played badly, and the more he frowned and glared during the performance, the worse it got. . . . I was supposed to answer letters for him this weekend, but after the things he said to me, I couldn't call him up. I just don't want to face him again. Thought maybe I would feel better today, but that sort of put a damper on my joy about vacation. [Of many low points this was perhaps the lowest of all!]

TABUTEAU CONDUCTS THE CURTIS ORCHESTRA

Tuesday the girls had a string rehearsal with Tab and they said he mentioned that he hadn't seen or heard from me in three days and where was I—that I should phone! So I called and went over Tuesday night only to find that then he was mad because I didn't come Sunday to get his letters. He said that had nothing to do with the broadcast. I don't care. No one else could have faced him after the scolding I got either. Anyhow, Mme Tab even said she liked the oboe in the *Danse Arabe* and she thought the whole program was o.k. So I wrote letters and addressed cards for Tabuteaus. When I left she gave me a present, which I opened when I got home. I was surprised to see inside a card with Tabuteau's own writing on it, especially after I had been writing "Cordially, Marcel Tabuteau" all evening. He never fails to get a kick out of my imitating his signature. It was a bank envelope with some holly on it specially made the exact size with an oval hole for Lincoln's face to look out and inside was a brand new $5.00 bill. I was really surprised. On the outside it said, "Pour la secrétaire. Bon Noël, Marcel Tabuteau."

I had an idea about fixing up something for him for Christmas and finally decided to go through with it—an ABC Book. I wanted to put one of his theories with each letter and draw a picture, such as A is for A-440; B for Barret, the oboists Bible; C for control; D for *distribution;* G you must be in gear; L for Lorée; V for vibrations, etc and some are funny like H—is what you get when you don't play well; R is for rebound and also for reed, and of course, T is for Tabuteau. I dashed all over trying to find a sketchbook. The stuff in the first stupid art store I went to was impossible, but then I luckily hit the real thing and found all the materials I needed: Gillette 303 pen points, a small tablet just the right size with twenty-eight or thirty pages for only 20¢, nine colored pencils—Art gum, India ink, colored paper, and then all of a sudden I really began to feel like Christmas. I guess because we always did such things at home. Yesterday I made little designs or pictures for all the letters of the alphabet that seem good enough to get the ideas across. It took me *forever* though and I still have to color it. I didn't do another thing except go over and wash Mme's blouses in the afternoon after which she asked me what I was doing on Christmas. She said I must not be alone and that if I had nothing more exciting to do, I should come over and have dinner with them. I hope it works out, as that would be wonderful. One Sunday night last month when I was at their place he was listening to the Philip Morris program on the radio. He likes to hear that funny oboe solo peeped out, *On the Trail* by Ferde Grofé. He is so crazy about it—sits there and grins. He didn't know the notes, so I decided to fix up a card with a donkey on it and wrote out all of the solo.

December 24, 1944

During the Intermission of last night's concert I went to speak with Mme Tabuteau and she said they expected to be alone on Christmas and she had asked him about it and I should be sure to come about 6:00 as they will eat late as usual. Tomorrow will be my second Christmas in Philadelphia. Today I went to watch the broadcast at the radio station. The String Ensemble did Corelli's *Christmas Concerto*, Bach's *Air for the D String* and a song, *Sleep, Holy Babe* by McCallin. It was fun sitting up in the booth and watch Tabuteau conduct. I realize that I couldn't even begin to appreciate or understand him when I first came here. Now I see a little of what he does anyway. During the rehearsal you could hear him singing along with the orchestra over the microphone while they were timing it. He puts so much more into it all than we can possibly give him back. I was glad to see Mme Tabuteau when she came in. I know she hates to see him using so much energy and working so hard. He's had gout for two days and has been miserable. Last night after the concert I saw him limping down the street on Minsker's arm and he had a cane. It was so unlike him and made me realize someday he will really be old and not his vital energetic self. I hate to think of it. Concert after concert, and he is never disappointing and *never* falls below a certain high standard of beauty and excellence. I know sometimes when I've been so mad at him, I almost wished he would play badly but he *never* does and to think he has accomplished that impossibility on the *oboe*. I wonder if anyone else can have the persistence and endurance to be as devoted to it as he has.

December 25, 1944

Christmas night with Tabuteaus. I went over about 6:15 and felt so honored as I was the only guest. Mme T was dressed in a long gown and looked so nice. Monsieur even shook hands with me and said 'Merry Christmas.' He was still getting over the gout and couldn't eat the food he fixed. The table was beautifully set. We had sherry soup, veal in sherry (juice was divine), potatoes, big green *salade*, two cheeses, white wine (Burgundy), fruitcake, mints, fruit, and tea. They were amazed how I could keep eating and eating but I can do it because they string it out so slowly and enjoy every bit. Before dinner, he opened my ABC Book and he enjoyed it beyond my highest

TABUTEAU CONDUCTS THE CURTIS ORCHESTRA

expectations. I really was pleased, because he roared and laughed at every letter and illustration. I do believe it even raised his opinion of me a notch. He said how clever and witty it was—better than anything he had seen or heard on the radio all weekend. Of course it flattered him because it was all about his theories. Every time he saw one of his familiar illustrations like a Car to represent being in "gear" or a Rocket bursting for the "Rebound," he would laugh more. Then I was really glad for once I had carried out an idea despite my doubts. He also liked getting the music for *On the Trail*. [When I found my fifty-five-year-old yellowed paper pencil draft of the ABC book, I could understand why Tabuteau had enjoyed it. It was, after all, a tribute to his ideas. Beyond the obvious "L is for Lorée," I had used his own words for "O is for Oboe—the damn stick of wood" and in "T is for Tabuteau who knows the oboe from A to Z" he got credit for the whole alphabet!]

After dinner they opened your sketches. Mme T loved the folder as soon as she saw it. She especially liked the cats and chickens and he loves trees. They both remarked on an oriental style or delicacy in your work, reminding them of Chinese drawing. Later, when I said you were good at Oriental designs, Tab said, of course, because there was a close connection between the West Coast and the Orient. Tabuteau likes San Francisco. He said it is a holiday for him when the Orchestra goes there and that he loves China Town. Your sketches were *très évocatif,* he said. Some of the tall trees in the valley view, probably eucalyptus, looked like the cypress trees of Southern France. And he also liked the *escargots* (snails). I suppose he would cook them! Come to think of it, only one thing was missing—cane! From talking to him last night, I was able to gather that the cane grows and looks the same as what we have in our backyard. In France it grows wild along the banks of streams near the Mediterranean and is not cultivated as I thought. Only a small percentage of the stalks are the right size for the oboe. He seemed to fear they would not see France in 1945. The war in Europe is terrible. They pulled a good joke on me. Madame T asked if I wanted to know what Tab got her for Christmas. She came out with a little box and I said why it weighs nothing. Inside, it was empty and they laughed and laughed. He said every day was Christmas with them and they didn't have to wait for one special day. He turns over every check to her. They are amused because they say I remember everything. Mme Tabuteau said they must write to you but you know them! You'll be glad, anyhow, that they gave me such a nice Christmas evening. We sat around and listened to a radio

MARCEL TABUTEAU

performance of *The Vagabond King* about François Villon. Drank tea and ate candy. Mme Tab gave me a box of chocolate covered mints. It was such fun and he really was in a good humor.

December 26, 1944

This morning I was over at the Studio fixing some cane for Tabuteau. He came in and was *still nice*! He had just received a letter from his brother in Toulon and said if there were any chance of getting back to France he wouldn't begin next season. Tabuteau is very strange in the things he says. He talked about France, the war, and gave his opinion on loads of subjects. Among other things, he said he didn't like French people and didn't feel he was French. At least he hates the ones in this country—Salzedo, Barrère, Bailly, etc. It seems he accuses them of the very things he appears to be himself. Grasping for money, etc. He said that, strangely, the most sympathetic people he'd known here were Germans, that they couldn't be bad. The trouble with a person who couldn't be bad was that he couldn't be really good either, etc. He went on and on. He said, no one, not anything in the world, has ever gotten him. He regards the whole world as crazy, but says he didn't let it get him. He could stand winters here because of being absorbed in the world of reeds.

Tuesday, January 2, 1945

[In the winter of 1944–45 I had the additional "job" of helping out as Tabuteau struggled with the planning of his radio programs.] I had to work with Tabuteau on his programs again from 11:00 a.m. to 2:00 p.m. and then Mme Tab took me to the Colonnade for lunch. In discussing something this morning, Tabuteau mentioned God—the first time I've heard him mention God other than in a *profane* way. He was saying he had to find his own rules for everything and his own way to God—not through Buddha, Mohammed or Christ. Well, I do remember that once in speaking of his musical concepts, he told us that we should contemplate the stars and how everything in the universe revolves in its order and place and that one time when he wanted to let someone know how much he admired that person's playing, he said, "God does not play with the stars more perfectly than you do with music."

Monday, January 8, 1945

I have a lot to write and don't know where to begin. I intended to stay inside all day yesterday and make reeds—with only time off to listen to the Curtis broadcast. About 1:45 I was in the kitchen having just finished my fried egg sandwich, when the doorbell rang. I begrudgingly

TABUTEAU CONDUCTS THE CURTIS ORCHESTRA

answered, expecting it to be Marion's boy friend or someone, anyhow not for me. To my utter amazement, it was Monsieur Tabuteau on his way back from the String broadcast. He's often walked by here with me, but this was the first time he's ever rung our bell! It was very cold and snowy, so he stepped in and said I should phone Mme T to let her know if I could come over later to help, as they were having *Monteuxs* for dinner (not broiled). Was I excited! Tabuteau was amused at my outfit. I had on my green corduroy slacks and my tan sport shirt and he said I looked like a boy. He said he'd like to dress that way! [Girls rarely wore pants (called slacks in those days), and most definitely never out on the street or to school.]

Well, *anyway,* at 5:15 I arrived at Tabuteaus. I peeled mushrooms, took ends off string beans and ran them through the slicer, washed and prepared the lettuce for salad, wiped off the glasses, silver and plates, set the table and peeled the potatoes, while Tabuteau was fuming around in their tiny kitchen over the artistic touches on his leg of lamb. Mme Tabuteau was mad at him for having a party when he doesn't know how much work it is. It seems Mme Monteux has a sister here, Mrs. Meyer Davis, whose husband is some big producer of plays or orchestras and entertainment and has scads of money. I know their son slightly, a clarinetist, but never knew the relationship with Monteuxs before. So the four of them, Davises and Monteuxs came to Tabuteaus for dinner. You have no idea what an amusing time I had. It seems Davis asked Tab if he had any good pupils and so they came and dragged "Lola" out. (Tabuteau finally has gotten that far with my name.) "Lola" was presented to Monteux and Mme as being from San Francisco, and they say *Storch*!! "Any relation to the bass player?" [Arthur Storch, a distinguished-looking elderly gentleman with white hair who looked something like Walter Damrosch, was a member of the San Francisco Symphony Orchestra for many years. We were not related, but I used to call him Uncle Storch.] They were all gabbing while I was still poking in the kitchen. Monteux seems a quite charming and delightful little person. Of course, being at Tabuteaus, it was all such a wonderful, familiar, very French atmosphere. Only six people can fit at their table, so I ate at the little low one in front of the sofa right next to Mme Tab and Monteux. They all called me "Lola" even though Mme T explained that wasn't *really* my name.

All I did was help Mme Tab take the plates off and on, and the rest of the time I sat stuffing myself on Tabuteau's own canned salmon, celery, carrots, mushrooms, string beans, mashed potatoes (he beat two

MARCEL TABUTEAU

eggs, butter and cream in with them), roast leg of lamb, salad, two cheeses and rye bread, then cake, fruit, and champagne. This was strung out through the whole evening. Monteux passed my plate to Tab and said, "Lola should have some more meat." I listened to all the conversation, mostly very amusing. Fortunately, I can understand French pretty well now, so I didn't miss much except the point of a couple jokes that happened to hinge on words not in my vocabulary. I kept wondering if I was just imagining things as for years I had gone all the way from Santa Rosa to San Francisco to see Monteux conduct, watch him arrive in a taxi at the Opera House—once I hid in a broom closet in some theater to watch him rehearse a Standard Oil Broadcast—and then I come to Philadelphia, go around the corner and see him eat dinner! When Tabuteau mentioned how I used to go seventy miles to hear him conduct, Mme Monteux said I had discrimination! Monteux is quiet and modest, but has a good sense of humor. Tab laughed his fool head off. "*Mon cher Monteux*—" "Marcel"— "Pierre!" They were all in excellent spirits, no doubt aided by the spirits in three bottles of champagne and some red wine. Tabuteau and Monteux talked quite a bit about incidents in France, the orchestra under Colonne and other things.[11] Mme Monteux talked mostly about Monteux and was altogether different from the impression I received of her San Francisco self as she sat in that front box. They all told a lot of stories: how once when Monteux was eating in a restaurant at Liège and saw a man comparing him with a picture in the newspaper, Monteux then proceeded to order his steak and potatoes in very crude terms. Another time, Monteux asked a horn player to play his A, and the horn player responded, "How do you want it, high or low?" There was also one about Horowitz who supposedly said, "*Il est très bon. Cela coûte très cher.*" (That's very good. It's very expensive.) They mentioned Mengelberg and what a good colleague he was. They spoke a lot about Monteux's recording of the Franck *D Minor Symphony* and how Admiral Nimitz has it and it was played when the boys went into battle on Bougainville. It was so funny when they all started to go to the "Ladies Room." Monteux comes back making the observation that Tabuteaus have three toothbrushes. He said he presumed one was for guests. Later he said he'd let the next person know which one he had used! So Tabuteau quotes a line from the opera *Manon*: "*Un homme très observant*" (A very observing person), and then they both sing it. What a riot!

I'm getting quite a collection of "conductors dinners" to my record. This was quite different from the Toscanini-Ormandy affair of last

TABUTEAU CONDUCTS THE CURTIS ORCHESTRA

A social evening and dinner in 1945 with Tabuteau, Mme Tabuteau, Mme Monteux, and Pierre Monteux, seated. Standing from left to right are first violist of the Philadelphia Orchestra, Samuel Lifschey; William Kincaid; composer Harl McDonald; an unknown serviceman; and flutist Albert Tipton. Photo by Adrian Siegel.

year. They stayed till 11:00—after which we (the Tabuteaus and me) discussed the success of the evening. Tab's cooking was superb and he is so proud of it. Tabuteau brought me home before midnight, but I didn't go to sleep for ages as I'd had two cups (though small) of coffee. Tabuteau thinks that Monteux knows very little about woodwinds and that he doesn't even hear intonation very well. He cited a lot of instances in last weekend's program and said Monteux did not care much about *phrasing* in the woodwinds. I think Tab was sort of disgusted at one rehearsal when Monteux asked him to play something "louder." This is a word not in Tabuteau's vocabulary and he has great disdain for it in connection with playing. Despite all this, however, he praised Monteux highly, saying he thought he was one of the two or three best conductors in the world and compared to some around here, a master. Mme Monteux was making a big speech about "who ever was the *imbécile*" (pronounced in the French way) who had the electric tuning note installed for the Philadelphia Orchestra which plays five minutes before the concert for tuning. Tabuteau was trying to say how no one ever took an oboe "A" anyhow. She kept talking louder than he was and I was laughing to myself, knowing he is mainly responsible for the electric A-440. All his life, he had the continual oboists' fight because no one liked his A, so he finally said, "Get a machine; then there is no argument," and now everything is beautiful and he is always right. The dinner for Monteux was a rare "throwback" to the early 1930s when, as Mme Tabuteau told me, they often used to invite people to their small apartment. Even Stokowski had been there with his wife of the time, Evangeline Johnson.

Once while writing to my mother I included a mock sample of the type of letter I was doing for Tabuteau in "his" handwriting and on Drake stationery.

The Drake
Spruce Street West of Fifteenth
Philadelphia

January 15, 1945
    I have been so busy with the Orchestra, Children's concerts on Saturday mornings, rehearsals for Curtis broadcasts, and then concerts in the evening, that I cannot teach on Saturday afternoons—and as I have never listened to any of my recordings since I've been playing in the Philadelphia Orchestra, I'm afraid I cannot recommend the best ones to you!
Cordially yours,
Marcel Tabuteau (*THE signature*)

January 20, 1945
    Our rehearsal on Thursday night was really fun. Tabuteau was in a rare mood—guess he'd had enough to eat and drink for supper. We're playing the Overture to *Oberon* and the first movement of Schubert's *Unfinished.* The clarinet and oboe play the opening in unison—it's hard to blend—and he approved of that. But he won't let us play the second movement—too difficult for us, he says. Then we are doing the *Blue Danube.* According to him we sound like the Dirty Schuylkill. Everything with Tabuteau is so interesting to play. No matter how familiar it is, it seems like new. He often alludes to animals in his explanations. About rhythm, he said that we should land back on the beat like a cat always lands on its feet when you drop it. Speaking of the large intervals in one of the études I was studying (Ferling No. 4), they should be "played like a jackass and for *you* that should not be so

— 327 —
TABUTEAU CONDUCTS THE CURTIS ORCHESTRA

difficult!" In orchestra, to demonstrate how my embouchure and jaw should be more forward "like an ape," he jutted out his chin in imitation of a monkey. He told us the two notes in the introduction to the *Blue Danube* should sound like a cuckoo and then said we were awfully sad sounding cuckoos. While trying to see two people at once, he said, "I am not crossed-eyed yet," and at one point he yelled at us, "You are out of tune! You can only do that in a big orchestra, but not in the Curtis ensemble!" Tabuteau was never at a loss for colorful ways to get his ideas across. "That first note is like stepping on a banana peel." "You are allergic to music—like you have a good waterproof raincoat on. All the drops go right off. You don't react." "Your tone gets away from you—like the jackass who follows the carrot around all day but never catches up with it." "No instrument is played 'poof.' It has to be 'Ta.' "We have to practice what we don't like. That is the irony of our profession." To a clarinetist whose attack was ahead of the others, "Tell me, why are you always ahead of time? Why do you come in too soon? You should get a patent on that and then all the people who are always late would buy it!" Another admonition was, "You don't know how to use your talent. It is like lighting a cigarette with a $1.00 bill." And in one of his classic mispronunciations, wanting us to do better in shaping or "modeling" our phrases, he advised, "You should go to a muddling class and learn how to muddle a little phrase."

During their years in Philadelphia, Sunday was a day of relative relaxation for the Tabuteaus, a day when considerable time was dedicated to cooking a substantial evening meal. Every Saturday morning there was the ritual shopping expedition to the Reading Terminal Market. For years, Tabuteau patronized his favorite suppliers of fresh poultry, rib lamb chops, special cuts of roasts for *gigot provençale,* and fine, fresh vegetables. While I was at Curtis, he made a brief attempt to have either me or Martha Scherer do his shopping—we would be let in to the apartment by hotel personnel and put the food into the tiny refrigerator—but after a couple of mishaps such as the one recounted below, he decided we were useless and returned to doing it himself. One day before the start of ensemble class, he called Martha over to the side of the floor in Curtis Hall where we rehearsed. I saw him upbraiding her, gesticulating wildly, his jaw jutting out and the saliva flying. She turned ashen white and came back to her seat next to me thoroughly shaken. When there finally was a chance to ask her what had happened, she explained that on stopping at the usual stall to pick up the weekly chicken, there were none available. Thinking to do the next best thing, she got one from another shopkeeper. Apparently it had been a very inferior fowl, and Tabuteau was screaming at her, "Say, that chicken was so *coriace* (tough and leathery), do you want to pois*on* me or what? Don't you know you should never do *that*?" An earlier student, Robert Davison, fared better. He had studied for a while at the Paris Conservatoire, spoke French, and therefore, supposedly could be "trusted" with the shopping. But even he told me how Tabuteau had once telephoned him about some unsatisfactory string beans, "Are you trying to strangle me?" to which Davison apologetically replied, "*Mais Maître, j'ai fait de mon mieux*" (But maestro, I did my best) which must have had a calming effect, as Tabuteau then said, "Well, come o-vair for dinner." Tabuteau was sufficiently fond of Davison to take him along on several fishing trips to Nova Scotia.[12]

Food was of the utmost importance to Marcel Tabuteau and the delicious meals he cooked were at least partly due to his insistence on the best quality and freshest of ingredients. In the 1950s when he returned to France, he was disappointed in the chickens. He was convinced they were being raised artificially and not allowed to run loose and eat the grass. As I look back, I think that his cooking was neither too elaborate nor dependent on rich and fancy sauces. It was the balance of flavor, tenderness of the meat, and his creativity that always made a Tabuteau meal a special feast. In Philadelphia, I was often asked to help, which was not easy in their minuscule kitchenette. I had to push the string beans through the slicer and shake the salad greens in the basket until the leaves were completely dry. He always used romaine, in the 1940s not the common item it is today. There was a special touch to his mashed potatoes. He boiled a clove of garlic in the water with the peeled and cut-up potatoes. When they were cooked, drained, and the garlic clove removed, he quickly smashed them, adding hot milk, an egg yoke, the egg white stiffly beaten, and large lumps of butter. Sprinkled with parsley and accompanying a couple of slices of tender gigot rôti with its juice spooned from the roasting pan, followed by the thinly sliced haricots verts, this was a mouth-watering treat. For dessert, he would sometimes send me out to buy ice cream, usually a good quality vanilla, but would turn it into a special creation with some slices of fruit, even canned pears,

— 329 —

TABUTEAU CONDUCTS THE CURTIS ORCHESTRA

and a couple tablespoons of rum. From Tabuteau, I learned to put a spoon of vanilla ice cream into the after-dinner coffee in place of regular cream or milk.

When he prepared a chicken (always referred to as "the bird"), he would rub it inside and out with cut pieces of garlic, stuff a few cloves of garlic under the skin, put a sprig of rosemary in the breast cavity, and then begin the roasting after draping several slices of bacon over the top to be left until crisp. Often he served a light Rhine wine, Sylvaner or Traminer; he liked the robust California Zinfandel in place of the fine French reds that were unobtainable during the war years. During the week, the Tabuteaus ate slices left over from a roast beef or cold chicken. Or they would quickly broil rib lamb chops, always adding freshly ground white pepper corns. The only contribution I ever saw Madame T make to the cooking was to prepare a light vegetable broth with celery and carrots if he did not feel well.

Around the middle of January 1945, the girls in the Hannah Penn House had the idea of inviting the Tabuteaus to dinner. This was a daring step, in which our pianist, Heather Halsted, largely encouraged us. She loved to cook, and not being at Curtis, she was not intimidated by Tabuteau. It was, however, far from a simple undertaking. First of all, the Hannah Penn House was not really set up as a home with a real kitchen. There *was* a kitchen which sufficed for the teas and meetings that took place in the normal running of this Republican Women of Pennsylvania stronghold, but we, the roomers, were not supposed to make use of it. Other difficulties were that essential items for preparing such a dinner were completely unavailable during wartime. We could not even buy a potato masher. The Tabuteaus loaned us theirs, along with a string bean slicer, pepper grinder, olive oil, and French vinegar. Heather felt that she would be able to cook the leg of lamb. Tabuteau seemed intrigued by the thought of our wanting to have the dinner but warned us that he would have to approve the menu and that it would "cost us a lot." He also offered to bring his own canned Canadian salmon for the first course. Now we had to raise the necessary funds, use our ingenuity to fix an attractive enough setting, and find time to do the shopping and make the preparations.

Carried away by all the excitement, when I described the event, I dated my letter in French:

29 janvier, 1945

Dear Mother, Our dinner for Tabuteaus last night was a success beyond my wildest hopes or dreams of how we could do it here. Last week with exams and all, Marion and Shirley paid no attention to the fact we were having a dinner, so Heather and I did *everything* and shopped for all the food and little extra items. We went to Reading Terminal Market and bought all the same things he does. Mme T ordered the Leg of Lamb from his own butcher. Heather picked it up Saturday for $3.50 plus about 55 points. [We were still on wartime food rationing.] Each girl in the house put in $4.00 of which Shirley advanced what we didn't have. Tabuteau had said a dinner like that would cost us at least $15.00 so we were prepared, but then for seven people it averaged less than $3.00 per head and we had to buy so much stuff. We had a pound of butter hoarded and we bought Canadian Oka cheese. Fruit costs a fortune here. Red and white California wines are $3.75 a bottle. We bought French chocolates for her and salted nuts for him—duplicated the ingredients of the Toscanini *Salade*—Fennel, cress, radishes, Romaine and Endive. Garlic for the lamb, onion, potatoes, and we had to buy candles and paper napkins. We got two cloth ones for them. A wooden salad fork and spoon for 15¢ in Woolworths and silver polish. Heather borrowed small salad forks and a tablecloth. We put card tables together in a square in Heather's room and it looked wonderful all set with a fruit centerpiece of apples, tangerines, and persimmons, two pears and green leaves. We had to pay 60¢ for a bunch of huckleberry leaves from Washington State. This will all sound like a horrible extravagance to you, but it's something we'll do once and remember forever and think of all the wonderful meals I've had at Tabs. Now I know what it means to put one on.

Our broadcast yesterday went well and afterwards Marion and Shirley suddenly realized we were having a dinner, so they got worried and really pitched in and helped. We cleaned up the room, washed all the dusty dishes (there are loads of dishes in the H.P.H. kitchen closets) and arranged a table to put the serving things on. The kitchen is down three flights of stairs from Heather's room! Heather and I prepared the vegetables and at 6:30 on the dot the Tabuteaus arrived. They wanted to see the whole house and loved it. They didn't

TABUTEAU CONDUCTS THE CURTIS ORCHESTRA

realize what a grand set-up we have. He used to know people who lived in the house thirty years ago. They raved over every room. We put their coats in Marion and Shirley's room; they saw the Club Room downstairs, the dining room, which we don't dare use, the Library, and then he said but he wanted to see "my quarters." I knew they did, so brought them up to the attic and he liked it, especially as I had put a print on my wall which I bought for 25¢ last Fall of a wharf and boats and houses and it turns out to be Toulon. He swore he recognized the actual section and even his brother's house. He was so excited. Then he said, "Now where is the kitchen?" He went downstairs and met Heather and helped chop up everything for the sauce for the salmon, told us to put on the potatoes, and peeked at the lamb. He brought rum and fixed rum cocktails like he drinks in Canada every day. He loved the kitchen and so did Mme. Then we all went upstairs, sat down and had two helpings each of salmon with celery and olives, rye bread and butter. They were in such good spirits and acted so at ease, just as at home. I had fixed place cards on some of Heather's little folded sheets of paper with the date and name on the outside, and inside, the menu in French. They loved that touch:

Saumon du Canada
Gigot provençal
Haricots verts
Pommes de terres purées
Salade romaine
Fromage
Fruits
Café
Vins blancs et rouges

All the food was perfect. He went downstairs again and helped us fix the Lamb and carried it up and he mashed the potatoes. All went smoothly and was hot, and everybody ate *everything* and practically nothing was wasted or left over which pleased me. We had grapes in a bowl of ice water for him afterwards and he loved them. We absolutely duplicated a Tabuteau dinner at our house and they had a wonderful time and appreciated it all. He talked continuously and they didn't realize the time and it was midnight when they left. With all of us working together, it took exactly one hour to clean up the almost incredible mess and put things back so you'd never have known there had been a dinner. Heather, Shirley and I collapsed in my room until after 2:00 a.m. and raved and marveled at how it went and could hardly believe it. I felt like it was a dream. Tab said so many funny and many serious and interesting things too. It was a grand chance for the girls to see him as he is outside of class. He was crazy about Heather and her enthusiasm for cooking. He said he would expect more of us musically now that he saw what we had and could do in the house. Mme T said I'd had good training at their place when she saw all the Tabuteau customs: grapes in water, parsley on the salmon etc. It couldn't have been more perfect and the satisfaction of a dinner like that is, you eat so slowly, you don't get uncomfortable or too full, but thoroughly enjoy it all. We got along without champagne but he thought the wine Heather bought was *excellent*! And I swear he drank almost all the half gallon of red himself, which he said after all, was only *two* quarts. It was a very dry red from Lodi [California]. What pleased us so much was that he said in thirty years in Philadelphia, he'd never seen an atmosphere like this or thought it possible here. He said it was like the *Quartier Latin* in Paris and the fact that it was *un*-American pleased him. He really had a good time. Wished you could have looked in on us last night.

Mainly concerned with the food that night, it was one of the few times I did not record every story told during the evening. In my diary notes I *did* find one about Rachmaninoff. In the 1920s and 1930s, his works were played very frequently by the Philadelphia Orchestra. As Tabuteau told it, while Stokowski and the orchestra were rehearsing his Second Piano Concerto, Rachmaninoff was sitting at the back of the hall listening. At the end, he walked up to the edge of the stage and said in his long-faced manner, "Puleeze Maestro, my music is sweet enough! Don't make it any sweeter." In reminiscing about his days of touring with Damrosch, Tabuteau spoke of the significant advance in standards of woodwind playing since he came to the United States. I did not feel too flattered by his comment, "Why, forty years ago, you could have been second oboe in any orchestra!" I later realized later that under the circumstances, he probably meant it as a compliment. Perhaps most important of all was his statement about "how he was hired by Stoki after hearing a performance of *Tristan* in 1915."[13]

January 30, 1945

When I returned from school today, I found that Mme Tab had come by with a ticket for Heather to hear Casadesus. Later, Tabuteau himself had stopped in to see if we had any parsley left, as he was

TABUTEAU CONDUCTS THE CURTIS ORCHESTRA

inviting Robert and Gaby Casadesus for dinner after the concert. When I was at Mme Tabuteau's, she gave me a big print from the Museum of Modern Art in New York of a Maurice Utrillo, "Paris Street." She had seen the pictures in my room and had no place for it herself. She told me that he (*le maitre*) really had a fine time at our dinner and said again how perfect all the food and everything had been. I returned her things, including a third can of salmon that we didn't use. She gave it back again and I'll try to send it to you, as you've never tasted such good salmon. Here is the recipe for the sauce he made: You chop up some parsley, fine like a mash, plus some garlic, white onion or shallot (which you probably can't find). Tab added some celery and tomato when he was over here. Then some salt, regular mustard, oil and vinegar. It is really good on the salmon . . . You eat it cold. The Tabuteaus usually just leave the salmon in chunks on a serving dish and put parsley around it. No lettuce, just the sauce. I suppose if you wanted lemon too, it would be o.k. They serve it with *very thin* sliced rye bread and butter. For appetizers before the salmon we had celery and big green olives. This was all before our main meal, but it really makes a meal in itself. For people who drink wine, a chilled white, Chablis or Rhine type.

In early March I was happy to be called for second oboe in La *Traviata* with the Philadelphia La Scala Opera Company. "I just had to count measures and play a little here and there and I made $20.00. At last I have made in one day what we used to live on for a month."

March 8, 1945

One thing has been settled as of today. I will graduate May 12, at the same time as a lot of my friends and with the understanding that if Tabuteau is still in this country next year I could continue to study with him. He told the secretary I had made such good progress and was doing so well, he wanted me to graduate. I can hardly believe it. You know, as a rule I don't care a snap for diplomas but it really does mean a lot to me to graduate from Curtis . . . Remember the card from Tabuteau saying he wouldn't take a girl? And now there is a certain sense of satisfaction to know I'll be the first girl to graduate on oboe from Curtis. Just think, I'll be on the same list with Bloom, the Gombergs, de Lancie, and all. Hallelujah! [As always the "good news" was soon followed by the "inevitable aftermath."] At my last lesson he became so furious when I was playing a Brod étude that he took my pencil and scratched and marked so hard on my music, the page practically tore through. The lead broke and he grabbed my shoulder and I thought he was going to break every bone in my body. [I used to show my own students the page of Brod Étude No. 7 where in raging fury, he said "Punctuate, damn Fool!"] The other two kids sitting there had their mouths hanging a mile open while he was roaring and screaming at me. The funny thing was my reaction. I could hardly keep from laughing, as I thought what on earth could he do to me anyhow. He's being harder on himself than on me. Well, if he didn't get in a real rage like that once in awhile, I'd feel I'd missed him in his rare form!

[I was extra worried about Tabuteau's latest fit of anger, as I could imagine him saying, "This stupid girl—she cannot even play two notes, and she wants to graduate!" Feeling I absolutely must play well in the next class,] I stayed home last night and worked on a reed with a certain idea in mind. Perhaps playing with that former Curtis student at the opera helped. We had the whole orchestra this afternoon instead of just woodwinds and I decided to make a tremendous effort to play well. All of this added together, work and determination must have had some effect because I had one of my rare successes. First he said, "Good, oboe! I never heard you play so well." Later, in the *Invitation to the Dance,* "Play faster. You have plenty technique. You have more technique than I have." Of course, with his tongue in his cheek because he can afford to joke about his playing. But I must have hit the tone quality he likes (if I could just keep it!), because everything I played he said, "Good!" Once he turned to Marion and Shirley and asked, "What happened to her?" Afterwards, he said to me, "what kind of a reed is that? Where did you get that reed?" I said it was *not* one I stole from the studio. Anyhow, he said it "was the best I'd done—exactly that!" and he really was *so* pleased. He even said he wished we wouldn't play so well (!) or he couldn't stand it anymore in the Philadelphia Orchestra. [The rest of our rehearsals went relatively smoothly, and I earned an even more extravagant compliment, a *bravissimo,* for the *Invitation to the Waltz.*] During a fast part, he said, "I wouldn't want to challenge her to a competition on that right now." Everyone laughed but it worried me. I am always afraid of the reaction.

March 30, 1945

Tuesday I had a letter from Washington D.C. [I had played an audition for Hans Kindler, thinking of it only as a possibility for a summer job, but now I was being offered a contract as second oboe for the next season.] Tab had said that Kindler is a "bad egg" as a conductor. My inclination is to take the job because while it isn't the most desirable thing in the world, it's something definite and you have to

TABUTEAU CONDUCTS THE CURTIS ORCHESTRA

start somewhere. It's twenty-two weeks next winter, $75 a week, which doesn't sound too bad at first, but when you consider what it costs to live in Washington, taxes taken out of it, and transportation back to Philadelphia for lessons, it is not anything to get excited about. I don't think Tabuteau is averse to my accepting this. His only other advice to me is "go to Hollywood and play in the Studios, make a lot of money and be in California," but that I refuse to do. I didn't come here in order to go back and do that!

1:00 a.m., April 13, 1945

The news about Roosevelt's death is almost too much to really comprehend at once, and we had to have our rehearsal as usual. I think it is extremely sad. Almost unbelievable regardless of what anyone may think of him—who can take his place right now? We didn't feel like playing and a sort of pall seemed to hang over everything. All the flags were at half-mast; but as a whole, I don't think Philadelphia acted very bereaved. You know, in "historic" Philly most of the bigwigs are die-hard Republicans. When we heard the news, we were eating in a drug store and we didn't believe the man who announced it. A couple of women just said, "Well whad'ya know, Roosevelt's dead!" Saturday night the Orchestra played the *Eroica* of course, in his memory. I think a foreign country would make more fuss over it than we do, but then considering, it was all handled very well and I admire Mrs. Roosevelt very much. I'm glad I saw him once when he came through here last November. You could feel his personality. The final Curtis broadcast is postponed until next week along with all commercial broadcasts.

April 23, 1945

Yesterday the long series of Curtis broadcasts finally breathed its last with a popular program including the Carmen *Aragonaise* with the oboe solo—so I had nightmares again, but he said it sounded "pretty good." [We had only done a small part of the immense symphonic repertoire but the intensity of the work with Tabuteau as conductor, left a lifelong impression on all who shared the experience. It gave us an approach for our future way of thinking about whatever music we would study. At the time, I wondered why he considered the second movement of the Schubert *Unfinished Symphony* too difficult for us. Later, I understood better that the interpretation, level of control, finesse of phrasing and rhythm he demanded, would really have been beyond our abilities. The season was not yet at an end. Several of us played a quintet written by the Philadelphia composer, Vincent Persichetti, as a test for the new medium of "Frequency Modulation."]

MARCEL TABUTEAU

We rehearsed at his house, a very quaint place on a typical Philadelphia Alley—bricks, white steps and all—very artistic little street—his wife served us ginger ale and pretzels afterwards. I don't know how great an improvement the new type of radio transmission is.[14]

April 24, 1945

It was exciting for me to play second oboe in *Tosca* with the Philadelphia Opera Company. Luigi Di Fulvio, who is in the orchestra with Tabuteau, played the first part and was very amusing. Lots of the orchestra men were in the pit, including Anton Horner, who has been in the Philadelphia Orchestra for over forty years and has taught many of the best hornists in the country. I had a chance to talk with him during intermissions and it really was an inspiration. He seems to be such a fine man and I'm glad to hear someone speak of music as he did. After he quit playing first horn, he continued as fourth just because he loves music so much. He said he dreaded to think of the day when he will have to give up playing altogether. It was fun to rehearse on the *stage* of the Academy. Chambers, the first horn of the Philadelphia Orchestra, was also playing. I am not yet so spoiled but what this gives me a thrill—to sit on the same stage! The conductor was Baccolini, husband of Bruna Castagna, and *very* Italian.[15] I could understand some of the things he said. *Avanti, andiamo!!* It was the first time I've ever been the *only* girl in an orchestra!

Tabuteau won't be back from tour in time for graduation but Mme T will be there. Ordinarily, when they had the woodwind ensemble at school, the Spring recital of that group counted as your graduation performance, but now, I imagine they will consider all the broadcasts we've done with Tabuteau—thirteen of them with woodwinds. Regardless of what I say about Tabuteau, he's really been very nice on the average this winter. I've had dinner there practically every Sunday and I've been very lucky to know them so well. When I see how he coops himself up in that Studio and works on his reeds and gougers for hours on end and realize he's been at it forty years, I guess the miracle is that he's as human as he is!

Monday night there was a good graduation recital—George Walker and Pierrette Alarie. I walked home with Mme Tab and we met him returning from the orchestra at the door of the Drake. They had me come up and he gave me a bag full of *French cane*. I think it's some that one of his pupils who was with an Army band brought back from Paris—but then the old story about my being a girl came up again. I guess that's why he thinks I should go to Hollywood, because all the boys will be back here. Of course, he said I should have a

TABUTEAU CONDUCTS THE CURTIS ORCHESTRA

better oboe before I play "first" anywhere. For my lesson yesterday we played a Sellner duet.

[There were more end-of-the year programs.] Marion played very well last night. I'd never heard her do the Brahms *E Minor Sonata* better. The box was full of "celebrities." Primrose, Zimbalist, Piatigorsky—quite a lot for one small audience. [One recital] lasted from 5:30–7:00. Two whole violin concerti. The mother of one of the little geniuses was sitting next to me and I could see and feel her pushing her child along every time a rhythm lagged a bit. After being at Curtis awhile you get rather tired of prodigies, especially those who just get up and rattle off a lot of notes and technique with absolutely nothing in back of it and they are the majority. I can't help but think of Tabuteau speaking of the empty clamshell—good on the outside, but inside—empty. There are a few exceptions, like Sylvia Zaremba, but she is an all-around intelligent girl and can hold her own with people any age.

[Although the whole school year had been dominated by the Tabuteau broadcasts, I had some awareness of the momentous events taking place in the world and signs of the approaching end of the war began to appear in my letters.] I heard the opening of the San Francisco conference last night and was so excited. Then tonight I heard Molotov speaking Russian and just the beginning of Anthony Eden, as I had to leave for a concert. It's so wonderful that it's being held in the San Francisco Opera House. I think I'll buy a paper every day so I'll know at least a little of what's going on for a change. It really is wonderful to see an international group like that coming together. [This was the beginning of the United Nations.]

April 30, 1945

Friday I had dinner at Tabuteaus and he celebrated the end of another season. We had caviar! On Saturday he left for two weeks tour so I have a little breathing spell. I surely need it to study some of my other subjects. Martha and I are cleaning Tabuteau's studio—but completely! We started Saturday and spent about four hours there. The thick layer of coal dust hasn't been removed for years. Papers and cane are messed and jumbled all over the place. It is rather amusing 'cause you never know what you'll pick up next.

May 8, 1945

As far as I'm concerned, VE Day here is just a big mess. "Philthadelphia's" streets are always dirty enough but now they're littered with so much paper and other mess and on top of it all, it

MARCEL TABUTEAU

rained . . . Martha and I went to the Studio anyhow, as we had planned to finish the cleaning and then I prepared about seventy pieces of cane. On my way back from school about 4:30 p.m., I had stopped outside the Hannah Penn House and Mme Tab came by and talked awhile and then asked me to come over. We ended [up] having dinner together at a new Chinese place I knew of and she liked it. Then we also talked some more afterwards at the Drake and I left about 11:00 p.m. I was pleased because she said there was no one else she'd really rather be with as Tabuteau is away and VE Day means so very much to her. Our orchestra picture is on the bulletin board at school and I ordered two as I thought you'd like one. We don't _look_ so pretentious, but it will help me to remember everyone.

May 11, 1945

My last official day at Curtis was really very nice. At 4:00 we had tea with Mrs. Zimbalist serving. At 5:00, a recital by the graduating composition students. There were three sonatas, all well played. I liked George Walker's especially. Primrose had invited his two string quartets (eight students including Marion and Shirley) for dinner, which was very nice of him, I thought. Guess who is sleeping in our house tonight? though I haven't met her yet as she had also gone to the Primrose dinner. Mrs. *Feuermann*! She came for Marion and Shirley's graduation. I hope I'll meet her tomorrow, as it would mean a lot to me to meet the wife of someone I admire as greatly as Feuermann. To my mind, he is one of the greatest artists. Every time I hear one of his records, it's an inspiration . . . there's a cast of his hands in the Curtis Library.

3:30 p.m., May 12, 1945

I can hardly believe graduation is over and it really happened. I wish you could have been here. When Zimbalist read out my name and said "from Santa Rosa, California," I sort of felt you were. We had a rehearsal at 9:00 a.m. and when I saw the caps and gowns, I began to feel it was important. Mrs. Feuermann took Marion and Shirley and me to breakfast, so I'll always remember that. She is a _wonderful_ person. She is so charming, so sweet and natural. I was so glad that when they announced Marion and Shirley's names, they said "student of Mr. Feuermann *and* Mr. Piatigorsky." They are Feuermann's only students ever to graduate from Curtis, unfortunately, the first and last. All the candidates for diplomas stood and then walked up as Zimbalist announced our names. I was in the first row with not far to go and was relieved that I didn't trip when I had

TABUTEAU CONDUCTS THE CURTIS ORCHESTRA

to walk up the steps to the stage. I remembered to take the diploma in the left hand so I could shake Zimbalist's hand with the right. First, there were two speeches, by Samuel Barber and Mrs. Zimbalist. Barber's talk was excellent.[16] Both he and Gian Carlo Menotti were awarded honorary Doctor of Music degrees. Barber spoke of music and all the other arts, of how we should not be narrow, but know literature, painting, etc., etc. He threw slams at the "fast finger" experts and said after awhile they had no one to amaze anymore. Tabuteau wasn't there because the orchestra isn't back from tour but he's never attended a graduation anyhow. So many people were crowding around with congratulations. Mme T gave me her good wishes in French and I think she has a book for me. I wish you could see the diploma. It is tied with a red and white ribbon and all rolled up in traditional style. Piatigorsky shook my hand afterwards and wished me luck, and said if I ever need anything, pointed to himself! (Of course I expect to take him up on it immediately!!) After getting rid of the heavy mortar boards and *wool* gowns—(incidentally, they were beautifully made ones, with such very stiff white collars that it was a struggle to pin them in evenly), Mr. Trepel (Shirley's father from Winnipeg) took us to lunch at the Warwick Hotel which is right across from Curtis. There were *nine* of us at a big round table. Mrs. Feuermann was with us. She called me "Laila" and was so friendly. She is young, only about thirty, and didn't want to sit in the box at the graduation, but just be with the other people. She hates form, but Zimbalist insisted.

May 15, 1945

Everyone is leaving our house. Tabuteau is back and Sunday evening I went over to visit them. He was tired but in a good humor. They gave me a wonderful book of poems by Baudelaire and what I like is what they wrote in the front: "*à l'adoptée du dimanche en souvenir des heures . . . avec nos voeux affectueux pour l'avenir,*" and both signed it with the date. The meaning is 'to the Sunday 'adopted one' in remembrance of many hours—(I can supply any adjective I want)—with our wishes for the future.' Hard to translate exactly.

Tabuteau taught yesterday and I was at the Studio for hours fixing cane. He is letting me copy some duets from an old manuscript that belonged to Georges Gillet and has his writing on the front. I think they are arrangements of piano sonatas, but in very classic style. Tabuteau says he has never even played them. Gillet's widow gave him the music. He said Gillet was a strange man. No one ever went to see him. He died of a cerebral hemorrhage while making an English horn reed.

MARCEL TABUTEAU

He made all kinds of reeds. Short, long, always changing, but his playing was always the same. Tabuteau was really in a great mood because guess what else I got? Most exciting of all, the fingering for high C which he attacks out of thin air at the end of a C major arpeggio. It doesn't quite work on my oboe because of the automatic octave key but by holding one key down, I can get the same combination.[17] I walked back with him to the Drake carrying a bottle of Seagrams Whiskey he'd left at the Studio. Mme fixed me a sandwich and then I returned to school to read through the Mozart and Beethoven Quintets.

May 17, 1945

Another hot sticky day. I put cane in to soak at the Studio at 10:00 a.m. and Tabuteau was there making a reed before taking the train to the Bethlehem Bach Festival. He spent half the time telling me how he's had to put up with Kincaid being so jealous of him all these years, and how he pushes in his flute to make it sharp so Tab can't play. It seems Bruno Walter praised Tab in Mozart, saying, "it couldn't be better," and Kincaid was furious and was swearing under his breath and horribly jealous. (At least so Tab says.) Anyhow, it seems they are having a big feud now and Mme T says he's vain and stupid, and she doesn't want Tabuteau to give him his whiskey. I'm sure I don't know how it really is. Then I went to the Reading Terminal Market to pick up their meat and do the shopping as since Martha left it seems I've inherited the job. This is Gillet's birthday. He was born in 1854. Tabuteau said he gave up the oboe at fifty due to losing his teeth and then said no one had any business playing after age fifty—Tab said Gillet was very "egoic" (egotistic). I don't think I told you I found out why I think Tab had such a mania on straight teeth. It seems just as recently as 1937 he had a lower front tooth which protruded and turned more and more so he couldn't play and had to hold the oboe on an angle. He finally had it pulled and was of course worried, thinking he might not be able to play at all any more. I guess they were even ready to retire then, if necessary. But the space filled up and his teeth are perfect now. While cleaning up the Studio, we ran into a plaster cast of his lower jaw in a drawer and I could see how his tooth was. Practically the same as mine. No wonder he had the subject on the brain.

More letters to write for Tab. One refusing to take a boy who studied with him before. Tab even says the boy is talented, but he wants nothing to do with pupils. He won't take any more at Curtis or privately either, if he can help it. By the way, they say not to tell anyone, but this time it is definite. Next winter they pack and go to France in

TABUTEAU CONDUCTS THE CURTIS ORCHESTRA

the following summer of 1946. If so, I am more than fortunate. He will continue next season with the Philly Orchestra but it appears there will *not* be Curtis broadcasts. PSFS (Philadelphia Savings Fund Society) wanted him to form his own orchestra but he can't do everything. He may conduct four or five broadcasts, but even so, they probably won't be through Curtis. Tab feels he did the right thing by urging me to go to Washington and having me graduate. If I do well next year, I'm sure I can get something better and maybe I can yet convince him I can do more. After all, it isn't easy to get him to say you're ready. He told me I'd have to help them pack next spring and said he'll give me a lot of his music. I hate to think they'll go back to France, but I know it's the only thing they want to do and I'm lucky to have known them so well. [Tabuteau remained in the Philadelphia Orchestra for eight and a half more seasons!]

May 20, 1945

Madame Tabuteau promised to take me to the Bach Festival at Bethlehem *if* it didn't rain. Yesterday morning it was dark and threatening and windy so I didn't think we'd go *but* after I came back from the Reading Terminal Market with eight lamb chops, six pears, a half pound of cream cheese, one-half dozen eggs, two heads romaine, and one of leaf lettuce, Mme T insisted I go to Bethlehem anyhow. She gave me $5.00 and told me to hurry up—so I got "*le train*" and right away saw Mme Miquelle.[18] She was alone so I sat with her and had an interesting visit all the way up. I got her to talk about her father and it was very fascinating. I never knew much about Longy who was also a Gillet pupil. When we arrived at Bethlehem, I went with some other musicians who were on the train and ate lunch in the basement of the Moravian church that was turned into a cafeteria. Then afterwards, I heard the famous trombone choir playing Bach Chorales from the church tower. The church is on the campus of Lehigh University and all the buildings are of gray stone with lots of trees and grass all around—really an ideal setting for Bach. I saw Tabuteau before it began and he said I should get tickets for the building across from the church where the whole mass is broadcast. The church itself is sold out long before and usually in nice weather people just sit around outside on the grass. But I could hear very well in that auditorium and otherwise I would have frozen. The *B minor Mass* was given in its entirety in two sections, from 2:00–3:30 and then 4:00–5:30. I was lucky that Tabuteau got me a ride back in a car with the librarian of the Philadelphia Orchestra. During the Intermission, I saw all the musicians. Now I know so many of the Philly Orch men as well as I

MARCEL TABUTEAU

Madame and Monsieur Tabuteau on the steps of Packer Memorial Chapel at the Bethlehem Bach Festival in the 1940s. Photo by S. Franklin Mack.

ever knew those in San Francisco. Tabuteau was quite the idol of the hour, speaking to many friends and signing autographs. He had played the day before in things that really had much more for oboe. Wish I'd heard them. All the connoisseurs come with the scores. Tabuteau asked me if I noticed how all the Bach enthusiasts had the faces of the *Moyen âge* (Middle Ages). As he said, "long and stern and serious." I replied, "Very Gothic," which was apparently the right remark. Then he was admiring the wonderful trees. He loves *trees* and said the form of a tree was like the most beautiful symphonic structure and even more perfect than Bach. He also admired a squirrel and said he used to be bored playing at Bethlehem, but now that he knew there was hope for him to really go back to France, he enjoyed it."

May 22, 1945

I've just had my last lesson of the season. Tabuteau made me play all the exercises he's been giving me recently, arpeggios etc. Then we did a movement of a Ferling duet. Finally, after we played it several times, he said it wasn't bad. We looked at part of the Bach *B Minor Violin Sonata* that he told me to work on in the summer.[19] It is wonderful

TABUTEAU CONDUCTS THE CURTIS ORCHESTRA

music—the way he *phrases* it. Then I split some cane for him and he told me if I worked well on what he'd given me, I'd be pretty sure to be in good shape for playing next year. He said I had some material to work with now, the *clay,* and it is up to me to see what I can do with it. He said in Washington I should copy all the first oboe parts and study them at home, and next year "I'll try to get you a job with some Sinfonia." So maybe he will yet! He has given me some exercises lately that do marvels for me and says I must practice softly, piano, with a dolce tone and not _blow_ and make it sound like I'm stretching my neck. It was an encouraging note for a last lesson and considering how little I've been practicing the last few weeks, it could have been worse. He was playing parts from the *St. Matthew Passion* that he will do here with the Philadelphia Bach Festival on Saturday. I never cease to marvel at how he makes it sound.

May 29, 1945

Tabuteau practically insisted I go home to California and I have to follow orders. And so after two-and-a-half years in Philadelphia, I was on my way back to California (again by bus), to stay for the summer.

MARCEL TABUTEAU

12 TABUTEAU'S SUMMERS IN CANADA

Salmon Fishing in Nova Scotia

THE WAR YEARS

The outbreak of the war in Europe in 1939 brought about a complete change in the way the Tabuteaus spent their cherished vacation months. Gone were the visits with family and the long summer lunches on the terrace of their little house near Toulon, the Pingouinette. It is not recorded exactly when or how Tabuteau first decided to go to Cape Breton, but John Minsker thinks he must have already spent the summer of 1940 in Canada. Shortly after the beginning of the war, Minsker heard Tabuteau "talking about the flame-throwers and that was when he realized he could not go back to France." By the time I came to Philadelphia in 1943, a new routine had been established; it was the yearly summer trip to Nova Scotia for salmon fishing. Tabuteau would take the Cadillac he kept stored in a Philadelphia garage during the winter, and drive for more than two days up through Maine, New Brunswick, and then go by ferry to Cape Breton from Mulgrave to Port Hawkesbury. Later on, with the onset of gas rationing, he sometimes left a car in Canada.

It was when I began to write letters for Tabuteau that I learned something about his preparations for the summer months. There were orders to suppliers in Wisconsin and Minnesota for special flies and hooks and correspondence with the people he had come to know in Cape Breton. I remember especially the names of Joe Aucoin, Ralph and Claire Dieltgens, and, above all, Rose Tompkins. Both Tabuteaus always spoke with great fondness of Rose. They rented one or two rooms in her simple farmhouse in the Margaree Valley and lived a quiet life, doing their own cooking. Madame Tabuteau read books and Tabuteau was usually up before dawn to get to the streams before the other fishermen.

In the Margaree Valley, the name "Tabuteau" conjures up a picture quite the opposite from that of the eminent Philadelphia oboist. The Margaree Salmon Museum in North East Margaree, Cape Breton, sponsored by the Margaree Anglers' Association, is dedicated to the preservation of trout and salmon fishing in the Margaree River. There, in the midst of a collection containing old-time fishing equipment, information about famous people who came to the area, and stories of noted guides, one can see a photograph of Marcel Tabuteau wearing sportsman gear, holding a fishing rod in one hand and a very large salmon in the other. If the name Tabuteau is legendary in the music world, it is Tabuteau the salmon fisherman who is still a subject of conversation in the Margaree Valley.

Fifty years after Tabuteau's visits to Nova Scotia, I unexpectedly came in touch with Rose Tompkins' nephew, Dr. Kevin Tompkins of Hamilton, Ontario. He was able to fill in many details of the Tabuteaus' life in his aunt's home.[1]

> In the early 1930s, Aunt Rose opened a "tourist home" which catered to a summer school for landscape artists from New York. They would come with their students and spend the summer teaching and learning the art in idyllic surroundings. A little paint shed was built to accommodate their supplies. Rose was running a mixed farm, tourist home, and post office in order to survive. Come the war years, the artists faded away and many of the local able-bodied men and potential farm help went to war. When I was ten or eleven, my father drafted me to leave school a month early and to spend my summers helping Aunt Rose with the farm chores. I am not sure when Mr. T. first came to stay with Aunt Rose. It was my understanding that

MARCEL TABUTEAU

Marcel Tabuteau happy with his salmon "catch" in Cape Breton, Nova Scotia, in the early 1940s.

earlier in the season, he fished the Chéticamp River which borders the south border of Cape Breton's Highlands National Park that, to this day, is a wonderful place for hiking and photography. Even now they catch a few salmon there. Perhaps another attraction for the Tabuteaus was the fact that besides the Irish and Scottish cultures, the French who were expelled from Acadia by the British in 1759 also settled the area. Their patois might well have been very foreign to the Tabuteaus, but no doubt they felt some kinship with these locals.

Aunt Rose's house had one bathroom and the Tabuteaus spent a lot of time in their room; perhaps two rooms. They were rather like prisoners once the sun went down. Despite the arrangement that the Tabuteaus would do their cooking, they intruded minimally on the lives of others in the house. Aunt Rose died in 1964, and later the house was demolished. Any semblance of mixed farming in which she engaged is lost. The countryside is still beautiful, but alas, the river no longer teems with salmon as it did in the 1920s and 30s.

One of the other "artist guests" and fly fishermen who stayed with Aunt Rose was Mr. Bryant Baker, who sculptured *The Pioneer Woman.*

Mr. Baker, like Mr. T. was a very aggressive, competitive fisherman. Most of these men gradually began to feel that they owned the river and they resented anyone intruding on their reserve. There were stories of disagreements almost resulting in fisticuffs. My brother Greg, at the time a medical student, was invited by Mr. T. to go out fishing early one morning. As they left Aunt Rose's house before sun-up, Greg let the front door screen slam, much to Mr. T.'s annoyance. "Sh-h-h, you'll wake up Mike." But as they proceeded along the brookside path to the river, whom should they meet on his way home with a salmon in each hand? You guessed it, Uncle Mike.

I was the boy who cleaned any salmon that were caught. Mr. T. did almost all of his own cooking in Rose's kitchen. I recall him happily fussing around with his cigarette holder in his mouth. He reminded me of a younger F. D. R. (Franklin Delano Roosevelt) I seem to remember that veal was one of his favorite meals. He would take out his pocketknife, skewer the meat in many places, and stuff in slit cloves of garlic. After use, he would ceremoniously wipe the knife with a thumb and forefinger, close the knife and drop it back into his pocket. Mr. T. was always most kind to me without being patronizing. Mrs. T. could not be otherwise. He taught me how to swim in the cold North Atlantic. They usually went for a swim at the time evening chores were to be done, so he was not too popular with Aunt Rose when he took me away and she was left to milk my two cows in addition to her two cows. Alone and spending most of her life with her back to the wall, she was much less understanding of the needs of a twelve-year-old boy than were the Tabuteaus. Mr. T. would pick up beer bottles along the river, and when he had collected sufficient numbers, he would sell them and turn the proceeds over to me.

There was little or no music in Margaree. We did have a large radio and the C.B.C. News Reports by Matthew Halton of the progress of the war were our only interest. Mr. T. would sometimes walk around humming "Bonb, Bonb, Bonb," but I did not hear him play his oboe more than a couple of times, and then only for a minute or two. Mme T. liked to sit on the lounge in the kitchen by the wood-burning stove and watch and listen to Aunt Rose. Mr. T. did most of the cooking. He loved to cook veal perhaps because the local beef was so tough. He would sear it on top of the stove and then plop it in the oven till done. I had heard of garlic but had never seen it. He would stab the veal in a half dozen places and bury the garlic in the meat. I remember one autumn Sunday when my mother and father were away and we had our usual prime rib roast. I insisted on fixing it with garlic à la

MARCEL TABUTEAU

Tabuteau. After a lifetime of bland food, my brothers and sisters would not touch their main course. This did not make Mr. T. more popular in our house!

Once I wrote to Dr. Tompkins stating my opinion that "the summers Tabuteau spent in Nova Scotia were probably the only ones in which he did not go to the Casinos! I guess the fight for the salmon completely replaced his compulsion for gambling." This idea was dispelled by Tompkins's reply in which he told me how his older brother Greg had reminded him of a session with some of his pals. "Don't you remember the night we were playing poker in the cabin with Patrick (Mike's son) and for one hand Mr. T. put up the keys to his Cadillac? I don't know what he was holding, but you can be assured that all his opponents folded." Apparently the lure of the Nova Scotia salmon had not completely suppressed Tabuteau's desire to gamble. In this rural setting, a far cry from the casinos of the south of France, there were poker games, sometimes involving three first cousins, all of them nephews of Aunt Rose. No one had any money. Some were struggling university students whom Tabuteau would occasionally stake to a few dollars in order to keep the game going. One of Rose's tourist cabins was once rented out to a couple on their honeymoon. The new groom got into the game, and it soon became obvious that he was a quite a good player and the "locals" were down on their luck. They were playing a game called "Chicago," which was supposed to be penny ante, but it got out of hand and went on for several nights. On the third night, after everyone had scraped up enough money to continue, the new groom was still winning. Although he naturally wanted to bow out when 11:00 p.m. rolled around, Tabuteau persuaded him to keep going since the poor country folk were down. About 5:00 o'clock the next morning when everyone was about even, the game broke up.

Dr. Tompkins asked his brother if the rumors were true that there had been fistfights among the fishermen. Greg confirmed that they were a very competitive and aggressive lot, jealously guarding their "rights" to different pools and streams, and that arguments often led to blows. Dr. Tompkins thinks that his father, "Dr. Greg, also an avid fisherman, with a quirky Celtic heritage, did not have much use for Mr. T., but then he did not have use for a lot of people. Loved and respected, nevertheless, by a given number of the local inhabitants for his straightforward manner, he did not hesitate to come to the aid of a fellow fisherman, when one day Mr. Tabuteau found himself in an urgent situation with an incarcerated hernia. Dr. Greg successfully treated Tabuteau for this problem, enabling him to wait until his return to Philadelphia for surgical repair. Dr. Tompkins observed that Tabuteau could make enemies with his competition, but be very easy going and friendly with almost any other group of people; 'Aunt Rose types,' medical students, fishing guides and little boys for whom he collected and sold beer bottles." These benign aspects of Tabuteau's personality were perhaps more evident during his relaxing summer life than in the winter when he was constantly engaged in a battle against reeds, students, and conductors.

I had learned how much Tabuteau disliked writing and realized that I would receive no news from Canada. I devised some "multiple choice" letters which were dutifully completed and returned to me in the summers of 1944 and 1945. Some words were crossed out; phrases in italics indicate words filled in the blank spaces or added by either one of the Tabuteaus.

Nova Scotia, Canada
June, July or August 1944

July 20th 1944

Dear Lola:

This is to let you know that we are having a fine vacation here. The weather is (cool, hot, perfect) and the fishing is (fair, good, marvelous). So far I've caught _20_ salmon*s* the largest weighing _20_ pounds. You'll be glad to know that I found the car, the Dieltgens, and Joe Aucoin all (in top-notch condition, happy, ready for action). There is (plenty, not enough, too much) good Scotch, and I am not letting any go to waste. The best thing we've had to eat so far this summer was *what I am cooking*. I get up about _6_ a.m. and fish until _noon_, and have (completely, almost) forgotten there is such a curse in existence as an oboe.

Madame Tabuteau is (bored, playing solitaire, *she did it once!* eating candy). She is having a good rest, but wishes that you were here to (wash her blouses, answer the mail, clean the fish) *and have a good time.*

Be good, don't get careless, and keep practicing at least (one, two, three, four) hours a day. Write to us (soon, seldom, whenever you have time to answer it yourself).

Best wishes,
(sign here) *Marcel Tabuteau*
Louise André Tabuteau

Occasionally Tabuteau wrote a few lines himself. The following summer a letter from the Acadian Inn in Chéticamp dated June 24, 1945, made it clear that he fished that area of Cape Breton before proceeding on to the Margaree Valley:

> Dear Lola,
> Received your card and letter; I am glad to know you enjoyed your trip, also, you are happy to be home again in beautiful California. At Chéticamp the first few days had wonderful weather and exciting fishing but—since, too much rain and poor luck; nevertheless I am very satisfied, no music or musicians around!! In a few days will leave for Margaree.

For the rest of this letter he left a blank page "to be filled by secretary's imagination" and then later in the summer he sent the "fill-in."

> *August 15, 1945*
> Dear Lola:
>   We are having a _wonderful_ time here at Margaree. The main news of course, concerns le saumon. So far the score on this year's catch is _30_ and the weight of the largest _20_ pounds. We (are) (~~are not~~) going to have some canned. Compared with other seasons, the fishing is _poor_ this year. The condition of flies, rods, lines and all other paraphernalia de pêche, is (satisfactory) (~~could be better~~). Joe Aucoin and Ralph Dieltgens are (still on the warpath) (~~have become bosom friends~~). The other fishermen around here are (a nuisance) (~~not causing any trouble~~) (finding difficulty challenging my title "Champion of the Margaree.")
>   The food and liquor situation is (good) (~~bad~~) (~~fair~~). We have (plenty) (~~not enough~~) meat, mostly (lamb) (beef) (~~chicken~~) (hamburger) (~~elk~~) _lobster._ Miss Tompkins still has her (dog) (chickens) (vegetable garden) (fruit trees) and bakes (cakes) (cookies) (pies).
>   We spend a lot of time (reading) (swimming) (loafing) (eating) (drinking) (~~writing letters~~) (~~listening to summer symphony concerts via T. S. F.~~). We have (newspapers) (radio) and think the news is generally _bad._ We hear (~~Walter Winchell~~) (~~Raymond Gram Swing~~) (Gabriel Heater) (~~Drew Pearson~~) (~~Frank Sinatra~~) (The Crime Doctor).
>   There has been (some) (~~a lot~~) (~~no~~) mail from France.
> Any special news: _War prisoner nephew back home Compiègne._
> As things look now, we will see the "grapps and pêches trees" about _1946._

TABUTEAU'S SUMMERS IN CANADA

During the coming winter I will probably tell the following to go to——:(Ormandy) (Curtis) (PSFS)[2] (Hilsberg) (the oboe) (pupils) (the world).

Now we will have to close this letter, because our secretary is getting too lazy to write anymore.

Don't forget to take it easy, and practice like #-*5$.

With best wishes,

Marcel Tabuteau

News of the war naturally assumed great importance at that time. Fifty years later, the secretary of the Margaree Salmon Museum, Ralph Watts, asked a passenger on the ferry to Sydney, Nova Scotia, if she remembered Tabuteau and she recounted the following incident: "At the local corner store owned by Jake Sode, there was a radio. It was early in the war and a number of the local residents were listening to the war news. Tabuteau came in and said 'Hello—what's new? etc.' No answer from the locals who were so intent on the war news. He remarked, 'Can't any of you talk?' and walked out." This left quite an impression. Considering Tabuteau's heavy French accent and the fact that the storeowner was Lebanese, there was no doubt ample room for misunderstanding!

Dr. Tompkins told me that the Tabuteaus had purchased property overlooking Whale Cove near Margaree Harbour with the intention of building a home there. Several of Rose Tompkins relatives knew what eventually became of Tabuteau's land. One of her nephews, Nicholas A. Miller, was able to confirm exact dates of the Tabuteaus' visits from an old register kept by Aunt Rose. Tabuteau had acquired his property from Howard MacKay. Rose Tompkins MacKay, wife of MacKay's son, Alexander, sent me a photograph with an arrow marking the original Tabuteau acreage that ran from the ocean to the foot of the mountain. Rose MacKay also had personal memories of the Tabuteaus: "Around 1943 my brother and I lived with my grand-aunt, Rose Tompkins. I can remember Mr. and Mrs. Tabuteau. The one thing that stands out in my mind is going to the beach with them. That would be about eight miles from Rose Tompkins' house. I can remember a storm came up with thunder, lightning and hail and Mr. Tabuteau was in swimming when the storm was going on. I can still remember his laugh. We went up to the house just above the beach that was Howard MacKay's home where

I *live* today. So the first time I was ever in this house was with Mr. and Mrs. Tabuteau. I would have been four years old then. I have been living in this house thirty-three years as I married Howard's son, Alexander. Mr. and Mrs. Tabuteau were good friends of my husband's parents. The beach is owned by us now. The Tabuteaus used this beach frequently and I believe that is how they became friends with my husband's parents. My husband can remember Mr. Tabuteau buying a lamb and then he would cook the whole lamb in this house and on different occasions invite the Dieltgens for the meal."[3]

In 1992, I spoke by telephone with Ralph Dieltgens's widow Mayme. She clearly remembered the days when Tabuteau and her husband fished the Margaree River. She was not exactly sure how Ralph had met Tabuteau, but believed it was just while they were fishing the streams. They soon became very good friends. Ralph spoke both English and French, and they exchanged funny stories and information about little-known pools and good spots to fish. In the same way that Tabuteau searched compulsively for the ideal reed or the winning hand in a card game, he also pursued the biggest salmon. The strength of his personality was such that even without the oboe, it impressed itself on children and adults alike. Tabuteau was respected as a "serious" fisherman and was accepted as one of the people of the Margaree Valley. They did not realize until many years later the extent of his fame as a musician, even though he had presented Ralph with a copy of his 78-rpm recording of the Mozart *Sinfonia Concertante* made by the Philadelphia Orchestra in 1940. When Ralph married in 1946, Tabuteau was his best man, and Ralph's sister, Claire, the matron of honor. After the ceremony, Tabuteau arranged a festive champagne supper for the newlyweds.

It was to Ralph Dieltgens that Tabuteau eventually left his Cape Breton property. According to Ralph's daughter Linda, "It was about fifty acres of deeply-wooded land with a beautiful stretch of waterfront reaching up into the hills to an area formerly known as "St. Rose." The Tabuteaus felt that Ralph was the person who would appreciate it to the fullest." In the early 1990s, Alexander MacKay's son, Gordon, bought half of the land and built a house there.

Tabuteau usually sounded happy when he spoke of the summers in Margaree. He would only be upset at the thought that some other fish-

TABUTEAU'S SUMMERS IN CANADA

erman might get to the choice spots before he did. It is perhaps a tribute to the environment they found in Nova Scotia that the Tabuteaus could enjoy it there while having so many worries about their families in wartime France. We may wonder what in Cape Breton (aside from the salmon and the friendly straightforward people) was so attractive to the Tabuteaus that they returned again and again, even after the war was over. Despite the turbulence of the world situation in the 1940s, it seems the Nova Scotia summers brought Tabuteau as great a degree of contentment as he would ever know. In contrast to his long-preferred Midi of France with its dazzling sunshine and intense colors, Cape Breton, a land of cool, green rolling hills laced by quickly flowing streams, lies between the cold Atlantic and the Gulf of St. Lawrence. Aside from one or two industrial towns in its southern half, the inhabited spots were little more than modest villages. In the 1940s, this peaceful countryside had not yet been "discovered" and exploited by tourism. Margaree Harbour, Margaree Forks, and Fordview all lay on the Margaree River, not more than a few miles apart. Chéticamp, only twenty-three miles to the north, was originally settled by French-speaking people who were largely engaged in commercial fishing. The Atlantic salmon, totally different than the Pacific salmon, do not die after spawning, but live to return to the sea. The lure of the salmon was that as they entered the river from the very cold sea to spawn, they were very frisky and provided the fisherman with a challenge. For years after Tabuteau retired to live in France, he continued to correspond with Ralph Dieltgens about salmon fishing, a subject on which they obviously shared the most serious thoughts. But in 1959, the one time he returned to Nova Scotia, it proved difficult to recapture the idyllic days of the Cape Breton he remembered.

MARCEL TABUTEAU

13 ANOTHER YEAR OF STUDY WITH TABUTEAU

1945–1946

NATIONAL SYMPHONY ORCHESTRA, WASHINGTON D.C.

In the spring of 1945 Hans Kindler had held auditions at the Curtis Institute, and I was offered the job of second oboe in the National Symphony Orchestra. Tabuteau suggested I accept the position and use it as an opportunity to learn repertoire. At the same time he cautioned me to stay for only one year and arranged for me to continue with "post graduate study" at Curtis that the relatively short trip back and forth would make possible. Thus, in October I began my third year of lessons with Tabuteau. The focus was now on Ferling and Brod études in their original keys and in transpositions.

My first season of professional orchestra playing was far from inspirational. After the atmosphere of Curtis with Tabuteau's elevated goals and constant emphasis on achieving the highest possible level of finesse, it was disillusioning to be thrust into a milieu where there was no thought of style and to be surrounded by a motley crew of colleagues, some pleasant enough, but others sloppy and crude. Early in the season I wrote to my mother: "Tabuteau always says you have to be an aristocrat to play the oboe, but my oboe colleague is the farthest opposite you can imagine. He comes slouching in, turns to the clarinetist and says 'Shuddup.' Then he always wants to borrow my knife or feather." I was accustomed to seeing Tabuteau warming up on the stage at least forty minutes before a concert. My new colleague arrived five minutes before rehearsals began and announced that he had just swallowed a raw egg for breakfast before rushing to the hall. Around my third day in the orchestra he asked if he could try my reed. When Tabuteau asked to play on our reeds it was like a royal command and we felt it to be almost an honor, no matter what his verdict might be. But now with this unwashed-looking individual beside me, I had to think fast, and so I primly announced, "I never let *anyone* play on my reeds." In a disgusted tone of voice he replied, "Oh, you Curtis students are all the same." But I was never asked again.

The trips to Philadelphia and the lessons, even when an ordeal, became my salvation. And there was also the opportunity to hear the concerts that the Philadelphia Orchestra played in Washington, D.C. Letters to my mother continued with details of my "new life." On October 24, 1945, I wrote:

> I went to Constitution Hall and practically ran right into Tabuteau. I hadn't been able to get a ticket for love or money as the whole series is sold out by subscription. I finally ended up hearing the concert from a hollow place under the stage—the pit is covered over and I could hear quite well from there. Of course, it was pitch dark like a cellar. Anyhow, Tabuteau even sounds wonderful from that angle. After two days of hearing my new Washington colleague, Tabuteau sounded like a stream of crystal spring water and as for Kindler, in the first place, I don't think he's such a great musician, so I'm not afraid of him. He just says, forte—sing, play it beautiful—mezzo forte—that note longer— or shorter—only surface remarks, and never seems to penetrate the broader meaning of the music. It makes me realize even more what a wonderful musical experience orchestra with Tabuteau was last year. I wish more people, especially conductors, had his vision of music.

Despite living in Washington, I managed to partly continue my old life in Philadelphia. Soon thereafter I wrote:

> I had my first regular lesson yesterday at the studio—an hour lesson. The first always seems the worst. I was sandwiched in between two boys. One soldier had just finished a lesson and Tabuteau was giving

MARCEL TABUTEAU

him the line about all the things wrong with him and another fellow who has returned to Curtis after being released from the army, was there during my whole lesson. He was cleaning out Tabuteau's desk drawers and sharpening all his knives and acting like a general lackey and stooge and I thought *I'd* been a slave! This fellow even holds Tabuteau's coat for him. I played an étude and about two lines of Bach. He said the way I play Bach, he shouldn't even speak to me but that my reed was all right—I just didn't know how to play. He played a lot of things for us with brilliant technique and said he had played all his lessons like that when he was seventeen or eighteen—as fast as anything—but that he couldn't attack a note in the orchestra."

November 3, 1945

Thursday afternoon I went to listen to the Curtis woodwind ensemble rehearsal and then over to Tabuteaus. They asked me to come to dinner Friday night and also to do the shopping. Friday morning I practiced and then went to the market. I lugged a veal roast back to their apartment with two pounds of grapes, cheese, and romaine. When I got there he was dressing for the concert and the maid was cleaning. I had to speak to him about some lamb chops and he comes out in his shorts and shirt. It was really funny. Too bad I didn't have my glasses on so I could have seen him better. Then I went to the Friday afternoon concert. I was just getting in line when a lady came up with a ticket she wanted to give away. She said she was going to pick the last person at the end of the line to give the ticket to and I was the lucky one! It was a $3.16 downstairs seat with all the Friday afternoon hoi polloi Philadelphia Society! It was not a very good program. Lea Luboshutz from school played an uninteresting modern concerto by Lopatnikoff . . . Then I walked home with Tabuteau. He stopped and bought some string beans and I went on to the Hannah Penn House and made a reed. [I was able to stay with friends there on my short trips to Philadelphia.] Back to Tabs at 6:30 and had a delicious meal. Rolled roast veal, spaghetti with the meat juice, butter and cheese, tea, the beans, salad, and "grapps." I told them all about Washington. They talked of France; he said I'd better stick around, as I'd probably get a lot of books from them when they leave! I wonder if he *really* will leave this time? We all went out and walked around several blocks and I got to the Hannah Penn House about 11:00 p.m. The kids were playing Beethoven quartets with Seymour Lipkin looking on. The next morning I went to the Studio at 11:00 a.m. and had an hour lesson . . . Lately my reeds are better than *I* am. An unheard of development! And he said that after this year with my experience, I should be able to

ANOTHER YEAR OF STUDY WITH TABUTEAU

'make pretty good' if I only would *think* right. I don't know if he meant money or music! Then he talked about the world, 'What a bunch of fakers.'" Now accustomed to his actions so that even once when he yelled at me so loudly that I actually jumped, it did not prevent me from feeling it had been a good lesson. He seemed to think I was practicing better and had understood "a few things." He again mentioned that he was "telling me all his little secrets that he doesn't tell everyone and said I must promise to send him some money if he gets broke when he is old! It is true though, I have heard him give a lesson and say practically nothing.

Sunday, November 24, 1945

Thursday when I arrived [in Philadelphia for the Thanksgiving weekend], I called Mme T. They had received a sudden invitation that they felt they must accept, even though they had already bought their own "bird." They were worried about me and asked me to come over and fix my dinner there. I had three potatoes, five slices of cold roast lamb, a big salad, tea and toast, and really had a good time, eating at their table in state. I left at 5:00 and met Shirley who had already had her dinner with Mrs. Piatigorsky . . . Tabs had asked me to have turkey with them the next night, if I would still be here. On Friday morning I stopped by Curtis and went to the record library searching for recordings of Tabuteau that Mme T wants to take back to France. But she doesn't know if he is really ready to quit. He was supposed to make a transition this year—take it easy, go for walks, not make so many reeds, or take extra jobs, but he's still at it the same old way. She wonders if he'd know what to do with himself if he quit. One day at the studio, he said he sort of hated to think it would be all over, to know he couldn't spend all this money and then come back and earn some more. Probably no oboist (at least, an important first chair like he is) has ever gone on playing at fifty-eight, but he plays better than ever, so from that standpoint there's no reason why he shouldn't continue.

[For the delayed Thanksgiving dinner,] I peeled chestnuts for the stuffing. They had a couple of French people there when I arrived and they asked the young doctor to come back for dinner. He'd been sent over lately to do some research, a sort of government exchange student. He was very bright and they liked talking with him. He looked thin and told a lot about what happened in France during the war. I guess what we've heard has been no exaggeration, probably just the opposite. The turkey (*dinde*) tasted perfect and Tabuteau dished out very generous portions. The stuffing of sausage filling (fried first) and boiled chestnuts was good, but rich. I basted the bird every ten minutes.

MARCEL TABUTEAU

He put loads of salt, pepper and butter on it before roasting and cooked it for one and a half hours. It really looked fairly simple and they never make gravy, but just use the juice from the bottom of the pan as it is. We also had cranberry sauce, which I guess is definitely *Américain,* as the Docteur hadn't had it before. I had to leave at 9:30 to catch my train, but it was surely a marvelous meal—worth waiting for.

December 1, 1945 11.30 p.m.

From the train: I didn't get to Philadelphia until about 3 p.m. yesterday, but had quite a time anyhow. He had correspondence for me to answer. Decided he should have various form letters already prepared and then just say, "Form 1 to so-and-so" etc. And then dinner last night. I'm trying to remember now what he fixes, so please preserve my letters as usual. It may aid my memory sometime in the future. We had what is called veal cutlet—mostly all meat, no bone. He cooks it in a pan with quite a lot of butter and when you buy it, it must be light in color, not pink and juicy or it's no good. Then he mixes some water with the juice and pours this on spaghetti that has been cooked with several garlic segments in it. It is really delicious. We had the usual *salade* and some wonderful cheese—*port salut.* Fresh pears for dessert. Mme Tab gave me a marvelous present. She heard I needed mittens and said she had several pair she bought in Canada two or three years ago—*Angora* glove style, and so heavy and warm and soft. They were about $2.50 then, but you couldn't even find them for ten dollars now. I took the black ones, as they'll go with everything I own.

I had another good lesson. It seems for the first time, I'm beginning to have a musical reaction. So often Tabuteau has said there must be a certain inclination; you must have a musical reflex. When you see a group of notes, you should immediately see what to do with them. He says "You must answer the little call." Trouble was, I really didn't feel any little call! That's why I hardly dare to believe what seems to have happened. Suddenly music has begun to take on real meaning in terms of form and color and I see so much to do. It's like beginning to see the grammar or structure of a language as a whole after having learned only little pieces of it.

December 5, 1945

This afternoon I wrote about six letters for Tabuteau. I wish I'd kept track of all the pupils I've had to refuse for him. It really is sad. Think how I would have felt once to get one of those letters. I probably would have pestered him just as much as all these others do.

ANOTHER YEAR OF STUDY WITH TABUTEAU

I continued to be unhappy with my new employment. "Touring with this orchestra and these musicians, would almost finish me on music if it weren't for Tabuteau. When I compare it to the wonderful work we were doing last year! Ugh! It seems like my best days are *behind* me and yet to the average person, because I am connected with a *known* organization, they automatically think it means something, as you said, 'arrived.' But for real musical quality I wouldn't take all the performances we've given for *one* number done with Tabuteau last year." In contrasting the difference in training of most of the musicians in the National Symphony Orchestra with what we had received at the Curtis Institute, I was beginning to see Tabuteau in the perspective of his wider influence on American orchestral playing. It was only during the past fifteen years, since the early 1930s, that his oboe students and other wind players from his classes had been joining U.S. orchestras—and, of that time, almost five years had been lost in the war. Nevertheless, the impact of his teaching was already having an impressive effect and was soon to spread further.

As the Christmas holidays approached, I could look forward to spending almost two weeks in Philadelphia. There were visits, concerts, dinners, and lessons, all of which was more like "real" life to me than being in Washington. Everything concerning the Tabuteaus went into my letters.

Sunday, December 9, 1945
I am *so* glad you fixed the Christmas box for Tabuteaus. They will love it—especially plain fresh nuts too, as I think Tab is sometimes afraid to eat salted ones, because of his mouth for playing. What *can* I give them this year? I can't outdo my inspiration of the ABC book from last year! I did send Mme T a box of chocolates for her birthday November 28.

December 24, 1945
Saturday we were speaking of things French and I said I wish I *were* part French on account of the oboe and all. Tabuteau said he's changed that tradition. You don't have to be French anymore to play the oboe and that anyhow, after three years with him, I was part French. He was quite definite. So that's that. I guess it's about the best thing he could say, because then I'm supposed to have absorbed some of that whole way of thinking . . . Tabuteau said he'd play duets with me during the holidays, so I said, well, I'll practice some. And he said, "don't practice *too* hard. You know you must always manage not

— 360 —
MARCEL TABUTEAU

to play better than I do." As if that would even be possible! . . . We were discussing oboists and his students and if Harold Gomberg played like he did. When I mentioned that no one had his intensity of tone in the upper register, he said that he had kept that for himself and hadn't taught it. He said none of them have that and he gave so much, he had to keep something for himself! It's precisely what makes him different from all the rest, as far as tone goes.

December 26, 1945

I went to Tabs about 4:30. I had gotten a nice French card and a Swiss hanky for Mme T and a French magazine with articles about Pierre Bonnard for him. Mme T loved the card and kept saying I was too artistic, had too good taste etc. and I'd be unhappy in an orchestra and he yelled, "Say wait a minute—*too* artistic—you should hear the things she does in her less*ons!*"

[Now that we have reached the beginning of the twenty-first century and see women filling major oboe positions in a number of American symphony orchestras, it may be difficult to remember that fifty years ago a girl oboist faced almost insurmountable hurdles. Tabuteau had been accustomed to the fact that solely giving his word about one of his students was sufficient recommendation and a firm guarantee to any symphony conductor that the person was qualified and prepared to fulfill the obligations of a principal oboe career. But now, as he had finally "taken on" training a couple of girls, he was sometimes forced to think about their dubious futures.] We had a long talk on the subject of girls and careers in music . . . It started out by considering the girls in the Hannah Penn House, marriage and everything—the eternal problem. It was practically an argument and it all seemed so hopeless. I could only wish I were a boy. He doesn't say so much now about it being physically impossible, but the Tabuteaus' viewpoint is just so different. I can't even write it all out. It's depressing anyhow. I got the idea that he figures if a girl gets married it's the end of her music—all wasted—and she carts babies around and yet he said the question of the importance of your career should never stop you from getting married, i.e., if a nice young man should want you to marry him, you shouldn't refuse because of "your career." And he even mentioned people who would be *nice* for me. I said, "Say, what are you trying to do? Get rid of me?" It made me so mad. I just felt like I'd really like to show him. If necessary, I would not even look at a boy—that's probably the best way—to just avoid them altogether. I'm sure if I were a boy, Tab would make more effort to push me oboistically or would feel more sure of me.

ANOTHER YEAR OF STUDY WITH TABUTEAU

Tabuteau dictated a whole bunch of letters—some in French. I am writing to a M. Delacroix in France about some cane. Tab's French seems much clearer than many Frenchmen—or at least I can understand it better. He doesn't seem to speak so much through his nose, like Charles Boyer, for instance. They had to go out for dinner but told me to stay and fix my supper which I thought was certainly very nice, as eating out in Philadelphia on Sunday is awful. It was their idea to send you a telegram and they made it up too. (Not me.) The kidnapping idea was Tabuteau's. [The telegram carefully saved by my mother read, "HAPPY NEW YEAR OUR LOVE GREETINGS AND FORGIVE US FOR KIDNAPPING LOLA = TABUTEAU."]

Before my "vacation" was over, there were more serious talks about my "future" and Tabuteau again returned to his idea that I should go and play in the movie studios in Hollywood. But now he added a new element to the conversations, that before he would recommend me for *anywhere*, I would absolutely have to get a new oboe with covered keys. I was still playing my open-holed Lorée and he said I was working against something that I couldn't possibly beat. My reaction to all of this was, "Oboes are practically *impossible* to find now and of course if you *do* locate one it's about $500!!" At the end of the war, all oboes, and especially Lorées, were extremely rare items. There had been only minimal production during the war years and after Lucien Lorée's death in January 1945, good oboes had become scarcer than the proverbial hens' teeth. My problem was eventually solved. MacLean Snyder, one of the students returning from the Army, had picked up a YY series Lorée oboe while he was stationed in Scotland. Tabuteau talked him into selling it to me and after Hans Moennig made some repairs, it became my first covered key Lorée.

Shortly after the New Year in January 1946, I met the original Mr. Graf who made the machines that Tabuteau and some of his students used for gouging oboe cane. Ernest Graf was a machine shop expert who worked for Exide Storage Batteries. John Minsker remembered that he had one finger missing from an early workplace accident. I had the impression that he enjoyed using his expertise to create the unusual tools needed by an oboist, but Minsker said that Graf was often unhappy with Tabuteau. Graf held to a high standard of precision in finishing the machines. Then Tabuteau in his impatient way would take a file to the guide, insert dimes under the posts, and do anything to get the results he wanted. Later, after a lapse of many years in the production of Graf machines, they were made again, first by Graf's son and then his grandson. For me, the opportunity to meet the man I had heard about but never seen, was an important occasion.

January 4, 1946

Saturday afternoon Tabuteau sent me out to see Graf, a mechanic who makes his gougers and tools. Evidently they've worked together for about twenty-five years. I knew Tabuteau was always sort of secretive about this Graf and was rather surprised to be asked to pick up some tools. I guess Graf was even more surprised to see me as he said, "Tabuteau must think an awful lot of you, because you're only about the third or fourth person he's sent out here in twenty-eight years." Graf had done work for very few of the students. I really felt honored and as if I'd been admitted to the inner sanctum . . . He explained a lot of things to me and Tabuteau had said I could have him make me a cane splitter, a planing board (for the rough work), and a shaper— for my Christmas present. Isn't that terrific? I feel now, it's just up to me what I do as Tabuteau is giving me every opportunity.

January 8, 1946

In between two rehearsals I went to a liquor store here in Washington with a note from Tabuteau (which I had written myself) and a $15.00 check. It's a store that all the Philadelphia Orchestra men patronize and they know Tabuteau well. Scotch is extremely hard to get now but they came through with two bottles for him and before I left I was acquainted with the men behind the counter and they were calling me "Lola." They said I should send the Boston Symphony in too. It was really a riot, but as Tab said I should get acquainted with them so I could get Scotch for him, I did my best. Tabuteau drinks Scotch everyday, else he said he couldn't keep going—he would have no pep or energy. His system or circulation is very low. Even the doctor tells him to drink. He doesn't drink much wine anymore. I wouldn't be surprised if his heart is not too good—though he doesn't talk about it. He goes to a doctor anyhow. One thing, Tabuteau is careful about his drinking and will never drink before a concert.

January 16, 1946

Just returned from our second concert with Fritz Kreisler. It has been worth the whole season just to play with him. Experiences like this once in awhile make you still believe in music. He was so wonderful.

ANOTHER YEAR OF STUDY WITH TABUTEAU

He is seventy-one and doesn't play technically perfectly anymore, but musically he plays the violin like no one I've heard. There's really nobody just like him. He's more like Tabuteau is on the oboe—he plays every phrase and note with meaning and color and interest—and it was such pure Beethoven! I just felt we weren't really worthy of playing with him. It couldn't be good enough. His playing is so much more beautiful than all these perfect virtuoso violinists—the Russians—with their brilliance. Last night in Baltimore, he spoke to everyone in the orchestra who came by his door. So natural and friendly—no standoffish aloof business like so many great artists. I had a chance to say just a few words to him. But tonight was my big moment. I was backstage when he came out of his room and asked me for an "A" and in French, mind you! Isn't that fantastic! I have no idea what made him speak French to me. I was so surprised; I could hardly get the reed in the oboe. Anyhow, I've played an "A" for Fritz Kreisler that is something for the record and me only the *second* oboist. It just isn't done. The first oboe always does the A-giving. I remember exactly what he said: "*Mademoiselle, voulez-vous me donner le La?*" This was a concert in celebration of the orchestra's fifteenth year under the illustrious Dr. Kindler and no tickets were for sale. They gave us two each in a moment of unprecedented generosity.

January 22, 1946

[On Drake paper] I am writing from Tabuteaus'—an un-dictated letter, as he is in New York with the orchestra and I came to do Mme's blouses like the old days. She gave me a lamb chop, potatoes fried in butter, *salade,* cheese, peaches with rum poured on top and the last of the fruitcake from Christmas, tea, and unrestricted candies. This was just a *little* dinner for the two of us—not like last Sunday when I came over and wrote letters and we had chicken and ate so much we could hardly move afterwards. I seem to keep busy enough doing their correspondence even though I don't live in Phila. I must tell you what Mme T said. You have a date for dinner with Tabuteau when the orchestra comes to San Francisco on their tour in the spring. It is practically certain he'll go—only one chance in one hundred he won't. What brought it up—some rich dame called tonight, a relative of that Mrs. Sloss in S.F., and she started out about how Tabuteau must be sure to visit their beautiful home and so I said, 'Well, I hope he has time to meet my mother.' Mme Tab said that was *far* more important—that you absolutely must meet him and hear the Philly Orchestra and that all those men belong to *you* too. I'll have to try to send you some extra money.

[In the end, the "one chance in one hundred" happened, and Tabuteau did not go on the 1946 tour. But my mother finally met him two years later in 1948 when he made his last trip to the West Coast with the Orchestra. He thoughtfully sent a few lines on a postcard of the Hotel Mark Hopkins-Atop Nob Hill, surprisingly postmarked May 23, her birthday: "Took your mother for—a Coc. [cocktail] to the 'Top of the Mark.' Of course she never had been there. M. T."]

January 27, 1946

Segovia played the Ponce guitar concerto with us. He was very fine but the guitar does not carry very well. Under his coat he wore a black velvet vest with silver buttons on it and with his big dark rimmed glasses and rather longish hair, made quite a picture wandering onto the stage with his guitar. General *Eisenhower* was in the Presidential box, as was also former ambassador to the Soviet Union, Joseph P. Davies. Finally I see some dignitaries at a concert.

With love,

Your Washington correspondent, Laila

The last couple of months of the season continued in much the same way with a few more lessons and chances to hear the Philadelphia Orchestra. On March 2 it was the Mendelssohn *Scotch Symphony* that Tabuteau played impeccably and the *Rosenkavalier Suite* with its lilting oboe solos. On March 9 Sol Schoenbach walked into the Studio while I was having a lesson, and I had to play my Brod étude in front of him. As students, we looked up to all of the Philadelphia solo players with such awe and respect, that not surprisingly, Brod *Étude No. 12* remained forever associated in my mind with Schoenbach's unexpected visit. That same night, Artur Rubinstein was the soloist with the orchestra in the Brahms *B-Flat Concerto*. "There were no tickets left but Tabuteau was good enough to get me in through the back door and I was able to sit in the Curtis box with all the piano students. Seymour Lipkin was there, and I had a little visit with him during intermission. He treated me to a glass of water. You have to stick a penny in a slot to get a cup."

Sometimes Tabuteau, Kincaid, and other men from the Philadelphia Orchestra took part in "Pops" concerts conducted by Max Leon, the owner of a local candy factory. I was grateful for the opportunity to hear Tabuteau play the big solo in Johann Strauss's Overture to *The Gypsy Baron* but sometimes wondered why he played in those concerts. When

ANOTHER YEAR OF STUDY WITH TABUTEAU

I heard him remark, "You know, he is the only conduc*teur* who has ever given me a turkey and a bottle of whiskey for Christmas," it was easier to understand.

In early April everything was winding up. I was to go on tour for five weeks with the North Carolina Symphony and have the opportunity to play first oboe. On a last weekend in Philadelphia, "Tabuteau gave me a lesson on the orchestra parts for North Carolina and told me so much. He let me play on one of his old reeds with the new oboe. Mme Tab was in the kitchen and when I finally got going decently, she said 'There, that sounds like Tabuteau!' She is a sharp oboe critic and was absolutely right about when it sounded good and when not . . . If I could only be under his influence another year! He worked with me for almost two hours and then we had a marvelous chicken dinner and fresh pineapple for dessert. I heard the Pension Fund concert—all Wagner with Helen Traubel.[1] Tabuteau played part of the time on 'my' oboe and he likes it very much. A couple notes still have to be adjusted and he says I'll have not a 'good' instrument, but a *beautiful* instrument—a Stradivarius. He has been wonderful to me really. He gouged twenty-five pieces of cane for my North Carolina tour. Imagine him going to all that trouble. It shows he really has a very kind streak or he'd never do so much."

At this point my detailed reports of what the Tabuteaus said, ate, wore, and maybe thought came to an end. Although the intense period of studying in Philadelphia was over, by now the Tabuteaus had become almost like family to me. They often addressed me as *notre fille* and referred to themselves as *la Famille*. In 1946 Madame Tabuteau made the decision to return to France for the first time after the war to see all their relatives and check on their property. The comfortable transatlantic steamship service to which they were accustomed had not yet been restored so she courageously decided to fly over in a Constellation. Tabuteau, who never wanted to get in a plane, planned to go to Canada again for the salmon fishing. During that summer I received letters from both of them.

On June 29th he wrote from Margaree in Nova Scotia:

> I enjoyed your picture of Madame Tabuteau's take-off on a sister ship of the "Sacred Cow."[2] I felt I was there in person. You should give up music and become a reporter. This year the fishing is *very very* poor,

MARCEL TABUTEAU

the worst for years. Reason, no snow last winter, no rain. Rivers are low and so is—Tabuteau.

P. S. Just received your last letter; am glad you had a nice time in New York and a possible engagement to Kansas City. It will do you good to play English horn. Although I wrote to you, send me the questionnaire, I always enjoy it. Think of . . . me . . . feeling like a "sacred bull." M. Tabuteau

Mme Tabuteau wrote from Paris that the first thing she noticed was the change of "mode." Women had suits with long jackets. Prices were astronomical. The theaters were barely beginning to reopen. "There are taxis again, busses also, but they only run until 9 at night. The Metro until midnight." She remarked on the patience of the French people who wait in lines for everything. In August she went to Toulon and the Pingouinette, where she found things "somewhat less bad than she had feared. We will come and spend the summer of 1947 there."

On her return to Paris Mme Tabuteau stayed at the Hotel Monsigny next to the Banque de France. She went to the opera, *La Flûte Enchantée* (The Magic Flute). "Gromer played oboe; naturally it is not the same thing." Knowing I was spending the summer in Philadelphia, she asked, "*Le Drake est-il encore debout?*" (Is the Drake still standing?) and if the cane sent by André Tabuteau had arrived. She said Tabuteau was "*bien malheureux*" (very unhappy) in Canada. Don't forget to send him the newspaper." From Tabuteau himself came more complaints about poor fishing, attacks of gout, boredom, and a request for some *books*. I was to "inquire at the Drake if they received a parcel or a *bag from France* containing oboe canes. If so, tell them to keep it with great care! Also, try to see Graf and tell him to do his best to have machines and shapes ready for me; expect to be back Phila. about the 10th of September. Please have the Studio in good order."

In the fall of 1946 I had to get ready to play English horn in the Kansas City Philharmonic Orchestra. I was not thrilled about this new job. After auditioning for solo oboe, I had received the standard answer that "they had a man in mind." But when Tabuteau reminded me that he had begun his career on English horn, it made me feel somewhat better. He gave me a little help, showing me how it required more wind to play this instrument, and he made a couple of colorful observations

ANOTHER YEAR OF STUDY WITH TABUTEAU

that I would never forget. He said not to "tell anyone" but that in reality "the English horn was an 'alarm clock' and the oboe, 'a micrometer.'" To play the English horn was "like walking on a six-foot-wide plank as opposed to balancing on a tightrope." I was impressed how he picked up the English horn and brilliantly dashed off the oboe passage in triplets from the last movement of the Beethoven *Trio*. I often heard him run through it on the oboe but did not know that there was a chance it might have been recorded. With John de Lancie playing second oboe and John Minsker, English horn, they had performed the first movement at a student concert.[3] They began to rehearse the whole trio with recording in mind, but because by then Tabuteau had experienced a backstage fall which precipitated a second hernia operation, his physician felt the project was too risky and advised against it.[4]

In those days one did not casually go to the telephone and call long distance. Tabuteau, who always disliked writing letters, complained that he "no longer had a secretary." Sometimes they would send a telegram to me in Kansas City. In November 1946 when I was thinking of getting a cat, there came a wire, first mentioning that all my letters had been enjoyed, and then: "also think cats situation worth going into but don't forget the poor dogs here—stop—reeds hellish as ever and everything else too—have already booked reservation for May and sold piano studio=LES TABUTEAU" (The Tabuteaus). Since 1943 I had been with them for every holiday season. Now at Christmas time I mailed a box with a variety of small gifts and received another telegram. "Just opened the box—enjoyed every gift and will miss Lola for Christmas but trees and reindeer will shine at your place . . . though we don't answer, write often—a very happy Christmas and love = les tabuteau." When the Tabuteaus *did* write, there were bits of news about their life in Philadelphia (which continued in much the same way), but more often they told of their plans for returning to France. Now that the war had ended this finally became a real possibility.

14 SUMMERS IN FRANCE

The Pingouinette; Back to Philadelphia, 1948

Although the Tabuteaus were now seriously considering their permanent retirement and return to France, postwar conditions made life there far from attractive. As late as 1948 there was no white bread—(a catastrophe for the French); baguettes were made from heavy, dark gray flour; bridges throughout the country still lay in ruins, and there was strict rationing of gasoline. They were eager to again be able to enjoy the spot where they had spent so many long summers in the decades between the two wars. But it would take several years before their little house, the Pingouinette, could be put back into livable shape.

After the end of the First World War, Tabuteau was increasingly drawn to the Midi and especially to the sunny south coast of France, the Côte d'Azur. He felt at home there, and in the 1920s Mme Tabuteau (at that time still Louise André), located a simple stucco one-floor Mediterranean style, tiled-roof cottage at La Lèque on the Cap Sicié. A tiny settlement, even smaller than a hamlet, La Lèque was situated in the dry piney hills not far from the sea above the fishing village of Le Brusc. After buying the property, they enlarged the house, adding the modern conveniences of a good kitchen and bath, and were very

La Pingouinette, Tabuteau's summer home at La Lèque near Le Brusc, Cap Sicié, from the mid-1920s until 1951. Photo by Laila Storch.

comfortable there. The Pingouinette was named after the master of the house, *le Pingouin*. Tabuteau loved to cook outdoors on the terrace, where they could have their meals in the shade of the grape arbor. Flourishing in the reddish-brown Provençal soil, an orchard of fruit trees baked in the burning southern sun while the bright blue rim of the Mediterranean shimmered in the distance. In the 1920s and 1930s the Philadelphia Orchestra season lasted only thirty weeks, so that even with the addition of the festival in Ann Arbor, Michigan, Tabuteau was usually able to leave for France in May. He went on ahead of Mme Tabuteau, who had to finish her teaching schedule.

Before the Tabuteaus could settle in for their several months' stay at the Pingouinette, they had to make the ritual visits in the north of France: his family in Compiègne, her relatives in Paris and Blois, and everyone at the Lorée firm, where he always ordered oboes to be picked up in the fall. In 1996 I rode from Paris to Blois with Mme Tabuteau's nephew, Dr. Jacques Budin. Along the way, he reminisced about the period in the 1930s, *avant la guerre* (before the war), when "the Tabuteaus

Tabuteau consulting with his good friend Lucien Lorée, whose oboes he played from his earliest years until his last days.

stayed on the Left Bank at the Hôtel Littré in the Rue Littré. That was their *quartier* in Paris, the area of the Boulevard du Montparnasse. It was only later after World War II that they chose the Hôtel Louvois on the Right Bank. Tabuteau would have his breakfast at *La Coupole*, and sometimes he took us (his nephews), for a 'Coupe la Coupole,' ice cream with hot chocolate. I remember that he gave money to the musicians in the café so that they would go away and play somewhere else on the terrace." On a Paris visit in May 2001 I decided to look for the Hôtel Littré. An almost invisible four-star establishment, it still stands at 9 rue Littré in the sixth arrondissement, marked only by the polished brass initials H L on the rather austere, heavy, front door. From there, I walked the short distance to *La Coupole* at 102 Boulevard du Montparnasse, where one can see the newly restored pillars painted by the artists who frequented the brasserie in its heyday of the 1920s and 30s. A few days later, together with a group of American oboe players in search of their French background, I enjoyed a festive dinner at *La Coupole.*

Jacques Budin continued to recount his memories while retracing the route taken by Tabuteau. "Sometimes he rented a car but in 1936 or 1937, he brought over with him from America, a Buick Roadster with a '*spider*' (rumble seat), which made a big impression on us. I was about twelve years old then and to be allowed to ride in the back was a special reward as he wasn't too fond of children. After 1945, he would rent a Citroën." We headed south via the Porte d'Orléans, passing through the small town of Longjumeau, where a statue of the coachman immortalized by Adolphe Adam in his operetta *Le Postillon de Longjumeau* stands in the main square. Jacques explained that this road was called the *Route des Boeufs*, as the oxen used to be driven up on foot (or hoof!) from the Valley of the Loire all the way to the Paris markets. Orléans was the northernmost city of the valley, so everything that came up the river by boat would then continue by road for the remaining one hundred kilometers to Paris. Jacques described every detail of the trips with his uncle: "We left Paris at 8:30 a.m. About an hour later we stopped at a roadside restaurant in Montlhéry, L'Escargot de Linas, and there, at 9:30 a.m., Tabuteau would eat two dozen escargôts. Further on, there was a stop for lunch at the Auberge de la Montespan and then came a siesta. It took all day until about 6:30, to get to Blois, a trip we make today in two or three hours." Now that names are being given to the highways of France, perhaps we should call this '*la Route Tabuteau!*'"

Mme Tabuteau's family, the Andrés, were from Blois in the Département de Loir-et-Cher. The imposing château in the middle of this city on the Loire river harbors shades of François I and Anne de Bretagne. In a later century, the Chocolat Poulard factory was established on the banks of the Loire. Perhaps the enticing aroma wafting through the air contributed to Mme Tabuteau's love of chocolate and her nickname of *Chocolat.* By the end of the nineteenth century, there had been Andrés in Blois for about a hundred years. Louise Marie Henriette André (the future Mme Tabuteau) was born in Blois on November 28, 1891, the third of five children, from oldest to youngest: Jean-Louis, Claire, Louise, Pierre, and Denise, mother of Jacques. Madame Tabuteau always proudly signed her name "Louise *André* Tabuteau," and it was from her, and later from Denise, that I learned something about their parents. Their father, Edmond André, was in the same business as his father before him, *papier peint* (wallpaper). He also painted viaducts, bridges, railway stations, and large commercial buildings throughout France. This profession required a good deal of travel, which he loved. His wife took care of the books, using a front room of their house as an

MARCEL TABUTEAU

office where she answered the telephone and tended to the business correspondence. Denise remembered their mother, born Jeanne Marie Benard, as being "*très gaie et vivante*" (lively and cheerful) despite having a disability, possibly the result of childhood polio, which caused her to walk with difficulty. "She was a very good manager and kept the household running smoothly during father's frequent absences."

The Andrés were rather in advance of their time in respect to the education of girls. Louise graduated with her baccalaureate in 1910 and continued her studies at a "Normal School" in Gueret to be an English teacher. Her parents arranged for an exchange with a young lady from Glasgow, Scotland, who would spend summers in Blois to teach them English. Later, Louise and Denise visited the family in Glasgow to further improve their language skills. Both of the André brothers became active in government. Claire lived for many years in Algeria. Denise, aside from raising her family of three, studied art and was a dedicated painter during all of her long life. Louise, who excelled in her academic studies, was sent by the French government after the war of 1914–18 to teach in a school in the American Midwest. She later became head of the French Department at the Shipley School in Bryn Mawr near Philadelphia. At that time this select school was open only to girls. From 1938 to 1954 she taught French language courses and French diction at the Curtis Institute of Music. An energetic and effective teacher who used every minute of the class time, she brought her students an ample view of French culture, as well as drilling them on irregular verbs. The many books and beautiful furniture she had stored in Blois were unfortunately lost when bombing raids during the Second World War destroyed the André family home.

One version of how the Tabuteaus met was told to me by Madame herself. It must have been in the early 1920s. She had gone to a Philadelphia Orchestra concert with another young woman teacher from her school. After the concert, they stopped in at the drugstore on the corner of Broad and Locust Streets across from the Academy of Music. It was the typical drugstore of the era with a soda fountain and other amenities. They were taking turns weighing themselves on the scale, at which point Marcel Tabuteau came in, heard the two young ladies speaking together, and addressed Louise with, "*Vous êtes française, Mademoiselle?*" How long it took for their friendship to develop we do not know, but for a time in the 1920s they lived together in the western part of Philadelphia at Sixty-third and Walnut Streets in what was then a pleasant neighborhood with many trees known as Woodside Park. In 1929, the same year that the Drake Hotel was built, they moved into an apartment on the fourteenth floor. This thirty-one story, narrow, reddish-colored apartment-hotel with its Mexican-Spanish ornamentation and distinctive rooftop, towered for many years over any other structure south of Market Street. They were less than a two-block walk from 1512 Spruce Street to the Academy of Music, and Tabuteau could arrive on the stage just a few minutes after leaving his apartment. Today, following a long period of neglect, the Drake is being refurbished and, with its proximity to the new Kimmel Center for the Performing Arts, may well again house musicians and others who wish to be at the center of the city.[1]

On July 11, 1934, when Marcel Tabuteau was forty-seven and Louise André, forty-three, they were married at the *mairie* (town hall) of the tenth *arrondissement* in Paris.[2] An ornate Gothic-style building on rue du Faubourg Saint-Martin, the *mairie* is located only a few steps from the corner of rue du Château d'Eau where Lucien Lorée had his oboe establishment for many years both before and after World War I. The old Conservatoire, rue de Bergère, where Tabuteau studied under Georges Gillet is also nearby. His marriage, therefore, took place in a part of Paris closely allied to his life with the oboe. The witnesses were Louise's sister Denise and her husband, Dr. Pierre Budin, who remained the Tabuteaus closest friends for the rest of their lives.

Every summer the Tabuteaus would spend several days at Molineuf where Denise had restored a picturesque twelfth-century cottage. At the edge of the forest of Blois, about nine kilometers west of the city, the tiny village of Molineuf is not far from the great château of Chambord, François I's monumental hunting lodge. After their visit, the Tabuteaus were off to the Midi, usually by car, but occasionally they took *le train bleu* with its comfortable Wagons Lits. This was the most modern and luxurious way for well-to-do travelers of the 1930s to speed through to the Riviera. The Tabuteaus could get off the train in Toulon and head for the Cap Sicié. Tabuteau's Compiègne nephew, François Létoffé, told me what life was like at the time of his early visits to La Pingouinette. "In *le*

Midi, it was all much more natural and tranquil than now. The country-side around La Lèque was quite wild and unspoiled. There was really no one there. In Le Brusc a fisherman would just ask, 'Do you want to come fishing with us?'—a stark contrast with present day conditions where everything is highly organized, even to having a refrigerator on the boat. There were grapevines and peach trees all around the Pingouinette and a fireplace on the terrace where we cooked outdoors. And a very lucky thing, there was a well on the property. Now there is water everywhere, but in those days it was very rare and the local people would rather give you a liter of wine than a liter of water." Even Leopold Stokowski was entranced by the unspoiled, rural atmosphere of Cap Sicié and La Lèque. Once while traveling in the south of France, he wrote a note to Tabuteau expressing his interest in buying property there.[3]

While there is no doubt that Tabuteau found the casual summer life at the Pingouinette to his liking, there may well have been other reasons which added to his affinity for the area. It was not far to Fréjus and the best fields of oboe cane, nor to the nearby casinos, ranging from the relative simplicity of Bandol to the elegance of Monte Carlo. The long winter hours spent at the reed desk were replaced in the summer by his even more compulsive attachment to the gambling table. Then in Toulon there was Tabuteau's brother, André, only eighteen months younger, but totally different in character. Père Tabuteau had insisted that André enlist at age seventeen in the École d'Armes in Joinville where he became a fencing expert, eventually earning the title *maître d'armes*. In 1919, Marcel brought André to the United States for the second time.[4] He stayed for about three years playing clarinet and English horn with a certain degree of success, but he became homesick for France and returned to marry Augusta Pery. They settled in Toulon, where he played first violin in the local opera house orchestra. He was also a professor of violin in La Seyne at a college of the Marist Brothers religious order, a school attended by future high-level generals and admirals. (Remember that all the Tabuteau children had first played string instruments, schooled by their brother-in-law, Émile Létoffé.) André's wife, Augusta, was an outstanding *cuisinière* specializing in the preparation of fine Provençal dishes. François Létoffé told me that even the "experts" from Compiègne had never eaten such delicious mushrooms as those cooked by Tante

Augusta. They all enjoyed many memorable meals on the terrace of André and Augusta's little red-tile-roofed villa with its corner tower at 39 Avenue du Vert Coteau. Between the house and the gate that opened onto the street, there was a small orchard of citrus and peach trees. François recounted, "One time we were on the porch eating oysters and needed some lemon. Someone just extended an arm and we had a lemon picked right off the tree!"

Mme Tabuteau's first post-war visit to France had been in 1946. A year later in May 1947, they both made the trip. It was now almost eight years since Tabuteau had been in France, the longest single stretch of time away from his home country since he left in 1905. On May 24 John and Andrea de Lancie drove the Tabuteaus to New York where they were to board the Queen Elizabeth at the Cunard Line's Pier 90. I had never seen anyone off on an ocean liner, and as their thirteen pieces of luggage left no room in the car, I went over on the train. We all met in the Tabuteaus' Cabin Class accomodations where I noted that "they had a nice room but no porthole." I was impressed, however, by the ship's general resemblance to a luxury hotel. With its almost three thousand passengers, one realized that travel was returning to pre-war levels. Before they left, Mme Tabuteau had written to me, "Le Pingouin is delighted to go back and see his France but we don't yet know what we'll do for the winter of 47–48. In any case we are taking a return ticket." At the end of June a note arrived from "Blois, where we are spending the day. We are en route towards the Midi and the Pingouinette. Found a good Citroën. Voyage on the Queen Elizabeth was a big success." They spent almost all summer at the Pingouinette. Although conditions were still difficult (they had brought boxes of food with them from Philadelphia), they nevertheless seemed very happy to be in their old familiar surroundings. In her letter of July 17, Madame reported on the details of a typical Tabuteau meal, which included "hors d'oeuvres, gigot, salad, cheese, a *gâteau*, coffee, three kinds of wine and liqueurs followed by a long nap . . . The weather is beautiful and le Pingouin is happy. *He* has decided, I think, to return to France for good in '48."[5] At the end of August on a postcard, other news: "Le Pingouin, carried away by temptation, here we are at *l'usine*[6] *de Monte Carlo* where he is applying the number system to the rhythm of the Roulette. So far so good, and we just had a delicious champagne lunch."

MARCEL TABUTEAU

Tabuteau selecting oboe cane with Marius Audino on the Biasotto property outside of Fréjus, 1951. Photo by Laila Storch.

SUMMERS IN FRANCE

André Tabuteau in uniform as a master fencer of the École d'Armes, Joinville. Photo by René Gautier, Compiègne.

The year 1948 arrived, and despite their expressed intention of returning to France "for good," the Tabuteaus decided to again spend the summer in Canada. But now *I* was in France with introductions to their families. Ever since my Curtis days I had been eager to learn more about their home country, but for several years following the end of World War II it was almost impossible to find any type of transatlantic transportation. Finally, through the Institute of International Education, I managed to get passage on a student boat, the *Marine Tiger,* a former Liberty ship. The Spartan accommodations had barely been converted from its earlier function as a troop ship. It took ten to twelve days to cross the ocean. I later learned that some of these ships had cracked in half during their years of service in the North Atlantic.

In Paris I met Mme Tabuteau's sister Denise, her husband Dr. Pierre Budin, a dentist, and their three grown children, Jacqueline, Jacques, and André, known as Dédé. The Budins invited me to lunch at their apartment, 6 rue de Maubeuge in the ninth *arrondissement*. Mme Tabuteau had given me a long list of special items she wanted me to bring back: Caron perfume "Bellogia," feather-down powder puffs, leather gloves—all these luxury goods available even in a time of general austerity. From Tabuteau, I had a letter addressed to Raymond Dubois at Lorée, to help me in ordering an oboe and English horn. The Lorée firm was only now beginning to resume production, and it was far from certain that I would be able to get an instrument. Buying perfume and doing other errands were the "required" tasks, but it was visits to Lorée and the prospect of getting to the cane fields that I really anticipated. It seemed providential that the Tabuteaus had given their niece Jacqueline, a medical student, permission to spend some vacation time at the Pingouinette. She invited me to come along, which meant I would be close to "cane country." First came several weeks in Paris and a trip with Mme Budin to Molineuf, where at the sight of her little cottage, called La Vallée, and Chambord, the most spectacular of all châteaux, I felt transported into a land of fairy tales. Then in early July, I climbed the steep steps of a third-class carriage with Jacqueline and her six-year-old daughter for the all-night train to Toulon. The hard wooden seats were not conducive to sleep, but with early dawn and my first glimpse of Provence, my excitement at seeing the slender, dark silhouettes of cypress trees, the ochre-colored houses and red-tiled roofs of Avignon, Arles, and Valence made all further thought of rest seem unimportant.

As soon as we arrived in Toulon, we made our way to André Tabuteau's house. I was glad to see a "Tabuteau" and found André to be jolly and easy going with a temperament diametrically opposed to that of his brother. Probably today he would be called "laid-back." I was soon to learn more about his easygoing ways when it came to oboe cane. Travel along the Côte d'Azur in those years was very uncomfortable and time-consuming, with many changes of busses and long walks to the cane fields under the burning mid-day sun of the Midi. As the result of an accident, André always had to walk with a cane; the operation that should have improved his condition had only made it worse. For a long time he was bedridden, but he had remained cheerful with an always-ready friendly smile. It was, therefore, perhaps understandable

SUMMERS IN FRANCE

that he asked why I should "bother to go all the distance to Cogolin or Fréjus" when one could just as well get cane much closer at Hyères. But because his brother Marcel, albeit rather reluctantly, had parted with some information on where to locate the best cane, I would not have dared ignore his suggestions. Furthermore, the cane I had seen from Hyères seemed of inferior quality and rather soft and grainy. Now I could better understand an incident which took place in 1946 shortly after the end of the war. A packet of good oboe cane which André sent from Toulon had finally gotten through to Philadelphia. André had soaked the cane, split, and cut it to size, but not allowed it to completely dry out. When Tabuteau opened the precious parcel and found the moldy pieces of cane, he was almost in tears and, bewailing his brother's ineptitude, lamented, *"Mon pauvre frère"* (My poor brother). If André was a bit casual about oboe cane, this attitude did not, however, extend to the question of food. Immediately after our arrival in Toulon, we were served a delicious impromptu lunch of a mushroom omelette, cold roast lamb, fresh crusty bread, local cheeses, and ice cream. Great meals were a regular part of life at 39 Avenue du Coteau and would prove a welcome respite from the austere conditions in which we were to spend the next three weeks at the Pingouinette.

Friends of the Toulon Tabuteaus hauled us in a paint truck the twenty-some kilometers to La Lèque to open up the house. We must have looked like a band of gypsies: Jacqueline, Francine, and me, André Tabuteau, with his wife Augusta, two of their friends, two dogs, and Marie, the faithful maid who always worked for the other Tabuteaus when they were in France. I felt as if we were taking part in a scene from a foreign movie of the 1940s. We rattled through the villages of La Seyne and Six-Fours where we bought potatoes and vegetables. Tabuteau had asked me to lug a fishing rod and lure all the way from Philadelphia which I managed to deliver to one of the locals. When a neighbor finally brought the key and let us into the Pingouinette, we found it looked very much as it must have before the war except that the little house had been stripped of every piece of hardware, plumbing, and movable household appliance. For us, it would be almost like camping. Nothing functioned—neither the refrigerator or the bathroom—but at least there were a couple of metal frame cots to sleep on. Even though

MARCEL TABUTEAU

Tabuteau had apparently had an enjoyable time there in 1947, he had been disillusioned by the behavior of his neighbors who, he believed, had ransacked his place. Some of the damage had, of course, been caused by the various marauding armies that had crisscrossed the south of France during the war. But we *did* hear stories about the local *paysans* taking things. As I wrote home, "They say the peasants are *des voleurs* (robbers). It's true in a way. They all take everything for themselves. If a tree falls on someone else's property, they chop it up and carry it away to sell as their own property. The gardener plants vegetables for Tabuteau and then takes them himself. There are hundreds of stories, all the same. In Philadelphia, when we heard that Tabuteau had iron bars on his windows in the south of France, we thought how untrusting he was. Now I understand better and am very glad the bars are there! There's a phrase, *'les gens de ce pays'* simply, the *'people* of this region,'—they are really different."

I compared the countryside to where I had grown up in California. It reminded me of Sonoma County with its grapevines, olive trees, plums, peaches, the dry hills, and intense blue sky. The water in the shallows of the sea varied from shades of deep cobalt blue to light aquamarine. It was so clear, one could see through to the gravely bottom. Flowering wild broom added even more yellow to the rows of acacia trees (*mimosa*) which lined Tabuteau's driveway. A thick hedge of fragrant lavender formed a border with the neighbors' property, and the air was sweet with the scent of the sun-drenched pine trees. All day long the *cigales* (huge cicadas) kept up a loud and persistent chorus. Goats grazed in a nearby field. By day we saw colorful lizards and at night, a caterpillar with a green light gleaming under its tail. It was all very rural and had none of the trappings of so-called civilization. Fortunately, one could not then foresee that fifty years later it would be impossible to even find Tabuteau's old house among the forests of condominiums and development that had overtaken the whole region.

In that long ago summer we had to descend almost two miles on foot to Le Brusc to buy our groceries. With the houses painted yellow, blue, white, or pink, fishing boats tied up along the wharf, nets stretched out to dry, and the fishermen in their bright blue togs conversing lazily with other "*types*," it was a colorful scene. But I felt I must not lose too much time enjoying the surroundings; it was imperative to get to Toulon and begin the search for cane. In 1948, a "cane excursion" along the Côte d'Azur was not a simple undertaking. Starting out at 6:00 a.m., I had to first walk down to Le Brusc to catch the bus for Toulon. Toulon was a lively port town full of French sailors with their jaunty caps topped by red pompoms. The palm trees, hot sun, and strings of hanging beads which clattered as you entered the doorways made one feel the closeness to North Africa. From Toulon, I took another crowded bus which inched its way along the Côte; the slow tempo of the trip allowed plenty of time to admire the eucalyptus trees, mimosa, purple bougainvillea, cacti, and the long avenues of rose and white oleanders. The cane "industry" had never been highly organized, and during the war it was completely neglected. Unless one knew somebody, it was almost impossible to find really good cane. Fréjus, for many decades the traditional source of the best cane, was Mecca to oboists. Once when Tabuteau had asked me to write a letter about cane to a Monsieur Audino in Fréjus, I was told to "forget the address." But I felt I should go there first and could already picture myself with clippers and measuring tools, picking out my cane from the "the Source!" Only Fréjus was said to have just the right combination of elements for growing top-quality oboe cane, cane with a hard varnish-like outer surface that grew wild in the valley of the Reyran along the banks of its little stream.

From the windows of the bus I saw signs along the roadside, "*Marchand de roseau: cannes à pêche, paniers à fleurs, cannisses brise-vent, instruments à musique*" (Cane merchant: fishing rods, baskets for flowers, barriers against wind, music instruments). "Music instruments" in last place indicated our ranking. Most of the cane merchants were very secretive, and all claimed that their cane was the best. They would say the cane from Ste. Maxime and Cogolin was too dry, and the cane from Hyères, too soft. There was nothing already cut to size; they complained that cane for the oboe was too much trouble—too difficult to sort and cut because it was so small—as opposed to the larger stalks used for clarinet, bassoon, and saxophone. When I finally approached Fréjus, I was thrilled to see the huge stacks of cane drying in the fields outside of the town. By an uncanny stroke of luck I walked right into

MARCEL TABUTEAU

Monsieur Audino's general store. As commanded, I had managed to forget his address but not his name! Marius Audino was a friend of the Biasotto family, and through his help I would be able to meet them. (Many of the people who worked with cane were of Italian descent.) But at present, the Biasottos were not at home; it was going to require a second trip to Fréjus. I came back a week later and took a taxi (far too expensive for my budget) out to the farm where I met the Biasottos: two brothers, Dante and Ange, and their old father. They had nothing cut to the correct length, but they allowed me to choose long stalks of ten-and-a-half millimeter diameter cane still covered with shreds of dry leaves which I then tied into large bundles. The Biasottos generously invited me to share their lunch under an outdoor shelter made of woven cane. Chickens were running in and out of the house while ducks and rabbits wandered about the yard. It was several miles from the Biasotto farm to the train, and I had no idea how I would get there with my unwieldy bundles of cane. My luck held when a clarinet reed manufacturer, Victor Olivieri, from the island of Majorca, stopped by and gave me a ride in his truck to the Fréjus railway station. Again, I climbed into a third-class carriage, this time filled with dirty little children who were all chewing gum which they rolled into balls and stretched into designs with their filthy hands, dropped it on the floor—always returning it again to their mouths. It might have seemed an amusing sight, but I found it impossible not to think of the germs.

For those interested in history, there was more to Fréjus than oboe cane. Founded in 49 B.C. by Julius Caesar as Forum Julii, it would later be on the great Aurelian Way which ran from Rome via Nice, Antibes, and Aix, to the colonial city of Arles. Fréjus can still boast of its Roman ruins: the aqueduct, amphitheatre, and arena. Napoleon landed in Fréjus in 1815 when he returned from his first exile on the island of Elba, and in 1944, allied troops came from North Africa to disembark not only in Fréjus, but all along that section of the coast. Aside from its former military importance, Fréjus possesses a cathedral, a beautiful cloister built between the tenth and thirteenth centuries, and a baptistery which dates from the end of the fourth century. An unexpected surprise inside the church is the outstanding organ from the famous nineteenth-century

My first cane "expedition" outside Fréjus in 1948. L to R: Victor Olivieri, Laila Storch, Ange Biasotto.

firm of Cavaillé-Coll. On a later cane excursion, I had the unforgettable experience of hearing Gustave Bret,[7] then in his late eighties, play Bach organ sonatas and toccatas and fugues on that magnificent instrument.

I searched for cane not only in Fréjus but also at Ste. Maxime and Cogolin. At first the dealers would say they had nothing and would only bring out a few pieces when one was about to leave. It all seemed so difficult that I was "tempted to see if I can grow it in California." My first cane "expedition" was coming to an end. I bought several long flower baskets (the size for shipping gladiolas), and after a few days at André's sawing cane into manageable-length pieces, shipped off about fifteen kilograms (approximately 33 pounds) to Paris. After a final delicious feast with André and Augusta Tabuteau on their veranda, it was goodbye to Toulon, the Mediterranean, Le Brusc, and the Pingouinette.

During my stay in France, I had sent letters to the Tabuteaus in Nova Scotia telling them how the summer was going. From Fordview they wrote to tell me how glad they were to know that I was happy to finally be in France. I had sent them a small piece of acacia (mimosa) from one of Tabuteau's trees. He responded that "The idea of beginning to blow again is repugnant to me—especially in comparing the *infecte* (stinking) Academy of Music with the beautiful mimosas of the Pingouinette. Thank you for sending us a little souvenir twig." Madame added, "Your first letter from the Pingouinette describing your arrival à la gypsy just reached us. We had no idea how you were managing. We are happy that you had that little visit there and now you know the 'grapps and pêches' first hand . . . Don't forget the powder. Caron Sweet Pea, *naturelle.* If possible, two boxes rather than one. Also perfume . . . a small box from a good *maison* for a Christmas present, and a Lanvin, not too big. Don't forget powder puffs, cologne, and as many small bottles of perfume as you can bring for little gifts. I envy you to be in Paris, but our turn will come soon. Here the summer was dull but pleasant, especially for *le Pingouin* who is still tormented by the passion for fishing."

At the end of August the Tabuteaus sent another letter from Fordview in care of my boat, the *Marine Jumper.* "We can imagine you on the "Jumper" in the middle of the ocean and hope that you do not "jumpiez" too much and that you have good and entertaining company." They announced the date of their departure from Nova Scotia as September 9 and their plans to arrive in Philadelphia three days later on Sunday evening, the twelfth. "Le Pingouin seriously recommends that you do not say anything about what you have seen or found in the Midi. He wants to be the first to know . . . We are impatient to see you and hear all." As always, seemingly worried that some good "secret" source of cane or oboes would be disclosed, he wrote to me in Philadelphia only a few days later with more admonitions and cautions, asking if I had received the letter sent to the boat. "*Do not show anyone any* of the things you have brought back, *especially oboe and cane.*"

RETURN TO PHILADELPHIA

Now followed the unloading of all the booty from my nine pieces of luggage. There was a violin for Tabuteau and two baskets of cane, much of which I still had to saw into proper lengths. My main fear was that the oboe Dubois had made for me was "too good" and that Tabuteau would want to keep it for himself. Even Monsieur Graffen, the "finisher" in the Lorée shop, had said that "Tabuteau will surely want it."

My fears soon proved to be correct. "Tabuteau has developed a real passion for my new oboe and I will be glad to leave town with it actually in my hands. I *knew* it from the first five minutes I blew in it. He said it is the best oboe he's seen in the last twenty-five years and I was lucky that Christopher Columbus discovered America so I could go back to France and get an instrument like that." Interesting reasoning!

During the next month I was able to see and hear Tabuteau in action again with the wind and string classes at Curtis. I also had a number of extremely intensive sessions on orchestral repertoire. I was about to begin playing first oboe in the Houston Symphony Orchestra, and he probably wanted to make sure that his reputation as a trainer of solo players for so many of the country's orchestras would not be dimmed by sending out into the world such a rarity as "a woman oboist." He said that I must play "Robust," because if I have a nice, sweet, small tone, "they'll say, like a woman." He told me that I "had the boat" but now I "must cross the ocean." Sometimes I felt like an athlete going into training; other times, it seemed that "he was like Svengali standing over me saying, 'more on this note, faster the trill, slower, longer, the wind like this,' and on and on." I played for him at every opportunity—at the studio—at the apartment—all the orchestral parts I had copied out by hand and memorized. The cadenza of the *Bacchanale* from *Samson and Delila*, solos from *Don Juan*, *Till Eulenspiegel*, and *Don Quixote*, *Tombeau de Couperin*, *Scheherazade*, *Daphnis and Chloé*, the Schubert *C Major Symphony*, the Beethoven *Fifth*, *Sixth*, and *Eighth Symphonies* and the Violin *Concerto*, *Escales*, *Afternoon of a Faun*, Tchaikovsky *Fourth Symphony* and the Violin *Concerto*, Sibelius 5th, the Dvořák *New World*, Stravinsky *Firebird*, the Brahms Symphonies and Violin *Concerto*, the Johann Strauss Overture to the *Gypsy Baron* and the Grieg *Norwegian Dance*. In between all this we worked again on the Barret *Grand Studies*, especially Nos. 13, 15, and 16, in different keys and rhythms. The first two lines of No. 16 were to be played in every feasible key, *piano*, both staccato and legato, also one octave apart, always remembering to sing the melody. Then we spent time on the Mozart *Oboe Quartet* and the *Sinfonia Concertante*, the Bach *Concerto for Two Violins* (yes, on oboe), and the Paladilhe *Solo*. Clearly, he wanted to help me, but as I wrote home, "Right now my head is turning. He's told me so much, I can't straighten it all out. I spend my evenings sawing and sorting cane." I often wondered what any neighbors may have thought if, through the thin walls of my Spruce Street room, they heard the sawing followed by the 'clink, clink' of pieces of dry oboe cane dropping into a box.

Occasionally I managed to play something to Tabuteau's satisfaction, but other times were close to traumatic. There was a particularly difficult Sunday at the Studio with a lesson I would never forget. It was on the solo passage shortly after the opening of the Brahms *First Symphony*. He insisted that the intervals progress in an almost inexorable manner so that in the octaves G to G and D to high D, the lower notes build enough intensity to allow the octave above to emerge and soar effortlessly upward. There must be intensity on the high C followed by a leaning inflection (in a *piano* dynamic) on the descending A-flat. The F and D have to grow out of the A-flat and be played with an "up" inflection so that one can lean on the C before the diminuendo on the final B natural. He was pulling it out of me note by note and then screamed, "The *tragedy*—it is C minor—Damn fool! I told you to take the C key. The high D and C must ring. Tense! Practice *a tempo* with a metronome." And I was supposed to use other fingerings for the final C to B.

Shortly before I was to leave for Houston there was a bit more praise than cursing. "He wanted Madame Tabuteau to hear me and keeps saying 'how well I play.' In fact, tonight he asked me to play *Tombeau de Couperin* for her and said he'd never heard anyone play it like that in twenty years and that I play absolutely as well as anyone he knows. When Mme T said that I can never hope to get in any of the top orchestras like New York because I am a woman, *he* said he didn't know about that because I played so well. This afternoon he told me if I keep on this track and practice correctly now and work, there is a hundred percent chance that I will do something that no one expects me to, and I will really show them something. But he also said, 'you know I am against women in music, but the way you play——etc., etc.'" For Tabuteau to make these statements five years after he had reluctantly decided to teach me represented a striking change of attitude. The degree of his support was evident in the letter he wrote to Efrem Kurtz, the conductor in Houston. (Kurtz later gave me the letter.)

> September 19, 1948.
> Dear Mr. Kurtz,
> We have just said goodbye to Miss Storch, who is on her way to Houston with such a marvellous oboe that I would like to own it myself. For a few weeks, she has been working with me and I want to tell you that I find the trip to France has been a great inspiration to her and it shows immensely in her playing. She is in perfect form and I am sure she will come up to all your expectations. Confidentially, she plays as well as any of the boys I have had . . .

In lauding the new oboe and giving me his "seal of approval" in comparison with the "boys," he obviously wanted to reassure Kurtz, who had, after all, taken a considerable chance in hiring a woman.

Despite all this, Madame Tabuteau's prediction proved to be closer to the truth. It would still be several decades before any woman was admitted to the oboe section of a major U.S. symphony orchestra.[8] In 1947, one other woman oboist, Martha Scherer, graduated from Tabuteau's Curtis class. However, he saw that even though we found some work, the odds were against us for further advancement. He therefore accepted no more women in his remaining six years of teaching at the Curtis Institute. When Evelyn McCarty applied for an audition in early 1954, the secretary of admissions, Helen Hoopes, replied that the school was sorry to tell her they were not hearing girls who wished "to major in Oboe because of Mr. Tabuteau's feeling that he can accept boys only for his class. He has a very few students . . . together with the fact that boys are given preference by the major symphony conductors, for which his graduates are in demand."[9] Only a few weeks later, with Tabuteau's decision to retire and the appointment of John de Lancie, the policy changed, and Evelyn received the news that "Since Mr de Lancie is willing to consider girls for his class at the Institute, provided they surpass boys in talent, we are sending the enclosed application." But there was an added admonition. In taking over Tabuteau's class, "Mr de Lancie will be able to select but one new Oboe student. We therefore suggest that you give serious consideration to the length of the journey for an audition."[10] In April, Evelyn McCarty heard that she had been accepted to study with John de Lancie for the next school year, 1954–55, becoming the first of the women oboists to benefit from this new program.

As I wrote on my way to Houston by train, from "somewhere in Mississippi: No one could have given me a better send-off than the Tabuteaus—a midnight supper after the Saturday concert—and then on Sunday afternoon we went for a ride in their car. Afterwards, I had a cold lamb dinner and Tabuteau made me a big sandwich to take on the train. He played my oboe on the stage a little on Saturday and still keeps raving about what a beautiful thing it is." Those few weeks before I left for Houston were one of the most concentrated periods of study I ever experienced. The advice Tabuteau gave me at that time covered every aspect of oboe playing. I tried to write down as well as I could the essence of his remarks.

1. Wind control and numbers: He returned to the things he had emphasized in my first lessons of five years earlier. Practice 1-2-3-4-5-4-3-2-1 on one note and then in fifths (A-E-A) detached and slurred. From a low C, play 1-13 (to high A) and then the opposite. Do the same, playing all the notes in between. Practice all the intervals, then when you have a little solo, you have something to play on. Exaggerate—but in the right direction. Always let the *music* determine the numbers and try to come as close as possible to what fits you and the music the best. Don't *force* the pattern on the music.

    Always keep the line. Each note must take its cue of placement from the note you are on. You must get beyond just playing the notes on the oboe.

    There must be distribution and form and then the real spirit and life besides.

    Play to the last fellow in the balcony. *Travel!!*"

2. How to practice: Don't waste your time playing foolishly. Never play anything valueless. Every little prelude must have a meaning. Play every arpeggio and interval exercise as if it were a beautiful solo. Your mental ideal must be *better* than you. You must try to meet it. Play little exercises to keep in form. Practice articulation in slow motion. Some are "ta" and some are "ti." "Ti" is sharper than "ta." Practice striking notes at exactly the spot on the range that you want.

    Practice the skeleton of everything. FORM—ROOT."

3. Suggestions for a division of practice time: Play exercises for embouchure and wind for one half hour. Then forty-five minutes on studies, forty-five minutes on solos to develop style. Practice scales and thirds—staccato and legato.

Practice Gillet Studies sometimes for the acrobatic embouchure. Play them *slowly* and always with *line* and purpose.

Practice in front of a mirror. Make it look easy. Don't frown and make faces.

Always imagine Tabuteau is behind a curtain listening to you.

4. About reeds: Get the feel of the reed before you play and *make* it sound as you want it to. If reeds play low-C#,—F#"—E'" they are not false.

Always put five or six reeds away that play well to keep on hand for emergency, but don't depend on them. Then try to make one.

This final counsel was optimistic indeed and very likely wishful thinking! From my memory of the agonizing reed crises I saw Tabuteau suffer each time he had a solo performance in the offing or even a demanding orchestral part, I doubt that he was able to follow his own good advice. During that Houston season I also received an occasional letter with suggestions for surviving orchestral life such as: "Don't let the pitch bug get the best of you and don't forget if the others see you are really disturbed, they will tune still sharper." Or speaking of contracts, in December 1948: "Naturally, try to obtain as much as possible, as there is money there (referring to Houston), but always do it prudently and above all, intelligently. Being there yourself, you can judge the situation better than anyone else. As they appreciate you, it seems to me that $150 would be a minimum, but base it on what the *others* manage to get. The oboe must always be '*parmi les mieux considérés*' (among the highest paid) so good luck and keep us au courant."

Other good pieces of advice were:

1. Never play to please no matter whom. Only for *you.*
2. Never discuss problems of interpretation with your colleagues, but play with a degree of mastery and conviction that most of your "*antagonistes*" (adversaries) cannot do better than *imitate* you.

Tabuteau began his own season at his usual level of intensity. On October 22 Madame Tabuteau wrote that le Pingouin had begun to play again "only too well and with too much enthusiasm. I don't see us yet next winter with the 'grapps' and the rest." A month later he was getting accustomed to the "new régime" which he found quite pleasant. With his "associate John de Lancie now in service," Tabuteau would play only the first half of the season but would continue to teach at Curtis for the full school year. At this point, he made one of his periodic remarks about perhaps needing help in his old age from his students. It came in a letter complaining that some steps taken by then-president Harry Truman were "costing me dearly. Stocks have just fallen by five billions in two days. If this continues you will soon have to support me. Better get ready and become famous."[11] I never took his various comments of this type seriously, considering them to be his version of a joke. But apparently some of his students were offended by the idea that he might one day really expect some financial aid from them.

Tabuteau rarely wrote about concerts. But when he let me know that "Mme Tabuteau will go to the only Max Leon concert of the season as there will be *On the Banks of the Nile* scene from *Aida*" [with the big oboe solo], it was also to say, "the reeds are always capricious and am eternally searching for a good gouge. Are you having more luck than I am?" In November 1948 the Orchestre Nationale of France came to Houston on their tour of the United States. Monsieur Beurrois, who played second clarinet to Gaston Hamelin in this orchestra, was the proprietor of the Hôtel de Chevreuse where I had stayed in Paris. During the summer he had invited me to listen to some rehearsals, and now I was happy to see and hear the orchestra again. He asked me to take some of the women violinists shopping so they could buy nylon blouses, still an unobtainable luxury in France. They were traveling everywhere by bus but said they found it bearable because the wonderful hotel bathrooms always had plenty hot water for showers (a rarity for them). Only later I learned that one of these violinists, Jeanne Haskil, was the sister of the great Romanian pianist Clara Haskil, who I was soon to meet in Prades.[12] When the Orchestre Nationale played in Philadelphia I received reports from both the Tabuteaus. First, Madame: "Tabuteau was in New York at the time of the Orchestre Nationale but I had a loge and invited Mme Bonade. After the concert the oboist Goetgheluck and clarinetist Hamelin came over for a *few* minutes but at 3:00 a.m. were still there. That is to say, we had a charming evening. Cold leg of lamb, Rhine wine, and assortment of cheeses. Pingouin had the chance to see and talk with them after his return from N.Y. at 1 a.m. I found Goetgheluck to be charming and even almost

SUMMERS IN FRANCE

distinguished. He was all complaisance to the point of flirting with Mme Bonade which made her very happy." Tabuteau added, "I heard the French orchestra, but not in Philadelphia; we went to Atlantic City. We spoke with the proprietor of your Paris hotel. It was raining *à torrents* (pouring). A very small audience, but how beautiful it was! As you remarked, everything is different from what we do, but I was very interested by the result. Strings, winds, all were admirable. Even the oboe, who exhibits the opposite of what I try to do, was very pleasing to me." These words from Tabuteau himself show that he did not always dislike what he heard from the French musicians who came decades after the legendary performers of his student days.

15 TABUTEAU'S LAST YEARS AT THE CURTIS INSTITUTE

1946–1954

With the end of World War II, a type of renaissance took place in Tabuteau's classes at the Curtis Institute of Music. Two major aspects of this "renewal of life" in Tabuteau's last eight years of teaching there were the return of the young men whose studies and careers had been interrupted by the war years of 1941 to 1945, and his increased work with string players. There was no longer any necessity to accept "young ladies" into the oboe class. Once the single feminine "holdover" from the war years, Martha Scherer, finished her studies and graduated in 1947, Tabuteau was able to enforce his preferred policy of "no more girls" for the remainder of his tenure. This discrimination finally ended only after Tabuteau retired and his successor, John de Lancie, took over the teaching at Curtis.

Among the brilliant "last wave" of Tabuteau students at Curtis were John Mack, Marc Lifschey, Alfred Genovese, Louis Rosenblatt, and Laurence Thorstenberg, all of whom went out to fill solo oboe or English horn positions in major American symphony orchestras. Felix Kraus, Donald Hefner, Theodore Heger, and Richard Kanter spent less time with Tabuteau, but they also contributed to carrying his influence

The oboe students at Curtis in April 1949 on the steps in front of the school. From the left: Louis Rosenblatt, Laurence Thorstenberg, John Mack, Marcel Tabuteau, and Walter Bianchi. Laila Storch is visiting after the end of the Houston Symphony season. Photo by Daniel Sagarman.

on into the twenty-first century. By the end of 2006, Marc Lifschey, John Mack, and Felix Kraus had passed away.[1] The others are retired from their major positions but are still busy with teaching, performing, and other activities. One member of the 1948–49 class, Walter Bianchi from Brazil, was the only oboist from a foreign country to study with Tabuteau at Curtis. He came recommended by the musicologist and flutist Carleton Sprague Smith, who had spent time in South America as a lecturer and cultural relations officer for the U.S. State Department. Bianchi never forgot the year he spent in Philadelphia. In 1972 while touring with the Soni Ventorum Wind Quintet, we arrived in the far south of Brazil for a concert in Porto Alegre to find Walter Bianchi sitting in the lobby of our hotel waiting to meet us. He belonged to an orchestra there and had seen our names in the local paper. Even though I was very jet-lagged, I could not refuse his wish to immediately go across town to his house and play Sellner Duos!

In the latter part of the 1940s, Tabuteau was gradually lightening his responsibilities with the Philadelphia Orchestra. John de Lancie joined the oboe section in the fall of 1946 after having played first oboe for the

Orchestra's spring tour. At the beginning of the 1948–49 season he officially became associate principal. After the early 1950s Tabuteau would play until Christmas and then go on "vacation" for the second half of the season. If, theoretically, Tabuteau could now begin to take life easier, he nevertheless continued to give his total energy and enthusiasm to his students and to conducting the Curtis ensembles until the end of the school year. Nor was the oboe neglected. Along with these final years of teaching, Tabuteau took the unusual step, for him, of playing in the summers by participating in the Casals Festivals of Prades and Perpignan. In 1952, he made his rare solo recording of the Handel *G Minor Oboe Concerto* with the Philadelphia Orchestra under Eugene Ormandy for the benefit of the Pension Fund.

It was the second new element in Tabuteau's classes, the addition of string players to the wind ensembles, that brought a greater breadth and sparkle to the repertoire studied and performed in the yearly concerts. In one way, it was a continuation of the "orchestral" season of 1944–45, although most of the works played were on a smaller scale. I continued to return to Philadelphia in the late 1940s and was able to hear many of the spring recitals of the combined ensembles. The oboists who took part in these concerts remain my friends to this day. On April 18, 1946, "Music for String and Woodwind Ensemble" repeated several of the old French standards from 1930s programs by composers Paul De Wailly, Gabriel Pierné, Luigi Hugues, and Adrien Barthe of the famous *Passacaille.* New was the Bach *Double Concerto* played by violinists Norman Carol and Viviane Bertolami accompanied by string orchestra and Ernest Bloch's *Concerto grosso* with Seymour Lipkin the piano soloist.[2]

The spring of 1947 was a difficult time for Tabuteau. When I returned from my short Kansas City season in early March, I was shocked to see how thin he looked and learned that he had lost twenty-five pounds. The very night I arrived in Philadelphia he played a concert but was scheduled to enter the Lankenau Hospital two days later on March 3 for an operation. Several painful attacks had been diagnosed as gallstones. Mme Tabuteau told me he was "obsessed with the idea that something else was wrong with him . . . sure they would discover cancer or something." He had "worked up to the last" he said, and next week he would "probably be in a box." In the end the operation

TABUTEAU'S LAST YEARS AT THE CURTIS INSTITUTE

went very well. His appendix was removed along with the gall bladder. The doctors found that "his liver is not bad, and being in such general good health he should now take a new lease on life again." He would "only have to be in the hospital about ten days." I was, of course, disappointed not to have the lessons I always hoped for on returning to Philadelphia. Instead, I went to visit him almost every day in the hospital, usually staying several hours in an effort to cheer him up. He wanted me to play cards . . . "For money! I won $1.25 one day and lost 65¢ the next." After about a week, despite a painful attack of gout, he was "getting his energy to talk and gesticulate and be amusing and enthusiastic again."[3] When he returned home to the apartment, I was kept busy replying to all the letters and flowers he had received . . . with some of "the ones we *didn't* send being inevitably funnier than the actual answers." A few days later the Tabuteaus went off to Atlantic City. News came on a postcard that "they were installed in a beautiful room facing the sea, but no sun!" Mme Tabuteau's note of March 23 said, "*le malade* is doing as well as possible. Do not give our address to anyone."

Tabuteau's slow recuperation made it impossible for him to prepare and conduct the annual concert of combined ensembles. Seymour Lipkin, who was about to graduate, was in charge of the program for May 9 that was more heavily weighted with orchestral repertoire than usual. It contained only a single work for winds: the Pierné *Preludio and Fughetta* of the famous 1937 recording venture. This time Martha Scherer was the oboist for the part played on the record by her former teacher, Rhadames Angelucci. A Handel *Concerto grosso* with Aaron Rosand and Burton Fine as the solo violinists and the *Classical Symphony* by Prokofiev led to the concert's glowing conclusion—the participation of Rudolf Serkin in Beethoven's *Concerto No. 5* in E-Flat Major, the *Emperor.*

Seymour Lipkin told me his favorite Tabuteau story more than once—in 1997 and again at the Curtis seminar of May 2003. He had even shared it with his teacher, Rudolf Serkin. It was about the car. "You wake up one day and you go into the garage and you turn the key and the car shake—and the car goes hrr-room, hr-room, hrr-room—and the whole garage shake, h-r—rrrrr, but you do not go any*where.* Nothing! That is your playing. You forgot to put yourself in gear." Seymour remembered

MARCEL TABUTEAU

that all of Tabuteau's explanations were "very vivid. The great thing we learned was this intense concentration on the direction of the phrases, where they were going, and the meticulous molding of the phrases. He taught us how to concentrate, and that the music must be a living thing. The music must 'dance.' He would be so meticulous about the intensity of each little part of the phrase. 'It is a finger—it is a wrist, and then the whole thing make an arm.' It was very vital. Eventually after you pick it apart it has to coalesce into a totality. I learned that you had to concentrate on these things in great detail. I had no idea before. I thought you just played—you sort of emoted and it came out. I keep quoting him all the time. Just this week I was in Toronto with a conductor, a gifted fellow who seemed to sort of sit on the music, and I told him that Mr. Tabuteau used to say, 'you know, you have to let the music *take* you. Do not impose your mediocrity on the music!' I find myself being extremely detailed now in talking to my own students. Sometimes I think I am really inhibiting them but then I remember how it was with Tabuteau; at first, terribly inhibiting, but in the long run it is liberating. It allows you to really make these things dance and do what you want them to! He was an incredible influence. My other big influences were Toscanini and Serkin. Serkin never spoke about these things. He talked in grand terms. He did them but he never mentioned them, and with Toscanini—for me, it was just a question of listening."[4]

Another of the gifted Curtis pianists was Isabelle Vengerova's student Jacob Lateiner. Like Seymour Lipkin, he filled in missing string parts on the piano during Tabuteau's wind class rehearsals and sometimes conducted the orchestra. Over half a century later he reminisced, "I don't remember his being nasty. I know at the final class of the year, he had a decanter that he used to always pour his water from and we emptied out the water and filled it with gin." When I asked what happened, Jacob replied, "Nothing. He just kept on drinking it with never a word. And then when the rehearsal was over he said 'Hah! You thought you fooled me! Do it every week!'" Whether this is the same or a similar "gin in the water pitcher" incident as the one described earlier by Abba Bogin is uncertain. On a more serious note, Lateiner stated, "I learned more about music from Tabuteau than anyone else in my life. He was the greatest influence." Sometimes after the school orchestra

TABUTEAU'S LAST YEARS AT THE CURTIS INSTITUTE

rehearsal Jacob would stay longer and play for Tabuteau the piano pieces he had learned with Vengerova. Once he asked Tabuteau about the oboe passage in the Scherzo of the *Eroica*. Tabuteau already had his coat and hat on and, as Jacob said, "was thinking of his beloved food waiting at home." But he took his hat off and spent forty-five minutes explaining his phrasing. Jacob could not quite "get it" on the piano, but finally he changed a fingering that helped achieve the type of articulation Tabuteau wanted. Tabuteau exclaimed, "That's it!!" and only then did the food win out. To Jacob, this was "an illustration of the importance of music to him. It was his religion."[5]

These three pianists, Seymour Lipkin, Jacob Lateiner, and Abba Bogin, students of preeminent Curtis teachers, each credited Tabuteau as the prime source of their musical knowledge. In Abba Bogin's words, "There were some wonderful teachers in the school. William Primrose taught chamber music, and his classes were unbelievable. I studied with a marvelous piano teacher, Isabelle Vengerova, but I would say my primary influence in how I make and play music probably comes more from Tabuteau than from any other instructor at the school." Abba Bogin's opinion of Tabuteau's ensemble classes and his role in the orchestra agreed with the many others who felt it was "the focal point of the school, what Curtis was all about (and what the Philadelphia Orchestra was all about). I think that Tabuteau . . . was the pivot at both places. He was the center of the world. Everything revolved around him in terms of phrasing . . . Everyone who played or sat down next to him was influenced by him . . . When a similar passage came up that Tabuteau had just played, one was influenced to play it that way. Even when he was sitting in the middle of the stage and not conducting, there were ways he influenced the rest of the orchestra across weeks, months and years."[6]

Tabuteau's Curtis recital of April 20, 1948, opened with the Bach Chorale Prelude: *Kyrie, Gott Heiliger Geist,* a transcription by Hershy Kay for eighteen winds and double bass. Mozart's *Eine kleine Nachtmusik* and Barber's *Adagio* gave prominence to the strings. For winds, it was Gounod's *Petite Symphonie* and two movements of the Thuille *Sextet,* Opus 6. As a finale, the combined groups performed the Beethoven *Septet.* The oboists in this concert were Marc Lifschey and Laurence Thorstenberg. Among the string players were violinists Joseph Silverstein,

MARCEL TABUTEAU

Giuseppe Cusimano, Burton Fine, and Diana Steiner, and cellists Robert Sayre and Hershel Gordon.

An anonymous author reviewed this concert for the May issue of the *Woodwinds* magazine. It presents a fair picture of Tabuteau as conductor: "So far, we have been writing only of the sounds that reached the ear. But the star performer of the evening was Mr. Tabuteau himself. His engaging personality, his patent joy in making music permeated the concert and delighted the audience. Sometimes it was his pleasure at the way the music was being played; at others times, as a result of a fancy note, it was the pointing to his ear, a grimace and the inevitable hopeless shrug of his shoulders. And who could resist when Mr. Tabuteau turned around and smiled while still conducting the group as much as to say, 'Come, let's all enjoy making music together!' The honors were his—and the audience too."

From his days in the ensemble classes, John Mack remembered that he played in two different groups with both beginners and seniors. "We were three new people, Lou Rosenblatt, myself, and Walter Bianchi from São Paulo, Brazil. Larry Thorstenberg was already there. He was *very* mature compared to us. He had been through the Battle of the Bulge, had dreadful experiences, and could not help but see many things differently." In 1949, at the end of John Mack's first year in Curtis, he was a soloist in the Mozart *Sinfonia Concertante* for winds and orchestra with Harold Wright as the solo clarinet, Leonard Hale, horn, and Norman Kasow, bassoon. Laurence Thorstenberg was the oboist in the Hindemith Quintet, and Thorstenberg, Mack, Walter Bianchi, and Louis Rosenblatt all participated in the Strasser transcription of the J. S. Bach *Passacaglia in C Minor.* The strings contributed a *Sarabande, Gigue,* and *Badinerie* by Corelli, the Waltz from the *C Major Serenade* of Tchaikovsky, and the Prelude to *Le Déluge* by Saint-Saëns, this time with Giuseppe Cusimano as the violin soloist. A year later in April 1950, John Mack and Marvin Morgenstern were the soloists for the J. S. Bach *Concerto for oboe and violin,* while Laurence Thorstenberg was the oboist in Samuel Barber's *Capricorn Concerto.* He also played in Saint-Saëns's *Caprice sur des airs Danois et Russe,* (the work composed for Taffanel's *Société* and performed by Georges Gillet in their famous 1887 tour of Russia). Thorstenberg played in the *Pastorale variée dans le style*

TABUTEAU'S LAST YEARS AT THE CURTIS INSTITUTE

ancien by Pierné and was joined by John Mack in the Richard Strauss *Serenade in E-flat major,* Opus 7, for thirteen winds. An equally lengthy program was prepared for the following year with everything from Igor Stravinsky's *Pastorale* in the version for violin, oboe, English horn, clarinet, and bassoon and the Mozart *Quintet* for piano and winds to the Bach *Brandenburg Concerto No. 1.*[7] Louis Rosenblatt had clear memories of this recital. For the Stravinsky, he was playing the English horn and John Mack, oboe. The violinist was Toshiya Eto, the first Japanese student to come to the Curtis Institute after World War II. He was also soloist in the *Brandenburg Concerto* with the three oboists, John Mack, Louis Rosenblatt, and Alfred Genovese. This concert, which took place on April 18, 1951, was followed the next day by the usual Tabuteau summing-up of how everyone had played. As Lou described it "He went down the line chastising each student for his shortcomings. 'You did this and that wrong—after I told you!' etc. etc. and then he came to Eto, the last in the line. 'And you, Monsieur Eto, you are a wonderful artist.' It was a supreme moment. Eto blushed almost to a dark red and all the others regarded him with appropriate awe."[8] Toshiya Eto was later to have a distinguished career in Japan as a soloist and teacher.

There were but two more class recitals, those of 1952 and 1953, before Tabuteau returned to France in February 1954. The program of April 23, 1952, opened with the Bach *Suite for Orchestra* No. 1 in C Major, a work that Tabuteau had played and recorded in Prades with Pablo Casals in 1950. I well remember the challenge of playing the second oboe part and having to stick with Tabuteau like glue, especially through the rapid tempi Casals took in the C minor section of the *Bourrée.*[9] For the Curtis performance, the two important oboe parts were played by Alfred Genovese and Felix Kraus with Otto Eifert, the bassoonist. Traditional wind pieces followed: Felix Kraus played in the De Wailly *Aubade,* and Alfred Genovese was the oboist in both the Roussel *Divertissement* and the Hindemith *Quintet.* Strings and wind combined to finish with what was beginning to seem not only a favorite of Toscanini's, but also Tabuteau's—the Beethoven *Septet.*

Although Tabuteau was probably not aware that it would prove to be the "farewell" recital, his final Curtis concert took place on March 27, 1953. It was almost exactly twenty-three years from the debut

MARCEL TABUTEAU

Bassoon student Arthur Grossman captured Tabuteau on film while he was conducting a rehearsal of the woodwind ensemble in Curtis Hall, 1953. Photo by Arthur Grossman.

performance of "Students of Mr. Tabuteau in Wind Ensemble" on February 10, 1930. Interestingly enough, whether by intent or coincidence, two works were repeated from the historic program of 1930; the Beethoven *Quintet*, Opus 71, which throughout the years had provided so many traumatic memories for wind students, and the Pierné *Pastorale variée dans le style ancien*. Alfred Genovese was the oboist in these two pieces as well as for the Sonata for piano, flute, oboe, and bassoon by Vittorio Rieti. The strings predominated in the opening Bach *Concerto for Two Violins* in D minor with soloists Michael Tree and Enrique Serratos. The concert closed with the *Symphony No. 5* in B-flat major by Schubert, the work that would become the cause of so much discord in the Prades Festival later that same year.

Pamela Gearhart, who entered Tabuteau's string class at Curtis as a sixteen-year-old violinist in 1951 and stayed until he left in 1954, kept detailed notes on his "comments." Although she said she found them to be "so dead on paper and only come to life if you hear his voice," I

TABUTEAU'S LAST YEARS AT THE CURTIS INSTITUTE

nevertheless believe they convey a good deal of the atmosphere of the classes and testify to the impression he made on string players who were usually less "terrified" of him than the wind students were.[10] Writing of her later marriage to Livingston Gearhart, who Tabuteau had been so fond of in the 1930s, Pamela said, "It was such a bond with Livingston that we shared that influence—it was electric!"

Excerpts from her notebook follow:

> I don't know how you can collectively produce such a proletarian sound. Let the music get the best of you . . . by putting your best in the music. Don't be so self-conscious in playing. Forget yourself. *Let the music take the best from you.* [This was one of Tabuteau's common refrains.]
>
> I don't know how people can stand it if they don't have that inward fun of doing things well and correctly. It is like a divine communion with truth. If I didn't have so much fun from music, I would have quit long ago.
>
> Stop thinking of the *violin.* You have all day to play the violin . . . play *music* now!
>
> Don't play everything like *violin* music . . . à la Pennsylvania, à la New Jersey, à la Connecticut . . . (Makes a sour face.) When it is *à la russe,* then *à la russe!* Make up your playing [as with cosmetics]—Play like a Slav even if you come from New Jersey!
>
> Don't bow your notes—place the notes on the bow.
>
> Teach yourself to <u>think</u> well. Playing is a reflection of your thoughts . . . Combine intelligence with humility and good thinking. The day of playing only with feeling is gone. What if you have a cold or a stomachache? A fine performance you would give! But if you think well, you will have a chance.
>
> We are here to establish an inward standard of beauty. [Tabuteau often used the term "Inward Giving."] One person in a thousand will notice it [a musical pattern], but when you find one person that does . . . Ah, . . . That is basis for faith and this is truth.
>
> All that I know is from seeing, hearing, and from others. Like the rolling of the waves . . . so beautiful. And if we would only look—but alas, it's always there, so we never see it. We could learn <u>so</u> much by looking.
>
> If we are willing, then we learn in spite of ourselves, but if you are indifferent, then—No!!
>
> Don't play notes—play what is *between* the notes.
>
> Bach is pure music—not violin music.

MARCEL TABUTEAU

In music we have two important elements: mood and mode. The absence of both makes *mud*!

Don't blow—*play*! We are here to play as well as *anyone* else.

If you don't enjoy music—extract teeth.

From my education as a young man, I realize that the trouble is we do too many things imperfectly. Don't be elated by what people think of you. Be polite—say "thank you," but *you are your best friend* and *you know* when you play well. I'm like wine—right now I bore you—but in 20 years, you will begin to think these are good ideas.

That's all right if you are playing for human beings, but you should play for that which you worship.

Music is like flying. Take-off and landing are the most difficult.[11]

Music is like a horse or a bronco. It will throw you unless you learn these tricks to keep riding. Be your own judge.

You try to hide in your mediocrity. Don't be afraid. Play out.

How can you play so . . . in this Temple of Art??

I am not nervous in front of you so why would you be nervous in front of me?

You zigged when you should have zagged.

There is nothing so correct as a metronome and yet nothing so stupid . . . We must be *both* correct and smart.

You know when people smile, they sometimes do it because they want something . . . but when a child smiles, he smiles because he *means* it.—That's what is so wonderful.

Make yourself distinguished . . . otherwise you will just be like everyone else and after all, what is the use of being just like everyone else. Then _anyone_ can take your place!

That's the joy of being a conductor. You just need the idea. You don't have to *produce* it.

It is a shame, a great calamity, when you are just as _medioc_ (mediocre) as you were 15 minutes ago—you should be better than you were then.

A diminuendo is _ascending_—ah—oh well, I don't have to tell you about the cigar and the smoke which must go upwards. I've already said that.

If you think beautifully, you will play beautifully, but if you think *medioc*, you will play that way.

You play but you don't go anywhere like the car when it's not in gear.

Music is part of the universe—part of the system. If you are not part of the system . . . well, then you are out of luck.

TABUTEAU'S LAST YEARS AT THE CURTIS INSTITUTE

> After playing in an orchestra for many years you become like a horse . . . anyone who pays can ride you. I pay $3.00 so this horse is mine for one hour.
>
> Take a pattern, even if you are wrong, for you have all your life to correct it, but *do* take a pattern.

Several of Tabuteau's last Curtis oboe students shared their personal memories with me. Louis Rosenblatt told of coming back for a visit after he had left school and watching Tabuteau make a reed. Lou thought that it was "perhaps for sentimental reasons" that he was working with an old gouger that may have once belonged to Georges Gillet. When Tabuteau said, "That's the tone he used to get—*poetic*," Lou found it to be more "*champêtre*, lighter and not like the way they play now." This was fascinating to Lou as he felt "here's a clue as to how his teacher sounded and what he may have been doing when Tabuteau was a student. I was curious as to what extent Tabuteau had developed his own ideas of how an oboe should sound. What he learned by himself and what did his teacher, Gillet, think was the right way? Had he actually changed a great deal? He made more than one reed that way and just kept saying a number of times, 'Yes, that's the way my teacher sounded.' Then all of a sudden he advised me that I must practice Handel and Bach violin sonatas to study form. That's what Gillet had always told him. It was a very cordial visit, not like a teacher-pupil sort of thing."[12]

Marc Lifschey had studied oboe for three years with Engelbert Brenner and then for a half year with Fernand Gillet, traveling from New York up to Boston by train for his lessons. He heard Tabuteau play for the first time when the Philadelphia Orchestra came for one of their regular concerts in New York. "That changed everything for me. That sound!! That was it. From that time on I worshipped Tabuteau." While still in high school he studied with Tabuteau for one year. I remember seeing Marc sometimes on Saturdays at the studio when he was only seventeen, but he soon disappeared—drafted. The year he came out of the army, there was no room at Curtis so he played first oboe in Buffalo for one season. He entered Curtis in 1946 and graduated only two years later in 1948. During our conversation, I mentioned that Tabuteau had once said he felt one of the most important things he was able to do was to "get back on the track." Because an oboist constantly has to make new reeds, it is easy to feel the lack of a stable pillar in one's work. Marc's response, "He was on a unique track. His imagination . . . !!"[13]

After retirement from his position of solo oboe in the Cleveland Orchestra, John Mack continued an intense round of activities as educator and performer. Throughout his long years of devoted teaching at the Cleveland Institute of Music and his summer Oboe Camp in North Carolina, he had a major influence on several generations of young oboists. In the late 1940s we used to work together gouging cane and tying reeds in Tabuteau's studio. I knew him as "Jack" then, and so he remained, but with the understanding that it was only a small circle of old friends who were allowed to use that name! I had never known much about the beginnings of his oboe study or how he came to the Curtis Institute. In 2000 he told me how in the tenth grade he had taken lessons from Bruno Labate in Linx and Long's music shop in New York. When Jack expressed the wish to audition at Curtis, Labate obligingly wrote a letter to his old friend, Marcel Tabuteau, saying that Mack had studied with him for several years, when in reality it was more like six months. While playing his audition, Jack ran out of breath during the last in a series of three pieces by Arthur Foote. He remembered how Tabuteau rocked back and forth on his heels and roared with laughter. (Again, an example of the perverse things that made Tabuteau laugh. He had a disconcerting way of finding someone else's discomfiture amusing.)

Jack's father, Silas Franklin Mack, a devotee of the Bethlehem, Pennsylvania, Bach Festivals, had heard Tabuteau play and met him there. It was sometime after the audition episode that "my father tried to persuade Tabuteau to teach me. His reply was, 'Tell the boy not to play the oboe.' My father said, 'I'm sorry Maestro, you'll have to tell him yourself. He wouldn't take that from me!' By then I was sixteen and in the 12th grade." Eventually Tabuteau agreed to take Jack as a private student. When his good friend Marc Lifschey, who was already coming to Philadelphia for lessons, heard this news, he said, "Oh John, just try to remember everything he says. You're going to be in such awe. Your head is going to be swimming. You won't be able to see straight." I began to take private lessons every other Saturday in 1944–45. All these fellows in uniform were coming in those years. My lessons were at 1 p.m. and as Tabuteau knew my train didn't leave until after 6:30 (we lived in

TABUTEAU'S LAST YEARS AT THE CURTIS INSTITUTE

Somerville, New Jersey), in bad weather he would just let me sit in the far right-hand corner of the Studio. This did not make these service men particularly happy because if they were going to get yelled at they would prefer it to be in private." Years later Earnie Harrison, who used to come up from Washington, D.C., for lessons, spoke of "some kid sitting over in the corner." "Yeah—that was me," said Jack.

Before Tabuteau left for Canada in the summer, Jack had gone through all thirty of the preliminary articulation exercises in Barret . . . He described what was almost the mystification we felt when first confronted with the impact of Tabuteau's playing. "He did things that one simply did not hear from an oboe player! I was hearing it all but I just couldn't get it. Up and down impulse—that was pretty easy to understand, but then came the big twelve articulation studies and the melodies. After that, I did not re-audition for Curtis but went part-time to Juilliard as I was waiting to be drafted. The war was over by then but the draft wasn't, so I had my physical and was classified 1A. Four days before my induction my parents received a telegram from the government saying that my older brother, David, had died in the Navy. As the sole surviving son I was now reclassified 4A.

"Soon I was put into the first oboe chair of the Juilliard Orchestra. I studied with Carlos Mullenix the first year and in my second year I went to Philadelphia for lessons with John Minsker. Harold Gomberg did not arrive to teach until 1947–48, my last year at Juilliard. What trouble it caused! In 1948 my mother saw in the paper that there were auditions at Curtis. I decided to play for Tabuteau again. It was just one night before he left for the big tour of 1948 so I had to go to the Drake Hotel and sit around in the lobby because his masseur was there. Finally came the command, 'Send the kid up,' and he asked me to play the solo from the Brahms *Violin Concerto*. By now I had had almost a year with Gomberg who wanted me to 'go out into the field' but I mentioned that I didn't feel I was ready to graduate. 'You're telling me!' was Tabuteau's response. He then expressed his willingness to take me and I said I had always wanted to go to Curtis but understood that he had already held auditions and accepted someone. 'You silly boy. You want to go to Curtis. I will tell Mme Tabuteau to go to school tomorrow and tell them I accepted you and they'll send you an application and you fill it out and

MARCEL TABUTEAU

send it back right away—but you must tell Mr. Gomberg about this and if he is unhappy with me, I will have nothing to do with you.'" John now had the difficult task of telling Gomberg who became very upset and accused him of having "planned this for a long time." John now became "persona non grata" both for lessons and ensembles, but he *did* graduate with a diploma. Gomberg never spoke to John again until the Tabuteau Day concerts at Curtis in 1979, thirty-one years later. John later thought the fact that Gomberg did not get upset with Tabuteau, but with him, was what had made it possible for him to go to Curtis after all.

Already in the fall of his first year at Curtis, John started to work in Tabuteau's studio. "Tabuteau knew that I was sort of handy and he began giving me things to do. At first it was just to select cane, split the cane and chop it to size. He didn't let me gouge cane or tie reeds. He was the one who was going to do that, but it was obvious to me early on that he wanted company. I couldn't take an outside job as Marcel Tabuteau might telephone and say, 'Meet me at the Studio.' I was on call at any time. [This was the period when I used to come back from Houston in the spring and spend four or five weeks in Philadelphia. If I wanted to do some reed work in the Studio, Tabuteau would say I could only go there at night 'if Mack were there.']

"Tabuteau was meticulous as always about gouging, meticulous about shaping, and meticulous about tying and about starting to scrape the reeds. But sometimes *three minutes later,* like a flying missile, a reed would go spinning against the wall. One time he said, 'say Mack, pick up this reed, the one I dropped.' 'Oh yes, the one you dropped *against* the wall.' Tabuteau: 'Yes, yes . . .' If he had stayed too long in the studio, to avoid problems he would say, 'Mack, tell me when it is 6 o'clock.' Then, 'Yes, I'm coming.' 'It's 6:30,' 'Yes, yes, I know.' 'Maestro, it's 7 o'clock.' 'Mme Tabuteau is going to give me Hell and she is right.' 'Maestro, it's 7:30!' 'Yes, I'm coming.' So finally we get to the Drake and he says, 'I want you to come up. We worked *so hard* today.' And we'd get in the elevator and he'd take out his key and go tap, tap, tap on the door of 1405. 'Open up . . . C'est moi and *Mack* is with me!'—trying to keep her off his back until she would calm down. As soon as I could see that things were O.K.—well, goodbye."

TABUTEAU'S LAST YEARS AT THE CURTIS INSTITUTE

"Gradually, as he saw that I was getting more and more adept at all of this, I was allowed to start some reeds and by the time of the first Casals Festival in 1950, I was making reeds for him. During my last year in Curtis (1950–51), I made every reed he played for the first eleven weeks of his half-season with the Orchestra. He had managed to get a good setting on his gouging machine and he would not touch it for anything. [In contrast to the days Minsker remembered when Tabuteau would make changes in the machine after gouging two or three pieces of cane.]

For weeks he didn't even go to the Studio. Mme Tabuteau wanted him to get used to what retirement would be like. I would go on Monday evenings, soak the cane, split and chop it, shape and tie five or six reeds which I would then finish during the week at my own place. On Friday I took them to Tabuteau's apartment between the Orchestra's morning rehearsal and the afternoon concert. Often he would play on them right away." (In a letter of 13 November 1950, Tabuteau showed his appreciation of the current situation.[14] "Imagine that since the month of February I have not yet made a single reed. The good Mac [Mack] has freed me from this infernal nightmare; It doesn't sound exactly as I would like, but everyone is happy and I have now only to wait for the benefits of "Social Security." It seems, they say, that the orchestra may join the plan. Enclosed is the program for next week (*Tombeau de Couperin, Milhaud Symphony No. 1, Beethoven "Emperor" Concerto with Serkin*). I'll let you know how it goes; if the reeds are up to the task, I'll tell Mac to think of you. He is really splendid (*épatant*) notre Mac." But the welcome respite from reed inferno could not last forever, even with the help of "le brave Mac," whose own account continues: "Around the ninth week something happened and a couple of the reeds did not close well on the sides. Tabuteau immediately accused me of having changed the gouge. But by then I was learning how he was, and had taken the precaution early on of gouging eighteen pieces of cane which I dated, put in a little box, and stored away in one of his desk drawers. Now I could show him this cane. When he tied some reeds on his original gouged cane, I was vindicated. However, then nothing would stop him from getting back to the Studio and beginning to fuss with the gouging machine again. I used to worry about how much he did with that."[15]

MARCEL TABUTEAU

Like those students of the decade before him, Theodore (Ted) Heger said he felt that "Tabuteau is still around. Whenever I make a reed, it's as if he is there listening and I'm glad he's not! In the fall of 1953 we had two lessons a week, on Monday and Wednesday so Tabuteau could fulfill his Curtis contract. The only edge I had was that I had no trouble transposing Barret and Ferling études. My father, who had studied with Alexandre Duvoir, passed on to me the Paris Conservatoire requirements and made me play every exercise in three keys. This amazed Tabuteau, because, of course, he considered me to be 'so stupid.'" Just like the students of twenty years earlier, Ted dreaded the high B-flat entrance in the Beethoven Quintet. "Those ensemble classes were almost scarier than lessons. Even in the Marine Band with a conductor who was like a Prussian officer, it was nothing compared to Tabuteau. He used to say that when he was younger he would have cared, but now he didn't care anymore. I remember seeing him on the stage at his last concert with the Orchestra. It was for the Pension Fund. He was laughing and fooling around the whole time and it really seemed he didn't care. I also remember that by the time I came to Curtis, Tabuteau had quit smoking and was always chewing some little candies. During the final classes he talked a lot about Gillet, saying that he was the greatest musician he had ever known."[16]

In 2003 Donald Hefner told me his own version of an oft-repeated anecdote from his student days. It has been told and retold with slight variations, but Don said the original story was "burned" into his memory. It was during a wind class rehearsal in one of the Curtis upstairs studios. The class was playing through a new composition for nine instruments by George Rochberg. There came a pause in the music, and looking ahead in the score, Tabuteau saw a low B natural for the oboe to be very rapidly articulated in sextuplets with a dynamic marking of pianissimo. He glanced over and addressed Rochberg who was there to listen to his own composition. "You know, young man, what you have written here for the oboe is impossible!" He then pointed to Don who promptly proceeded to toss off the passage perfectly. Tabuteau exploded, "Damn fool, you are always against me! I told him [Rochberg] it was imposseeble!!" Then to the class all sitting there in stunned silence, "Did you ever hear him do anything that difficult before?"[17]

TABUTEAU'S LAST YEARS AT THE CURTIS INSTITUTE

Alfred Genovese gave me his view of "how we stood it!" "I feel that Tabuteau is very present in all that I've tried to do . . . What I owe to that man . . . because even when he was rough on me, and he was very rough at times, I just took it and said, o.k., that's my dues—that's what I pay—but look what I'm getting. There is a story that shortly before Angelucci retired from the Minneapolis Orchestra in 1982 over forty years after he had left school, he was musing over just how to play a certain passage, and he turned to the other oboist, looked at him, and said, 'Jesus, I wonder if Tabuteau would approve?'" Al continued, "In my last year in Curtis, Tabuteau showed me another side. He would call me up about 10 o'clock at night when he was alone in the Studio and ask if I was doing anything. I'd say 'No,' and he'd ask if I'd mind coming over and keeping him company. I'd get on the trolley car and be there in a jiffy. He was working, gouging cane, and I used to look over his shoulder. He never stopped me from seeing everything he did. It was just a very friendly situation. He used to hint all the time how much he would like an invitation to my house—to come down and eat a dinner with us. At one holiday or another, practically all the Curtis students had been there, and he had heard by word of mouth what a great cook my mother was. But I was embarrassed. We were in such modest circumstances and I didn't want to put my mother through any added pressure or stress . . . He was not a snob. I know he would have loved it, but I felt awkward. To this day I regret it." I thought of our unforgettable dinner at the Hannah Penn House and regret along with Al that he missed having the memory of Tabuteau enjoying a meal at his home.[18]

From time to time Tabuteau spoke of putting his "system" into written form. One of his last students at Curtis, Felix Kraus, remembered that "he talked about writing a book about it himself, writing that is, if somebody wrote it for him. He applied to various of us, myself included, 'Would you write something about the number system for me?'" Felix recognized the difficulties involved and felt that Tabuteau's "abilities as a communicator would be essential" if one hoped to present his ideas as "transcendent a teaching method as it was for him."[19]

Richard Kanter entered Curtis in the fall of Tabuteau's last year at the school. He heard stories from the boys who were there slightly before him about bringing Tabuteau a gift at Christmas time. Tabuteau

MARCEL TABUTEAU

saw the square box (recognizable as containing Scotch) and exclaimed, "How did you know what I wanted?" When Mme Tabuteau asked if he had offered a drink to one of the boys, he cried out, "Don't give him any! He is just a little boy!" Dick remembered that Tabuteau had taken someone into the class that fall who stayed only a few months. He was not like the other students, being perhaps "a sort of jazz player," spoke in quite a different way, and had "no fear of Tabuteau. But he did have trouble in the ensemble class and one day spoke up to Tabuteau, saying, "Hey man, the oboe's cracked—see for yourself." Tabuteau, quite contrary to what one might have expected, did not explode but took the instrument, looked at it, and said, "It reminds me of the one I used to play when I was a student."[20]

Despite his decision not to accept any further women oboists at Curtis, Tabuteau *did* make an exception for a private student, Joan Browne (later known as Joan Shallin). In February 1952, at the suggestion of Felix Kraus and Raymond Dusté, she made the long cross-country trip from Oakland, California, in the hope of having lessons. When she met Tabuteau in the lobby of the Drake Hotel, he asked her the classic question, "Why do you want to play the o*boe*?" and then added, "Why don't you take up ballet? They *need* women there." Having seen the difficulty of finding jobs for even those "young ladies" he had taken the trouble to teach, he was no doubt convinced that his original idea of not encouraging girls to play the oboe was the right one. But he finally consented to listen to Joan and then to give her lessons at the Studio until he left for France early in the summer. The next fall she continued with regular weekly lessons, which were $10.00 for forty-five minutes, not too great a change from the $5.00 I paid for half-hour lessons ten years earlier. Nevertheless, it took about a third of what she was able to earn per week selling music at the Theodore Presser retail store—a job which earned her Tabuteau's comment of "How can you sell music at Presser's when you are so stup*eed*?" Joan endured many of the other same indignities as those students who came before and after her. There was Tabuteau's propensity to switch oboes. She managed to save $500.00 to buy a Lorée oboe, only to have him decide that it was better than the one he had kept for himself. She had to accept another in exchange. And once as a "reward" after a particularly good lesson, she was "allowed" to sweep out the

TABUTEAU'S LAST YEARS AT THE CURTIS INSTITUTE

studio after he left. But in the end, gratitude outshone any other feelings, and in reflecting on her studies with Tabuteau, she said, "It was difficult—challenging, but inspiring. I remember his comment that 'when I correct you, I don't expect you to change in five minutes or a day. I merely want to hear that you understand. I'm not teaching you for *now* but for ten years from now.' To me, this is the mark of a great teacher—that the lessons shape one's concepts for all time. To study with Marcel Tabuteau was one of the great privileges of my life."[21] After freelancing in Philadelphia, Joan Shallin played alongside Alfred Genovese and, later, Wayne Rapier, in the Baltimore Symphony Orchestra. She eventually changed her focus to the baroque oboe.

During the final years of his teaching, Tabuteau's influence on wind players other than oboists was no less profound than it had been during the decade of the 1930s. Bassoonist Arthur Grossman, my long-time colleague in the Soni Ventorum Wind Quintet, began his studies at Curtis in the fall of 1952. By the time of Tabuteau's departure at the end of February 1954, he had spent somewhat less than two full seasons in the wind class. (In his third year William Kincaid led the wind class.) However, his evaluation of his relatively short period with Tabuteau was that "musically, he probably had more influence on me than any other person." His experiences mirrored those of many earlier students. "Those wind classes made us more nervous and we had to work harder than for our own lessons. He was much more picky and often much more demanding than the individual teachers. It's true that Schoenbach was very demanding, but Tabuteau was so terrifying." I remembered how I had felt only ten years earlier—exhausted at the end of a rehearsal. According to Arthur, "You were stunned after one of those rehearsals; a one hour class, it seemed like it was ten hours long."

As those before him, Arthur had memories of the notorious Beethoven *Quintet*. "I think he used to enjoy making us feel uncomfortable. All we ever did was the first ten measures, and he would begin, 'Rea—dy! You are sharp! You have not played a note and you are sharp!!' Well, after that you couldn't even *start* to play. You were so nervous and all tight. Of course when you managed to squeeze out a note, you were sharp. And then he said, 'I *told* you, you are sharp!' It was just impossible to play in that class. One time we actually got past the intro-

MARCEL TABUTEAU

duction of the Beethoven to the first measures of the *Allegro,* and Tabuteau says, '1221-2332-3443. Or you could do 1221-2332-1221,' and he turns to Bob Bonnevie, 'Say, young fellow, repeat that.' Bonnevie tries, '1-2. 1-2-3—no, 1-3-2.' Tab shouts, 'No! Back*wards!*' Talk about making people feel uncomfortable! That's what he did all the time."

I agreed with Arthur that we all lived with that terror, and yet most of us, and that includes Alfred Genovese, John Mack, Marc Lifschey, John de Lancie, John Minsker, almost all his students, everybody had ended up worshipping the man. To a person who never had the experience, it is difficult to explain. Arthur reflected, "Even in the classes, although we were terrified, he made you learn your instrument . . . I don't think most of us learned to do what he wanted while we were *in* the class, but if you kept these demands in the back of your mind, later on you eventually learned how to control your instrument in a way that you never would have otherwise."

Arthur also remembered how Tabuteau spoke of Georges Gillet. "He worshipped him even to the point of having German shepherd dogs. It was the dog he had to have when he retired to France. Obviously, a lot that he was doing was to imitate Gillet . . . That was how they treated students in the nineteenth and early twentieth century, especially in Europe, and he just acted in the same way. You ground them into the dirt, and those who could survive would be able to get through anything." Many decades after our Curtis years I began to see a pattern in Tabuteau's interaction with his students and colleagues. The lowest level of disdain was reserved for his own oboe students, especially those at Curtis. (An exception was made for members of the armed forces who came to him during World War II.) According to Professor Jean Paul Narcy, who knew Tabuteau well, it was not an unusual way of teaching and continues until today in some French universities.[22] While wind students were treated quite harshly, the string players saw a different side of Tabuteau and found him to be amiable and good-natured. (Was this related to his own beginnings as a violinist?) With his colleagues in the Philadelphia Orchestra he was usually a cordial comrade. And when someone like the well-known Danish oboist Waldemar Wolsing sought him out and came to study in the south of France, a positive, warm and even jovial friendship developed.[23]

TABUTEAU'S LAST YEARS AT THE CURTIS INSTITUTE

In 1958 Arthur Grossman visited Tabuteau in France. It turned out to be quite a different story from the Curtis classes of only five years earlier. "I spent about ten days there. I stayed in a hotel but ate my meals at his place and, being there all day, got to know him much better. He used to have me unpack my bassoon and then he would take out the oboe. 'Say, listen, you know—Sibelius 2nd Symphony! Let's play that part,' and we'd play together, and he'd say, 'it sounds very good.' Nothing like he had ever said when I was in the class, but instead, 'It was a pleasure to play with you. Now, say listen, let's play Beethoven 2nd,' and so we'd play the slow movement. No music. All by memory— oboe and bassoon together and answering each other—we just played everything—Beethoven symphonies and Brahms. Then I told him what a pleasure it was. 'It's so nice to be here and get to know you and play these things because when we were in school we were so terrified at all times we couldn't play at all.' He said, 'you were not frightened of *me*? No-o—o!' and then started to chuckle. Everything was wonderful. Not a word of criticism, and off he went to the kitchen to cook!"

Arthur recounted a non-musical incident from his visit. "Tabuteau had that enormous black Citroën. Gasoline was extremely expensive then in France. I had come down to the south of France from Germany in my car, and I had Army coupons so I could get gasoline very cheaply. He asked if I could take his car and fill it up for him or if he could have some coupons. I explained that it was not possible for him to use the coupons but that I could take his car into town and buy the gas. Then Mme Tabuteau said if I'm going to town she would like to come too as she had some errands to do. Tabuteau was willing to let me drive his *car* into town, but he wasn't sure that he was going to let me drive it with *her* in it so he decided to test me. His leg was bandaged from an attack of gout, but we went out into the big field in back of his place, and he stands in the middle of the field directing me like he would order a sheep dog. 'Turn Right. *Now Left!* Back*wards!*' It was a driving test first before I could take Mme Tabuteau into town to do the shopping and fill up his car."

In almost any conversation about Tabuteau, some mention is made of the effect he had on peoples' lives. Arthur summed up his recollections with "many years after all of this, in 1998 when we were on Orcas Island for Aloysia's wedding, John Mack and I were sitting having a glass of wine in the hotel, and Leah [Arthur's wife] was there, and we talked for about an hour or so. Afterwards Leah said, 'That man must have been *really* something for two men who are old enough to be grandfathers to spend all that time speaking only about him.' There was Casals—but I would *never* say that Casals had the kind of musical influence on me that Tabuteau did." Arthur then laughingly concluded that Tabuteau would "probably be pleased to know that we are still talking about him!"[24]

16 THE CASALS FESTIVALS IN PRADES AND PERPIGNAN

1950, 1951, and 1953

Toward the end of Tabuteau's playing career in 1950, 1951, and 1953, he took part in the Casals Festivals in Prades and Perpignan. If for no other reason than the fact that these festivals gave us a few outstanding recorded examples of his solo work, they are of significance in any account of his accomplishments. They marked not only the first time in many years that he played in the summer, but the first time that he performed in France since his departure in 1905 almost half a century earlier.

Tabuteau remembered Pablo Casals from his early appearances in Philadelphia and New York. When Alexander Schneider invited Tabuteau to take part in the 1950 Bach Festival, Mme Tabuteau wrote that, "*Le Pingouin*, in spite of his frequent negations, still loves music it seems. He is exhilarated by the idea of spending a month in the company of the famous Pablo." And Tabuteau, despite his oft-expressed less than complimentary opinion of phonograph records, was actually looking forward to the opportunity provided by Columbia's intention of recording all the performances. Coming at the beginning of the use of magnetic tape, the festival LP recordings did result in a more faithful reproduction of the oboe sound than most of the earlier 78rpm disks. It was not too surprising that Tabuteau accepted the invitation to play the *C Minor Concerto* for violin and oboe under Casals's direction. He had always loved the music of Bach and had enjoyed the spring ritual of playing in the Bethlehem, Pennsylvania, Bach Festival. I had read in *Time* magazine the news of Casals's forthcoming reappearance and could not believe my luck when in January I heard from Tabuteau that three oboes would be needed for the Brandenburg Concerto No. 1. "They asked me to choose two of my students to play in the Orchestra. Knowing that you will be in France, I suggested your name thinking that it could interest you. In all of America musicians are vying for the honor to go and play with the great maître Casals. The artists will not be paid for their services but you will be offered $300.00 for the expenses of staying in Prades." He said that he did not intend to be there for all the rehearsals but come only in time for the recordings and concerts. John Mack was to be the other oboist, and we were told to "prepare to work" and "manage" until he arrived.

Although later Casals Festivals would each have their high points, the particular spirit of the 1950 Festival would never be duplicated. The confluence of Bach—it was the two hundredth anniversary of his death—and the special circumstances of Casals's reentry into the music world after his long voluntary "exile" from his home country of Catalonia in Spain united to create a unique atmosphere from both a musical and emotional point of view. Casals had made a brief appearance in London in 1945 when he reemerged still in magnificent form to play several concertos. But then he returned to Prades to continue his protest against the countries which despite their victory in World War II did not take steps against the Franco regime. The idea of a festival came about in the summer of 1949 when a group of musicians gathered around Casals to study and play chamber music. They performed one public concert in the church on the town square. Later when Alexander Schneider visited Prades at Christmas time, plans were made for "*un Festival de famille*" to take place the following year. Casals was refusing all invitations to participate in world celebrations in honor of the two hundredth anniversary of Bach's death. Pointing to the mound of mail he was receiving by then, he said that publicity was *inutile* (unnecessary), just "let the friends know." He wanted it to be a "Festival of friends."

THE CASALS FESTIVALS IN PRADES AND PERPIGNAN

Solo artists from Europe were contacted, for the most part old colleagues and friends of Casals: pianist Clara Haskil, whose important career had been interrupted by the war and by illness; Parisian pianist Yvonne Lefebure; Hungarian violinist Stefi Geyer, a colleague and close friend of Bartók; and the Swiss pianist Paul Baumgartner. From the United States: Rudolf Serkin, Leopold Mannes (son of Casals's old friend David Mannes), Alexander Schneider, Joseph Szigeti, and young Eugene Istomin and Isaac Stern. Representing both Europe and the U.S. was Casals's oldest friend, the pianist Mieczyslaw Horszowski. They had first met in 1905 in Italy when Horszowski was thirteen years old and Casals was twenty-nine. Even in his seventies Horszowski always referred to his friend as "Mr. Casals." The stellar wind players were John Wummer, solo flutist of the New York Philharmonic Orchestra, Marcel Tabuteau from the Philadelphia Orchestra, and bassoonist Maurice Allard, famous professor at the Paris Conservatory. The rest of the orchestra was put together in about equal numbers from Europe and America. Alexander Schneider was the concertmaster and also a soloist. Sidney Harth was a member of the first violin section,[1] and Casals's brother, Enric, from Barcelona sat on the first desk of second violins. Among the violists were Karen Tuttle and Milton Thomas. The cellists of the Festival Orchestra were led by Paul Tortelier and included Daniel Saidenberg, Rudolf von Tobel, Leopold Teraspulsky, and Madeline Foley. Fernando Valenti played harpsichord. Not all the musicians were of such a distinguished level, but even with this less than homogeneous group, Casals achieved remarkable results in performances of exceptional musical perception and intensity of expression.

An international committee had been formed combining dignitaries from French musical and cultural life: composers Georges Auric, Francis Poulenc, and Nadia Boulanger, with a sprinkling of comtesses, princes, barons, and governmental figures. From America came benefactresses Elizabeth Sprague Coolidge and Rosalie Leventritt. All were under the high patronage of Vincent Auriol, president of the Republic and Monsieur Herriot, president of the National Assembly. There were other eminent personages among the supporters: M. Delvincourt, director of the Conservatoire Nationale, and prefects and mayors of the Prades-Perpignan region. From the clergy, the bishop of Perpignan.

The lengthy list of patrons included many old friends and admirers of Casals: Gustave Bret, founder of the Société J. S. Bach de Paris, and Dr. Albert Schweitzer, who had been the organist of Bret's group and was known for his writings on Bach long before he became the famous missionary doctor of Africa. In honor of the festival a special medal was cast with J. S. Bach on one side and Pablo Casals on the other.

The village of Prades in the Département of Pyrénées-Orientales lies some forty-five kilometers west of Perpignan in the foothills of the Pyrenees.[2] In 1950 a little train with hard wooden seats chugged up from Perpignan via several Catalan settlements to finally reach Prades at the foot of the snow-capped peak le Canigou. This magnificent mountain, celebrated in legend and song (its name alone resonates in the hearts of all Catalans), stands guard over the red-tiled rooftops of the town below. The central square is dominated by the fourteenth-century church of St. Pierre with its iron filigree bell tower typical of the region, while inside the church the ornate retable is crowded with gilded saints flying about over the altar. At the center of this golden sanctuary, St. Peter was about to look down on one of the most extraordinary tributes devoted exclusively to the music of Bach that would ever take place.

In Prades one heard as much Catalan spoken as French. From the window of my room I saw horses being shoed in the blacksmith's shop across the street. The town crier came by on his bicycle calling out from his hand-held horn, "*Poissons de la Méditerranée à la Nouvelle Poissonerie!*" (Fish from the Mediterranean at the New Fish Store). To get to the post office I often had to make my way through a flock of sheep or herd of cows that came crowding through the narrow streets. A block away, an old-time artisan who crafted all manner of fine leather articles would soon be filling orders for the festival musicians. It was cold and damp inside the buildings. John Mack, John Wummer, and I were living in the same house where we were cheered by our morning chocolate and croissants in the landlady's garden. Her old pet turtle would come out in the sun and bang its head against the side of our shoes. We had running water, but it was cold, as cold as the snowy slopes of the Canigou from whence it came. The public baths cost the equivalent of thirty-five cents and entailed an inconvenient walk along the Route Nationale to the other end of town. One day, John Wummer, who had the second floor "suite" with a bathtub (but only the same icy cold water), announced that he had taken a bath. We all asked how this was possible! "By drinking a whole bottle of cognac and then jumping in" was his reply.

All the rehearsals and recording sessions took place in the Collège Moderne de Jeunes Filles on a hill slightly above the main streets of Prades. Part of the low-ceilinged cafeteria had been partitioned off with heavy maroon-colored velvet drapes, and one of the washrooms was labeled "W.C., Orchestre Jean Sébastien Bach." The festival was an international news event covered by *Life*, *Time*, and *Paris Match*, who sent their leading reporters and photographers. In *Life* magazine there were large photos of Casals conducting and playing, of Paul Tortelier carrying his cello uphill to the school, and of Wummer and Tabuteau seated in front of the resplendent altar of St. Pierre. During rehearsals we had to be careful not to trip on the maze of cords and wires lying on the floor and twisting around the base of our music stands. Between the Columbia engineers and famous photographers Gjon Mili and Margaret Bourke-White, all crawling about the room bent on recording every moment of the festival on tape and film, we had to take our cue from Casals in order to concentrate. Thrilled to have an orchestra under his baton after so many years, he presided benignly from a high stool on his podium, unperturbed by any of the goings-on except the music. In an old flannel shirt, brown sweater and baggy trousers, holes visible in the soles of his otherwise neat shoes, Casals showed some signs of his years of material privation but no lack of musical fervor and energy. I noted that his understanding of rhythm and his musical explanations were exactly the same as Tabuteau's but expressed "not so screamingly."

Groups of townspeople hovered around puzzled by the sight of the recording vans, the tangles of discarded tape, and the sounds pouring out of the schoolhouse windows. They discussed listening in as "something to do," and one local commented "it must be very bad because they have to stop so often." The grocery store shopkeeper swore he knew nothing about music, but then he sang Bach's "Air on the G String" in solfège. Talking about the musicians created a diversion for the inhabitants of Prades. They learned all our names and were expectantly waiting to see Marcel Tabuteau. John Mack and I had been there since early

May but the Tabuteaus came only three weeks later, proceeding directly to the aging but elegant spa hotel in Vernet-les-Bains, twelve kilometers distant from Prades. Their arrival was accompanied by the usual turmoil over reeds and general arrangements. Casals was happy when Tabuteau came to the rehearsal the next day, and it gave the little orchestra an additional boost to have him there. It was evident that Casals felt here was someone who understood all of the musical ideas he was expressing.

The 1950 Prades Festival unrolled in an atmosphere of rare exaltation. When the crowds of local people gathered before the portals of the church for opening night, the interior was already bulging with concertgoers. The festival had attracted celebrities from the world of music, politics, the arts, and aristocratic society. There was no room for another soul to squeeze inside to hear the person who for them was not the world famous cellist, but their friend and neighbor, Don Pablo. Old Catalan friends of Casals had even come across the Pyrenees on foot. Later on, an extra concert was added only for the people of Prades. The account I sent to my mother recalls the ambiance of that night:

> On the evening of Friday, June 2, before the first concert, I arrived early on the square in front of the church. Red and yellow banners with the Catalan colors hung from all the lampposts. There had been a rainstorm but it cleared just in time for the Spanish-style buildings to turn a rosy pink in the last rays of the sun. The clouds lifted from the peak of the Canigou and with people milling about in the foreground, it all looked like the stage set for an opera. One could imagine the chorus might begin to sing at any moment, but instead it was the Prelude to the Festival Bach. If there is ever a night in my life I shall never forget, it is certainly this one. We went in the "musicians' entrance" through the Sacristy and there was Casals tuning along with all the orchestra players. Finally they dusted out a little side room for him. Two high officials of the church, the *évêques* (bishops) came in and donned their purple robes that were hanging in the costume (vestment) room. I'm sure it's the only time their antechamber served as a warm-up room for symphony musicians. We were all to sit on the "stage" while Casals played the opening Suite. The concert began late—it was at least 9:30. After we were all seated, the Bishop came out and made a speech officially opening the festival. His subject was the power of music and of a great maître. Using this theme, he touched on Casals, Bach, and *Dieu* (God). Also, how Bach *had* to

THE CASALS FESTIVALS IN PRADES AND PERPIGNAN

be played in a church, explaining that his religious spirit was so great he was performed even in the Sistine Chapel.

The audience was perfectly quiet and sat in an atmosphere of harmony and peace. There was nothing to break the spell as if all the out-of-tune things had already erupted before. When Casals came in, the orchestra and the whole audience rose and stood quietly. There was no applause at all but the silent tribute was so eloquent and moving. As Casals got up on his platform, I heard him saying, "*C'est gentil*" (How kind). There is no use trying to describe how he plays. It is the rare combination of *everything*. No question of age—(He is 73—but never one sign of a bow shaking). Perfect control and effortless technique throughout and musically it is impeccable. One cellist said the other day, "He plays like a young man of thirty." Perhaps you could say that, but I never heard anyone of *30* play like *that*!! When he finished, the whole audience stood again.

He stopped us from doing that when he came out next to conduct the *Brandenburg No. 2*. Later, back stage I heard Casals say that after not having played in public for so many years, he didn't know what would come out. Mr. Schneider said when Casals first came off after the cello Suite he thought he'd played badly. Can you imagine? I think he was very nervous before, but it didn't show for an instant. I sat in the first row of the audience for the final two numbers and it was really fantastic. The spirit and the way the *Brandenburg No. 3* was played is something I will probably never hear again.

Afterwards people all crowded back and everybody was kissing everyone else. Schneider was crying half the evening, as after all, it is largely the realization of his dream and work. In a way, it all seems a miracle. Prades changed over night into a real sanctuary of music. All the musicians were invited to the *Mairie* (Town Hall). It was already almost midnight. The tower of the church was illuminated and made a beautiful picture on the square. In the crowded hall of the *Mairie* Casals sat at a table at one end, and just by luck I happened to be near by, so heard and saw all. The Mayor made a short appropriate speech and then Ernest Christen, a pastor from Switzerland, made an eloquent speech exactly expressing the sentiments of everyone there, after which they popped some champagne corks and served wafers. Casals stayed until the end, greeting and kissing all his old friends and colleagues. All evening he looked so happy and his joy was contagious to everyone. In his speech Mr. Christen said how he had observed that the musicians were so happy to be playing for Casals, and that their love for him showed in their eyes. When I walked home up the

MARCEL TABUTEAU

cobblestone street after watching Casals being driven off in a car, there were beautiful dark clouds with bright streaks of moonlight behind them all around the Canigou. It would be impossible to imagine an event like this. I think one would have to be a stone not to feel, at least in some measure, the super-normal qualities of the whole evening. To say it was a splendid concert would not even give the most superficial idea of it all.

The festival followed a format of six concerts of works for orchestra and six concerts of chamber music. Casals began each orchestral evening with one of the Bach Suites for unaccompanied cello, playing them in the order of one through six. On the festive opening concert described above, he began with the Suite No 1 in G Major that was followed by the exuberant *Brandenburg No. 2 in F Major.* Although Tabuteau was one of the four soloists in this work which features violin, flute, oboe, and trumpet, strangely enough the only name listed on the program was "Dennis Clist, Trumpet, of the Philharmonia Orchestra." On an earlier page in the same program booklet, Paolo Longinotti is named as the trumpet soloist. Perhaps this would be a good place to dispel the story that has persisted for years: "How could Casals use a saxophone in the Brandenburg *Concerto*?" I was witness to the consternation that set in during the early days of rehearsals when Columbia was already there with trucks and technicians ready to begin recording all the works to be played in the festival. We learned that Longinotti had not come because he had already recorded the work for Columbia and was not allowed to do so again. In those days high trumpet players were a very rare breed. Hurriedly, the British engineers brought in someone from London who for one reason or another found the part impossible to play and left almost immediately. Casals was sitting there on his podium not knowing what to do when Paul Tortelier came up to him and said, "Don't worry Maître. I have an idea." Tortelier made a telephone call to Paris, and the next day two people arrived on the train, the brilliant saxophonist Marcel Mule, accompanied by an E-flat clarinetist from the Garde Républicaine band. Tortelier assured Casals that Mule had played this part before and that the small C saxophone made a very good substitute for a high trumpet. The few notes that were out of its range would be inserted by the E-flat clarinet player! Casals was in no position to question this

THE CASALS FESTIVALS IN PRADES AND PERPIGNAN

solution and appeared happy that everything could go ahead according to schedule. And so the work was both recorded and performed in this version on the first concert. Tabuteau wanted doubling in some of the forte passages. Therefore, I sat between him and the E-flat clarinetist who was assisting Mule. I witnessed the absolute coolness with which the E-flat "expert" could suddenly inject a high "peep" into the middle of a quickly moving sixteenth-note passage—and Casals's tempi were fast indeed. In fact, Tabuteau, who objected to very little in the first festival, was quite taken aback by the sudden speed! A new program printed on a single sheet listed all the soloists with "Trompette: Marcel Mule." This is the true story of Casals and the *Second Brandenburg Concerto* as I saw and heard it in 1950.[3]

On the second orchestral concert of June 5 Tabuteau played in the Cantata No. 82, *Ich habe genug*, with Doda Conrad as vocal soloist. The concert concluded with the *Concerto in C Minor for Oboe and Violin* with Tabuteau and Isaac Stern. A full-page photo of Casals conducting this concerto with the audience in the church looking raptly on was featured in *Life* magazine as the opening of the festival. This was a slight twisting of the facts, as in between the concerts the recording sessions had continued, with several days spent on the Bach Double. When the LP recordings appeared in December 1950, Roland Gelatt wrote in the Saturday Review, "One of the glorious moments at the Prades Festival was the middle movement of the C Minor Concerto for oboe and violin. And—astounding good fortune!—here it is again to savor repeatedly with all the magic of that original performance. Just as Caesar saw cause for distrusting men with lean and hungry look, so I would have misgivings about any person who could listen unmoved to the sweet melancholy of this movement. Marcel Tabuteau's oboe is the very essence of restraint and nobility, and Isaac Stern comes within a hair's breadth of equaling him." The Cantata *Ich habe genug* with its eloquent oboe solo was also recorded but not released; the master tapes were never found.

On the third orchestra concert of June 9, Tabuteau played in Cantata No. 204, *Ich bin in mir vergnügt*, with the Swiss soprano Helene Fahrni. After the concerts, John Wummer promptly disappeared to sit and have a drink at the Café Lewitas. Nor was Tabuteau anywhere to be seen. During a week when there was not much for oboe, he took off and went back to Toulon for three days, returning in time for the conclusion of the festival. He *did* attend one special event, the christening party for baby Maria de la Pau Tortelier. Rather than miss the festival, Tortelier's wife Maude had come to Prades and waited there for the birth of her baby in the local hospital. Casals was the godfather. Both Tabuteaus attended the ceremonies at the church and in the mayor's garden. Tabuteau declined playing Casals's *Sardana* outside in the garden, so I had the pleasure of doing it. However, at the end of the festival he both played and recorded the *Sardana* oboe solo.[4]

Parties and gatherings in the garden of the Grand Café punctuated the busy schedule of concerts and recording sessions. The orchestra gave a surprise dinner for Alexander Schneider in appreciation of his having organized the festival. Casals came after the dinner, and there were again many speeches. When Casals spoke, he said that at first mention of a festival, he feared it would be too much of an undertaking for him, but that now he was so happy to be in the middle of music again and he felt better than ever. It had given him a second youth. A Cobla performed Sardanas at the party.[5] When they played the Catalan national anthem, Casals conducted. I played in a trio with the Torteliers that Paul had composed for oboe and two cellos. Then Tortelier sang *Perpetual Motion* in very rapid solfège accompanying himself on the piano. Ruth Draper was there and gave four "sketches" from her one-woman shows.[6] Burl Ives pulled out his guitar and entertained us with "Jimmy Crack Corn" and other country songs. Lily Pons and André Kostelanetz dropped by. Later everyone wanted to learn to dance the Sardana. Casals came forward and separated the big circle of dancers so that we could see and follow the Catalans in the center. Then everyone threw serpentine confetti, and as all the colors mixed and twisted in with the dancing, the Cobla continued blaring away while Gjon Mili dashed back and forth to get his angle shots for *Life* and *Time* magazines. As Casals was leaving, we sang the *Brandenburg Sixth,* which amused him. The party went on until almost 3:00 a.m. with Schneider giving imitations of violinists and mocking the way each member of various well-known string quartets walks out onto the stage.

Rudolf Serkin and Joseph Szigeti arrived while the festival was already underway. Although Fernando Valenti was there for the harpsichord,

THE CASALS FESTIVALS IN PRADES AND PERPIGNAN

Serkin played the keyboard solo in the *5th Brandenburg Concerto* on the piano. Those who heard it never forgot the drama and excitement Serkin conveyed in the first movement cadenza. Isaac Stern wrote about it in his autobiography, and later his words were quoted in a book about Rudolf Serkin.[7] Serkin wished he could have stayed in Prades for all the rehearsals if only to play the "continuo" piano in accompaniments to the Brandenburgs, but he had promised to return to Vermont where some friends and students were planning to get together for chamber music. This would prove to be the pre-beginning of the famous Marlboro Festivals. In Prades I found it "amazing to see Serkin, Casals, Szigeti, Stern, and Tabuteau all in one small room." Casals came to all the chamber music concerts, sat in the first row, and enjoyed every minute. After his superb performance of the 5th Suite for cello, Tabuteau was in the clouds and said he'd never heard anything like it in his fifty years of music. One night a crowd of about two hundred people tried to push their way in to the concert. It was almost a riot, and people seemed to have gone Bach-Casals crazy! Finally we gave a special concert for the population of Prades, and I found it "very interesting to see all the Catalan faces in the audience, instead of New Yorkers and continentals."

A number of pianists turned up in Prades: Gary Graffman, Leon Fleisher, and my old Curtis friend Seymour Lipkin. Seymour and I had lunch with the Tabuteaus and Enric Casals at a rural restaurant, La Bonne Truite. Afterward, we convinced Tabuteau to drive up into the hills on the rocky road to the isolated twelfth-century Abbaye of Serrabonne, one of the architectural gems of the region. Its finely sculptured marble columns crowned with grotesque and grimacing imaginary figures, half animal, lion, or man, gave Tabuteau the opportunity to hold forth on the strange thoughts in the minds of the medieval monks. Seymour and I climbed to the top of the tower and tolled the bell. We could easily have spent more time in this fascinating spot, but we had to get back for a rehearsal, as the horns and bassoon had arrived for the *Brandenburg No. 1*. On June 18, a special concert was given at the Abbaye of St. Michel de Cuxa. Lying in the fields a short distance outside of Prades, in 1950 this thousand-year-old abbey was still in a semi-ruined state. Most of the pink marble columns from the cloister had long since been removed and sold to the Metropolitan Museum of Art, where they stand at Fort Tyron Park on the Hudson River and are known as "The Cloisters." The audience for this concert filled the whole main area of the church and overflowed into the side transepts. As the abbey had not yet been restored, it was lacking a roof, and only the vault of the blue sky was above us. I found it more beautiful than any cathedral. Looking across to where there would ordinarily be a stained glass window, one could see the clouds above the green hillside and from time to time hear a bird song or a cock's crow in the distance. Grass was growing near the top of the crumbling sidewalls, but nothing disturbed the atmosphere of beauty and peace except the flash bulbs of Margaret Bourke-White. The acoustics were excellent. Tabuteau's solo in *Ich habe genug* never sounded better. John Wummer played the B Minor Suite, and after a rousing performance of the *Brandenburg No. 3*, Casals ended the program with his own *Sardana, St. Martin du Canigou*, this time with Tabuteau playing the oboe melody. In the shadow of the Canigou so close to the border of Spain, it was particularly moving to hear Casals's encore, the Catalan folk song "El Cant dels Ocells" (Song of the Birds), filled, as he played it, with nostalgia and longing for his homeland.

The last concert on June 20 began with the most demanding of the cello suites, *No. 6 in D Major*. The rehearsals and concerts had been so tiring that Casals told his brother he felt he wouldn't be able to play. But he did, and magnificently. Then followed, one after the other, works with extended parts for two and three oboes; Tabuteau excelled in the *Orchestral Suite No.1 in C Major*, the *Brandenburg Concerto No. 1 in F Major*, and finally Cantata No. 32, *Liebster Jesu Mein Verlangen*, sung by Helene Fahrni and Doda Conrad, with its flowing oboe solo in the opening *Sinfonia*. "After the final Cantata, the Bishop (*évêque*), who was sitting in the first row, held up his cap in the air and the whole audience exploded in spontaneous applause. I guess that had never been heard in the church. It seemed they had to make up for the silence during the whole festival. Casals came back and played again, the *Chant des Oiseaux*, and that was the end. [This began the tradition of "The Song of the Birds" ending every festival.] We all went to the *Hôtel de la Sous-Préfecture* where there was a wonderful farewell party with all sorts of sandwiches, cakes and cookies and champagne. I was rather amused when I arrived to see the two bishops in their vividly colored robes,

FESTIVAL J.-S. BACH
sous la direction de
PABLO CASALS

Mardi 20 Juin, à 21 h., en l'Église Saint-Pierre à Prades

6ᵐᵉ et DERNIER CONCERT d'ORCHESTRE

6ᵐᵉ SUITE, en ré majeur, pour Violoncelle seul.
　Prélude - Allemande - Courante - Sarabande - Gavotte I et II - Gigue.
　　　PABLO CASALS.

1ʳᵉ SUITE D'ORCHESTRE, en ut majeur.
　Ouverture - Courante - Gavotte I et II - Forlane (Danza Veneziana) -
　Bourrée I et II - Passepied I et II.
　　　Hautbois : M. TABUTEAU et L. STORCH.
　　　Basson : M. ALLARD.
　　　Clavecin : F. VALENTI.

1ᵉʳ CONCERTO BRANDEBOURGEOIS, en fa majeur.
　Allegro - Adagio - Allegro — Menuetto alternant avec Trio I, Polacca
　et Trio II.
　　　Cors : L. THEVET et G. COURSIER.
　　　Hautbois : M. TABUTEAU, L. STORCH et J. MACK.
　　　Violon solo : Alexander SCHNEIDER.
　　　Basson : M. ALLARD.

CANTATE Nº 32 : "Liebster Jesu, mein Verlangen"
　pour Soprano, Basse et Orchestre.
　ARIA. RECITATIVO. ARIA. RECITATIVO. DUETTO. CHORAL.
　　Hélène FAHRNI et Doda CONRAD.
　　　Hautbois : M. TABUTEAU.
　　　Violon solo : A. SCHNEIDER.
　　　Violoncelle solo : P. TORTELIER.
　　　Clavecin : F. VALENTI.

The program for the final concert of the 1950 Casals Festival in Prades. Tabuteau plays in three big works: the Orchestral Suite No. 1, the First Brandenburg Concerto, and Cantata No. 32.

already sitting at the long table in the garden munching on a couple of ham rolls. They made quite a picture under the colored lights of the garden. Dr. Puig gave a fine speech and Casals spoke, again thanking everyone. They mentioned the hope for another festival next year of Bach and Mozart." It was difficult to decide what to do after the end of the festival. Almost everyone left and the remaining people sat around talking in the Grand Café drinking *limonades* with Gjon Mili, Clara Haskil, and Enric Casals. There was a luncheon at Schneider's "villa," but the very air seemed changed, and Prades began to look more like just an ordinary dusty little village in the Pyrenees.

The 1951 Casals Festival in Perpignan, which celebrated the music of Mozart and Beethoven as well as Bach, took place in the Palais des Rois de Majorque, one time capital of the Catalan realm. The palace testified to the grandeur of the Catalan kingdom that reached from the south of what is now France to the island of Majorca. Centuries before, the courtyard between the chapels had seen great festivals of poetry and music. Dr. René Puig, a proud resident of Perpignan, now dreamed of renewing this greatness with his friend Pau Casals at the helm. In early May 1951 the Tabuteaus arrived in France, heading to the South after a few weeks in Paris. They planned to spend some time at the Pingouinette before coming to Perpignan for the beginning of rehearsals in June. I decided to stay in Prades until it was necessary to be in Perpignan. During the month of May the most popular subject of conversation in Prades was about the imminent move of "their Festival" to Perpignan. The shopkeeper at the delicatessen waxed eloquent as to the fact that the musicians "had made simple people love the music of Bach—that everyone in Prades was happy because it was *Casals'* festival." Now in Perpignan it would be another type of thing. "The Perpignanais are jealous. They're jealous of our Rugby team; they're jealous of our climate; they're jealous because we're nearer to the Canigou than they are." He took it all to heart and said they considered people like Madeline Foley and Rudolf von Tobel, who had been coming there for years, as Pradeeans. The saddle-maker, M. Gourse, said he would greet Tabuteau with the theme from the oboe and violin concerto and proudly demonstrated how well he could remember and sing it. As more musicians began to arrive, they all lamented having to go to Perpignan. Even Casals did not want to stay in Perpignan during the festival but intended to travel back and forth, making the fifty-kilometer trip by taxi or chauffeured car every day. There was a mix-up with housing for the Tabuteaus, and they went to stay at Canet-Plage on the beach about twelve kilometers away. Later they moved to a modern and comfortable house in the middle of town. I was fortunate to find lodgings with the Collonge family, former Berlitz language teachers who had lived in England, Egypt, and Constantinople and were now semi-retired in a lovely house and garden on the edge of Perpignan. They were housing two other musicians from the festival and were always generous if we wanted

THE CASALS FESTIVALS IN PRADES AND PERPIGNAN

to invite guests to join in the delicious meals they prepared for us. The Tabuteaus found the atmosphere and the food at *chez Collonge* to their liking and came to lunch several times during the festival. A typical meal was roast filet of beef, potatoes *en croquette,* stuffed *courgettes* (squash) or tomatoes Provençal style, salad, cheeses, and dessert. Tabuteau was very impressed that M. Collonge brought afternoon tea to my room while I was making reeds. Room and meals (including homemade marmalade at breakfast) was one thousand francs that summer (about three dollars).

An English Committee of Honor had been added to the festival with conductors Sir John Barbirolli as president and Adrian Boult as vice-president. New patrons included William Primrose, Lionel Tertis, and Sir William Walton. Most of the soloists from 1950 returned, but new to the Perpignan Festival were the mezzo-soprano Jennie Tourel, the Danish tenor Aksel Schiøtz, and the beloved English pianist Myra Hess. Isaac Stern and Alexander Schneider were again the solo violinists with the addition of Erica Morini.[8] There were very few changes in the orchestra, as Casals wished to keep the same musicians from the year before. Rehearsals and recording sessions took place in the Théâtre Municipal, a rather neglected but formerly elegant small theater with faded red velvet seats, dating from the Napoleonic era of the early 1800s. For Tabuteau, the major works in the 1951 Festival were the Mozart *F Major Oboe Quartet* K. 370, Mozart *Wind Quintet with piano* K. 452, *Divertimento No. 11 in D Major* K. 251, and Bach *Cantata No. 189* with Aksel Schiøtz. He also played in the orchestra for most of the Mozart piano concertos, the *Symphonie Concertante* for violin and viola with Stern and Primrose, and the *Symphony No. 29 in A Major* K. 201. All were recorded except the Piano Quintet. As the year before in Prades, recording sessions were sandwiched in whenever possible. The conditions were far from ideal, but at least something of Tabuteau was captured that might otherwise never have existed. On his sixty-fourth birthday, July 2, he recorded the Mozart *Oboe Quartet* with Isaac Stern, William Primrose, and Paul Tortelier. The Columbia engineers who had their van parked in an alley behind the theater told Tabuteau to play each section straight through two times. Tabuteau asked me to follow the score and mark the good takes—the ones that should be used for the final recording—which I did. There was a perfect version of each movement, but after the

MARCEL TABUTEAU

tapes were taken to England, they were stuck together, totally ignoring the best choices and giving Tabuteau no opportunity to hear the results. Small things, such as a missed attack here and there, needn't have been released. A few years later, recording engineers could edit tapes by clipping out or inserting individual measures and even single notes. In this case it would only have been a question of using the proper take for a complete movement, but unfortunately it was not done.

On July 7 Casals opened the first concert of the festival as he had in the previous year with the Bach *Suite No. 1 in G Major* for unaccompanied cello. Afterward, Tabuteau, searching for a lofty enough way to describe the performance, said that Casals had played like a Michelangelo or a Rembrandt. His own part in that concert consisted of playing in the orchestral accompaniments for three Mozart concertos. Two of them, K. 271 in E-Flat Major with Myra Hess and the *Symphonie Concertante* with Stern and Primrose, were recorded. Isaac Stern also played the *G Major Violin Concerto* K. 216, on the same program. As a concert hall, the church of St. Pierre where we had played in Prades was far from perfect. The acoustics were so over-reverberant that volunteers had strung hundreds of yards of string in dangling rows from the dizzying heights of a walkway near the ceiling in an attempt to break up the echoes. By comparison with the Palais des Rois de Majorque in Perpignan, however, it would rank as a world-class auditorium. The Palais stood on a hillside far from the center of town and was often in the path of a brisk wind that made it extremely difficult to keep the music on the stands. There were no facilities at all for the musicians, but worst of all, the committee had not taken into consideration the possibility of bad weather. Everyone said, "It never rains in Perpignan in July," so that no provisions were made for alternate performance space. That summer, the first chamber music concert on Sunday, July 8, should have been Tabuteau's big night. He was scheduled to play both the Oboe Quartet and the Quintet with piano. He had conscientiously come early to try the acoustics on the stage. Between four and five o'clock in the afternoon it poured rain, but then stopped, so the concert went on. During the opening number, when Stern, Primrose, and Tortelier were playing two Bach *Adagios and Fugues* in Mozart's arrangement, they had to move back under the stone arches by the side of the stage. With such

THE CASALS FESTIVALS IN PRADES AND PERPIGNAN

bad weather, the audience began to drift away. It was proposed to cancel the concert, but Tabuteau wanted to go ahead and play. Stern and Primrose had to leave the next day so the oboe quartet was played in the same uncomfortable spot under the arcades with the rain coming down and the remaining people crowding in so closely that the artists could barely move their elbows. Considering the circumstances, Tabuteau played beautifully. The next day, explaining why he had insisted on playing under such adverse conditions, he said that he had "felt like a lion with a thorn in his foot and he had to get it out."

The *Quintet for winds and piano in E-Flat Major* K. 452, with Tabuteau, the highly respected French clarinetist Louis Cahuzac, Van den Bulcke on horn, Sennédat on bassoon, and pianist Mieczyslaw Horszowski, was scheduled for the same July 8 concert. Because of the rain it was postponed until the next night, but without enough publicity about the change, very few people attended. Nevertheless, in his notes for July 9, Horszowski considered the concert "a success." Arguments between Tabuteau and Cahuzac over intonation prevented the recording of this work.[9] By now, Tabuteau was thoroughly unhappy and disgusted. Realizing how he felt, the next day Mme Tabuteau urged him to go back to the Pingouinette for a week. Again, John Mack and I were left with everything to play and record including the *B-Flat Concerto* K. 595 with Horszowski. I did not relish the idea of playing after Tabuteau. It was a relief to me when he returned the following week.

A few nights later when Horszowski played K. 595 Concerto at the Palais, the wind was blowing so hard that everyone was struggling with clothespins to try to keep the music on the stands. Casals was bundled in his overcoat with a wool scarf around his neck. Instead of the performers being able to warm up, our instruments only got colder. Even with cold hands and music blowing away, the concerts were excellent. On Sunday, July 15, Casals, totally unruffled, played the Second Unaccompanied Bach Suite magnificently despite the dreadful weather. There was no choice but for the rest of us to do our best. After her Mozart *A Major Violin Concerto*, Erica Morini said she had barely been able to keep her bow on the strings because of the wind.

A high point on the concert of Saturday, July 21, was the seven-movement Mozart *Divertimento* K. 251 for oboe, two horns, and strings.

Rehearsal at Théâtre Municipal, in Perpignan. Casals Festival, 1951. L to R: John Mack, Marcel Tabuteau, Laila Storch.

Fortunately, this time the exquisite phrasing of Tabuteau's oboe solos was caught in the recording.[10] Casals decided that the three low Ds interjected several times by the solo oboe in the Rondo (allegro assai) were not sufficiently robust for his taste. He asked all three oboists to play them unisono, both on the recording and in concert. On the same evening as the *Divertimento,* Clara Haskil created a sensation with the *F Major Piano Concerto* K. 459. For Casals at age seventy-four, it was a Herculean task to play the five Beethoven Sonatas and three sets of Variations with Rudolf Serkin as he did on the concerts of July 22 and 25. He also took part in six Beethoven trios, performed the first three Bach unaccompanied cello suites as well as two of the gamba sonatas with piano. Add to this all of the conducting during the rehearsals and concerts

THE CASALS FESTIVALS IN PRADES AND PERPIGNAN

for the three-week festival period. A person half his age could well have been exhausted, but people who had known him for years confirmed that he had never played better. On July 28 there was a special concert in the rather austere cathedral of Perpignan with the organist Marcel Dupré as soloist. On the same program Tabuteau again played the Cantata *Ich habe genug* with Doda Conrad as the bass soloist.

In Perpignan there was no central gathering place like the Grand Café in Prades, so the festive parties and sociability of the year before were lacking. One time we all went to a château south of Perpignan, a massive and overly ornate house built in the early 1900s by someone who had made a fortune manufacturing cigarette paper. Mrs. Leventritt paid for the cold buffet that was served outdoors on the terrace looking toward the mountains of the Spanish border. Serkin was in friendly form talking with everyone, and the Tabuteaus came, bringing with them Miss Soffray, our solfège teacher from the Curtis Institute. After the last concerts in Perpignan we went back to give another performance at St. Michel de Cuxa. Casals conducted *Eine Kleine Nacht Musik* and ended the festival as before with the "Cant dels Ocells." He also played an aria from Bach's *Organ Pastorale in F Major*, as everyone said, like "the King of the Angels." Following the concert, a table decorated with greens and the yellow and red Catalan colors and set with sandwiches and champagne appeared in a half-ruined vaulted stone room on one side of the abbey. It seemed like Prades again with the trees, air, and sun, a more fitting setting than the hot and stuffy center of Perpignan. After a farewell dinner at the Grand Café, Casals continued going down to Perpignan in the July heat to record the several sets of Beethoven Variations with Rudolf Serkin.

Despite his high praise and eulogizing of Casals's cello playing, in 1951, Tabuteau was beginning to show some ambivalence about his character. On a cane-hunting trip to Fréjus in August, all during lunch I had to listen to Tabuteau's tirades detailing what he considered to be Casals's flaws. "He can't fool me." Tabuteau found him "weak" because in the first festival he never criticized anyone but said that everything was "beautiful." This year he was "weak" because he criticized some but not others. Then he was "not a real conductor but had become infected by the public—the applause and the adoration." If this were true, it seemed to me that instead of sitting in Prades, Casals had only to go back into the world at any time and play concerts. But as I had found out years earlier, Tabuteau's unerring logic in musical concepts did not always carry over into questions of human psychology.

There was no full orchestra in the 1952 Casals Festival, and Tabuteau spent his whole summer at La Lèque. He again returned to Prades for the festival of 1953. The same composers were featured as in Perpignan with the addition of Schubert. This time all the rehearsals and concerts took place in the Abbaye of St. Michel de Cuxa. From the very beginning there were complications. Horszowski arrived early to record with Casals, but the Beaux Arts Society of Paris that was carrying out repair on the abbey had not given their workmen the order to stop and let the festival preparation begin. Then the piano arrived but not the piano tuner. The piano tuner eventually came but not the recording men and equipment. Eugene Istomin made a special trip to Paris to see the deputy from the Département of Pyrénées-Orientales at the National Assembly to persuade him to intervene. After everything was supposedly smoothed out and several technicians came to unpack the piano, an architect from Beaux Arts refused to let them enter the abbey. Much drama ensued, as both Horszowski and Serkin had other engagements to fulfill, and it appeared that their recordings would not be done. Finally on May 25, one half hour before rehearsals were scheduled to begin, with workmen still shoveling piles of debris out of the abbey, the musicians of the orchestra gathered together. Tabuteau, however, had not yet arrived. The first item on the agenda was to record the Schumann cello concerto. Casals had thought he could play and conduct it from where he sat, but that did not succeed. Nor did having his brother conduct work out. Jacob Krachmalnick, who was the concertmaster that year (and also concertmaster of the Philadelphia Orchestra), made a telephone call to Switzerland where Eugene Ormandy was vacationing and convinced him to make a quick trip to Prades. When it was known that he would come, they tried desperately to get in touch with Tabuteau but could not reach him at La Lèque. We recorded the Schumann without him. I played the rather small oboe part, and in a few

THE CASALS FESTIVALS IN PRADES AND PERPIGNAN

Marcel Tabuteau and flutist John Wummer. Tabuteau is wearing a beret as it was very cold in May in the Abbaye of St. Michel de Cuxa rehearsing for the 1953 Casals Festival. Photo by Laila Storch.

hours everything was smoothly expedited under Ormandy's direction. For many years, however, his name could not appear on the record due to his commitment to another company.

In 1953 there were concertmasters on almost every stand of the orchestra and a fuller complement of wind players. It was very chilly in the Abbaye of St. Michel de Cuxa in May. Casals wore a knit cap and conducted rehearsals in his topcoat. At first there was an atmosphere of joy to be making music again with Casals. There were some wonderful new soloists in the persons of William Kapell, Arthur Grumiaux, and Lillian and Joseph Fuchs. But after a couple of weeks, dissension set in over the question of recording. Meetings were called which only augmented the discord. The orchestra had not expected to record more than the Schumann *Cello Concerto* and came to an impasse on whether to allow other works to be done. The Schubert Symphony No. 5 in

MARCEL TABUTEAU

B-flat major was a particular source of contention.[11] Tabuteau was very unhappy with the results of a meeting with Casals and decided that he would only play his solos and then leave. On June 19 he played the beautiful Bach Cantata 202 *Weichet nur, betrübte Schatten* with the Swiss soprano Maria Stader and a week later the Mozart Quartet, this time with Jacob Krachmalnick, Karen Tuttle, and Paul Tortelier. The live recording of this concert from tapes of radio broadcasts found in Italy was first issued in LP format in 1982 by Discocorp[12] and more recently on CD.[13] Both issues list Orea Pernel, whose name appears on the printed program, as the violinist. She did not, however, play in that performance. I took a photo of the group that did.

John Mack and I shared the oboe parts for the remainder of the festival. On June 29 Tabuteau wrote from La Lèque, "Returned in *grand vitesse* (very quickly). The sun as rare here as in Prades but all the same, very happy to be home *chez moi*." So ended his association with Pablo Casals.

17 TABUTEAU AS SEEN BY HIS PHILADELPHIA ORCHESTRA COLLEAGUES

As the twentieth century drew to a close, I was able to talk with a number of Philadelphia Orchestra musicians who had played on the same stage with Marcel Tabuteau. I had never really known how he was regarded by rank-and-file members of the string section, and I wanted to add the memories of violinists, violists, cellists, bass players, and other wind players to those of the oboists who knew him so well. Two constants stood out in their reminiscences. Without exception, they praised his magnificent oboe playing and the superlative level of his artistry. Highly trained and skilled performers themselves, most said how much they could learn by listening to Tabuteau. They also remembered his great love of gambling; almost everyone had a story connected with his card playing. Sometimes they spoke first of his gambling and only afterward about his musicianship; sometimes it was the other way around. In his long years with the Philadelphia Orchestra, Tabuteau seemed totally preoccupied with two kinds of playing: oboe and cards.

Many of their colleagues spoke of Tabuteau and Kincaid almost in one breath as if they were two parts of the same musical body. At the same time, they noted a certain element of rivalry that existed between the two. They also frequently mentioned the relationship of Tabuteau and Kincaid with Eugene Ormandy. Most of the orchestra men felt that Ormandy was afraid of Tabuteau and Kincaid. Some from the Stokowski era suggested that after that vibrant period, it cannot have been easy for Ormandy to arrive and find these two dominating personalities facing him from where they sat in the very middle of the stage. "They were the gods!" was a refrain repeated by many of the orchestra members with whom I spoke. Ormandy had little choice but to accept their long-standing eminence in Philadelphia and their importance to the stature of the orchestra.

According to one violinist, "Ormandy didn't like them and they didn't like him. When he came, they were already great stars and he arrived as a relatively untried conductor. Tabuteau and Kincaid were the last of those great players from Stokowski days—Guetter, Bonade, Schwar, and Torello, who played the bass like a cello. But it was a different story then. I remember hearing how Stoki would fire people on the spot if they didn't do what he wanted."[1]

There were differing opinions about Tabuteau's behavior on the stage. John de Lancie considered it a type of "myth" that Tabuteau more or less ruled the orchestra. "I sat next to him for eight years and I never heard him give a conductor a bad time. By the same token, I never saw a conductor try to give him a bad time. He minded his own business." Mason Jones also found Tabuteau to be "quiet in the Orchestra. You wouldn't know he was there except for his playing. Once in awhile he'd come to me if he thought I was playing a sustaining note where he had a solo, and he'd say, 'Mr. Jones, would you mind playing that a little bit softer?' And, of course, he was always interested in the pitch. He was pretty hard with the concertmaster about the 'A' and also [about] how the pianos were tuned."

What was it like for Mason Jones as a student, to find himself suddenly playing with his teachers? Jones had auditioned for the Philadelphia Orchestra in 1938 in the middle of his second year at Curtis. He was asked to join the orchestra immediately and go on tour. "I was third horn for one season. I didn't have any experience but I sat right next to Anton Horner, my teacher . . . He was a good father in the routine of the orchestra . . . I did nothing but concentrate on my part, counting

TABUTEAU AS SEEN BY HIS COLLEAGUES

bars, coming in, and getting the transposition right . . . I learned very soon after getting into the orchestra that you never talked shop, whereas when you're a student that's all you do. Although I had played in Tabuteau's woodwind classes, he never was chummy. There was a big age difference between us. In the orchestra he kept his distance and I kept mine. He played the concerts, went to Curtis, went to his studio and made reeds."[2]

Tabuteau did not always conduct himself as politely as he did with Mason Jones. Irwin Eisenberg sat on the first stand of second violins next to Irvin Rosen, not far from Tabuteau. Eisenberg remembered how "he couldn't stand it that the violins were always too high, so when he tuned he would purposely play low. The woodwinds would play a chord; he'd be so mad that everybody else was high, so he'd play his note out of tune. He would never do that with Stokowski, but Ormandy was afraid of him. Really afraid of him *and* Kincaid, both of them. They were the gods . . . I heard him playing right there in back of me. He was the Maestro of the Orchestra, that's all. He might play out of tune in a rehearsal, but at the concert when he and Kincaid played something together in unison, it was absolute perfection—always."[3]

Jerome Wigler, another violinist, had similar memories. "The two of them were sitting there like gods . . . Tabuteau was a wonderful oboe player, a great musician, and a great teacher. I remember *Ports of Call.* That was beautiful." *Ports of Call* (*Escales*) also made a deep impression on violinist Morris Shulik. "The phrasing, the atmospheric pictures that he was able to draw—I tell you, when he played *Ports of Call*—it took you right back to the souk in Morocco. Every time in rehearsals—you could smell the place; you could see the place; you could feel it." Shulik was not only eloquent in his praise of Tabuteau and Kincaid but also attempted to explain something of their place in musical history and the period that nourished their artistry. "About Tabuteau, he was more or less like a Dr. Jekyll and Mr. Hyde. When it came to his *playing,* he was the greatest. I played with him for about five years and knew him quite well as a colleague—I mean as well as anybody could. I used to marvel at what I was hearing and then Kincaid right beside him. When they played *Afternoon of a Faun,* they were 'in sync' musically, even if they weren't always good friends. I sat there and listened to these two people

MARCEL TABUTEAU

day after day after day, and I learned a lot. The way they answered each other, you had to hear it. Tabuteau and Kincaid—they were giants."

In attempting to explain the phenomenon of these musical personalities, as well as the changes throughout his years in the orchestra, Shulik continued, "They were a product of their times. Fritz Kreisler . . . I used to hear him often. Nobody plays like that today. It's not part of our culture. It was that beautiful Viennese style, the phrasing, the charm, and the idiosyncrasies of the Viennese School. Today it is all more mechanical. If you hear one soloist, the others are almost similar. I'm in the orchestra a half a century now and I see these young people—violinists, and horn players too, and they play better actually, technically better. When I came into the Philadelphia Orchestra, the string section was definitely not as good man for man as it has been in the recent past. But something has happened. There's this high level of performance but it doesn't touch you at all. They play the *notes* and they play the notes superbly . . . its science and television, but the next generation will be different than this one. Things keep changing." Shulik was not the only one who said the great style of the Philadelphia Orchestra was gone. Some blamed Riccardo Muti, saying that he wanted a virtuoso orchestra and had remarked, "There is no such thing as the *Fabulous Philadelphians.*[4] He tore down the sound and then he left. He didn't let you play really; he restricted your playing. Stokowski liked individuality. It's gone today. There are a lot of remarkable musicians but the style is gone."[5]

There are many stories about the rivalry between Tabuteau and Kincaid. Sol Schoenbach said there was an "ongoing contest, fighting all the time for who is 'Number One.' Once we were playing in Richmond, Virginia—the Brahms *Second Symphony.* It was in the first movement after the development section where all of a sudden everything is very quiet. At the end of the flute and oboe unison passage, suddenly you hear this voice saying, 'It's a funny world. He wants the same salary but he does not want the same pitch!' It was incredible because just that day Kincaid had gone up to the office and demanded that he should get the same amount as Tabuteau. It was always money, but also prestige—ego. Well, Tabuteau was a rare character, the most unforgettable I've ever known."[6] Sol Schoenbach had managed to establish a relationship of respect and mutual admiration with Tabuteau that was to endure to the

TABUTEAU AS SEEN BY HIS COLLEAGUES

end of their lives. When Sol first joined the orchestra and was introduced by the manager, Tabuteau commented, "I don't know how you
play, but you're the best *looking* bassoonist I ever saw." Shortly afterward,
however, an incident occurred which forced Sol to take Tabuteau's measure. Sol told the story: "I remember the first time we did *Scheherazade*
where the bassoon opens up the second movement. I started playing and
I wasn't very happy because there was this pip, beep, boop, and F-sharps
going on, so I stopped playing. Ormandy said, 'Mr. Schoenbach, what's
wrong?' I replied, 'I'm not running a testing ground here,' and everybody
started to laugh. Then Tabuteau said, 'Young man, what do you mean by
that?' I said, 'I don't like anybody to test their notes on me like that!' and
Ormandy, sensing that there was a storm coming, said, 'Intermission.' So
everybody ran off the stage, and Tabuteau and I went off too, and we
were exchanging verbal blows. I maintained that I didn't want anybody
tampering with reeds while I was playing my solo, and he said, 'I've been
doing this for years and you don't tell me—that's the way it is,' and so on,
like that. And while he was gesticulating and talking away, he took out
his cigarettes, *Virginia Rounds,* which he smoked in those days. They
were more expensive than the average, and he took one and put it in his
long cigarette holder made from a piece of oboe cane, and I just reached
over and took one too. When he saw that, he screamed, 'You're *imposseeble*!!' and stalked away. Everyone was watching this and waiting for the
blood, 'Oh, you took his cigarette!' but I never had any trouble with him
after that."[7]

Tabuteau apparently did not maintain much personal contact with his
fellow orchestra men. According to John de Lancie, he was more or less
in a world by himself. "He'd come out on the stage—he was always there
early—and he would try to intimidate people to stay away so that he
could try out his reeds without having anybody else playing. Or, he would
hear someone and if it was sharp, he would go over and give the person
hell. But to the best of my knowledge there was no socializing with other
orchestra members. Of course, he used to gamble with a bunch of the
guys. David Madison, the assistant concertmaster, spent a lot of time
with Tabuteau. And then there was Emmet Sargeant and Robert
Gomberg . . . He must have been very friendly with Hans Kindler because he's the only person who I ever heard *tutoyer* with Tabuteau. When

MARCEL TABUTEAU

Kindler came to the Philadelphia Orchestra to guest conduct, in the intermission of the first rehearsal he immediately got off the podium and said, 'Oh, Marcel, *comment va tu?*' and Tabuteau responded, '*Et toi, comment ça va?*' So they obviously had a close relationship.[8] In the early days, Tabuteau was also very friendly with Tony Torello and was present at the christening of the Torello sons."

Many people have wondered about Louis Di Fulvio, who played second oboe with Tabuteau for thirty seasons. In the mid-1920s when someone was needed for that position, two people showed up, Di Fulvio and Ernest Serpentini. Tabuteau favored Serpentini and told Stokowski that he was the better oboe player. But Serpentini was very quiet, almost mousy in manner, and Stokowski liked the idea that Di Fulvio seemed more lively. So he hired Di Fulvio. After a few years Stoki felt that he'd made a mistake. He called Tabuteau in one day and said, "You know, I think we ought to get rid of Di Fulvio." But by that time, Tabuteau had grown very fond of Di Fulvio. They really got along well, and he was the best card player in the orchestra, a fantastic card player, and everybody knew it. As Tabuteau related the story, "So do you know what I told Stokowski? I said, 'Maestro, Di Fulvio is a *very unusual* person.' Stoki asked, 'Oh?? How *is* that?' and Tabuteau answered, 'You know, he is the only oboe player in America who hasn't tried to imitate me.' Stokowski laughed and Tabuteau laughed even louder. From then on Stokowski kept Di Fulvio and seemed to find him, if not exactly like a court jester, nevertheless amusing."[9]

Clarinetist Anthony Gigliotti remembered that Di Fulvio did everything for Tabuteau—held the feather for drying out the oboe, had cigarette paper ready if water got in a key, and counted bars. Di Fulvio often played with the various opera companies in Philadelphia. Once when there was a big oboe solo and he was giving a fittingly emotional interpretation, the conductor stopped and said, "Please, Mr. Di Fulvio. Follow me! I have the stick." Di Fulvio replied, "Eh Maestro, you gotta da stick, but I gotta da solo!"—a retort worthy of his famous compatriot Bruno Labate of the New York Philharmonic, who was never intimidated by conductors. About his own experiences with Tabuteau, Gigliotti said, "I felt I learned more by playing and sitting behind him during my first four years in the orchestra than any other time in my life."[10]

TABUTEAU AS SEEN BY HIS COLLEAGUES

Harry Peers, the trumpet player who heard the Mozart *Concertante* with the improvised cadenzas, was not a regular member of the orchestra, but while still at Curtis he occasionally came in as an extra player. First, he had to join the Musicians' Union. He described his audition at the dingy union headquarters on North 18th Street as an example of the low level of expertise required to become a "certified" card-carrying member of Local 77 of the American Federation of Musicians. "They took a whole bunch of us, saxophone players, clarinet players, flute players, and violinists into a room and passed out dance arrangements. The cacophony of those players was so awful, you can't imagine it. Afterwards, the fellow who was listening said, 'Ok, you're all members.' I couldn't believe it." When Harry returned home, he received a call from Paul Lotz, the personnel manager of the Philadelphia Orchestra, asking if he would be free for the following week to play *Ein Heldenleben.* As Harry recalled that experience, "What a band it was! Caston, my teacher, was first trumpet. Harold Rehrig and Melvin Headman played the two E-flat parts and Saul Caston and Sigmund Hering and I played the B-flat parts." I asked if he had any contact with Tabuteau or ever spoke to him at rehearsals. "Never. Remember he was a god-like creature to me. Most of those men in the Philadelphia Orchestra at that time were either my teachers or my teachers' associates. I was a seventeen-year-old boy. But I never forgot what I played with them; not only *Ein Heldenleben,* but also *La Mer* and *Harold in Italy.*"[11]

Roger Scott joined the orchestra in 1947 and became principal double bass in 1949. He remembered "the fuming that went on" when his good friend, Marilyn Costello, came on the stage to tune her harp. "Of course, Tabuteau didn't like this at all and you could see him stewing around and muttering to himself. I admired both Kincaid and Tabuteau. They were the big stars when I was in school and now to sit on the stage with them and to listen to them play so wonderfully! It was tremendous. I was not aware until I got in the orchestra that Tabuteau led the wind chords. With all due respect for Mr. Ormandy, his beats were sometimes less than precise. During my first season, all of a sudden at the end of *Don Quixote,* I thought how in the world do they play those last couple of chords like that? I used to get called in and he would lay the law down to

— 444 —
MARCEL TABUTEAU

me. I was too loud, too soft, too short, too long, too sharp, too flat, too soon, too late . . . I would simply say, 'Well, I'm trying to second guess you every step of the way and once in awhile I miss.' But Tabuteau led the chords. Then when he left, it was Kincaid, and after he left, Mason led them for a while. As a listener, you're unaware of this, but as a player you're keenly aware. You see the head dip and everybody just plays along with him."[12]

Lorne Munroe, principal cellist in the orchestra from 1951 to 1964, also found Ormandy's beat puzzling and difficult to follow. "When I joined the orchestra and saw the beat was always late, I soon realized that even the string section was relying on Tabuteau to bring them in." Scott remembered the Christmas party at Curtis when Tabuteau came out with an alpenhorn. It had been in the instrument room, and no one even knew what it was. "Tabuteau put an oboe reed in it and he was laughing so hard I was afraid he was going to have a heart attack right on the stage. I had never been subjected to either his scathing wit or his praise, but just to see someone whom I had admired for so long having so much fun with this whole shebang was amazing. I had never heard an alpenhorn but with the oboe reed buzzing inside of it, you can imagine it was not like a later point in my career when we actually had a Swiss Alpenhorn soloist!"[13]

Violinist Isadore Schwartz, a Curtis graduate from 1931 and a forty-year veteran of the Philadelphia Orchestra, found that "Tabuteau was a very complex character. He always had a feud going on with Bill Kincaid. At times it got out of hand. I remember one day when they waited until they were outside the hall on the steps at the stage door and they almost came to blows. I was standing right there listening to it, the two of them, and I thought they were going to actually fight." I asked Mr. Schwartz what he thought was the source of their rivalry—if it was about musical matters or questions of salary? His answer was that "Tabuteau would tell Kincaid how to play something or Kincaid would tell Tabuteau, and there was often a difference of opinion. But all in all, when Tabuteau said something it was sound, there was no question about that. You always learned if you listened to Tabuteau . . . one thing I did when I came into the orchestra, I always listened to my elders— Tabuteau, and Bill Kincaid, too. For instance, if I was noodling and

TABUTEAU AS SEEN BY HIS COLLEAGUES

Tabuteau said 'don't do it that way,' he was right. They were the greatest I ever heard. They were masters. That's all."[14]

Violinist Irvin Rosen joined the Philadelphia Orchestra in 1945 and stayed forty years. Rosen, who sat very near to Tabuteau and Kincaid, described the impressive way in which they matched their playing in the unison triplet passage in the last movement of *La Mer*. "Whenever we played *La Mer* they were both out there maybe half an hour or more before the concert. When I became principal of the second violins I used to come on the stage to look at some of the difficult passages in my music, and there were these two great artists going over this passage time and time again. They met right in the center, and it sounded absolutely fabulous. On that first note, the double B-Flat—it wasn't like either a flute or an oboe. It seemed to be some sort of extra-terrestrial instrument."[15] I remembered hearing that ethereal phrase seemingly emerge from nowhere as it floated up to where I sat in the top balcony of the Academy of Music. To me, it was fascinating, so many years later, to learn how Tabuteau and Kincaid had prepared for each performance, leaving nothing to chance.

As a double bass student at Curtis, Edward Arian had attended Tabuteau's classes as often as possible. When he became a member of the Philadelphia Orchestra he came in closer contact with his oboe playing and his interaction with Ormandy. "It was well known that Ormandy was uncomfortable with those holdovers from the Stokowski years. By that time I joined the orchestra in 1947, Ormandy was fairly secure, but even then, occasionally during a concert he would get sort of confused. Of course, the orchestra just went right on and the listener couldn't tell, but we saw that he was having problems because he would get very red and start to perspire and begin pulling at his sleeves that was a nervous habit he had . . . I have memories of Ormandy looking out at the orchestra like someone hunting for a life boat in a panicky way and Tabuteau sitting right there in front of him quietly shaving an oboe reed. When Ormandy looked at him he would look back at Ormandy and give him a big smile as if to say, 'Don't worry, you'll get it.' I'm sure Ormandy did not appreciate it, but he knew Tabuteau was leaving soon."[16]

Seymour Rosenfeld played trumpet in the orchestra from 1946 to 1988. His wife told me a story from his Curtis days of almost sixty years

MARCEL TABUTEAU

earlier.[17] He was yet another student who had came to grief by saying "hello." "One day he greeted the Maestro with, 'Hello Mr. Tabuteau.' Tabuteau wheeled around with fury and said, 'Hello, hello, hello! This you say to your friends and your companions. To me, you say 'Good Morning, Mr. Tabuteau.' Later, every time he saw Tabuteau in the orchestra, he said, 'Good morning, Mr. Tabuteau' with that same inflection, and made sure to do that as long as Tabuteau was there . . . Speak to any musician who played at the time of the great Marcel Tabuteau, and you will hear the same thing, that his phrasing was the controlling influence in Ormandy's handling of a musical work. He was totally dependent on the combination of Tabuteau and Kincaid."

For tuba player Abe Torchinsky "the greatest thrill when I joined the Philadelphia Orchestra was to play with both Tabuteau and Kincaid. I had been taken to the concerts when I was a small boy, and I heard all those great players. My father was a tailor, and we got the fifty-cent tickets. When I went to Curtis I was in Tabuteau's classes—the winds and percussion with Eugene Istomin playing the string parts on the piano. I learned more from Tabuteau than any other teacher."[18] Several of the musicians (two cellists and a bassoonist), whose realm is primarily in the bass clef, spoke primarily of Tabuteau's helpfulness and good humor. Perhaps they were not as directly involved in pitch battles as the violinists, who, in their striving for brilliance, often edge toward the high side. Bassoonist John Shamlian had also been in Tabuteau's wind classes at Curtis and remembered him as "a very fair man . . . I always found him to be a direct personality. He taught me to listen and how to be rhythmic. And he was encouraging to young people in the orchestra. If suddenly I had to play first bassoon, he would turn around and nod in a helpful way. Sometimes he had trouble with gout and had to play while having his leg on a stool. Eventually he had difficulty with his hands and carried around a rubber ball which he kept squeezing all the time when he wasn't playing."[19] This reminded me that I had quite often seen Tabuteau flexing his fingers while holding corks between them. He would also exercise his fingers on the dinner table as if at a piano keyboard.

Cellist Elsa Hilger was the first woman to play in the string section of a major U.S. orchestra. She was hired by Stokowski in 1935 and remained until 1969. She was almost ninety-six when I visited with her

TABUTEAU AS SEEN BY HIS COLLEAGUES

by telephone in December 1999, and her first remark about Tabuteau was that "he had a very good sense of humor which was delightful. No matter what happened—sometimes in traveling you don't get good rooms or good food or the halls are not what you are used to, but he just had a laugh about everything." When I said that wasn't exactly the side of him I had seen, she laughed, "Oh no, you would see the other side!" And about his playing? "Oh yes, beautiful, beautiful. He was one in a million or two." Cellist Harry Gorodetzer also entered the orchestra in 1935. At that time Stokowski was still very much in charge. Gorodetzer spoke in a similar vein as the others from that era. "It's not the same orchestra. They've changed direction. The attitude is different. Everybody had such pride in those days. You had total devotion to your work. We were thrilled to be in the Philadelphia Orchestra—to be a part of its great success. Now the musicians take it so casually as if they're doing you a favor by being in the orchestra. And we were very lucky. We had all the great conductors in their prime—Toscanini, Beecham, Dimitri Mitropoulos, Bruno Walter, and with Stokowski, it was always magical. There was such imagination and with Tabuteau too; he wasn't just playing an oboe. You listened to him and you melted, it was so beautiful." Gorodetzer said that when he used to warm up, often sitting on a chair backstage near the door from which the cellos entered, Tabuteau would sometimes come by and speak to him. "He would be trying a reed and he'd come over and criticize what I was doing, and then I would play for him. He was very nice about it, and I took it gratefully . . . One time when we were returning on the train from Pittsburgh, I stayed up all night putting compresses of liquid laudanum on his leg above his ankle for the pain—he had the gout so badly. Robert Gomberg and I made a seat with our hands to carry him into the train. He couldn't even walk up the steps."[20]

Bass clarinetist Leon Lester remembered all the legendary Philadelphia wind players. "The *sound* those people got!" Lester never forgot the thrill it was for him to hear Bonade in the *Pines of Rome.* For a Saturday night concert, he was sitting in the Curtis box only about forty or fifty feet away from the stage. "One of the men in the percussion section put on the record of the nightingale—after the bird, the clarinet

— 448 —
MARCEL TABUTEAU

comes in. The way Bonade played that solo—you'll never hear anything like it again."[21] Later when Lester himself played in the orchestra, he noticed how Tabuteau prepared for the difficult passage after the pizzicato section in the *Scherzo* movement of the Tchaikovsky Fourth Symphony where the oboe enters on a high "A." "Each and every time he had to play that solo (it would be on the second half of the program), he would go out on the stage ahead of time and practice it."

Aside from his glorious playing, Bonade was apparently a prankster. Tabuteau told de Lancie about one of his indiscretions that did not go over too well with Stokowski. "Once they were playing a piece by Schoenberg. They rehearsed it on Monday, Tuesday, and Wednesday, and when on Thursday they were going through it again, all of a sudden Bonade asked, 'Mr. Stokowski, is my part for an A clarinet or a B-flat clarinet?' Stokowski looked down at the score and said, 'Well, it's for A clarinet.' Then Bonade spoke out and laughed, 'Ah ha, ha, ha—I've been playing it on B-flat all week!' Instead of keeping quiet he made it into a big joke."[22]

Joseph Primavera, who played viola in the orchestra from 1951 to 1967, remembered Tabuteau as "an extraordinary musician—a remarkable person, a remarkable teacher. Most of us learned a lot from listening to him. I also played cards and gambled with him . . . I was very young, only twenty-five or twenty-six years old, and he and Kincaid were already in their sixties. Even so, Kincaid and I were very close. When we went on tour, if we were in a dry state he would give me twenty to forty dollars and say, 'Go buy me some Scotch.' He always drank *Three Brothers.* Sometimes it was difficult to get liquor, and I'd have to take a cab and bribe the driver to help me. Kincaid and I would sit in the Pullman car on the bench, and Tabuteau would come and sit in between us, and Kincaid and I would have a drink of Scotch. Tabuteau loved to eat and drink but he had to be careful because of his gout. Kincaid would turn to me and say, 'Hey Joe, wasn't that lobster delicious tonight?' and Tabuteau would get so upset. 'You are picking on me. Stop! Stop! I love the lobster and I cannot eat it!' We used to tease the life out of him about food and drink." I asked if he thought there was ever rivalry. "Oh yes, absolutely. That was on and off, because both wanted to be The Star."[23]

TABUTEAU AS SEEN BY HIS COLLEAGUES

GAMBLING

Everyone had stories of Tabuteau's gambling. It was common knowledge that he would sometimes be broke by the end of the summer in France and would have to borrow against his next season's salary to get back to Philadelphia. John Minsker could remember as long ago as the early 1930s when Tabuteau had big books that were published in Monte Carlo showing every number that came out on the roulette table for a year. He had seen scraps of paper with long lists of numbers lying around Tabuteau's studio and even tried to help him figure it all out by taking one of the books home to study over the summer. Tabuteau and Bonade gambled a lot together. They both pored over the Monte Carlo books during the winter and tried to figure out a system. Then in the summer they went to the casino with the idea that they were going to break the bank. When their "system" didn't work, Tabuteau in his customary fashion, blamed Bonade.

Many of the musicians remembered Tabuteau sitting up all night on the train, especially on the long tours, playing poker with five or six other orchestra men. Gambling was then illegal everywhere except in Nevada. When Tabuteau found a place where he could gamble, he would, as John de Lancie described it, "ask me to come along as a sort of body guard. Some of these places were just joints. If I was in a room when he was winning and I decided to leave, even for a few minutes, and then he started losing, he would accuse me and vice versa. If he was winning when I was out of the room and I came in again and went over to stand near him and watch what was going on and then he'd begin to lose, he'd start yelling at me . . . He was very superstitious about all that. It was no joke." Mason Jones remembered how it was on the trains to New York. "We went there ten times a year, and right after the concert Tabuteau would get on the train, and the poker game would start as soon as possible. Often it would be with Serpentini and Di Fulvio. They played all the way home. Tabuteau was kind of rough and gruff about it. If things weren't moving along he would say to 'come on, ante up.' Apparently you had to watch him like a hawk because he took advantage of every situation."

Roger Scott described how they arranged the games on the trains. "We had two cars. One was a smoker and one was a non-smoker, and it

MARCEL TABUTEAU

seemed that the smokers all played poker. They would turn the seats around and some of them would just sit on the edges. If you wanted to play badly enough you'd find something to play on, even a piece of cardboard. The cards were thrown away at the end of each trip because they were so gummy from being handled so furiously." Leon Lester didn't play but remembered being on the train "about two seats ahead of Tabuteau, and when he was winning everything was lovely, but as soon as he started losing, all you could hear was, 'Shansgh the deck—shansgh the deck.' He thought he'd have better luck with a new deck." Irwin Eisenberg told of what happened when a violinist who was also a heavy gambler joined the orchestra and got in debt to Tabuteau. "Tabuteau was furious. He went to Ormandy. He went to the Association. The violinist owed Tabuteau about $700.00 which was a lot of money in those days, and he couldn't pay." Edward Arian also remembered how angry Tabuteau would be if he were losing and characterized him as becoming "almost apoplectic." Arian served for a number of years on the orchestra committee. He was in charge of a little fund to which each orchestra member made a yearly contribution of the modest sum of three dollars. This was to take care of sending flowers or for mailing and other orchestra business. "Tabuteau was the last person I got the money from and finally the only way was to wait for the poker game. I would literally force him—if he won a pot, I would grab the money. It was quite funny."

The game was usually poker, but violist Joseph Primavera reminisced about shooting craps on the floor of the train. "On an occasion when Louis Di Fulvio had injured his ankle and was unable to go on tour, we took Al Genovese who was still a student at Curtis . . . It was by Pullman in those days, and we would go back to the club car and play cards. Genovese had never been on tour with us before, and somebody said, 'Look, a lot of the fellows are back in the Club Car.' 'Oh,' he said, 'where's that?' and they told him, 'Go all the way through the Pullmans.' So Al came through, and there he sees his teacher. We're all dirty because of the floor, and Genovese got so upset. He loved that man; he was so afraid of him and respected him so much and then to see his teacher down on his knees with his necktie loosened shooting craps and arguing with us! It was a real shock." Al Genovese had his own stories about Tabuteau's gambling. One concerned cards and another, the

TABUTEAU AS SEEN BY HIS COLLEAGUES

oboe. He was watching a card game one time when Di Fulvio was playing, and Al saw that he had the winning hand. Tabuteau proposed,
"What do you say, Luigi? We'll split the pot." (Of course, Tabuteau was
holding not as good cards.) Di Fulvio was very loyal, but he knew what
was going on, and he was squirming in his chair and said, "I'm so sorry
Maestro, I have to play the cards." Tabuteau was furious, but Di Fulvio
won the money. Al also had memories of Tabuteau's rare admission of
an element of gambling in his oboe playing. Although today the lowest
level of oboe playing is much higher than it was in the past, there is now
a type of uniformity that Al described as "One size fits all." Tabuteau
once told Al, "I gambled. Sometimes I make it and sometimes I don't."
Occasionally Tabuteau cracked on a few of the repeated B-flats in the
third movement of the Sibelius Second Symphony, but as Al continued, "if he'd taken it easy and careful all the time, that wouldn't have
happened, but there wouldn't have been that excitement either."[24]

A story not connected with gambling but involving train trips was
told by Jerome Wigler. "A few key players from the orchestra, including
Marcel Tabuteau and trombone player Charlie Gusikoff, would occasionally go up to Montreal to play for conductor Wilfred Pelletier. You
weren't allowed to bring liquor across the border during the war. The
orchestra men had upper and lower bunks in the sleepers. Charlie was
in an upper bunk and Tabuteau was in the one beneath him. Evidently
Tabuteau put a bottle of Scotch under Gusikoff's mattress to smuggle
it in when they came back across the Canadian border. When Charlie
got into bed, he felt this lump under the mattress. He checked and
there was the whisky. So he took it out and kept it. Then late at night he
felt a hand under the mattress looking for the bottle. It was Tabuteau,
of course, but the bottle wasn't there. Gusikoff had hidden it and
Tabuteau couldn't say anything because of the customs."

TABUTEAU'S FAREWELL SPEECH IN FEBRUARY 1954

In his last few years in the orchestra, Tabuteau stopped playing in January although he continued to teach at Curtis until the end of the spring
term. His farewell speech to the Philadelphia Orchestra has been
recounted with differing variations (some of them improbable) by a

number of the men who were sitting there on the stage and heard it. On February 25, 1954, I wrote to my mother that I had "called the Tabuteaus yesterday. They are really leaving and he was on his way to say goodbye to the orchestra." It was before the days of personal cassette machines and regrettably the speech was not recorded. I have given John de Lancie's version as he repeated it several times in almost identical fashion. It had been quite indelibly imprinted into his memory.

"Tabuteau came in to see Ormandy and told him he'd like to say goodbye to his colleagues. So he came out and Ormandy followed him onto the stage. Tabuteau got up on the podium and thanked Ormandy for giving him a few minutes of his precious time and started to talk. It wasn't very long before we realized that this was probably going to be something special! First of all, he made a few comments to some of the old timers, like Kincaid, Sol, and one or two others. There were still a number of men who went *way* back to the early 1920s. And then he said, 'You know, when I came to the orchestra as a young man in 1915, I was delighted to come, and here we are in 1954, and I'm delighted to go.' Now that immediately set the tone, and we thought, what's going to happen—what's he going to say next? Then, among other things, he turned to Ormandy and said, 'You know, Maestro, it has been my experience that the more the men hate the conductor the better they play for him, and Maestro, your orchestra has been sounding very well lately.' Of course, all the guys broke up laughing. Ormandy turned white and red, and then Tabuteau went on and I can't remember it all except that there was nothing complimentary. Then he waved and said 'Good luck' and he left. Ormandy called an intermission. We waited about a half an hour but he didn't come back on the stage for a long, long, time."

Already in my Curtis years I felt that Tabuteau had what might be considered a rather distorted sense of humor. While many of his remarks were truly amusing, some could only have seemed funny to him. In 1955, a year after his famous "farewell speech," the Philadelphia Orchestra made its first long tour of continental Europe. After hearing a broadcast of the orchestra from Bordeaux, Tabuteau had sent Ormandy a congratulatory telegram saying how glorious it had sounded and was upset when he received no acknowledgment. As de Lancie put it, "here was a person so acutely aware of what was going on and so perceptive

TABUTEAU AS SEEN BY HIS COLLEAGUES

about everything and yet he couldn't understand that if he insulted people, they didn't necessarily come back to him." Sol Schoenbach commented that "he observed everything and everybody and he was a good student of human nature. Only he didn't examine his own too well." This characteristic also made his name "mud" in France for many years. One time in the early 1930s during his summer holiday, he was invited by a colleague to listen to the oboe concours at the Paris Conservatoire. When at the conclusion, he was asked by one of the members of the jury, "What did you think of the *concourrants* (the contestants)?" he replied, "They should declare a Day of National Mourning!"[25] While no doubt to him a witty statement, it was hardly calculated to endear him to his former countrymen. It would be many decades before oboists in France would begin to speak with some moderation about Marcel Tabuteau.

MARCEL TABUTEAU

18 RETIREMENT IN FRANCE

La Coustiéro, 1954–1959

While staying at the Pingouinette in the summer of 1948 I had wandered through the fields toward the Mediterranean and stumbled upon several lovely, but derelict, villas in the pinewoods. Some were inhabited, but others were little more than empty shells. I learned that interesting "aristocrats" were living in the neighborhood. Just beyond the olive trees there was a Russian, Prince Galitsin, of pre-revolutionary days. Formerly there had been some Habsburgs and a noble old French family. I saw two deserted villas facing the sea that must have been very beautiful but certainly would now be more costly to repair than to buy. This entire region near Toulon had been ravaged during the World War II occupation by Germans, Italians, and Americans. Little could I guess that only a couple of years later Tabuteau would buy one of these very villas.

In 1949 the Tabuteaus decided to go to France immediately following the Philadelphia Orchestra's "historic" May–June tour of England. No American orchestra had visited Europe since the New York Philharmonic went with Toscanini in 1930. I watched Tabuteau furiously making reeds to prepare for the extensive repertoire: *Don Juan*, Sibelius No. 2, Brahms No. 2, Beethoven No. 5 and No. 7, *Firebird* Suite,

Scheherazade and more. On some days he spent as long as ten hours at the Studio working on his gougers—almost like a madman! He decided the bell of my oboe was better than his, and he would have to use it for the tour. The orchestra was to play twenty-eight concerts in twenty-seven days including a concert version of *Madama Butterfly* conducted by Sir Thomas Beecham. The opera took place in Harringay Arena, a huge facility in North London seating up to 10,000 spectators, usually used for boxing matches and Greyhound dog racing.

The orchestra was to sail from New York on Friday, May 13. I had to help pack up Tabuteau's reeds and fill out the baggage labels for his trunks. He didn't begin to pack his suitcases until 11:00 p.m. on Thursday and to me seemed quite disorganized and rather in a daze. On Friday morning I went with the Tabuteaus on the train to New York. There was a festive air at the pier with assorted celebrities, reporters, and photographers from the press on hand to see the musicians board the S.S. *Parthia.* James Petrillo, president of the Musicians' Union, was there, as were President Harry Truman's daughter Margaret and her voice teacher, Helen Traubel, who came with Eugene Ormandy. I took pictures of all of them and also of Schoenbach, Kincaid, and Tabuteau, as they walked up the gangplank. Mme Tabuteau planned to leave a few days later on the Cunard R.M.S. *Caronia,* meet Tabuteau in London at the end of the tour, and then continue on to Paris.

A little news about the Tabuteaus' summer reached me in California. At the Pingouinette things had gone somewhat better than during their 1947 visit. He had been able to get oboes from Dubois in Paris and cane from Biasotto in Fréjus. As their vacation was ending he said that he hated the idea to return to *le biniou.* (Tabuteau often used the name of this Breton folk instrument when referring to his oboe.) According to Madame Tabuteau, "ten days ago he started to work and despite his protestations, blows with enthusiasm." In November I received a letter from Tabuteau with the first intimation of some important changes in their future plans. He began by describing their return trip to the U. S. on the *Queen Mary:* "An excellent and rapid crossing but terrible food— perfect English style cuisine." Then he described how life in Philadelphia continued in its usual manner on the fourteenth floor of the Drake with "*bonne table, bon pinard et le fameux fauteuil*" (good cooking, good wine, and the famous armchair). There were a few words about the "artistic side of things. They smell as bad as before if not worse. Today came a fresh breeze to purify the air. Robert Casadesus was with us. He played his own concerto and the Liszt No. 2. *Admirable!*" And finally, "The surprise which concerns La Lèque is not yet *officially concluded* to my great regret. *If* things work out the way we arranged them before we left Paris, here is what waits for us—a mansion at the edge of the Mediterranean! Perhaps you remember the property that borders on the sea, *chemin de la fossé,* and was damaged during the war. I took these photos of the garden myself. When I receive confirmation of the purchase I promise to let you know."

Less than two months later came another letter with the heading "Jan 2, 1950, Holy Year(!)" that announced, "As to La Lèque, we are happy that it is definite. Here we are *châtelains* (Lord and Lady of the manor). Now we need only go plant our *fesses* (backsides) in the sun. While waiting, I am on my third week of vacation. The weather is very beautiful and I'm taking advantage of it by driving the Cadillac to the seacoast; unfortunately I go back to work the ninth of January— Orchestra and Curtis the same day. I tremble a little at the idea." On January 25 Mme Tabuteau wrote, "We are preparing our departure, but news from the Midi is very scarce. No sign of life from the architect chosen to take care of the *château.*"

They were encountering the common difficulties of having repairs made at a distance. But by summer 1950 before they left La Lèque to drive to Prades for the first Casals Festival, they were writing on letter paper with the printed heading, *La Coustiéro, La Lèque par le Brusc, Var.* Although the move to their new villa appeared imminent, when I visited them in July they were still at the Pingouinette. Returning a year later I found that little had changed except that this time I was given a detailed tour of the new house. Some progress was being made. The windows were now protected by attractive new iron grillwork, and there were railings in a similar style on the inside staircases. To me it seemed "a huge place to get in order, but the views are incredibly beautiful. It is the type of villa you dream about. Big, but livable and artistic—not stiff and pretentious." I felt that by the next summer they should surely be able to live there.

RETIREMENT IN FRANCE

Tabuteau could finally contemplate retirement in this magnificent setting. But for over two more seasons in Philadelphia he continued the same round of complaints, agonizing over his work and reeds. His message on a Christmas card in 1950 was: "The reeds are very bad, I work like a crazy man and no good results. I really think it is time for me to quit!"[1] He had, however, become accustomed to having an assistant and playing for a fewer number of weeks. In March 1952 when John de Lancie became ill, Tabuteau had to return to full action in the orchestra. From Madame, "de Lancie is in bed two weeks already and can't come back before Easter. So it's le Pingouin who blows and suffers! (*qui souffle et souffre!*) No use saying how happy he is—because of this we had to change many things . . . and now there is no space on the boat." They had hoped to leave for Paris on April 16, but at the end of the month he was on tour with the orchestra in Hamilton, Ontario, something he never expected to do again. It was during this period on April 5, 1952, that he recorded the Handel *G Minor Concerto* for the "First Chair" album that was made and sold for the benefit of the Philadelphia Orchestra Pension Fund. Issued in LP format by Columbia and featuring eight principal players of the orchestra, it included William Kincaid, Sol Schoenbach, Mason Jones, and Lorne Munroe, as well as Tabuteau. A novelty for its day, the pinkish-lavender cover with Adrian Siegel's medallion-shaped photos of the soloists became a familiar sight to record collectors.[2]

When the Tabuteaus finally arrived in France, Madame had her complaints: "Naturally 'La Coûtchéro' is not yet ready to receive us—it probably never will be." (They had begun to use this nickname for the Coustiéro based on the French words *coûter* and *cher*, "to be expensive.") But eventually it *was* ready. The big move took place on Tuesday, August 5, 1952, at four o'clock in the afternoon. Mme Tabuteau was very specific about the date and time when she wrote months later with the whole story: "Moved out and moved in by friend Lanza, and one should have seen the D.P.s in Lanza's truck.[3] We took great care to see that le maître Pingouin could sleep in his old bed and have <u>his</u> things around him right away, so he felt happy at his 'Coûtchéro' and was even able before the end of the summer to go by his Pingouinette without emotion."

That fall and winter she described how *he* was continuing to do battle in the Philadelphia Orchestra. "The orchestra played in New York

MARCEL TABUTEAU

yesterday. Hartford tonight. Le maître of the house returned only at dawn. He is in the eleventh week. The eleventh 'round' he says, and as he only has to do fifteen, he _should_ be arriving at the last weeks of his career—but after the enthusiasm with which he blows in that horrible stick (_sale truc_) and the beauty he gets out of it, I don't see him yet in the ranks of the pensioners. And then he is so happy to be annoying all those who are impatiently waiting, but with such patience, the day of his adieu. All this only to tell you that for news we are still and always with the same old story!! The only new things perhaps would be that his headaches are less intense, or rather the pain has moved—the crises of gout have returned. One at the Coustiéro and another on the boat, and the last about a month ago. He had to miss a rehearsal. Gout comes back, head gets better. What a man! His appetite is marvelous. He is gaining weight—especially in front——and the reeds are no good— what more can I tell you?"[4] Later in the same letter, "At the l'heure _des petits cadeaux_ [time of little gifts] I want to let you know that I would really appreciate it if you could make an enlargement for me of the photograph you took of the balcony below my window. I had not yet told you but I really like it and _du reste_ [besides] we have none of the new house."

During the next Philadelphia winter of 1953 there was more of the same. Tabuteau wrote on December 6: "Here, for me, it is always a fight to the death with the reeds. Fortunately, the tenth week has just ended and _there are not more than . . . five!_" Madame added the measured words, "_De quoi demain sera-t-il fait?_" [What will tomorrow bring?] to speak like Victor Hugo. We have tickets on a Queen—I don't know which one—leaving New York on _February 26_! I have not yet told anyone. Keep this _possible_ news for yourself. But if _he_ ever makes a _final_ and interesting decision, I'll tell you. Life on the fourteenth floor continues more or less the same and pleasant. The weather has been superb all this fall. Last Friday was the Curtis Christmas party and next Friday begins vacation. As always the cursed _séances_ of the reeds——reeds——La Coustiéro is still there and we receive regular news."

At the end of December Madame described the winding down of Tabuteau's time in Philadelphia. "Here, the grand maître has become a Pasha for the past eight days. Gets up _after_ 11 o'clock. Doesn't do anything with his day and seems perfectly happy!! Le 26 février is still

RETIREMENT IN FRANCE

until now the day of departure. *He* has given notice to the landlord of the studio and has sold *all* the contents, everything that is in there, music, cane, the grindstone, the whole lot, *en bloc,* to be able to leave with his hands in his pockets. *But* officially he has not yet said anything. Therefore until the official announcement, do not say *anything*—or believe *anything*. We'll see! But I am preparing to move as in any case we will not be keeping 1405. From time to time one must make serious decisions . . . There has been lots of music: Boston—Detroit with Paray. Le Pingouin went to hear them and also his Philadelphia with E. van Beinum who he likes very much and Philadelphia came out the winner in the tournament." Before long came the moment of Tabuteau's famous "farewell" speech to the orchestra (see chapter 17). On February 26, 1954, he sent me a telegram from New York, stating simply, "I have to believe it myself." They had really left!

A month went by before I heard from Mme Tabuteau about their departure from Philadelphia. "Heroic! To say the least. Our old Cadillac took us to N.Y. Starting out after 8 a.m. we arrived at 10 a.m. The boat was to leave at noon. In the cabin there were oboists en masse. Cognac, champagne, flowers, etc. It was *épique!*" (epic). She continued with news of their new life. "We are at la Coûtchéro, not yet definitely settled in, but happy in the sun. Warm by day, cool at night. The house is pleasant because it is *heated.* The central heating works beautifully— a miracle! The dog is big and handsome and every morning dog and master make a long walk around the countryside. So far no one misses Philadelphia and the oboe. Are you coming? Dr. Moennig wrote that you will leave for Europe in April.[5] Naturally you must bring us some precious American products that we forgot." She included a list of things for le maître: "4 *tubes* brushless shaving cream *Benex. No* other brand. If you don't keep your whole ration of cigarettes for your friends bring them to the Maestro. Pall Mall or Lucky Strike." If I was coming on the Cunard Line, "in the shop buy several *State Express* in yellow boxes of 25. Also, six boxes or more please, of Allenbury *Glycerine Black Currant Pastilles.* We love these pastilles even if they are English."

It was a big leap in lifestyle from the simple quarters of the Pingouinette to the Coustiéro with its twenty-five rooms and a tower. Originally built by a Paris aristocrat who had intended adding yet

MARCEL TABUTEAU

another wing to accommodate her large family, this sprawling tan stucco red-tile-roofed villa was the equivalent of two complete dwellings. Set among the aromatic Mediterranean pine trees, the house was designed in such a way that almost every window of its two stories faced the sea. John de Lancie once told me that he felt sure Tabuteau expected to receive eminent personalities of the music world in his splendid new home. My impression was that the Tabuteaus wanted neither a lot of company nor pupils coming to study in the summers. Madame used to say, "We are not running a hotel." Although guests were rather infrequent, Tabuteau did enjoy the company of his wife's sister, Denise, with her husband, Dr. Pierre Budin from Paris, as well as his own Toulon family, André and Augusta Tabuteau. Not long after their arrival in spring 1954, Mme Tabuteau described a visit from the Budins. "We drank well, ate well together, and the two "*docteurs*" *se sont bien eng——* (swore at each other) during their games of cards and backgammon. [Mme Tabuteau in her cultivated way did not write out the whole word *engeulé*.] Le Pingouin lost all his money.[6] The other (*Budin*) is so lucky and while all that was going on, Madame, my sister, was painting! Two good canvases of the trees. The days pass quickly and are full of nothing. But, 1: We have acquired a second dog, a love of two months, (Daring) 2: We have installed a telephone: Number 59 at Brusc. 3: The fisherman Pingouin, just today has ordered a boat. A *merveille* (marvel) naturally, which will be ready in June. One can sail and dream by moonlight." In their first year at La Coustiéro, life did perhaps have a dreamlike quality.

The Budins came again in February 1955. Madame Tabuteau brought me up to date: "No escapades since the beginning of November '54 to Monte Carlo. The Budins are here now since fifteen days. The *docteur* has also retired, (sold his practice to son Jacques), and has nothing to do now but wander about followed by his wife. No question, we now belong to the oldsters. Next week we will return to the home of the civilized. A trip to Paris. I hope to see some good plays and maybe a movie but don't even speak of music. I would never be able to drag him (*Le Pingouin*) to a concert."

In the spring of 1955, I was still in Houston but was becoming disillusioned and thinking of leaving the orchestra. In thanking me for my letters, Tabuteau said the reason I did not get much news from them was

RETIREMENT IN FRANCE

The Tabuteau's twenty-five-room villa by the sea, La Coustiéro, at La Lèque.

that "Lola" was not there to keep up his correspondence. This time, how-ever, he *did* reply: "I notice that you are a bit discouraged by the conditions and intrigues around you and you ask my advice; personally I experienced a half century of this kind of torture and I never had the *cran* (pluck) to make the decision to look for more hospitable realms. Where are you with the Fulbright? That would be an interim solution. You might even find work in Europe *but* if you then had to find another spot as first oboe in the U.S., I fear that you would have a great deal of difficulty . . . All goes well here and I am proud of myself. I know how to do nothing."

A few months later in May 1955 I did receive the Fulbright grant, arrived in Europe, and stopped by Toulon to see the Tabuteaus. They met me at the train station, and I noted that "they look as if life in

MARCEL TABUTEAU

Madame and Monsieur Tabuteau at La Coustiéro. Photo by Tofte-Hansen. Courtesy of Claus Johansen.

retirement agrees with them . . . The first thing we did was to go to a pastry shop and eat some cakes and candy. Then on to shopping for ham, cheese, vegetables, cherries etc. The emphasis is still in the same place!" On earlier visits, I had always stayed down the road in a small auberge near Le Brusc and made the hot walk up the hill to their villa. Now for the first time I was invited to stay in the house. I can still remember waking up in a second-floor bedroom, looking out the windows through the sweet-smelling pine trees toward the intense blue sea. I felt as if I were staying in Ali Khan's villa—at that time his name was synonymous with luxurious Mediterranean living! But I noticed, "even though this place is so beautiful, the Tabuteaus seem to be having their troubles." It was a problem to find satisfactory domestic help. They were so busy running about, shopping for food, closing other property deals, and there was much talk of "boundaries." A fight was going on about people who wanted to camp in the vicinity, and Tabuteau was furious that ships from the fleet in Toulon took part in naval drills in his "front yard" (the Mediterranean Sea!). I questioned whether the

RETIREMENT IN FRANCE

Tabuteaus were able to fully enjoy their new situation. He was already beginning to talk about "how wonderful it was in *Canada* in the summer so I guess they just never will be satisfied." By now I had some sense of their reactions, and although I could not "imagine a more ideal setting than this house, I wouldn't be too surprised if they'd sell the whole thing after a couple of years. They have put it in such perfect condition—hot water—[at that time still not common in that area]—all is so comfortable it could be sold to anybody—exiled royalty, Texas millionaires—or a movie star."

In the fall Tabuteau wrote about hearing Fidelio on the radio on the night of the reopening of the Vienna opera house and added news of his relatively inactive life. "Here, all goes well. I eat and drink much too much. That keeps me from attaining my ideal to melt and harmonize into the vegetable kingdom (*règne végétal*), I mean the beautiful trees that I love so much. Even though we are so lazy about writing don't be influenced by us. Write often with many details about what you are doing in Vienna." Every time I visited at the Coustiéro, it would go smoothly for the first day or two, but soon everything would revert to the old pattern. If I played a few notes for him, he vociferously made me aware of all my shortcomings. And when I was put to helping in the kitchen, he found me equally inept and roared, "How do you expect to play the oboe if you can't peel a mushroom?" Despite such traumatic moments, however, there *were* culinary compensations during these visits. The dining room at the Coustiéro was in the middle of the house situated exactly between the two sections of the villa. When seated at the long table, one looked toward the terrace and on out to the sea. Afternoon meals could last for hours. A favorite starter was melon with thin slices of *saucisson de Lyon,* a type of fine salami. Or sometimes it would simply be ripe tomatoes surrounded by piles of finely grated carrots. Tabuteau often prepared his roasts on the outdoor grill in back of the house using grapevine cuttings to make the fire and coals. The courses proceeded at a very leisurely pace and included the excellent French cheeses and wines of the region that he bought in Toulon, Sanary, or Bandol. Afterward, demitasse was served outdoors on the terrace. It was after such a lunch that I first heard about the curé in the family.

What I had foreseen almost as soon as the Tabuteaus had settled into the Coustiéro appeared to be happening. He couldn't spend all his time cooking and eating; restlessness was driving him back to the gambling tables. Sometimes he would head off at 10 p.m. after dinner for the casino at Bandol and stay until the early hours. It was not long before they began to feel that their beautiful new place was too big for them. When Tabuteau first returned to France he said he had no oboe with him and professed to not want to teach anymore. At Christmas he sent me a photo of his dogs with a note, "These are the kind of pupils I really enjoy. They obey and have faith in me." An American flutist, who played in a wind quintet with me in Vienna, asked if I would approach Tabuteau for her about lessons. He refused to consider it, saying something to the effect that, "I would only make these young people feel badly—now they are happy thinking they play well." (This had not seemed to worry him ten or twenty years earlier!) Although Tabuteau pretended to have little interest in music, it was not long before he began to sit outside on his terrace gouging cane, with an oboe and several bells lying on the table.

In 1953 Waldemar Wolsing came from Copenhagen to spend the month of July studying with Tabuteau. He had already made an earlier visit in the summer of 1950. As well as being solo oboist of the Danish National Radio Orchestra, Wolsing was an important figure in the general cultural life of Denmark. Chairman of the orchestra committee, he worked untiringly to improve conditions for his fellow musicians, gave lectures on art, nature, and literature, and once during a political crisis in Denmark even arranged for his orchestra to make a "peace mission" to the Faroe Islands. In 1949 when Eugene Ormandy came to Denmark as a guest conductor, he was favorably impressed by Wolsing's musicianship and suggested that he arrange for some lessons with Tabuteau. Ormandy knew that Tabuteau was to play in the Casals Bach Festival in the summer of 1950 and later be at his home near Toulon. As Wolsing himself described it: "He (Ormandy) liked my playing but said that he would like it more *mouillé* (liquid) and more flexible . . . I went to France to this little place up in the mountains. I stayed there six weeks! . . . I learned something different when I heard what Tabuteau

RETIREMENT IN FRANCE

Tabuteau with the two dogs he loved so much, Boss and Daring, 1957. Photo by Tofte-Hansen. Courtesy of Claus Johansen.

could do with his oboe! He showed me his way of scraping a reed—it changed everything . . . When I asked him about something I always got a completely honest and logical answer. But of course he would always begin by saying, 'C'est un grand secret!' He was like that!" It was a sign of Wolsing's open and inquiring mind that at the age of forty-five, with his established orchestral and solo career, he wholeheartedly embraced learning not only new ideas about phrasing, but was ready to make basic changes in all aspects of playing the oboe—wind and lip control and reed making. His lessons were at the Pingouinette and to him, almost as impressive as the opening of new vistas in oboe playing was the luxury of a meal on Tabuteau's terrace. Coming from the austerity of postwar Denmark, he described how "we were eating under a large tree with yellow flowers. There was some ham from Provence, red wine, and melons, so small and juicy. Tabuteau prepared the gigot himself, and afterwards we had the most delicious cheeses. Then the gardener came with a huge basket of perhaps thirty to forty peaches. Tabuteau said only four of them are ready to be eaten exactly in this

MARCEL TABUTEAU

In "retirement" Tabuteau continued to work on reeds and try oboes, often at an outdoor table at La Coustiéro, 1957. Photo by Laila Storch.

RETIREMENT IN FRANCE

quarter of an hour. He selected those four and just threw the rest, all thirty-six, away." [Mme Wolsing was shocked!]

In July 1953, Wolsing returned to La Lèque for a still more intensive period of study. This time he asked for three sessions a week. He was happy to get his favorite room again, No. 5 at the Grand Hotel in Le Brusc. Now his lessons took place at La Coustiéro and often lasted from four to five hours. A very friendly relationship was established between Tabuteau and Wolsing. For the next fifteen years Wolsing addressed letters to his "*cher maître*" and signed them as "*votre petit élève reconnaissant*" (your grateful little student) or often simply "*votre petit élève.*" For his part, Tabuteau always wrote to "Dear friend Wolsing," or "*Mon cher collègue et ami.*"

Despite Wolsing's great desire to work more frequently with Tabuteau, either due to his heavy concert schedule or for reasons of health, he could not come back for many years. However, he was so deeply influenced by Tabuteau that he arranged for several of his Danish oboe colleagues to make the trip and study in the south of France. Paul Tofte-Hansen and Erik Hovaldt were at La Coustiéro in the mid-1950s, and in 1963 Jørgen Hammergaard had lessons in Nice. Oboist Claus Johansen, who was a student of Hammergaard, considered that "because of Waldemar Wolsing, Danish oboe playing has never been the same. For a while the whole section of the National Radio Orchestra was sounding rather American. Something is still left among us second generation Tabuteau students in Denmark but now the younger players play with a different sound, more or less in the German tradition and most people use Marigaux instruments." [Tabuteau had selected Lorée oboes for them.[7]] Wolsing and his colleagues were the only European oboists who sought out Tabuteau in the twelve years of his retirement in France.

Gradually a few American pupils found their way to La Lèque. Marjorie Jackson had been there in 1950 and returned on and off before going to play in Louisville. Frank Stalzer stayed a whole winter from October 1954 until May 1955. While teaching at Louisiana State University he had taken a few lessons from John Mack in New Orleans. In an after-dinner conversation Mack told him he thought Tabuteau would be "interested in anyone who really wanted to improve himself," so Frank borrowed the necessary money and managed to get to the south

MARCEL TABUTEAU

of France. For eight months he lived in a little cabin that belonged to a farmer down the hill from La Coustiéro. He had a bedroom and a tiny kitchen but no bath, only an outhouse in back of the farmer's place. Half a century later Frank Stalzer told me about those months of his lessons. "They were on Monday afternoons in one of the downstairs rooms of the Coustiéro. I think it was because that was the day the gambling places were closed. He asked me if I had THE Book. I had brought Barret and Ferling and that's what we used the whole time. We also did a lot with numbers and there was a great deal of emphasis on articulation. Sometimes when I forgot to use numbers and just played blindly he would jump all over me. At my very first lesson he said, "Let me see your oboe." At that time I had a Laubin with a Lorée bell I had found in Wally Bhosys shop in New York . . . I'd heard about Tabuteau and his temper so when I showed him the oboe and he could see that the top and bottom joints were a Laubin and the bell was a Lorée and he asked, 'Why did you do this?' I was waiting for the lightning to strike and a hole to open up so I could fall into it and replied, 'Well, because I felt it helped the intonation and opened up the sound.' He just handed it back to me and said, 'Oh!' Sometimes I'd go in for a lesson and he'd say, 'Let me see your reed,' and then he'd scratch on it and give it back, 'Here! Play.' In a couple of instances I realized he was making the reeds worse. I think he did this deliberately just to force us to play on a reed that wasn't up to par. Once when the reeds weren't very good, I started to apologize, and he said, 'Look, any idiot can play well on a good reed. The trick is to play well on a bad reed.' Of course I know he worked constantly on reeds and he mentioned how when they went on tour some of the fellows would play golf or tennis and he had to stick with his reeds. He wouldn't allow himself to play on anything other than absolutely the best reed he could find, even if it was some little town in western Nebraska . . . About gambling? He never talked about it. His wife got sick one time and he realized there was no doctor in Le Brusc. I think he was frightened and that's when he sold his place and got the apartment in Nice."

Whether in his Philadelphia studio, a Curtis classroom, or under the pine trees at La Lèque, Tabuteau's approach to teaching had not changed. Looking back on his studies, Frank said, "I owe him so much.

RETIREMENT IN FRANCE

In one of my last lessons I asked him about the stories we've heard of people whose playing was so beautiful that the birds would stop their singing to listen and about clarinetists whose phrasing was so incredibly beautiful that the brook would stop running. Were they really as fine players as these stories have led us to believe? Tabuteau answered that when he came to America in 1905, the people who were at the *very* top of their profession *then,* would have a hard time now [specifically the wind players], and that in the next forty-five years [this would be the present], the standards would have risen that much more."[8]

Perry Bauman, a student from Curtis days, came to visit. He made the 1955 and 1958 European tours with the Philadelphia Orchestra as an extra oboist and found time to spend five days with Tabuteau. "Of course, he never stopped teaching me and I was a nervous wreck by the time I left." Later, on tour with the Toronto Symphony, Bauman felt "fortunate that the last concert was in Lyons so that I was able to fly down and see him in Nice. I took my colleague along, the second oboist, who had never met him. I had caught a bad cold in London and Tabuteau said, 'Bau*man*, what's the matter with you? Here, I'll fix you,' and he poured two straight 8 oz glasses of Scotch. Of course it did fix me! I missed the plane back to Orly airport the next morning."[9]

In the middle of May 1959 I received the last letter from the Tabuteaus headed "La Coustiéro." They were planning to leave Toulon on the night of May 17, *le jour de Pentecôte* (Pentecost), always an important spring holiday in France, in order to arrive at the Hotel Louvois in Paris the next morning. It appeared that they were giving up the Coustiéro. Mme T referred to the enormous amount of work to empty "this big house, so full of useless possessions," and was grateful that her sister Claire had come from Nice to help. For their first, and as it turned out, last, trip back to the United States, the Tabuteaus were to sail May 28 on the *Queen Mary* and arrive in New York on June 2. They were not sure of all their plans but knew that John Mack would meet them at the boat. One thing was definite; shortly after arrival, "le Pingouin" intended to head for Canada and the salmon fishing. John Mack remembered driving them from the dock in New York to Philadelphia and Tabuteau's insistence that they stop at a restaurant along the way to "get a steak for the young man." They took temporary quarters in their old home, the Drake Hotel. When I saw them there on June 9 he was busy arranging to get a car for the trip to Canada. Two weeks later Mme T wrote from Margaree Forks describing their rushed departure from Philadelphia. They had barely been able to sort out which baggage to leave in the hotel and what to take with them before they were on the road. Tabuteau, impatient as always, had not even allowed time to see the manager to secure their return lodgings. She had hoped to visit with some of her old friends but instead at 4:00 p.m. on Wednesday, "we took off at high speed through Connecticut, Maine, the frontier at Calais, to arrive in Canada the next day at 5:00 p.m. in Margaree where everyone was astonished to see us—especially Rose. [An entry from Rose's guest register for June 12, 1959 confirms how quickly they had gotten there.] We stayed for two days and then following his old custom, went to Chéticamp for the opening of the little river on the 15th. We found old friend Joe Aucoin and all his family, but either the fishing was not what it used to be, or maybe the fisherman. In any case, until now the salmon have not taken the bait. It is cold, 45°—50°, raining; the sky, gray, and closed in by mist. The river is too high and muddy, etc. etc., a disaster. I have the impression that we are on our last trip to the Margaree. Illusions are falling like ripe fruit." After Chéticamp they rented a house in Margaree Forks for two months. "You know why he needs a house . . . he wants to cook and not have fixed hours. Anywhere else one must, after all, get there more or less on time for meals—and then the meat is over done and there is always pie for dessert! Fortunately I found a woman to come at eight in the morning to clean and do the dishes . . . We'll see later on if life in the Margaree has any charm, interest and beauty but . . . *j'en doute* (I doubt it)."

There were other complaints. They had to pay seven dollars a night while staying at the Acadian Inn in Chéticamp which Mme T remarked was the same amount as in the States—in other words, for those days, expensive. And "the dining room has remained the same; one eats badly, but must not say so. The little river is about five miles from the village and once there, one still has to go about eight more miles _on foot_ to get to the fishing." By the middle of July nothing had improved. "The river continues to be miserly and so far not even the first salmon. He is beginning to be less fond of fishing! Fortunately there is 'la cuisine' to distract him. In a few minutes we are going to Inverness to look for a gigot." This fishing trip of 1959 did not turn out in the way Tabuteau had hoped. It was now eleven years since he had last been to the Margaree. Although he did find his old friends still there, the scarcity of salmon was a serious disappointment. In Philadelphia he was also somewhat disenchanted. His former colleagues were pursuing their busy lives and had little time for visiting. He was glad if he occasionally saw a former student. One day Donald Hefner had left his oboe at Hans Moennig's to be adjusted and was told to telephone at 1:00 o'clock. Don called on time and then "trudged over to Moennig's. There was Tabuteau, very cordial, who said, 'Come walk with me back to the Drake Hotel so I can talk with you.' After a block or two, we came across a rather disheveled looking newspaper salesman who recognized Tabuteau. The man greeted Tabuteau as if they were old friends and Tabuteau responded just as cordially." They walked on a bit further when Tabuteau, noticing Don's inquiring look, commented, "I like to keep good relations with ze press!"[10]

Madame Tabuteau had hoped to spend several months in Philadelphia "living like before the retirement," but in early November they left for France, this time on the *Queen Elizabeth*. From the boat Tabuteau wrote to his good friend Ralph Dieltgens referring to salmon as always with an "s" at the end. "Many thanks for your good letter which reached me just before sailing . . . I was not surprised to hear about fishing being poor for the rest of the season, but the unsuccessful scores were not altogether the Margaree's fault. *Many times* I have seen salmons at the Seal Pool, *none caught,* and I can assure you it was 100% the fishermen faults. They were walking in the river with their *famous waders deep to their neck with* the salmons *resting in two feet of water!*"

Was the sale of the Coustiéro and the return trip to the U.S. partly intended to see if they would after all prefer to "retire" to Canada, where they owned a large piece of land? But now the salmon fishing was disappointing. And only a year earlier he had said that he was "fed up with France, *French people, etc.*" The truth seemed that it was difficult for him to be really happy anywhere. After arriving in Paris, the Tabuteaus again stayed at the Louvois for about three weeks. There were "telephone calls, shopping, couturiers for new furs, dinners in restaurants, etc., etc. *une*

MARCEL TABUTEAU

valse sans arrêt—et la valse du portefeuille [A waltz without stopping and a waltz of the pocket book]. We have rented an apartment at the Résidence Négresco like last winter, but this year's is bigger and we'll have room to put all our trunks. We'll leave by train Monday night (November 30) and go directly to Nice—and later on go back to Toulon and La Lèque." In Paris they had "dined with the Silveras—the buyers of the Pingouinette. They'll be there for Christmas and maybe we will also."[11]

RETIREMENT IN FRANCE

19 TABUTEAU'S FINAL YEARS IN NICE

1959–1966

The Tabuteaus had barely settled in at the Négresco when in the middle of December they made their first return visit to the Coustiéro. They wanted to see the "new proprietor, the successor, while he was there on his way to Dakar," and Tabuteau was anxious to check on his dogs. Mme Tabuteau described in some detail the circumstances in which this trip took place, prefaced by telling me what had happened on the day following their arrival in Nice on Tuesday, December 1. The "tragedies" began with the "*raz de marée*" (a tidal wave) at Nice and the bursting of the dam with ensuing flood at Fréjus. She thought that "our old friend, Gustave Bret,"[1] and Ange Biasotto would have escaped the worst as they lived on high ground toward the outskirts of Fréjus; Ange's brother, Dante Biasotto, however, whose *établissement* (cane business) was in the valley of Fréjus Plage, had his house washed away and all his stock of cane wiped out. The world's oboists who depended on the precious cane of Fréjus would be affected by this catastrophe for years to come.

From his Domaine de Sainte-Croix, Gustave Bret wrote to me on December 6, 1959, confirming what Mme Tabuteau had surmised: "The relative high situation of our house protected us from the horror of the breaking-out of the flood waters but very near to us many people we knew well disappeared in frightful ways! I don't have to tell you more as the newspapers in the whole world are surely giving the harrowing details which are sadly only too true . . . It was on Wednesday December 2, towards 9:30 in the evening that the disaster took place. We were in my studio listening to a new phonograph record of the Mozart *Sinfonia Concertante* for violin and viola performed by Joseph and Lillian Fuchs, when there was a strange sound. Was it some large trucks in the distance? But it became a grumbling—unforgettable—that came closer, constantly louder. The lights went out. Gabriel, our farm hand, was able to call us on a direct phone line and tell us that the dam had broken . . . What to do in the dark of night in the middle of sixty-foot high water in the valley below us? Nevertheless, Gabriel went out by the Route de Cannes with three or four faithful neighbors and succeeded in saving some people who had taken refuge on the roofs of their houses. It was only the next day that one could have even a limited idea of the extent of the disaster. Since then the rain has come down without interruption undoing all that the indefatigable teams of workers have been trying to salvage." A week later, Monsieur Bret wrote again to say that as he had feared, all the cane at Dante Biasotto's had "been destroyed but the family was alive. Much of the cane from the banks of the Reyran that Dante had already cut and harvested, washed into my property but with the continuing rain I do not know if he can salvage it."

The Tabuteaus rented a car to drive from Nice to Le Brusc. (He had gotten rid of the two cars he owned and had not yet decided what type of new automobile to buy.) Mme Tabuteau described their trip. "The morning we left was nice but very, very, cold and barely six kilometers from Nice we ran into snow, a lot of snow, and icy roads. But the 'stubborn one' kept on going! It was a difficult, in fact hair-raising, trip, but the 'gods' were good to us. In spite of everything, numerous jammed roads, and frequent long waits, (I thought we were going to have to spend the night outside on the road—thank goodness the car was heated), by nightfall we arrived at Le Brusc. We decided to stay in a little hotel by the post office, *Chez Francis,* where the food is good. We only finally managed to get there because after St. Raphael, the roads were clear. Yes, but at 6:00 a.m.

TABUTEAU'S FINAL YEARS IN NICE

the next day, there was snow at Le Brusc and all around the whole countryside. It was so cold in this hotel that is only good for the summer. *He* swore never to return. I did not think it possible to see so much snow on the Côte d'Azur—and to be so cold. After the snow, came a deluge of rain for more than twenty-four hours, but Le Pingouin went up to La Lèque just the same. He saw everybody—the proprietor, his old caretaker, Jean, the neighbors, and his dogs. He was pleased enough I think, and found La Lèque beautiful as ever."

Three days later the Tabuteaus managed to get back as far as Toulon. They were afraid to be marooned in Le Brusc and left as soon as the sun came out. After a brief stop to see André and Augusta, they continued toward Fréjus, where they looked for the Biasottos. "We found Dante and his family still alive and full of courage, but very beaten down by this misfortune and with little hope of any financial help. As you and I know, it is always those who have nothing, the simple people, the good ones, the honest ones—his type—who suffer. For everyone who knows oboe cane, this is a disaster. I don't think much is left. Fortunately, Mother Nature recovers." At the end of her letter Mme T added, "The Pingouin says, 'Above all *keep* your cane—preciously. Do not sell it!'" He knew I had a large supply. On every trip to the Var during the past ten years, I had always gone to Fréjus and picked out top-quality cane. Eventually he asked me to send him a couple of kilos back to France.

The Tabuteaus were happy to return to their comfortable apartment in Nice. They had now more or less settled in at the Résidence Négresco on the Promenade des Anglais and seemed to be enjoying their "new" life, which was actually closer to their "old" life at the Drake Hotel in Philadelphia. Mme Tabuteau even compared their apartment of two rooms and a kitchen to the one they had rented at the Drake in the summer of 1959. It gave them the convenience of being in their own home but with the services of a big hotel—and the price was exactly the same. She was glad to have a maid come for two hours every day to do the housekeeping, and they both were pleased with the closets and storage space as "he was tired of seeing all the suitcases." Since the beginning of their trip to Canada the previous summer, they had been on the move for over half a year. Tabuteau never stopped thinking about his friends in Canada and the salmon fishing. In April 1960 he wrote to thank Ralph Dieltgens for a copy of the *Atlantic Salmon Journal* and added that he would love to go fishing with him in Spain. He said he had even made inquiries about fishing in Norway, but "nothing there like the old Margaree."

Eventually, life began to take on a certain rhythm, albeit a leisurely one. Tabuteau was again gouging cane and making reeds, always trying to find what Mme T referred to as the "unreachable note." He taught an occasional student and at night, with no concerts to play, made his regular visits to the local "Usine," the casino of Nice. During the summer of 1960 they made a few short trips around the region. Then finding the roads too crowded for driving, they decided to take the train for a two-week visit to Paris, where they stayed at their old *pied à terre,* the Hotel Louvois. Félix, the concierge, still presided at the front desk, and their only disappointment was "the bad weather, cold and rainy, which made going out for festive evenings in the Bois de Boulogne impossible."

By August 1960 they were still at the Négresco, but now in a large studio with kitchen. The only serious drawback was the noise from the street. They had already moved from the dark north side and were planning to move again in September to a quieter part of the building where they would have more space. They appreciated the central location with the ease of going out at night, and they liked having a balcony with fresh air blowing in from the Mediterranean. Warm days and cool evenings made summer in Nice very pleasant. In the afternoon Tabuteau often sat in the sun on a bench along the Promenade while waiting for the opening hour of the "Usine." In the nearby market he found "excellent fish, as good or even better than at Le Brusc," and everything else he needed to cook delicious meals. For awhile that summer he had thought of going fishing in France, but when he learned it would be necessary to rent his own section of a river in an unknown area long in advance and find a place to live, he decided it was "not his style—not enough freedom," and gave up the idea. They did not go anywhere, but Mme Tabuteau found plenty to do in Nice and was never bored. She noted the many concerts being given along the Riviera: "At the palace in Monaco all the same people, Casadesus, Isaac Stern—only Casals is missing, but the day will come." Tabuteau followed his routine of blowing the oboe and making reeds by day and going to the casino at night.

TABUTEAU'S FINAL YEARS IN NICE

It was a rare diversion when Philadelphia Orchestra harpist Marilyn Costello and her husband, Daniel Dannenbaum, came by Nice to visit. With them were conductor Efrem Kurtz and his wife, flutist Elaine Shaffer, whom Tabuteau remembered well from Curtis wind classes of the 1940s. They had dinner in a hilltop village where the chef cooked on an outdoor wood fire as Tabuteau had done at the Coustiéro. The excellent food, wine, and conversation made for a convivial evening. According to Mme T, "Le Pingouin was in form, in good humor and amused everyone." No doubt he relished this now rare opportunity of reminiscing and joking with musical colleagues.

Only a few months later in November, they made yet another move, this time leaving the Résidence Négresco and taking a sixth-floor apartment at the Miramar, 111 Promenade des Anglais. On February 1961, "projects for the future are not yet ripe," but aside from a few minor bouts with health problems, they were continuing to enjoy life in Nice. The winter was mild. Their new apartment was flooded by sunshine, and they had a view of the sea and the airport. Tabuteau loved watching the planes take off and land, likening them to one of his favorite comparisons: the "take off and landing" required to produce a perfect note on the oboe. He decided that their new location "might even be better than the Coustiéro." At least it was more "*pratique*" (convenient). However, as at the Négresco, he complained about "the noise of all the people and the trucks." They spent a day in Cannes with the Bonades, but Mme Tabuteau was finding it difficult to arrange get-togethers, even with old friends, as he did not want to budge. She felt that although they were comfortable in their sixth-floor apartment, it was foolish to spend another whole summer there. He had again written to Ralph Dieltgens about Canada. "Unfortunately for me I don't think I will make the trip this year. I realize (to console myself) the fishing there will never be like during the war when the salmons [in his usual plural form] came to the Margaree in great numbers and fishermen were few. Nevertheless, I know the beautiful country is there with the lovely people, not like here where I feel like being in the jungle with ugly wild beasts around . . . Don't fail to write to me about you, the Margaree and . . . . . . the fishing. Affectionate thoughts to all your family—the children, and old friends." Months went by, and they still had no definite plans. Tabuteau

MARCEL TABUTEAU

sat on his balcony looking at the sea and absorbing the sun. A few visits from American friends broke the monotony. Several Philadelphia Orchestra violinists who were traveling along the Côte d'Azur stopped in to see him, and the de Lancies came with their two children. In October, the sudden death of their sister-in-law, André's devoted wife Augusta, was a shock to both Tabuteaus. They rushed to Toulon when they heard that she had suffered a stroke that totally paralyzed her left side. A niece who was a nurse came from Bordeaux, but only a week later Augusta passed away. Tabuteau tried to help his brother reorder his life. The disappointments that come with old age were piling up, and the loss of this close relative caused Mme Tabuteau to reflect that his or her own *départ* might arrive unexpectedly. She said they were going to make an effort, or at least "think about," organizing their affairs.

On July 2, 1962, Tabuteau celebrated his seventy-fifth birthday. Madame Tabuteau referred to it as the "day of the arrival on the planet of the famous T." In the morning they were awakened by a cable from old orchestra colleagues. There were messages from Hans Moennig and their faithful friend Jane Hill, the Curtis registrar, and I had sent a card with a little "poem" which seemed to please him.

ODE à la MODE

In order to fittingly celebrate
The advent of such an illustrious date
75 oboists, (you've surely trained more)
Should take up their oboes, (no need of a score)
And play in crescendo, 1-9 would be best,
Happy Birthday to him who has taught us to know
That music is more than just do-re-mi-do.

But in lieu of a concert of dubious worth
We wish him instead a day filled with mirth
May he eat, drink, and be merry
From morning 'till night
Enjoy life's real pleasures with all of his might
Let others have speeches and tributes galore,
It bolsters the ego and fulfills their needs,
They think they're important, but
they never made
REEDS

TABUTEAU'S FINAL YEARS IN NICE

Mme T commented that now he had "joined the Club of . . . Antiquities."

In December of that same year I saw the Tabuteaus for the first time since their 1959 visit to the U.S. On my way back from a tour of the Soviet Union with the Robert Shaw Chorale, I left the plane in Glasgow and went down to Nice by train. Now I could see for myself how their current living style compared with the years at the Pingouinette and the Coustiéro. It was only a couple of weeks before Christmas. The air was slightly crisp, and the streets of Nice were animated and cheerful. With shop windows full of colorful displays and luxury items, it was a sharp contrast to the drab storefronts I had just seen in the Soviet Union. Mme Tabuteau took me shopping and bought shiny foil Christmas tree ornaments, French children's books, records, and a beautiful red velvet dress for my three-and-a-half-year-old daughter, Aloysia. She remembered seeing Aloysia as a baby in 1959 intently listening to the sound of the oboe and wondered, "might she have the 'misfortune' to become an oboist?" Perhaps she would be relieved to know that Aloysia is a violinist! And she would surely be pleased that Aloysia's daughter Sophie wore the same red velvet dress at Christmas forty years later when she was three and a half! During that visit I took color slides that have been seen by many people. In one, Tabuteau, wearing a black and white checkered flannel shirt, is holding his oboe while standing on the balcony in the winter sunshine. In another, he is sitting at a table surrounded by tools, cane shavings, and several oboe bells, proving as Mme Tabuteau once said, that he could "still be amused by making reeds that sound as if they could not be surpassed by *Dieu le Père*" (God the Father).

Since the Tabuteaus' return to France, I had been sending them packages of American items they missed—everything from Miss Saylor's Coffee-ets (a hard candy they were fond of) to Band-Aids. Mme Tabuteau loved getting boxes from Bonwit Teller or Wanamaker's, where she used to shop. In the summer of 1963 before making what would prove to be my last visit to the Tabuteaus, I asked if there was anything they needed. She replied that this time there was nothing to bring: "He has enough aspirin for five years and *moi des pansements*" (Band-Aids for me). Later I learned that they had enlisted another "shopper." A young violist and aspiring conductor from the Philadelphia area, Marc

In 1962 I took advantage of the bright December sunshine in Nice to photograph Tabuteau on his balcony. Photo by Laila Storch.

Mostovoy, had begun to study with Tabuteau in France during the summer of 1962 and was taking care of the errands. Earlier in the year he had already shipped huge quantities of aspirin and Band-Aids. How did Marc Mostovoy (who was only nineteen at the time) find his way to Nice and convince Tabuteau to give him lessons? Indeed, if not for a valuable piece of advice he had received from Philadelphia horn player Ward Fearn, he may never have gotten past Tabuteau's doorstep. While Marc was studying at Temple University, he also took some lessons from Fearn, a longtime Tabuteau devotee. After a year Fearn suggested that Marc "study with the master himself." He wrote to Tabuteau but, typically, never received a definitive response. Marc described what happened next: "Not one to accept defeat, I took it upon myself to go unannounced to Nice and let the chips fall where they may. Fearn had armed me with the 'key' to success—a bottle of Haig and Haig Scotch Pinch Bottle which I brought with me in June of 1962." After quickly freshening up from the overnight train trip from Calais to Nice, Marc went directly to Tabuteau's apartment at 111 Promenade des Anglais.

TABUTEAU'S FINAL YEARS IN NICE

Tabuteau holding oboe with Lorée oboe case on the table in the Nice apartment, December 1962.

When there was no response, Marc was heartbroken. "Perhaps he had gone away for the summer? I was just about to leave, when an angry voice from inside said in French "Who is it?" Obviously I had waked him up, and he wasn't happy about it." Marc managed a few words of introduction, who he was, and why he had come. After he referred to Ward Fearn's letter, Tabuteau opened the door. "He was in his bathrobe and scowling. He told me that he had no time and to go away. Just as he was closing the door, I quickly handed him the Pinch bottle of Haig and Haig . . . the situation changed dramatically. He was obviously very pleased with this gift, and told me to return that afternoon at 2 or 3 o'clock and we would discuss the matter further. That's how it all started."[2]

Marc was exuberant about the beginning of his work with Tabuteau and the beauties of Nice. He wrote to his parents that Tabuteau had agreed to see him every few days and that "the climate is really perfect. It never rains and it is always sunny but there is a nice breeze. There are

MARCEL TABUTEAU

palm trees and other tropical plants everywhere. I have been working hard and practicing my viola every day. Madame Tabuteau even went with me to try and find a place for me to live which isn't too expensive." By July 18 Marc was bubbling over in his admiration for Tabuteau. "He has a great mind and is a great musician. The only trouble is that some of what he says is too far above me and I don't understand what he means. He says that this is only natural and I will have to think about the ideas he gives me for years, and that someday I will understand. He says he was about forty years old when he started to understand what music was about . . . They are so nice to me. He even recommended that I go and take a few courses at the Conservatory. He has a terrific sense of humor and says that I should come to him and learn what to do and then go to the Conservatory and learn what *not* to do."[3]

After Marc returned to the States he continued to send the everyday items that Tabuteau wanted from Philadelphia, but he now added the scores of oboe concertos by Vivaldi, Handel, Marcello, Albinoni, Telemann, and Cimarosa. In November he suggested "It would be so wonderful if you could record some of those beautiful oboe works. What an enormous contribution to music it would be. Now that records have been perfected, I think they could really do justice to your playing . . . when you did most of your earlier recording the equipment was not highly developed enough to pick up the great sensitivity of your playing."

Marc spent the next two summers in Nice absorbing Tabuteau's philosophy and as many of his musical ideas as possible. Tabuteau always said he did not like to write letters, but he corresponded frequently with Marc Mostovoy thanking him "for his interest and scouting for oboe concerti." Full of enthusiasm at the thought that Tabuteau might consider recording some of these solos, Marc told him of his plans to "form a first class chamber ensemble which would be at your disposal and which could accompany you whenever you would want to play a concerto. These would all be younger musicians who will listen to you and respect what you have to say and who could be taught to play the way that you want them to." Toward the end of May 1963 Marc telephoned Tabuteau, who replied by mail, "As always, found myself deficient when talking on the phone, you must now be convinced of that . . . I probably will be at Nice this summer and of course you would be welcome but

TABUTEAU'S FINAL YEARS IN NICE

I fear I already told you all about my secrets; I came to the conclusion the only one now for you to approach would be Almighty God (!) but you are indeed too young . . . to afford that." In a P.S. he requested and gave measurements for "an abdominal hernia belt, if you decide after all to come." On June 19 he thanked Marc for sending the Marcello Concerto. "You are really a nice boy. I knew the work and had it in my folio but gave it away to a friend of mine when I retired. It has a splendid slow movement and is altogether very oboistic. I am looking forward to the pleasure to see you again but somehow I regret I did not have the courage to warn you I am not at present in the mood to philosophize about music and if you come you will have to take me as I am. Anyhow, you will have the international musicologues 'vacationing' in Nice this summer and I feel you will be rewarded." (Marc was planning to attend classes at the *Académie de Musique d'Été* in Cimiez). In another P.S. he asks, "If you could bring me a pyjamas, 'cotton' striped bleue (*sic*) and white, not too loud, Size D, it means the largest size . . . Thanks MT."

Despite Tabuteau's warning that he was not "in the mood to philosophize about music," Marc Mostovoy and others, too, would have the benefit of Tabuteau's counsel in the summer of 1963. From time to time young oboists would either write or turn up in Nice hoping for lessons. David Dutton, who was in Salzburg with the Oberlin "Study Year Abroad" program, had driven down to Nice in November 1962. He arranged to come back the following summer bringing another oboist, Don Baker, with him. They often had their lessons in the novel setting of Tabuteau's balcony. When he grew impatient, he would yell "*merde*" and throw pencils over the railing. Other times he would say "sh-sh," not wishing Mme Tabuteau to hear, and with a sheepish look sneak quietly into the apartment to get a "booster" of Scotch. Certainly one of their most colorful sessions must have been the occasion when Tabuteau decided the two young men should stand at opposite ends of the balcony, while from the middle he gesticulated and conducted as they played the *Allegretto grazioso* movement of Brahms Second Symphony.[4]

Another young American oboist drove to Nice in 1963. Joseph Robinson was at the University of Cologne on a Fulbright scholarship. As the proud possessor of a new Volkswagen Bug, he headed for Paris on his spring break to visit the Lorée Company. There, he was given

MARCEL TABUTEAU

Marcel Tabuteau's address, and in the company of another student, he headed south. He felt that his former studies with both Ralph Gomberg and John Mack should provide him with an introduction to the retired master. Arriving at the apartment door he found no one at home but was told by the maid to return at 8 p.m. When he came back, he was surprised to find the table set and ready for dinner. Tabuteau's first comment was "you don't look like an oboe player!" He was dismayed to see two young boys instead of the one he was expecting. Fortunately, they had already eaten an ample meal in a restaurant, so that being told they would have to "divide up the food" was more of a relief than a sacrifice. An awkward silence was broken when Joe pulled out a list of cane growers he had been given by John Mack. Tabuteau became very animated, making comments such as, "you won't get any cane there. This man has been dead for twenty years. That one is in the furniture business," and so forth. When Joe showed him a kilo of tube cane he had bought from the Paris dealer Maurice Deriaz and stashed away in his car, Tabuteau was eager to try it. Now an "expedition" to Fréjus was quickly arranged for the next morning. The boys were told to pretend to be Germans. Tabuteau apparently believed that being American could hinder their chances of getting good cane. They visited four Var villages and by mid-afternoon were in Cogolin. This "cane day" ended with Tabuteau agreeing that Robinson could come back in July for lessons.

The five weeks that Joseph Robinson spent studying with Tabuteau revolutionized his concept of what is required to become a good oboe player. Having been given excellent reeds by John Mack made his early oboe years less of a struggle than that faced by many students. But now in Nice, after a rather mild and friendly beginning, he was soon subjected to the "Tabuteau treatment" and had to cope with huge adjustments in thinking and practice. Saying, "I think I know the cure but you won't like it," Tabuteau told a little story: "Consider all the tiny mollusks in the sea: how they squirm from the invading grains of sand. A few will become pearls. It's up to you to make the pearls. I am not going to withhold the irritant." The application of the "prescription" addressed questions of embouchure, angle of the reed, wind pressure, the concept of not blowing directly in the reed, articulation, and "scaling" of notes. Joe was required to practice in front of a mirror using a reed "adjusted on a tube of cane" in lieu of the oboe itself, making sure there was no neck movement. He wrote out the short exercises which, if followed religiously, were guaranteed to bring exceptional results. These lessons illuminated for Joe, as they had for many others, the possibility of a range of expression not previously considered achievable on the oboe. When Robinson returned to the United States, he wavered between music and academic studies. Music won out, and after six years as first oboist of the Atlanta Symphony Orchestra, he joined the faculty of the new North Carolina School of the Arts. From 1978 until 2005 he was the highly respected principal oboist of the New York Philharmonic.[5]

In Nice, with easy access to the post office, Tabuteau continued to do some "business." Already several decades earlier, he had attempted to establish a cane enterprise with his brother in Toulon and had gone so far as to have stationery printed with the heading "Frères Tabuteau." They would sell not only oboe cane but also, as is usual along the Côte d'Azur, *cannes à pêche* (fishing rods) and other items made from *le roseau*.[6] Perhaps because the "Brothers Tabuteau" had started out as string players and André continued to play violin in local theaters, Tabuteau never lost an opportunity to acquire a violin or two to sell in Philadelphia. I hauled one back for him in 1948, and he was still organizing "deals" later on during the Casals Festivals. From his earliest years in the United States, he sold oboes to his students and colleagues; it was a "sideline" he never abandoned. Long after his death, Mme Budin gave me a packet of papers and photographs that, aside from a shopping list for groceries and his 1965 entry card for the casino at Monte Carlo, included a pile of his personally filled-out receipts for oboes or bundles of cane mailed to various oboists in the United States. He was also sending huge quantities of cane to the oboists in Denmark. In June 1963 he let Waldemar Wolsing know about a shipment of "3000 pieces selected and prepared for gouging for 200 dollars." Tabuteau's brother in Toulon did all the work of preparing this cane that Tabuteau referred to as "a part of the reserve I had in mind to take along for the last journey to charm St Peter." In the same letter he asked for the precise dates he should expect "your colleague, Mr. Jørgen Hammergaard" and adds "will gladly do my best to help him if he comes to Nice." Tabuteau's letters to Wolsing continued on August 3 with "It was for me a great pleasure to meet Mr. Hammergaard with whom I had a too short but interesting time. I regret you are so busy and unable to afford a visit. I would have loved to see you again and discuss little problems which are so dear to us." Although Tabuteau missed seeing Wolsing in 1963, he expressed the wish "if you could arrange to come to Nice in the spring . . . it will be marvelous because I have to leave for the States about [the] end of May to coach a woodwind group for six weeks in the summer. Whenever you decide to come it will be [a] joy to see you again and '*chat*' about oboes and. . . . reeds." Tabuteau never failed to include his "meilleurs souvenirs à vos charmant collègues." Nothing, even periodic attacks of his old enemy, the gout, would stop his trips to search for cane. On one trip to Fréjus to see Dante Biasotto he found no cane ready for him. Mme wrote that he "worked like a '*mercenaire*' (mercenary) cutting and preparing the stalks himself and came back with some good cane—but also the gout. Dante invited him to eat dinner with them—and the main dish was '*sanglier,*' wild boar—far too rich for him but of course he could not refuse their hospitality."

In August 1963 on my last visit to the Tabuteaus, I traveled with my husband, Martin Friedmann, and our little daughter, Aloysia. We rented a Deux Chevaux (two horsepower) Citroën in Paris. After a stop in Molineuf to see Madame Budin, we bounced on down to Nice. We wanted to take the Tabuteaus out to lunch at the best possible place, perhaps the Hotel de Paris in Monaco, but he would not hear of it. According to him, the food was not good anywhere. "I will cook," he announced. The next day while he was preparing lunch, I took the very special photo of Tabuteau standing on his balcony at noon in apron and pajamas, playing a folk tune on the oboe to the enchantment of four-year-old Aloysia. After a superb meal, the afternoon gradually came to an end, and the *maître* prepared to leave for the casino. Martin, long fascinated by the legendary gambling stories, asked if he could go along. We decided that he would be limited to playing, and probably losing, the sum of $20.00. The next day I learned what happened. By the time they had been at the casino for about a half hour, Tabuteau had gone through all of his money and asked to borrow some from Martin. Martin reluctantly gave him $5.00 and then soon lost what he had left at the roulette table. The next day he was upbraided by Tabuteau, who,

TABUTEAU'S FINAL YEARS IN NICE

while handing him a five-dollar bill, said, "You see, if you had loaned me all of your $20.00 you would still *have* your money!" Now Martin had his own "Tabuteau gambling story," albeit simpler than one of decades earlier when Tabuteau and his nephew Jacques Budin went out together after the funeral of Mme Tabuteau's older brother, Jean-Louis André. They had rather too much to drink and before continuing on to the "Usine" Tabuteau gave Jacques his wallet for safekeeping. Seeing that it contained 800,000 francs, a huge sum at that time (it was during the postwar inflation of 400 francs to the dollar), Jacques held back half and handed 400,000 francs to Tabuteau. The next day when Jacques returned the half he had kept, Madame Tabuteau, rather than being pleased, was furious. She scolded her nephew, saying, "You had no business not to let him lose his own money!" Such were the unpredictable reactions of both Tabuteaus![7]

Already in the fall of 1963, Tabuteau was responding to Marc Mostovoy's suggestion that he think about making some solo recordings. Despite Marc's opinion "that the oboe you have now is a beautiful instrument," Tabuteau felt, as always, that before taking on such a project, he must have something better. In September he wrote to Marc: "I expect to go to Paris within a couple of weeks. If I find the instrument I am looking for, will let you know; all my future activities depend on that." Two years later Tabuteau was assiduously practicing the opening bars of the second movement of the Cimarosa Concerto in a variety of rhythmic patterns.[8]

Always thinking of a return to Nova Scotia, in December 1963 Tabuteau wrote to Ralph Dieltgens: "Now the chances are that we could have again a few good days at the Margaree next summer. A group of talented young artists invited me to coach them for six weeks, so I selected Cape Breton, the Margaree, with all my old friends, as my headquarters to work with them . . . Will be quite busy with the group from the middle of July until the end of August . . . We are looking forward to the pleasure to see you all and to the good time we will have together . . . fine fishing or . . . not." The "talented young artists" were the members of the Soni Ventorum Wind Quintet, at that time Felix Skowronek, William McColl, James Caldwell, Robert Bonnevie, and Arthur Grossman, resident at the Conservatorio de Musica de Puerto Rico. In a letter to Marc

MARCEL TABUTEAU

Tabuteau on the balcony of his apartment in August 1963 playing a folk tune for Aloysia Friedmann, age four. She is wearing a pink dress and holding a toy cat that Mme Tabuteau had sent her from France. Photo by Laila Storch.

TABUTEAU'S FINAL YEARS IN NICE

Mostovoy, Tabuteau mentioned his plans for Nova Scotia. "How about you coming along? I am looking forward to meet the group and the talented oboe player you know" (James Caldwell). But only a few weeks later, in early January 1964, he wrote, "The meeting with the Porto Rico musicians is——OFF . . . their schedule and dates interfered with Nova Scotia. So if friend Marc wishes to see me he will have to come to Nice again. Of course he will be always welcome P.S. I only hope you did not herald my going to the States too much."

As Mme Tabuteau expressed it, aside from the few trips to Paris, they had not "budged" in the past four years. The Tabuteaus declined to accompany the Budins on an organized tour to the U.S. by plane. Mme Tabuteau was not interested in such a short visit but said that if *he* should decide to return for the salmon fishing, they, "the antiques," would go by ship. Although the 1959 trip had not been a great success, he was still thinking about Canada and the fishing. At Christmas 1964, in mixed French and English, Tabuteau sent one of his last messages to his friends in Nova Scotia. "Noël 1964—To old friend Ralph, Mayme, and the lively charming daughters! Our best wishes and affectionate thoughts. If you have time please let me know about the Margaree salmon fishing in the summer 1964. It is always good to think of all of you and the wonderful times we had together." For Tabuteau, Cape Breton, the Margaree, and all it stood for, would always remain a dream of happy earlier days.

Tabuteau's letters of 1964 and 1965 to both Marc Mostovoy and Waldemar Wolsing increasingly refer to health problems. On February 23, 1964, to Marc: "Again and again thanks for your devotion and faithfulness . . . About our health, Mrs. T and I are going to—pieces. Last December when in Paris Mrs. T fell flat on her back from a taxi; as for me, for more than two weeks I have been unable to dress, write, cook, etc. as my right hand was paralyzed with rheumatism: so you can easily picture what is going on at the Miramar. Fortunately the Winter has been very sunny." On June 4, 1964, "I hope this will reach you before you sail. I should have written sooner but had lots of trouble with my health. Nevertheless I hope to manage to be in good shape to welcome you . . . The sick man would like you to bring him *two boxes* of 100 Bayer Aspirin. Also to call Moennig on 21st Street between Chestnut and Market. Don't forget to forward my warmest greetings and ask him for three plates (*plaques*) to scratch reeds."

In 1965 Tabuteau became ever more concerned about getting his ideas onto paper. To Marc he wrote, "We both often think about you and I am delighted you still believe your meeting me was worthwhile . . . but . . . keep the secrets to yourself because if I ever write a short essay about the T. system I would not enjoy to be accused of plagiarism!" According to Marc, Tabuteau had once said, "Before someone else lays claim to my ideas! . . . Now don't forget I should receive soon from you a written composition about our discussions on musical aesthetic. I remember what my celebrated teacher told me: 'If you bring a healthy looking brute on the stage without any makeup *he will look cadaveric* under the stage lights.' I am afraid I will have to give up whiskey. I am too often on crutches. Your old friend won't be so expensive."[9] A month later, on March 26, Tabuteau reminds Marc about writing the paper, "Thanks for your last but you forgot to say anything about my *request* concerning the little essay, composition, summing up our conversations inspired by you and the celebrated brand of Scotch. I want you to do your best about it, or, would have someone else to do it—with—perhaps a cheaper brand." This remark, no doubt an example of "Tabuteau humor" referring to the high-quality expensive Scotch Marc had been bringing him, could also be seen as a type of "threat" to take away the project. Marc had expressed concern about the daunting task of putting these "conversations" into suitable form, and on April 26 Tabuteau wrote again, "Don't be upset about the 'Essay.' All I expect from you is a check up, 'memorandum,' of all I tried to inoculate you with, 'musically speaking.'"

Unable to travel to Nice in 1965, Marc sent a cable and gift that arrived exactly on July 2, Tabuteau's birthday. "How could you time it so perfectly? Your friend Gnam (Adrian Gnam) brought me the belt. I hope someday to make good for all you are doing for an old man going to pieces . . . I am going to weigh the question of going to the States and take advantage of your sponsorship. Do you really think they would be interested in what I have to offer?" By then, Marc had organized Concerto Soloists, a sixteen-piece string orchestra with harpsichord, ready for Tabuteau to perform with and conduct.

TABUTEAU'S FINAL YEARS IN NICE

Adrian Gnam had indeed arrived in Nice in the summer of 1965. He had been on tour with the Cleveland Orchestra under George Szell for almost two months in the Soviet Union and in Western Europe. Again, it was the Philadelphia horn player Ward Fearn who suggested that Adrian should try to study with Tabuteau. But Adrian was given somewhat more "coaching" in his preparation for the "assault on the citadel" of Nice. From Paris he wrote to Marc that "I have purchased three bottles of Russian Cognac for him and will buy two more bottles, one from Fearn, of Grand Marnier, and also one bottle of Haig and Haig as you suggest." Adrian had also been entrusted by Marc to deliver the very personal gift of the much-needed hernia belt. Marc was relieved when a "progress report" arrived from Adrian beginning with July 9: "Tomorrow afternoon after 2:00 I'll pay a visit to Tabuteau . . . Wish me luck. I'll continue this after I see M. T." On July 10 he was getting closer: "Went to Tabuteaus this afternoon. He was out, but his wife welcomed me and asked me to come back Monday at 2:00 p.m. which I shall do with fingers crossed." Adrian obviously felt that the recounting of these maneuvers merited the exact time of day: "July 12th noon . . . Well, it is done . . . M. Tabuteau accepted me for lessons and we started today 'from the beginning.' He made a reed for me and, oh— what a reed! This man is truly a master. I can't thank you enough for writing to him. I gave him your gift and also mine which he was very happy to receive."[10] In replying to wish Adrian "a very happy and rewarding summer," Marc added, "Practice well and absorb as much as you can of what he tells you for you might never get it again."

Years later I heard about this auspicious beginning from Adrian Gnam himself. When Tabuteau opened the door of his apartment, he had immediately said, "Ah, Monsieur *Ahg*-nam, I've been expecting you." (And *Monsieur Ahg-nam* he was to remain in Tabuteau's roll call of names!) Thinking there would be many oboists competing for Tabuteau's attention, Adrian was surprised to find that he was the only student. For the next eight weeks he went to the Miramar almost every day, spending from 11 o'clock in the morning until late at night with Tabuteau. "Time out," as he put it, only for Scotch, dinner, and roulette. They conversed in French, and Tabuteau must have found him a congenial companion, not only someone who was eager to learn but a

MARCEL TABUTEAU

willing "foil" or "sounding board" for expounding his ideas. Tabuteau always seemed at his enthusiastic best while talking about how to form a musical phrase, explain his numbers, or any of the principles to which he had given so much thought. Reminiscing that "there isn't a day I don't think of that man," Adrian described how he had worked on the obligatory Barret studies and reeds as well as transposing and reading from different clefs. Learning that Adrian had an interest in conducting, Tabuteau required him to sing extensively and said he "must be able to sing everything right." At 4 p.m. they stopped playing or gouging cane, and Adrian would pour a glass of Scotch for Tabuteau. Johnny Walker Black Label was the preferred drink at that time, and Adrian made sure to bring him a new bottle every few days.

Tabuteau was going through the orchestral excerpts that would eventually become "The Art of the Oboe" LP album, and Adrian was able to help him work with the tape recorder. It was a large reel-to-reel Sony machine brought by Wayne Rapier. In comparison with later models, this new equipment with its separate microphone was cumbersome and a challenge for Tabuteau to use. He nevertheless succeeded in getting a quite a large amount of material onto tape.

Adrian especially remembered hearing parts of *Coppélia*, arpeggios and the famous high "C." After getting up into the third octave Tabuteau would say, "Not bad for a man of seventy-eight." One time out on the balcony he proclaimed, "I will make the ground shake." Then he played his favorite arpeggiated figure, and just as he reached the lofty note, there came the great roar of a plane taking off from the nearby Nice Airport. Tabuteau exulted, "See, I told you I could make the ground shake!" Before Adrian left Nice, Tabuteau gave him one of his old French gouging machines that he had adjusted by pushing French francs under the posts, even as he had done thirty years earlier in the United States with dimes. From January 1965 until the end of the 1967–68 season Adrian Gnam shared the solo oboe position in the Cleveland Orchestra with Robert Zupnik. Later, he also became a conductor and director of the music program at the National Endowment for the Arts.[11]

By now the Tabuteaus had been in the same sixth-floor apartment of the Miramar for almost five years. Then in August 1965 there occurred

TABUTEAU'S FINAL YEARS IN NICE

what Mme T referred to as "*un désastre*" (a disaster). For some unknown reason they were required to move. He wrote, "We are in a mess here as you can imagine. We must vacate for September 1." They were to take a third-floor studio apartment until the end of September and then look for something better. In the middle of September, Tabuteau laments, "I hardly survived the ordeal of moving end of August, same operation to be performed end of this month. Will still be at the Miramar until further notice." A postscript from Mme T, mostly in English (unusual for her), stated that "*le grand homme* [the great man] is 'dejected' and in a bad mood. Let us hope for better days." In October Tabuteau wrote to Marc of his distress. "I have been so upset by having to move twice in a month. I miss the balcony very much."

Just at this time I heard from my flutist friend Elaine Shaffer, telling of her ten-day visit in Nice and how wonderful it had been to see the Tabuteaus almost every day. She played for him and was "inspired" by all the things he told her. "It was not really anything new or different from what we'd heard twenty years earlier at Curtis, but the ideas seem to be more comprehensible than they were when I was in the class. And then, I *never* had him concentrating on just *me.* Sometimes when I would arrive he would look pale and tired but as soon as he began talking about music he would be transformed . . . One day we took him a few of the Japanese felt pens he liked. When he first saw them he said, 'Do these make a *crescendo,* or are they like those horrible ball-points'? So he took a card in the restaurant and wrote '*Merde T.*' on it."

Elaine later wrote to tell of something that he said could be considered the "Tabuteau Coat of Arms." "The three things he gave me were a micrometer, an *eating* fork, and a little paint brush. The fork was to explain that you play *between* the prongs and not on the points, and the brush was to make the *curves* in the music: up and down motion, and of course, the micrometer, as he often used to mention, for precise 'scaling' of the notes . . . He suddenly got the idea that these three things contained *all* the secrets in music, so he put them together in a little plastic bag and tied it with a blue ribbon from the chocolates we had taken to Mme T from *Marquise de Sévigné.*"

During Elaine's visit "Tabuteau had been drinking heavily, but Efrem [Kurtz] had some influence on him to drink less . . . He wanted Efrem to teach him how to win at the casino but he is a hopeless case—he jumps from one table to the other. Efrem did help him though, and he *won* on the last three days by going home before he lost it all again. He told so many amusing stories of the old days, with Kincaid and Stoki. One about a young girl pupil to whom he was explaining the numbers system and squeezing her arm to illustrate. She said 'If you do that once more I'll punch you in the nose.' That became Efrem's line all the time and Tabuteau was laughing each time he heard it . . . We had supper at their place one night; he was tired of restaurants. They didn't want us to come to their new apartment as it's only one room, but we went anyway . . . Mme T is an extraordinary woman—she complained a lot to me about her life with him. He *is* difficult. He is still heartbroken that he sold his house near Toulon and said that if we had gone to see it that time we may have bought a piece of land there and he would still be there!" Yet another example of Tabuteau's original way of reasoning!

Tabuteau had been thinking of making a commercial recording. The idea was discussed with Efrem Kurtz, who had a contract with Angel records. Efrem and Elaine encouraged him to go ahead with plans for a disk that he intended to entitle "Tabuteau's Audition with St. Peter." Rowland Floyd, who was studying with Tabuteau that fall, confirmed how this title had come about. "It was Tabuteau's claim that the Philadelphia Orchestra from time to time would send out little cards saying things such as 'Do you have any change of address?' and then as a sort of P.S., 'How are you?' They really did not require an answer but Tabuteau replied saying that he was doing just fine; in fact, he was working on his Audition for St. Peter and if he didn't get first oboe in Heaven he was sure he'd have no trouble in Satan's Orchestra since he'd spent so many years with Eugene Ormandy."[12]

Rowland Floyd came to Nice in September 1965 and was the only oboe student working with Tabuteau at the time of his death in early January 1966. Originally from Huntsville, Texas, Rowland had studied with me for a short time in Houston when he was only sixteen. Now retired from his position as first oboist with the National Arts Centre Orchestra of Ottawa, Canada, he described his experiences during those last few months of Tabuteau's life. In the 1960s Rowland was studying with Marc Lifschey in San Francisco. When Lifschey decided to go to

TABUTEAU'S FINAL YEARS IN NICE

New York for the summer of 1965, Rowland asked what he should do next. Lifschey said that he had heard "via the grapevine that Tabuteau is doing a little teaching these days. You might want to consider going over. You know, he's very temperamental but I'll make some inquiries." When Rowland received a telephone call at three o'clock in the morning from Lifschey (who had overlooked the time change from New York to the West Coast), he was barely able to focus. But he did understand Lifschey's words: "I've been in touch with Tabuteau who says, 'Tell the young man if he thinks he can stand it, to come ahead.'"

With nothing more than Lifschey's verbal contact, Rowland determined to somehow finance the trip and go to France. A flutist friend who had taken classes with Jean-Pierre Rampal at the Summer Institute in Nice helped him find a place to live, and he managed to pay for his plane ticket only a few hours before leaving San Francisco. Arriving in Nice after the long flight, he felt it was "a good omen" when he saw some blue ageratum flowers in the little garden below the Tabuteaus' apartment. "Everywhere I'd lived—from Texas to California, even in Maine—they had these flowers and here they were in Nice."

A cordial note from Tabuteau was waiting for him:

> *Sept. 30th, 1965*
> Dear Mr. Floyd,
>   Welcome to Nice for a young man who takes the trouble from San Francisco to Nice to master the ungrateful oboe. With my best wishes and admiration,
> Marcel Tabuteau
> P.S. Let me know before you expect to meet me. M. T.

Soon the work began: "I had three lessons every week, lessons which sometimes lasted several hours. It was a priceless, unforgettable experience because nobody else was studying with him then. I would go right after lunch every day at 1 or 2 o'clock and stay until 6. It was a heavy dose and I didn't have that much time to assimilate it all. Saturdays were a particular treat and at the same time somewhat contradictory. He wouldn't allow the maid or Mme Tabuteau to do anything by way of cleaning up his studio. That was my role. It turned out to be a no-win situation. He would be sitting at the desk playing and if I stopped to listen I would be chastised because I was there to clean up. If I found anything on the floor,

MARCEL TABUTEAU

a piece of cane or one of his old reeds, I got to keep it. I would be rummaging around dutifully trying to clean up and then he'd scold me because he was playing. How dare I work when I should be listening."

To me, this type of *inconsistency* sounded totally *consistent* with the way we were treated twenty or thirty years earlier in the Philadelphia studio. Rowland agonized over reeds, feeling that he was not "gifted" in this direction. Here again, Tabuteau continued his old habits: "Occasionally when he couldn't make a reed play the way he wanted, he would cut the cane off the tube, save the tube, then bind the two pieces of the cane together and tell me to take them home and make it work. Usually it didn't succeed except once when I got a really nice reed and was very pleased. Now I'd been there about six weeks. It was raining and I was somewhat homesick. I felt this was going to be a trying day, so I showed him the reed hoping to cheer *him* up. He tried it and said yes, it was good. Of course, the deal was if I made it work he got to keep the reed, so then I had nothing to play on. He took back the reed, then insult to injury, said I was like this tough old bird who was hard to teach—very talented, but like a high-powered rifle that I was shooting all over the place. I needed Tabuteau to teach me how to aim. It was a difficult day."

Rowland related that "He was also working on the tapes. He would practice and then want to write down what he was going to say. On one particular day, I said something about a sheet of paper and he asked, 'A what?' so we had to sit there and practice the difference between 'sheet' and 'shit.' I tried to convince him to just talk because if I corrected everything then it wouldn't be him. I didn't yet realize that with such a personality he wasn't going to listen to anybody. He wanted to write other things too, and would dictate letters, so on occasion I was also his secretary."

In those few months at the very end of Tabuteau's life, Tabuteau gave Rowland a condensed course covering all aspects of oboe playing. In a little notebook Rowland jotted down the main points that were stressed in his lessons. Tabuteau was teaching with the same intensity and continuity of ideas as he did twenty years earlier. He was passing on the same precepts and illustrating them with his rich imagination and pictorial examples. Sometimes he provided new or different examples. To explain the "loop" in changing direction, he now spoke of the natural action of a

TABUTEAU'S FINAL YEARS IN NICE

brush. Using a light feather against the wall, it goes up, and then when turning to start the downward direction, the tip of the feather takes a moment to follow in the down motion. An athlete does the same thing while "chinning" on a bar. When he lifts his arms up, he can only go to the chin position. If he wants to go higher he must make the transition and push the arms above the bar. Tabuteau wanted this transitional motion to be produced and heard at the right point in a note on the oboe.

In emphasizing the importance and universality of Tabuteau's musical concepts, one may forget how particular he was about every aspect of oboe playing. While presenting his philosophy of music to me he also elaborated on the elements of physical application necessary to reach these lofty goals. He spoke of phrasing, motion, and direction in a musical line but did not neglect fundamental details, beginning with the position of the hands and how to hold the oboe correctly. He would not tolerate any hint of contortion or an unusual or awkward angle of the arms. The fingers, arms, and wrists all had to be integrated in such a way that the instrument looked like an extension or a part of one's body. No shifting of the reed to one side of the mouth was allowed. He recommended looking in a mirror to control the position and to make sure there was no "mouthing" of individual notes in articulated passages. No frowning. No wrinkled forehead. It should "look easy." He used to say that you must "plant your feet on the ground" (or floor). The playing comes from the ground up. Watch a singer. You cannot slouch and play well.

Rowland's notes indicated that

> The angle of the oboe should not be flat against the chest. No extremes. There should be no "barbaric" wild sound [created] by holding the oboe out at too straight an angle. The fingers should be curved. No right-hand straight fingers. Don't puff out your cheeks. It is more difficult to undo bad habits than to learn new ideas.
>
> Too often technique refers only to fingers and speed. Breath is to the oboe player like the violin bow. A violin player is not great because of his left-hand technique but because of the work and concepts he (can produce) with the right hand, the tone and color—variety. One does not just play on the fingerboard. Each note must have its color and often one must play an ugly note to bring out the beauty of the others. If all have the same color, it is boring. A beautiful tone in and of itself is not more useful than having a fine rifle and not being

MARCEL TABUTEAU

able to aim it in the right direction. Even if a man has great and noble thoughts and not the wherewithal or technique to write them down, he is not much use to the world as a philosopher.

About reeds: Never finish a reed on the same day. The cane doesn't like to be forced around that little hole (at the top of the tube). Make necessary adjustments later on. You must be able to make a *ppp* attack—not airy, [fuzzy] but as clear as when you strike a thin-lipped glass. Playing on a hard reed is like sitting on a hard chair. You might as well be comfortable. There is no such thing as a good reed, just a reed that is less bad than others. The concept must be in your mind (points to ear) and if it (the reed) is bad, then you need to work harder. *If* you have the concept in your mind especially about the reed, but for the tone too, then you can find a way to produce it. Let the sound ring in your head before you actually play.

The diagram of lip pressure 9-1-9 with the wind doing the opposite, 1-9-1. [Exactly the same diagram I was given in my first lesson.]

Don't blow directly in the reed but from the nose (where the eyebrows come together). Most of his students have forgotten this. They blow directly into the reed.

Say Ah-a-a-a, sustaining the sound and abruptly close mouth. The pressure and support are still there as it should be when you begin to play. [Tabuteau can be heard illustrating this concept on the Wolsing CD.]

Pianisississimo is not all on zero. That equals death. Even at the lowest dynamic level there must be some direction. One does the same work as if the passage were double forte.

There is no point in noodling. You *must prepare.* Don't just pick the instrument up and play with a loud raucous tone. Support the tone before attacking the note.

There is always a reason for everything. There is *one* reason why you make it and *fifty* why you don't. You are in command. Don't let the oboe command. At Curtis, Tabuteau was the boxer who punched his students for four years.

Tabuteau said he learned something every day from the knowledge he had. If one cannot learn from what one knows, then it is not worth knowing. "Discipline yourself as if I were with you telling you what to do all the time. Scales and articulations every day for thirty or forty minutes each. It takes a lifetime."

If Tabuteau gave Rowland a wealth of valuable advice about how to play the oboe, he also made some remarks that recalled the sense of

TABUTEAU'S FINAL YEARS IN NICE

paranoia that existed in the earlier days of American symphony orchestras. For even the finest instrumentalist, a fear of losing one's job seemed always to be lurking in the wings. "Give the man in front of you (the conductor) the feeling you admire him. Therefore, heads up and eyes up! Look straight ahead—at *him*—the conductor. Don't look down to the ground. He [Tabuteau] always keeps something to himself (in teaching), never tells all, especially in America with conductors as they are." I remembered that twenty years earlier I had heard Tabuteau speak of how he would "shine up" a certain pupil to "go after" another one when he gets too cocky.

Toward the end of 1965, possible commitments for Tabuteau in the coming year were beginning to pile up. Joseph Robinson had contacted Dr. Vittorio Giannini proposing to invite Tabuteau to be "in residence" at the newly formed North Carolina School for the Performing Arts in Winston-Salem. Robinson suggested to Tabuteau that "he would teach musical interpretation to groups of chamber players both wind and string, possibly host high-level symposiums by some of your famous professional oboe students, and play some yourself if you wanted to . . . the schedule could be tailored as flexibly as you would like." He described the pleasant living conditions in "the most beautiful and progressive city in the South—both far enough from the old rat-race—but close enough to the mainstream of professional music-making." The idea must have appealed to Tabuteau, as on November 26 he replied, "Considering the potentiality of the opportunity you offer me, I do feel inclined to go back to the U.S. It would be interesting for me I am sure, and I really thank you to have thought of me as an inspiration for American Youth." He also refers to the question of writing the "codicile" (an outline of his theories), something he had discussed earlier with Robinson, but expresses one concern: "The only question is, will I be granted older days!" Prefaced by the word "Confidentially," he also told Robinson about an invitation from Oberlin that he was inclined to accept.

By mid-December Tabuteau found himself in a situation of having to write more letters than he probably wished to in attempting to coordinate his various invitations for 1966. On December 13 he told

MARCEL TABUTEAU

Robinson, "I feel it is fair to let you know I have just today accepted the invitation of the Oberlin College to stay with them as a guest for their Centennial Celebration from Oct 17th to Nov 12th. I received the official invitation a few days ago; felt I had to answer now." Tabuteau's letter of December 16 to Marc Mostovoy included congratulations for his written summary "of the chats we had together. You did a good job, bravo! If I were a Dean, I would give you a Doctor's degree! Keep on the *direction* indicated and I am sure you will make the grade. For your presentation of the T. system you forgot (a) few illustrations; One of them dear to me. It is about *playing in gear.* You should have mentioned the *motor running slow fast* but the car not moving. As I hope to see you next summer, we will give a final touch to the T. system before some one else claims paternity to my ideas." Always secretive about his projects, he adds: "*Confidentially* the Oberlin Conservatory of Music invited me to participate in the celebration of their Centennial, I have accepted, *but, please keep this to yourself.*"[13] He gives Marc the dates and adds, "Before my stay in Oberlin I plan to go to Canada and hook a few salmons; I hope you will join me." At the same time, Wayne Rapier, who was a member of the Oberlin faculty, was trying to juggle the Oberlin stay with arrangements Marc Mostovoy was making for Tabuteau and his new Philadelphia Chamber Orchestra. Wayne wrote to Marc: "The Conservatory will probably want him here first and in consideration of your plans, I'll try to push for an early date although for the students' sake a few weeks of local professors taking off the summer's rough edges might make his visit more pleasant and beneficial for all concerned. Could you come here with your players maybe late November?" A third letter flew from Nice to Philadelphia. On December 17 Tabuteau wrote to Curtis secretary Jane Hill thanking her for the "delightful obligato of Phila. gossip, always entertaining to us," and added news of another possible engagement: "About Buffalo, I was quite surprised to receive early in November a long cable with a prepaid answer, inviting me to work with them next summer. I answered I was not allergic to the idea and asked for more particulars, terms . . . then not a word, a strange bug must have stung them! In spite of this set-back, there is a chance we will have the pleasure to see you in 66." The invitation to

TABUTEAU'S FINAL YEARS IN NICE

Buffalo had come from Livingston Gearhart, one of Tabuteau's pupils from the 1930s. Gearhart had given up the oboe and become a fine pianist and composer. He had gone to France, studied with Nadia Boulanger, and now in the 1960s was a professor at SUNY Buffalo. Both he and his wife Pamela, a violinist who had been in Tabuteau's string classes, held Tabuteau in the highest regard, and it is not surprising that they would want him to return.[14] Why this project did not materialize is unknown, but from these various letters it is obvious that Tabuteau was looking forward to the idea of coming back to North America, not only to visit old friends and "hook a few salmons," but, above all, to be involved again in musical activity.

Tabuteau's correspondence from late December 1965 indicates even more extensive teaching possibilities, both at Oberlin and North Carolina. On December 22 he wrote to Joseph Robinson about "planning for my future (!) [exclamation his] in the U.S. I do not expect to work in the summer, never did it," but said, "if Dr. Gianinni has in mind something interesting for me to do with the students in Winston-Salem and the conditions are tempting and not in conflict with what I have to honor, I would be glad to consider going to N.C. We found Winston-Salem on the map and saw it was not too far from Phila. Or New York." Robinson, full of enthusiasm at the prospect that Tabuteau might really come to North Carolina, described the school in more detail and expressed his conviction that it was headed for a rosy future. "Your association with it would, of course, speed it even more quickly to eminence within the Conservatory field." He mentioned that one of the school's first oboe students, David Weber, had been complimented for his playing in Bizet's *C Major Symphony*. This was the "young David," whom Tabuteau had hoped could come to Nice the previous summer.[15] Robinson closed with the hope that the "cheery spirits" he perceived in Tabuteau's letter would carry on through the winter and spring, and "send him to the U.S.A. full of good health and energy." It is quite unlikely that Tabuteau ever received this letter.

Rowland Floyd had been in Nice several months when one day he went for his lesson only to be told by Madame that Tabuteau was ill and could not see him. When he returned the next day she said, "Well, go in and have a chat but he's really not well at all." It was not long afterward

MARCEL TABUTEAU

that Rowland received a hand-delivered note dated January 5, 1966, 111 Promenade des Anglais:

> Dear Mr. Floyd,
>   Something dreadful happened! Mr. Tabuteau died yesterday around 8 p.m.—a heart attack!
>   Could you do something for me? To come tomorrow Thursday around 11–12 a.m. so we could hear again his voice and music. I do not dare touch the *magnétophone* [tape recorder].
>   I know you will be upset but do come please.
>
>   THANK YOU,
>   LOUISE TABUTEAU

Rowland went to the apartment not quite knowing what to expect. He had brought a few flowers and arrived to find a group of ten or twelve relatives and friends all dressed in formal black sitting in the small room. Tabuteau was lying in state on his day bed, and Rowland realized it was to be a type of memorial. Madame Tabuteau turned to him and said, "We're ready now." He turned on the tape recorder. As Tabuteau's voice and oboe were heard, people began to cry and faint. Rowland felt it was anguishing for everybody and was relieved when Mme Tabuteau finally said, "I think that's enough." Thirty-four years later Rowland could still see it all clearly. "Wires and telegrams were arriving from around the world, and while I was there, yours came. As each message came in, she would go over, kiss him, read it to him, and then lay it on this sort of pyre—the pile of telegrams." About a week and a half later Rowland went back to pick up some music that Tabuteau had borrowed from him when he was thinking of making the "St. Peter" recording. "To my great amazement, he was still there. The telegrams were gone. He was whiter but still there in his formal suit, lying on this little couch with the painting that Harold Gomberg had done over his bed. I saw my music and the music stand on a bookshelf right above the bed. Madame Tabuteau said 'I don't know anything about this; does he have anything of yours?' I said I didn't want to disturb him, and she said, 'Well you won't.' I felt a little uncomfortable leaning over him, attempting to retrieve my music. There was a little rug on the floor and I slipped. My knee landed right beside him so the

TABUTEAU'S FINAL YEARS IN NICE

whole body rocked and almost rolled on top of me. I think I probably turned as white as he was. What if he rolled off on top of me, not just a dead body, but *Marcel Tabuteau!* I was most upset, but Madame didn't bat an eye, just said to try again. This time I went from the foot of the bed and with a trembling hand got the music." Rowland would never forget seeing this man who was always so full of life, now lying there in complete stillness.

It was long before the time of everyday, let alone hourly, instant communication. The news of Tabuteau's death on Tuesday January 4, 1966, reached us in Puerto Rico by way of a January 6 Philadelphia newspaper clipping which fell out of an envelope along with a short note from Jane Hill of the Curtis Institute. It was a dreadful shock. Jane's husband, Felix Meyer, who suffered from an incurable disease, added a few words: "He's spared all the old age things we have to go through." A message came immediately from my old friend Heather Halsted of 1940s Hannah Penn House days: "We have lost another link in the chain that connects us to a world that seemed less chaotic than today's, when values were more stable. Maybe it was our youthful way of seeing things—but Tabuteau's playing seemed permanent and World War II was a transient thing. Now chaos seems the order of the day, and you wonder how long things of beauty and good and worth will be able to survive. Tabuteau was a symbol to all of us. Now he's a legend."

Joseph Robinson saw the notice in the New York Times and wrote to Mme Tabuteau the next day: "The news of your husband's death came as a great jolt to his friends here in the States who were looking forward so eagerly to your return to this country in the summer." He felt that Tabuteau's recent letters were "full of the sparkle and vitality that made every encounter with him unforgettable," and was "glad that he enjoyed buoyancy and hope in his last months." From Copenhagen came a tribute from Waldemar Wolsing. "Every time I take my oboe in my hands I think with gratitude of the greatest oboist and artist I have met."

Madame Budin wrote to me explaining that she did not want to leave her sister alone "at this painful time. To reply quickly to your telegram received this morning, I am copying the message she sent to the Kurtzes who telephoned from Switzerland . . . and then perhaps I'll add a few personal words about the dear old friend we loved—the qualities and the faults. Truly he departed as he would have wished it. If Louise dared, she would say, 'The Gods loved him.'"

Mme Tabuteau's letter told of his last two days: "On Monday, January 3, he was still searching as always; Bach on the *magnétophone*. I recorded several notes and he said, 'I will call this Truth through Music,' and in speaking of a phrase he wanted to correct, he said, '*le 'la' doit se fondre*' [The A must blend (*or melt*) into the B-flat]. In the afternoon he had to do an errand and went out about 5 o'clock; naturally the d. . . . [*devil*] led him to the *Mediterranée* [the casino] to return at 20:30 and a late dinner. Tuesday morning about 10 o'clock he didn't feel well and seeing him so pale, I was frightened. His eyes had an ethereal look. His doctor came and called a cardiologist. He spent the afternoon quietly, lying down, with orders not to move. In the evening at 7:30 the doctor came back; a few minutes later our Pingouin felt a sudden malaise. The doctor did everything he could to help—a shot—massage of the heart . . . but all of a sudden he told me 'His heart has stopped.' It was dreadful. Fortunately for him, I don't believe he felt anything; the expression on his face was serene. Two seconds and our cathedral had crumbled. Think of him often—that's all I can tell you." Mme Tabuteau added a personal note: "My dear Lola, We did everything as he would have wished it . . . I hope he is in peace with himself, the heavens and the universe. One must think of him often, perhaps he still has need of us. Fortunately I have a wonderful sister who is here with me and a devoted brother who came immediately to help me. *à bientôt* and please also thank your artist colleagues for their telegram. Louise Tabuteau."

Tabuteau's sudden death was a shock to everyone. He was looking forward to new projects—offers to give master classes at Oberlin, conducting and recording of baroque concertos with the chamber orchestra Marc Mostovoy had formed, teaching at the new school in North Carolina, and now so unexpectedly, he was gone.[16]

At the end of July 1966 Mme Tabuteau announced her decision to move to Toulon, where she still had many friends. Crushed by her loss, she "had left *le Pingouin* in his little urn at Nice, situated on the side of the hill looking toward the rising sun where only the rustling of the wind in the trees broke the silence of his corner. The noises of the crowd (*échos des hommes*) don't reach up there. Perhaps he is happy—but I am very sad and cannot yet comprehend what happened on this fourth day of January for which there was no warning of tragedy . . . If it were not for my family, I'd still be on my fourth floor in Nice where I like my solitude." After several bouts of illness Madame Tabuteau could not remain alone in Toulon. She spent her last few years in a sanatorium near Paris at Saint-Germain-en-Laye. Louise André Tabuteau died on October 31, 1973, shortly before her eighty-second birthday, and is at rest alongside her Pingouin on the hillside Cimetière de l'Est in Nice.

MARCEL TABUTEAU

20 PHILADELPHIA POSTLUDE

Tabuteau's Playing; His Musical Ideas and Influence

In November 1967, almost two years after Tabuteau's death, Mme Tabuteau returned to Philadelphia accompanied by Denise Budin. Her main goal was to take part in the creation of the Marcel Tabuteau Memorial Scholarship Fund and to make sure that the tapes Tabuteau made in 1965 would be edited. Already in February 1966 many of her old friends, Sol Schoenbach, Mrs. Adrian Siegel, and Mrs. Philip Klein, began working to make this a reality. A letter was sent out on February 17 expressing the plan "to provide scholarship and grant-in-aid for talented oboe students." For a number of years the Marcel Tabuteau Memorial Scholarship Fund was able to offer help to oboe students in the form of living expenses and sometimes even the purchase of a good instrument. Eventually what remained was absorbed into general Curtis Institute funds.

During this same visit to Philadelphia, Mme Tabuteau gave me a copy of notes written by Marc Mostovoy. At that time I knew nothing of his work with Tabuteau, but feeling there must a reason she wanted me to have the paper, I added it to a drawer with other Tabuteau "memorabilia," where it remained for thirty years. One of the first tributes after Tabuteau's death was a concert given in March 1966 by Marc Mostovoy's recently formed group, Concerto Soloists. *Elegy* by Philadelphia composer Harold Boatrite with the dedication "In Memoriam," Marcel Tabuteau, 1887–1966, was added to an all-Vivaldi program. Samuel L. Singer of the *Inquirer* wrote in glowing terms of the orchestra and praised the *Elegy* as "appropriately somber . . . it ably contrasts different groupings of string instruments as it establishes and heightens the elegiac mood. It ends with a soaring passage for the solo violin."[1] Mostovoy's dream was to have Tabuteau himself as a soloist and conductor with these young musicians. It was not to be, but throughout the following decades, Concerto Soloists (later named the Chamber Orchestra of Philadelphia) provided valuable opportunities for aspiring string and wind players.

Several years later the Rittenhouse Square Women's Committee commissioned David Amram, long an admirer of Tabuteau's artistry, to compose a work in his memory. Amram based his composition, *Trail of Beauty,* on the "poetry, prayers, and speeches of the native American people." In a preface to his score, he wrote of the "quality of timelessness" in the spirit world of the first Americans and of how their tradition "best expresses the feeling all of us in music have when we honor a musician." *Trail of Beauty* for solo oboe, voice, and large orchestra with the addition of Native American percussion instruments was given its première on March 3, 4, and 5, 1977. John de Lancie was the oboe soloist and Rose Taylor the mezzo-soprano, with Eugene Ormandy conducting the Philadelphia Orchestra. Daniel Webster of the *Philadelphia Inquirer* commented on Amram's "intensely lyrical, long-lined style" and the unusual combination of voice and oboe "flowing through the varied orchestra sounds which include authentic Indian music. The oboe—played by John de Lancie with elegance and projection, unifies this thirty minute work with its return to intervals of descending fourths and fifths."[2]

Two years after these performances, John de Lancie, then director of the Curtis Institute of Music, announced a special celebration to honor the memory of Marcel Tabuteau. On March 4, 1979, Studio II-B on the second floor of the school was to be renamed the Marcel Tabuteau Room. Previously honored in this Faculty Commemorative Series were Efrem Zimbalist, violinist and former director of the Curtis Institute, and the illustrious harpist and teacher Carlos Salzedo. An exhibit of photographs, display panels with an outline of the major events of Tabuteau's career, his Paris Conservatoire Premier Prix medal, and a box of his reeds (all of varying lengths!) were on view throughout the festivities. From Copenhagen came a telegram signed by Jørgen Hammergaard, Paul Tofte-Hansen, and Waldemar Wolsing: "For the memorial concert for the great oboist Marcel Tabuteau on March 4th his Danish pupils from the National Orchestra, Radio Denmark, send their warmest greetings in deep gratitude and admiration of the master as teacher and artist." Seven Tabuteau students from the years 1935 to 1953 returned for two programs of varied solo music for oboe, one in the afternoon and the other in the evening. Robert Bloom performed his own composition *Requiem for Oboe and Strings* accompanied by a group of Curtis students led by John de Lancie. Ralph Gomberg played the Mozart *Quartet* K. 370. Boris Goldovsky and Jorge Bolet shared their fascinating reminiscences from the early 1930s when they had both been associated with Tabuteau. Mention was made that Tabuteau's Curtis students had held positions of solo oboe or English horn in eighteen American symphony orchestras.[3] Two films were shown, one of early movies of Philadelphia Orchestra rehearsals onstage at the Academy of Music (without sound) and the other an interview given for Public Television in 1959 during Tabuteau's return visit to the United States. These films brought back to life some aspects of his colorful speech and expressive gestures. John Mack presented a group of short French pieces by Murgier, Barraud, Auric, and Planel, ending with the famous Paladilhe *Solo de Concert*. I chose to play *Légende* by Louis Diémer, the little-known Paris Concours solo of 1904, the year Tabuteau was awarded his Premier Prix. Faithful Curtis pianist Vladimir Sokoloff was our accompanist for all of these works. Louis Rosenblatt played Mozart's *Adagio for English horn*, K. Anh. II, 94 supported by a string quartet of current Curtis students. Curtis Hall was crowded not only with oboists but with other former members of Tabuteau's classes and Philadelphia Orchestra colleagues for the day John Mack referred to as "The Glorious Fourth." I caught a glimpse of flutists Julius Baker and Albert Tipton, clarinetists Bernard Portnoy and Anthony Gigliotti, and violinists David Madison and Frederick Vogelsang. Mitchell Miller of oboe and conducting fame was there. Other Tabuteau students came with *their* students. The beaming presence of Hans Moennig, a man so

PHILADELPHIA POSTLUDE

important to all of them, completed the gathering. Everyone who played felt the pressure of stepping out once again onto the Curtis stage where they had been the "beneficiaries" of Tabuteau's stringent criticisms. At one point during Ralph Gomberg's performance of the Mozart *Oboe Quartet,* an ominous rumbling sound almost like an explosion was heard from the direction of a neighboring building. Those of us who were hovering backstage all whispered, "*Tabuteau!!*"

On behalf of the Rittenhouse Square Women's Committee, Mrs. Philip Klein presented an award for the Marcel Tabuteau Chair of Woodwind Studies to John Minsker, the first recipient. The dedication of the Marcel Tabuteau Room had been entrusted to me. I spoke of the Curtis catalog for the year 1924–25 which had announced the courses in Orchestral Instruments (see Curtis catalog, chapter 8), with its statement about the "serious lack of players of woodwind, brass, and percussion instruments" in the United States—that there were "more excellent positions, waiting to be worthily filled, than there are players ready to fill them" . . . and how it was the "plan of The Curtis Institute of Music to build a school to supply this demand." The teachers were to be the solo players of the Philadelphia Orchestra, each "a master of great reputation." In declaring that "this studio will henceforth be known as the *Marcel Tabuteau Room,*" I referred back to that early announcement and how, little over a half a century later, the art of woodwind playing in the United States had become such, that the supply of excellent players is now greater than the number of positions worthy of being filled. I also said that this was without doubt "in large part due to Marcel Tabuteau's thirty years of teaching at this corner of Eighteenth and Locust Streets. The extent of his influence in the area of musical understanding, his conception of phrasing, line, and style, reached far beyond the ranks of the oboists he taught. In the woodwind ensemble classes, students of all other wind instruments came under his guidance. Violinists, violists, cellists, and pianists have all attested to the impact that Tabuteau had on their musical lives. His ideas were passed on, gradually establishing an approach and a tradition that has become a standard across the whole country. Of a more tangible nature, however, beyond a few phonograph records, and the memories of his students, there is little that remains." In conclusion I expressed our gratitude to John de Lancie "for having chosen this most appropriate way to perpetuate the memories of those artists whose names and creative teaching are synonymous with The Curtis Institute of Music."

A festive social hour and banquet was held next door at the venerable Barclay Hotel, where Adrian Gnam of the National Endowment of the Arts, "Mitch" Miller, Jacob Lateiner, John Mack, and Ronald Reuben spoke of the many facets of the amazing personality who left such an imprint on so many lives. Then there was the evening concert with Alfred Genovese, violist Burton Fine, and Vladimir Sokoloff playing Charles Martin Loeffler's *Deux Rapsodies.* Some afternoon performances were repeated, and the night ended with Harold Gomberg, returned from retirement in Italy, to play the Cimarosa *Concerto for Oboe* accompanied by the Curtis strings. The principal Philadelphia newspapers reported on the event, their headlines stating quite appropriately: "Oboists Pay Homage to Tabuteau" and "A Great Artist's Legacy Is Often Those He Has Taught." Samuel L. Singer of the *Inquirer* offered his personal tribute by writing "despite the moving performances by the seven live oboists, the highlight for many was the playing of a Tabuteau recording of Handel's Oboe *Concerto in G minor.*"

In the next few years, Tabuteau's memory was kept alive in a number of ways. The tapes he recorded in Nice were edited by John de Lancie and John Minsker and issued by *Coronet* in a two-LP set, entitled *Art of the Oboe.* Levering Bronston's review written for the April 1971 publication *The New Records* demonstrates a fine grasp of Tabuteau's distinctive qualities. He called this recording a "fascinating document." Tabuteau, "discoursing, analyzing, exemplifying, expounding his beloved "numbers" method, ruminating, playing, joking, teaching," all of this from a man "who dominated orchestral woodwind playing in America to such a degree that today every major orchestra in this country has a solo oboist who is a Tabuteau product; but his influence goes much deeper than that . . . There has never been disagreement over the extent of Marcel Tabuteau's realm—he was the supreme master of that aspect of the performer's art which is surely the soul of music-making: the spinning out of a series of notes, with each individual note being considered in relation to the notes preceding it and following it—being considered, that is, in a manner to make the entire series of notes a continuum in sound—a phrase—having a 'meaning,' or 'point.'" After commenting that the one thing Tabuteau never mastered was his French accent, Bronston congratulated *Coronet* for including "the complete text: a kind of line-by-line English-English libretto." He ended his review with one of the finest tributes to the far-reaching value of Tabuteau's ideas: "Of course the appeal of this set may be limited. I should think it will be of interest mostly to oboists and flutists, clarinetists and bassoonists, horn players, trumpeters and some trombonists, perhaps an occasional tuba player; all manner of woodwind students; violinists and violists, cellists and bassists, perhaps even one or two inquisitive opera tenors; an enterprising timpanist here and there, concert pianists who are musically adventurous, music schools, libraries, various record collectors and sundry music lovers." If Tabuteau had still been around, I cannot help but wonder what he would have said when he noticed there was no mention of *conductors*?

After the LP recordings had been out of print for many years, they were reissued in 1996 in CD format by Boston Records as *Marcel Tabuteau's Lessons.*[4] In July 1997 the *American Record Guide* called it "an invaluable document," adding that "Marcel Tabuteau enjoyed a pristine reputation in the music world such as few orchestral musicians ever attain," and credited his forty years in "what may have been the greatest orchestra in the world at the time" for helping him "to lay the foundation of all modern oboe performance." This review (unlike the one of twenty-five years earlier) mentions that the recordings were made in Tabuteau's apartment in Nice from memory, as he had no music there with him. It also refers to the "poignant moment" where he speaks of his audition with St. Peter, "an audition he was to keep in January of 1966, depriving us of what he now graces heaven with, except for these sterling seventy-two minutes."[5]

CONCLUSION

Only three days before his sudden death, Tabuteau was recording a phrase from the Bach *Brandenburg Concerto No. 1* which he intended to call "Truth through Music." These words could well stand as a motto for his whole life. Despite the contradictory elements of his nature,

MARCEL TABUTEAU

there was one constant—his steadfast pursuit of an often seemingly unreachable musical goal. He had to fight the endless battle of the reeds while always striving for a higher level of nuance and expression. Reflections on Tabuteau's musical ideas and attempts to describe the way he played have been scattered throughout these pages. How can it be explained to someone who never heard him in person? John Minsker, who played alongside Tabuteau in the Philadelphia Orchestra for almost twenty years, felt that "There *is* no basis for comparison. He was one of these people who come along every century or so—outstanding artists—like Paganini and Liszt—Kreisler, Casals, and Callas. They are just *so* outstanding; they are in a class of their own. Tabuteau had everything. He had the tone, he had the articulation, he had the conception of *music*—how thorough he was in that—in his analysis of the groupings—how two notes are grouped together, then put into a larger group of four, and how this phrase is connected to the next phrase. He analyzed those things and got us all thinking about it."

Minsker described what it was like to sit so close to Tabuteau in the orchestra. "He could take a tone and he could just do anything with it—he could pull it to the left, he could pull it to the right, he could lift it up, he could put it down. It was constantly in motion—the color and the intensity always changing. There was nothing static about it. You felt that it was suspended in the air." After all these years Minsker still spoke with wonder of the oboe solos in the *Eroica Symphony*, not only the *Marcia funebre* but also "those in the last movement which were so incredible—it was *just fantastic* how he could bring a note from nowhere . . . Then there were the concerts with Toscanini—*Ibéria*, how Tabuteau played in *Ibéria*, and the Schubert *C major*. And the beginning of *Don Quixote*—My God, you just sat there and you held your breath . . . and he could turn around and play the other Strauss—Johann—the *Zigeunerbaron* Overture. Oh, how he played that—maybe not the greatest music, but what a performance! He took that just as seriously as he would the *Eroica*." The ability to play a piece of musical "fluff" with exquisite style is a quality shared by many great artists. I thought back to the year Tabuteau conducted the orchestra at Curtis. How difficult it was to play to his satisfaction the series of oboe G's an octave apart at the beginning of the *Emperor Waltz*! Minsker elaborated on another aspect of Tabuteau's playing. Less obvious than the larger solos were accompanying, or obbligato, passages that would barely be noticed out in the audience. But sitting next to Tabuteau in the orchestra, Minsker could hear how "Tabuteau approached those parts with the same care he gave to a major solo. No matter how unimportant something might appear, he played it with absolute dedication." Tabuteau followed his own advice to us: study everything from the score and be familiar with what everyone else is playing.

In a book celebrating one hundred years of the Philadelphia Orchestra, Daniel Webster wrote that Tabuteau is credited "with having shaped the entire Orchestra's sense of phrasing and even its sound . . . His standards resonated beyond Philadelphia. His playing presaged an 'American school,' a style of playing that was admired, studied and learned by two generations. It combined the elegance of French musicianship with a more robust but eloquent sound that differentiated an American orchestra from those of other countries when heard on recordings."[6] John Minsker felt "his great sound was the basis of Tabuteau's playing" and said he "would give anything to hear it again. It began with a small sound, but one that he could make so big; he could expand and contract and add color. It was a dark sound but a lightweight dark sound. The top register would shimmer and the low notes were smooth and rich. It was always great, but some of the most marvelous playing would be in the rehearsals when perhaps there was just the perfect combination of a reed and how he felt. How much he could put into two or three notes!" Tuba player Abe Torchinsky spoke of the thrill it was for him to sit on the same stage and hear Tabuteau. When he played, "the hair stood up on the back of my neck." Few artists are able to produce such a frisson. Others who heard Tabuteau, both from sitting near to him in the orchestra or from the perspective of the concert hall, testified that unfortunately for posterity, the real character of his playing was not caught by the recording techniques of the time. Sol Schoenbach also tried to define the impression made on him by Tabuteau's playing. "It was expansive. It was a complete *thought,* not something you just throw away like a side remark. I'll never forget after the beginning of the Brahms *First Symphony* when the oboe comes in and how he would curve that solo.

From that point on, the other players began to move and mold their own phrases—it spreads—something is going to happen to the people around you like what happened to me, and not only the woodwinds. I would say that Tabuteau was the most *profound influence* on American music that exists."[7]

These attempts to describe Tabuteau's playing are perhaps best summed up by someone, not an oboist, speaking of his memories from over seventy-five years ago. Iso Briselli, a violin prodigy from Europe, who came to study with Carl Flesch, entered the Curtis Institute on the day the school opened in 1924. Through the rest of the 1920s and into the early 1930s, he went to all the Saturday night concerts of the Philadelphia Orchestra. "When I first heard Tabuteau in the Orchestra, I was amazed at the approach he had—his music—and the way he phrased things. Everything he did was towards perfection. I always had the feeling that when he had even a small solo . . . it was a kind of performance he gave. Whether it's a single note or a phrase or a whole movement, you felt that nothing was left out—it was polished— chiseled—and a perfect kind of expression. I felt he took an attitude that he was giving a message, a very personal message, when he played. All the woodwinds looked to him to set the atmosphere they would fit into. He was the leader, whether admitted or not. He was the deciding force." Asked about "tone," Briselli said, "It was a unique kind of tone. It was so perfect in its projection. Every note fit into the whole phrase. You sat there hypnotized waiting for the phrase to finish. His sound was so unique, and yet he fit in perfectly with the rest of them. The other woodwinds—Kincaid, the clarinetist [probably Bonade], were all excellent musicians, but you felt Tabuteau set the atmosphere. He gave the direction. You were always aware of that background of his sound. Very extraordinary. It's hard to describe."[8]

Already in 1947 I was pondering the question of "what it is actually that makes Tabuteau? The most intangible things. It's that when he plays the Strauss tone poem *Death and Transfiguration*, you feel the most complete distillation of the essence of the whole piece and its meaning and even though you can't take what he plays away with you, you've had the feeling—the spirit."[9] After several years of hearing Tabuteau in the

PHILADELPHIA POSTLUDE

orchestra, one realized that he created a distinct color, tonal approach, and style for each composer. There was the special intensity of his Wagner sound; a tinge of poignancy for the solos in Schumann, and a depth of sound one could only call "Brahmsian" in the famous four symphonies. Every measure of Mozart and Beethoven was treated with infinite care and attention to the variety of character inherent in each phrase. His articulation added sparkling humor or dramatic emphasis as the music demanded. And he always made his reeds specifically for the music of that particular week's program, continually testing and trying them on the measures he would have to play. One can search for the core—to try to explain the fascination—what made Tabuteau's playing unique. It was in part the rare combination of color and imagination linked to a clear sense of structure and form, even as a great architect places elements on the façade of a building that would already stand firmly without the décor. Beyond that, there was the intensity of total physical involvement—not projected through any excess of bodily motion, but a way of playing that came from within. He obeyed his own precept: "The oboe should be a part of you. In itself it means nothing. *You* should speak." It was the same as the actor who projects a moving speech from a Shakespeare play or the singer who gives his all in a Verdi aria. But there was also the indefinable.

Trying to find a word to express how I remembered Tabuteau's playing in *Don Quixote,* I once said it was "of another dimension." John de Lancie was assistant to Tabuteau in the Philadelphia Orchestra in December 1949 when two concerts were given in memory of Richard Strauss. He heard Tabuteau play the solos in *Der Bürger als Edelmann, Till Eulenspiegel* and *Don Quixote* and agreed, "It was a different dimension—exactly that." He then recalled "a Beethoven work, *The Creatures of Prometheus,* a series of pieces with important oboe solos and a narration. I can only tell you that it was breathtaking—absolutely transcendent. Even Hilsberg said to me as he was leaving the stage, 'the way Marcel played tonight!' Well, it *was* a different dimension." John remembered reading a book where there was a line about the great nineteenth-century pianist Anton Rubinstein that said "to have heard Rubinstein play the piano is a considerable consolation for growing old. (Or for having lost our youth.)" John felt this was relevant for us in the sense that we, too, had something of true greatness to look back on. The esteemed violinist and venerated pedagogue Josef Gingold addressed the same question when he wrote of his teacher, the peerless Belgian, Eugène Ysaÿe: "The impression an artist makes upon his listeners somehow cannot be expressed to others. Books and articles can only attempt to describe it—they are unable to recreate it."[10] Even as we have to believe the written reports about the legendary nineteenth-century performers—singers, pianists, and violinists—who left no record in sound at all, we must trust those who tell us that Tabuteau was one of that league—the dimension beyond, the indefinable transmission by an artist of the innermost message of the music.

In May 1997, inspired by flutist Julius Baker, a "sixtieth Anniversary" reunion was held at Curtis for the graduates of 1937. In writing about the weekend event, director Gary Graffman, evoked his 1920s and 1930s predecessor Josef Hofmann's words that the purpose of the Institute was "To hand down through contemporary masters the great traditions of the past; to teach students to build on this heritage for the future." Graffman was struck by how much of the 1937 graduates' discussion "centered around memories of the renowned oboist, Marcel Tabuteau—funny anecdotes,—naturally, but also descriptions of his unique teaching methods. Tabuteau's influence as a musician was, and still is, remarkable . . . it's particularly amazing, because Tabuteau influenced not only oboists and wind players, but also musicians in all disciplines. What can an oboist teach a pianist? Performers of all kinds still remember Tabuteau's "phrase-making" seminars . . . One of our newest alumni, a violist, commented that during his years at Curtis scarcely a lesson went by without his teacher (Karen Tuttle) telling him something that Tabuteau—(an oboist, remember!)—had told her!" . . . Music and musicianship—MUST be—learned from great artists of all kinds, and fine musicianship transcends not only time but also instruments."[11] Six years later in May 2003, another Curtis Alumni Reunion featured a series of performances and a panel discussion that focused completely on the influence of Marcel Tabuteau. Five of the participants—Seymour Lipkin, Laila Storch, Martha Scherer, Norman Carol, and Jacob Lateiner—had taken part in the unforgettable 1944–45 season when Tabuteau conducted the Curtis Orchestra for the KYW broadcasts.

PHILADELPHIA POSTLUDE

In thinking further about Tabuteau's influence which extended throughout the twentieth century and now into the twenty-first, I asked myself a question and came to a conclusion. As no fewer than fifteen pupils of Georges Gillet came to this country, among them the outstanding Georges Longy and Alfred Barthel, why, of all of them, did Tabuteau evolve as the major force in the development of oboe schooling in America? I believe it was the confluence of two main currents—first, his own performance during the long period when the Philadelphia Orchestra became known for its sumptuous sound, its recordings, its tours, and creative programming, with superb players in the solo chairs, all under the leadership of the charismatic Leopold Stokowski; and second, following his initial decade in the orchestra, the creation of the Curtis Institute of Music, where he was able to choose students of high caliber from anywhere in the country, knowing that they would be on full scholarship. This provided Tabuteau with the ideal ground to develop and expound his ideas of teaching, not only the oboe, but music in general. Through these two parallel channels of his musical life, Tabuteau became known as both a superb oboist and a masterful teacher. Of the other fine French oboists, Georges Longy of Boston, whose fame cast a shadow over Tabuteau's first few decades in America, did not teach.[12] Georges Gillet's own nephew, Fernand Gillet, who followed Longy in Boston, had a very analytical mind and contributed the valuable "practice method" for his uncle's "Advanced Studies." He *did* teach, but without the widespread results achieved by Tabuteau. Other Gillet students—Alfred Barthel, Alexandre Duvoir, and Pierre Mathieu—were respected teachers in Chicago, Minneapolis, and St. Louis. However, the orchestras of these cities in which they played could not compare with the renown of the Philadelphia Orchestra in the 1920s and 30s. Added to all of these elements was Tabuteau's own innate ability, already recognized in 1904 by Georges Gillet, when he wrote: "*Nature exceptionelle d'hautboïste*" (An exceptional temperament for the oboe). I also believe that of all the Gillet students, Tabuteau was the one who, throughout his lifetime, pondered most deeply his teacher's observations and comments about natural phenomena and developed them into a comprehensive philosophy of musical phrasing.

MARCEL TABUTEAU

Tabuteau used to maintain that it "took seven years to make an oboist." If one considers the months of work he required on basic concepts of attacks, dynamic range, slow scales, and broken thirds in all articulations, inflections, and tempi, the Barret Oboe Method, with every study in the book transposed into other keys, the Ferling 48 Études, also transposed, as well as the Brod 20 Études, the Sellner Duos, not just played through, but studied as thoroughly as any étude, with all the Allegro movements in brilliant tempi, and finally, if you were still there, a few solo pieces and at least the first few of the Georges Gillet 25 *Studies for the Advanced Teaching of the Oboe*—it could easily take seven years. Working on orchestral repertoire, which he insisted must be done from the score, was left largely to the individual. Most of his Curtis students had an average of four years of lessons. The intense level of work, however, which also included the ensemble classes, can scarcely be measured in normal time. It was a reservoir on which you could draw for the rest of your life.

By now, many elements of Tabuteau's teaching have filtered into generally accepted concepts of how to play the oboe. Today the ability to attack a note with security in any dynamic range and play low notes softly is assumed. Seventy-five years ago, placing an attack was more like a lottery ticket—you were lucky if you won. Tabuteau's approach has been passed on by his students and has taken most of the guesswork and feeling of uncertainty out of oboe playing. It has been aided by the general adoption of the long-scrape or so-called Tabuteau-style reed— called such because rather than being completely his own invention, it was the result of his incorporation of other ideas already in use. However, very few of the generic long-scrape reeds portrayed as Tabuteau style truly deserve that name, as the character of his sound depended more on the interior proportions of the gouged cane than on the exterior appearance of the scraped reed.

The day is long past when to have a pleasant sound and a reasonable degree of facility is enough to guarantee an oboist almost certain employment. The present general higher level of purely instrumental competence brings with it much greater expectations of refined artistry and musicianship. Whereas in the 1940s and 1950s only a few oboists would appear to audition for an available position, there can now be between one and two hundred applicants. It has become more like the violin world, with the difference that orchestras need only three oboes, while there are places for at least thirty-two violinists. With so many oboists now playing in a basically acceptable manner, it becomes essential to do more—to demonstrate real musical style, distinction, and individuality. What better way than to follow Tabuteau's oft-repeated exhortation: "Play the life of the note—Have something to say!"

APPENDIX 1.
INTRODUCTION
AND TEXT TRANSCRIPTION FOR
THE TABUTEAU-WOLSING CD

On March 3, 1964, Marcel Tabuteau wrote from Nice to his "Cher ami Wolsing" in Copenhagen: "I am glad you could arrange to come from March 21st to March 29th so we can celebrate pre Easter together; also with pleasure will entertain you with latest reeds problem and. . . . . . . blowing technic" (ellipses in original). He followed this with another letter two days later: "If you possess a recording machine or if a friend could lend you one I think it would be a good idea to bring it with you. We could make few yards of tape you could take home and have home with you concrete ideas and few notes played by old T. and his friend Wolsing." Wolsing managed to borrow a Nagra tape recorder along with a high-quality microphone, the best he could obtain, from Danish Radio. This led to Tabuteau's first attempt to narrate a few of his ideas for a "machine" and to record some orchestral excerpts. He seemed impelled to talk and told Wolsing that he should get "a kind of testament" from him. It was now ten years since Tabuteau had left the Philadelphia Orchestra, and he was close to his seventy-seventh birthday. He played everything from memory as there was not a piece of music in his apartment for reference. Some slight differences of articulations and even of notes appear in works I heard him play many times in Philadelphia. One example of his excellent recall, however, is the phrase (originally for soprano voice) in *Tristan und Isolde,* Act 2, from Leopold Stokowski's *Symphonic Synthesis* which he had recorded in 1935. And it is unlikely that he had played a note of the Colin solo since his student days.

In transferring Wolsing's tapes to CD, their experimental nature has been preserved. One hears Tabuteau ask, "Let's hear that now," and there are background sounds of street traffic in Nice, an occasional auto horn, some foot tapping and squeaking of chairs in the apartment. The only changes made were to link some subjects and solo excerpts into a reasonable sequence. Many of the listed "excerpts" are little more (or even less) than one whole measure and are preceded or followed by an improvised flourish. Others are quite complete. Aside from the excerpts, there are Tabuteau's own explanations of several concepts he considered as most fundamental to his way of oboe playing: Track 9, Wind control; Track 11, Up and down inflections; Track 13, Using numbers and speed of the wind; Track 15, Playing with pressure of the wind.

This recording differs from later ones in that Tabuteau is interacting with another person instead of speaking alone into a microphone. One can hear the excitement in his voice when he begins to talk of possibly going to Copenhagen to record all the orchestral solos in a professional studio. One also hears him say that he did not like anything he had just played. He was looking forward to Wolsing's return in the following year and wrote to him in April 1965: "I am glad that you are considering coming to Nice this summer . . . Don't forget to bring your recording equipment . . . I have learned a lot about reeds lately." It was a disappointment to Tabuteau when he found that Wolsing was unable to make the trip. On July 2, the day of his seventy-eighth birthday, Tabuteau sent this message to Wolsing: "I hope the Future will allow us to meet again," adding, "We will have to make another [recording] and be well prepared." But it was not to be. After Tabuteau's death, Wolsing felt that despite Tabuteau's dissatisfaction the tapes should be heard. He gave them to his friend Claus Johansen, whose careful guardianship has now brought us this belated surprise of a unique "almost live" contact with Marcel Tabuteau.

APPENDIX 1

Tabuteau-Wolsing text with track titles 1–16

All indications of "*Plays*" are Tabuteau. Conversation is noted by T. (Tabuteau) and W. (Wolsing). Audio editor, Gary Louie.

1 Prelude

> T. Did you make a tape on it?
> W. Oh yes. We can—
> T. No,—No, but, no—but—W. Oui? T. All right W. Do you like—do you like to hear it?
> *Plays*: Delibes, *Lakmé* (ballet). Massenet, *Élégie*. T. All right. Strauss: *Don Juan.*
> All right—let's hear that, you see. Rimsky-Korsakov: *Scheherazade.*

2 Brahms, *Third Symphony*

> T. I'll do it three different ways. You see—and see if you can hear the difference. W. Yes. (*Plays*) See, that's one. One version. (*Plays*) Two version. All right—let's hear that now. (*Plays*) See. Up—Down. Now I can hear the difference. (*Plays*) You see—Up, the last C#. . . . W. Yes. T. All right. See if you can hear the difference. (*Plays*) You see what I mean? You see, because I do it three different ways there—the first time I play the C# up and the C# down. The second time I play the G# up and the C# down. Do you understand what I mean? W. Yes, yes, yes. T. You see? Now I like to find out for people who are not prepared, you know, to know what I am doing, if they notice the difference. That's the problem. W. Yes. (*Plays*) T. You see—all right, let me hear that once more. (*Plays*) You see, that's why—you know it is *so*—you know, the register is bad—you know what I mean? To those C#, you know what I mean? And it is a bad register for the oboe—so, when the notes come out, we call it a victory. You see what I mean? (*Laughs*) Don't you understand? W. Yes. T. It's a *victoire!* When the note comes out, never mind if it is up or down. W. Up or down. T. You understand? You know—W. Yes. T. Because—you never know how that C# is going to come out of that. You know what I mean? (*Plays*) You see, to feel the A to the C#, it is a—a terrible problem. You see what I mean? Not to have a break between the A and the C#. W. Oh yes, the continuity . . .

3 Two high C's

APPENDIX 1

4 Distribution

Dancla *Étude.* Ends with a phrase of *L'Italiana in Algeri.* W. Thank you. T. (*Plays*) See? No, no dancing. (*Plays*) Dancing—No dancing. (*Plays*) See what I mean? W. Yes? T. Then I dance on the last part. It's to show you, you can make—the same group, you can make a different interpretation. Don't you understand? W. Yes, yes. (*Plays*) You know, the numbers—you can change it. You don't change the music. You see what I mean? W. Yes, yes. T. (*Plays intervals*) Or—(*same intervals again*) You see? W. Yes. T. (*Plays again*) Or—(*Plays*) See the difference? W. Yes. T. You see what I mean? Like, like Mahler, you see? Like Mahler. If I play it placid, you see, I am going to play it different way, you see. (*Plays Mahler Symphony No. 1*) Now you take—(*continues the solo*) T. Now, another interpretation. (*Plays*) T. You see what I mean? W. Yes, yes. T. It's all different, you see, my distribution. W. Yes. T. Same melody—but different a-appliance, you see.—W. yes, on the *fantaisie.* T. Yeh, you see? It all depends how—you see, how you have a reed that responds, if you have a reed—you know sometimes you have a reed you can't do anything you, you want to express.

5 Nine excerpts

Bizet: *Carmen*

Wagner: *Tristan und Isolde* Liebesnacht (Symphonic Synthesis, transcribed by Leopold Stokowski)

Ravel: *Daphnis*

Strauss: *Der Rosenkavalier*

Paladilhe: *Solo*

Bach: *Brandenburg No. 1*

T. Oh, that's what I'd like to play for you. Stravinsky, W. Oh yes. T. Because there is a progression, I'd like to see how it sounds there. W. Oh yes. T. You know, I play it for you.

Stravinsky: *Pastorale*

Tchaikovsky: *Fourth Symphony*

Charles Colin: *Solo de Concert, No. 5*

Arpeggio to high C

6 Five more excerpts

Tabuteau talks: You know, I should make a, a recording of all the oboe solos W. Yes. T. And sell—W. And sell, yes. T. Do you think? To help me to make money. W. Yes. T. You know, I would go to Copenhagen—

W. And make a—T. And make a—all the solos, phrasing, my phrasing, and play. W. Yes, yes.

Beethoven: *Fifth Symphony*
Bizet: *C Major Symphony*
Ibert: *Escales*
Strauss: *Don Juan*
Shostakovich: *Fifth Symphony*

7 Tabuteau and Wolsing reminisce

T. Well, friend Wolsing—it was good to see you again. How nice it is to remember the few good days we had together about ten years ago, isn't that it, ten years ago? W. Yes, yes, ten years. Yes. Eleven years ago. T. Eleven years ago? W. Yes T. It's too bad that we did not see each other more often. W. I—I—I hope it I could come back to you again here—T. A-ah! W. in Nice—and study some more. Too short. Too short time here. T. Well, of course you know, I congratulate you for your desire to do well and to understand thoroughly what we all—what we are all trying to do. W. Oh yes, I hope it too. Until last time your idea to play the interval thus will be clear for me for—T. Ah—I am sure you understood now. I am sure. W. *You* are sure? T. Yes, I am sure you did. W. I thank you so much for all what you have done for me. T. Well, it was a pleasure to do it.

8 Brahms, *Violin Concerto*

9 Georges Gillet. The Wind

T. It *does* this. You see? The wind. (*Plays*) See? W. Yes. T. I increase, I increase in the speed. W. Up, up. T. That sound, you see? W. Yes, yes. round—T. The loop. You know, like my teacher, when I was a boy, you know, to explain that to me, he explained to me, Gillet, W. Gillet. T. The greatest man I ever met, you know—better than all the *conducteurs* together. You know? W. Yes? T. He said to me, "When you go in the country and you find a snail, pick it up, I mean, and look at it very thoroughly. You will see the snail, the shell, you know?" All right. That's the shell. You see, the shell goes this way (*sketches on paper*) double, double track. You see? That's the wind. You see? He said, "Make your wind do that," you know? and—and place your note—note here, note here, note here, note here, note here and note here and note here. You see what I mean? W. Yes. T. You understand? W. Yes. I think I understand. I think—and then you can place the note, there and there and there and there and there. T. That's right. You see what I mean? W. Yes. T. You see? W. Yes. T. And—the wind goes faster. You know, when you loop

— 525 —

the loop, if you go to a fair. You know, when I was a kid, I went to a fair, and you take a seat, you know, with a little carriage on two rails, and you go *this* way, you see? W. Um-hm. T. Well! My teacher explained to me, if you go, you take the ride. You know, it goes fast. Zz-z-itt, Slower—up. Zz-z-itt, slower—up. You know? Don't you understand? W. Oh, yes. So—? T. That's right. You see what I mean? Look here. We start here. You know, that was the track. We were here. Ten cents please, boys. You know the man collects money. W. Yes. T. All right, then he let loose the little *char* (*chariot*). You go down this way. Wo-o-oof! You see what I mean? W. Yes. T. And then you go—somewhere else. Another loop. Wo-o-oof! You see? It goes—it goes faster here—slow here—you know? From here, slow. Faster again—Slow—and so on. So, when I change—I make (*sings interval*) W. *Oui.* T. Don't you understand? W. Yes. And you—you-you—T. I press. I—I have more speed! W. Yes. T. There is more speed here. See what I mean? That's right. At the direct time—you know what I mean? At the right moment! W. Yes. T. If you do that at the wrong moment, it's you know—? W. And that makes that—? T. That's right. W. And here? Faster? T. Slower. Faster, W. A variation? T. That's right. W. Of the—T. That's what determines the up and down. W. Yes. Well! T. Don't you understand? That's why very few people play like I do, see what I mean, on a wind instrument. Don't you understand? W. Yes, yes. I see.

10 Rossini, Overture *L'Italiana in Algeri*

(*Plays*) T. Ah! You know, I—I—I—I traced—I traced the *Italienne* in Algiers—W. Oh. T. You know, I figure it out. You see—W. Yes. T. Did you figure out what I gave to you? (*Plays opening*) Oh, you took that? Let me see. Let me try a prelude. You know I want to fix the reed good so I play just those few bars. You know, all what I've played, I do not like it. You see what I mean? W. You don't like it? T. I don't—I did not like anything that I have done. I would like to play just few notes the rea—the way—the real way I want to play them. W. Hm? T. You understand the idea. So let me get in shape. (*Prepares*) Let's try it, huh? (*Plays*) Can I hear that? (*Plays*) T. You see—W. Yes . T. That's what I should have put on my, on my sustained note. You see. W. Yes. (*Sings repeated notes*) I played—and then, I collapsed. W. Yes. Yes, yes, yes. T. And that's why it sounded bad and I was unhappy. (*Plays again*)

11 Patterns. Up and down. Logic.

T. The pattern is two "down" and one "up." (*Plays*) Now, one "down"—two "up." (*Plays*) Let's hear that. (*Sings*) Up, down—up, down. Up, up.

down. That's my distribution W. Yes. (*Plays Massenet: Élégie*) You see, Let's hear that. T. Don't you think it is interesting? W. Yes. Very interesting . . . the life . . . T. Sure. If you play only one, one way traffic—you see—it's meaningless. You understand that? W. Of course. T. To make it short, life is like our system. It exhale and inhale. You see, that's what I mean by up and down. It is like breathing. You see what I mean. Taking a breath to keep alive. When you don't do that your music is dead. Like you would die, or would be dead if you don't—if you stop breathing—breathing, I mean to say. I must not pronounce it "breathing" and "brething." It is not the same thing, you know. You can play soft—you can play forte—you can play slow—you can play, you know, volume—sixty footer—thirty footer. Small . . . But it is dead, because you always play on one jet. It never—it never—it does not belong to an orbit. It's like a—it's like a star who don't belong to the system. It's called a comet, you know. All right. The organ music is like a comet-sshht!, and you never see it again, except maybe thousands of years—But when you have the right distribution, you know, that you—you, you play down, you play up—it's like breathing, I mean to say—you see? Up and down. It's like inhale and exhaling, you know? W. Yes. T. That means life in your music. T. That's all. You see what I mean? W. Yes. T. That's all the understanding that we should all have. W. Yes. T. And it is easy to see that way. Very easy. It does not mean a crescendo. On the contrary. When I go up, I think of smoke who is lighter than air and goes up, you see. W. Yes. T. Most of people they go up, they play louder, you know, crescendo going up—diminuendo going down. I do exactly the contrary. To me, a diminuendo—it's a sign of ascending. W. Umm? T. Like this. (*Plays Don Juan*) You see? My notes are going up: d—e-f#-g. Going up, but I go up and make a diminuendo. You see that. W. Yes. Yes, yes. T. It's like a crossing move. W. Yes, yes. T. That's why I know—I had so much fun in music. You know, I really had fun, because there is all the keys of logic and truth in music, you see, when you are willing to feel it the right way. W. Yes. T. (*Plays*) You see, I don't make a crescendo. My notes are going up but I don't make a crescendo. (*Plays Lakmé*) I want to—up—up. Now I am going to do—(*Plays*). That was up and down, you see? You see the two different ways. W. That's clear. T. You understand that? W. Yes. T. You see? Look here. (*Plays*) Up—I don't—W. Diminuendo—Up is speed and down is slow. T. That's right, like that, you see. (*Sings*) Faster here and slower and faster. You know when you turn a wheel, you push. Going up you don't have to push. The weight of the machine takes it up. You only have to push it

— 527 —

APPENDIX 1

down. W. Yes, yes. That's the same thing. That's why we could learn so much only with a willingness to go with logic. That's all.

12 Conversation outdoors in Nice

W. Beautiful parkway. T. Beautiful, but—so noisy! W. So Noisy? T. Yes,—and too many people. W. How many people are living here in Nice? T. Yes, yes. W. Oh, how many are here in Nice? Three hundred thousand? T.—oh, not as much. W. How much auto? How much? T. Oh, automobiles? W. Yes. T. Hundred of thousands every day. W. Oh, yes, yes. (*Sounds of traffic*) It's very nice weather today. Very nice weather. T. Do you live from the sea—far from the sea where you—W. No, I have the sea just under my window. I can see the docks and the piers and the ships there—over there—I sent you—one time I sent you some photos . . . T. Yes, that would be very interesting. W. Yes, they have there a great, a great boulevard there. Andersen's Boulevard. You know, the Fairy Tales. T. I see.

13 Horn call with numbers

Siegfried's Rhine Journey. Numbers. Speed of wind.

T. I would say—when they had something to play—a call—a horn call—(*Sings*) I would explain to them that—(*Sings*) 1-1 1-2, 2-2, 3-3, 3-4. See, and then I would say, never mind the horn. Put your horn—put your horn on your knees and simply for few minutes say: 1-1 1-2, 2-2, 3-3, 3-4. No, no notes, no melody. 1-1 1-2 123-234. 1-1 1-2-1-1 1-2 1-1 2-2 2-3 1-1 2-2 3-4 for the continuity, you see what I mean? And after doing that for one minute or two, I said, "now take your horn." Would you believe that they would play it as well as any, as any professional? You understand the idea? W. Yes, yes, T. Because they had, the, the, the directive of their mind. You see? (*Sings again*) Bon bon, bon-bon. Bon-bon con-nect. Bon—1, 2-2, 2-3 or 1-1, 2-2, 3-4. You see, the distribution as you want. 1-1, 1-2, 1-1, 2-2, 2-3-1-1, 1-2 and then the second one: 2-2, 2-3, 3-4, 4-4, 4-5. See, there is always a progression and you keep your line. W. Yes. T. You see. So, I only say that to you to explain that the little problem, the little game of distribution and speed of the wind with the pressure of the lips, you know? W. Yes .T. It works for every wind instrument. It works with any kind of wind instrument. You see, because when you, you increase the, the speed of the wind, you don't have to press so much with your lips.

You know, it's like the train on the railroad track. You see? W. Um hum. T. The train is at the stop in the station, but it is going to receive the order from the *chef de gare* to—to go again. You know, to run again.

APPENDIX 1

So, watch the locomotive. The locomotive—you know? It's heavy on the track . . . psssh -pssh-pssh . . . (*imitates the engine gaining speed*) You know when they have the speed, there is not so much weight on the track as when they start. Well, it is the same thing with your embouchure. Do you understand? W. I must start? T. With pressure.

W. With pressure? T. Because your wind is not at full speed. When the wind is at full speed—full speed—full speed (*pronounces more exactly!*) W. Yes, yes, yes. T. You can open your lips. It's like the, the, the train on the track is less—has less weight as when it starts to pull the twenty cars behind the locomotive. You understand? W. Yes. T. When they have the speed, they almost *fly* on the track. W. Uh hum. T. So it is the same *principe* for any wind instrument. (*Blows on reed*) You see when I play on "one," I press more. I press more when I am going to reach twenty or ten or nine—you see, I press here, because I have no speed, but (*demonstrates*), I open my-my, my, my lips like a carp—W. Yes. T.—taking air out of the water. You see what I mean? W. Here? (*Wolsing doesn't understand T's pronunciation, "hair" for "air"!*) You see, I don't pinch. The speed of the wind push the tone up! W. Yes, yes, yes. T. You know, like the train when it goes ninety miles an hour, has less weight on the track as when it start to, to roll. That's exactly—when I was speaking about logic a little while ago, that's what I mean by logic. W. Yes. T. That's all. (*Plays Siegfried again*) You see? 1 2 2-3, 2-2, 3-3, 3-4. (*Plays*) You see. Now I sustain the ta-ta-ta-ta-ta. (*Plays*) You see what I mean? W. Yes. T. You keep the line and you have the swing to—Hum-m? (*Blows on reed*)

14 Conductors. Reeds.

T. Against the accompaniment—against the bass. You see now, it is like if you play—try to fill a bottle with no bottom. You see what I mean? There must be a bottom to play against. W. Yes, yes. T. To fill the bottle. W. Yes. T. You fill the bottle because there—there is a bottom. If there is no bottom you never fill the bottle. W. No. T. So, that's what—that's what I mean by that. I have to play—I have to be the bottom. W. (*unintelligible*) T. You know—I should—I should have said again, the conductor must be the bottom!

Strauss: *Don Quixote* T. You see, that's my inner work. You see what I mean? W. Inner work? T. Inner work, you see. You see, I don't *play* that, but that's what I—I—I express, you see. W. Yes, yes. T. You see? That's all. W. That's all. *Lakmé* (*Demonstrates intervals*) And that's why, you know, I have, I have had so much fun. W. Yes. T. You know? When you—you, you almost can do what you wish to do, I think it—it was worthwhile to be alive for a short while. You see what I mean. W. Yes, yes.

T. (*Crows reed*) Well, you see that's the kind of reed you should play. You know, you should have always control even without the oboe. You, you understand? All right. (*Plays with reed alone*) That's what you have to do on the oboe. But it's a good *principe* for the reed. You almost have that figure eight of the reed I gave to that Ledet—you know what I mean. W. Yes. T. You know when I was young I used to play those—heh-heh—strong reeds, you know. Now I play old woman reeds. You know?

15 Pressure of the wind

T. He would say now before playing you have to exhale. Get the air out of your lungs. So I would say Ah-a-a-a-a-a-ah—He would say to me, no, no, don't inhale. Take your oboe—Play. That's the pressure. You see what I mean? W. Oh, yes. T. You don't play with the wind. You have to play with the *pressure* of the wind. So, for a few months, every time I (*unclear word*) a lesson, Ah—a-a-a-a-a-a-a-a-h -to empty the lungs -a-a-a-ah—Play! Tah. So I had to play with the pressure. You see what I mean? W. Yes. T. You understand that. You *blow* in the reed. W. Yes, yes, yes. T. You must not *blow* in the reed. Look here. Ah—a-a-a-a-a-a (*Attacks*) But if I would play Tah—see what I mean? (*Plays Sibelius: Symphony No. 2*) You see when I, I,—I—I spoke about—I need somebody to play against. Because the conductor would give me the downbeat. You see what I mean? W. Yes. T. Now when I play alone it sounds like I start on "one." You see—against—instead of playing against "one." W. Yes. Yes, yes. T. That's why I need a conductor. Rea—dy. (*Plays Sibelius again*) Do the conducting now so that I can play. (*Plays Sibelius a half-step lower*) All right.

16 Message to the Danish oboists: Tofte-Hansen, Hammergaard, and Hovaldt

Well, it was good to be with all my friend of Copenhagen again through the medium of our mutual friend, Wolsing. Of course we spoke about you and how nice young men you are. Please, be sure I was thinking of you when I play five or six notes from Sibelius beautiful sentence that I played in your machine.

Wolsing: Thank you so much, cher maître.

Tabuteau: You are all welcome.

APPENDIX 1

APPENDIX 2.
THE STUDENTS OF
MARCEL TABUTEAU AT THE
CURTIS INSTITUTE OF MUSIC

From 1925 to 1954 listed in chronological order:

Bernard Raphael
Guy Shortz
Llewellyn Reynolds
Adrian Siegel
Lloyd Ullberg
Robert Bloom
Frederick Compton
Abraham Krupnick
Paul Bartholomew
Robert Hester
Sidney Divinsky
Harold Gomberg
Rhadames Angelucci
Isadore Goldblum
Arno Mariotti
John Rigano
John Minsker
Albert London
Leo Esral

Martin Fleisher
Harry Shulman
Don Edwin Cassel
Livingston Gearhart
Edmund Jurgenson
Edwin Kosinski
William Kosinski
William Vitelli
Perry Bauman
John de Lancie
Charles Gilbert
Joseph Lukatsky
Ralph Gomberg
Victor Molzer
Robert Davison
Thelma Neft
MacLean Synder
Kenneth Van der Heuvel
Charles Morris
William Criss
Laila Storch
Martha Scherer
Marguerite Smith
Charles Edmunds
Marc Lifschey
George Thomas
Laurence Thorstenberg
Walter Bianchi
John Mack
Louis Rosenblatt
Dominique-René de Lerma
Alfred Genovese
Felix Kraus
Theodore Heger
Issac Hilles
Donald Hefner
Stewart Davis
Richard Kanter

Note: List provided by Elizabeth Walker, librarian of the Curtis Institute of Music

APPENDIX 2

APPENDIX 3.
THE TABUTEAU SYSTEM:
ESSAY AND OUTLINE
BY MARC MOSTOVOY

Introduction

At various times throughout the years Marcel Tabuteau spoke of his desire to put his thoughts on performance and teaching into written form. He often appeared to be searching for someone to help him organize and codify his ideas. Both Waldemar Wolsing in 1964 and Wayne Rapier in 1965 brought tape recorders to Nice to help Tabuteau attempt such a project. But it was a string player, not an oboist, who transcribed Tabuteau's principles onto paper. Marc Mostovoy, a young violist and aspiring conductor, spent the three summers of 1962–64 in France studying with Tabuteau. In 1965 at Tabuteau's request, twenty-three-year-old Mostovoy wrote a summary of his lessons that Tabuteau referred to as "the chats we had together." He based the "essay" on the extensive notes he had taken and sent it to his teacher for correction and approval. Following Tabuteau's favorable response, Marc sent him an expanded version in outline form: "A Résumé of the Tabuteau System." These documents remain the only representation of Tabuteau's teaching beliefs that were being codified with his cooperation. *L. S.*

Contents

Marcel Tabuteau's Ideas on Music, Music Performance and Interpretation

Essay by Marc Mostovoy

> Read, annotated, and approved by Marcel Tabuteau shortly before his death.

Music is life, a living art. It is governed by natural laws [of logic]* as are all living things. Music should not work contrary to nature but in accordance with it and with all those forces that have a continuous effect upon us. As a living being must breathe, so must music. It must inhale as well as exhale. Music can be described as a combination of inhalations and exhalations; as life is in continuous movement, so must it be with music. There is constant motion all around us and within us. Music being life must have this continuous movement, pulse, and direction to remain alive. When these elements cease to exist, the music dies.

---

*Tabuteau's penciled annotations are noted in brackets. They were reminders to himself of the changes he wished to have incorporated into the final version.

APPENDIX 3

Music is life, a living art. It is governed by the natural ~~facts~~ LAWS *of logic* of our ~~universe~~
as are all living things. Music, therefore, is not something that s\should work contrary

Music being ~~life~~ must have continuous movement, pulse, and direction to remain al~~ive~~
and when they cease to exist, the music dies. *noise remains / picture cars when not in gear with motor running but does not move*

rebound must be considered when interpreting a piece of music. We must transfer those
little black notes on the page into a living, vital force. *must serious handicap of our elementary learning is the ⅜ etc.) 2 notes = 1 interval, 2 notes = 1 passing value*
    What shall be our approach to the problem ? First, we must analize the rhyth~~mic~~

the phrase will lose its form or backbone. The phrase must always retain a definit~~ely~~
form of skeleton to it. *n 4 Rousseau idea we too often believe we are doing the expressing thing by placing the 16th note yet wrong, keep To th notes fixed like they are*
    We cannot, of course, number in any haphazard fashion but rather in logical and

*Section of Marc Mostovoy's 1965 "essay" with corrections written in pencil
by Marcel Tabuteau.*

[Noise remains. Picture a car that is not in gear with motor running, but does not move.]

Music can be compared to a language. It has its own forms of grammar, sentence structure, and punctuation, all of which must be utilized correctly. It is a very difficult language to master. One must arrange the letters or notes very carefully and group them into words with the proper spelling; then into sections and phrases, sentences, and paragraphs, and finally into an entire composition. During that process, the punctuation marks must be chosen and placed where needed to clarify the meaning of each phrase so that no ambiguity remains. The truth of each word must be recognized. Commas, colons, dashes, question marks, and exclamation points have to be used in the right places. The notes are your alphabet and they must be properly phrased. It is indeed no easy task to play a piece correctly; no easier than writing a novel.

With these thoughts in mind, let us approach the musical phrase. In reality, what we see in the score is the negative of a picture where black is white and white is black. We must develop the picture into its positive form, which is its true form. It is not enough to play the notes with good intonation, correct rhythm, [division] proper dynamics, et cetera. Anyone with some intelligence can be taught the mechanics of music, which are only the prerequisites to achieving good phrasing. Their importance is, of course, paramount, but beyond this, one must apply

— 535 —
APPENDIX 3

correct articulations, note spacings, and above all, give the phrase life by applying color to the music. Direction, inflection and rebound also need to be considered. We must transfer those little black notes on the page into a living, vital force. [Most serious handicap of our elementary training is the wrong logic; two notes = one interval. two notes = one positive value. To each one tonality.]

How shall we do this? First, we must analyze the rhythmic structure of a given phrase and have a complete understanding of what the composer intends. We then take the notes and divide them into the most logical group patterns for expressing the feeling of the particular phrase. After doing that, we observe a very interesting fact. Almost always, the last note of a group pattern falls on the first beat of the following measure. Contrary to popular belief, the groups usually do not start on the first beat and end on the last. For example, in a 4/4 measure of quarter notes, you do not count them as 1-2-3-4 but rather as 4-1-2-3 with 4 occurring again on the first beat of the next measure (4-1-2-3 / 4). This is a natural procedure and can be shown to work in nature. For example, to take four steps, you must actually take five. On the fourth step, your legs are still apart so you must take the extra or fifth step for your legs to come back together to complete the action. You are then again in the starting position. So it is with the grouping of notes. We almost always start the grouping with the second note and treat the first note as the ending of the preceding group.

We find also, that notes in different time signatures can be grouped in various patterns according to what sounds best. If there are five or more beats to a bar, they should be grouped or divided into combinations of the basic divisions of two, three and four. For example, a five beat measure could be divided into 3+2, or 2+3. Six can be 3+3, 2+4, 4+2, or 2+2+2. Many times there will be only one set of group patterns that sound right for a phrase, but other times a number of groups could work equally well. It is then up to the performer to use whichever pattern seems to do the most justice to the music. In many instances it is even possible, and in fact necessary, to change from one group pattern to another in the same passage. For example, in a series of 6/4 measures, your groupings can go from 3+3 to 4+2 and then to a 2+4 pattern all in one passage. However, this possibility is unfortunately very rarely considered.

An example of Tabuteau's own notation of his number system.

Note grouping is only the beginning. Our next step is to combine or synchronize the group patterns with varied colors, inflections, et cetera. Let us use numbers to represent the amount of color a certain note is to receive. This is perhaps an artificial way of expressing the color but it is good for getting the idea across, as we must have some unit of measure. The higher the number, the more color or density the note will have and the lower the number, less color. There should be constant variation. However, it is not good to give every note a different color or number, as the phrase will lose its backbone. The phrase must retain a definite form or skeleton. Our main object is to give the phrase life and yet to keep it on as smooth a curve as possible. We must both ascend and descend in the most even and musical way we can. We should also constantly be on guard not to play on the "zero" level or to use the same numbers over and over again in succession. The music would then stand still and die. It could be compared to a man trying to go somewhere but who marks time in place instead of walking ahead to his destination. The music must remain in constant motion. It must stay alive. [J. J. Rousseau idea: We too often believe we are doing the expected thing by playing the right note, yet we neglect to do justice to the real life of the note—vibration.]

We cannot use numbers in any haphazard fashion but rather in logical and consistent patterns combining the grouping patterns with the coloring of each note. The numbers may either ascend or descend according to what the phrase calls for rhythmically, harmonically, and melodically. Whenever we desire a group change or when the rhythm definitely calls for one, we apply the same number to the last note of the preceding group and to the first note of the new group, thereby serving a three-fold purpose: to distinguish between the two groups, to give backbone to the phrase, and to help give the phrase a smooth curve. The second repeated number automatically calls for a type of rebound. We could compare it to a billiard ball bouncing off the side of the table, or when someone reaches for a piece of food, which is too hot; he touches it and quickly pulls his hand back. This is what we mean by a rebound.

Other notes in the phrase require what we call inflections because of the part they play either rhythmically or harmonically in the phrase. These inflections are opposite in feeling to the rebound. Notes with inflection are played with a slight nudging feeling or small push such as when a child playfully nudges his friend during a game. Both the inflection and rebound are inward feelings or reactions, something that must be felt—not done with obvious accents. Each note can have an "up" or "down" feeling or what we may call inhalation and exhalation. The rebound can usually be considered as an "up" feeling and inflection as "down," although it is possible to have rebounds on notes that are "down" and inflections on notes with "up" feeling. The amount of coloring each note receives and the proper distribution of inflections and rebounds must be carefully considered. We usually find that the numbers increase to a certain point and then decrease with the same pattern so they can ascend once again. It is good to keep the color changing in as consistent patterns as possible. Correctly combining the groupings and coloring make the music bubble over with precious life. Of course, these ideas are only the beginning. Much more is involved but this is the basis or foundation for all that is to follow. Music must stay alive!

A word of caution at this point: The amount of coloring or density a note receives should not be mistaken for the dynamic level which is something else again. Numbers or coloring may increase over both a crescendo and a decrescendo and vice versa. The two have no definite relationship to one another. The basic difference between dynamic and color can be illustrated as follows: On a stringed instrument, the amount of color is related to the speed of the bow across the strings and at what point between the bridge and fingerboard the bow is being drawn. The dynamic level is directly related to the amount of pressure being exerted by the bow on the string. Therefore, it is possible to have a fff with little or no color and quite dead, or a ppp with a high number bursting apart at the seams with color and excitement. Of course, the reverse could be true.

On a wind instrument, the changes of color are achieved by the speed of the air blown through the instrument, by the position of the lips, and the amount of pressure applied to the reed or mouthpiece. The dynamics are affected by the amount of air forced through the instrument. On either a string instrument or a wind instrument, therefore, we can see how we get various tone colors over many different dynamic levels. It stands to reason that the more proficient the player, the more coloring he is able to produce. It is extremely important not to confuse the two terms, dynamics and coloring.

Taking all of this into consideration, we must always realize that there can be more than one way of phrasing a line. It is up to the musician to think of the above concepts as a basis upon which to build. He must find for himself the most logical and musical way of interpreting the phrase. The good string player learns to place the notes on the bow and the wind player to place the notes on the wind. The poor musician makes the notes with his bow or with his wind. This is a very important distinction. It is not an easy task and it will take years of study and experimentation to learn how to apply these concepts.

Technically, musicians are playing better than ever, but musically there can often be a lack of true communication. Musicians should apply the concepts of grouping, coloring, inflection, and rebound to help give real meaning to what is on the written page. We need artists who

APPENDIX 3

will not rely solely on their natural ability but who will also apply musical logic to their playing. We must all strive to raise music to the highest levels, where its true splendor, unobstructed by mediocrity, can radiate to all and become an ever-vital living force.

Marcel Tabuteau's Teaching

A unique aspect of Tabuteau's colorful approach to teaching was his uncanny ability to pull out of the air, on the spur of the moment, imaginative expressions to help get across an important musical idea. A never-ending wealth of analogies and examples poured forth as if from a geyser, producing vivid imagery to demonstrate or amplify the concept at hand. Tabuteau's principles were inspired by life, nature, motion and other natural phenomena—or as he himself often said—"the natural laws of nature and logic." These basic tenets ran as a thread through his teaching and although he expounded on favorite examples over the years, he continually added to his verbal "repertoire," finding creative new ways to express his ever-expanding ideas.

The following notations (the first seven sections of a total of forty-eight) were written in longhand during my lessons with Marcel Tabuteau during the summers of 1962–64. They capture, in Tabuteau's own words, his ideas about music. His colorful explanations were accompanied by demonstrations using his oboe, voice, and animated body language. Some of Tabuteau's musical concepts are abstract and not easy to understand, especially without benefit of his personal demonstration. Often he would verbalize the same thought slightly differently at a subsequent lesson. I have generally included one version or a consolidation, but the words and syntax remain his. As I recorded his ideas over a period of three summers, there are certain inconsistencies and points needing clarification which I planned to resolve with him during the summer of 1966. For the record, however, I felt it important to present all of the principles as he stated them with the hope that every musician reading this would glean something of value. Because of my string background (I brought my viola to lessons), and interest in conducting, Tabuteau verbalized many of his concepts with that in mind.

The headings in bold type are my categorizations—an attempt to organize his thoughts in the most comprehensible manner possible. A quote encompassing more than one topic may be repeated in the relevant section. In lengthier sections, I have introduced subheadings for easy reference. Words in (parenthesis) are his; words in [brackets] are my edits, inserted only for clarification or informational purposes. It should be remembered that Tabuteau stated there could be exceptions to his "rules" even when he says "always."

d = down; u = up

T = Tabuteau

The "Tabuteau system" (his term) is T's unique method of analyzing and explaining the (very difficult to explain) art of music performance by breaking music down into its smallest and most vital components and relating it to life itself. *M. M.*

1. INHALE/EXHALE

It is always two elements that create a meaning. Your line [phrase] is a continuous disturbance of inhale and exhale. Music is living and must breathe.

Everything occurs in pairs: High tide/low tide, day/night, inhaling/exhaling, etc.; that is life.

2. UP/DOWN INFLECTIONS (impulses)

You can have up inflections and down inflections. Inhales are up in feeling, exhales are down in feeling. Up equals energy—down equals weight.

An oboist always blows out, yet he must make ups and downs.

Downs are heavier than ups. Before you have a down inflection, you should go up.

An inflection up is suspense; when you go up you must come down unless [you wish to remain] suspended.

Even though the up is more intense, you must make the down sound down. The inflections must be correct—up and down.

Practice up-down and down-up; there's a world of difference.

Sometimes you have an up and a down [inflection] on [within] the same note.

If you think down on the wrong note, then you are cooked!

APPENDIX 3

Stravinsky, for example, wrote music in complex time signatures and changing ones, so that the up and down inflections fall at the right place.

3. "HELPING" UP/DOWN (for string players)

It is not enough for the bow [just] to go up [or down]; you must help up to be up and down to be down [to effectuate a difference]. Help the bow go up: Lift—go up with it.

On a slurred [or tied] upbeat to downbeat, think up and down and move the instrument to show up and down, even though the direction of the bow is the same.

4. UP/DOWN BOWING

Whenever possible, use down-bows on downs and ups [up-bows] on up; e.g., in ¾ time, the first beat is down-bow and the third beat is up-bow; the middle beat is your choice.

Change direction with your bow when needed. The point is not whether your down note is on your down-bow, but whether you are changing the bow when you should. This is of extreme importance as it is not good to keep the same direction of the bow for notes that need the bow in the opposite direction.

Rather than having all different [random] bowing [in string sections], have all bow one way [unified bowing], whether right or wrong. [T said he did not agree with Stokowski's idea of free bowing.]

You can only give and take—you only have ups and downs. You must bridge the gap between an up and a down with your bow wrist; the wrist is the link. Like a paintbrush, connect up and down strokes.

5. BOWING OPPOSITE

In bowing, you often have to play down inflections up-bow and up inflections down-bow when the bowing is impossible to match. Use an up-bow on a down inflection and vice versa only when there is no other choice.

If you are on a down-bow on an up inflection or vice versa, move the violin in the right direction so the inflection is correct.

When playing downs [down inflections] on up-bows and vice versa, use your [bow hand] index finger to give weight to the downs.

Practice down inflections on up-bows and vice versa. You must overcome the technical deficiencies of instruments.

APPENDIX 3

6. SIDE INFLECTIONS (impulses)

Some notes cannot be classed as up or down inflections but feel to the side—to the left or to the right. North and south are not enough—you must [also] have the east and west. [T example: Beethoven's 1st symphony, 2nd movement, third note]

7. PLACING NOTES

The good musician places the notes on the breath or on the bow; the poor one makes the notes with his breath or bow. Don't wind or bow your notes! [A favorite T expression]

Carry your breath through [on an articulated passage]; your tongue moves and articulates the stream of air; i.e., play the note legato and touch the wind to make the articulation.

Practice the wind first then place your notes. Always place the note on the line both as far as dynamics and color. (The wind doesn't change; it's the mouth that works.)

The distribution of your bow is extremely important; place the notes correctly on the bow.

Exercise [practice] on one note first.

You play your notes against silence, not on silence; you must make opposition.

The introductory page of "A Résumé of the Tabuteau System"

Purpose of the Tabuteau System

- To bring the elements of life, naturalness and good taste to music
- To present and encourage the use of some relatively unexplored concepts in music performance
- To provide musicians with the essential skills needed to shape the music as desired
- To teach musicians how to think creatively and be witty with music
- To instill knowledge enabling a musician's interpretation to stand apart from others
- To help take away monotony from music performance by giving direction and color to the musical phrase
- To remove the element of mere chance or luck in music performance by approaching it with a much greater degree of thought and understanding
- To eliminate the bar-line as a sign of division
- To incorporate the "dance step" into music performance

APPENDIX 3

- To bring out to the fullest what has always been there in great music while helping lesser music succeed by means of creative treatment
- To raise the level of audience understanding and appreciation of classical music by performing only at the highest level
- To show musicians how to practice and activate all of the above

APPENDIX 3

GLOSSARY OF TERMS
USED BY OBOISTS

Cane: *Arundo donax,* plant from which oboists make their own reeds. It grows in all Mediterranean-type climates, but the cane most favored for the past two hundred years has been that from the region of Var, France, particularly near Fréjus. It is cut, dried, and prepared according to specific traditional standards. Depending on soil, wind, and sun, like wine, the quality of cane from the banks of a stream or field near one village will differ from that twenty kilometers further on. The same type of cane is used for the reeds of all woodwind instruments (clarinet, bassoon, saxophone, but in varying diameters, with the oboe using the smallest, between 10 and 11 millimeters).

French scrape reed: also called "short scrape." The manner of scraping a reed historically favored by the Paris Conservatoire–trained oboists who came to play in American symphony orchestras in the early part of the twentieth century. Marcel Tabuteau was largely responsible for changing this style of reed making during his years in the Philadelphia Orchestra and teaching at the Curtis Institute of Music. The most noticeable characteristic of his changes was the use of a longer "scrape." During several decades as his students gradually spread from the East

Coast toward the West Coast, taking their reed skills with them, the last "pockets" of the short scrape eventually disappeared.

Gouger: a small machine (approximately 5×7 inches) with a curved blade in a guide bar. It is pushed back and forth by hand to remove the center pulp of the cane and must be set to a precise inner curve which is largely responsible for the eventual tone quality and response of the finished reed.

Oboe bell: the small flared end section of an oboe can make a difference in the tone quality of the instrument. Tabuteau, always seeking something better, frequently tried different bells, had the inside dimensions changed, or borrowed them from his students.

Shaper: hand-held hardened steel tool which clamps the piece of gouged and folded cane (after soaking in water) to create the exact form or "shape" of the finished reed. A sharp knife or razor blade is employed to remove the excess cane from the sides of the shaper. The shaped cane is then tied onto a 47-millimeter-long metal tube with cork around its base. Using very sharp special knives, the oboist must then trim and scrape the reed to playable state. This may require anything from fifteen minutes to reworkings over a period of several days. Shapers are made with many different dimensions, which greatly affect the tone quality and pitch of the reed.

NOTES

PREFACE

1. David Blum, *Casals and the Art of Interpretation* (Berkeley: University of California Press, 1977), pp. 18–19.

1. COMPIÈGNE AND THE TABUTEAU FAMILY

1. Edward Blakeman, *Taffanel* (New York: Oxford University Press, 2005), pp. 207–208.

2. It is not known whether this Grumiaux family was related to the family of well-known Belgian violinist Arthur Grumiaux, but Tabuteau himself wondered about this.

3. As I was unable to find Létoffé's name in Paris Conservatoire records, I do not know what institution granted his prize.

4. Claudette Paul and Jean-Claude Lecru, *Compiègne à La Belle Epoque* (Brussels: Éditions Libro-Sciences SR, 1973), no. 117 (photograph of the inn).

5. *Compiègne à La Belle Epoque*, no. 11.

6. The clock can be seen in postcard no. 3 in *Compiègne à La Belle Epoque*.

7. Letter to Laila Storch from François Létoffé, July 22, 1980.

2. PARIS CONSERVATOIRE

1. If not for this white marble plaque, I would never have been able to find Gillet's tomb when I first searched for it in 1976. Covered with moss, its inscription eroded through time and neglect, it was indistinguishable from the long rows of other gray tombstones. Now, with help from American and French oboists, the Association Française du Hautbois has seen that Gillet's grave is cleaned and restored.

2. Paul Taffanel (1844–1908, b. Bordeaux, d. Paris), flutist and conductor, professor at Conservatoire, and conductor of Société des Concerts du Conservatoire and Opéra de Paris.

3. For this concert, Louis Bas was the oboist in the première of the Novácek *Sinfonietta,* while Gillet played in the Beethoven *Quintet* for piano and winds, the Handel *G Minor Sonata,* and the Mozart *Serenade for Thirteen Winds.*

4. The French word *mécanisme* to denote facility of execution has always seemed more reasonable to me than our commonly used term *technique,* as true technique is not simply fast fingers but must include control of all the elements required to play well.

5. Philip Bate, *The Oboe,* 3rd ed. (New York: W. W. Norton, 1975), pp. 204–205.

6. Longatte was to become a respected professor at the Conservatoire of Valenciennes and Pontier, who played in Concerts Colonne and the Opéra-Comique and who experimented with making oboes and with various ways of scraping reeds. Information from Gaston Longatte *fils,* 1976, and Étienne Baudo, 1998.

7. Sol Schoenbach, principal bassoon, Philadelphia Orchestra (1937–57); later, director of the Settlement School of Music, Philadelphia.

8. According to a folk saying, the inhabitants of Compiègne were often referred to as *les dormeurs* (sleepy people) because they inhaled so much ozone from the famous surrounding forest. (Thanks to François Létoffé.)

9. Conversation with John de Lancie, 1996.

10. Archives Nationales, Série AJ37.

11. At the time Tabuteau attended the Conservatoire, there were four progressive awards possible in the *concours;* in ascending order, they were *second accessit, premier accessit, second prix,* and *premier prix.* The two former correspond to honorable mentions.

12. According to Gaston Longatte *fils,* Mercier would become soloist with the Garde Républicaine, while Balout played in the Opéra-Comique.

13. The Société des Concerts du Conservatoire, featuring the professors of the Conservatoire along with some of the outstanding students, was arguably the best orchestra in Europe at the time. The lofty pronouncement issued in 1846 by M. de Kératy, a peer of France, does not overstate its eminence: "These concerts of the Conservatoire, have they not merited a European reputation? Has one not heard of them up to the banks of the Danube, the Sprée, the Tiber and the Neva? The admirable symphonies of Beethoven, have they been as completely understood and interpreted anywhere else?" Constant Pierre, *Le Conservatoire National de Musique et de Déclamation* (Paris: Imprimerie Nationale, 1900), p. 940.

14. Paul Rougnon, *Souvenirs de 60 Années de Vie Musicale et de 50 Années de Professorat au Conservatoire de Paris* (Paris: Editions Margueritat, 1925).

15. Archives Nationales, Série AJ37, 248.

16. *Le Ménestrel,* July 31, 1904, p. 247.

17. However, he once told me that when he graduated from the Conservatoire and went into an orchestra, he couldn't attack a note—Gillet's reeds were wonderful for lessons but not for orchestra playing.

18. Program from Bibliothèque Historique de la Ville de Paris, with thanks to Nancy Toff.

3. ARRIVAL IN AMERICA

1. First steps were taken to unionize musicians as early as 1878 with the formation of the Musical Mutual Protective Union of New York. Invitations to join with the American Federation of Labor were refused until 1896, when a number of local unions attended the AFL convention in Indianapolis and voted to found the American Federation of

Musicians. For the next two or three decades, its main concern, aside from fixing wage scales and work conditions, was the restriction on importing players from Europe to fill U.S. orchestra positions. Joseph Weber, with whom Damrosch had extensive dealings, became the second president of the AFM in 1900, serving until 1940.

2. Some decades later guests included Karen Blixen of *Out of Africa* fame and the British actor John Gielgud.

3. Damrosch Collection, New York Public Library (hereafter cited as Damrosch Collection), MNY Box 20, Folder C.

4. Damrosch Collection, Amer Box 33, Organizations, Musicians Union, Folder A.

5. Damrosch Collection, 3, Composers and Performers, Box 8.

6. Damrosch Collection, 3, Composers and Performers, Box 8.

7. Laurence Ibisch, "A French Bassoonist in the United States: Auguste Mesnard," *Double Reed* 1, no. 2 (October 1978).

8. Barrère Autobiography, Nancy Toff Archive.

9. National Archives Microfilm Publication, T715, Reel 573.

10. Walter Damrosch, *My Musical Life* (New York: Charles Scribner's Sons, 1926), p. 213.

11. Damrosch Collection, MNY, Amer Box 33, Folder A.

12. Nancy Toff, *Georges Barrère and the Flute in America*, exhibition catalog, New York Public Library for the Performing Arts, 1994.

13. Damrosch Collection, Box 20, Folder B, Barrère contract.

14. Damrosch Collection, Box 20, Folder D.

15. David Whitwell, *The Longy Club: A Professional Wind Ensemble in Boston (1900–1917)* (Northridge, Calif.: Winds, 1988), p. 5 n. 7.

16. After leaving New York, Addimando became the first oboist of the San Francisco Symphony Orchestra. A program résumé from 1922 shows that he played the Beethoven *Trio* in the orchestra's sixth season, 1916–17.

17. Recounted by San Francisco oboists to John de Lancie.

18. Damrosch did not hesitate to threaten musicians who tried to break their contracts. He told Addimando, "Do not act hastily. If you deliberately break your contract you will find it impossible to accept any other engagements . . . as both the laws of the State of New York and the laws of the American Federation of Musicians would prevent that." Damrosch Collection 3, Composers and performers, Box 8.

19. Damrosch, *My Musical Life,* p. 204.

20. If it seems that undue emphasis is being given to the rare occasions between 1905 and 1915 when Tabuteau's name appears, it must be remembered that personnel lists of musicians for either orchestra concerts or operas were not routinely included in the printed programs. The importance of the Beethoven *Trio* lies in the confirmation it provides of Tabuteau's presence during the far-flung peregrinations of the Damrosch orchestra.

21. Damrosch Collection, 5, Concerts and Recitals, Folder A.

22. Damrosch Collection, 3, Composers and Performers, Barrère.

23. Damrosch Collection, 3, Composers and Performers, Box 8, New York Symphony members.

24. Bruno Labate appears to have been in the English horn position for Damrosch during Tabuteau's year of absence for French military service. The following year (1908) in New York he played second oboe in the Beethoven *Trio* with Tabuteau again on English horn. They were to remain good friends. Arthur Statter remembered that much later when Toscanini and the New York Philharmonic came to play in Philadelphia, Labate and Tabuteau would meet at the stage door of the Academy of Music and walk down the street toward a bar "jabbering away a mile a minute."

25. Damrosch Collection, 3, Composers and Performers, Box 8, New York Symphony members.

26. Damrosch Collection, Box 33, Organizations, General, Musicians Union, Folder A. Weber conveniently overlooks the fact that Tabuteau was replaced not by an American-born musician, but by an earlier "import" from Europe.

27. In May 1908 Tabuteau was not yet twenty-one years old.

4. THE METROPOLITAN OPERA

1. The Belgian oboist Albert de Busscher was the younger brother of the better known Henri de Busscher. See chapter 6, note 8, regarding the spelling of his name.

2. Famous American soprano Lillian Nordica had changed her name of Norton to a more Italian-sounding one. She became especially famous for Wagnerian roles.

3. New York Public Library, Damrosch Collection 3, Composers and Performers, Box 8.

4. It is not known exactly why Tabuteau pretended to be Belgian, but possibly in his determination to advance in his profession he felt a connection with the prestigious opera in Brussels could benefit him.

5. "Brief of an Artist," *Woodwinds Magazine* (ed. James Collis), February 1948.

6. Interview with John de Lancie, April 1999.

7. Damrosch Collection, 3, Composers and Performers, Box 8.

8. Louise Homer, an eminent American contralto, was the aunt of composer Samuel Barber.

9. Tabuteau, therefore, must have played in that historic opening of the 1908 season. It seems unlikely that such a meticulous conductor as Toscanini would have entrusted the important Nile Scene for oboe and soprano to an untried player, even considering the dearth of fine oboists. Perhaps there was some sort of rehearsal, even if not a complete run-through with orchestra and all singers. Tabuteau's perception sixty years later could easily have been that there was essentially no rehearsal.

10. Martin Mayer, *The Met: One Hundred Years of Grand Opera* (New York: Simon & Schuster, 1983), p. 103; Max Smith, writing in the *Press*.

11. Aldrich and Krehbiel quoted by Harvey Sachs, *Toscanini* (Philadelphia: J. B. Lippincott, 1978), p. 106.

12. Mayer, *Met*, p. 99.

13. Mahler's three seasons at the Met were 1907–1908, 1908–1909, and 1909–10. Toscanini had seven seasons there, 1908 through 1914–15.

14. Marcella Sembrich later became Tabuteau's colleague on the faculty of the Curtis Institute of Music.

15. Mayer, *Met*, p. 81.

16. Article by Bert Lucarelli, based on an article by Margaret Downie Banks, *Newsletter of the American Musical Instrument Society* 19, no. 2–3 (June–October 1990).

17. All information about Met contracts comes from the Metropolitan Opera Archive.

18. Story told by Tabuteau to John de Lancie. Recounted to the author by de Lancie in 2000.

1. Visit with Brooks Parker, Seattle, 1976.

2. Archives of the Philadelphia Orchestra, Academy of Music, Philadelphia.

3. Archives Départementales de l'Oise, Rp 963, Registre Matricule du Recrutement, Marcel Paul Tabuteau-Guérineau, Classe 1907, Bureau de Recrutement de Compiègne, vol. 3, no. 1291.

4. *The Architecture and Landscape of the Exposition* (San Francisco: Paul Elder, 1915), p. 20.

5. In this discussion, I have relied for information upon Frank Morton Todd, *The Story of the Exposition: Being the Official History of the International Celebration Held at San Francisco in 1915 to Commemorate the Discovery of the Pacific Ocean and the Construction of the Panama Canal,* 5 vols. (New York: Published for the Panama-Pacific International Exposition Company by G. P. Putnam's Sons, the Knickerbocker Press, 1921), vol. 2.

6. The eminent Boston music critic Philip Hale wrote a glowing "Appreciation" of Saint-Saëns for one of the exposition programs. "The fact that Camille Saint-Saëns will visit the Panama-Pacific Exposition as guest and in the capacity of composer, conductor, pianist and organist, is a matter of international importance . . . He comes, not only as one of the greatest composers now living, but as an ambassador from a sister republic, whose friendship has been constant and sincere since the days of the Revolution." Hale devotes two more paragraphs to Saint-Saëns's wide range of accomplishments beyond that of music. (San Francisco Library of Performing Arts)

7. Fair booklet and daily programs, San Francisco Library of Performing Arts.

8. The famous Richter, who did not wish to cross the ocean, had refused all offers to conduct in the United States.

9. James J. Badal, "The Strange Case of Dr. Karl Muck," *High Fidelity,* October 1970, pp. 55–60.

6. THE PHILADELPHIA ORCHESTRA

1. Told to John de Lancie (July 26, 1921–May 17, 2002) by Tabuteau. Related to me by John de Lancie, April 24, 1999.

2. Bate's statement appears in *New Grove Dictionary of Music and Musicians,* ed. Stanley Sadie, 20 vols. (New York: Macmillan, 1980), vol. 18, p. 516, entry for "Tabuteau, Marcel."

3. Notes from my diary, January 28, 1945. See chapter 11, p. 333.

4. Oliver Daniel, *Stokowski: A Counterpoint of View* (New York: Dodd, Mead, 1982), p. 290.

5. Leopold Stokowski interviewed by Gordon Stafford, March 1956, quoted in Daniel, *Stokowski,* p. 291.

6. Tabuteau to Laila Storch in Prades, 1950.

7. In the 1920s Doucet was known to be playing in the leading movie theater of Minneapolis, where the salary was $65 a week as opposed to the Minneapolis Symphony Orchestra wage of $35. Letter from Theodore Heger to the author, January 2000.

8. De Busscher's name appears in various spellings—De Busscher, Debucher, or de Busscher. The generally accepted form is de Busscher.

9. There were three de Busscher brothers. Henri de Busscher, solo oboist of the Queen's Hall Orchestra in London, left in 1913 to be succeeded by Léon Goossens. Melvin Harris, "Oboist Extraordinary," *To the World's Oboists* 3, no. 3 (1975), p. 1. Henri was the middle brother, François the oldest, and Albert the youngest. All three studied the oboe with Guillaume Guidé, the great Belgian master. They were also boy singers. The de Busscher discussed in the Damrosch papers is Albert. He is listed as solo oboist in the Cincinnati Symphony Orchestra programs of 1906 and 1913, but he may not have been there continually between those dates. Henri de Busscher is named as fourth oboe in Cincinnati for the 1913–14 season. Did his brother Albert help him out after the failure of the Philadelphia negotiations? Albert was in Cincinnati in 1908 when Damrosch engaged him for the New York Symphony Orchestra. He could therefore have come to New York at the same time that Tabuteau joined the Metropolitan Opera (see chapter 4). Albert was considered a very gifted oboist but supposedly drank too much and led such a reckless life that he often could not play at all. Tabuteau told John de Lancie that Albert would come to see him in the middle of the night and beg him to fix a reed as he had nothing to play on. For more detailed information on Henri de

Busscher and his brothers, see Beth Antonopulos, "Oboist Henri de Busscher: From Brussels to Los Angeles," DMA diss., University of Washington, 2002.

10. It would not have been acceptable or even legal for the union to admit someone knowing that the orchestra already wanted him for the first oboe position. The correspondence between Wheeler and Stokowski is preserved in the archives of the Philadelphia Orchestra.

11. Eugene Devaux had been a member of the Philadelphia Orchestra oboe section in 1910–11, before Stokowski arrived.

12. C. Stanley Mackey, tuba player in the Philadelphia Orchestra from 1900 to 1904; also acted as personnel manager, 1905–15, and as principal librarian, 1907–15. Archives of the Philadelphia Orchestra.

13. It would be a number of years before Tabuteau incorporated the letter *h* into his spelling of *which*.

14. Although Tabuteau was not officially accepted into the oboe class at the Conservatoire until he was fifteen, he probably felt that he could truthfully state the total number of years he studied with Gillet as dating from his first audition in 1900, when his lessons began.

15. Oscar Shumsky (1917–2000), telephone conversation, November 1999.

16. The Heckelphone was probably the bass oboe the Philadelphia Orchestra purchased in 1917.

17. William Kincaid (1895–1967) was a graduate of the Institute of Musical Art, where he studied with Georges Barrère. For more information see John C. Krell, *Kincaidiana: A Flute Player's Notebook,* 2d ed. (Santa Clarita, Calif.: National Flute Association, 1997).

18. Letter from John de Lancie, March 2000, recounting anecdote told to him by William Kincaid.

19. Archives of the Philadelphia Orchestra.

20. Archives of the Philadelphia Orchestra.

21. From Jacqueline Razgonnikoff, archivist and librarian at the Comédie-Française, December 2003.

22. Samuel S. Fels was a member of the Administration Committee of the Philadelphia Orchestra as well as a member of the board of directors. An industrialist, Fels was the head of Fels Naptha Soap, a philanthropist, and a supporter of the arts.

23. The correspondence quoted here is in the archives of the Philadelphia Orchestra.

24. Letter from Arthur Judson to Tabuteau, Felix Kraus personal archive, Cleveland.

25. John Minsker remembered that when he joined the orchestra in 1936, a clause in the union agreement gave the conductor the authority to require any player to use a particular instrument. However, he did not believe it was ever enforced during his tenure. Note from John Minsker, September 2003.

26. The Ondes Martenot was one of the earliest electronic musical instruments, invented by French composer Maurice Martenot and first demonstrated in 1928.

27. Michael Kennedy, *Richard Strauss* (New York: Schirmer Books, 1996), p. 71.

28. Ibid.

29. Mrs. Frederick Shurtleff Coolidge was better known as Elizabeth Sprague Coolidge.

30. Letter of November 9, 1943, to my mother.

31. Conversation with John de Lancie, who was in the orchestra for the broadcast of December 21, 1947.

32. Letter of December 21, 1947, to my mother.

33. In 2001 the 1934 *Scheherazade* was re-released on CD as a part of the handsome Andante Collection, issued by Andante Productions, Ltd., France.

34. *Public Ledger* review in the archives of the Philadelphia Orchestra.

35. John Minsker has a copy of the original Red Seal 78-rpm disk, No. 7380. More recently it appears with recording dates listed as 2–3 May 1929 in the same Andante album, *Leopold Stokowski, Conductor,* as the 1934 *Scheherazade.* For details concerning the English horn in the Philadelphia Orchestra, consult the seven-part account by Michael Finkelman, "Philadelphia Story," in *Double Reed* 24, no. 3 (parts 1 and 2); 25, no. 3 (3 and 4); 25, no. 4 (5); 26, no. 3 (6[1]); 26, no. 4 (6[2]); and 27, no. 2 (7), which appeared from 2001 to 2004. These articles are available online at http://idrs.colorado.edu/publications/Journal/Journal.Index.

36. Conversation with Sol Schoenbach, October 1996.

37. Told to John de Lancie by Sol Schoenbach.

38. Comment made to the author, in Prades, 1950.

39. Boris Goldovsky, *My Road to Opera* (Boston: Houghton Mifflin, 1979), p. 199.

40. Telephone conversation with Tabuteau, 1954.

41. Letter from John de Lancie, March 2000.

42. Marc Mostovoy, a violist, studied with Tabuteau in Nice, 1962–64. He later became conductor of the Philadelphia Chamber Soloists (see chapters 19 and 20).

43. Clipping in the possession of Guy Baumier, Tabuteau's great-grand nephew in France.

44. Comment made to John de Lancie.

45. Philip Hart, *Fritz Reiner* (Evanston, Ill.: Northwestern University Press, 1994), p. 70.

46. Luigi Di Fulvio played second oboe in the Philadelphia Orchestra, 1925–58.

47. Telephone conversation with John Minsker, September 26, 2003.

48. Kincaid's version as related to John de Lancie.

49. Conversation with John de Lancie, 2000.

50. Sol Schoenbach in B. H. Haggin, *The Toscanini Musicians Knew* (New York: Horizon Press, 1967), p. 129; Haggin, *Conversations with Toscanini* (New York: Doubleday, 1959).

51. Sol Schoenbach in William Ander Smith, *The Mystery of Leopold Stokowski* (Rutherford, N.J.: Associated University Presses, 1990), p. 135.

52. Ibid., p. 135.

53. The performance of April 11, 1932, at the Philadelphia Metropolitan Opera House was recorded and is available on CD in the *Andante Collection*.

54. Benjamin de Loache's essay appeared in Edward Johnson, ed., *Stokowski: Essays in the Analysis of His Art* (London: Triad Press, 1973).

55. The Philadelphia Orchestra played summer concerts in Robin Hood Dell in Fairmount Park.

56. Conversation with John Minsker, 1995.

57. Letter from Emmet Sargeant to John de Lancie, 1993.

58. Myrtile Morel, Premier Prix, class of Georges Gillet, 1909. Morel was the brother of timpanist, Juilliard professor, and conductor Jean Morel.

59. This opinion was expressed in 1976 by Gaston Goubet, who often played in Paris orchestras with Morel in the 1920s and 1930s.

60. Conversation with Patricia Morehead, IDRS conference at Banff, 2002.

61. Conversation with John de Lancie, March 30, 1996.

62. Conversation with John de Lancie, April 1999.

63. Minsker had gone directly from Curtis to play English horn in the Detroit Symphony Orchestra for the two seasons between 1934 and 1936, when he was engaged by the Philadelphia Orchestra.

64. Conversation with John de Lancie, 1999.

65. Telephone conversation with Alfred Genovese, February 8, 1998.

66. Letter from Tabuteau, December 21, 1954.

67. Letter to my mother, May 17, 1955.

68. French text of letter from Tabuteau postmarked Toulon, November 15, 1956: "'La Famille' reçoit toujours bien les nouvelles. Merci. Celles de ce matin m'ont attristé, the decaying Stoko—en pleine forme et jeune, il sentait déja le cadavre, qu'est ce que ce doit être maintenant! En toute justice il me faut admettre qu'en mon demi siècle d'expériences avec les chefs d'orchestre il était le plus doué de tous mais il possèdait tel pouvoir de destruction qu'il n'a pu n'échapper ni s'épargner—"

7. TABUTEAU AS SOLOIST WITH THE PHILADELPHIA ORCHESTRA

1. The dates of Tabuteau's first three solo performances are in the Archives of the Philadelphia Orchestra. The Lefebvre *Andante and Tarantelle*, dedicated to Georges Gillet, was the Paris Conservatoire solo for 1897 and 1902. The two reviews of the Mozart Oboe Quartet have only come to light in 2007. Among other material left by Tabuteau in his studio when he retired in 1954, they had remained for over fifty years in the possession of Felix Kraus. After his death in December 2006, they were given to David McGill, who, recognizing their importance, sent me copies. They provide documentation of Tabuteau's collaboration with the first chair players of the orchestra in the currently only known Philadelphia performance of the Mozart in its original quartet form. (Thaddeus Rich, concertmaster 1906–1926, Emile Ferir, principal viola 1918–1919, Hans Kindler, cello 1914–1920, principal,

1916–1920). Unfortunately, the titles of the newspapers were cut off, but the first quote has "1918" at the top and a heading of "Rich Quartet Heard In Fine Concert." The other article ends with the reviewer's initials, "F. L. W."

2. *Press,* May 1, 1920. All newspaper reviews are from the archives of the Philadelphia Orchestra.

3. *North American,* May 1, 1920.

4. *Record,* May 1, 1920.

5. *Public Ledger,* May 1, 1920.

6. *Evening Ledger,* May 1, 1920.

7. *Philadelphia Inquirer,* May 1, 1920.

8. *Evening Bulletin,* May 1, 1920.

9. *Concours* solo, Paris Conservatoire 1907. Tabuteau's score of the Ropartz *Pastorale et Danses,* which is in my possession, indicates that the piece was played beginning at the section, Vif et gai. For the purpose of the program it was apparently called simply *Danse.*

10. Michael Finkelman, "Philadelphia Story," part 1, *Double Reed* 24, no. 3 (2001): 62, note 30.

11. *Record,* October 22, 1927.

12. *Public Ledger,* October 22, 1927.

13. *Philadelphia Inquirer,* October 22, 1927.

14. *Evening Bulletin,* October 22, 1927.

15. Leon Lester played bass clarinet with the Philadelphia Orchestra from 1938 to 1966.

16. Sol Schoenbach died on February 25, 1999.

17. The Simfonietta was led by Fabien Sevitsky, a nephew of Serge Koussevitzky. He later became the conductor of the Indianapolis Symphony Orchestra.

18. Edwin H. Schloss, identified by Marc Mostovoy.

19. Although he was usually known as Georges, Longy's full name was Gustave Georges Léopold Longy.

20. A comparable instrument today would cost between $4,000 and $6,000.

21. See full questionnaire in chapter 6, above.

22. *Philadelphia Inquirer,* October 28, 1939.

23. *Evening Bulletin,* October 28, 1939.

24. Olin Downes in the *New York Times*, November 8, 1939.

25. Conversation with John de Lancie, April 24, 1999.

26. Archives of the Philadelphia Orchestra. *Evening Ledger*, November 2, 1939. The weeklong tour was "sandwiched" between the Mozart performances in Philadelphia and New York. Tabuteau later told de Lancie that Olin Downes had been influential in suggesting the programming that made it possible for Tabuteau to play the Mozart on Friday and Saturday in Philadelphia and then on the Tuesday concert a week later in New York.

27. *New York Sun*, November 8, 1939.

28. *Evening Bulletin*, October 21, 1950.

29. *Philadelphia Inquirer*, October 21, 1950.

30. *Philadelphia Daily News*, October 21, 1950.

31. Harl McDonald's Mozart *Quartet* arrangement is preserved in the Eugene Ormandy Collection of Scores at the Van Pelt Library of the University of Pennsylvania.

32. Tabuteau had played the Mozart *Quartet* in the summer of 1951 at the Casals Festival in Perpignan.

33. Preben Obbery, *Leopold Stokowski* (New York: Hippocine Books, 1982), p. 164.

34. Letter of December 12, 1962, to Marc Mostovoy, violist and conductor who studied with Tabuteau in Nice.

35. Charles O'Connell, *The Other Side of the Record* (New York: Alfred A. Knopf, 1947), p. 125. Quote brought to my attention by Michael Finkelman.

36. The RCA Victor Red Seal 12-inch record No. 17900 was made on December 8, 1940, exactly two weeks before the *Concertante*. The label, *A Night on Bare Mountain-Fantasia* (orchestrated by Stokowski), explains the change of title from *A Night on Bald Mountain*, as well as the instrumentation which gives the oboe an important solo toward the end of the piece.

37. The Bethlehem Bach Choir, founded by J. Fred Wolle in 1898, gave the first full performance of the *B Minor Mass* in the United States. It was strongly influenced by the Moravians who settled in that area. The Bethlehem Bach Festival, held in Packer Memorial Chapel on the

campus of Lehigh University, with a trombone choir playing traditional chorales in the church tower, has had a loyal following throughout the years.

38. The complete Philadelphia Orchestra recordings with Arturo Toscanini (1941–42) include Schubert, Symphony No. 9 in C Major; Richard Strauss, *Tod und Verklärung;* Debussy, *La Mer* and *Ibéria;* Respighi, *Feste romane;* Berlioz, *Roméo et Juliette, "Queen Mab" Scherzo;* Mendelssohn, Incidental Music to *A Midsummer's Night Dream;* Tchaikovsky, Symphony No. 6 *Pathétique.* Musical Heritage Society, 5386461.

39. One hundred years earlier in 1837, yet another eminent oboist, Henri Brod, whose études were valued and taught by both Gillet and Tabuteau, had received the same award. See André Lardrot, "Henri Brod," *Revue de l'Association Française du Hautbois* 8 (2001): 27.

40. Archives of the Philadelphia Orchestra, *The Journal of the Philadelphia Orchestra, Season 1935–36, RCA Victor Tour and Résumé.*

41. Telephone interview with Joseph Santarlasci, December 4, 1999.

8. TABUTEAU AT THE CURTIS INSTITUTE OF MUSIC

1. Cohen would later be known as Saul Caston.

2. Gardell Simons, principal trombone, 1915–30.

3. John de Lancie, who came to Curtis in 1936, was able to remember almost all of the early students. I have identified others from Curtis archival lists. See appendix 2 for more details.

4. Telephone conversation with Ralph Gomberg, younger brother of Robert, August 1999. Ralph's comment after his own long career: "It was the survival of the fittest." Ralph Gomberg died on December 9, 2006.

5. Telephone conversation with Oscar Shumsky, November 1999.

6. Telephone conversation with Zadel Skolovsky, January 19, 1997.

7. Leon Lester and Arthur Statter, now both deceased; Lester in 2003 and Statter in June 2004. John Minsker died on August 5, 2007.

8. Adelchi was the bassoonist member of the operatically named Angelucci family, the others being oboist Rhadames and Ernani, who played French horn.

9. Letter from Theodore Heger, September 2002.

10. Visit with Leon Lester, Philadelphia, December 1999.

11. Caston was principal trumpet of the Philadelphia Orchestra, 1923–45.

12. Conversations with Arthur Statter, October 27, 2000, and February 5, 2001.

13. Reno was attorney general of the United States from 1993 to 2001.

14. Casimir Hall was named for Casimir Hofmann, the pianist father of Josef Hofmann. When Efrem Zimbalist became director of the school, he changed the name to Curtis Hall.

15. Boris Goldovsky (1908–2001), pianist, opera coach, and conductor, also known for his many years as the popular moderator of the Saturday Metropolitan Opera broadcasts.

16. Boris Goldovsky, *My Road to Opera* (Boston: Houghton Mifflin, 1979), p. 143.

17. At the beginning of the Nazi regime in Germany, the name was changed to the Curtis String Quartet.

18. Telephone conversation with Perry Bauman, January 18, 1997. Bauman died on August 16, 2004.

19. Pierné *Prélude and Fugue,* Opus 40, No. 1. Issued on Victor Red Seal 10-inch 4332-A /B: The Curtis Woodwind Ensemble under the direction of Marcel Tabuteau.

20. Telephone conversation with Mitchell Lurie, December 8, 1997.

21. Conversation with Mason Jones, December 3, 1999.

22. Edward Arian, Philadelphia Orchestra, 1947–67. Telephone interview, December 4, 1999.

23. See chapter 19, p. 493.

24. Telephone conversation with Wally Bhosys, May 1997. Bhosys died on April 27, 2006.

25. Philip Kirchner was born in Lithuania in 1892, came to the United States in 1906, and played in the Russian Symphony Orchestra and the New York Philharmonic before going to Cleveland. Donald Rosenberg, *The Cleveland Orchestra Story* (Cleveland: Gray, 2000), p. 63.

26. Ferdinand Del Negro, bassoon and contrabassoon, Philadelphia Orchestra, 1922–62, principal 1944–45, in conversation with John de Lancie.

27. Letter from Theodore Heger, November 12, 2001.

28. Telephone conversation with John Minsker, July 22, 2003.

29. E-mail notes from Bert Gassman's daughter, Carol Gassman-Proud, November 23, 2000.

30. Telephone conversation with William Arrowsmith, April 10, 2006. Arrowsmith died on June 5, 2006.

31. Telephone conversation with Earl Schuster, February 4, 2000. Schuster died on November 5, 2003.

32. E-mail note from Grover Schiltz, April 2006.

33. Notes from Daniel Stolper, April 2006.

34. Conversation with Earnest Harrison, May 2001. Harrison died on July 13, 2005.

35. Telephone conversation with Richard Blair, August 5, 2006.

36. E-mail notes from Marilyn Zupnik, January 2000. Marilyn Zupnik studied oboe with her father, Robert Zupnik, and later with John de Lancie at the Curtis Institute of Music. She became principal oboist of the Minnesota Orchestra in 1980.

37. Telephone conversation with Robert Lehrfeld, September 12, 2006.

38. Letter from Raymond Dusté, April 18, 2005. Among Dusté's California students were Felix Kraus, Richard Woodhams, Patrick McFarland, and Joan Browne Shallin.

39. The Philadelphia Orchestra played in Birmingham, Alabama, on February 11, 1948, during a week-long tour of the South.

40. From account written in 1996 by A. Clyde Roller. Roller was an internationally known and honored music educator who began his career as an oboist. He was a conductor at Interlochen Center for the Arts and a professor at the Eastman School of Music and the University of Houston. Roller died in 2005.

41. Telephone conversation with David A. Ledet, August 1, 2006. *Oboe Reed Styles* was reprinted by Indiana University Press in 2000.

42. Albert Debondue, 1885–1984, awarded the Premier Prix in 1919, was the author of numerous études for oboe.

43. An excellent oboe costs around five thousand dollars, while a violin may range from thirty thousand to several million dollars.

44. Rudall-Carte was a woodwind instrument firm in London known primarily for flutes.

45. Lucien Lorée continued to take an active part in the company owned by Raymond Dubois after 1925. Robert de Gourdon, married to Dubois's daughter Raymonde, later became the proprietor of the firm. His son, Alain de Gourdon, is the master oboe maker and current owner of the firm. See Laila Storch, "100 Years F. Lorée: 1881–1981," *International Double Reed Society Journal* 9 (June 1981).

46. The 1900 model instruments were probably Conservatoire system without *plateaux* keys. System No. 6 *bis* with *plateaux* 1906, sometimes also known as the Gillet system, came into use in 1906.

47. From logbooks of Lorée oboe sales beginning in 1881.

48. Telephone conversation with Donald Hefner, May 23, 2003.

9. LESSONS WITH TABUTEAU

1. Personal interview with Orlando Cole, November 1, 1996. Cole entered the school in 1924, the year it opened.

2. Telephone interview with Roger Scott, double bass, Philadelphia Orchestra 1947–95, principal 1949–95.

3. "Bands" refers to the fact that my teeth were being restraightened following my audition, when Tabuteau had said it was impossible to play oboe with teeth like mine.

4. W. R. Lym, Los Angeles oboist and mechanic who made shapers, gougers, and oboes.

5. Miss Hoopes was the secretary of admissions I had met at my audition in 1941.

6. This 1917 portrait was left in the Studio when Tabuteau returned to France in 1954. In 1975 John de Lancie gave it to me on the occasion he had helped to organize for the fiftieth anniversary of the Curtis Institute. It is now in my "reed room."

7. Tabuteau rented the Studio, room 404 in the Ludlow Building at 36 South Sixteenth Street, from the mid-1920s until he left Philadelphia in 1954.

8. William Sargeant and Merrill Remington were oboists in the San Francisco Symphony Orchestra. Lois Wann and Mitchell Miller were both well-known oboists in New York.

9. By now the seasonal work at Burpees Seeds had ended, and I had begun to work at a camera shop in Germantown where I could practice in off hours without disturbing anyone.

10. Eleanor Mitchel, a flute student of William Kincaid, had just graduated from Curtis.

10. MY FIRST YEAR WITH TABUTEAU AT THE CURTIS INSTITUTE

1. Marion Davies was from Hayward, California, and Shirley Trepel from Winnipeg, Canada.

2. Claire Dameron, Mme Tabuteau's older sister, and her family had lived for many years in Algeria.

3. Tabuteau regularly read the bass line in the Barret studies and played it along with us in the treble clef.

4. From time to time MacLane changed the spelling of his last name. In the book *The Philadelphia Orchestra: A Century of Music* edited by John Ardoin, he is listed as Ralph McLane, clarinet, 1943–51 principal (p. 225). In the November 7, 1943, Town Hall Beethoven program for the New Friends of Music, he was Ralph MacLean. He continues as Ralph MacLean in the personnel lists of Philadelphia Orchestra programs for 1944–46, but by 1948 when he was a soloist in the Mozart *Sinfonia Concertante,* he had become Ralph McLane.

5. Harry Harris, "Musician Cooks Like a Composer to Achieve Harmony with Foods, *Philadelphia Evening Bulletin*, April 28, 1948. Available at http://idrs.colorado.edu/Publications/DR/DR12.1/DR12 .1.Tabuteau.html.

6. This was the Tabuteaus' address as printed on Drake stationery.

7. From written note notes by Martha Scherer, April 2001.

8. Fritz Reiner was a member of the Curtis faculty from 1931 to 1941.

9. Telephone conversation with Thelma Neft Geller, June 29, 2002.

10. When Tabuteau retired in 1954, a trunk with assorted belongings, including the court records, was left in Philadelphia. It was acquired by Tabuteau's student Felix Kraus.

11. As will be seen in later chapters, Tabuteau would continue to suffer from hernia problems.

12. George Walker, a distinguished pianist and composer, received a Pulitzer Prize for composition in 1996.

13. Melissa A. Stevens, *Pedagogical Concepts and Practices for Teaching Musical Expressiveness: An Oral History* (Columbus: Ohio State University, 1999), interview with Abba Bogin, p. 66.

14. For a more extended account, see Laila Storch, "My Dinner with Toscanini," *Double Reed* 18, no. 3 (1995): 65–70.

15. I only learned the vulgar usage of this word decades later from a dictionary of "Argot" (French slang) in the University of Washington Library.

16. This was before I played the Concertante recording for him in 1945.

17. While I was in Philadelphia, Tabuteau smoked either Philip Morris English Ovals or Richmond Straight Cut No.1; both came in small cardboard boxes he used for storing his gouged oboe cane.

18. Abe Kniaz was a horn student at the Curtis Institute.

19. At that time, James Petrillo, the president of the American Federation of Musicians, was known as the czar of the music world.

11. TABUTEAU CONDUCTS THE CURTIS ORCHESTRA

1. The total number of broadcast concerts in the 1944–45 season stretched to twenty-two; woodwinds took part in thirteen.

2. The "singer" was Pierrette Alarie, a young soprano from Quebec, who later sang at the Metropolitan and the Paris Opera.

3. The program also included the Boccherini *Minuet,* Gounod's *Ave Maria,* and the Bell Song from *Lakmé* sung by Pierrette Alarie, and ended with the Strauss *Emperor Waltz.*

4. This comment refers to the series of repeated Gs played in octaves by the two oboes at the beginning of the *Emperor Waltz.* Tabuteau pronounced "note" more like "nut."

5. Domenico Vittorini, professor of Romance languages at the University of Pennsylvania, taught Italian and literature courses at Curtis.

6. Conversation with Seymour Lipkin, Seattle, September 27, 1997.

7. Alexander Hilsberg, concertmaster and assistant conductor of the Philadelphia Orchestra, conducted the full Curtis Orchestra after the end of the war.

8. Taped memories of Tabuteau sent to me by Diana Steiner, 1997.

9. Telephone conversation with Charles Joseph, July 11, 2005.

10. Telephone conversation with Hershel Gordon, January 31, 2007.

11. Edouard Colonne, 1838–1910, violinist, conductor, and founder of *Concerts Colonne* in Paris; conducted in London, Russia, and the New York Philharmonic in 1905. Monteux had played viola in Colonne's orchestra.

12. Telephone conversation with Robert Davison's widow, Olga-Rita Davison, 1995.

13. Hurriedly written down after the dinner, this note contains the essential truth that Tabuteau was *hired* in 1915. However, as he left the Metropolitan Opera at the end of 1913–14 season, the Tristan performance would have been in 1914.

14. Vincent Persichetti's quintet written especially for us to play on an experimental FM broadcast from the Franklin Institute was later published with the name *Pastorale*. Two other students who took part in the broadcast were Elaine Shaffer, flute, and Robert Cole, bassoon.

15. Bruna Castagna (1905–1983), Italian contralto who sang at Teatro Colón in Buenos Aires and made her Metropolitan Opera début in 1936.

16. Samuel Barber was in U.S. Army uniform.

17. I was still using an oboe with an automatic octave key favored in the 1930s in California. Tabuteau strongly disapproved: "You cannot play the harmonics!" But it was impossible to get a new instrument during the war.

18. Renée Longy Miquelle, daughter of Georges Longy, the famous oboist of the Boston Symphony Orchestra from 1898 to 1925, had taught solfège at Curtis before I attended the school. This was the first and only time I met her.

19. In assigning this sonata Tabuteau was following the suggestion of his own teacher, Georges Gillet, who recommended that his students study the Bach sonatas for violin and piano.

12. TABUTEAU'S SUMMERS IN CANADA

1. See Laila Storch and Dr. Kevin J. Tompkins, "Marcel Tabuteau from a Different Angle," *Double Reed* 15, no. 3 (Winter 1992).

2. PSFS was the Philadelphia Savings Fund Society that sponsored the series of Curtis Institute Orchestra concerts conducted by Marcel Tabuteau.

3. All information based on correspondence with Dr. Kevin J. Tompkins, Ralph Watts, Nicholas A. Miller, Alexander and Rosie McKay, Carol, Linda, and Mayme Dieltgens, 1992.

13. ANOTHER YEAR OF STUDY WITH TABUTEAU

1. Helen Traubel was an American soprano noted for singing Wagner roles after Kirsten Flagstad was no longer available.

2. "Sacred Cow" refers to the nickname for the special aircraft that flew President Roosevelt to the Yalta Conference and was later inherited by Harry Truman. It was the type of converted army plane that later became known as Air Force One. ("The Story of Air Force One," History Channel, January 20, 2001.)

3. Michael Finkelman believes this was the children's concert of February 22, 1947, conducted by Alexander Hilsberg, who was inclined to insert unscheduled "surprise" numbers not documented in the programs. Michael Finkelman, "Philadelphia Story," part 6, *Double Reed* 26, no. 4: 60.

4. Both John de Lancie and John Minsker remembered the circumstances of Tabuteau's fall. Ormandy had asked them to listen to some playbacks, and while coming out of the backstage sound booth, Tabuteau tripped on a small step.

14. SUMMERS IN FRANCE

1. Joshua Silver, "Many Roles for Many Purposes: A History of Philadelphia's Drake Hotel" (1998).

2. Mairie de Paris, copy from *actes de mariages* of the tenth *arrondissment*, Paris.

3. Letter in possession of Guy Baumier.

4. Ellis Island records show that André Tabuteau arrived in the United States for the first time in 1913.

5. Letter from Mme Tabuteau to Laila Storch, July 17, 1947. Postcard from Mme T., August 15, 1947.

6. *L'usine:* the factory. The word was used by Tabuteau for a gambling locale.

7. Gustave Bret—eminent organist, founder of the Société Bach de Paris in the early 1900s, friend of Albert Schweitzer and Pablo Casals—was retired and living on his family estate in Fréjus.

8. When I became solo oboist of the Houston Symphony Orchestra in 1948, it would not have been considered a "major U.S. orchestra."

9. Letter to Mrs. Robert H. McCarty, Evelyn's mother, January 29, 1954. Courtesy Evelyn McCarty.

10. Letter from Helen Hoopes to Mrs. Robert H. McCarty, April 22, 1954. Courtesy Evelyn McCarty.

11. Original quote in French and ending in English: "Cette nouvelle lumière de Harry me coûte bien cher—les stocks viennent de baisser de cinq 'bbbillions'[*sic*] en deux jours, si cela continue, vous devez bientôt avoir à me 'supporter,' better get ready and become famous." In the same letter he showed concern for my new living arrangements in Houston: a "garage apartment." "We are anxious to know about the garage, inside and outside, take pictures; is it safe for a girl, and especially for the 'unique instrument'?"

12. The three Haskil sisters, Clara, Lili, and Jeanne, share a tomb at the Cimetière Montparnasse in Paris. There Jeanne's name is written as "Jane."

15. TABUTEAU'S LAST YEARS AT THE CURTIS INSTITUTE

1. Marc Lifschey died on November 8, 2000, John Mack on July 23, 2006, and Felix Kraus on December 14, 2006.

2. Norman Carol later became the concertmaster of the Philadelphia Orchestra, a position he filled from 1966 to 1994. Seymour Lipkin continues his career as concert pianist, teaching piano at the Curtis Institute and leading the Blue Hill Summer Chamber Music Festival.

3. Excerpts from my letters of March 1947.

4. Visit with Seymour Lipkin in Seattle, September 27, 1997.

5. Visit with Jacob Lateiner in New York, 1997.

6. Melissa A. Stevens, *Pedagogical Concepts and Practices for Teaching Musical Expressiveness: An Oral History* (Columbus: Ohio State University, 1999), p. 69.

7. Tabuteau had recently performed and recorded the Brandenburg No. 1 with Pablo Casals in the Prades Festival of 1950. Was he therefore perhaps inspired to include it in his own students'concert?

8. Visit with Louis Rosenblatt in Philadelphia, May 2003.

9. The original 1950 Prades Festival recordings of the Bach Brandenburg Concerto No. 1 in F Major and the Suite for Orchestra No.1 in C Major (Marcel Tabuteau, Laila Storch, and John Mack, oboes) have been released on CD by Pearl, Gems 0200 and 0201.

10. Letter from Pamela Gearhart, July 2002. Livingston Gearhart studied oboe with Tabuteau in the mid-1930s. He later studied composition in France with Nadia Boulanger, played as part of a two-piano team, and became a prolific composer.

11. Tabuteau often used the example of a plane taking off and landing to illustrate the difficulty of making a perfect attack and ending of a long tone and said that anyone can fly while in the air. In 2003 I mentioned this to astronaut Bill Anders, who gave over the controls for a short time to pianist Claude Frank on the way to Seattle from the Orcas Island Chamber Music Festival. Anders chuckled and seemed to fully appreciate the analogy.

12. Visit with Louis Rosenblatt in Philadelphia, 1976.

13. Conversation with Marc Lifschey in Bloomington, Indiana, November 1995.

14. Letter to Laila Storch, November 13, 1950.

15. Conversation with John Mack, Orcas Island, Washington, September 2000.

16. Letters and telephone conversations with Theodore Heger, 1998–2003.

17. Telephone conversation with Donald Hefner, May 23, 2003.

18. Telephone conversation with Alfred Genovese, February 8, 1998.

19. Stevens, *Pedagogical Concepts and Practices,* interview with Felix Kraus, p. 113.

20. Telephone conversation with Richard Kanter, March 18, 2004.

21. Telephone conversation with Joan Shallin, July 10, 2004.

22. Professor Narcy used the word "contempt" to describe the attitude of teachers toward their students. Conversation in Compiègne, 1990.

23. Note the laughter in the Tabuteau-Wolsing CD—which was not a normal part of our lessons!

24. Personal interview with Arthur Grossman, Seattle, Washington, April 2, 2000.

16. THE CASALS FESTIVALS IN PRADES AND PERPIGNAN

1. Sidney Harth, later a prizewinner in the Wieniawski Competition, was concertmaster of the Chicago Symphony and Los Angeles Philharmonic and was also known as a conductor.

2. In 1950 there were about five thousand inhabitants in Prades, but it had the atmosphere of a village.

3. In 2003 all six of the Brandenburg Concertos, the Orchestral Suites Nos. 1 and 2, and many other of the historic 1950 Bach Festival recordings were released in three 2-CD sets by Pearl Gems, 0200, 0201 and 0202.

4. The *Sardana* was issued only as a "special bonus" with festival recordings.

5. A Cobla is a Catalan band-orchestra consisting of 12 instruments: flaviol, tambour; double reeds: 2 tiples, 2 tenores, and a solo tenore; brass: 1 trombone and 2 fishhorns; plus a contrabass which plays for dance or concert versions of the Sardana.

6. Ruth Draper, 1884–1956, was an American monologist and monodramatist whose art was acclaimed throughout the U.S. and Europe.

7. Isaac Stern, *My First 79 Years* (New York: Alfred Knopf, 1999), p. 91; and Stephen Lehmann and Marion Faber, *Rudolf Serkin: A Life* (Oxford: Oxford University Press, 2003), p. 46. Isaac Stern's quote: "I will never forget hearing him in that rehearsal: all of us in the orchestra just sitting there and listening to his cadenza start slowly and begin to build, and then build and build, and suddenly march across the musical landscape with giant boots, and end with a musical volcanic eruption of sheer ecstasy, a climax that leaped out of the piano and roared its way into the coda, at which point we made our orchestral entrance, playing the final few measures, and then finishing the last chord and suddenly jumping to our feet and screaming like crazy, 'Bravo! Bravo!' It was one of those astonishing musical moments when everything that could be done with a phrase was done—and a little more."

8. Erica Morini, 1904–95, a Viennese violinist, was a child prodigy who made her début at age twelve and had a major concert career in Europe and the U.S., with tours of Asia and South America.

9. Bice Horszowski Costa, *Miecio—Ricordi di Mieczyslaw Horszowski* (Genova: Erga edizione, 2000), p. 352.

10. Available on CD Sony SMK 66569 "Casals Edition." In 2002 the *Divertimento* was released on Pearl GEM 0175 in one of four volumes of Casals Festivals, Perpignan 1951.

11. Tabuteau did not play in the recording of this work that was made on July 4, 1953, and only finally released forty years later by Sony records in their 1993 "Casals Edition."

12. Educational Media Associates, Berkeley, Calif., RR 547.

13. Music and Arts Programs of America, vol. 2.

17. TABUTEAU AS SEEN BY HIS PHILADELPHIA ORCHESTRA COLLEAGUES

1. Telephone conversation with Morris Shulik, December 1999.

2. Conversation with Mason Jones, December 3, 1999.

3. Conversation with Irvin Eisenberg, April 30, 1999.

4. The comment refers to *Those Fabulous Philadelphians,* a popular book about the Philadelphia Orchestra by Herbert Kupferberg.

5. Telephone conversation with Jerome Wigler, December 3, 1999.

6. Conversation with Sol Schoenbach, 1998.

7. Conversation with Sol Schoenbach, 1997.

8. *Tu* and *toi* are the familiar "you" form in French. Tabuteau always used the formal *vous* with all his pupils and even with Mme Tabuteau.

9. Tabuteau told this story to John de Lancie, who related it to me in 1999.

10. Visit with Anthony Gigliotti at the Curtis Institute, March 1999.

11. Visit with Harry Peers in New York, 1999.

12. Telephone conversation with Roger Scott, December 5, 1999.

13. Telephone conversation with Lorne Munroe, May 9, 2004.

14. Telephone conversation with Isadore Schwartz, December 5, 1999.

15. Telephone interview with Irvin Rosen, December 5, 1999.

16. Telephone interview with Edward Arian, December 4, 1999.

17. At the time of this interview in 1999, Seymour Rosenfeld was unable to speak following a stroke two years earlier.

18. Abe Torchinsky, tuba, 1949–72, in a telephone conversation in 1999.

19. Telephone conversation with John Shamlian, February 2000.

20. Telephone interview with Harry Gorodetzer, April 1, 2000.

21. Conversation with Leon Lester, December 1999.

22. This story originally told by Tabuteau to John de Lancie.

23. Telephone interview with Joseph Primavera, December 7, 1999.

24. Telephone conversation with Alfred Genovese, February 8, 1998.

25. Telephone conversation with John de Lancie, July 1994. This account was given to him by both Tabuteau and Jean de Vergie.

18. RETIREMENT IN FRANCE

1. Original text on 1950 Christmas card to Laila Storch: Les anches sont très mauvaises, je travaille comme un fou et pas de bons resultats. I really think it is time for me to quit! Bonne chance et meilleurs voeux, Marcel Tabuteau.

2. Adrian Siegel was the official photographer of the Philadelphia Orchestra and cellist in the orchestra.

3. " D.P.s" refers to Displaced Persons who lost their homes following World War II.

4. Letter from Mme Tabuteau, December 9, 1952.

5. The Tabuteaus always referred to Hans Moennig as Dr. Moennig.

6. The two *docteurs* refer to Dr. Budin and to Tabuteau, who had received an honorary Doctor of Music degree from the Curtis Institute.

7. From material provided by Claus Johansen in March 2006. Baroque oboist Johansen, currently a senior producer at Danish Radio, was Waldemar Wolsing's good friend. He made several taped interviews with Wolsing. As Wolsing neared the end of his life, he gave away his large collection of music, reeds, tools, and cane to various oboe players and to the conservatory in Copenhagen. Aware of Johansen's interest in oboe history, Wolsing gave him all the material about Tabuteau including letters from both of the Tabuteaus, carbon copies he had made of his own letters, and the tapes he had recorded in Nice.

8. Notes from Frank Stalzer, May 2000. Frank Stalzer became a professor at Arizona State University in Tempe. In 1962 he made a return visit with his wife and daughter to see Tabuteau in Nice.

9. Telephone conversation with Perry Bauman, January 18, 1997.

10. Telephone conversation with Donald Hefner, May 23, 2003.

11. Letter from Madame Tabuteau, Paris, November 25, 1959.

19. TABUTEAU'S FINAL YEARS IN NICE

1. Gustave Bret wrote to me frequently throughout the 1950s both about musical subjects and with news of his family and the region of Fréjus.

2. Letter from Marc Mostovoy, September 26, 2003.

3. Marc Mostovoy, letter to his parents, July 18, 1962.

4. Telephone conversation with David Dutton, February 27, 2002.

5. Telephone conversation with Joseph Robinson, March 17, 2004, and Robinson notes.

6. Paper in possession of Guy Baumier, Tabuteau's great-grandnephew in France.

7. Recounted by Jacques Budin in 1996.

8. Tabuteau recorded the Cimarosa passages on the tape recorder brought to him by Wayne Rapier in 1965. Boston Records 1017CD, "Marcel Tabuteau's Lessons."

9. Letter from Tabuteau to Marc Mostovoy, February 14, 1965.

10. Letter from Adrian Gnam to Marc Mostovoy, dated July 9, 10, and 11, 1965.

11. Telephone conversation with Adrian Gnam, August 11, 2003.

12. Telephone conversation with Rowland Floyd, May 6, 2000.

13. A letter from Wayne Rapier to Marc Mostovoy dated November 15, 1965, confirms that Tabuteau had "formally agreed to accept Oberlin's invitation next school year."

14. Information about Livingston Gearhart and Buffalo from conversations with John de Lancie, 2001.

15. Tabuteau wrote to Joseph Robinson on June 5, 1965: "I am heartbroken about you and young David not coming to Europe this summer. This nice young man bombards me with his enthusiasm and long letters . . . a few days ago I sent him few pieces of gouged cane, five of my

old reeds and a shaper as a reward for his good taste, he has———— [*Tabuteau's dashes*] so much admiration for me!"

16. Mme Tabuteau told Marc Mostovoy she was convinced Tabuteau's heart attack was caused as a result of his having played for seven hours without stopping. She begged him to put the oboe down and rest, but he refused. In her opinion, at his age, playing the oboe for so long was too much for him. Whether this contributed to the cause of his death, we cannot know. For some months he had not been feeling well. His nephew, François Létoffé, recalled World War I when Tabuteau had been diagnosed with a heart murmur and thought it may, after all, have caught up with him.

20. PHILADELPHIA POSTLUDE

1. *Philadelphia Inquirer,* March 9, 1966.

2. "Important Premieres," *International Double Reed Society: To the World's Oboists* 5, no. 3 (December 1977): 7.

3. Laila Storch, *Curtis Institute Alumni Association Newsletter* 5, no. 4 (Winter 1979).

4. *Marcel Tabuteau's Lessons,* Boston Records, 1017 CD.

5. Review signed by "Ritter" in 1997 July–August issue of *American Record Guide*, p. 216.

6. John Ardoin, ed., *The Philadelphia Orchestra: A Century of Music* (Philadelphia: Temple University Press, 1999), p. 161.

7. Conversation with Sol Schoenbach, October 1996.

8. Iso Briselli: from an interview with Marc Mostovoy in Philadelphia, December 16, 2003.

9. Letter to my mother, March 4, 1947.

10. Josef Gingold, "Ysaÿe's Solo Violin Sonatas," in L. S. Ginsburg, *Prof. Lev Ginsburg's Ysaÿe,* ed. Dr. Herbert R. Axelrod (Neptune City, N.J.: Paganiniana, 1980), p. 525.

11. The Curtis Institute of Music, *Overtones* 21, no. 3 (June 1997): 2.

12. Georges Longy was known for educational activities connected with the Longy School and with conducting but not for oboe students. He was reported to have said: "Je ne veux pas élèver des chiens pour me mordre aux chevilles" (I don't want to raise dogs to bite at my heels).

SELECTED BIBLIOGRAPHY

Ardoin, John, ed. *The Philadelphia Orchestra: A Century of Music.*
     Philadelphia: Temple University Press, 1999.

Bartlett, F. C., M. Ginsberg, E. J. Lindgren, and R. H. Thouless, eds.
     The Study of Society. New York: Macmillan, 1939.

Damrosch, Walter. *My Musical Life.* New York: Charles Scribner's
     Sons, 1926.

Dandelot, A. *La Société des Concerts du Conservatoire (1828–1923).*
     Paris: Librairie Delagrave, 1923.

Daniel, Oliver. *Stokowski: A Counterpoint of View.* New York: Dodd,
     Mead, 1982.

Fletcher, Kristine Klopfenstein. *The Paris Conservatoire and the Contest
     Solos for Bassoon.* Bloomington: Indiana University Press, 1988.

Ginsburg, L. S. *Prof. Lev Ginsburg's Ysaÿe.* Ed. Dr. Herbert R. Axelrod.
     Neptune City, N.J.: Paganiniana, 1980.

Goldovsky, Boris. *My Road to Opera.* Boston: Houghton Mifflin, 1979.

Haggin, B. H. *Conversations with Toscanini.* New York: Doubleday,
     1959.

———. *The Toscanini Musicians Knew.* New York: Horizon, 1967.

Hart, Philip. *Fritz Reiner.* Evanston, Ill.: Northwestern University Press, 1994.

Hefner, Donald L. "The Tradition of the Paris Conservatory School of Oboe Playing with Special Attention to the Influence of Marcel Tabuteau." Ph.D. diss., Catholic University of America, 1984.

Johnson, Edward, ed. *Stokowski: Essays in Analysis of His Art.* London: Triad, 1973.

Kennedy, Michael. *Richard Strauss.* Schirmer Books, 1996.

Kupferberg, Herbert. *Those Fabulous Philadelphians.* New York: Charles Scribner's Sons, 1969.

Martin, George Whitney. *The Damrosch Dynasty: America's First Family of Music.* Boston: Houghton Mifflin, 1983.

Mueller, John H. *The American Symphony Orchestra.* Bloomington: Indiana University Press, 1951.

Obberby, Preben. *Leopold Stokowski.* New York: Hippocene Books, 1982.

Philip, Robert. *Early Recordings and Musical Style: Changing Tastes in Instrumental Performance, 1900–1950.* New York: Cambridge University Press, 1992.

Pierre, Constant. *Le Conservatoire National de Musique et de Déclamation.* Paris: Imprimerie Nationale, 1900.

Puritz, Gerd. *Elizabeth Schumann.* Ed. and trans. Joy Puritz. London: Andre Deutsch, 1993.

Roman, Zoltan, comp. *Gustav Mahler's American Years, 1907–1911: A Documentary History.* Stuyvesant, N.Y.: Pendragon Press.

Shanet, Howard. *Philharmonic: A History of New York's Orchestra.* New York: Doubleday, 1975.

Smith, William Ander. *The Mystery of Leopold Stokowski.* London: Associated University Press, 1990.

Whitwell, David. *The Longy Club: A Professional Wind Ensemble in Boston (1900–1917).* Northridge, Calif.: Winds, 1988.

Wister, Frances Anne. *Twenty-five Years of the Philadelphia Orchestra, 1900–1925.* Philadelphia: Women's Committee for the Philadelphia Orchestra, 1925.

SELECTED BIBLIOGRAPHY

INDEX

INDEX

Eugénie, Empress, 2
Evening Bulletin, 140, 144, 147, 151, 154, 163
Evening Ledger, 139, 154, 155

Fahrni, Helene, 424, 427
Falstaff (Verdi), 66
La Fanciulla del West (Puccini), 67
Fantasia, 169
Fantasie (Colin), 30
Farrar, Geraldine, 62, 65, 67, 73–74
Fels, Samuel S., 104, 105, 555n22
Ferir, Emile, 136
Feuermann, Emanuel, 115, 254
Fiala, Josef, 164
Fine, Burton, 396, 399, 511
Fine, Vivian, 235
Finkelman, Michael, 141, 568n3
Flagstad, Kirsten, 117, 568n1
Fleisher, Leon, 426
Fleisher, Marty, 191, 198, 201
Flesch, Carl, 73, 98, 177, 180, 515
Fleury, Louis, 37
Floyd, Rowland, 63, 495–500, 502–504
Foch, Marshal, 3
Foley, Madeline, 418
Foote, Arthur, 405
Francescatti, Zino, 98
Frankenstein, Alfred, 169
Fremstad, Olive, 65
Fricke, Harry, 71
Fricsay, Ferenc, 134
Friedmann, Aloysia, 480, 487, *489*
Friedmann, Martin, 487–488
Friendships of Marcel Tabuteau, 438, 442–443
From the New World (Dvořák), 44, 47, 56
Fuchs, Joseph, 436, 475
Fuchs, Lillian, 436, 475
Fuller, Loïe, 86
Furtwängler, Wilhelm, 117

Gabrilowitsch, Ossip, 118, 120–121
Gadski, Johanna, 65, 66
Galimir, Felix, 283
Ganz, Rudolf, 48
Gassman, Bert, 206
Gatti-Casazza, Giulio, 58, 72
Gaubert, Phlippe, 51
Gaudard, Charles, 25
Gauthier, Eva, 110
Gautier, M., 3

Gearhart, Livingston, 191, 402, 502, 570n10
Gearhart, Pamela, 401–404, 502
Gelatt, Roland, 424
Genovese, Alfred, 133, 202, 393, 400–401, 410, 412–413, 451–452, 511
Georges, Albert, *13,* 14, *15,* 16
Gershwin, George, 82, 121
Geyer, Stefi, 418
Giannini, Vittorio, 500
Gieseking, Walter, 116
Gigliotti, Anthony, 273, 443, 509
Gilbert, Charlie, 191, 192, 198
Gillet, Fernand, 25, 204, 214, 404, 518
Gillet, Georges, 14, *35,* 91, 141, 190, 341, 548n1; assessments of students, 27–30; becomes oboe professor at Société des Concerts du Conservatoire, 25; death of, 340–341; impact on students, 25–26, 256, 518–519; influence on Tabuteau, 21–22, 260, 265–266, 404, 413; Légion d'Honneur award, 171; Lorée oboes and, 212–213; Marcel Tabuteau's study under, 27–31, 40, 96, 130; Myrtile Morel and, 129; performances of, 22–25; reviews of, 23–24; Société de Musique de Chambre pour Instruments à Vent and, 22–23; Tabuteau-Wolsing CD and, 525–526
Gingold, Josef, 517
Gittelson, Frank, 180
Glantz, Harry, 82, 104, 105
Gli Uccelli (Respighi), 112
Gluck, Alma, 66, 117
G Minor Concerto (Handel), 24, 151–152, 395, 458
G Minor Symphony (Mozart), 168
Gnam, Adrian, 491–493
Godard, Benjamin, 91, 141
Godowsky, Leopold, 73
Goetgheluck, Jule, 160
Goldblum, Harold, 190
Goldovsky, Boris, 117, 189, 283, 509
Gomberg, Cela, 199
Gomberg, Harold, 184, 190, 199, 201, 274, 361, 403, 406–407
Gomberg, Leo, 199
Gomberg, Ralph, 182, 198–199, 273, 485, 509–510, 561n4
Gomberg, Robert, 199, 442, 448
Goossens, Eugene, 118, 163
Gordon, Hershel, 318, 399

INDEX

New York Symphony, the, 95; east coast
tour of 1906, 50–51; Marcel Tabuteau
offered a job with, 37–38; Marcel
Tabuteau's first season with, 44–51;
Marcel Tabuteau's second season with,
55–57; musicians recruited by, 40–44;
rivalry with the Boston Symphony
Orchestra, 39, 43–44; Walter Damrosch
takes over, 39–40; western states tour,
57; Wind Instrument Club, 50. *See also*
Damrosch, Walter
New York Theatre Roof Garden, 43
New York Times, 43, 48
New York Tribune, 36
Nice, France: Adrian Gnam in, 491–493;
Elaine Shaffer in, 494–495; Laila
Storch in, 480–481, 487–488; Marc
Mostovoy in, 480–484; Rowland
Floyd in, 495–500, 502–503; the
Tabuteaus residences in, 476–479,
493–494; the Tabuteaus trip to Le
Brusc from, 475–476
Nicholas II, Czar, 2
Night on Bare Mountain (Mussorgsky), 168
Ninth Symphony (Wagner), 87
Nordica, Lillian, 62, 551n22
North American, 138–139
North Carolina School for the
Performing Arts, 500–502
North Carolina Symphony, 366

Obberby, Preben, 167
Oberlin College, 501–502
Oboe Reed Styles, 211
Oboes: cane for, *377,* 380, 382–384;
growth in professionalism and
popularity of, 519–520; language of
music and, 534–544; lesson notes of
Laila Storch, 245–247; Lorée, 32–33,
153, 203, 212–216, 385–386, *482,*
564n45; prices, 563n43; solo material
for, 24, 109–112, 163–165; Tabuteau's
method of teaching, 540–544;
terminology, 545–546
O'Connell, Charles, 148–149, 167, 174
Octet (Beethoven), 22
Offenbach, Jacques, 36–37
Olanoff, Max, 106
Olivieri, Victor, 383, *384*
O! Ma Tendre Musette, 25
Opus 103 (Beethoven), 22
Ormandy, Eugene: Arturo Toscanini
and, 291–294; Casals Festival and,

435–436; Doctor of Music conferred
on Tabuteau presented by, 171–172;
Marcel Tabuteau's farewell speech to
the Philadelphia Orchestra and, 453;
Marcel Tabuteau's relationship with,
439, 442; musicians interactions
with, 444–445, 446; Philadelphia
Orchestra and, 110–111, 118, *142,*
156, 157, 158, 160, 162, 174–175,
259, 395, 508; recordings, 170; tours,
174–175, 456; Waldemar Wolsing
and, 465
Overtones, 188

Paderewski, Ignace Jan, 100
Paladilhe, Émile, 27, 47
Panama-Pacific International Exposition
of 1915, the: attractions, 79; Camile
Saint-Saëns at, 81–85; Exposition
Orchestra, 80–87; facilities, 77–79;
Marcel Tabuteau at, 75–77; U.S. vessel
Jason at, 79–80
Paray, Paul, 122–123
Parès, Gabriel, 41
Paris Conservatoire. *See* Société des
Concerts Conservatoire
Parisian Sketches (James), 36
Parker, Brooks, 75–76
Parker, Horatio, 72
Pastorale (Hanson), 160, 162
Pavlova, Anna, 66
Pěemanová, Sonia, 317
Peers, Harry, 147–148, 198, 209, 444
Pelletier, Wilfred, 452
Penha, Michel, 108
Pernel, Orea, 437
Perpignan, France, 429–434
Persinger, Louis, 165
Persischetti, Vincent, 336–337
Petite Symphonie (Gounod), 23, 56
Petrillo, James, 456
Pfeiffenschneider, Justus, 71
Pfeiffer, Georges, 32
Philadelphia Bach Festival, 344
Philadelphia Conservatory of Music, 200
Philadelphia Daily News, 162
Philadelphia Inquirer, 139–140, 147, 150,
151, 152–153, 163, 508
Philadelphia La Scala Opera Company,
334–335
Philadelphia Musical Academy, 200
Philadelphia Opera Company, 257–259;
Laila Storch with, 337–338

Philadelphia Orchestra, the, 26, 37, 46, 202, 205–207; Administration Committee, 555n22; chamber music, 165; concerts in Washington, D. C., 356; conductors, 117–124; *Eighth Symphony,* 99–101; English horn in, 112–114; Ensemble, 165, *166; G Minor Concerto,* 151–152, 395, 458; guest soloists, 114–115; Henri de Busscher and, 91–95; hires Marcel Tabuteau, 96; Howard Hanson and, 160, 162; Laila Storch's attendance at, 295–296; under Leopold Stokowski's leadership, 88–106, 124–135, 439, 441; Marcel Tabuteau offered a job with, 88–89, 96; Marcel Tabuteau's early seasons with, 97–106; Marcel Tabuteau's farewell speech to, 452–454; Marcel Tabuteau's solo performances with, 98–99, 558–559n1; movies of, 509; Mozart Quartet, 136–140, 152–160, 162–163; musicians drafted during World War I, 102–103, 104–105; musicians who played with Tabuteau in, 438–454; new compositions first performed by, 106–109; Norman Carol and, 569n2; oboe section, 100–101, 109–112; operas, 117; *Pastorale,* 160–162; Pension Foundation, 289–290, 458; recordings, 167–170, 174, 458; *Second Brandenburg Concerto,* 141–142; Sergei Rachmaninoff and, 333–334; *Sinfonia Concertante,* 143–150; singers appearances with, 116–117; solos by oboists, 109–112; tours, 172–176, 455–456; wages and contracts of musicians with, 101–102. *See also* Stokowski, Leopold
Philadelphia Rapid Transit Company, 46
Philadelphia Savings Fund Society, 306
Philadelphia Woodwind Quintet, 14
Phillips, Edna, 124–125
Piatigorsky, Gregor, 115, 254, 282, 285, 290, 299
Pierné, Gabriel, 190, 395
Pittsburgh Exposition, 47–48
Pleasants, Henry, 112, 122, 147, 155
Pohlig, Carl, 91
Poland, Bernie, 207
Pons, Lily, 425
Pontier, Jules, 26

Portnoy, Bernard, 145–148; Curtis Institute and, 183, 187, 193–195
Poulenc, Francis, 418
Prades, France, 419–428, 435–437, 570n7
Press, Michael, 180
Price, Guernsey, 51, 52–53, 61
Priests, 3–4
Primavera, Joseph, 449
Primrose, William, 280, 282, 398, 430–432
Private students of Marcel Tabuteau, 203–211
Public Ledger, 143, 151
Puccini, Giacomo, 67
Puerto Rico Symphony Orchestra, 202
Pugno, Raoul, 48
Puig, René, 428, 429

Rachmaninoff, Sergei, 73, 138, 333
Raho, Edward, 100, 141
Raho, Lewis, 100, 105–106, 141, 205
Rampal, Jean-Pierre, 496
Rapier, Wayne, 203, 412, 493, 501, 574n8, 574n13
Ravel, Maurice, 110, 165
RCA Victor, 167, 168, 172, 174, 194
Reardon, Casper, 121
Recordings: *Art of the Oboe,* 511; Bach Festival, 416–417; Casals Festival, 430–431, 435–436, 437; Curtis Woodwind Ensemble, 194; *G Minor Oboe Concerto,* 395; Philadelphia Orchestra, 167–170, 174, 458; *Scheherazade,* 111; *Sinfonia Concertante,* 148; *Swan of Tuonela,* 113; of Tabuteau's voice and music, 403, 458, 511–512; Tabuteau-Wolsing CD, 521–530
Reger, Max, 111
Rehrig, Harold, 444
Reiner, Fritz, 117, 118, 119–120, 130; Curtis Institute and, 187, 192, 193, 196; *Sinfonia Concertante* and, 143; Thelma Neft and, 272–273
Reisenberg, Nadia, 116
Remington, Merrill, 235, 564n8
Respighi, Ottorino, 118
Reviews of Marcel Tabuteau, 34, 47, 136–137, *161;* after his death, 508, 511–512; in the Casals Festival, 424; as a conductor, 399; *G Minor Concerto,* 151; Mozart Quartet, 138–140, 152–160, 163; *Sinfonia Concertante,* 143–144, 147, 150

INDEX

André, 373–374; first performance, 31; gambling by, 438, 442–443, 450–452, 465, 487–488; *G Minor Concerto*, 151–152, 395; gouging machines, *232;* health of, 262–263, 276–279, 321, 350, 363, 395–396, 459, 490–491, 576n16; holidays with Laila Storch, 284–294, 301–302, 318–323; honors received by, 33–34, 170–172, 549n11; immigration difficulties, 52–54; influence of Georges Gillet on, 21–22, 130, 260, 265–266, 404, 413; interaction with Leopold Stokowski, 124–135; Laila Storch's study under, 217–244, 259–266, 269–270, 279–280, 296–303, 343–344, 386–387; at *Les Variétés,* 34, 36–37; Lorée oboes used by, 32–33, 212–216, *482;* marriage of, 103–104, 374; Max Leon's pops concert and, 365–366; Metropolitan Opera and, 63–68; military service in France, 51–52, *52, 53, 54,* 76–77, *78;* Mozart Quartet and, 136–140, 152–160, *156,* 162–163; on music, music performance and interpretation, 498–500, 534–544; new compositions first performed by, 106–109; New York Symphony and, 44–51, 55–57, 59–62; oboe cane selected by, *377,* 380, 382–383; oboes sold by, 486; oboes used by, 261; at the Panama-Pacific International Exposition, 75–76, 81–87; *Pastorale* and, 160–162; Philadelphia Orchestra and, 97–106, 394–395, 438–439, 513–515; Philadelphia Orchestra Ensemble and, 165, *166;* recordings, 167–170, 403, 458, 511–512; reeds used by, *230, 231,* 323–324, *467,* 469, 529–530; return to the U.S. in 1959, 470–472; return trips to France from the U.S., 16, 17, 51–52, 60–61, 369–372, 456–458; reviews of, 29–30, 33, 34, 47, 136–140, 143–144, 147, 150, 151, 152–160, *161,* 163, 399, 424, 508, 511–512; Rowland Floyd and, 495–500; San Francisco Exposition Orchestra and, 75–76, 80–87, *83;* Scholarship Fund, 507; *Second Brandenburg Concerto,* 141–142; 75th birthday, 479–480; *Sinfonia Concertante,* 143–150, 164–165;

socializing with other musicians, 442–443; at Société des Concerts Conservatoire, 27–31; solo performances, 98–99, 136–137, 558–559n1; students of, 181–187, 189–199, 203–211, 266–267, 317–318, 393–394, 401–415; studies violin, 8; summers in Canada, 345–354, *347,* 366–367, 384–385; summers in France, 369–371, 374–376, 380–381; teaching in retirement, 465–470, 480–486, 491–500, 531–532; teaching method, 389–390, 402–404, 469–470, 497–500, 518–519, 540–544; temper of, 307–308, 310–312, 313–314, 412–413, 469; tours, 172–176, *173, 175,* 455–456; tributes to, 507–512; unique talent of, 512–520; visits home from school, 17–18; wages and contracts, 71, 101–102; Waldemar Wolsing's study under, 465–468; William Kincaid's relationship with, 438–447, 449; Wolsing CD, 521–530
Tabuteau, Octave, 3, *5*
Tabuteau, Pauline, 6–7, *18,* 19–20
Taffanel, Paul, 4, 22, 30, 40, 50
Tansman, Alexander, 160
Taylor, Rose, 508
Templeton, Alec, 220
Teraspulsky, Leopold, 418
Terminology, oboe, 545–546
Terrasse, Claude, 36
Tertis, Lionel, 430
Tetrazzini, Luisa, 62, 72
Thomas, Milton, 418
Thomas, Theodore, 39
Thomson, Randall, 273
Thorstenberg, Laurence, 202, 393, *394,* 398–400
Thuille, Ludwig, 72
Time, 227, 238, 239, 279
Tipton, Albert, *142,* 509
Tod und Verklärung (Strauss), 107–108
Tofte-Hansen, Paul, 468, 509
Le Tombeau de Couperin (Ravel), 110, 170
Tomeii, Tony, 122
Tompkins, Kevin, 346–350, 352
Tompkins, Rose, 346–350, 352
Torchinsky, Abe, 447, 514
Torello, Anton, 82, 121, 152, 443; Curtis Institute and, 178
Toronto Symphony Orchestra, 193, 200–201

INDEX

LAILA STORCH is a graduate of the Curtis Institute of Music, where she studied with Marcel Tabuteau. She was solo oboist of the Houston Symphony Orchestra from 1948 to 1955, playing under conductors Efrem Kurtz, Ferenc Fricsay, Bruno Walter, Eugene Ormandy, Leopold Stokowski, and Sir Thomas Beecham. Following two years in Austria on a Fulbright grant, she spent one season as principal oboist of the Mozarteum Orchester, Salzburg. She took part in the early Casals festivals in Prades and Perpignan, 1950–53, and in later Casals festivals in San Juan, Puerto Rico, 1966–68. She also played in the Bethlehem, Pennsylvania, and Carmel, California, Bach festivals and has performed at Marlboro. In 1962 she toured the Soviet Union as oboe d'amore soloist with the Robert Shaw Chorale. As oboist of the Soni Ventorum Wind Quintet for twenty-six years, she toured extensively in the United States, Europe, and South and Central America and made many recordings. She has been a guest professor at Indiana University, the Oberlin Conservatory of Music, and the Central Conservatory of China, Beijing, and has given classes in Japan. Many of her articles have appeared in publications of the International Double Reed Society and in French translation for *La Lettre du Hautboïste.* In 1995 she was cited by the *New York Times* as "a revered chronicler of oboe lore." Now Professor Emeritus at the School of Music, University of Washington, Seattle, Laila Storch is an honorary member of the International Double Reed Society and in 2004 was elected to the Comité d'Honneur of the Association française du Hautbois